A Century of Social Work and Social Welfare at Penn

A Century of Social Work and Social Welfare at Penn

Edited by Ram A. Cnaan, Melissa E. Dichter, and Jeffrey Draine

PENN

University of Pennsylvania Press

Philadelphia

Publication of this book was generously supported by Florence Hart (MSW 65).

Published by
University of Pennsylvania Press
Philadelphia, Pennsylvania 19104-4112

Printed in the United States of America on acid-free paper
10 9 8 7 6 5 4 3 2 1

Library of Congress Cataloging-in-Publication Data

A century of social work and social welfare at Penn / edited by Ram A. Cnaan, Melissa E. Dichter, and Jeffrey Draine.
        p.   cm.
    Includes bibliographical references and index.
    ISBN 978-0-8122-4103-7 (alk. paper)
1. Social service—United States—History—20th century.   2. Social workers—United States—History—20th century.   I. Cnaan, Ram A.   II. Dichter, Melissa E.   III. Draine, Jeffrey, N.
HV91.C376   2008
361.30973—dc22   2008010437

Contents

1. Introduction: An Overview of the Journey   1
   Ram A. Cnaan, Jeffrey Draine, and Melissa E. Dichter

Part I. The Early Years

2. The Family and the Social Worker   13
   Mary E. Richmond
   Commentary, *Kevin Grigsby*   16

3. A Community Program for Child Care   20
   J. Prentice Murphy
   Commentary, *Ram A. Cnaan*   23

4. Avocational Guidance   26
   Karl de Schweinitz
   Commentary, *Ira Colby*   32

5. Personality in Social Work   38
   Porter R. Lee
   Commentary, *Ram A. Cnaan*   48

6. The Contributions of American Social Agencies
   to Social Progress and Democracy   51
   Frank D. Watson
   Commentary, *Ram A. Cnaan*   56

Part II. The Height of the Functionalist Era

7. The Time Element in Mental Hygiene Therapy as
   Applied to Social Case Work   61
   Jessie Taft
   Commentary, *Bill Silver*   69

8. Social Work Processes   71
   Ruth E. Smalley
   Commentary, *Mark Frazier Lloyd*   78

9. The Influence of Otto Rank in Social Work: A Journey into a Past   82
   Virginia P. Robinson
   Commentary, *Kathryn Rossé*   102

10. The Cause in Function   105
   Harold Lewis
   Commentary, *Beth Lewis*   110

11. The Black Instructor: An Essential Dimension to the
   Content and Structure of the Social Work Curriculum   114
   Louis H. Carter
   Commentary, *Nicholas Roush*   121

12. Institutional Change as a Creative Process:
   Some Educational and Practice Considerations   123
   Howard Arnold and Tybel Bloom
   Commentary, *Anthony F. Bruno*   147

13. Social Work and Social Action   149
   Kenneth L. M. Pray
   Commentary, *Carol W. Spigner*   158

Part III. Writings on the Influence of the Functional Approach

14. Functional Theory: Its History and Influence on
   Contemporary Social Work Practice   165
   Martha M. Dore
   Commentary, *Martha M. Dore*   179

15. The University of Pennsylvania School of Social Work:
   Reflections of a Graduate   182
   SaraKay Smullens
   Commentary, *SaraKay Smullens*   198

16. Jessie Taft and the Functional School: The Impact of Our History   200
   Rich Furman
   Commentary, *Rich Furman*   205

Part IV. Representatives of the DSW Program

17. An Integrative, Intersystemic Approach to Supervision
    of Couple Therapy   209
    Stephen J. Betchen
    Commentary, *Stephen J. Betchen*   218

18. Reflections upon University Retirement:
    With Thanks and Apologies to James Joyce   221
    Gerald L. Euster
    Commentary, *Gerald L. Euster*   229

19. Boundary Spanning: An Ecological Reinterpretation of
    Social Work Practice in Health and Mental Health Systems   232
    Toba S. Kerson
    Commentary, *Toba S. Kerson*   244

20. Challenging Injustice and Oppression   248
    David G. Gil
    Commentary, *David G. Gil*   267

21. Partnering with the Jewish Community of Romania and
    Transitioning from Holocaust and Communism to Modernity   271
    Zvi Feine
    Commentary, *Zvi Feine*   285

22. Introduction to a Dissertation: Posing Questions on Perceived
    Empowerment and Community Problem Solving   288
    Jacqueline B. Mondros
    Commentary, *Jacqueline B. Mondros*   296

Part V. Contemporaries: Recent Ph.D.s and Faculty

23. The Role of Social Disadvantage in Crime, Joblessness, and
    Homelessness Among Persons with Serious Mental Illness   305
    Jeffrey Draine, Mark S. Salzer, Dennis P. Culhane, and Trevor R. Hadley
    Commentary, *Jeffrey Draine*   319

24. The Social Services of African American Congregations
    in the Welfare Reform Era   322
    Stephanie C. Boddie
    Commentary, *Stephanie C. Boddie*   328

25. Education for Social Development: Curricular Issues and Models   333
    Richard J. Estes
    Commentary, *Richard J. Estes*   350

26. The New African American Inequality   354
    Michael B. Katz, Mark J. Stern, and Jamie J. Fader
    Commentary, *Mark J. Stern*   389

27. How Evaluation Research Can Help Reform
    and Improve the Child Welfare System   391
    Richard J. Gelles
    Commentary, *Richard J. Gelles*   406

28. On Becoming a Scholar-Practitioner   409
    Kenwyn K. Smith
    Commentary, *Kenwyn K. Smith*   425

29. Neighborhood-Representing Organizations:
    How Democratic Are They?   428
    Ram A. Cnaan
    Commentary, *Ram A. Cnaan*   446

30. Moving from Psychoeducation to Family Education for
    Families of Adults with Serious Mental Illness   450
    Phyllis Solomon
    Commentary, *Phyllis Solomon*   463

31. Postmodern Feminist Theory and Social Work   466
    Roberta G. Sands and Kathleen Nuccio
    Commentary, *Roberta G. Sands*   476

32. A Cross-National Study of Adolescent Peer Concordance
    on Issues of the Future   478
    Vivian C. Seltzer and Richard P. Waterman
    Commentary, *Vivian C. Seltzer*   495

33. The Journey Toward Intercultural Sensitivity: A Non-Linear Process   500
    Joretha N. Bourjolly, Roberta G. Sands, Phyllis Solomon, Victoria Stanhope,
    Anita Pernell-Arnold, and Laurene Finley
    Commentary, *Joretha N. Bourjolly*   516

34. Occupational Social Work for the Twenty-First Century   519
    Roberta R. Iversen
    Commentary, *Roberta R. Iversen*   536

35. Where the Homeless Come From: A Study of the Prior
    Address Distribution of Families Admitted to Public
    Shelters in New York City and Philadelphia   539
    Dennis P. Culhane, Chang-Moo Lee, and Susan M. Wachter
    Commentary, *Dennis P. Culhane*   565

Part VI: Recent Former Faculty

36. Risk Classification and Juvenile Dispositions:
    What Is the State of the Art?   571
    Peter R. Jones, David R. Schwartz, Ira M. Schwartz,
    Zoran Obradovic, and Joseph Jupin
    Commentary, *Ira M. Schwartz*   604

37. Organizational Learning and Change in a
    Public Child Welfare Agency   606
    Burton J. Cohen and Michael J. Austin
    Commentary, *Michael J. Austin*   618

38. Lessons Learned About Working with Men: A Prison Memoir   621
    Jack Sternbach
    Commentary, *Jeffrey Draine*   633

List of Contributors   637

Index   639

Chapter 1
Introduction: An Overview of the Journey

Ram A. Cnaan, Jeffrey Draine, and Melissa E. Dichter

This volume is a unique collection of social work research and thought from faculty and alumni of the University of Pennsylvania School of Social Work (now the School of Social Policy & Practice) over the past century. We have selected key contributions from individuals important to the social work profession and affiliated with the School from the early pioneers in 1908 to recent alumni and current faculty in 2008. Some of the articles included here have been previously published; some make their debut in this book. Accompanying each article is a commentary reflecting on the author's work in the context of the field and the School. When possible, the commentary was written by the article author; in other cases, we selected other members of previous or current student or faculty communities to comment based on their experience with the work.

We focused on three key groups of contributors. First are papers written by previous faculty, many of whom are deceased. This set of articles represents the body of knowledge and wisdom that is the history of the School and the profession. Almost all the people who led the School in its first seventy years are no longer with us. Many left behind intellectual heritage and societal imprints that continue to shape the fields of professional social work, social welfare, and policy. We selected many of them to be represented in the earlier chapters of this volume. All their chapters are accompanied by commentaries written by people who are strongly affiliated with the School. Second, we invited a select few School alumni to submit an article that represents a substantial intellectual contribution and that is related to the education they obtained at Penn. Members of this group include a few who obtained their Master's (MSW) at Penn and even more who received their doctorates here. From the latter group the majority received the DSW and a few received the newer Ph.D. Third, we approached every School of Social Policy & Practice faculty member who has been with us for more than five years and asked them to submit the article that best represents their intellectual contribution.

A century ago, society struggled with waves of "unruly" new immigrants, not "well-suited" to be Americans. Their adaptation to the New World was painful and was perceived to threaten an American way of life. Poverty, overcrowdedness, alcoholism, unemployment, prostitution, and diseases were major concerns while society was seemingly searching for ways to make new immigrants more "American" and help to ameliorate the pain and suffering of acculturation. Being part of the Progressive Era, the practices of charity, good will, and friendly visiting were considered insufficient. They were mere band-aid solutions that might abate the acute pain but would not solve the problems and their persistence. The country was looking for scientific answers to these and other social problems. It seemed clear that if only our great minds could be harnessed to help the immigrants, solutions would be found and the immigrants would become model Americans. Ironically, at the time that we are compiling this volume to celebrate the century of the School, immigration and the rights of immigrants are once again high on the national political agenda. Unfortunately, the voice of social work in this debate today is largely unheard.

While the ideal of being able to eradicate poverty and fully solve all social ills was naïve and unattainable, it served as the basis for systematizing the practice of help and attempting to make help more professional, methods-based, theory-related, and empirically tested. Across the country, social services transitioned from being staffed with good-intentioned middle- and upper-class women to a cadre of hired staff aiming at running the services efficiently and vowing to eradicate poverty and other social ills. Amid these social trends emerged the need to form a coherent body of knowledge and train those helping the poor, immigrant, sick, and needy in a systematic manner. The call swept the country, and those engaged in providing the services recognized the need to start systematically training people to become professional social workers.

It was in 1908 when the beginning of training for social work education emerged with the birth of what was then called the Philadelphia Training School for Social Work and has since joined the University of Pennsylvania, expanded and become the University of Pennsylvania School of Social Policy & Practice. Through the leadership efforts of Benjamin Franklin Pepper, under the directorship of John Prentice Murphy and with the financial support of the Seybert Institution, funds and programs became available for the organized training of social workers. What made this training unique was that a group of social workers from various social services agencies were pulled out from their regular work and attended a set of lectures and courses that lasted a year. It was a cross-agency new training for social work. The first year's curriculum of the "Course of Training in Child-Helping" sought to provide both a broad overview of the profession of social work and an in-depth study of its several areas of expertise. It was divided into four sessions and led by the social work professionals of the three cooperating agencies: the Children's Aid Society of Pennsylvania, the Pennsylvania Society to Protect Children from Cruelty, and the Seybert Institution.

The inaugural lectures were given by Mary E. Richmond, director of the Philadelphia Society for Organizing Charity and one of the most prominent social workers of her generation. A decade earlier, she had famously advocated the establishment of training schools for social workers. She must have felt enormously rewarded as several such schools were founded in the last years of the nineteenth century and first years of the twentieth, especially as she was part of the founding forces of the Philadelphia Training School for Social Work.

As one of the oldest and most well-respected social work programs in the country—indeed, the world—the Penn program has been home to scholars, educators, and practitioners dedicated to first-rate social research, advocacy, and practice, always at the forefront of progressive innovation towards social justice. Long before other schools thought it worthwhile, the Pennsylvania School of Social Work had a social research unit, emphasized social justice, professionalized community practice, and developed the functional approach to social intervention that is the foundation for modern day direct practice. As Roy Lubove has written in *The Professional Altruist*,[1] Philadelphia's school "was not viewed merely as a substitute or alternative to apprenticeship but as a concrete demonstration of the 'scientific' character of social work and a turning point in the transition from vocational to professional status."

This era of growing pains and learning by experience is reflected in this volume by articles and commentaries that featured the School's original leaders. The first articles presented here—those by Mary Richmond, J. Prentice Murphy, Karl de Schweinitz, Porter Lee, and Frank D. Watson—are a reflection of this era. The commentaries written especially for this volume set these original leaders in context and relate them to the School's heritage.

The commentary on the chapter by Mary Richmond, who is considered by many as the mother of social work, is written by Kevin Grigsby, who graduated from the School with a DSW and serves at the time of writing as president of the alumni board. Another DSW alumnus, Ira Colby, who serves as a dean of the School of Social Work at the University of Houston and is also current president of the Council of Social Work Education, wrote the commentary to accompany the article by Karl de Schweinitz. The commentary about J. Prentice Murphy, the School's first director, was written by Professor Ram A. Cnaan, who directs the doctoral program in social welfare and serves as an associate dean for research; Dr. Cnaan also contributed the commentary to accompany the articles by Frank Watson and Porter Lee.

Never dormant, the School was continually reinvigorating and assessing social work. Indeed, it even changed its name a few times. and then embarked on one of the most ambitious undertaking in the history of social work in America. In the era between 1930 and 1960, almost every school of social work in America turned to a diagnostic (e.g., psychoanalytic) approach, while at the University of Pennsylvania the School of Social Work ventured into what is known as the "functional approach." This undertaking was the fruit of the combined efforts of Jessie Taft, Virginia Robinson, and Ruth E. Smalley. Now, many years after the initial struggle between the diagnostic and functional schools, it is clear that modern day social work is heavily functional, although not labeled as such.

What was the theory and practice of the "functional school"? John H. Ehrenreich, in his 1985 book, *The Altruistic Imagination: A History of Social Work and Social Policy in the United States*, wrote an excellent account of the social work movement, from Freudian psychology-based intervention on behalf of the client to a strengths-based focus on the interactive and function-oriented relationship between client and worker. The Functional Approach, based on the theories of Otto Rank, was developed by Penn colleagues Virginia Robinson and Jessie Taft. In fact, Ehrenreich attributed the "turning point" in social work to Robinson's 1930 publication, *A Changing Psychology in Social Work.*[2] Ehrenreich describes the ensuing controversy between two social work factions:

Caseworkers began to split into two "schools": the "functional school" and the more orthodox Freudian "diagnostic" (or "organic" or "psychosocial"). Although the functional school remained a small minority, the debate it provoked has had an enormous influence on social work methods and principles. Continuing for more than fifteen years, the debate quickly grew extraordinarily bitter, even vitriolic. By the late forties, graduates of "functional" schools (e.g., the University of Pennsylvania and the University of North Carolina) had trouble finding jobs in agencies that adhered to the diagnostic school, and vice versa.

This volume includes seminal works from founders of the functionalist approach, including Jessie Taft, Ruth E. Smalley, and Virginia Robinson. These articles are followed by a group of articles by people who were trained in the School and used the functionalist approach. These individuals were invited to be faculty members and carried the functionalist approach for many years after the founders retired. Among these students are Harold ("Hal") Lewis, Lewis Carter, Harold Arnold, and Tybel Bloom.

DSW alumnus Bill Silver, who now teaches practice at the School, wrote the commentary on Jessie Taft's work. Another practice teacher, Kathryn Rossé, wrote the commentary accompanying the chapter by Virginia Robinson. The commentary on Ruth Smalley was written by Mark Frazier Lloyd, a historian who conducted extensive research on the school's legacy for the centennial commemoration. Another leader at the time, although not writing specifically on the functional approach, was Kenneth L. M. Pray, who became director of the Pennsylvania School and moved it into the University. Pray applied concepts from the functional approach to planning, administration and social action. The commentary author for his article is current faculty member Carol Wilson Spigner, who holds the Kenneth L. M. Pray Chair and directs the new program of Master of Science in Social Policy.

Those directly influenced by the functional school students wrote commentaries on those mentors. Beth Lewis, who was on the faculty for ten years, wrote the commentary to the article by her father, Harold Lewis. Nick Roush, who received his MSW from the School, wrote the commentary for Professor Louis Carter. And Anthony Bruno, who received both his MSW and DSW from the School and, in addition to being a professor at Philadelphia Community College, currently teaches courses in the School, wrote on Howard Arnold and Tybel Bloom's work.

A former faculty member, Martha Dore, was invited to contribute an article that reviews the origins and influence of the functional approach. A student who graduated in the 1960s and was trained in this approach and used it in practice, SaraKay Smullens, was invited to submit a paper describing how the functionalist approach and the School's philosophy was applied in social work practice. Another article about the impact of Jessie Taft and the functionalist approach was contributed by Rich Furman, a student who attended the MSW program in the early 1990s.

The early years of social work education throughout the country did not emphasize research and theory building. As Roy Lubove noted, "these early schools were established and controlled by social workers [which] virtually guaranteed a conflict between the ideal of the school as a scientific laboratory, offering a broad professional education while expanding the boundaries of social work theory and research, and the need to satisfy agency demands for trained workers."[3] Atypical of social work education programs, the Pennsylvania School of Social Work, from the first cohort onward, offered a course on the research and theory of the social sciences. In this regard, the School's work was at the cutting edge of the new profession of social work. The need to create a new body of knowledge for social work required the formation of a doctoral program to train young social workers to become researchers.

In 1935, the School was engaged in discussions of merging with the University of Pennsylvania. In "Proposal for Affiliation," we find the following:[4]

Upon recommendation of the School, the University shall award the following professional degrees:

(A) Master of Social Work to candidates who are graduates of a recognized college or university, who have completed two years of professional training, including class instruction and practice under supervisors approved by the School, and who have submitted a thesis indicating knowledge and competence in some phase of social work to be approved by the faculty of the School. No less than fifty per cent of the work in the first year or ten per cent in the second year shall be in class room instruction.

(B) Doctor of Social Work to candidates who have completed two years of work in an accredited school of social work; two years of practice in social work in a competent social agency; a third year of work in residence in Pennsylvania School of Social Work; and thereafter an additional year of practice at the end of which there shall be submitted a thesis in the candidate's major subject which will be a contribution to the theory or practice in that field.

This document is the foundation upon which one of the most prestigious programs of doctoral education was built. The University's *Catalogue for the Session of 1935–1936* contained the following description of the School: "A Doctorate may also be awarded to qualified students who have engaged in advanced study and practice." The plans for the doctorate were laid in the 1930s but lack of faculty with doctorate degrees and the university's reluctance caused a delay and doctoral education was not offered until 1949 and the first degree was not awarded until 1951.

University president George McClelland announced the appointment of 44-year-old William Donald Turner as dean of the School of Social Work in May 1948. Turner was a psychologist, not a social worker, but he had been a student of Jessie Taft and had adopted the theory and practice of the functional school for use in his work in human resources management. It was Turner who, within a year, was successful in winning University approval of the School's doctoral program, which led to the professional degree of Doctor of Social Work. He created within the School a Doctoral Council of Social Work and placed the degree program under its direction. Membership of the Doctoral Council was limited to the four faculty members who had earned doctorates: Isabel Carter, Virginia Robinson, Jessie Taft, and Turner himself. The Doctoral Admissions Committee consisted only of Robinson, Taft, and Turner. The Admissions Committee promptly opened the program to four junior members of the School's faculty: Anita Josephine Faatz, Associate Professor of Social Planning and Administration; Goldie Basch Faith, Associate Professor of Social Casework; Elizabeth Alston Lawder, Assistant Professor of Social Casework; and Rosa Lee Schneider Wessel, Associate Professor of Social Casework. In June 1951, these four were the first to earn the DSW degree at Penn. Professors Robinson and Taft had mentored all four and they were seen as the future of the School. Dean Turner immediately invited the foursome to join the Doctoral Council of Social Work, and Faatz also joined the Doctoral Admissions Committee. Robinson and Taft had already announced their intention to turn over their work to their successors, and in June 1952 both retired. The award of Penn's DSW to its first class of recipients fulfilled perhaps the most important of their long-held goals and simultaneously guaranteed the continuation of their functional school.

Indeed, the first cohorts of students were graduates of the School's MSW program who could advance the functionalist approach. Many of those graduates, upon completion of their degree, were invited to stay and join the faculty. A 1952 evaluation report from the Council on Social Work Education raised concern about "the concentration of degrees from the Pennsylvania School," noting that the faculty consisted almost exclusively of Penn-trained professionals.[5] This problem was soon resolved when a cohort of doctoral students was admitted from outside the School and graduates of the DSW program took positions in local agencies, other universities, and research institutions. Ever since, the mission and practice of the DSW has been that the School's doctoral program was to focus on scholarship and candidates for the doctor's degree were required to present a thesis based on original research pertinent to the profession and reflecting satisfactory research methodology.

The DSW program yielded many of today's leaders in social work education; at least ten graduates became deans, among them Ira Colby. Included in this book are works from a small sample of these noted scholars. Tybel Bloom and Harold Lewis both graduated from the School with a DSW and then joined its faculty. Their papers were discussed above, as they focus on or represent the School's functional approach. Among the other graduates of the DSW program whose articles are included in this volume are: Stephen J. Betchen, Gerald Euster, Toba S. Kerson, David G. Gil, Zvi Feine, and Jacqueline B. Mondros.

As time passed, what was once revolutionary and successful came to be seen as regressive. While in the 1950s and 1960s the DSW degree was most prestigious and designed to enhance social work theory and empirical research, it slowly lost its appeal. Other professions developed degrees that were not research-oriented and distinguished them from the traditional Ph.D. with disciplinary related degrees such as Dr.P.H. (doctor of public health), D.Min. (doctor of ministry), Psy.D. (clinical degree in psychology), and Ed.D. (doctor of education). Newer schools of social work embraced the Ph.D. degree as their terminal degree and the significance of the DSW as a terminal degree in social work diminished.

In response to this trend, many schools that offered a DSW as the terminal degree in social work applied to their respective universities to convert or replace their DSW program with a new Ph.D.; Penn was no exception. In the late 1980s, a task force was formed and, together with the university, decided not to close the DSW program but to cease admission and accept new students only to a new Ph.D. program. It took over ten years for all of the DSW students to graduate and for almost 20 years only the Ph.D. program accepted students. Many graduates of this new Ph.D. program are now faculty members in prestigious schools across the country and are representing Penn as a premier source for social work researchers. In this volume, we are proud to present articles by two of the graduates of this program: one of them, Jeffrey N. Draine, is currently a faculty member at the School; the other is Stephanie C. Boddie.

Interestingly, now twenty years after the last student was admitted to the DSW program, it has been resurrected into new life. In the academic year 2007/8, a cohort of 18 students started a new DSW program designated to produce practice experts, policy leaders, evaluators, and practice researchers. This clinical DSW program is yet another innovative step taken by the School of Social Policy & Practice to enhance the status and quality of social work education nationwide. This new program coexists along with the continuing—and thriving—Ph.D. program for those more interested in an academic career in social welfare scholarship.

The latter part of the book is mostly composed of contributions by the current standing faculty of the School of Social Policy & Practice. In the past quarter century, the focus of the School shifted from building and advocating for the functional approach to representing the best that social sciences can offer social work. Through a slow process that spanned the deanship of Michael J. Austin, Ira M. Schwartz, and Richard J. Gelles, new faculty members were hired who were not trained in the School, many of them with non-social work degrees. The focus of the school, as well as the ideal of social work education, shifted to rigorous empirical research on what best helped people in need. These new faculty members all shared commitment for betterment of human conditions locally, nationally, and worldwide. Each came with his or her research focus and individual perspective and served as trailblazer for the profession to follow. Today, faculty members at the School are the most academically productive in terms of producing new academic knowledge and in terms of generating research articles and research grants. It is with no surprise that when the *Chronicle of Higher Education* rated doctoral programs in social work based on faculty productivity, in 2007 the School of Social Policy & Practice at the University of Pennsylvania nationally was ranked second.

Today's faculty members, as with those in the past 100 years, represent a variety of philosophies and methodological approaches, all contributing innovative research impacting human well-being and the social work profession. For example, Richard J. Estes, one of the most senior members of the faculty, and an alumnus of the MSW program, developed and popularized the fields of international social work and comparative social welfare. Mark J. Stern, a historian by education, runs an innovative program on the impact of the arts on the community as well as running the university's urban studies program. Professor Stern is also a major contributor to the field of social policy and his text co-authored with the late Professor June Axinn, who was a long-time member of the faculty, is an ongoing best seller. Our past dean, Ira M. Schwartz, and our current dean, Richard J. Gelles, along with Professor Carol Wilson Spigner are leading experts in child welfare. They are the first to be called upon when expert opinion is required regarding child welfare, their publications in this field are considered cutting-edge, and their views are well-respected across the world. Professor Kenwyn K. Smith, who developed and leads the new Master's degree in Nonprofit Leadership, is an international expert in organizational dynamics and group processes. Ram A. Cnaan contributed the link between social work and religion and is considered the country's expert on social services provided by religious congregations. Along with Professor Femida Handy, he is also an internationally renowned expert on volunteerism. Professor Phyllis Solomon is a top-notch community mental health researcher and a leader in social science research methodology. Her work in this field paved the way for many policy changes and she is internationally known as one the country's top scholars in this field. Jeffrey Draine, who received his Ph.D. at the School, is also an expert in community mental health and his contributions and studies in the areas of mental illness in the justice system place him as a national expert and leader. Another expert in mental health is Professor Roberta G. Sands. Her article chosen for this volume is an example of an innovative and critical thinking and a model for keeping social work abreast of conceptual developments. Professor Vivian C. Seltzer is completing her fourth book in a series beginning with contribution of an original theory of adolescent psychological development and behavior. Benchmarks of normative and deviant growth are included. It rejects the psychoanalytic model of rebellion and redefines peers as adolescent "attachment" figures. Each models criteria for decision making of others towards "Identity." Comparison and evaluation can disappoint. Some adopt deviant defenses. Basic premises are supported in studies with 6,000 U.S. and foreign adolescents. The fourth book is a model for practice with adolescents using the theoretical model.

Professor Joretha N. Bourjolly is currently associate dean for academic affairs and among the School's experts in health. The field of medical social work suffered many losses in the past twenty years and Professor Bourjolly's contributions and collaborations with the Nursing and Medical schools keep the School at the front line of new knowledge. Many faculty members are involved in the University's new and growing interdisciplinary program in Public Health. Professor Roberta R. Iversen, who served as associate dean, specializes in poverty and especially on the impact of welfare and workforce policy reform on the quality of life of low-income parents and their families. Her work in this area proved that these reforms had numerous consequences unforeseen by our national policy makers. Professor Dennis P. Culhane is the national authority on the scope and nature of homelessness and related policy reforms. His large scale studies on homeless people settled years of arguing about how many and who are the homeless. He also pioneered with using Geographic Information Systems (GIS) technology in understanding social issues and the Cartographic Modeling Lab (CML) he chairs is a national model of data integration and visual presentation.

We also invited or selected papers from former faculty members. Such is the case with our previous two deans, Michael J. Austin and Ira M. Schwartz. Dean Austin selected an article he wrote with Burton Cohen who served at that time as a research faculty member. One who in many ways represents the switch from the functional school to today's School of Social Policy & Practice is Jack Sternbach. The commentary about Jack, written by Professor Draine, illustrates how different he was from the traditional functionalist culture of the School and, although he did not last long in the School, his spirit and the trend he represented is still with us.

As you can see, the writings contained in this collection represent the broad spectrum of theory, content expertise, and philosophical and methodological approaches contained within the School's heritage. The format and content reflect its core tenets and perspective, based on social work values: (a) a clear understanding of and respect for the past; (b) thoughtful analysis of current and professional issues; (c) a vision of the future that reflects a commitment to social change; and (d) knowledge appreciation and knowledge generation on local, national, and global issues. When you read this book, you will surely be impressed and inspired, as we are, with the significant contributions to the field of social work and, ultimately, the well-being of society, emerging from the School's founders, current faculty, and alumni.

Preparing this collection has been an exciting and intriguing endeavor. Through this work, we have had the opportunity to comb through the most esteemed to the more obscure publications to find historical, seminal, and cutting-edge writings. In doing so, we recognize the vast number of influential and ground-breaking social work leaders who are or were members of the School's community. With sadness we declined many others excellent articles from alumni and past faculty members that could have add another volume to this impressive collection of articles. It has been a challenge to pair down these thinkers and writings into a manageable list. And it has been a joy to be in touch with former colleagues and peers, and to collaborate with contemporaries, as part of this process.

This book serves as a representative sample of social work's development in its formative years and the Penn School's central role in that growth. On this centennial anniversary, we present you with this book to commemorate the School's intellectual history to date. Undoubtedly, this marks only the beginning of a long legacy of social work theory, research, and thought at Penn.

Notes

1. Roy Lubove, *The Professional Altruist: The Emergence of Social Work as a Career, 1880–1930* (Cambridge, Mass.: Harvard University Press, 1965), 140.

2. John H. Ehrenreich, *The Altruistic Imagination: A History of Social Work and Social Policy in the United States* (Ithaca, N.Y.: Cornell University Press, 1985), 124–38.

3. Ibid., 141.

4. Typescript in the collections of the University Archives, News Bureau—Subject Files (UPF 8.5, Box 268, File Folder 2): Social Work, School of, I (1935–1959).

5. "Report of Evaluation Conducted Under the Auspices of the Middle States Association," 12 pages, in File Folder labeled "Pennsylvania, Univ. of, Studies Reviews Consultation," Box 135, Record Group 29, Council on Social Work Education (CSWE) records, Social Welfare History Archives (SWHA), University of Minnesota.

Part I
The Early Years

Chapter 2
The Family and the Social Worker

Mary E. Richmond

You, who have come together at the end of a busy winter and during a period of financial depression to consider methods of charitable work, should greet with enthusiasm an institution that needs no subscription list for its support, no board of directors for its management. I refer, of course, to the institution of the family. Someone has called it "the first great practical syllogism, two premises and a conclusion—father, mother and child." There are those, I know, who rebel against the conception of the family as the great social unit, the fundamental social fact. There are those who feel that the family as a moulding and controlling factor in human affairs has had its day. They maintain that its form is largely fortuitous, depending not so much upon the nature of man as upon the nature of the food that he eats, the character of his occupation, etc. But the cock crows and the sun rises, and the connection between the two events is not always as intimate as the cock himself imagines. These disparaging views of the family, of its origin and its functions, will have their day and cease to be, while the family itself continues to be the pivotal institution around which our human destinies revolve.

This is mere commonplace, of course. The air itself is commonplace in the sense that it is everywhere, but when it is bad we become unpleasantly aware of it, as we do of contaminated family life. To all here present, however, the great formative influences, the processes that have made us what we are, have gone on within our own homes quite unconsciously, for the most part. The way in which each one of you has entered and will leave this church, your feeling about the place itself and its associations, the greater or less degree of tolerance with which you are listening to what I am saying this moment, what you will think about it afterwards, if you ever think about it at all, and what you will do about it—these things have been determined far more by the family into which you were born and in which you grew up than any single one of you has any conception of. I am making no wholesale claim for heredity as against, environment in saying this, but I am making a claim for the overwhelming force of heredity plus the environment that we inherit.

Approaching my subject with these convictions, it naturally follows that I do not stand here to-night to plead with social workers to "do something" for the family. I plead rather, for the sake of the immediate ends we have in view—for the sake of the life, liberty and happiness of all the disadvantaged and oppressed—that we may see to it that the family "does something" for us. In other words, we can progress only a little way unless we learn to work at every turn with nature rather than against her. If we could once realize that, whatever else may fail or succeed—industrial systems, forms of government, societies, nations, races—that whatever may happen to these, the family will persist as long as there is human progress; if we could once grasp the fact that in the long view it is never family life which suffers, but that everything else suffers, including human beings, whenever its claims are ignored; if we could once fully realize this, then all of our work would take on a new dignity and significance.

Let me try to illustrate, not so much from the details of our charitable work as from current happenings in industry and education.

In one of the counties of a far southern state to which the railroad penetrated only a few years ago, it was found that men working on the farm at fifty cents a day were tempted away by the dollar a day of the railroad. Removed farther and farther from their families and homes, many of them have become what is locally called "quitters," or what we know as wife-deserters. On the face of it, this development of industry would seem to have been bad for family life, and incidentally it was, but I am not indulging in mere paradox when I maintain that in the long run, through the fact that it clearly was bad for the workmen, it was also bad for the railroad and for industry. Any form of industry that brings about such results is unstable in its organization and such instability implies loss and the waste that precedes inevitable reorganization.

We need renewed faith in certain very elementary things at the moment. We need to look far enough ahead to see that no large industry which ignores the fundamental facts of family life can continue to prosper. Inevitably the reaction must come, its methods of employing and using labor must be reorganized. It would be no difficult matter to prove the short-sightedness of those industries which depend upon child labor, for instance, or of those others which deliberately seek to work a large number of adults for a short season rather than a smaller number for a long season. The neglect to provide safety devices and other protections against industrial accident gives death his harvest of many thousands yearly in this country, and would seem on the face of it to be more destructive of family life than almost any other one factor in modern industry. But here again a larger view, a larger faith in the persistence of the family, ought to make it clear that industry itself must suffer. Whenever this faith, reasserting itself, recognizes the family as the fundamental social fact to which all other social facts must adjust themselves, industry either must break or must yield.

Industry is yielding reluctantly but inevitably in the matter of the hours of women's work. An English chaplain in the mill town of Preston noted half a century ago that infant mortality was reduced sixteen per cent during a long cotton strike which kept the women operatives at home. Though the standard of living was materially lowered, probably, the chances of life were raised. But it was only a few months ago that our Supreme Court established the principle for all time, as we hope, that, in the interest of family life and public health, the hours of women's work may be regulated by statute. No gathering of those who love their fellow men held in this year of grace should fail to give thanks for that decision. It marks the greatest single step yet taken in this country in a saner adjustment of claims as between industry and the family.

In education also, the adjustment needs to be made. Those who are shaping the school of to-day are realizing more and more that teacher and parent must co-operate in all educational plans. The problem of school feeding that has agitated England so much of late can be regarded as a school question and can ignominiously fail of solution, or it can be regarded as a family and school question, and on that basis can be solved. No educational system can be successful which ignores the family. Family life will suffer undoubtedly from mistaken educational ideals, but, in the long run, the failure will be an educational failure.

Illustrations are everywhere, but I must hurry on to the one practical suggestion for social workers toward which this leads. It is unquestionably true that we may hinder for a little while the life of the family, we may contaminate it, we may reduce its effectiveness, we may break it up altogether here and there; and our social work has succeeded often in doing all of these things. The one practical suggestion that I can make to you is that you ransack all your work for a year, say, from top to bottom with reference to its influence upon the particular families from which your beneficiaries have come and to which they go. Examine every admission to your institution and every discharge from it, every item of the daily lives of its inmates, with reference to this central fact. Ask yourselves, Have we made this man a better or worse husband and father? Have we made this woman a better or worse wife and mother? Have we at least set plans in motion that will make the children better heads of families than their parents have been? Has the burden-bearing capacity of each one concerned been weakened or has it been strengthened by the way in which we have borne our burden of caring for him or for those who have a right to look to him for care? Whether you are dealing with infants in foundling asylums, or children in day nurseries, or the sick in hospital wards, or defectives in state institutions, or prisoners in their cells, or families fallen into distress, or the aged in homes, or the dead awaiting burial even—I care not what form of need or distress or weakness you are dealing with—you cannot afford to forget the family that looms forever in the background. The conditions of normal family life, and all the variations which you are forced to note there from—these two groups of contrasting facts bound the stage of your operations.

And all of our work both for children and for adults needs to be subjected to a far keener and more searching analysis from this point of view. One of the weakest spots in the administration of justice in America to-day is found in the absence of any well-defined standard of parental responsibility, any minimum requirement below which no child's life shall be permitted to fall without prompt and effective interference. It is useless to expect the enforcement of such a standard on the part of magistrates and judges when social workers themselves are not agreed upon it. We need to secure such a standard for ourselves by a closer scrutiny of our own work, and then to educate the public up to it.

At the very moment that we are smugly saying to ourselves that we must never break up families, in that very moment we may be scattering the contagion of dismemberment far and wide. The worst things ever done to the family are done in the name of family life and ostensibly to perpetuate it. While we are arranging creches and school lunches, for instance, in order to make it easier for the woman of the normal family to become a breadwinner, we are building up family life with two fingers and tearing it down with eight.

At this point we need the trained worker for whom your chairman has been pleading. There is a great deal of sentimental and vague talk about the sacredness of the family. One may say very true things, moreover, and apply them very falsely. We need to go beneath the names of things, for not everything that calls itself a family is truly so. There are sham families, and unstable families, and broken families, and families (so-called) that are mere breeding places of vice and crime. The trained worker, instead of juggling with words, will deal clearly with facts and conditions; will strive to answer truthfully of each charitable act that it has allied itself with the forces that make for a deeper and stronger family life. One who recognizes this supreme obligation will work to break up sham families and will work to keep together real ones, and will do all this in the interests not so much of family life as in the clear recognition that only so and with the aid of family life may we accomplish any of the things that we have set out to accomplish for our human kind.

To such a one, the practical syllogism of father, mother and child becomes the symbol of everything humanity has dreamed of or striven for. The family is not merely a place where bodies are reared to maturity, where laborers are trained for the industrial markets of the world, where freeborn men are prepared for the duties of citizenship, but it is the cradle of immortal souls, no less. Toward this, the ideal family, the approach is inevitable and overwhelming; none of us can delay it, none of us can hasten it very much. How glorious a thing to have helped its coming in ways however humble, and how pitiful a thing to have hindered its arrival by so much as a single day!

Reprinted from Mary E. Richmond, The family and the social worker, *National Conference on Social Welfare Proceedings* (1908).

Commentary

Kevin Grigsby

Mary Richmond is a familiar name to most professional social workers. Whether we learned about Miss Richmond in a history of social work class or encountered her work while researching a class assignment, it was evident that she was one of the pioneers of our profession. Her influence on the profession of social work has been strong. In fact, she was very influential, if not instrumental, in the establishment of professional training in social work. In the spring of 1908, Miss Richmond addressed the National Conference on Social Welfare in Richmond, Virginia, on the topic of

"The Family and the Social Worker," arguing "the family itself continues to be the pivotal institution around which our human destinies revolve." This commentary is based on a rereading of the text of her remarks and offers an interpretation of my own "connection" with her legacy at the Penn School of Social Work, now the School of Social Policy & Practice.

Miss Richmond's remarks were made a century ago. She made them in the same year that what is now the Penn School of Social Policy & Practice was founded. Although some of the language sounds dated, for example, "defectives in state institutions," the crux of Miss Richmond's remarks remains not only relevant but profound. That is, professional social work training is necessary if we are to "accomplish any of the things we have set out to accomplish for human kind." She recognized the complexity of the challenge to improve the human condition through philanthropy and charity and understood that it takes more than a well-meaning person with "a good heart" to adequately make a difference in people's lives. The influence of psychoanalytic theory and the theory of evolution are clearly evident in her comments about "great formative influences" occurring "quite unconsciously" and about the "overwhelming force of heredity." But rather than adhering to a single theoretical perspective, such as the determinism of Freud, to try to reconcile the "nature versus nurture" argument, she was clearly ahead of her time in making the claim that both heredity and the environment make us what we are. She argues we should learn to "work at every turn with nature, rather than against her." In her view, the nature versus nurture argument should be abandoned and replaced with a nature *and* nurture perspective. Understanding the person in the context of the environment has become a cornerstone of contemporary social work practice.

Her remarks of a hundred years ago reflect an understanding of the critical need to understand not only the person, but *the family* in the context of the environment. In her brief remarks, she goes on to address the impact of the workplace on family life, noting that progress had been made only recently through the hours of "women's work" becoming regulated by statute. Regarding education, she was prescient in understanding that schools would only be successful when teacher and parents cooperate in educational planning. Today's Individualized Educational Plans (IEPs) and Individualized Family Support Plans (IFSPs), fundamental building blocks of the federal Individuals with Disabilities Educational Act (IDEA) and its amendments, recognize and demand involvement of the family in educational planning. She also addresses the issue of parental responsibility, or perhaps it is better stated as parental irresponsibility, in her comments about the absence of "any well-defined standard of parental responsibility . . . below which no child's life shall be permitted to fall without prompt and effective interference." Our standard of parental responsibility is still very crude, if it exists at all. In today's environment, the prevailing standard of parental responsibility is that children should not be maltreated. How one defines maltreatment remains a conundrum. The complexity of knowing when to intervene in families—and when not to intervene—requires great skill when the desired outcome is "a deeper and stronger family life" as she stated in her address.

Fundamentally, Mary Richmond advocated for trained social workers at time when our profession was in its infancy. She believed that only professionally trained social workers could truly ally "with the forces that make for a deeper and stronger family life." Many years later, Harold Lewis was far more explicit in his discussion of the nature social *work*.[1] But it is clear from these comments and her later writings[2] that Miss Richmond laid the foundation for establishing a scientific basis for social work practice.

Seventy-five years after she made these remarks, I finished my MSW degree and went to work as a professional social worker. I did not attend Penn as an MSW student. The MSW program I attended stressed the "scientific practitioner" approach and included very little content about the history of social work. Walter Hudson's seminal article "First Axioms of Treatment" postulated, "If you can't measure the client's problem, you can't treat it."[3] In a nutshell, our training was based on this premise and I became very adept at measurement. Even so, I felt something was missing. My aspiration entering the MSW program was to become a family therapist, likely working in a comfortable office at a hospital or clinic. Fortunately, my experience as an MSW student opened my eyes to the plethora of career options available to professional social workers. As a social worker assigned to a county jail in the rural South, my charge was to provide mental health crisis intervention to inmates and to function as an expert advisor to defense attorneys in cases where competence to stand trial was in question. To say I was astounded at the number of inmates I met who had experienced out-of-home care as children is an understatement. If social workers in child welfare were really helping children and families, why was a history of out-of-home placement so common in a correctional population? Before long, I was actively involved in creating therapeutic foster care programs in three rural counties. This required my "full immersion" into the child welfare and foster care system. My recollection of the full immersion experience was much more like baptism by fire than in the baptismal pool! In many ways, my early years of professional social work practice created more questions than were answered for me about the role of the social worker and the family. Before long, I made the arrangements to come to the Penn School of Social Work to begin working on the Doctor of Social Work degree. I wanted to find the answers to my many questions. In searching for those answers, I became acquainted with the writing of Mary Richmond. In short, I found harmony in her perspective on the family and my own. I regard the family as the "fundamental social fact" and agree that even when other social institutions fade from view, the family will continue to be the "pivotal institution around which our human destinies revolve." I assumed that the scientific basis of social work practice and need for professional training had been in place from the earliest days. At Penn, I learned about the "friendly visitors," the orphan trains, the asylum movement, and other historical precedents of our profession. As I learned more about the provision of child welfare services in this country, the lack of professional social work training for so much of the child welfare workforce astounded me. One of my questions was: How was it that some children entered foster care for a period of time, but then returned to their families of origin and remained with them *without* a subsequent return to foster care? In fact, this question became the topic of my dissertation research—but that's another story.

My "discovery" of Mary Richmond and so many of the other pioneers of our profession led me to a much greater understanding of the history of our profession and of myself. I'm not sure I could have had the same experience at other schools of social work, as most of them do not offer the rich history of Penn. When I was on campus at Penn, the Social Work Library comprised the second floor of the Castor Building; I clearly remember the unique environment where students and scholars were literally surrounded by the rich history of our profession. I remember writing a paper on the well-being of children working in the oyster industry in the later part of the nineteenth century—a topic that came to light as I browsed the original journal articles in bound volumes nearly a hundred years of age. Because of the richness of the library and the curriculum at Penn, Mary Richmond, Ruth Smalley, Kenneth Pray, Jessie Taft, and Harold Lewis are as a much a part of my understanding of social work as are more recent "icons" of our profession including Walter Hudson, Enola Proctor, and Bruce Thyer. In effect, I don't think I was fully socialized into the role of being a "real" social worker until I came to Penn. Although I never had a chance to meet Mary Richmond face-to-face, it's true we were introduced at Penn. I'm thankful the school provided me with the opportunity to meet her—and so many others.

Notes

1. Harold Lewis, *The Intellectual Base of Social Work Practice* (New York: Haworth Press, 1982).
2. Mary E. Richmond, *Social Diagnosis* (New York: Russell Sage Foundation, 1917).
3. Walter W. Hudson, First axioms of treatment, *Social Work* 23 (1) (1978): 665–68.

Chapter 3
A Community Program for Child Care

J. Prentice Murphy

As the children's needs of any community are related to and interwoven closely with all the other social needs of the place, no definite start in the shaping up of a children's program can be made unless there is a careful inventory of all the community's social needs.

There should be a survey, so far as the children's end is concerned, of actual conditions, of needs and resources. Before the first step in the formation of a program is taken one should know of the different kinds of children needing care in the community, and how they are being provided for; whether there is a generalization of work by each agency with inefficient methods, or whether there is specialization and efficiency.

Some five years ago, with the opening of the trust funds of the Seybert Institution in Philadelphia, the trustees planned a careful study of the children's situation in the city before taking any steps in the creation of a new institution or agency for children. The things they found in Philadelphia, and which had been presented to them through a state committee that had considered children's conditions throughout Pennsylvania, are the things that probably exist in every community that fails to plan wisely and comprehensively for its future citizens. There was a multiplicity of children's institutions, most of which were well filled, all working independently of each other, and no one covering anything like a comprehensive part of the field. Certain groups of children were entirely uncared for, as for example, illegitimate children. Very young children under four or five were poorly provided for, but whole orphaned children, the smallest in number and the least pressing for care, were more than amply provided for. There was no coordination of work, no stimulation of ideas, no proposals for better methods of work, and an almost yearly request for new institutions to care for more children, gave the community the impression that although sheltering many children's organizations, Philadelphia was still far behind in providing adequate and complete care for those whose homes were unfit, or which had been broken up.

The Seybert trustees made a study, such as has been recommended above, covering the particular functions of every children's society in the city, of the provisions for the three general classes of children, and of that other and most necessary feature, the placement of such children in family homes.

With the needs and the resources for meeting them well plotted out, the first step on the part of the trustees was to make overtures to the Pennsylvania Children's Aid Society, an efficient child placing society in the community, for the creation of what has been called the Children's Bureau. This bureau, as was noted in the announcements issued at the time of its organization, was to centralize and focus the children's activities of the community in one place, and to strive to do for all children's agencies what an Associated Charities does for all charitable agencies in any given community. It was hoped also that the Bureau would be able to standardize investigations and methods of care, to arrange an extensive placing-out program by the institutions, this work if possible to be co-ordinated with the placing-out work of the Pennsylvania Children's Aid Society, to show that more institutions were not necessary, but in fact, fewer; that careful investigation work with each family problem would indicate less need for the separation of children and parents, less extension of institution care, and more emphasis on prevention.

The bureau was likewise to be a center of information about any local child problem, and was to maintain a group of experts qualified and equipped to diagnose any child problem, and to advise with those immediately concerned, upon it.

Shortly after its organization, the Pennsylvania Society for the Protection of Children from Cruelty joined the Executive Council or committee of the bureau, and became likewise responsible for its direction. Through this close working organization the three sustaining societies began very gradually to change their programs and to harmonize their work with that of the city. The same may be said for the work of the institutions and other children's societies co-operating through the bureau, but not directly represented on its board.

There are many communities in which institution care must be used for the present until the placing-out facilities have been extended. This work of extension of child placing can only be worked out definitely and helpfully when it is a part of the whole scheme of community child care. In Philadelphia institutions will be necessary for some time. They might exist indefinitely but for the progressive ideas now being proposed by the group immediately concerned with the Children's Bureau.

In the re-shifting of institution plans it was possible to arrange for better medical and physical care, for a more careful reception of children, for a quicker moving of institution populations, for a merging of work done by institutions so that there would not be an overlapping of one particular phase of work. The idea of the Bureau may be carried further so that in its council there will be an extensive representation of all the children's charities. This program has been concerned today solely with the care of children apart from their homes, and such as are on probation or under preventive supervision in their own homes. The community program must still be worked out for a wider use of the schools, for a more extensive development of play grounds, and for a tying up of the children's problem with the larger social problems of the community.

Last summer a few of the leading social agencies in Philadelphia shaped up an inventory of the more urgent present social needs for Philadelphia, with the results noted in another paper. It was not the first time that such a study had been made, but the changing conditions made a new one necessary. For special reference as to what the original community plan was as worked out by the Seybert trustees, the first Seybert Institution report, issued three years ago, is worth study. Certainly the planning of the whole job has given the children's field its proper emphasis. The community now knows of the needs for infant hygiene, baby saving work, and of greater and more extensive convalescent care; and is thus supplied with the facts (which in turn have received the widest publicity) for the prevention of some of the unwise charitable bequests devised for children's work in Philadelphia during the past six years.

It hardly seems possible or likely that seven millions of dollars will be left again for groups of children which the community now knows do not represent a serious problem. I am referring specifically [sic] to the Carson bequest of four millions for the founding of a college or school for orphaned or half-orphaned white Protestant girls between the ages of nine and thirteen, and also to the Ellis bequest of almost three millions for institutional care for dependent children. This money released for more necessary fields of work would make the children's situation in Pennsylvania much different from what it has been, and will continue to be, inevitably, for some time to come.

It is the responsibility of every intelligent social worker to be able to plan for his community as wisely and as comprehensively as the engineer plans when he starts to build a railroad or a shop. The contributing public will look increasingly to social workers for expert advice in this field. No social agency worthy of repute will continue in the future to work out a social problem without relating it to the work of the other children's societies about it.

To summarize the above, an efficient program for child care means:

(1) A study of conditions and of resources, both public and private.

(2) The federation of the children's activities so that they will meet community problems as one.

(3) A central bureau to standardize investigations, and to do the diagnosing work for the small agencies, thereby bringing about desired mergers.

(4) The confidential registration of all cases treated.

(5) The proper development of needed agencies, this including facilities for the care by public authorities of those dependent children whose condition involves long and costly treatment.

(6) Private societies for the care of such dependent children as do not fall within the classification of those referred to above.

(7) The gradual closing up of institutions, the adoption of the placing-out method in their stead.

(8) Adequate facilities for the care of the defective children, and for the training of certain of the delinquent children.

(9) Adequate Juvenile Court and probation provisions, and the proper correlation of this work with that of the private societies.

(10) A proper relation of the children's program with other social programs of the community, with a constant emphasis on the preventive side.

Reprinted from J. Prentice Murphy, A community program for child care, *National Conference on Social Welfare Proceedings* (1912).

Commentary

Ram A. Cnaan

John Prentice Murphy (1881–1936) attended the Wharton School of the University of Pennsylvania, Class of 1908, but did not graduate, choosing instead to become General Secretary of the Children's Bureau of Philadelphia. Murphy enjoyed a distinguished career in social work, including nine years as secretary of the Children's Aid Society in Boston (1911–20) and sixteen years as executive secretary of the Children's Bureau of Philadelphia and of the Seybert Institution (1920–36). He was president of the Child Welfare League of America from 1932 to 1934, and at the time of his death he was president-elect of the National Conference of Social Work. In 1934, the University of Pennsylvania honored him by conferring upon him the degree to which he would have been entitled if he had graduated with his class, that is, the B.S. in Econ., retroactively "as of" 1908.

The University of Pennsylvania School of Social Policy & Practice is one of the oldest social work programs in the world. This book celebrates the school's hundred years of social work education, and John Prentice Murphy is instrumental in this endeavor. The school's origins date to 1908 when a "Course of Training in Child Helping" was developed under the direction of the Children's Bureau of Philadelphia. J. Prentice Murphy, director of the Children's Bureau and a national leader in social services to children, was the program's director and Carl Kelsey, professor of sociology at the University of Pennsylvania, was consulting director. Unfortunately for Philadelphia and the school, two years later, Murphy accepted a job in Boston and left the city for a decade. However, upon his return to Philadelphia in 1920, he resumed his connections with the school as an instructor and member of various committees.

Murphy was one of the first to work on models of intervention and outcome assessment in social work. In an article in 1915, he and Ruth Lawton studied the practices and outcomes of child outplacement by the Boston Children's Aid Society. They found that the procedures mandated by the agency were rarely followed and the outcomes were less than promising.[1] Their findings led to the agency changing its practices and the field of child welfare becoming more research oriented.

One of his key assertions was that while we learn how to forecast societal trends, we know too little about individual behavior and change. In an article in *Time* magazine (June 23, 1930) about illegitimate children and policewomen, he was quoted as saying, "We cannot be strictly logical about human beings. We can prophesy with accuracy about masses of people—but not about individuals. Approximately 70,000 illegitimate children will be born in the U.S. in 1930, but no community can foretell who of its people are to enter this arena of suffering."

In the Depression Era, Murphy was one of the first to call for the federal government to take an active role in helping people in need. He testified before the congress and encouraged the federal government to come to the aid of the people. In a review article in *Time* (January 11, 1932) it is reported: "Executive Director J. Prentice Murphy of Philadelphia's Children's Bureau testified that 970,000 were out of work in his city, that people in some States would get no relief unless it came from the Federal Government." In many of his public appearances and writings, and irrespective of his illustrious career in many private agencies, J. Prentice Murphy was adamant that real welfare cannot come from private charities but must come from the federal government. He reasoned this viewpoint as many agencies are incapable of doing so, many communities have too few private charities, in large cities their funds were running low, private contributions were diminishing and unreliable, and only the federal government can channel funds to all parts of the country. This lesson from the Depression was lost on many of us after World War II, but Murphy's writing on this matter can still be relevant for social work today.

Murphy was a prolific author. In an era when few social workers engaged in academic writing, he continuously published, especially in the areas of child welfare and corrections. He was the editor of *New Values in Child Welfare* and *Postwar Progress in Child Welfare*. Among his many writing are the following articles in the *Annals of the American Academy of Political and Social Science*: "The Foster Care of Neglected and Dependent Children"; "What Can Be Accomplished Through Good Social Work in the Field of Illegitimacy?"; "Children in the New Deal"; and "The Juvenile Court at the Bar: A national Challenge."[2]

In many ways, John Prentice Murphy exemplifies what an ideal social worker is and ought to be. He worked with the neediest people of his time. He ran social services agencies that provided cutting-edge care. He advocated in popular media and in congress for social reform. He authored numerous academic publications including the one in this book. And, he was a respected lecturer in the Philadelphia School of Social Work in its early days. His legacy holds strong and serves as a compass for the current generation of social work educators at the University of Pennsylvania, School of Social Policy & Practice.

In 1936, *Social Service Review* informed its readership that "Prentice Murphy Leaves Us." In a short eulogy, the editor of the journal reports that on February 2, 1936, Murphy died of pneumonia at the young age of fifty-four when he was ready to embark on the task of presiding over the National Conference of Social Work. I end this commentary with the words of the editor of *Social Service Review*: "Mr. Murphy was greatly beloved by those who knew him. He was a spiritual leader, the social conscience, on whom many had come to rely."[3] In this spirit, we present one of his key publications.

Did he know that the school he served as its first director would become a social work powerhouse? Did he envision social work education so established and central to the profession a century later? We do not know the answers to these questions, but we do know that without his leadership and courage the Pennsylvania School of Social Work may have not come to be. Thank you John Prentice Murphy.

Notes

1. Ruth W. Lawton and J. Prentice Murphy, A study of results of a child-placing society, *Proceedings of the National Conference of Charities and Correction* (New York: Department of Child-Helping of the Russell Sage Foundation, 1915), 164–65.

2. J. Prentice Murphy and James H. S. Bossard, *New Values in Child Welfare* (Philadelphia: American Academy of Political and Social Science, 1925); Murphy and James H. S. Bossard, *Postwar Progress in Child Welfare* (Philadelphia: American Academy of Political and Social Science, 1930); The foster care of neglected and dependent children, *Annals of the American Academy of Political and Social Science* (May 1918): 117–30; What can be accomplished through good social work in the field of illegitimacy? *Annals of the American Academy of Political and Social Science* (November 1921): 129–35; Children in the New Deal, *Annals of the American Academy of Political and Social Science* (November 1934): 121–30; The juvenile court at the bar: A national challenge, *Annals of the American Academy of Political and Social Science* 145, Part 1: Law and Social Welfare (September 1929): 80–97.

3. Prentice Murphy leaves us, Editorial, *Social Service Review* 10 (1) (1936): 128 (photo p. 1).

Chapter 4
Avocational Guidance

Karl de Schweinitz

Every now and then during the last six weeks this letter has been mailed from the office of the New York School of Philanthropy to some one of the students in a special course for volunteers.

My Dear Miss. . . . . :
   We are following the field work of each student very closely and if we find a student's practical work is not likely to reach the standard required for our certificate, in the short period of training we are able to give, we are asking the student to resign from the course.
   We are doing this in a number of cases, and among several others we think that you are not especially fitted for this kind of work, and that it would be more profitable for you to devote your efforts to some other form of work. On this account we are asking you to return your card.

That is a significant letter. It marks the closing of one epoch in social work and the opening of another. It is the emancipation proclamation of the volunteer.

For years the people who have been making social work their avocation have been struggling for just the sort of recognition that this letter implies. That same atmosphere of prevarication which has been used to content women with being merely objects of chivalrous solicitude in masculine leisure has intentionally or unintentionally been permitted to pervade the world of avocational service, tempting its wayfarers to become lotus eaters, dabblers, dilettanti, and to be satisfied therewith. We have been sentimental about volunteers. We have given them credit where credit was not due. We have told them that we could not work without them and then in the next instant we have asked ourselves with a fear of showing unsophistication in the face of an assured negative, "Do you really believe in volunteers?"

Just as women have been under the necessity of demonstrating their fitness for admission to business and politics on an even footing with men, so have volunteers been obliged to prove their capacity for assuming all the rights and privileges of social work. This letter is the measure of their success. It is a letter of dismissal. In employment there may be opportunity for favoritism, but in discharge all men are equal. Moreover, this notice comes in a time of war to people who wish to offer their services to their country. Instead of being allowed to do this immediately, they have been told that they must enter a training class for volunteers, that they must attend twenty lectures, that they must complete three days of field work a week for ten weeks, and that they must do this to the satisfaction of their instructors.

Dismissal under such circumstances would not have been possible a few years ago. It is one thing to allow a volunteer gradually to lose her interest and to fade away slowly from social work, like a Cheshire cat in a leisurely mood; it is quite a different thing to discharge a volunteer because he or she is not making good. This has become possible only because social workers have learned through experience with volunteers what high standards can be expected of those who wish to make social work their avocation—standards that often are higher than those which many agencies require of their professional staff.

It is now antiquated and irrelevant to contrast the professional with the volunteer worker. We are all social workers, each striving to do the thing for which we are best fitted. Likewise is it short-sighted to speak about obtaining a large staff of volunteers as if that were an end in itself. The end is the job.

I wish, indeed, that we could abolish the words, professional and volunteer. They are not accurate terms. Salary has nothing to do with the quality and quantity of an individual's contribution to social work. A certain associated charity, for example, includes upon its list of volunteers the name of a man who has always been a professional social worker and excludes a woman who during all of her long connection with the society has not been on salary for even a day. What counts in social work as in anything else is the amount of time, thought, and ability that an individual expends upon the job. Those who know most about social work and who can do social work best, who regard social work as their vocation, will, whether professional or volunteer, form the nucleus of every social agency. Obviously, the men and women whose energies are not exclusively applied to social work, who consider it rather as an avocation, will expect direction and leadership from those who are devoting themselves wholly to the task. Vocational and avocational explains this relationship more nearly accurately than does professional and volunteer.

Now that avocational workers have shown themselves willing to submit to the possibility of discharge, now that they have emancipated themselves from coddling and have proven themselves capable of taking a definite part in the organization of social work, they are entitled to the same measure of guidance in the choosing of their tasks that is afforded the vocational worker. Why not avocational guidance? The avocational workers are demanding that we consider not their convenience and their feelings, but the job. They recognize that the important thing is not who does the work but that the work is done. Why not, therefore, assign them to service upon the basis of what the task requires and what they are able and prepared to give?

Case work uses more avocational workers than any other form of social work. Where, for example, does the charity organization society as a typical case working agency find them essential? Where does it find them to be, if not essential, at least of great importance?

The friendly visitor is necessary to family work—in fact to almost all case work. But experience has shown that the friendly visitor is most successful when she has not made the investigation and when she does not give relief. Her relationship with the family must be a personal, not a professional one, that of the neighbor running in from across the street, not that of the doctor calling to diagnose and cure. Inherently, friendly visiting is an avocational service.

The case conference is an inevitable part of charity organization. Case work is the most intimate of all professions. So vitally does it affect the human beings with which it deals, and through them all society, that its practice becomes possible only with the support of an intelligent and ardently interested body of citizens. The case conference, therefore, must have avocational workers upon its membership and not for this reason alone. They are needed also to represent to the vocational workers the attitude of the lay public. This is a function that transcends the decision of the individual family problem. The great contribution of avocational workers as members of case conferences is the subtle influence which their point of view expressed week after week has upon the work of the district visitors.

A certain organization has a committee on home economics. The home economists upon this committee might be called the vocational workers and the case workers the avocational workers. Recently the committee discussed ways of educating the women of a tenement neighborhood in the preparation of budgets. The home economists were inclined to talk in terms of calories and proteins until the avocational workers (in this instance the case workers), being themselves unable to think in that language, pointed out that technicalities would have to be abandoned for the common ground of what the average person knows about the things he eats.

In much the same way the avocational members of case committees interpret the public to the vocational workers, just as, also, they interpret the vocational workers to the public. Moreover, as soon as they appreciate what good case work is they insist upon securing the sort of vocational workers who are able to achieve the standards they desire to see maintained.

Lack of money will doubtless always prevent the employment of as many case workers as ideally would be desirable. The use of avocational workers, therefore, makes possible on occasion an intensive work which otherwise would not be achieved. In many other ways they supplement the activities of the vocational workers.

While when organizations are being started or when they are being reorganized avocational clerical work has been imperative, it is not, in charity organization societies at least, likely to develop into a long continued service. The clerical tasks done by avocational workers are more often a matter of convenience than of necessity for the district visitor. Clerical work should rather be considered as introductory to the various forms of avocational work just discussed.

To recapitulate: avocational workers are essential as friendly visitors and as case conference members. In case work, particularly in intensive case work, they are important while clerical work is for them largely a means of education preparatory to other activities. With an understanding, then, of the relation of the avocational worker to the various tasks involved in helping families, avocational guidance now becomes possible.

Avocational guidance at present is so haphazard as frequently to be non-existent.

John Jones after hearing a talk upon social work by Thomas Brown, of the charity organization society, greets the speaker at the platform after the lecture and asks whether there is any way in which he can be of use. "Oh yes, Mr. Jones," replies Mr. Brown, "wouldn't you like to come to our case conference tomorrow?"

Of all places in social work, the case conference should almost always be the last to which to introduce a prospective avocational worker. To him the case conference will mean nothing. It may discourage him altogether. The avocational worker is supposed to be an intelligent representative of the lay public. Unless he has some foundation of experience in case work he will have neither the courage nor the background to interpret the public to the vocational worker, for an interpreter must know two languages, the language of the speaker and that of the auditor.

What Mr. Brown ought to say to Mr. Jones, prospective avocational worker, is, "Miss White, our superintendent of case work, will be glad to see you tomorrow afternoon."

And when Mr. Jones calls to see Miss White she should remember that he deserves as much consideration as would a vocational worker, and that he must be placed where he will be most useful even if that means in some other organization than her own.

She should bear in mind, also, that from the point of view of social work the world has two kinds of people, those who are interested in dealing with things and people in the mass and those who are interested in dealing with individuals. The former will not find in case work their niche. They will be happier with some organization devoted solely to the passage of legislation or the education of people in groups. It is useless to attempt to employ either as an avocational or vocational worker any one who does not like to deal with people one by one and who does not feel that that is the way in which he or she can be of greatest service.

Attention must also be paid to the experience, to the ability, and to the interest of the prospective avocational worker. Thus a person of action who cannot appreciate the value of time spent in discussion should not be assigned to a committee engaged in a statistical study. Again there come to social agencies people without any practical experience who at the same time are anxious to do something that in their opinion is definite and practical. Do not attempt to train such persons surreptitiously by placing them upon case committees. This is particularly true in dealing with a certain type of young woman who has been attending lectures and classes until she yearns for something that means work, not education. Assign her to the simpler kinds of visiting-carrying allowances, taking children to dispensaries; or, if there is clerical work to be done, let her do that. But do not manufacture work for avocational workers. If you have nothing for them to do, perhaps somebody else has. No longer do we tolerate such employment for vagrants as carrying bricks from one pile to another and back again. Why, then, should we practice a similar subterfuge upon an avocational worker? Yet, I suspect that this is not infrequently done. I wonder whether, in the desire to establish a record for vocational service, district visitors are not tempted to develop more avocational tasks than the work really demands. In doing so are we not perhaps keeping many people from useful work either elsewhere in our own agency or with some other organization?

On the other hand, there are certain office tasks which if not performed by avocational workers would not be performed at all, with a resultant loss in the efficiency of the district visitor. I have been told, for example, of one avocational worker whose criticisms of case records have greatly stimulated the case work of a certain district visitor.

We are handicapped in the making of any pronouncement upon avocational guidance by the lack of collected experience. There is need for material upon which we can base plans both for placing and for training avocational workers. Mr. Porter R. Lee suggested that the experiment of keeping a case record of an avocational worker be attempted. This case record would have an appropriate face card, showing the background, experience, and affiliation of the worker. The record itself would begin with the first interview, telling the impression made upon the district visitor by the avocational worker, what task was assigned to her and why; then it would show the history of their subsequent relations.

Of course there are difficulties in this. Yet beginnings are being made. Only a few weeks ago in a certain agency, not the C.O.S. by the way, I saw an admirable method of keeping record of the characteristics and assigned activities of avocational workers. We have had, moreover, enough experience to know that training is essential for the avocational worker. Even the young woman who has had a surfeit of education will be reconciled to a certain amount of class work or individual tutoring if it is plainly supplementary to practical work.

Certainly, before avocational workers engage extensively in case work they should understand its philosophy. Once they have grasped the outlines of this philosophy they will be able to work more intelligently; they will understand the reason for the method that they are asked to follow. It is not fair to expect the avocational worker, solely through the visiting of two or three homes, to attain a point of view that is the development of the experience of many case workers with the problems of many thousands of families.

Give her some inkling of the philosophy of case work. If it does not answer the questions that arise in her mind, if it does not meet the test of actual conditions, then let her abandon it. But start her out at least with a working formula.

Training in method and introduction to our point of view is important for every avocational worker. There are, however, doubtless many who need it in less degree than do the majority of those who enter service with us. I think, for example, of one type of woman who needs little training, for she already instinctively understands our methods. She is seldom to be found in our large cities. Her home is likely to be in a town. Her children are now grown and she is past middle age. Although in comfortable circumstances, she has for a large part of her life done her own housework. She has been a good practical mother. When she visits her married daughter she is likely to busy herself darning the curtains or upholstering the davenport. Her common sense prevents her from giving advice about the care of the children, but their sweaters and mittens are evidence of where the product of her needle goes.

She is the true democrat. To her the butcher and baker are not tradespeople, but Mr. Brown and Mr. Smith. She is genuinely interested in the snatch of conversation she has with them as they serve her before her door. Of course she does her own buying. Doubtless she has traveled widely. Probably she has been across both the Atlantic and our own continent. Yet, whereas such experience has given to the aristocrats of the town a veneer and a mannerism which mark them as apart from their neighbors, she, having more real culture perhaps than they, is still one with the people of the town.

Because she is welcome in every household she is unconscious of class distinction. Knowing the humble origin of even the wealthiest family in town, she is not impressed by any show which they may make and is, therefore, the more respected by them. She has kept the common touch. Instinctively the family which she may visit feels this. In one conversation her simple, friendly interest has frequently learned more about the household, its past, its relationships, its troubles, its hopes, its prospects, than we with all our method.

Her self, the product of years spent in the daily performance of household tasks and of acquaintance with many kinds of people in whom she has always seen the good, tells the family that here is a woman whom they can receive as an equal and with whom they can talk as to an intimate acquaintance. Such a woman is, I think, the ideal friendly visitor, the true democrat of whom there are few indeed, for they do not develop in our segregated city and suburban life.

If it is of women that I have largely spoken, that is because more women than men are engaged in avocational service. The proportion is probably as two-thirds are to one-third. Considering the engrossing demands of business, perhaps this is not a serious disproportion. We need more men for avocational work, however, and I believe that more can be secured.

Why not, for instance, take advantage of the movement for home defense? Home defense not only demands military preparedness but also requires the strengthening of the sinews of citizenship. Fundamentally, Germany's power has been her people. She has been able to accomplish what she has done largely because she has successfully nourished their stamina and physique. What would happen to us if we limited our home defense to drill and the manual of arms? Is it not essential that every family which is in danger of losing its moral or physical vitality be saved from this disaster? What work can a man do that would be more important than home defense of this kind? Moreover, such work is not without its own reward. In a speech upon "The Personal Relation in Industry" John D. Rockefeller, Jr., said: "Heretofore the chief executives of important industrial corporations have been selected largely because of their capacity as organizers or financiers. The time is rapidly coming, however, when the important qualification for such positions will be a man's ability to deal successfully and amicably with labor."

The appreciation and understanding of the point of view of the families with which case work brings one into contact is precisely what is required for the development of the ability to which Mr. Rockefeller refers. Furthermore, case work is an opportunity to get out of the rut of one's own routine, the rut of acquaintance with the same kind of people. It means an introduction to a new part of the world, a world that is always interesting and which always challenges.

An appeal of some such sort as—this contains the four elements that are needed to cause a man to engage in avocational work—the element of fear, the element of importance (the importance of the work), the element of self-interest, and the element of adventure. One element that should be omitted from every effort to attract men to avocational work is the element of sentimentality. Sentimentality, for that matter, will not attract any greatly desirable avocational worker.

A friend of mine who spent several weeks in a hospital had during his stay twenty-five different nurses. All but one were efficient, capable young women. He asked them why they had chosen their vocation. All but one told him that it was the kind of work they liked and that it was an interesting way of earning a living. Only one had entered the hospital in order to nurse fevered brows and to smooth the pillows of the sick. She was the only one who did not make good. The kind of person who is likely to be most successful in social work is so well balanced and has such a fund of common sense and innate sympathy that the least departure from what is true sentiment will make her distrustful of the real value of the work that is being done. Beware, therefore, of too emotional an appeal.

Let us remember, also, that social work has not a corner in altruism. No profession has. Altruism, like religion, should be a part of everyone's life. No matter what one's job, whether it be the collection of ashes or the instruction of the young, it should always be selected because it offers a means for the expression of one's ideals. Altruism should not be the determining factor in the selection of social work as an avocation, any more than that it should be the determining factor in every act of one's life. The real reason for making social work one's avocation is interest in social work and the liking of the details of the job. The person who enters social work from this point of view, who makes social work his hobby, will be the most permanent social worker.

And is it not true that social work is the most fascinating job in the world? Is there anything more gripping than the problem of human relationships? Is there anything more interesting than human beings? Who, indeed, would exchange for the responsibilities of a halo the plea sure of doing the thing one likes?

Reprinted from Karl de Schweinitz, Avocational guidance, *National Conference on Social Welfare Proceedings* (1917).

Commentary

Ira Colby

Setting the Context

Karl de Schweinitz lived a renaissance life. Following a short stint as a journalist for the *Philadelphia Public Ledger*, in 1911 he began a passionate lifelong career in social services when he became executive secretary of the Pennsylvania Tuberculosis Society. Later, he served as general secretary of the Family Society of Philadelphia (1918–30) and as director of the University of Pennsylvania School of Social Work on two separate occasions, 1933–36 and 1938–42. Following consulting positions with the Social Security Administration and the American Council on Education, de Schweinitz joined the social work faculty at UCLA, from where he eventually retired. A prolific writer, de Schweinitz explored a variety of topics including civil liberties, health, housing, industrial and labor relations, international affairs, race relations, recreation, social insurance, social work, and unemployment. Not one to stay away from controversy, his 1929 children's book on reproduction, *Growing Up: How We Become Alive, Are Born and Grow*, is listed on the Mountain & Plains Booksellers Association banned booklist (http://www.mountainsplains.org/bandf.htm).

On the surface his 1917 paper, "Avocational Guidance," presented at the 44th Conference of Social Work, created a dialogue around the role of and the relationship between the volunteer and the professional. His paper was included in the Conference's session, "The Family and Community, Volunteer Service" (*Proceedings*, 118–25). But to fully appreciate de Schweinitz's comments we must consider the context, the zeitgeist, of the period.

Two months prior to the opening of the National Conference of Social Work Conference in Pittsburgh, Pennsylvania, the United States Congress had declared war on Germany. In his address to Congress asking for a declaration of war, President Woodrow Wilson stated, "It will involve the immediate addition to the armed forces of the United States . . . at least five hundred thousand men, who should, in my, opinion, be chosen upon the principle of universal liability to service, and also the authorization of subsequent additional increments of equal force so soon as they may be needed and can be handled in training" (Wilson, 1917). Wilson's clarion call was heeded by Congress, although fifty members voted against the declaration of war, including Jeanette Rankin, a social worker and the first woman elected to the United States House of Representatives.[1]

To achieve victory, a military mindset was needed to directly support the war effort. As Wilson stressed to Congress, there was an immediate need to increase the armed forces with a half million soldiers who would leave their day-to-day obligations to serve in the war effort. By the summer of 1918, more then one million so-called American "doughboys" were in Europe (Stallings 1964; Meade 2002; Keene 2001). Certainly the war would impact social welfare, but to what level no one knew or completely understood. As William Cross, General Secretary for the National Conference of Social Work, wrote in the 1917 *Conference Proceedings*, "Who could foretell the transformation of social movements and organizations, and their new relationships, under circumstances of war?" (*Proceedings*, iii)

With the war effort at its beginning stage, what then was the import of de Schweinitz's comments? Why would one of the era's great social welfare leaders raise in discussion matters related to staff as an avocational or vocational pursuit? Was de Schweinitz directly concerned with the growing tensions between professionals and volunteers or was he hinting to the repercussions that a massive "draft" of men and women into the military and its support services would have on social welfare services?

Overview of de Schweinitz's Paper

The purpose of the de Schweinitz paper is somewhat ambiguous at its outset. There is a hint that he will discuss suitability and appropriateness issues among volunteers. Abruptly, de Schweinitz redirects the audience to consider the working relationship between the professional and the volunteer. He builds an argument that supports the strengthening of the volunteer's role and argues that the terms "professional" or "volunteer" be discarded because "we are all social workers" (*Proceedings*, 119). de Schweinitz felt that the differentiation between the two was based on the type of work performed rather than the title or salary for the worker (119). He asserts that the workers should be categorized as either "vocational" (professional) or "avocational" (volunteer). The avocational worker, de Schweinitz puts forth, can provide critical basic services—they "are essential as friendly visitors"—which in turn frees the vocational worker to delve into other matters (120). He believes that vocational workers do not know how to appropriately or effectively use avocational staff; they are assigned tasks for which they are not prepared rather then attempting to assess the attributes the volunteer offers a client or organization.

De Schweinitz somewhat apologetically notes his references to the avocational worker as women, noting "more women than men are engaged in avocational service" but goes on to say that "we need more men for avocational work" (*Proceedings*, 124). This reference midway through the paper recognizes the critical juncture that gender equality had reached by 1917. With the war effort on the nation's doorstep, women's traditional role as a "home" person or volunteer was about to significantly change. The war, out of necessity, provided opportunities for women that in the past had been the principal domain of men. Women moved into factories including the dangerous work of building munitions and ships, they took on greater importance in the medical arena, they moved into journalism, and many became conductors on trams and buses (Zeinert 2001).

The war, as feminist Carrie Chapman Catt noted in 1914, "falls on the women most heavily, and more so now than ever before" (Goldstein 2001). At the end of the war, Harriot Stanton Blatch (1918) argued that the positive role women played during the war should not go unrecognized. Without a doubt, the war provided women a significant national venue to demonstrate their abilities and in 1918 ultimately resulted in voting being extended to women (Zeinert 2001).

De Schweinitz concludes his remarks by noting that altruism is a common denominator for many life experiences and not the sole province of social work. He goes on to note that altruism plays little to no role in selecting social work as an avocation but "liking the details of the job" will sustain a person's long-term interest and involvement in the profession (*Proceedings*, 125).

In summary, de Schweinitz's position is threefold: first, avocational workers, whose work can augment vocational workers' efforts, should be viewed as social workers; second, avocational workers' activities are valuable to the client; and third, vocational workers must identify and fit the avocational worker's particular strengths and potential contributions to a specific client and/or organizational need, not vice versa.

Alternative Perspective

There is little room to disagree with de Schweinitz's central thesis that avocational workers are important to the social services enterprise and that their expertise and potential contributions should be matched with clients' needs. Today, at the outset of the twenty-first century, social work has matured into a complex profession, supported by more than a century worth of experiences in both education and practice. The literature is filled with robust discussions around volunteers, their significance to social welfare agencies, strategies to recruit, and mechanisms to maintain an active volunteer base. The notion of civic responsibility is carried out through volunteer work and is embraced through formal national programs that encourage and recognize volunteers, such as Points of Lights Foundation (www.pointsoflight) to the common university-based service learning programs (www.compact.org). We can also reason that there are distinct differences between professionals and volunteers, often influenced by legal considerations and state licensure laws.

At the time de Schweinitz delivered his paper in 1917, however, the social work profession was still in its infancy (Herrick and Stuart 2005); the reliance on volunteers and friendly visitors was still fresh in the profession's memory bank; university-based degree granting social work educational programs had only begun a few short years earlier; and the Association of Training Schools for Professional Social Work, the first university member association for social work education programs, was organized in 1919, two years following de Schweinitz's paper (Kendall 2002). Considering his remarks solely in the context of an evolving profession, we can appreciate his plea to reconsider the volunteer as an avocational worker who too is a member of a fledging profession and one who should be treated with respect and appreciation for their contributions.

On the other hand, de Schweinitz may have been indirectly encouraging his colleagues to reassess the volunteer's role given the war's impact at the local community. He may have understood that the war effort would require an infusion of hundreds of thousands of individuals into the military and scores of others into supporting roles. de Schweinitz may have conceded that the war would severely deplete volunteer pools and that social services would be competing with the national government and industrial sector's human capitol needs, which were being crafted within nationalistic patriotic themes. Considering these points, de Schweinitz may have concluded that the only way to maintain a minimal social services voluntary pool was for social services organizations and their professionals to dramatically modify their ways of interacting with volunteers.

Was de Schweinitz that clever to foretell the future and the staffing predicament that social services could face? Was he reconceptualizing an extremely politically sensitive issue within the guise of a social services matter? Did he believe that framing the looming volunteer crisis as a threat to the survival of social services would have a hollow ring, as did the vote of the fifty members of Congress who opposed the war? Did he recognize that challenging the war effort could have a reverse negative effect on social services?

Or, was de Schweinitz simply addressing a nagging organizational issue of the time, one that continues to plague the social welfare community today? Did he really deem that volunteers and professionals shared an equal sphere of expertise? Was de Schweinitz's opinion solely influenced by his observations and direct experiences with professionals and volunteers?

We certainly do not know the answers to these questions, though we can state with relative confidence that Karl de Schweinitz brought to the table a growing staffing issue shared by social welfare agencies. While his 1917 presentation was somewhat disjointed, his comments should prompt today's social work community to recognize the constant mandate to strengthen the relationships and interactions between volunteers and professionals. Our responsibility to continually attend to and assess the relationships between volunteers and professionals is a direct result of two client-centered imperatives: first, we do this because agencies will benefit from a growing volunteer pool; and second and most important, we work to clarify and enhance the roles of both professionals and volunteers with the ultimate objective to provide quality, competent and ethical client services.

Notes

1. A member of the Republican Party, Jeanette Rankin was gerrymandered out of her House district as a result of her vote against entering World War I. In 1918, she mounted an unsuccessful campaign to represent Montana in the U.S. Senate. During the ensuing years she was active in the Women's International League for Peace and Freedom, the National Consumers' League, and the American Civil Liberties Union. She was again elected to the House of Representatives in 1940 and was the sole member of Congress to vote against the 1941 declaration of war on Japan. Prior to her vote that day in 1941, Rankin said on the House floor, "As a woman, I can't go to war and I refuse to send anyone else" (Cronau 1919, 289; Felder 1999, 82–86; Stuhler 2000, 139; Yellin 2004, 281).

References

Blatch, Harriot Stanton (1918). *Mobilizing Woman Power*. New York: Woman's Press.

Cronau, Rudolf (1919). *Woman Triumphant: The Story of Her Struggles for Freedom, Education, and Political Rights*. New York: R. Cronau.

Felder, Deborah G. (1999). *A Century of Women: The Most Influential Events in Twentieth-Century Women's History*. New York: Citadel Press.

Goldstein, Joshua S. (2001). *War and Gender: How Gender Shapes the War System and Vice Versa*. London: Cambridge University Press.

Herrick, John and Paul H. Stuart (2005). *Encyclopedia of Social Welfare History in North America*. Thousand Oaks, Calif.: Sage.

Keene, Jennifer D. (2001). *Doughboys, the Great War, and the Remaking of America*. Baltimore: Johns Hopkins University Press.

Kendall, Katherine A. (2002). *Council on Social Work Education: Its Antecedents and First Twenty Years.* Alexandria, Va.: Council on Social Work Education.

Meade, Gary (2002). *The Doughboys: America and the First World War.* New York: Overlook Press.

Proceedings of the National Conference of Social Work (1917). 44th annual session, Pittsburgh, Pennsylvania, June 6–13.

Stallings, Laurence (1964). *The Doughboys: The Story of the AEF, 1917–1918.* New York: Popular Library.

Stuhler, Barbara (2000). *For the Public Record: A Documentary History of the League of Women Voters.* Westport, Conn.: Greenwood Press.

Wilson, Woodrow (1917). *War Messages.* 65th Cong., 1st Sess., Senate Doc. 5, no. 7264. Washington, D.C.

Yellin, Emily (2004). *Our Mothers' War: American Women at Home and at the Front During World War II.* New York: Free Press.

Zeinert, Karen (2001). *Those Extraordinary Women of World War One.* Brookfield, Conn.: Millbrook Press.

Chapter 5
Personality in Social Work

Porter R. Lee

The one qualification for successful social work, universally recognized as indispensable, is a good personality. For support of this sweeping statement the inquirer is referred to any executive seeking a candidate for a vacancy on his staff. Good personality. What do we mean by it? When we test the qualifications of a candidate we ask: Is he tactful? Can he work with other people? Is he dependable? Has he poise? Has he personal magnetism? Is he temperamental? And—the ultimate, invariable, all-inclusive test—has he a sense of humor? If he rates 100 per cent in all of these qualifications, he may be nonexistent, but he would seem to be, according to the current philosophy of selecting personnel, so far a perfect social worker. The search for good personality in candidates for social work reflects something more than a preference on the part of appointing officers for new associates who will be agreeable to work with. It is a recognition of the fact that the tasks of social work demand in their performance something more than technical proficiency. They present themselves to the social worker very largely in the guise of human personality; and they can be understood and performed only by those who have a gift for human relationships.

In active human affairs few programs carry conviction through their own intrinsic merit. They are accepted by constituencies chiefly because they are presented through the medium of personalities who carry conviction. In general, men are inspired less by facts and philosophy than by facts and philosophy presented to them by an inspiring individual. We are influenced in our standards and modes of conduct less by principle and precept than by principle and precept interpreted by personalities who beget confidence. Public support is enlisted for new movements less by the inherent merit of such movements than by conviction inspired by the magnetism of their proponents. An overburdened spirit will relieve its stress by confiding, not in one who is willing to listen, but in one who will listen with understanding. At heart, most of the tasks of social work involve stimulating change in entrenched attitudes, modification in beliefs, redirection of effort, alteration in the values ordinarily attached to the process of living. The most potent agency for this aspect of the task of social work is the interplay of personality upon personality. Settled conviction, rooted prejudice, entrenched habit, established routine—these yield to a variety of influences, but to none so readily as to the influence of man with man.

Where personality counts. At what strategic points in the administration of social work does success hinge chiefly upon the qualities of human personality and their expression? In the last analysis, all social work is concerned with the adjustment of individuals to their environments. This is most conspicuously true of the various forms of social case work. Strictly speaking, however, other forms of social work are also concerned with this problem. We seek social legislation for the purpose of modifying the environment of the individual in ways that will make his adjustment easier. We develop group effort in order to add to the environment elements which may enrich the life of all. We conduct research in order to have a basis for understanding the conditions of social life, and ultimately in order to modify them intelligently.

The adjustment of the individual to his environment as a general statement of the function of the social case worker suggests an intimately personal relationship. It involves two important elements. The first is a knowledge of human personality and its characteristic difficulties in social life. The second is that peculiar power of so conducting one's self with respect to another that assistance offered him in his own effort at adjustment will not only seem to him both authoritative and acceptable, but will in no way usurp his own judgment and responsibility. The most successful social workers are those who have, in addition to a thorough knowledge of human personality and of the processes of adjustment, such equipment of personal qualities as will inspire in their clients a disposition to trust their leadership. This is the one phase of social case work which is uniformly present in every case work experience. It is the first strategic point at which the success of the social worker depends largely upon personality.

The adjustment of the individual to his environment involves a knowledge of environment and its possibilities for the individual. It involves also an ability to work effectively with environmental factors. What is environment? The theorists are not agreed. For one engrossed in the problem of living, however, it has some practical aspects. It is a home. It is a school. It is a job. It is recreation. It is literature. It is a street, shops, laws, a hospital, the ideas of others, books, lectures, newspapers, conversation. It is the complete category of persons, things, experiences outside one's self. However defective this conception of environment may be from the scientific point of view, it has practical implications for those of us who are trying to adjust ourselves.

It has equally practical implications for the social worker. The adjustment of an individual to his environment with the help of a social worker means practically such modifications in his life as changes in his relationship to school or to job, a new neighborhood to live in, new forms of recreation, contact with medical agencies for specific services, training for new occupational or cultural outlets. To the social worker, the environment of the client presents itself through the medium of personality. In his efforts to be of service to his client through the modification of environment, his client's home is a group of parents, brothers, and sisters. His school is a teacher. His job is an employer. His recreation comes through a librarian, a club leader, a scout-master. He achieves health or hygienic living through his use of a physician or a nurse. In so far as the successful adjustment of a client demands a different relationship with these persons, the case worker's success depends not only upon his skill in suggesting the right modifications, but also upon his power to win parent, teacher, employer to a new interest in his client.

The importance of this personality aspect of environment cannot be too strongly emphasized. Success in dealing with it puts upon the social worker demands which cannot be met merely through ingenuity in devising for clients paper programs of saner living. It calls upon all of the resources of personality which the case worker can muster.

Leaving social case work for the field of community leadership, the importance of personality is equally apparent. Community leadership as a function of social work is concerned sometimes with public support for legislation, sometimes with the promotion of a greater degree of cooperative effort on the part of social agencies, sometimes with the galvanizing of an apathetic public attitude into live interest in social problems, sometimes with the organization of an entire community in the financial support of its social work. There was a period in the recent history of American social work when it was believed that to secure effective public action with reference to any evil nothing more was needed than to publish the facts. More recently, however, the conviction has grown that facts, even when accompanied by their social interpretation, do not necessarily lead to effective activity. So far have we swung from this rather passive form of community leadership that in some of our activities we have adopted such phraseology of the market place as "selling social work to the public," "putting the program across," etc. Repugnant as this phraseology is to many social workers as applied to social work, and I confess I wince when I hear it, it nevertheless implies recognition that effective community leadership must reach and influence human beings. This again is a task in the performance of which the most important process is the interplay of personality upon personality. In general, the degree of response which social groups make to proposals for community action is determined less by the inherent merit of those proposals than by the impression produced by the personalities of those who essay community leadership.

I should like to present a somewhat different problem as a fourth aspect of the task of the social worker in which personality plays a leading part. This is a by-product of organization. There are almost no instances of the individual practice of social work apart from organizations. Practically all social workers are employees of agencies. There are, of course, many places in which the complete staff of a social agency consists of one person, but most of us are working under supervisors or are ourselves supervisors. The efficiency of an organization is determined by many factors, none of which is more important than morale. Morale is a quality of group activity which is the expression of the relationship of the members of the group to each other and to their group organization. What determines the quality of the morale in a particular organization? In part, the conviction of the whole group of employees that the work of the organization is worth while. In part, the consciousness of the employees that their participation in the work of the organization is valued. How are conviction and consciousness such as these developed? Their development depends mainly upon the quality of the relationship which exists among all of the members of the group organization.

The most important factors in determining the quality of this relationship are those who occupy positions of authority. Organization in itself is a depersonalizing procedure. As a process it implies the establishment of routine for handling many matters which would otherwise be settled by the persons concerned through spontaneous discussion and decision. Organization may develop a smoothly running machine. A smoothly running machine in the sphere of administration does not necessarily imply an impersonal experience, but this possibility is always present. Whatever tests of efficiency may be legitimate for other fields of human activity, we must retain as a test for social work the degree of spiritual satisfaction which it yields to those who are concerned with it, whether as clients, as professional workers, as volunteers, as contributors, or as citizens. We have already suggested that the most important tasks of social work are tasks which call for the investment of personality. We shall not realize our fullest return from this investment unless the agencies of social work are so organized as to draw from the rank and file of social workers their fullest contribution to the morale of the movement. The basis of this contribution is maintenance within social agencies of a fine quality of personal relationship among their personnel. For the development of such a relationship, the duties of the rank and file of workers must appear not merely as assigned tasks, but as opportunities for creative contribution to a cause in which they have faith. Too often the employees, from the executive to the office boy, have no means of knowing whether their work is acceptable to their organization, except by the impersonal process of inference from the fact that they have not been fired. No staff will contribute its best under such circumstances. The responsibility for the development of morale is general throughout the profession; but, we may add, it rests most heavily upon executives and supervisors. We may take this responsibility as a fourth phase of social work in which personality is an outstanding factor.

Personality in the record of social work. What has been the success of social work with respect to the personality aspects of its task? If these aspects are as important as I have suggested, social work could hardly have written so impressive a record of success without substantial achievement on the side of personality. Like all movements born of a recognition of human need and carried out in an attempt to minister to it, social work has had its prophets. Its history written in books, in the Proceedings of this Conference, in more prosy annual reports, and revealed in vivid, if unrecorded, experience with the older leaders of our profession whose memory is treasured by many of us still living is largely a history of the achievements of personalities, some of them outstanding, some of them relatively unknown. The outstanding character of some personalities is in itself evidence of the part which personality plays in active affairs. Within recent years in social work we may seem to have had fewer such than formerly. This has been interpreted in some places as evidence that personality is playing a part of decreasing importance in social work. To some observers, also, the same tendency is indicated in our rapid development of technical methods and in the wider ramifications of organization in our field. Technique and organization have been necessary developments. Social work could not have met the challenge of a complicated modern social life without them, and if it is to make its greatest contribution to human welfare, these technical developments must be carried much farther.

This does not necessarily suggest the mechanizing of social work. Increase in our power of accomplishment increases our responsibility for high standards. I do not believe that we shall ever accept a substitute for the power of personality in our professional equipment. On the contrary, the remarkable development of organization and technical methods has given us new respect for human personality and has reinforced our traditional belief that it is indispensable to any social work worthy of the name.

Nevertheless, I doubt if we have been sufficiently aware of the extent to which our most highly perfected professional effort has been wasted effort because it has not sufficiently reckoned with the personal equation. There is, in my judgment, no more tragic form of waste than the waste of professional skill which occurs when the person in whose behalf it is exerted fails to make the maximum use of it. A physician brings to bear upon the need of his patient a professional judgment which is the product of a long period of education and long experience in studying and treating human ills. Each patient he treats is receiving the benefit of this investment of himself in his professional development. Over and over again this investment is barren of return because the patient does not follow the suggestions of the physician. Social workers experience constantly a similar lack of return on their own professional investment. To each task which the social worker undertakes he brings to bear the product of his total training and experience. Over and over again the result is less than it deserves to be because client or community does not follow his lead.

In the old days—gone forever let us hope—such failure could be covered by ascribing to the client an unwillingness to cooperate, or to the community a state of backwardness with which no human skill could successfully deal. Let us concede that no permanent improvement is possible in any individual or in any community unless individual or community does the lion's share of the work in his own behalf. It still remains true that failure to achieve the success which the professional skill of the social worker deserves frequently results from his own inability to reinforce a sound program of procedure with that art of human relationships which alone wins from human beings wholehearted response to stimulus from the outside. The waste for which such failure is responsible is the more tragic when contrasted with the brilliant total record of social work.

To this form of waste in the use of professional skill we may add another, which results from the same failure to develop the art of human relationships. This is the waste which occurs when, in the face of imperative need for concerted action, social workers find it difficult or impossible to agree among themselves. Differences of opinion, differences in general point of view, are not only inevitable, but desirable, particularly in those fields whose scientific development is only just beginning. In order to reduce this waste which is the product of disagreement, it is not necessary that disagreements be eliminated, but only that they be discussed and reckoned with on a high level without bitterness, without personal feeling, without that intensification of prejudice which in intellectual matters is too likely to be the product of a self-defensive attitude.

No profession makes heavier demands upon the personality of its practitioners than social work. No profession should be—no profession is—able to reveal to the world a greater measure of success in the personal aspects of human relationships. Nevertheless, I suggest that in all soberness we recognize rifts among groups in this Conference in so far as they have developed distrust, personal antagonisms, and a lack of professional cohesion for what they really are: evidences of our failure in the art of human relationships, in the practice of which we should be preeminent among the professions.

The development of personality for social work. To what extent is it possible for social workers to train themselves deliberately for the personality requirements of their professional tasks? Continuing success in social work implies more than growing technical proficiency. It implies growth also in the scope and usefulness of those personal traits which the tasks of social work peculiarly need. So far as I know, however, such development is usually a by-product of experience. Few educational projects are ever formulated for the direct purpose of developing the personalities of students, except on the purely intellectual side. Furthermore, doubt is often expressed whether the deliberate development of personality through any organized method of education is possible. We hear it suggested that, like poets, good personalities are born and not made. It is suggested further that the growth of self-consciousness in human relations which may seem inevitable in any direct effort to educate personality implies a contradiction in terms. It would tend to make artificial a form of expression whose usefulness depends upon its spontaneity and lack of self-consciousness.

We may agree that these difficulties are formidable, but we can hardly be content with a negative answer to this general question. What are the facts? We have seen that social work deals with situations which at heart involve problems of personality. We have seen that success in dealing with these situations calls for an unusual personal equipment. We have seen, further, that a considerable part of our failure to realize all of the potential results of our programs is due in large measure to failure in the personal aspects of our professional work. Furthermore, we are recruiting annually younger men and women whom we send into positions in the field of social work where we expect them to grapple with situations involving these very elements. Through schools, through apprentice-training, through association with older and wiser leaders in the field we are equipping them with a scientific understanding of our professional problems and with a mastery of proved technical methods. But with regard to this leading factor in successful work we are doing for them almost nothing. We can hardly set up a complete curriculum for the development of personality. As a first step, however, we can recognize that we have defined here a problem of professional efficiency which is as fundamental as any other, and set ourselves the task of trying to solve it.

What is this professional problem? In practical terms it can be stated as the problem of adapting human personalities to the specific requirements of the professional tasks of social work. This is no new type of educational project. What is the training of the diagnostician? It is largely the adaptation of his power of thought to a specific task. What is at its best the training of the teacher? It is in part the adaptation of his powers, intellectual and otherwise, to a specific task. So might we speak of the training of the diplomat. I do not pretend to understand the ways of diplomats, but I am under the impression that, having dedicated one's self to the diplomatic service, one becomes more proficient in that service by learning something of national traditions, something of international relations, something of international law, something of the specific subject matter of those questions, political, economic, and social, concerning which nations negotiate with each other. But beyond this, the man who grows in value to the diplomatic service has learned how to conduct himself as a personality in those peculiar ways that are essential to successful diplomatic intercourse.

If we mention in one breath the diplomat, the salesman, and the waiter, we have mentioned three types of vocations each of which calls for an adaptation of personality to specific vocational ends. These ends are not the same, and their significant variations suggest certain corresponding variations in the types of personality required to meet them. When we say variations in types of personality we do not suggest complete differences. Human beings are biologically more nearly alike than different, whether they are diplomats, salesmen, or waiters. Their personality make-ups are more alike than different. To be sure, their differences have already played a large part in determining whether they would become diplomats, salesmen, or waiters. I am not suggesting that a given individual could be equally successful in all of these occupations. I am sure there must be good diplomats who would not make good waiters. It seems true, however, that whatever the original personality equipment of a man who enters one of these occupations, he will, if successful, be found to have modified his personality—or, strictly speaking, his habitual expression of it—in distinctive ways that have contributed to his success in the vocation chosen. Had he chosen another vocation making demands upon his personality and achieved success in it, his personality development would have been no less marked, but in certain important ways it would have been different.

If there is at least a thread of reasonableness in this argument, it is significant for social workers. I suggest, as a first step toward the solution of our problem, recognition that the tasks of social work call for something more than a native equipment which includes a good personality. They call for the adaptation of such a personality to the specific ends of social work. We must determine, therefore, what are the peculiar and distinctive demands which social work makes upon the personalities of its practitioners.

Adjustment. As the first qualification to meet these demands we may suggest what our psychiatric friends call a well-adjusted personality. I leave it to them to carry on their service of educating us laymen to an appreciation of what this involves. They have put us forever in their debt by revealing the origin, nature, and scope of prejudices, fears, inhibitions, complexes—those marks of the fettered personality too often unconscious of its fetters or mistaking them for symbols of grace. Stubbornness, prudery, self-assumed omniscience, cruelty, cynicism, bigotry, autocracy, egotism—these are not new phenomena to human beings. Psychiatry has told us nothing new regarding their potentialities for evil, unhappiness, and conflict among men. None of them has ever been attractive; all of them have been condemned in the other man. The individual in whose own conduct they appear has called them by softer names and, at times, has exalted them to the plane of virtues.

Psychiatry can perform no miracles, and it does not claim to be a vehicle of revealed truth. It has made clear, however, the true nature of some of these less attractive expressions of personality and has suggested some new ways of reckoning with them in one's own conduct, ways which mean great individual satisfaction and less strain in human relationships.

Leadership. The adjustment of one's personality is not a complete solution of the problem of adapting one's self to the tasks of social work. Human relationships are dynamic. Their quality is determined, not only by the state of the personalities concerned, but also by the characteristic ways in which these personalities express themselves in their actual relationships. It is in what we may call "the functioning of personality in human intercourse" that the greatest demands upon the social worker are made. One may be genial, magnetic, winning, well-poised, objective, sympathetic, persuasive, and courteous and yet not gifted in the art of leadership.

By the art of leadership we mean that quality in human relationships which permits the exercise of personal influence upon others without weakening their initiative. In ordinary life those persons exercise an influence upon us whom we have reason to trust. This trust is not easily given. It is a product usually of slowly maturing acquaintance. The confidant, the guide, philosopher, and friend is usually the man or woman who, through such acquaintance, has been revealed to us as a person in whose hands the more or less intimate affairs of our lives are safe. Until this basis of confidence is established, influence, leadership—in the best sense—is not possible. The quality of leadership demanded in the relations of social worker to client or in the relations of social worker to strategic persons in the community whose support he seeks is not different from the quality of leadership which marks helpful personal relationships in private life. Leadership in social work is possible only on the same basis of confidence that makes it possible in non-professional relationships.

The task of leadership in social work, however, is more difficult, chiefly because between client and case worker, between strategic citizen and community organizer, usually no ready-made confidential relationship exists. There has been no slowly maturing acquaintance ripening into neighborliness or friendship upon which it may rest. The social worker must lay this foundation as he proceeds. He has not only a purpose to achieve with his client, but he must establish such a relationship to him as will enable him to achieve this purpose. The establishment of this relationship will tax all of the worker's personality resources. To play the role of dictator is not difficult, and the strategic position of the social worker is often such as to tempt him into it. It is less easy to display the leadership which abandons domination in favor of the stimulation of initiative and self-propulsion.

Here is a professional problem of the highest importance. Is it possible for social workers, through a conscious process of self-education, so to adapt their personalities as to give them a higher order of skill in the peculiar problems of leadership which are characteristic of social work? The answer obviously is "Yes." The answer is "Yes" because they have succeeded in doing so. We may make the fullest concession to specialized knowledge and other forms of technical proficiency as factors in the success of social workers. But this success has been achieved quite as much through personality.

I venture to suggest further that the personality of the successful social worker through his years of experience shows a progressive development. It is not only mellower, richer, and more persuasive, as any personality may become through maturing experience; it has also been adapted in quite specific ways which have been determined by the requirements of his professional tasks. Let me once more illustrate what I mean. We may assume two persons in their early twenties, each with personalities which would meet the most exacting requirements of professional positions where personality counts. Let us further assume that these two persons are as alike in their personal qualities as it is possible for two individuals to be. One enters the diplomatic service; one enters social work. Let us leave them for fifteen years and renew their acquaintance after a successful experience in their respective fields. As human beings, we should expect to find them more mature, mellower, ripened as personalities are through experience in life. We shall, of course, find differences in their development. Any two personalities would probably be less alike at middle age than in youth. I am inclined to think, however, that among the differences discernible after fifteen years we should find some significant ones that were products not merely of maturity, but of constant, and perhaps unconscious, adaptation to the respective requirements of diplomacy and social work.

I do not wish to overstress the differences between diplomacy and social work or to overstress the significance of the peculiar personality demands of any occupation. It seems clear, however, that some occupations require a greater degree of self-control, a different form of self-expression, a higher measure of patience, a more intimate, a more sympathetic, understanding of human need than others. Surely those who fill such positions, at least, would agree that the efficient dispenser of information at the information booth of a railroad station has a greater need of patience than, let us say, the driver of a team of mules. Indeed, I am told by those who know that for the latter occupation patience is a positive disqualification.

Suppose we grant all this; where does it lead us? I think it leads to the conclusion that part of the professional training of the social worker, part of his unceasing effort to increase his proficiency throughout his professional career, should be devoted to the study of the effective use of personality. Let me repeat that such study would not necessarily be a new factor in the development of social workers. It means only a more conscious and deliberate attention to a problem which they have been highly successful in solving. Thus far, however, our interest in the personality development of social workers has been undefined, unorganized, and casual. We have been satisfied with personality as is or with personality as developed through the natural maturing process of experience in life. We have not sufficiently realized that the task of leadership which social work imposes upon its practitioners requires not only a good personality, in the ordinary sense, but a good personality adapted to the specific requirements of that task.

At intervals throughout this paper I have distinguished between the personality qualifications of the social worker on the one hand and his special knowledge and technical proficiency on the other. At the risk of inconsistency I now suggest that in the practice of social work these aspects of proficiency can hardly be separated.

In so far as the social worker succeeds by deliberate effort in improving his personality equipment he is, in my judgment, adding to his technical skill. In so far as he makes himself master of the technique of social work I believe he is schooling his personality to express itself in ways that make for sounder, more helpful professional relationships. Technique means nothing but a better organization of one's powers for a particular task. Those powers may be intellectual; they may be manual; they may be temperamental. The demands of social work call for all three.

The skilled social worker, the social worker who is master of his own technique, is one whose collective powers have been schooled for his specific tasks. We have seen that these tasks involve personal relationships of the most delicate and strategic kind. We have come to believe that they cannot be performed except by the trained social worker. Just what the training of the social worker should be can as yet be only tentatively stated; but I am convinced that in the future it must include study of the functioning of personality in human intercourse. Such study involves the risk of making artificial what should be spontaneous and natural. One of our problems seems to be that of devising educational experiences for social workers which will eliminate this risk while enabling them to achieve steadily and consistently a richer development of their personalities for the task of leadership.

Personality and civilization. We have considered in this paper some of the ways in which personality is significant in the practice of social work. In conclusion, I suggest that if our professional development shows a steadily growing use of human personality, we may in the long run make an even more strategic contribution to our civilization. The accumulation of scientific knowledge and its application to the affairs of men by experts working through the medium of organization become constantly more intricate and widespread. These developments have greatly increased the scope of human life. It is, however, beyond question that they have at the same time tended to depersonalize it.

In certain ways, which formerly contributed powerfully to the sense of solidarity in our social groups, industry and trade have changed. Big business and mass production have contributed definite gains to our social life, but they are responsible also for some irreparable losses. Except in isolated instances, personal contact between merchant and patron, between employer and employee, is no longer possible. It is still possible for the owner or manager of a business to take pride in his plant and his product, but it is a pride which he can no longer, as once he could, share through face-to-face discussion with patron and employee. In education the standardized curriculum and the increased size of educational institutions have changed the character of the old education in which close contact between teacher and pupil was a leading factor. In the practice of medicine the development of medical institutions and medical specialists has limited the possibilities of a personal relationship between physician and patient. Even in the home the exigencies of modern urban life have restricted the area of vital personal relationships, and neighborliness, the first step in the extension of the personal interests of the home out into the community, has been almost eliminated.

These developments have taken place so gradually, they have been so covered with the revelation of new satisfactions which science and organization have made possible, that we have hardly appreciated their significance. To one who believes that the development of civilization has rested largely upon the cohesive power of human personality the steady contracting of the area within which this power is given scope is ominous. I do not see how it can ever regain its old significance in the world of business. It becomes, therefore, of critical importance that we retain it at its best in those fields in which it is indispensable to success. Social work is one of these. Without human personality as a guiding force, social work will be a sterile effort.

I do not believe that the force of human personality in the affairs of men is spending itself. There is, however, a real danger that our faith in the possibilities of efficient organization may lessen its opportunities for service. Those forms of human effort in which experts deal with human beings, education, medicine, social work may be so influenced by the depersonalizing trend of modern civilization that they may fail in the achievement of their own purposes unless they bring into their conception of what constitutes fitness for service a recognition of the indispensable contribution of the developed personality. Science and organization may make life safer, more rational, more convenient, broader in its scope. Personality alone can use science and organization to make life richer. Social workers throughout their history have demonstrated this truth. We can, by taking thought, add to its influence in our changing civilization.

Reprinted from Porter R. Lee, Personality in social work, *National Conference on Social Welfare Proceedings* (1926).

Commentary: Porter R. Lee, a Social Worker and Pioneer

Ram A. Cnaan

Porter Raymond Lee was born in 1879 in Buffalo, New York. He attended Cornell University and received an A.B. in 1903. He was a gifted public speaker with acclaimed leadership skills and was elected to the honorary Aleph Samach society of Cornell University. Upon gradation, he moved to New York City and attended the New York School of Philanthropy for a six-week course in social work. Upon completion, Porter R. Lee started his professional career as the assistant secretary of the Charity Organization Society (COS) of Buffalo. This COS was the first in the country and the model after which future American social work and services were based. Under the influence of S. Humphreys Gurteen, social care was removed from the auspices of the churches and from the hands of the friendly visitors. Gurteen also emphasized the minimal value of financial and in-kind support and the importance of advice and guidance. In the Buffalo COS, Porter R. Lee received the best socialization to the quest for scientific philanthropy. When he entered the building, he saw the famous sign stating: "No relief here!"

Lee moved to Philadelphia in 1909, where he succeeded Mary Richmond as the

General Secretary of the Philadelphia Society for Organizing Charity. In 1910, the "Philadelphia Training School for Social Work" retained the services of Lee as a senior faculty member; here, he lectured on conducting social investigation and group work. Lee is credited with being the pioneer of the "case method" of instruction, which for generations was the primary social work teaching tool. In this method, a real case of an individual or a family is carefully investigated and then presented to the class. Following the case presentation, the participants discuss opinions as to how best to help the person or family in need. The idea is that principles are elicited and the participants learn from these principles and can apply them to other people under their care.

In 1911, Porter Lee advocated and succeeded in transforming the school modus operandi from a collection of lectures by experts into an institution that requires its students to be engaged in field work. In a letter from March 13, 1911, he wrote the following:

Three years ago the Children's Bureau, which is maintained by the Children's Aid Society, the Society to Protect Children from Cruelty, and the Seybert Institution, conducted a series of lectures twice a week by notable out-of-town leaders in social work . . . requiring nothing of those who enrolled for the course except attendance. The Training School for Social Work this year has been in a way an outgrowth of these lectures. That is to say, we felt that the lecture courses lacked the practical field work which ought to go with them, and that no one society was able to give its new workers a broad enough training through a single class session of an hour a week. Our school this year, therefore, has been rather a merging of the various training classes of the different societies and the Children's Bureau class work.

Lee moved to New York City in 1912, where he became a member of the faculty at the New York School of Philanthropy (renamed the New York School of Social Work in 1918 and the Columbia University School of Social Work in 1940). He was named Director of the School in 1916 and became a national leader in the field of social work.

Lee was invited to be a keynote speaker at the 1915 meeting of the National Conference of Charities and Correction in Baltimore where Abraham Flexner delivered his famous challenge to social work to become a profession. As a keynote speaker, Lee suggested that "No organized activity . . . can claim professional standing until it rests upon scientific knowledge and has developed definite methods to reach its goals."

In 1919, at the call of Porter Lee, representatives of fifteen schools of social work met in New York and established the Association of Training Schools for Professional Social Work (ATSPSW), which would gradually develop into the first nationwide accrediting agency. This was the precursor for the Council of Social Work Education. This move was visionary and enabled the growing schools to straighten their lines as to what is social work education and find some coherence in the emerging helping profession. This group started the process of setting standards for social work education that had culminated in the accreditation and regular reaccredidation of schools of social work.

After years of social investigations and analyzing cases, as the editor of the Milford

Conference Report Social Case Work, Generic and Specific (1929), Lee established the first generic theory base for the practice of social case work. This book was the culmination of his intellectual heritage and set new grounds for viewing social work as a unified discipline with principles and testable guidelines of practice.

In addition to pioneering with the case methods and starting the Council on Social Work education and setting standards for what is and what is not social work education, Lee also pioneered in seeing the person in environment. In today's social work education, students are undertaking a course that explores the interaction between society and the person. This course is often known as "Human Behavior and the Social Environment." The foundations for this course came from Lee's landmark book, *Social Work Cause and Function* (1937). In this book, Lee explored the tension between broad social problems such as poverty, hygiene, and poor housing and the delivery of social work services. The "function" in Lee's title is not related to the Penn Functional School. In this case, he opened the discussion that will follow us for generations as to who are we serving? The cause-function debate involves the issue of whether social workers should help their clients comfortably accept (or adapt to) the social situations in which they find themselves or whether they should challenge (or attempt to change) the social situations of their clients, thereby participating in the alteration of society itself. It is the debate between the structural-functionalist and Marxist perspective of society. While Lee did not resolve the conflict, he definitely put it in the open and set the foundation for numerous debates and inquiries.

Lee also co-authored two books, *Mental Hygiene and Social Work* (1929) with Marion Kenworthy, and *Social Salvage* (1924) with Walter William Pettit, and his Collected Speeches and Papers on Charity Organizations are available in the Whitney Young, Jr., Memorial Library of Social Work at Columbia University in New York. Porter R. Lee was keenly aware that social workers of the nineteenth and early twentieth centuries lacked both systematic ways to work with clients and professional status. He tirelessly worked on advancing both missions until the end of his life. In 1938, Lee retired from his position at New York School; he died a year later in 1939.

Chapter 6
The Contributions of American Social Agencies to Social Progress and Democracy

Frank D. Watson

The role of the private social agency in America is unique. Not only is their number without parallel abroad but the range of activities undertaken is a constant surprise even to those long familiar with the history of social work in America. The National Conference of Social Work, about to celebrate its fiftieth birthday, with its membership of some five thousand representatives, mostly of private social agencies, and an attendance of three to five thousand at its annual meetings in recent years, has no counterpart in any foreign country. One of the outstanding impressions of American charity recorded by visitors is the quality of personnel in charge of these private agencies. With the advent of training schools for social work and vast foundations for the development of techniques for the improvement of social conditions, not to mention the growth of technical literature and the recent birth of a National Association of Social Workers, social work in America is well on the road to being professionalized, if indeed it has not already reached that stage. These facts should be recognized and utilized by departments of public welfare if they are to attain their greatest usefulness.

To the writer, American social agencies have made four noteworthy contributions to social progress and the achievement of democracy. It should not, however, be implied that each type of social agency is making all four contributions or that any one type is making equally significant contributions in each of the four roles about to be discussed in greater detail. If to some these contributions seem less outstanding than they do to the author, it should be recalled that the road of social progress has been a long and tortuous one and that while the path today is less difficult to travel, it nevertheless stretches on indefinitely. It should also be borne in mind that democrat is a relative term, the fulfillment of which lies in the future. In a sense everything that hastens social progress by ever so little or that brings us one step nearer achieving a more democratic society is noteworthy.

The Social Agency and Social Exploring

It is no mere accident that the work of one of the oldest and yet one of the most progressive social agencies of a large eastern city should be described in a recent five years' review of its work as "social exploring" and its executive secretary aptly compared to Christopher Columbus, bent upon his memorable voyage of discovery. Nor is it an accident that *The Survey,* the official organ of the social agencies of America, should choose as its symbol a picture of the ship that carried the great Genoan across the sea and that the National Association of Social Workers should claim as its emblem the compass, the sign of the pathfinder.

After making due allowance for the inertia to be found in all social institutions, one has failed to catch the spirit of social work in America to-day who does not sense its eternal flux. Social work has never been a static thing. It may be charged with making mistakes but taken in the large, it can never be justly criticized for standing still. Its tendency to strike out into new paths has sometimes brought upon its head the charge of instability, flightiness, professional busybodying when it did not evoke the more serious claims of undermining American institutions and prosperity.

To those who recognize that there can be no progress without change, this everlasting desire of social agencies to unearth evils and to offer new and better solutions is their crown of glory. It places them among the scouts out on the firing line of progress in the ancient warfare against poverty, disease and crime. It led them "to discover" the need for stamping out the great white plague and the social evil, even before the medical profession as such was aroused to concerted action against either of these allies of poverty and disease. It led them to champion better housing and wiser city planning long before municipalities were awake to these responsibilities, if indeed we may say that this happy condition has yet arrived. It has led them "to discover" the courts, especially the inferior ones, in their efforts to secure justice for the man of small means and the newcomer in our midst. Above all, it has revolutionized the procedure for juvenile offenders at a time when the legal profession in too few instances lent whole-hearted encouragement. It has "discovered" the child in the mill and mine while factory inspection departments frequently marked time and it has "discovered" the child in the public school while too often the school saw only the curriculum and dull children or mischievous ones.

These "discoveries" of social agencies are part of the American spirit of adventure as reflected in our economic, social, religious and political ideals. We are incurable experimenters and our favorable "place in the sun" has aided this experimentation. We are, if you will, childishly impatient. We do not take kindly to waiting for the wheels of government machinery to be set up. If we want to get some reform across, we organize a committee on the spot. It has been well said, although in jest, that no dinner party is complete in Boston which does not see some national movement launched before the coffee is served.

The social worker's desire to reform, coupled with this well nigh universal tendency to initiate and experiment, has been a great spur to progress and a real economy to the taxpayer. Not only has it brought public attention to needs the meeting of which was often a sound investment but it has often worked out in the laboratory, as it were, the solution of the problem. This has been the history of many important activities now carried on by the state. Thus it was private initiative and effort that demonstrated the need of public kindergartens, public schools, public hospitals, public libraries, public playgrounds, and a host of other activities now viewed as essentially belonging to the government.

The Social Agency and Public Opinion

Once having conceived the solution to a social problem and sometimes one fears, even before, the typical social agency goes out into the highways and byways to compel attention to its "program." Often inefficiency enters at this point and the public fails to pay attention or is mis-educated. Nevertheless the picture drawn a decade ago by Jacob A. Riis of present-day social work as the modern St. George slaying its dragon of poverty, disease and crime is not overdrawn. American social agencies are crusaders in their efforts to capture the citadel of what Dr. Richard C. Cabot calls the Kingdom of Evils. They have the true missionary spirit. Although much of their propaganda may too soon find its way to the waste paper basket, few will deny that their efforts to get a following are well nigh ceaseless. Nor are their efforts limited to the printed page and the multigraphed letters. Lecture platforms, pulpits and newspaper columns are all carriers of the message. No little time of busy executives of social agencies goes into addressing local clubs or speaking at state or national conferences of social work.

In addition to this distinctly propaganda work to influence public thought, social agencies have entered, often informally, the field of organized education. One only need recall the effective work of Cho Cho the health clown and the teachings of the Health Fairy, or study the charts and pictures of the National Child Welfare Association to appreciate the contributions social agencies are making to the education of the youth of the land. Their educational messages have not been addressed to children alone. Such agencies as the American Child Hygiene Association, the Child Health Organization, the National Tuberculosis Association and the American Social Hygiene Association have rendered invaluable service in the cause of adult education. No account of the influence of social agencies upon public opinion would be complete that failed to mention the significant contribution to American thought that is being made by *The Survey*, and *The Survey Graphic*, published by The Survey Associates, Inc., a volunteer body of public spirited citizens.

Although some of this educational seed falls on stony places and other in shallow soil, it would be belittling this second contribution of American social agencies not to appreciate the tremendous influence that the leaders of these voluntary social movements have exerted on public opinion in America. As the late Doctor Patten has well pointed out, "We could not have political conventions to advance the cause of social justice if social workers had not coined words and reshaped sentiments which these conventions evoke."

Contributions to Social Legislation

The amount of social legislation on the statute books of both state and federal government that is traceable either directly or indirectly to the efforts of social agencies is enormous. Activity in this sphere has been largely in the field of industrial reform, due to the recent trend among social workers to regard a low standard of living as giving rise to a large proportion of the problems of the social worker. So important is wise legislation in the field of industry that at least three of the voluntary social movements of America that have assumed national proportions, namely, the American Association for Labor Legislation, The National Child Labor Committee and the National Consumers League, devote most all their efforts to this end. Beside these organizations which have done yeoman service in writing on the statute books of the nation, workmen's compensation laws, child labor legislation and minimum wage statutes, are a host of other organizations such as family and child welfare agencies which have aided them in their efforts at industrial reform and another host of organizations such as state charities aid associations which have taken as their especial province wise legislation for those special wards of our state governments in America, the insane, the feeble-minded, epileptic and criminal. Many a state owes much of its progress in the care of these unfortunates to the consecrated efforts of "those who care" who have banded themselves together for the purpose.

In all fields of social legislation, the workers of the social agencies of America have a real contribution to make. Coming into day-to-day contact with the victims of either bad heredity or overpowering circumstances, they have a message for the legislator who lacks vision on the one hand or facts on the other. To these case workers, legislators seem sometimes to be dreamers, thinking about a changed order and neglecting the people who now suffer from it, and who must be reckoned with in an effort to change it. For them the social worker of our numerous case-working agencies drawing conclusions from the actual experience of individuals, are often much needed guides in social action.

Social Agencies as Free Lances, Standard Bearers, and Critics

One need not here enter upon any long discussion of the legitimate functions of government and private effort. For the most part Americans are not so much interested in the question of who does the job as in that of getting the work done. They are pragmatists in actions although many would not claim the title.

Were all social activities now undertaken by private enterprise transferred tomorrow to the government and what is more unthinkable, were there no longer any need for experimentation, there would still be a contribution which a voluntary organization of like-minded citizens could make to public welfare. That contribution would consist in serving as a free lance, "hitting anything and everybody when necessary for the common good." The free lance becomes what Francis H. McLean aptly describes as "the opposition, the everlasting opposition, friendly when officials and others are doing their best, but ready to buckle on the sword," the minute the revelations of their work require it. There is always the need for a careful study on the part of interested citizens of the kind of work a public agency is doing, but more important still is the need for evolving better and still better standards of work and the slow education of the public to a demand for the same. Adds Mr. McLean, "The official, through his administrative and legislative machinery, and the private citizen, working through his private agencies, are absolutely two equally necessary essentials for a proper development." Groups of like minded citizens, with such singleness of purpose as to combine voluntarily to carry through a given reform, are usually in most communities the standard bearers, developing techniques which the general public and governmental officials often only approximate.

Every community needs what someone has called "a community memory" and "a community conscience" that will function through changing administrations and political upheavals. These services such private social agencies as bureaus of municipal research and public charities associations admirably perform. It is an interesting paradox that with all the stress that the former type of organization places on improving the efficiency of government and its sympathetic attitude toward the extension of the sphere of government activities, it nevertheless finds its greatest usefulness is served by remaining itself under private auspices. Only so can it truly function as a free lance and "the everlasting opposition."

For the unfortunate wards of the state, public charities associations or state charities aid associations, as they more frequently are called, become largely the "community memory and conscience." Too often the typical citizen who is not anti-social but rather non-social, feels all is well once a sweeping reform has been accomplished and new and better laws placed on the statute books. He retires to "his castle" forgetting that the best of laws will not enforce themselves and that the best of statutes amount to little if the highest type of men and women are not chosen to carry them out. Serving as a searchlight playing on laws designed to protect the feeble-minded, insane, and criminal, groups too easily forgotten by the public, and in bringing into high relief the caliber of the men who can put at naught the best of statutes, public charities associations render a service of inestimable value to the body politic.

The typical American is too little doctrinaire, is too practical not to use every means at his disposal to accomplish his ends. If a governmental agency is ready at hand, well and good. If not or if it needs supplementing, equally well and good, for as Dr. Edward T. Devine has pointed out, the state is a social institution neither friendly nor hostile, without independent personality, but "a very vital part of ourselves," . . . "an extension of our will, our conscience and our strong right arm," . . . "a tool to work with. . . . The ideal is that of a society which is by no means entirely dependent upon the government for meeting its corporate needs, which uses the state increasingly . . . but uses increasingly also other instruments for executing the social will, which looks upon a voluntary association, a new chamber of commerce, a political party, or a newspaper as equally appropriate, within its limits, sometimes very wide limits, for accomplishing any beneficent purpose."

Reprinted from Frank D. Watson, The contributions of American social agencies to social progress and democracy, *Journal of Social Forces* 1 (1923): 87–90. Reprinted by permission.

Commentary

Ram A. Cnaan

Frank Dekker Watson was born in 1883. He attended the University of Pennsylvania and received a B.S. in economics in 1905 and later a Ph.D. in 1911. Upon his graduation from the University of Pennsylvania, he became a faculty member at Haverford College on the outskirts of Philadelphia. In 1914, as soon as the Philadelphia Training School for Social Work became stable and seemed permanent, Watson was invited to serve as a lecturer. Given that his dissertation was on Charity Organization Societies and his appointment at Haverford College was as a teacher of Sociology and Social Work, the choice was logical. In 1914–15 he taught "Survey of Modern Organized Movements in Social Work."

In 1916, the School faced a heavy financial burden and the board seriously considered closing it. It was a bleak period and one that threatened the future of social work in Philadelphia. In a special meeting of the board, Frank D. Watson reported for the Joint Committee on behalf of the School alumni and the area social workers. On the basis of his presentation, the board subsequently voted "that it is the purpose of the Board to operate a high grade professional school for the training of social workers in accordance with the submitted report of the Committee of the Alumnae and of the College Club [of Philadelphia]." Watson's report and enthusiasm on behalf of the young School carried the day and the board managed to recruit new members who provided financial support and who guaranteed the School's success.

In September 1918 the board elected Watson to the half-time post of director of the School. Watson, whose principal employment was at Haverford College, served the Pennsylvania School for three years, until his promotion to full professor of sociology and social work at Haverford, where he taught until his retirement in 1949. He served at the helm of the Pennsylvania School longer than any of his predecessors and transitioned it from infancy to the beginning of the modern era. He represented the Pennsylvania School at the formation of the Association of Training Schools for Professional Social Work (ATSPSW, the precursor for the Council on Social Work Education) and was elected chairman of the Association's Executive Committee in December 1920. The idea to form a body of the directors of the schools of social work was made by Porter Lee, another member of the Philadelphia School who at that time was the head of the New York School.

In his three years as director, Watson shaped the School for many years to come. First, he managed to secure the finances of the school. In 1921 the Welfare Federation of Philadelphia (predecessor of the United Way) admitted the Pennsylvania School to full membership. Watson and the Board of Trustees were successful in obtaining major funding from the Welfare Federation and the School was placed on secure financial footing. For an emerging profession and an educational institute that only five years before had been on the brink of collapse, this was a great achievement.

As director and knowing that financial affairs were under control, Watson started to look for strong faculty to lead the school. He recruited four new faculty members, each of whom made a significant impact on the School and the profession: Karl de Schweinitz, Virginia P. Robinson, Kenneth L. M. Pray, and Jessie Taft. These four pillars of social work education are featured in other chapters in this volume. Two of them led the School in different periods, and two of them set the foundations for the Functional Approach that shaped the education of the School for more than fifty years.

Watson separated his academic work as a professor at Haverford College from his work leading the Pennsylvania School. He held the position that the Pennsylvania School was, at its core and in its mission, a practitioners' school, rooted in the accumulated experience and wisdom of Philadelphia's leading social workers. As such, he did not see the possibility of an academic anchoring for the School. For Watson, the theoretical work was done in the university and the teaching of best practices was designated for the emerging schools that were unaffiliated with a university.

Among Watson's publications, one can find a seminal book based on his dissertation titled: *The Charity Organization Movement in the United States: A Study in American Philanthropy*.[1] This book was the authoritative review and study of the organizations that advanced social work from amateur good willing into a scientific endeavor. Watson's work documented their development and their structure in a detailed manner that serves scholars for many years after its publication. More than fifty years after its publication, Kenneth L. Kusmer wrote, in an article about Charity Organization Societies in *Journal of American History*, that Watson's book "is the only full-scale treatment of the subject."[2] Among Watson's many contentions is that volunteers are of central importance to the role of the professional social worker. The advantages of volunteers, he noted, are fourfold: (1) they supplemented professional services, (2) they communicated enthusiasm, (3) they provided additional community contacts, and (4) they educated the society about the lives of the poor and the causes of poverty. These same four are still hailed today by scholars of volunteering. Watson's work in the field was diverse, including an article titled "What Some College Men Wanted to Know About Marriage and the Family."[3]

In 1959, a year late, the School celebrated its fiftieth anniversary. The delay was caused because the School wanted the annual meeting of the Council on Social Work Education to take place in Philadelphia alongside the School's anniversary. In May 1959, it held a major event at the University Museum titled "Second Commemorative Address of the Fiftieth Anniversary Year." Ten people who had contributed significantly to the School received awards. Frank D. Watson, who had passed away a few months earlier, received his award posthumously.

Notes

1. Frank D. Watson, *The Charity Organization Movement in the United States: A Study in American Philanthropy* (1922; New York: Arno Press, 1971).

2. Kenneth L. Kusmer, The functions of organized charity in the Progressive Era: Chicago as a case study, *Journal of American History* 60 (1973): 657–78, 657.

3. Frank D. Watson, What some college men wanted to know about marriage and the family, *Social Forces* 11 (2) (December 1932): 235–41.

Part II
The Height of the Functionalist Era

Chapter 7
The Time Element in Mental Hygiene Therapy as Applied to Social Case Work

Jessie Taft

The word "therapy" is used instead of "treatment" because in its derivation and in my own feeling about the word there is not so much implication of manipulation of one person by another. "To treat," according to the dictionary, is to apply a process to someone or something. The word "therapy" has no verb in English, for which I am grateful; it cannot do anything to anybody, hence can better represent a process going on—observed perhaps, understood perhaps, assisted perhaps, but not applied. The Greek noun from which "therapy" is derived means "a servant"; the verb means "to wait." I wish to use the English word "therapy" with the full force of its derivation, to cover a process which we recognize as somehow and somewhat curative but which, if we are honest enough and brave enough, we must admit to be beyond our control. In fact, if it were not so, life would be intolerable. No one wants another to apply any process to the inmost self, however desirable a change in personality and behavior may seem objectively. One may be willing to let the physician cure a bodily ill, although even that is not so sure; but one's self is defended against every encroachment, even the most benevolent, which is not to say that resistance to cure is necessarily open, conscious, or violent. The most docile patient is often best able to demonstrate the worthlessness of the remedy and the helplessness of the doctor. In the face of my own personal realization of the impotence of the other to help me unless I let him—in fact, of my necessity to keep him impotent lest he use his interest in my welfare to interfere with me—I am forced to accept the full limitation which this recognition implies, in my own power to help others. I know in advance that no one is going to experience change—call it "growth" or "progress" if you have the courage—because I think it would be good for society, good for his family and friends, or even good for himself. I know equally well that no one is going to take help from me because someone else thinks it desirable. The anxious parent, the angry school teacher, the despairing wife or husband, must bear their own burdens, solve their own problems. I can help them only in and for themselves, if they are able to use me. I cannot perform magic upon the bad child, the inattentive pupil, the faithless partner, because they want him made over in their own terms.

This means not only a limit put upon those seeking help but a genuine limitation in myself, an impotence which I am forced to accept even when it is painful, as it frequently is. Here is a beloved child to be saved, a family unity to be preserved, an important teacher to be enlightened. Before all these problems in which one's reputation, one's pleasure in utilizing professional skill, as well as one's real feeling for the person in distress are perhaps painfully involved, one must accept one's final limitation and the right of the other—perhaps his necessity—to refuse help or to take help in his own terms, not as therapist, friends or society might choose. My knowledge and my skill avail nothing unless they are accepted and used by the other. Over that acceptance and possible use I have no control beyond the genuineness of my understanding of the difficulty with which anyone seeks or takes help, my respect for the strength of the patient however negatively expressed, and the reality of my acceptance of my function as helper not ruler. If my humility is actual, born of a conviction and experience too deep to be shaken, then at least I am not an obstacle to the person who needs help but fears domination. He may approach me without the added fear and resistance which my active designs for his cure will surely produce and find within the limitation which I accept thus sincerely—a safety which permits him to utilize and me to exercise all the professional skill and wisdom at my command. On the other hand, the person who seeks the domination of another, in order to project his conflict and avoid himself and his own development in resisting the efforts of the other to save him, is finally brought to a realization of the futility of his striving, since he cannot force upon me a goal which I have long since recognized to be outside my province and power. Whether such a person will ultimately succeed in taking over his own problem, since I cannot relieve him of it, is something which only the individual case can determine. There are those who are unwilling or unable to go further, which outcome every therapist must stand ready to admit and respect no matter how much his professional ego is hurt or his therapeutic or economic aim defeated thereby.

This is in no sense to be designated as passivity in treatment. As I conceive it, the therapeutic function involves the most intense activity; but it is an activity of attention, of identification and understanding, of adaptation to the individual's need and pattern, combined with an unflagging preservation of one's own limitation and difference. This kind of activity combines a steady maintenance of one's own will and integrity, with a simultaneous acceptance of and respect for the other's right and ability to heal himself in his own way if he is left free to use the therapeutic situation creatively.

With this preliminary explanation of the choice of the word "therapy" in preference to treatment, because of its relation to serving or waiting upon, not in the moral or religious sense, but in the realization of a psychological fact of limitation which must be accepted before therapy is possible at all, I am ready to discuss time in relation to the therapeutic process. It might have been discreet to limit my title to "Therapy as Exemplified in Social Case Work," since I intend to consider it for the most part in that connection; but what I have to say about time is true, as I see it, for all therapy, while my conviction and understanding of its therapeutic function is derived from analytic not from case work experience.

It is the type of work found in the child guidance, or psychiatric clinic, which I think comes nearest to what I mean by case work as individual therapy; and it is this kind of case work that I wish to consider in its relation to time. Here where there is no practical barrier, where the agency is set up to offer therapy, we are faced with the full responsibility for the time factor, the horror of unlimited time, visit piled upon visit, dictation upon dictation; on the other hand, equally the fear of having cut off too soon something that might have happened if only the worker had held on a little longer.

In the therapeutic case work with which I am acquainted it seems to me that the worker has finally accepted, at least intellectually, the fact that she can be of no use unless the client wants something, is willing to take her help and actively seeks it; but on the other hand she is not yet rid of her feeling of responsibility for his improvement. Why go on week after week if nothing happens to indicate progress; how justify herself for this piling up of time; how recognize when there has been enough therapy, except by results. Yet, for results she cannot be responsible without putting pressure on the client. As soon as she decides what ought to happen, must she not take command and decide, however tactfully, that the client should come longer, or has come long enough? This responsibility without control is the dilemma of therapeutic case work as now practiced.

Then there is the worker who has given up responsibility for the client's behavior in the world, for any final shaping of his personality, but who still cannot rid herself of responsibility for the interview in which she takes part. How can she go into it blindly and passively? She may be willing to be silent, to be very slow and patient; but is she not there to guide the process somehow to a result which will be therapeutic? If the whole affair is to be left to the client, where does she come in? It is no wonder she clings to history and the value of catharsis. If she cannot show the patient how to live, if she cannot give him moral, religious, or ethical instruction, at least she can see to it that he empties himself of his past, and even that he learns to interpret it in ways he never thought of. In other words, she can use the single hour or two of the weekly conferences to bring out material.

That this preconceived idea of what the hour should sooner or later bring forth, tends just as much to the control and domination of the client as if she had tried to reform his habits or his morals, very few case workers ever realize because, if they did, they would be greatly at a loss as to what function remains for them. Moreover, the reliving or rehearsing of the past plus the worker's interpretation of it seems to offer some kind of rational limit to an otherwise unlimited affair. If it is dangerous to use the disappearance of symptoms as a criterion, then what can be used? Perhaps the fact that all the material from the past seems to have been brought out and understood will provide a natural ending. Yet, as I know only too well from my own earlier efforts, it is a very baffling experience to see your patient with his past so clear before him and you, all his involved relations to his parents finally revealed and interpreted, and his problem of living as unsolved as ever. "Yes, I understand," he says, "but what can I do about it? I don't find it any easier to live." If you decide he should continue to come, what happens next? There is always something, there always will be something, to be found in his past that he has not brought out before. There is really no limit to the past either, with this approach; and the client may well go on until he rebels or you grow too weary to bear it, and end the struggle with or without therapy.

The futility of this type of relationship to the client has led certain case workers to the recognition of two other factors, which may be determinative of therapy and perhaps contain an inherent time limit or criterion for ending. The one recognizes the relation between worker and client as dynamic and present; the other recognizes time as a qualitative, as well as a quantitative, affair, valuable in and for itself when it is actually utilized in the passing moment without dependence on a next time. The first factor, the recognition of the reality of the relationship between worker and client and its dynamic changing quality has been quite completely accepted, at least verbally, among the more radical group of case workers.

But the cloven hoof remains, in my opinion, in the fact that the dynamics of the immediate relationship is often obscured by the concept of living out, reliving, or solving past relationships on the worker. The worker is being used, according to this concept, in the present to work out in immediate feeling experiences from the client's past. An utter confusion results, a practical denial of the reality of the present which is functioning for the sake of the past. Once more the worker is effectively hidden behind the screen of father, mother, brother, sister, while all the time her value for the client is that she is none of these and he knows it. He may be using patterns which were developed by him in birth, nursing, weaning, toilet training—Oedipus situation and what not—but he is using them now with all the changes wrought by years of living, using them afresh as they are in this present hour, in immediate reaction to someone who behaves as no one has ever behaved to him before; someone who understands and permits a use of herself, which determines for the client a new experience, valuable, if at all, in and for itself. He does not want a father or a mother, but he does want someone who will let him find himself apart from parent identifications without interference or domination, someone who will not be fooled, someone strong enough not to retaliate. The moment the worker confuses her own relation to the client with his relation to anyone else past or present, that moment she has again entangled herself with history, with external fact, with the static goal of definite material, and also has escaped her own responsibility for the present. The relation may be dynamic; but the client is unable to avail himself of its therapeutic possibilities because it is predetermined, set in advance, without creative opportunity.

According to this doctrine, which I am criticizing, the client is not really "cured" or through, until he has lived out all of his faulty biological and sociological relationships. If he has apparently worked through his use of the worker as a mother, he is not safe to go until the father relation has been lived through also, and so on. How long it should take before one can be sure that everything essential has been re-experienced consciously is as uncertain as material and relationships from the past are unlimited. Once more, therapy is defeated by the setting up of an external norm or purpose for which the case worker must assume responsibility willy nilly, but which unfortunately again contains no inherent time limit.

Driven into a blind alley by this limitless possibility in longtime case work, certain groups have taken refuge in what has come to be known as "the short contact." Here, for the first time in the history of case work, as far as I know, case workers are struggling with the fundamental problem of therapy; and it is interesting to see that they have been able to come to grips with the real issue only when they have set up for themselves an arbitrary limit in time. What happens, they ask themselves, to make a single or short contact meaningful, as it often is, for client and worker even if they never meet again. The fascination which the study of the short contact holds for our ablest workers indicates that somehow they realize that it contains the whole problem of therapeutic case work and its solution, if only it can be mastered.

I find the significance of this concentration on the short contact, by individuals who represent the experimental emphasis in case work, to be threefold: first, it indicates a self-confidence which has freed itself of fear to the point of taking responsibility for its own part in a process; second, it points to a growth and achievement in case work which can afford to admit a limitation; and third, it is a recognition of the fact that whatever takes place between worker and client of a therapeutic nature must be present in some degree in the single contact if it is ever to be there. If there is no therapeutic understanding and use of one interview, many interviews equally barren will not help.

In the single interview, if that is all I allow myself to count upon, if I am willing to take that one hour in and for itself, there is no time to hide behind material, no time to explore the past or future. I, myself, am the remedy at this moment, if there is any; and I can no longer escape my responsibility, not for the client but for myself and my role in the situation. Here is just one naked hour to be lived through as it goes—one hour of present immediate relationship, however limited, with another human being who has brought himself to the point of asking for help. If, somehow, this single contact proves to have value for the applicant, how does it happen? What in the nature of my functioning permits this hour to be called "therapeutic"—at least qualitatively?

Perhaps one reason we find it so difficult to analyze what takes place in the short contact is that there we are brought face to face with a present from which it is hard to escape and which, in consequence, carries symbolically and really our own personal pattern as it relates to time and the self-limitation which is involved in its acceptance. Not only is the client limited by this brief period of time, not only is he facing the possibility of being turned out too soon or kept on after he is ready to go, but I also am forced to admit my limited function as therapist, dependent as I am upon his right to go when he must or to deprive me of a second opportunity no matter how willing I may be to continue the contact, no matter how much he may need the help I have to give from an objective standpoint. My only control, which is not easy to exercise, is my control over myself in the present hour if I can bring myself to the point of a reasonable degree of acceptance of that hour with all of its shortcomings. This fact, that our personal reaction to time gives a clear picture of the real nature of our resistance to taking full responsibility for therapeutic case work, makes it necessary at this point to consider time and its relation to therapy more philosophically.

Time represents more vividly than any other category the necessity of accepting limitation as well as the inability to do so, and symbolizes therefore the whole problem of living. The reaction of each individual to limited or unlimited time betrays his deepest and most fundamental life pattern, his relation to the growth process itself, to beginnings and endings, to being born and to dying.

As a child I remember struggling with the horror of infinite space, but the passing of time was even more unbearable. I can remember my gratitude for Christmas, because at least presents remained, something lasted beyond the moment. There was deep depression in adolescence over the realization of this flow of time. Why go to a party, since tomorrow it will be over and done with? Why experience at all, since nothing can be held? On the other hand, there is equal fear of being permanently caught in any state or process. Fear of being bored is perhaps its most intellectualized form; panic in the face of a physical trap or snare, its most overwhelming and instinctive expression. As living beings we are geared to movement and growth, to achieving something new, leaving the outworn behind and going on to a next stage. Hence, we do not like a goal that can never be reached nor yet a goal that is final—a goal beyond which we cannot go. In terms of this primary double fear of the static and of the endlessly moving, the individual is always trying to maintain a balance, and frequently fails because of too great fear either of changing or of never being able to change again. To put it very simply, perhaps the human problem is no more than this: If one cannot live forever, is it worth while to live at all?

We see this problem and this double fear[1] reflected in every slightest human experience from birth to death, and consequently also in the case worker's, as well as the client's, attitude toward the long or the short contact. Whether or not she can face the reality of either, depends on whether life to her can be accepted on the terms under which it can be obtained—that is, as a changing, finite, limited affair, to be seized at the moment if at all. The basis for believing that life can be thus accepted, beyond the fact that all of us do more or less accept it if we continue to exist, lies in the fact that we are, after all, part and parcel of the life process; that we do naturally abhor not only ending but also never-ending, that we not only fear change but the unchanging. Time and change, dying and being born, are inner, as well as outer, realities if fear of external violence or compulsion does not play too great a part. Life is ambivalent; but so are we, "born and bred in the briar patch." And on this fact rests the whole possibility of therapy. We cannot change the fundamental biological and psychological conditions of living for others, nor for ourselves, but somewhere within each individual is this same life process which can go on for and of itself, if the fear which has become excessive primarily in birth and the earlier experiences can be decreased in quantity sufficiently to permit the inherent normal ambivalence to function and hence to provide its own checks and balances.

Time in itself is a purely arbitrary category of man's invention; but since it is a projection of his innermost being, it represents so truly his inherent psychological conflict, that to be able to accept it, to learn to admit its likeness to one's very self, its perfect adaptation to one's deepest and most contradictory impulses, is already to be healed, as far as healing is possible or applicable, since in accepting time, one accepts the own self and life with their inevitable defects and limitations. This does not mean a passive resignation but a willingness to live, work, and create as mortals within the confines of the finite.

So literally true even in the slightest situations is this description of our relation to time, and particularly to a time limit, that in any therapeutic interview where, in coming, the individual admits a need for assistance, it is possible to see the operation of this person's particular pattern, his own way of reacting to time, or, if you like, to the life problem itself. This one is at your door fifteen minutes too soon; the other keeps you waiting, or perhaps fails to turn up at all. The very one who makes you wait at the beginning of the hour may be equally loath to go at the end and leaves you to be responsible for getting him out. The other who comes before you are ready is on edge to be gone before the time you have allotted to him is up. Neither can bear the hour as it is, with limits set by the other, even though he has agreed to them beforehand. The one makes you bear the burden of his lateness and his lingering; the other tries to bear too much, both his own responsibility and yours, depriving himself of what is his, and you of the chance to contribute what you have already assigned for his use in terms of time. And so it goes, for every individual a slightly different pattern but with the same motivation. This is not in itself a serious matter to the analyst, who is paid for the hour in any case and should be skilled enough and courageous enough to protect his own time beyond that limit; but so deeply symptomatic is it of the individual's problem that one might fairly define analysis as a process in which the individual finally learns to utilize the allotted hour from beginning to end without undue fear, resistance, resentment, or greediness. When he can take it and also leave it without denying its value, without trying to escape it completely or keep it forever because of this very value, in so far he has learned to live, to accept this fragment of time in and for itself, and strange as it may seem, if he can live this hour he has in his grasp the secret of all hours; he has conquered life and time for the moment and in principle.

Here, then, in the simplest of terms is a real criterion for therapy, an inner norm which can operate from the moment the person enters your office to the moment at which he departs, more or less finally, whether he comes once or a hundred times. It is a goal which is always relative, which will never be completely attained, yet is solved in every single hour to some degree, however slight, if the client really wants help; and I present a situation in which limitation is accepted and acted upon at least for myself. If I believe that one hour has value, even if no other follows; if I admit the client's right to go as well as to come, and see his efforts and resistances in both directions even when he cannot; if I maintain at the same time my own rights in time as well as my responsibility and limitations and respect his necessity to work out his own way of meeting a limit even when it involves opposition to mine as it must, then I have provided the essentials of a therapeutic situation. If with this personal readiness, I combine self-conscious skill and ability to utilize the elements which make for therapy, the client may, if he choose, in greater or less degree, learn to bear this limited situation which as he finally comes to realize, is imposed by himself as truly as by me; by his own human nature, no less than mine; or, if you like, by the nature of the life process itself.

I have often heard discouraged case workers with much—perhaps too much—analytic information, question the value of case work, since only analysis seems to offer real therapy. In my opinion the basis of therapy lies in the therapist himself, in his capacity to permit the use of self which the therapeutic relationship implies as well as his psychological insight and technical skill. If this is true, therapy is potentially present wherever the therapeutic attitude is maintained, whether the contacts be one or many and whether the vehicle be case work or analysis. Analysis, as I understand it, is not case work and involves a training, personal discipline, and responsibility for self which the majority of case workers have not undertaken or achieved. Yet they are being forced into a kind of long time case work which seems to be nothing unless it is analysis in disguise—analysis carried as far as the case worker knows or dares under conditions involving practical responsibility for the patient which no analyst would accept. Few case workers are willing to be entirely responsible for this type of work. Either they do not let themselves know what they do or they rely upon a supervisor or psychiatrist to soften the responsibility which they are not able to carry.

The alternatives seem quite clear to me. Either the case worker should prepare herself to do analysis responsibly or she should learn to differentiate case work from analysis and to value it for itself.

Personally, I have never been so convinced of the value of case work as a therapeutic agent, which can go where analysis will never reach, once it learns to utilize analytic understanding legitimately without practicing a distorted analysis. Therapy is a matter of degree and may be present anywhere, but one has to control this quantitative element. Analysis is a particular, highly specialized form of therapy, which can no more be practiced by the case worker than dentistry by the doctor. If the case worker can learn to understand therapy in the short contact, if she can be willing to accept a limitation of function for case work and refrain from analysis unless she goes into it openly with preparation, she can solve the problem which now confronts every case worker and every social agency which thinks it should be doing therapeutic case work but is not and, from my point of view, ought not.

While the topic of this paper is "Time," I end as I began, not so much with concern for limiting treatment in time,[2] although that is one of the most valuable single tools ever introduced into therapy, but with the necessity for accepting deeply, not merely intellectually, but emotionally and organically in our daily living, the reality of personal as well as functional limitation. A time limit is a purely external, meaningless, and even destructive device if used by someone who has not accepted limitation in and for himself. It becomes, then, merely a weapon turned on the other, or a salvation to be realized through and by the other. In order to use time as a major element in therapy, then, one must first have come to grips with it in one's self; otherwise the limitations which it introduces as a therapeutic agent are unbearable, and what the therapist cannot bear in and for himself, the patient cannot learn to bear either—at least if he does, he succeeds in spite of, not because of, the therapist.

In the last analysis, therapy as a qualitative affair must depend upon the personal development of the therapist and his ability to use consciously, for the benefit of his client, the insight and self-discipline which he has achieved in his own struggle to accept self, life, and time, as limited, and to be experienced fully only at the cost of fear, pain, and loss. I do not mean that knowledge is not necessary, that technical skill is not necessary. They are, but they are of no value therapeutically without the person. To practice therapeutic case work, in the long or short contact, no less than to practice analysis, one must be a therapist, and only to the extent that this is true are the relationships one sets up therapeutic, regardless of the label, the number of visits, or the interpretation recorded in the dictation.

The distinction between therapeutic case work and analysis is primarily quantitative not qualitative, and rests upon the acceptance of their respective limitations, the nature of the task which is undertaken, and the capacity of the client to take the type of therapy offered, whether it be more or less. The next step for case work, as I see it, is not to become more analytic but rather to become responsible for therapy, for practicing it overtly or for refraining deliberately, but, in any case, for knowing and bearing its own strength as well as its weakness—in other words, for accepting itself.

Reprinted from Jessie Taft, The time element in mental hygiene therapy as applied to social case work, *National Conference on Social Welfare Proceedings* (1932).

Notes

1. See Otto Rank, *Technik der Psychoanalyse* (Leipzig: Deuticke, 1926–31), vol. 3.
2. Rank, *Technik der Psychoanalyse*, vol. 2.

Commentary

Bill Silver

Celebrating the centennial year of the Penn School of Social Work allows us to reflect on the unique contribution the school has made from its inception to the present. Having had the honor of being an MSW student in 1968, the year the school moved from Pine Street onto the University campus, a doctoral student in 1972 and an instructor to the present time, the school has been part of who I am.

This personal identification of the role of the social worker was a central concept of the functional approach—in the understanding that the helping relationship was embedded in the dynamics of the client/worker relationship. This significant and profound contribution to the field has stood the test of time. Effectiveness studies have consistently shown a correlation between the client's assessment of a positive therapeutic alliance and treatment success, rather than by any theoretical model.

It is with this sense of pride that I review Jessie Taft's 1937 article on "The Time Element in Mental Hygiene Therapy as Applied to Social Casework." As I review it, I'm first struck with certain assumptions about treatment in our current consumer society age of managed health care. The first is the magnificence of the concept of "choice" as central to human integrity. It is through the client's awareness of choice, or free will, that the healing process begins. Knowing and respecting this is what the therapist (servant) must do. This, as Taft points out, is not a passive venture, but a mindful attention to the spirit of what Martin Buber called the I/Thou relationship.

Training to be a social worker required an intensive process of personal introspection by which the student came to recognize and own his or her difference from others, which then allowed respecting that in the client. This concept is timely in our complex and troubled global society—how to incorporate and value difference without imposing our will on others. This takes care, patience, and most of all courage.

Taft applied this notion to the client/worker relationship, focusing on the use of time as a construct that helps both partners in this very unique relationship accept both the promise and the limitation that time implies. Taft's visionary understanding of the value of the limited (one session) context, as a way of accepting the present without becoming overwhelmed by boundless wishes or rendered hopeless by discouragement, was and is at the core of the healing relationship. This is both a challenge to the client "who has brought himself to the point of asking for help" as well as the worker. "I [worker] also am forced to admit my limited function as therapist . . . my only control . . . is my control over myself in the present hour." In this eloquent statement Taft poses the existential challenge of living, in confronting the dual fears of action, which can lead to loss or failure, or passivity, which can lead to hopelessness.

As Taft puts it, "If one cannot live forever, is it worth while to live at all?" This search for meaning, as Victor Frankel puts it, is at the core of our humanity. It is also this acceptance of our humanity with all its limitations, which is the core of social work training. "If he [the client] can live this hour, he has in his grasp the secret of all hours." Similarly the social worker facing and accepting his or her limitations as well as strengths is at the core of self-respect.

Taft's concept of social work training was as much a process of introspection and self-realization as it was a cadre of therapeutic skills the student utilized in practice: "therapy as a qualitative affair must depend upon the personal development of the therapist and the ability to use consciously, for the benefit of his client, the insight and self-discipline which he has achieved in his own struggle to accept self, life, and time as limited and to be experienced fully only at the cost of fear, pain and loss." Words to remember.

Chapter 8
Social Work Processes

Ruth E. Smalley

Just as the years have seen the emergence of "fields of practice" for social workers, so have methods for social work practice evolved, and in much the same rather ragged and haphazard yet "contributive-to-a-whole" fashion. Throughout this century social work literature has given an increasing amount of attention to method, more properly to the nature and characteristics of the specific *methods* through which social work purposes are carried out.

It is important at the outset of this discussion to define method, process, and skill as they will be used in this book. *Method,* in the sense of "a general or established way or order of doing anything,"[1] refers to the social worker's part, or to what the social worker is responsible for doing, in manner and timing as well as in content. In the how as well as the what, in order to discharge functional role and responsibility as a social worker in a specific situation. *Process* in the sense of "a course of operations, a forward movement . . . produced by a special method,"[2] refers to the nature of the interacting flow which results from the use of a specific method. The use of the casework method leads to the casework process in which worker and client are mutually engaged. So with each of the social work methods the use of each by the worker in relationship with the "other" leads to a characteristic process marked by engagement in movement toward a mutually affirmed purpose as that purpose finds expression in a specific program or service. *Skill* in the sense of "the familiar knowledge of any science (or) art . . . as shown by dexterity in execution or performance"[3] refers to the social worker's capacity to *use* a method in order to *further* a process directed toward the accomplishment of a social work purpose as that purpose finds expression in a specific program or service.

While this concept of social work method sees as central the engagement of some other or others in a relationship process toward a social work end, it includes all that is done "in behalf of" the other outside the face-to-face contact in the sense that whatever is done is related clearly and consciously by the social worker to what is eventuating through the relationship process, and in the sense that the same values and, to some extent, the same skill are operative in the extra-client situations.

The primary methods for the practice of social work, methods which reach clientele directly, have come to be identified as social casework social group work; and community organization. Secondary methods, or processes which facilitate an agency's operation and service without touching the clientele directly but require for their discharge a social work skill taught as such in accredited schools of social work, have been identified as supervision (one aspect of administration); administration (the process through which the agency's operation as a whole is carried out); research; and teaching or education for social work. It is immediately clear that each of the processes identified as "secondary" is employed in a wide variety of undertakings and is in no sense limited as process or skill to social work programs or purposes. However, such a method may be thought of as resulting in a social work process or a process in social work when it is used within a social agency auspice to accomplish a social work end. In such situations, in addition to the very considerable body of knowledge and skill required for its use in any setting, the method calls for the learned and conscious application of certain principles equally applicable to all social work processes. As a consequence there should be provision for its development as skill within the curricula of the profession's schools. It can readily be seen that any of the processes of social work may be used in any field of practice, if "education" as process is broadened to include programs of undergraduate social welfare sequences and staff development in social agencies and not limited to graduate professional education within schools or universities.

As pointed out in Chapter 1, a significant development in social work in recent years has been the identification of primary method (casework, group work, community organization) as more "differentiating" for practice than field (medical, children's, etc.). As a consequence of that identification, or perhaps as evidence of it, concentrations in schools of social work are by method or process rather than by field of practice as was once the case. And even though concentrations by method exist in schools, common curricula are required of all students, whatever their concentration, with the differentiating element in the educational experience limited primarily to the methods of practice sequence and to the method used in the field placement.[4]

Although the 1962 Curriculum Policy Statement of the Council on Social Work Education[5] identifies a concentration in a specific method as desirable for every student, there is ferment in the mid-1960s because of the recognition that all social workers serve individuals, groups, and communities. As a consequence, there is experimentation in some quarters on the practice of a single social work method or, in social work education, on the teaching of a single social work method or several methods in a single practice class, with relevant modification of the field assignment. In this chapter what is specific for the several social work processes, both primary and secondary, will be considered. This study makes their differentiation useful for practice and recommends concentration in a single method in the basic (master's degree) program of professional education. At the same time certain common characteristics or principles for practice which mark all social work processes as processes in social work will be identified; indeed it is the focus of this book to identify them.

As these generic principles are mastered for the development of skill in any one of the processes, they become transferable and usable in any other, whether primary or secondary. But their use does not constitute the whole of the process, each of which has its distinct characteristics growing out of its distinctive purpose, configuration of relationships, and consequent demand on the worker's use of himself in the particular situation. To deny the differences in the processes seems as impoverishing for social work practice as to deny the differences introduced by field of practice, differences which, as we have seen, need not obscure but can enrich the over-riding social work or social welfare purpose, whatever the specific program. Indeed one of the generic principles for practice to be presented is the consistent use of the focus and purpose that inheres *both* in a specific field for practice as represented by an agency function *and* in the specific method being employed.

Social Casework

The earliest social work method to be identified as such was social casework. It was conceived as an individualized method for administering a social agency's service. The agency in question was the Charity Organization Society, the forerunner of today's family service agencies under private auspice, and it is Mary Richmond who is generally credited with the first thorough going development of social casework as method. Although the one-to-one relationship between worker and client was emphasized as central in social casework, the family focus was never absent, even in the earliest writings, in the sense of an appreciation of the significance of the family to the individual, the place of the individual in his family, and the importance of family relationships for individual development and well-being. The family as *focus* for a service, a central social work concern of the 1950s and 1900s, was described in some detail by Jessie Taft and by Robert Gomberg, writing in 1944 in the *Journal of Social Work Process*.[6] Here the emphasis was on the way a focus on the family could serve as a dynamic in the helping process.

As early as 1899 Mary Richmond identified relationship or, at least, worker capacity for sensitive appreciation of another's feelings, as fundamental in casework:

Friendly visiting means intimate and continuous knowledge of and sympathy with a poor family's joys, sorrows, opinions, feelings, and entire outlook upon life. The visitor that has this is unlikely to blunder either about relief or any detail; without it he's almost certain, in any charitable relations with members of the family, to blunder seriously.[7]

In subsequent writing[8] Richmond specified the purpose of casework as being to effect better adjustments between individuals and their social environment. It is significant that in this same writing she identified other methods or "forms of social work" as group work, social reform, and social research, and counseled that "the caseworker should know something of all forms-the more knowledge he has of all the better-and should carry through his special task in such a way as to advance all the types of social work enumerated."[9]

In referring to the specific purpose of social casework, she said: "Examples of social casework show that by direct and indirect insights, and direct and indirect action upon the minds of clients their social relations can be improved and their personalities developed."[10] She found the test of social casework to be "growth in personality" as measured against such questions as: "Does the personality of its clients change and change in the right direction? Are energy and initiative released that are in the direction of higher and better wants and saner social relations?"[11] It was in this work that she wrote:

Human beings are not dependent and domestic animals. This fact of man's difference from other animals establishes the need of his participation in making and carrying out plans for his welfare. Individuals have wills and purposes of their own and are not fitted to play a passive part in the world; they deteriorate when they do.[12]

Her *Social Diagnosis*, first published in 1917, with its exhaustive presentation of the nature of social evidence required by the caseworker and the processes leading to its admission and use as a basis for treatment, stressed the importance of sources of information *about* the client other than the client himself (although he is not ignored). It developed also a content and form for diagnosis in a way that missed the intuitive spark and feel for the heart of social casework as a process in human relationship, so beautifully set forth in both her earlier and later works, to which reference has been made. The effort to be "scientific" gave the effect of deadening the spirit.

Richmond's formal definition of social casework is familiar to every social worker versed in his profession's history: "Social Casework consists of those processes which develop personality through adjustment consciously effected individual by individual between men and their social environment."[13]

The purpose of the casework relationship as Richmond saw it was clearly one of reform. Yet her interesting question, "Are energy and initiative released that are in the direction of higher and better wants and saner social relations?," speaks to her intuitive awareness that the sources for change lay in the client himself, and his own wanting, and that the intent of the worker was to release the wanting and the energy and initiative for its realization in socially desirable ways. She referred also to the method of social casework as leading to those *processes* which develop personality, and she appeared to glimpse the existence of a "process" in its qualities of interaction, engagement, and flow, purpose or end, which could lead to client change and growth, a concept which has since been developed with more sophistication.

Richmond worked on social casework only as it was developed and used in the charity organization societies. "The function of the agency" she appeared to equate with the purpose of the method, which was easy to do because of the particular focus and scope of family agency programs. This purpose (of both agency and method) she sees as inhering in her own person and in the person of every worker.

It remained for the historic Milford Conference,[14] in which Mary Richmond participated, to establish social casework as a "definite entity" and to conclude that "the outstanding fact is that the problems of social casework and the equipment of the social caseworker are fundamentally the same for all fields." In thus establishing the "generic" in casework method for use in practice in all fields, it is significant that the conference did not deny the difference introduced by a specific field. After the monumental work of this illustrious pioneer, and of her colleagues and contemporaries, social casework has been variously defined and developed over the years.

Almena Dawley, long Associate Director of the Philadelphia Child Guidance Clinic, early emphasized the understanding of human behavior as the essential part of the caseworker's task.[15] Virginia Robinson, for many years Vice Dean of the School of Social Work of the University of Pennsylvania, was one of the first writers to stress the significance of the relationship for the casework helping process:

If the history of social casework teaches anything it teaches this one thing outstandingly, that only in this field of the individuals' reaction patterns and in the possibility of therapeutic change in these patterns, through responsible self-conscious relationships, can there be any possibility of a legitimate professional casework field.[16]

If casework accepts squarely this responsibility for relationship, it has a field for research, for experiment, demanding the most untiring scientific accuracy and the most sincere, unceasing self-discipline.[17]

Jessie Taft added the concept of agency function, a more sharply defined concept of process, and the portent, for method, of their relationship in the development of skill in her epochal article "The Relation of Function to Process in Social Casework."

There is one area and only one in which outer and inner, worker and client, agency and social need can come together effectively; only one area that offers to social workers the possibility of development into a profession—and that is the area of the helping process itself.[18]

And, again, she wrote: "There is no escape . . . from . . . the necessity to establish ourselves firmly not merely on the basis of social need, but on a foundation of professional skill."[19]

Taft, in establishing the impossibility of basing the helping process (of social casework) on an understanding of need alone ("something that can never be known exactly or worked on directly"), suggested that

we limit our study of needs to the generally recognized categories (of social services) as they emerge out of the larger social problems and leave to the individual the freedom as well as the responsibility of testing out his peculiar needs against the relatively stable function of a particular agency. There remains to us a large and comparatively unexplored area for future development, an area in which to learn how to maintain our functions intelligently and skillfully and how to isolate whatever can be isolated from the particular situation in terms of the law, the nature of the general pattern of the helping process.[20]

Anita Faatz[21] refined and further developed the concept of social casework as an individual helping process given form and direction by social agency function. Prior and subsequent to that writing, in addition to the continued publications of Taft and Robinson, numerous articles in professional journals (notably by Aptekar, Dawley, Faith, Marcus, Pray, Smalley, and Wessel) identified, described, and illustrated social casework as the "functional school of thought" was developing it.

Meanwhile the impact of Freudian psychoanalysis on the practice of social work in this country and primarily, in the early years, on the practice of social casework had resulted in another development in social casework method commonly referred to as the diagnostic method in contra-distinction to the functional method, to which reference had just been made. The functional method was developed, originally, in what is now the School of Social Work of the University of Pennsylvania and in the Philadelphia community of social workers. The diagnostic method, as method, was perhaps first developed in its purest form in what is now the Columbia University School of Social Work and in the community of social workers in New York City. The profound insights developed by Freud and the analysts who were his colleagues and those who followed enriched all of social work, just as they revolutionized the practice of psychiatry.

However, a substantial body of the profession, in taking over psychological understanding in the specific form developed by Freud, were influenced by its somewhat mechanistic, deterministic view of man which saw him as pretty much prey to the dark forces of an unconscious, on the one hand, and the harsh restrictive influence of internalized parental dicta in the early years of growth, on the other. It was only in the middle 1900s that the Freudian analytic group, through its emphasis on ego psychology, reflected a more optimistic view of man which conceived him to be creator of himself as well as creature.

It is this view, first developed for psychotherapy by Otto Rank, a disciple of Freud, and later corroborated and elsewhere developed by a considerable body of writers and scientists in a variety of disciplines, which contributed to the thinking of the "functional school" from its beginning. This influence followed from Rank's serving on the faculty of the Pennsylvania School of Social Work and from his having been a dynamic influence in the lives of Taft, Robinson, and the community of social workers in Philadelphia. As was earlier suggested, in taking over the Freudian interpretation of human nature, the diagnostic group identified to some extent both with the purpose of psychoanalysis and with adaptations of its methods, with a resultant acceptance of responsibility to "diagnose a pathological condition" and to "treat it." This was close in spirit to Mary Richmond's emphasis on diagnosis of a social problem and assumption of responsibility for its treatment, with the substitution of a medical or quasi-medical "internal" focus for a more purely social "external" focus. The significance of the purpose of the agency and of the social service being administered became secondary to the purpose of treatment of socio-pathological conditions in individual clients. Indeed the agency's service was sometimes referred to as a "tool" in treatment.

To summarize, and all too briefly to do the "schism" justice differences between the diagnostic and functional schools of thought, reflected in the practice and teaching of social casework as method, were related to three kinds of understanding. (1) *Understanding of the nature of man.* The diagnostic school worked from a psychology of illness, with the worker feeling responsible to diagnose and treat a pathological condition, and with the center for change residing in the worker. The functional group worked from a psychology of growth and saw the center for change as existing not in the worker but in the client, with the worker's method consisting of engaging in a relationship process which released the client's own power for choice and growth. The functional group used the term "helping" in referring to its method, the diagnostic group "treating" or treatment. The functional group's view of human nature also took into account to a greater extent than did the diagnostic group in the early years of its development the effect of social and cultural forces in human development. This was due in part to Rank's emphasis on these forces, and in part to other influences. (2) *Understanding of the purpose of social work*. The diagnostic group saw it as the effecting of a healthy personal and social condition in the clientele served, with the specific purpose of the agency not only secondary but also sometimes in a curious way parallel to, or detached from, or even in opposition to the purpose of the worker. The functional group saw the purpose of the agency as representing a partial or concrete instance of social work's overall purpose and as giving form and direction to the worker's practice, with casework method constituting not a form of social treatment of individuals but a method for administering a specific social service in such a way, and with such psychological understanding of the helping process, that the agency service had the best possible chance of being used for individual and social welfare. (3) *Understanding of the concept of process itself*. This concept was not developed in the diagnostic group, some of whom have referred to social work method as a "repertoire of interventive acts" (apparently acts of the worker). The functional school developed the concept of social casework as a *helping process* through which an agency's service was made available, with the principles in social work method having to do with the initiating, sustaining, and terminating of a *process* in human relationship.

Reprinted from Ruth E. Smalley, Social work processes, Chapter 2 in Ruth E. Smalley, *Theory for Social Work Practice* (New York: Columbia University Press, 1967). Reprinted by permission of Columbia University Press.

Notes

1. Funk & Wagnalls, *Standard Dictionary of the English Language*, International Edition.

2. Ibid.

3. Ibid. For a penetrating analysis of *skill* in social casework, see Virginia Robinson, The meaning of skill, in *Training for Skill in Social Casework, Journal of Social Work Process* 4 (1942).

4. Parenthetical note should be made that in some schools a kind of emphasis in a field of practice is still possible and is available within today's generic curricula through the provision of field placement, locus for research and thesis, and specialized seminars in a given field, as well as through the planned inclusion in the commonly required courses of content with special relevance for a particular field.

5. Official Statement of Curriculum Policy for the Master's Degree Program in Graduate Professional Schools of Social Work, Council on Social Work Education, 1962.

6. Jessie Taft, Introduction, and Robert Gomberg, The specific nature of family casework, in *A Functional Approach to Family Casework, Journal of Social Work Process* 5 (1944); reprinted in *Family Casework and Counselling, Journal of Social Work Process* 6 (1948): ix, x, 82–132.

7. Mary Richmond, *Friendly Visiting Among the Poor: A Handbook for Charity Workers* (New York: Macmillan, 1889), 180.

8. Mary Richmond, *What Is Social Casework? An Introductory Description* (New York: Russell Sage Foundation, 1922).

9. Ibid., 259.

10. Ibid., 255.

11. Ibid., 260.

12. Ibid., 258.

13. Ibid., 98, 99.

14. *Social Casework, Generic and Specific*, a Report of the Milford Conference, 1929.

15. Almena Dawley, "The Essential Similarities in All Fields of Casework," *Proceedings of National Conference of Social Work* (Memphis, 1928), 358–60.

16. Virginia P. Robinson, *A Changing Psychology in Social Case Work* (Chapel Hill: University of North Carolina Press, 1930).

17. Ibid., 185.

18. Jessie Taft, The relation of function to process, *Journal of Social Work Process* 1 (1) (1937); reprinted in Virginia P. Robinson, ed., *Training for Skill in Social Casework*, Social Work Process Series (Philadelphia: University of Pennsylvania Press, 1942), and in Virginia P. Robinson, ed., *Jessie Taft, Therapist and Social Work Educator: A Professional Biography* (Philadelphia: University of Pennsylvania Press, 1962).

19. Ibid., 3, 5.

20. Ibid., 8.

21. Anita Faatz, *The Nature of Choice in Casework Process* (Chapel Hill: University of North Carolina Press, 1953).

Commentary

Mark Frazier Lloyd

Ruth Elizabeth Smalley was born in Chicago on November 14, 1903. She received her bachelor's degree in 1924 from the University of Minnesota, her master of social work degree in 1929 from Smith College, and her doctor of social work degree in 1949 from the University of Pittsburgh. She practiced first in the Bureau of Child Guidance in New York from 1929 to 1932 and was then was on the faculties of the University of Chicago, Smith College, and the University of Pittsburgh before coming to the School of Social Work at the University of Pennsylvania in 1950 as Professor of Social Casework.

Even in Pittsburgh, Ruth E. Smalley was a nationally prominent advocate of the functional school; her joining the Pennsylvania School significantly solidified the ranks of the functional school. In 1954, Dean William Donald Turner established an Administrative Council for the School and included both Margaret E. Bishop and Ruth E. Smalley among its members. Smalley joined Turner on both the Doctoral Council of Social Work and the Doctoral Admissions Committee. Smalley's leadership, in particular, was a major factor in reconstituting the School's faculty. In 1956 Turner named her vice dean of the School.

In May 1953, the Trustees announced the election of a new president of the University, Gaylord P. Harnwell, who took office in July. Harnwell soon announced his intention to conduct an institutional self-study that would extend to every School and academic resource center of the University. The "Educational Survey," as it was named, was funded in April 1954 and launched in October of that year. A faculty committee of seven, chaired by Professor of Law Paul W. Bruton, was appointed to study the School of Social Work. The Survey Committee worked for a year and a half, meeting with the dean, the faculty, the alumni, the agencies employing social workers, and experts outside the University community. The committee was initially unsympathetic to the school and only after much pressure the University administrators of the Educational Survey did add Ruth Smalley to the Committee's membership and she participated in its work for most of a year. Her influence on the committee was significant and many of the favorable recommendations were based on her initiatives.

Smalley became vice dean in 1956. In June 1957, Dean Turner announced his resignation and President Harnwell named her acting dean. In 1958, the University appointed her to the academic administrator position of dean of the School of Social Work. She was the first woman to be appointed dean of the School and the second woman to be named an academic dean at Penn.

President Harnwell and Provost Jonathan E. Rhoads strongly supported Dean Smalley's administration. She returned their confidence with vision, energy, and accomplishment. Within a month of the announcement of her appointment, Dean Smalley presented to the School's advisory board both an optimistic report on the state of the School and a sweeping set of initiatives. Likewise, within two months of her appointment, Harnwell and Rhoads were assisting her with an approach to the Russell Sage Foundation for the establishment of a research center at the School of Social Work. Though the grant proposal was ultimately unsuccessful and not all the initiatives were fulfilled, the tone of Dean Smalley's tenure was set. Cordial and mutually advantageous relations with the University continued throughout her eight years as dean.

At virtually every turn, Dean Smalley advanced the School's interests. She held closely to the school's functional theory and practice and made it a brand name for the Pennsylvania School of Social Work. Dean Smalley's determination to preserve and enlarge "the functional point of view" expressed itself most clearly in her selection of new faculty. Between 1958 and 1966, the School hired or promoted sixteen full-time instructors to its standing faculty. Thirteen of this number had earned the D.S.W. from the School itself. In this way Dean Smalley assured the maintenance of functionalism as the School's most notable characteristic.

She recruited intensely, raising the size of the graduating class from 55 in 1958 to 77 in 1966 (an impressive 40 percent increase). She expanded the teaching corps, raising the size of the faculty from 17 in 1958 to 24 in 1966 (also a 40 percent increase). She strengthened the School's administration, creating and funding the positions of associate dean and vice dean.

On her second try, in 1960, she established a new research center at the School. She successfully applied to the National Institutes of Mental Health a four-year grant to "further the development of a research center in the School and to augment faculty teaching in the doctoral program." The grant funded the hiring of a social scientist at the full professor level and an administrative assistant.

In 1963 she led the School through a challenging re-accreditation evaluation by the Council on Social Work Education. Her cultivation of major donors led to the School's first endowed professorship, the Kenneth L. M. Pray Chair. Over several years she negotiated a new building for the School, which was constructed at 3701 Locust Walk—the heart of Penn's campus—and occupied by her office and the School's faculty in June 1966. Hers was a winning administration.

In 1959, Dean Smalley celebrated the fiftieth anniversary of the School's founding and successfully lobbied the University to pay for it all. Beginning in 1958 and continuing through the first six months of 1959, she planned, organized, and carried out a magnificent celebration. She delayed the first event in the celebration until January 1959, so that it would coincide with the annual meeting of the Council on Social Work Education (CSWE), which met in Philadelphia that year.

An accreditation review of the school in 1963 summarized the progress of the school under Dean Ruth E. Smalley in the following manner:

A number of developments have been instituted during the past four years, all in the direction of improving the School's program. The research curriculum was strengthened, a Research Center developed, new faculty positions added, a cultural course introduced, a seminar for field instructors initiated. Extension of the curriculum in community organization is underway and there has been increased participation of faculty in professional and educational conferences (with an increased budget for this purpose), and an effort to broaden the base of knowledge of faculty through yearly seminars (one on the history of social welfare, the second on the relationship of law and social work). Partly as a result of such efforts, faculty publications and research activity have recently increased, and the groundwork laid for increased intellectual stimulation.[1]

With re-accreditation by the CSWE confirmed and the new building on Penn's campus assured, Dean Smalley felt that she had achieved her administration's chief goals. In January 1965, she submitted her resignation to President Harnwell, effective June 30, 1966.

In addition to her most successful tenure as dean, Smalley also served on national professional committees. She served as president of the Council on Social Work Education from 1960 to 1963 and on the Temporary Interassociation Committee that established National Association of Social Workers (NASW).

Smalley was a student of the founders of the functional approach and throughout her intellectual career felt a great debt to the foundations laid by Drs. Jessie Taft and Virginia Robinson. However, she did not accept the functional approach as a stagnate body of knowledge. She was active in attempting to improve and invigorate the functional approach to social work and her academic efforts culminated in her 1967 seminal book, *Theory for Social Work Practice*. Other publications include her 1956 brochure for the Council on Social Work Education, *Specialization in Social Work Education*. She also published many chapters such as "The Functional Approach to Casework Practice," in Roberts and Nee, eds., *Theories of Social Casework* (1970). In 1959 she was one of the presenters at the Colloquium on the Fiftieth Anniversary of the School of Social Work at the University of Pennsylvania. She also wrote "Today's Frontiers in Social Work Education," in Weaver, ed., *Frontiers for Social Work* (1960); "Attributes of a Social Work Educator, in Soffen, ed., *The Social Work Educator* (1969); and many articles including "School Social Work as a Part of the School Program" (1979) and "Social Work Education: A World View" (1968).[2]

On of the debates in social circles around the time of Smalley's tenure was about the ability of social work to be an international profession versus a profession that is distinctly different in every country. In her 1968 article listed above, she unequivocally stated that "Because the form that social work takes is so intimately related to any society's or country's goals for itself and its people, its values, its mores, it is inevitable that forms of social work should differ from country to country, and that its patterns of social work education should differ from country to country" (163).

Among the many awards and recognitions Dean Smalley received are the following: In 1961, Ruth E. Smalley's name was added to the Wall of Honor at the University of Minnesota. The names engraved on the wall are University alumni who have received the Outstanding Achievement Award. The University of Pennsylvania School of Social Work instituted the Dr. Ruth E. Smalley Award in International Social Welfare. This award is given to the member of the graduating class who, through writing, participation in class discussions, and experience, has demonstrated an interest in, and a working knowledge of, the international and cultural dimensions of social work practice, and the application of practice to research. In 1967, upon her retirement from the school, she was elected professor emerita.

Notes

1. Report of On-Campus Visit for Reaffirmation of Accredited Status of the School of Social Work, University of Pennsylvania, photocopied typescript, folder "Return to Penn . . . Studies," RG 29, Council on Social Work Education records, Social Welfare Archives, University of Minnesota.

2. *Theory for Social Work Practice* (New York: Columbia University Press, 1967); *Specialization in Social Work Education: A Review of the Report of the Committee on Specializations in Social Work Education of the Commission on Accreditation, . . . Some of the Implications for the Profession* (New York: CSWE, 1956); The functional approach to casework practice, in Robert W. Roberts and Robert H. Nee, eds., *Theories of Social Casework* (Chicago: University of. Chicago Press, 1970), 77–128; Today's frontiers in Social Work education, in W. Wallace Weaver, ed., *Frontiers for Social Work* (Philadelphia: University of Pennsylvania Press, 1960); Attributes of a social work educator, in Joseph Soffen, ed., *The Social Work Educator: Readings on the Preparation and Induction of Social Work Faculty* (New York: CSWE, 1969), 18–24; School social work as a part of the school program, *School Social Work Journal* 4 (1) (1979): 37–40; Social work education: A world view, *Social Work* 27 (3–4) (1968): 339–46.

Chapter 9
The Influence of Otto Rank in Social Work: A Journey into a Past

Virginia P. Robinson

[Editorial Note: This paper was written in part at the time when Jessie Taft was writing *Otto Rank: A Biographical Study* and was intended to be a chapter in that book. It soon became clear to us that it did not belong there. What I am using now in preparing a paper under this title for the *Otto Rank Association Journal* of 1968 consists of parts of the original paper of 1958 and parts of my biography of Jessie Taft written in 1960–61. It lacks the unity in feeling of a paper written as a whole from one focus in time. The span of time between the generation of the First World War and the Vietnam War is overlong to keep in focus in a search for the influence of one man's thought. The many individuals and many institutions and organizations that have played a part in the changes I summarize from the limited focus of the "I" of the writer can justly be disappointed or critical of what is omitted here as well as what is said.]

In the era of swift moving dramatic change in which we live today buffeted by violent forces operating in every direction we long for and seek peace while realistically we know that what we seek is control, if not of external circumstances, at any rate of our own reaction. We seek an anchor against attack and destruction, for stability in ourselves that can weather threat and confusion. The word *control* is in every mind, voiced continually on TV and radio. What can we hope to control and how? These are the persistent questions. Neither science nor sociology provides the answers. Answers will come only by experiment in imaginative thinking and responsible action in the long slow process of time.

Underneath the word *control* as we examine it the word *influence* comes to mind to challenge thought as it resists understanding and definition in its usage throughout history. One thing only stands out clearly, the sense of power it conveys. In primitive times this power was believed to emanate from the stars to men and could be all-powerful and pervasive while it remained magical and inexplicable. In present usage of the word this power is more direct, from man to man, from group to group. It may be good or evil but it remains inexplicable as in primitive times. We have not learned how to direct it or control it.

Among the questions that arise are how does one person influence another or a group; is it conscious and planned or does it occur only in natural association; when is it brief or sustained, can it be carried from its original source in one person to create a movement extending beyond itself as waves follow the stone thrown in a pond. Freud's influence is of this nature still powerful today in the technical magazines of psychoanalysis, effective as well in political, social and literary thought. In psychoanalytic theory and practice many differing groups have branched out, some called by the name of a leader in its practice. Two men in Freud's group and related to his brilliant discoveries were the earliest "defectors" from Freud's leadership and their names continue into the present to distinguish their followers. Jung and Adler of Freud's generation may be said to have established their difference perpetuated since in their names, Adler in the American Society of Adlerian Psychology and the *Journal of Individual Psychology*, Jung in the C. G. Jung Foundation. The main stream that emanated from Freud's genius is well described in *Psychoanalytic Pioneers*, its final chapter bringing this movement in the United States into the present era.

When Rank was forced to leave the "Ring" group around Freud with the publication of his *Trauma of Birth* in 1924 his activity as a therapist continued in America and later to some extent in Paris. His differentiation from Freud found expression in two books written, as he has said simultaneously, *Genetic Psychology* and *Technique of Psychoanalysis*. These contained the essence of what Rank, the youngest member of the Freudian group, had learned as a practitioner of psychoanalysis. It went far beyond and beneath Freud's theory in his understanding of the individual and his description of the creative, neurotic and average types. More important than *this*, he created a new form for the therapeutic process out of his comprehension of the dynamics of the positive and negative will with a brilliant use of time in an ending process that differed for each individual. His influence on social work began at the time when he left Vienna, established his residence in Paris and began to lecture at the New York School of Social Work, the Pennsylvania School of Social Work, The Graduate School for Jewish Social Work, and to take patients in New York and Philadelphia.

Among his patients in 1926–27 were two social workers whose relationship to him was an important factor in sustaining and carrying on his point of view. To describe this I must write autobiographically from my own memories still vivid and accessible to me today and from Jessie Taft's memories as she made use of them in 1959 in her book, *Otto Rank: A Biographical Study*.

At first it may seem an impossible task to disentangle the thread of a single individual born before the First World War from the tremendous world-wide changes that have brought us into the era of the Vietnamese War. One must discriminate among one's memories in order to focus on and find the turning points where influence can be said to determine choice and direction.

Born, raised and educated through high school in Louisville, Kentucky, my memories of childhood are of happy and uneventful school days and vacations shadowed only by the usual accidents and illnesses. Nature provided the forces to which a child could react with fear—flooding when the rivers rose, the Charleston hurricane, a tornado that devastated a section of the city. But even then, so it seems to me in retrospect, fear was not generalized but projected on a small experience as content, on a question that took the form, "would I be equal to it; would I get where I was going." I think of the society in which I lived as stratified by class, the upper social class distinguished by the family tree behind them. The middle class was the only one familiar to me, where education through high school was important, and a sense of security was derived from family background. Money was of less importance.

High schools were segregated as a matter of course by sex, not color, although Negroes lived in special sections of the city, had their own schools and were segregated in use of transportation and other services. This was taken for granted without discussion that I remember. Religious differences were much more important than color difference, the Catholic church bearing much negative projection. The Jewish families in this community were the distinguished families, among them Flexners, Brandeises, Dreyfuses. The Flexners were my playmates on my street and when I was older I visited in the family of "Uncle Louis" Brandeis when Mrs. Brandeis was president of the Women's Club and one of the girls was, like myself, getting ready for college. The only factor of difference that I was aware of as I grew up was between North and South. To be born north of the Mason and Dixon line or to talk like a "Yankee" was to be in some curious way inferior. I became conscious of this attitude as prejudice and reacted against it. I know that I felt my difference from the girls I knew in high school who were already going to parties with boys and looking forward to marriage. This sense of difference was balanced happily by the fact that my aunt who lived in our family was librarian of the only library in town (it was long before the days of Carnegie libraries) and I not only had the run of its books and beautiful garden close where tuberoses grew but a summer job when I was old enough to be useful.

I enjoyed school as I enjoyed this library and it was no surprise to me or to my classmates I think when I was offered the valedictorian scholarship to the University of Chicago. There seemed to be a tacit assumption on the part of my teachers that I would go to college but surprise when I refused the scholarship and made application to a small woman's college in the East, Bryn Mawr College, where standards were high and I was not sufficiently prepared to meet all its requirements. I needed help in making up enough credit to be considered by this college and an alumna who was a teacher of English in a private school who read Ovid with me once a week in the summer before college opened gave me something I had not found before among my teachers, an ego ideal, a standard, a distinguished personal quality, and a dedication to the content that she taught. Much older than I, she became a friend who carried my projection as long as she lived.

Four years in this eastern college followed by a fifth with a master's degree in philosophy and psychology gave me new experience and great personal satisfaction in my contacts with others whose interests were like my own but no sense of dedication to scholarship or to any particular career or profession. It was taken for granted in that era and particularly in that college that a college education, so rare for girls in the South, should lead to a career. My sense of *career* had always been teaching where my interest and opportunity for employment lay. Social work was unknown to me. Without experience or training in teaching I struggled through a year of not unsuccessful teaching in the girls' high school in my home town. Relationships with faculty, young and old, who, like myself, were baffled and absorbed by problems of teaching and administering a high school held me for a year.

It seems to me in retrospect more chance than choice that led me to enroll in the summer school of the University of Chicago in 1909, a decision that provided the dynamic that was to change the shape and direction of my "career" for the rest of my life. When I chose the small woman's college in 1902 I must have been guided by some inner wisdom away from the big university until I was ready to make use of it and what was being taught there.

This was a brilliant era in the University of Chicago. Dewey's influence still permeated its thinking: after he had left to go to Columbia, Tufts, Mead, and Angell were still active in the departments of philosophy and psychology. Even in summer school I was able to get classes with outstanding professors; one with Angell in psychology, one with W. I. Thomas well known for his work on *The Polish Peasant*. The house I lived in was rented to a graduate student for the summer use of a small number of graduate students by its owner, Dr. James Tufts. So I was surrounded by the sense of these creative men, the atmosphere of university life and the dynamic point of view that permeated it. *Pragmatism* was the word that identified it, used first by William Pierce and carried to popular knowledge by William James. It assailed everything I had been taught in college work in philosophy and psychology and the standbys I had built for myself or taken for granted in a conventional Protestant home and a Quaker college.

Surely it was chance that brought together in the small group of graduate students in Dr. Tufts' house that summer two students as unlike in externals as Jessie Taft and I, she from the Middle West, I from the South. Writing of her to a college friend I said, "I've never met such frankness in a mortal being. She is so frank and sincere and free from conventionality that she compels you to a like frankness and you find yourself telling her things in the most natural matter of course manner." Underneath the external differences we were drawn together by our interest in the courses we were taking and by a common dislike of the person in charge of the house. This likeness was to grow into a relationship life-long, determinative for our professional and personal development.

At the end of summer school I returned to my teaching position more interesting now in a smaller branch high school and with content I loved to teach, grammar and literature. Challenging too was an invitation from a small group of older professional women to teach them something about psychology. I used the abridged psychology of James that I had worn out in college courses and learned more, I expect, than my responsive students.

There must have been more protests against the management on the part of teachers in those days than I was aware of. Any interest in social or political problems of the times seems to have been completely lacking in me. Woman suffrage was the only movement in which I became involved when I was asked to become president of a newly formed College Association for Woman Suffrage in the city. I learned to argue and speak in public for this cause that seemed important and inevitable but I was never moved by it as were its leaders, Mrs. Park of England, Sarah Anthony, Anna

Howard Shaw, Mrs. Carrie Chapman Catt and others. It was their dedication and their quality that influenced me, not the cause itself. I marched in the suffrage parade in New York City because I was there and friends were marching but my feeling was not engaged as presumably it is engaged today in those who march in the civil rights marches.

After our summer together in Chicago, Jessie Taft had found an anchorage and a goal in the University of Chicago in a program leading to a doctor's degree but I was growing increasingly dissatisfied with the limitations in my experience and in the realization that, though teaching was what I wanted to do, I did not have the secret that would engage my high school students in a learning process. In letters that Jessie Taft and I exchanged we were expressing our desire to know "people" to get away from the academic atmosphere of school, college or university. When the person who was head of Dr. Tufts' house in the summer of 1909, who evidently had a confidence in us that we did not return, recommended us to Katharine Bement Davis, head of the New York State Reformatory for Women at Bedford Hills and the Laboratory of Social Hygiene, a research center, we agreed to come for a spring-summer trial experience. Here was the new experience we longed for, with people and problems utterly unfamiliar to us. Jessie Taft found in the job that Miss Davis offered her as assistant superintendent the opportunity to use herself with people that went beyond her expectations. As sociologist in the Laboratory of Social Hygiene I was a learner in a new undefined field offering all kinds of experience for me.

Of the greatest importance to both of us was the contact with the members of the board of the Laboratory of Social Hygiene who met at times with Miss Davis and her staff to hear reports and to advise on future steps.

These men were psychiatrists, some trained in Europe, all doing creative work with the mentally ill in institutions or clinics, Campbell, Hoch, Adolph Meyer, Salmon to name a few of them. In them we found the stimulus that led to the next step in what was now our own self-directed education. When we left the Bedford Reformatory after Miss Davis resigned to become Commissioner of Charities and Corrections of New York City, we had to find jobs to support ourselves but we knew with what we wanted to be associated. It was not social work as represented by Mary Richmond of the Russell Sage Foundation who had developed social casework but what seemed to us a more creative dynamic approach to human problems. We spared no pains in examining this field while we each got work on a temporary basis until we could find where we belonged. We had found assurance in ourselves and the opportunities ahead for this field that we now knew as *mental hygiene*. Jessie Taft described this movement as "epoch making" in a paper called *The Relation of Psychiatry to Social Work* and tells of her part in it at a meeting of the New York City Conference of Charities and Corrections in 1926. By this time she had found a specific job with the Mental Hygiene Committee of the State Charities Aid Association of New York where she had many speaking opportunities, a chance to experiment with a small school for difficult children and experience in helping adolescents in the Cornell Clinic of Psychopathology. Meanwhile I spent a year with a small group of teachers from the Public Education Association in New York engaged in defining a function for home and school visitors later known as school counselors. Following this year, I accepted a position in Philadelphia where a well endowed new institution was to be built for orphan children. It seemed to have much to offer but I found that in a paper planning stage it had no function to engage me and when the board of the Pennsylvania School of Social Work asked me to take over the direction and activities of the school whose small staff had gone to war, I accepted with alacrity. Jessie Taft had many offers of positions in Philadelphia and chose one that involved the opening of a new Department of Child Study in The Children's Bureau. This developed into the first mental hygiene work in Philadelphia. It gave us the opportunity we sought to be together, to teach and practice and use what we had to give. By this time we knew through reading something about what Freud was doing in Vienna. It was focused for social workers by William Alanson White in his books, *The Family Romance, The Meaning of Disease, Mechanisms of Character Formation* and his editorship of a great progressive journal, *The Psychoanalytic Quarterly.* We incorporated what we could use into our thinking, adding material we did not have from science, from Cannon, Herrick, Child, Kempf. My ignorance of social work meant that I had everything to learn about social agencies and resources in a community strange to me in order to help students in their field work assignments with family agencies and child placement agencies. Underneath the practical problems there was always the more fundamental problem I felt in the student in his need of help of some kind for himself as well as the client of the agency. We knew that these problems could not be understood by visiting in the homes of the clients of social agencies or giving financial aid to the poor or finding a home for a child. We were accepted for what we knew about behavior that was new and different and our conviction and our relation to people asking for what we knew gave us recognition and authority in the community. Jessie Taft had added to her equipment six months of supervised training in mental testing in order to have a tool for use in interview contact with individual children. She began to use her title of Doctor and her papers of this period describe what she could do in interview contact with the individual child, not only the children in placement agencies but with children of troubled parents in the community.

Education for social work was in a very early stage in this era and little was known as common knowledge by the few schools that existed when I became Associate Director of the Pennsylvania School of Social Work in 1920. The New York School, the Boston School, the Philadelphia School were among the first schools in existence; the Smith College School for Psychiatric Work developed in relation to the war experience as a summer school. Financial and organization problems were important to these schools as were relationships with sponsoring universities or colleges. Fundamental for all of us were the questions that concerned the individual student, supervisor and teacher, from selection of students through the learning-teaching process to accreditation. After several years of experiment with one or another part-time director, the Pennsylvania School was fortunate in obtaining a full time director in Kenneth L. M. Pray, a recognized leader in community social services. For him, too, the development of education for social work in the Pennsylvania School became a lifelong job until his death in 1948. This was the school where the impact of Rank's point of view was most directly felt and where his influence was sustained throughout his life.

These early years in Philadelphia with Jessie Taft at work in the Children's Aid Society and I in the Pennsylvania School of Social Work in retrospect seem the most active years of our lives. Were we impelled by our so recently acquired knowledge of mental hygiene with its promise of help for troubled children or by our pressing need to learn more for ourselves? Whatever this drive might have been, circumstances shaped themselves to fit our need in ways that seem to me now little short of miraculous. Soon after we came to Philadelphia while visiting a friend on the staff of Carson College for Orphan Girls in Flourtown, Pennsylvania, we did no more than look at the old stone house across a picket fence from her house when the aged owner died, the house was up for sale and we bought it on "Building and Loan" and borrowed money. These two houses stood alone on a road running from the Bethlehem Pike through country occupied only by cornfields and a railroad track carrying freight and two passenger trains a day from Ambler to Philadelphia. The house lacked water, electricity and heat and was in need of general renovation. We named it *The Pocket* for once inside of it the problems of getting out would be all absorbing. It asked all the strength and ingenuity we possessed but we did not grudge this expenditure of ourselves. House and garden thrived. I do not think our jobs suffered for both of us continued to be involved in the problems of children and child placement. When the house had been made habitable our good friend, Sophie Theis, in the Child Placement Department of the New York State Charities Aid Association suggested we take a child to board on a trial basis for a year. She described to us an interesting gifted boy seven years old whose mother had died and whose father had remarried. The year's trial as a boarding home led to adoption. A year later we took a second child, a girl of five, both of whose parents had died.

The house adjusted to a second child by the addition of dormer windows and a housekeeper. This constituted our family through thick and thin over the years until the boy was in college and the girl had completed her training as a dietitian at Drexel. We could not have done this without the help of unusual schools, Germantown Friends for the boy, Sunnyside Day School and public school for the girl, and two wonderful women in succession as housekeepers. Good child placing practice today would not have approved this placement of two children with two professional women but I think we survived this experience without harm to any of us. Grown up now, the boy with a good marriage and three children of his own, the girl with a responsible job as chief dietitian in a big hospital, would not repudiate their unorthodox childhood experiences nor did we as adopting parents ever regret our experience in living with children we loved whose problems of growing up became our own to learn from, to help with as best we could.

Jessie Taft describes her first meeting with Rank in the foreword to her book, *Otto Rank: A Biographical Study* (ix–xii):

My first contact with Otto Rank occurred on June 3, 1924, at a meeting of the American Psychoanalytic Association in Atlantic City where he was to give a paper in English on *The Trauma of Birth*, the title of his book recently published in German. As a clinical psychologist from Philadelphia working chiefly with children, I had no official right to participate in a psychoanalytic conference, but I was interested in psychoanalysis as a further training measure for myself in the future and I wanted to see who these analysts were and what they were like. An acquaintance who had worked in Vienna with both Freud and Rank had told me of something new and different in Rank's theory as well as in his therapeutic technique that had aroused immediate interest, although I had known nothing of Rank previously except his name and a title, *The Myth of the Birth of the Hero.*

I do not remember how I got to the meeting nor what was said there, but I still retain a vivid impression regarding the quality of the several speakers. With one exception all seemed to me unimpressive, if not actually dull, until the slight, boyish figure of Rank appeared beside the speaker's desk. He was the very image of my idea of the scholarly German student and he spoke so quietly, so directly and simply, without circumlocution or apology, that despite the strong German accent I was able to follow his argument and I thought to myself, Here is a man one could trust.

It took two years, with letters and a single interview, before I finally pinned myself down to a definite date for analysis with Rank in New York in the fall of 1926. Meantime, I had been saved from myself and my attempt to escape by engaging a substitute analyst, through the latter's untimely death. Later I was able to appreciate what a fateful accident it had been for me, as I remembered the two application interviews with their portent for the future of the analysis. The first man, in spite of his frank doubts of my suitability in terms of age and my limited time allowance, had ended by accepting me, but only after I had remarked, with full awareness of its possible influence on a man who had himself been analyzed by Rank, that Dr. Rank had previously agreed to take me. I left that interview knowing in my heart that I was the stronger of the two and had conquered in the first round.

In contrast, my meeting with Rank had been quiet, brief, without controversy. No doubts were expressed by him, no fear of my age, no interest in my life history, nor was there any contest regarding my rigid time limit. He did not promise anything. He merely agreed to try, on the basis of the time at my disposal. I can recall only one remark from that interview in response to something I had presented about myself. "Perhaps the problem lies there." And that was all, but on that one sentence I began to make myself over before anyone else should have the chance.

Coming to the point of being willing to subject myself to anything as strange as was psychoanalysis in the United States at this time was not due to any conscious personal need nor to lack of professional success, but to the deep awareness of being stopped in professional development. I knew that I had not the basis for helping other people, however deep my desire. Psychological testing of children was useful but, as I knew only too well, it was not therapeutic. Failure with the few neurotic adults who had been referred to me had filled me with guilt and fear. Psychoanalysis seemed to be the only resource, however fearful.

When I finally came to my first hour with Rank, while consciously submissive, afraid, and fully aware of my ignorance of psychoanalysis, my underlying attitude was far from humble. I was, after all, a psychologist. I had some knowledge of myself and my problems. I had achieved a point of view, psychologically. If there was anything in my unconscious in terms of buried memories, I would have to be shown. And so the battle was joined; but I soon found that it was a battle with myself. I was deprived of a foe. It took only two weeks for me to yield to a new kind of relationship, in the experiencing of which the nature of my own therapeutic failures became suddenly clear. No verbal explanation was ever needed; my first experience of taking help for a need that had been denied was enough to give a basis for the years of learning to follow.

At this time I had no idea of Rank's growing difference from Freud or of his alienation from the Vienna group. In cheerful ignorance, I combined with my daily hour a weekly evening lecture given by Rank for the New York School of Social Work, another by Ferenczi for the New School of Social Research, a regular seminar for social work students with a Rankian analyst, and still a third evening lecture course, by whom I do not recall. To this extreme activity on my part Rank offered no objection, but turned my naïve daily reports to good account in terms of their meaning for me in the therapeutic process. Never did I sense on Rank's part the bitterness or resentment that he might well have been feeling at a time when Ferenczi, who had but recently been his friend and collaborator, was refusing to speak to him. I did not try to account for the look of pain and constraint that characterized his appearance at the evening lectures, except by recognizing the hardship of reading such difficult material in English to a group no better prepared than myself to understand, and by projecting upon him my own exquisite embarrassment at these revelations of the secrets of the analytic hour.

At the end of an eight or nine week period—the time altered just enough to undo my original intent to control it—I returned to Philadelphia overflowing with emotion engendered by a vital experience, at that point quite innocent of theory of any kind, but eager to give to others the kind of help that had been given to me. It was not long before I realized that emotion and intuition were not enough. I had to earn a point of view by my own efforts, had to face Freudian difference, painful as it was, not merely through Rank but in my own thinking, reading, and use of the therapeutic relationship.

I turn now from Jessie Taft's account to my first contact with Rank in June 1924 when he was in the United States for the first time and came at the invitation of the Pennsylvania School of Social Work to be its commencement speaker. I was too responsible for the arrangements for that occasion, too involved in holding an audience which crowded the auditorium of the Social Service Building at 311 S. Juniper Street on a hot night while they waited an hour for his arrival delayed by the confusion in the change from Standard to Daylight time, to be able to listen to what he said but my impression of the importance of what he had to say, of the depth and significance of his thinking, of the quality of his conviction is unforgettable. Vivid too in memory is the impression of the intentness of his listening audience as they laid aside their discomfort and irritation with the heat and delay to try to the best of their capacity to hear and to understand something of what he was saying.[1] I had more freedom to listen the second time I heard him speak from the lecture platform of the New York School of Social Work in the fall of 1926. Again the sense of the tremendous significance of his thinking took precedence over the impression of his youth, his lack of freedom with the English language and the sense of his loneliness, his "difference" as he faced this strange, alien audience. The content of the lectures he read there and of those he was later to give in a lecture series at the Pennsylvania School of Social Work in the fall of 1927 came straight from the books he had written as his thinking began to differentiate itself from Freud's in his *Genetic Psychology* and *The Technique of Psychoanalysis*. This was formidable material and perhaps the very effort required to get any foothold in it was an additional stimulus in our struggle to find the meanings we could sense were embedded in every word he uttered. These lectures as he delivered them in English were multigraphed and distributed to the members of his audience. Later they were remultigraphed and bound for the use of students in the Pennsylvania School Library. In this form they continue to be used by faculty and students in the School and are the only English translations of *Genetic Psychology* available.[2] Happily, Jessie Taft's knowledge of German and her willingness to spare neither time nor effort in her struggle to comprehend the meaning of his *Technique of Psychoanalysis* resulted in translations, which, published by Knopf in 1936 under the titles of *Will Therapy* and *Truth and Reality*, made accessible to social workers the individual psychology in which they were interested.

When I applied for therapy in the fall of 1927, Rank accepted me within the framework of my position and my responsibility as head of the case work department of the Pennsylvania School of Social Work, without question for what use I could make of him in the analytic relationship. My picture of analysis was a naïve mixture of what was current in the social work community, especially in New York where friends had been analyzed and of what I had experienced through Jessie Taft's analysis as I spent weekends with her either in New York or our home near Philadelphia. My own analysis was completely different from anything I had heard from others. I began in the first hour with a description of my family where no problem existed for me and continued with family history until my interest flagged—as did Rank's. Dreams interested him and served me well to take me into the fundamental problems of relationship, the problems he was working on in his lecture series. These were problems of denial, identification and projection to show how the self builds itself up through likeness and difference in a search for its own identity. Figures in my current professional and living situations appeared in dreams for this purpose rather than figures from the past. I realize today more vividly than at the time how brilliantly and considerately Rank made use of these to show me my "patterns" in relationship. I remember today the sense of illumination when he said "perhaps what the self really seeks is identity; does it ever accept difference?" And the exhilaration when in response to a dream he said, "Perhaps you are really ready to leave." It would be the shortest analysis I have ever had.

How little I realized when I applied for "therapy" with Rank in 1927 that the experience which was to follow of one hour a day for six weeks, a time-limited, internal process, could possibly be the basis, the raw material, as it were, for an understanding of the problem of relationship, of self and other, professional as well as personal relationships. That it can be so remains always beyond explanation, often beyond belief, and certainly beyond proof when one approaches it intellectually or scientifically.

Dr. Taft recognizes and speaks to this dilemma in her article entitled "The Function of the Personality Course in the Practice Unit":[3]

Those few social workers who experienced something quite unlike classical psychoanalysis in their contact with Rank were saved in part from the tendency to put into practice with clients what they themselves had found helpful, by the fact that they were not at all sure what technique had been used with them. It was not anything they could grasp and formulate intellectually. Difference they had certainly experienced and were still experiencing, but they were unable to pin it down to anything definite enough to be used on their clients. They had learned that help comes from something more than intellectual knowing, that it goes beyond the facts or even the traumas of a life history, that it is a dynamic, present, swift-moving experience with an ending; but what to do with it in case work could not be determined so easily.

Our need, in truth our necessity, to get hold of something we could use in our understanding of the process of change that we had experienced in ourselves and of its applicability to our efforts to help our clients proved to be a powerful dynamic. But what Rank offered to an audience in his early lectures at the New York School and the Pennsylvania School of Social Work presented us with the barrier of his profound and difficult thinking complicated by his lack of ease in expressing himself in English.

My first opportunity to use what I had learned from Rank in addition to what I gave to students in classes grew out of a decision made earlier to work for a doctorate in the University of Pennsylvania department of sociology on a part time basis over the minimum acceptable time span of seven years. The faculty of the University of Pennsylvania were glad to have a closer connection with the School of Social Work that was associated with it and individual members could not have been more helpful in suggesting courses and planning a program for me. Nevertheless this period stands out as one of the most miserable periods of my life. All my interest remained in my students and my teaching and University courses got only the leftover crumbs of my time and energy. I did a minimum of required reading and went to classes feeling unprepared. But when it came time to write a dissertation I knew what I would do.

Using the Proceedings of the National Conference of Social Work as content I surveyed the development of social casework giving my own evaluation of its changing theories and practice from Mary Richmond's *Social Diagnosis* to the period of the thirties in which we were living and working. This was not research in the terms in which the University defined and expected it but the generous thesis committee accepted it and the University of North Carolina published it under the title of *A Changing Psychology in Social Case Work*. It contained the best of what I knew and what I hoped for in direction for this field. Its sale was unprecedented for a thesis in this field but it went beyond what practice in the field had attained and made enemies as well as friends for the School of Social Work and Rank's influence in it.

As I look back over thirty years in this effort to clarify my own comprehension of Rank's effect on social work, and as I follow Dr. Taft's account of the development of Rank's thinking, I realize in a new way that, at this critical time in the history of social work when social caseworkers were so eagerly and hungrily turning to psychoanalysis for some answers to the problems of helping individuals in need, Rank had already explored the problems of individual psychology and therapeutic processes to the bottom and reached his own solutions both in personal experience and in theory. His therapeutic gift remained for his use but he did not need further experience with therapy to enlighten him on the "Organization of the Self" or the problems of "Growth, Learning, and Change in the Development of the Individual," the title of two of the lecture courses that Dr. Taft organized at the Pennsylvania School of Social Work in 1936 and 1937 in which Rank participated and which she has described in Part III of her biography of Rank. Dr. Taft's account of his classes in the Pennsylvania School and Rank's letters to her during this period need nothing added to show the responsible nature of his relation to the field of social work, his responsiveness to the problems presented to him by social workers, his ability to share his experience and his thinking with them especially after he came to this country to live in 1935 when his own greater freedom with himself and his easier use of English permitted his spontaneous relation to a group to be manifest. However, even after he had an appointment on the faculty of the Pennsylvania School and took this appointment in all seriousness, he never thought of himself as a teacher in this field. In a class of caseworkers bringing their own cases as content for discussion, he lent himself fully and intently to the problems involved without at any time taking responsibility for the case from the worker to whom it belonged. It would have been utterly foreign to him to have supervised a worker on a case, as he might have supervised a therapist in a controlled analysis. But his slightest comment, spontaneous as it was, could touch an area of process the worker had failed to see, illuminating the case under discussion with his deep and penetrating comprehension of the dynamics involved.

It is interesting and characteristic of Rank's own understanding of differentiation in growth processes, that when the powerful influence which emanated from his therapy, direct personal teaching and writings began to be assimilated by the faculty and supervisors in the Pennsylvania School of Social Work where his relation to social casework was most fully expressed, there was no tendency to introduce into casework or supervision any imitation or adaptation of the therapeutic form or method of treatment. On the other hand, there began to appear a sharper sense of focus and responsibility developing around specific services or functions of agencies and deeper sensitivity to the feelings and movements of the clients in using those services.[4]

This development in social casework soon found a name for itself, functional social casework, under which all distinctive casework processes could be described. One book, *The Nature of Choice in Casework Process* by Anita J. Faatz, has traced this development from Rankian psychology to the authentic process of giving help in social casework. I turn to it now for two quotations which contain the precise recognition of what it is that carries the continuity. Recognizing the discovery of *function* by Dr. Taft and her definition of it in the first volume of *The Journal of Social Work Process*, as its authentic definition, Miss Faatz traces the continuity between this development of an authentic professional process which can be described in the different fields of casework, in supervision and in teaching, and the understanding of Rank's will psychology and helping processes. In the chapter entitled "The Discovery of Function" she writes:

But first, in order to give the focus and approach by which this development unfolds, I should like to state the thesis which constitutes, in these pages, the single strand of development to which all detail and factual content are related. It is this: that the important change, above all others, which functional casework embodies, is the shift of the dynamic center for the source of therapeutic results from the helper to the one being helped. From this all other detail of concept, method, process, and content flows. By this statement we do not intend to imply any denial of the determinative role played by the skill of the helper or lack of it: nor of the crucial importance of the helping process in affecting release of these vital elements in the self. But the quality of this skill does not arise from the caseworker's understanding of the facts and the problem, or from the competence of the diagnosis, or the control by the caseworker of the level upon which the self uses help; nor does it rest upon the accurate delineation of steps of treatment. It arises, instead, out of a primary acknowledgment that the source of understanding is within the self; that here, internally, is located the original upspringing of the impulse towards life, and here lies the control of change and growth.[5]

In the chapter on "The Search for the Therapeutic Factor" she adds to the statement quoted above the following:

The problem in 1930 was one of discovering where the control of the process lay: what distinguished casework from psychotherapy. In 1930 it was still believed that the caseworker somehow controlled the client's use of help and the extent and quality of the internal change which he experienced. The importance of the external reality factors of agency and client problem was fully acknowledged but not yet with clear understanding of where the significance of the outer reality lay. From this awareness of problem, explored and worked upon in the teaching process, in the supervisory process, in casework process in school and agency, it at last became clear that form bears a fundamental relation to the process; that the concrete reality of the helping situation carries the true projection of the deepest conflict of the self; and that help upon a practical, tangible life problem affords the potentiality for help which touches the core of the self and sets in motion an authentic process of growth.[6]

In addition to the historical development of functional casework which Miss Faatz' book follows with penetrating understanding of its continuity, the main body of the book authenticates her profound understanding of Rank's psychology by a description of the processes of giving and taking help that she practiced in her teaching and supervision of students.

Other references to the earlier literature of functional casework should include the *Journal of Social Work Process*, the first one of which, mentioned above, contains the definition of function in the article entitled "The Relation of Function to Process in Social Case Work." Other *Journals* which followed edited by Dr. Taft and other members of the faculty described the use of function in different casework fields, with illustrative articles and cases from the practice of the field work agencies of the Pennsylvania School of Social Work; also Dr. Taft's article published in the *Newsletter of the American Association of Psychiatric Social Work*, 1939, "Function as the Basis of Development in Social Work Processes"; "Conception of the Growth Process Underlying Social Casework Practice" published in *Social Casework*, 1950; and my own books, *A Changing Psychology in Social Casework*, 1930, *Supervision in Social Case Work*, 1936, *Training for Skill in Social Case Work*, 1942, and *The Dynamics of Supervision Under Functional Controls*, 1942.

As the use of the word *Functional* gained meaning in the field of social casework characterizing the practice of the Pennsylvania School of Social Work and its training agencies, Rank himself reacted against the use of the word as Dr. Taft describes quoting his letter of February 28 in which he says: "As to function I get more and more suspicious of words (or terms). It seems that besides clarifying something, they contain (or create) a new problem. I am afraid you will have to tell me whether I am function or 'need' (and which of the two Freud is)." Dr. Taft goes on to say that "Rank was the last person to understand function as used by the social agency . . . the only function he understood was a professional one but in his case self oriented and self maintained. Its importance as a support for the social worker was hard for him to realize or to conceive of as allowing for a truly helpful relation to the client." "At any rate," Dr. Taft says, "Rank should not be held responsible for the functional approach in social work which has been a bone of contention in social work discussions and often identified with the Rankian influence on the Pennsylvania School."[7] True as this statement is, I would add to it that the functional school of casework grew out of what had been experienced and learned from Rank and that its differentiation and growth were inevitable never just expedient as Ira Progoff suggests in his book *The Death and Rebirth of Psychology*. The concept of "limits" and the search for authentic limits in function and *in* the social agency service and structure which became the focus of the misinterpretations and hostility directed against functional casework grew out of the experience and discovery of limits in the self in a growth process and of the "voluntaristic acceptance of the inevitable" to use Rank's term.

Under the banner of the name *Functional* or *Rankian,* students in the Pennsylvania School waged war for what they were learning in their casework classes and field practice against the students from the Smith School and the New York School whose theory and practice stemmed from Freud and was beginning to be identified as *Diagnostic.* Nor were the arguments over point of view and practice confined to students. For the first time in its brief history, the field of social casework found itself no longer united by one approach and purpose, to do good to people in need, but divided by basically different approaches in its understanding of need and of how to help those who sought its services.

By 1947 the controversy between the two schools of casework in philosophy, principles and practice became particularly disturbing in the field of family casework to the point where the Family Service Association of America decided to sponsor a committee to study the differences between the two orientations calling it a "perplexing professional problem." Under the leadership of Eleanor Sheldon for the functional group and Patricia Sacks for the diagnostic group using case illustrations of practice, the committee worked faithfully over a two year period examining the differences in respect to concepts of personality theory, of methods of helping and of responsibility undertaken. They agreed in finding:

"widely divergent points of view in basic concepts," "opposing methods of appraising a client's need and of extending help" and "opposite views about the nature of responsibility undertaken in extending professional help."[8]

The report states in conclusion: "Because of the nature and profundity of the differences in philosophy, purpose, and method, the committee is in agreement in believing that these two orientations cannot be effectively reconciled or combined."[9]

In 1947, the year in which the Family Service Association of America initiated its study of difference in the casework field, the National Conference of Social Work took notice of this controversy and it was Kenneth L. M. Pray who, with "apologies for the fact that he was not a caseworker and never had been one" undertook to present to the section on casework a paper entitled, "A Restatement of the Generic Principles of Social Casework Practice." Mr. Pray was not only Director of the Pennsylvania School of Social Work, where admittedly the predominant emphasis of the faculty was on casework, but he was also regarded as the dean of social work, a man related to every field of practice. His dedication to the field of social welfare, both public and private, was known to be lifelong; his experience in teaching, board membership, committee work, with assignments on a national as well as a local level, as chairman of the Philadelphia chapter of the National Association of Social Workers, as President of the National Conference of Social Work, etc., had involved him constantly in a search for his own attitudes on the pressing problems of professional practice and of organiza-

tion and education for social work. While he was always open to what was new in practice or theory, he took nothing from another point of view superficially or facilely,
engaging only with what was pertinent to his own focus of inquiry where it had meaning for him until he could find use for it in his own thought organization. It is interesting to remember how responsive he was to Rank's philosophy, how much he enjoyed
a personal contact with him without any impulse to seek therapy for himself. His ability to accept the new point of view that his faculty were introducing into casework and
to deal with the criticisms of it that were projected on him in his contacts with other
schools of social work was amazing, understandable only in terms of a wholeness and
integration in himself and an undeviating respect for the other person, a balance
rarely found. As he struggled with the problem which occupied his mature life, the
problem of finding the limits within which professional helping could develop, he
made distinctive and important contributions to the literature of functional social
work, notably an article on "The Agency's Role in Service."[10]

His paper before the National Conference of Social Work on "Generic Principles
of Social Casework Practice" was eagerly awaited and accepted as a definitive statement of functional casework in its difference from the diagnostic school by his casework faculty and by practitioners in the field. I quote from the end of this paper where,
speaking of the difference he has described and which on the whole he regards as
promising for the future of social work, he closes with "a word of warning."

It is not, and cannot be, a matter of indifference either to the individual or to the profession,
what choice is made among these alternatives. . . . Either choice, any choice of basic concepts
of professional practice, involves giving up something of oneself, of one's own accustomed and
comfortable patterns of thought and feeling and action. Especially, perhaps—I am free to
admit—does the functional point of view demand this kind of change. For the individual, the
old personal freedom of professional purpose and achievement must yield to the limits of a
defined and controlled function and to the realization that the determination of the outcome
is within the power of another. This is not easy to accept and to make truly one's own. It involves
a discipline of the self which is probably unique among all professions, in its demands upon the
worker, both in training and in later professional practice.[11]

In this paragraph just quoted lies the most personal statement of the internal source
of his philosophy that to my knowledge Mr. Pray ever made. Inherent in this statement
is the recognition of the moment of internal change in the self in relation to "the
other" and realization of the discipline of the self which follows. This is a precise
description of what functional caseworkers experienced in the development which followed the impact with Rank's psychology.

Mr. Pray's death in March 1948 following this major speech at the National Conference of Social Work, the retirement in 1950 of the two oldest members of the faculty,
Dr. Taft and myself, was the occasion for major changes in the University of Pennsylvania School of Social Work. The New York School of Social Work had become Freudian
or diagnostic in its psychological orientation. The Graduate School for Jewish Social
Work where Rank's influence through Dr. and Mrs. Karpf was important had ceased
to exist. Rank's psychological point of view was carried into other schools of social
work notably the North Carolina School of Social Work and as far west as the Univer-

sity of Southern California where Rose Green, formerly of the Philadelphia Child Guidance Clinic and a patient of Rank's, held an important position on the faculty.

When the Pennsylvania School of Social Work found a new center of gravity in its relation to the University under the able Deanship of Ruth Smalley undoubtedly the influence of Rank continued to prevail and individual graduates carry the meaning of that influence into their practice. There is no way of assessing the extent of, and depth of that influence except through what comes back to those of us who represent the Otto Rank Association and edit its journals.

Rank has preserved folders among his papers for every class or lecture he has given, containing notes, usually on scraps of paper and often illegible, about some case or question presented by the group or class members; sometimes a complete outline of a lecture on a topic which he had prepared in advance for a particular meeting. Sometimes the choice of a topic was left entirely to him as was the case in an invitation from the New York School of Social Work Student Organization on November 16, 1935. An all day meeting of the conference was scheduled, the morning session to be on a philosophy of social casework with a paper and several discussions prepared by students. Rank was to be the afternoon speaker and though he was not expected to make any connection between his speech and the morning session, copies of the students' papers were sent to him in advance. His blue penciled marks in the margin of the papers indicate how thoughtfully he read them. He entitled his own paper, "Psychology and Psychologies" speaking very simply and directly to the point of the changing character of psychology saying:

That is the one idea I would like to impress upon you, psychology is not and never can be, purely scientific, i.e., absolute, in as much as it has to be human and not the experimental and laboratory kind. Theories of psychology are just as much a product of their civilizations as everything else, they not only change like fashions, I might almost say, but they have to change in order to be applicable to the understanding of the existing type of man.

This was the theme of his opening address to the Psychological Center in Paris, in the summer of 1934[12] perhaps his one attempt to use his influence directly to gather a group of professional workers from various fields, psychiatrists, psychologists, child guidance workers and general counselors who might come together to discuss the problems of counseling and helping under his leadership. This opening address was very important to him as evidenced by the number of copies he preserved, handwritten and typed, indicating various stages of rewriting before it satisfied him for delivery to the group that was finally assembled in Paris, its membership indicating the widespread extent of his leadership in the United States at that time. This interest in "changing psychologies" was his own, expressed in his *Seelenglaube und Psychologie* (written in 1930) and *Art and Artist* of the same period. *Beyond Psychology*, which was to carry on this line of thinking, was already beginning to formulate itself in his mind at the same time.

The focus of the problems that were of concern to social workers in the decade 1930–40 and where they turned to psychoanalysts for enlightenment can be read in an outline of a series of six lectures which Rank prepared for the Graduate School For

Jewish Social Work with the help of Dr. and Mrs. Karpf, at that time director and faculty member of the School, to be given in the spring of 1935. The outline was divided as follows:

Three lectures on theory:
  1) Activity vs. Passivity
  2) Denial vs. Repression
  3) Will as a Dynamic Factor
Three lectures on therapy:
  1) Time limit and the ending phase
  2) The role of the analyst as a type
  3) Illness and healing

The first topic was one of the most controversial issues in social casework at that time and Rank brought to it his own experience with the question of activity and passivity of the analyst in psychotherapy. He evidently discussed this topic in different groups of social workers and two rough copies of a lecture on this subject were saved among his papers. In this paper he gave a brief account of the changes he had seen in the attitude of the analysts towards their activity in the psychoanalytic process leading to "a movement in the past fifteen years towards a more active, more direct and more effective approach than orthodox analysis had to offer," beginning with his own separation of theory from therapy in 1921. Of his own attitude he says:

I allowed the patient a much more active part not only in the analytic situation but also in life by putting the whole emphasis of the process on an emotional, instead of an intellectual experience . . . I introduced the setting of a time limit to the analytic process on the basis of a philosophy of life in which the principle of separation plays the most important role. In this way the whole emphasis was shifted from the investigation of the cause to the present emotional situation in the analytic situation . . . analysts criticizing this approach as "suggestion" overlooked the fact that this dynamic activity called forth in the client an intense reaction—equally active—which left less room for suggestion than the analysts' explanation. . . . Their own reaction was due to fear, fear of suggesting something to the patient which had to be explained to him anyway and fear of his reaction, that is fear of his activity.

This fear was less or even non-existent in social work which was basically more active by its very nature and so could easily adopt the more active approach of the new therapeutic movement. This was first and foremost achieved by the Philadelphia School, the leaders of which were by virtue of their own approach attracted to my philosophy. But what they accepted from it was not only a confirmation of their own activity as social workers but the more essential and deeper meaning of the therapeutic process as an active, almost creative experience, on the patient's part. And because they try to permit the client to work out his own salvation, with their help to be sure, their approach was characterized as "passive" from the worker's point of view whereas it is "active" from the point of view of the client, that is, purely therapeutically speaking.

This point around passivity and activity in social casework has been confused by the same fundamental error which led Freud to the mixing up of theory and therapy. The whole psychoanalytic approach is centered around the therapist who is doing the research and the explaining on the basis of what he knows; while real therapy has to be centered around the client, his difficulties, his needs, his activities. It seems to me irrelevant whether the worker is active or passive as long as the client can be made active in a constructive way.[13]

Again and again in answer to the question which never failed to present itself in any audience of social caseworkers as to the nature of therapy, he made the point that therapy could not be based on causality but can only be based on spontaneity; that it was by its very nature anti-causal, an assertion of the individual against causality, that is creative.

The following statement which I take from his notes on this subject can stand today as a brief definition of therapy as he understood and practiced it.

Therapy, then, in its broadest sense is a process in which the individual is taught to accept limitations, an acceptance which ordinarily is brought about by the living experience in reality. Hence therapy, as said before, should be nothing else but a conscious and purposeful utilization of the normal growth in every existing relationship. Thus adjustment, which cannot be forced anyway, becomes acceptance, which, on the other hand, can only be internally achieved by a reevaluation of one's own past experiences.

From self-acceptance, which is the biggest change from self-denial, follows acceptance of others, the world at large that is of life. Therefore acceptance starts with the individual's own limitations within himself, limitations which his imagination tries to override (Ideal, etc.). This is necessary and helpful as long as he does not try to carry out his imagination beyond his own capacity. In other words, the imaginary expansion of one's own self has to be kept apart from real life inasmuch as it is impossible to carry it into life.

The danger in therapy is due to the same imaginative jumping beyond one's own self, because this leads to a vicarious living beyond one's own limitations in the other, the therapist, a phenomenon which has been described as identification or idealization. On the other hand, the more a therapist or a teacher is himself, that is, has accepted and remains within his own limitations, the more effectively will he enable his client or pupil to accept limitations in himself instead of projecting them and fighting them outside himself. This typical resistance of analytic therapy can be easily avoided if one does not demand more of one's client than oneself was or is able to achieve. As long as we do that we are just as much neurotic as is the other and are bound to accept all the other's projections and identifications. In other words, this kind of therapy becomes mutually vicarious instead of independent growth which finds its own limitations automatically in the individual himself.

Human relationship, common to all situations in all times and in all places, is the one basic element which forms the basis of social psychology as it is the sum and substance of so-called individual psychology which is in truth a relationship psychology. The only real individual psychology is a laboratory psychology in method and a biological psychology in content. Everything beyond that like emotion, intellect, language, etc. is relationship psychology which leads to social psychology of a new kind. The use one individual makes of the other in every relationship situation is the real subject of social psychology. So far only the relationship between doctor and patient has been made use of therapeutically until we discovered that every human relationship is therapeutic in essence, the parent-child relationship, the teacher-pupil relationship, marriage, friendship, love. The difference between therapy as a specially utilized relationship and other human relationships which operate therapeutically is then that in life the other becomes not only a part of the situation but of the other self as well.[14]

Rank carried this psychology to the many places in the United States where he was asked to speak in this period of his greatest popularity. Often the invitation came from a university, from faculty members and therapists, or from a school of social work. In Hartford, Connecticut, it originated in a clinic whose psychiatrist and chief social worker were present at the Psychological Center in Paris and here he gave what amounted to a continuous class or institute. At the University of Buffalo it was a week-end seminar organized by its faculty members. In Cleveland the enrollment for his lecture from both social workers and psychiatrists was so large that the group was divided into two parts. There were other lectures on his way west of which there is no record except a newspaper clipping. In California on the invitation of Dr. Lovell Langstroth he gave a week-end seminar of four lectures, one at Stanford University. Dr. Langstroth's interest in Rank's point of view stimulated a book of his own entitled *Structure of the Ego.*

California became Rank's goal as a place to find a new life for himself.

In the fall of 1938 Dr. Taft was in the hospital with pneumonia too sick to know that Rank had been to see her in the hospital. His letters have much to tell her of his ups and downs in writing, of his own illnesses, of his *Beyond Psychology.* During the two weeks he spent with us in our summer cabin in Vermont in 1939 he was absorbed in writing his *Beyond Psychology*—always cheerful, full of good humor in spite of bad weather. He was planning to go to California as soon as Estelle Buel then his secretary returned from Europe. The divorce from his first wife, Beata, long planned, came through in August 1939 and released him to marry Estelle Buel. His letters though he is not well are full of his plans to settle his affairs in New York and move to California as soon as possible. His letter to me October 22, 1939, expresses his farewell to the School. He died nine days later in Polyclinic Hospital, New York, of a sudden, undiagnosed infection.

Dear Virginia,

It was a real pleasure to receive such a good letter from you, especially at a time when I was beginning to feel a little better.

Though I was only a couple of days in the hospital for the removal of the stone—I was still for two weeks afterwards pretty much "hospitalized" but at least at home. The picking up is still rather slow and I am taking things easy. It seems to me the right time to go out West, not because I am not feeling quite well but because I want and need a different kind of life. This also applies to my relation to the School. I was glad to hear that things look so much better this year and I am sure the School has a unique function to fulfill. I am naturally proud of whatever I may have contributed to its present status and future significance.

At the same time I feel that that's all I had to give, not because I don't feel so strong at the moment but because my interests are decidedly narrowing down to some problems of which there is little use in either therapy or social work. I have to come to some peace within myself and with the world at large, which is a purely personal matter. Not that others may not benefit there from but it is not primarily meant for that.

Yet, it is still nice to hear that the help I could give to some people has borne fruit. I shall certainly make it a point to come to Flourtown before going West and probably wouldn't come anyway without Mrs. Rank and Spooky. I'll let you know in time.

With best wishes to both of you

Your Rank

This paper comes to an end while influence continues for wherever there is life as in Rank's contribution it can spring up anew in unexpected places. In working on these problems I have been newly impressed with the dynamic power of Rank's thought and the wholeness it achieved in expression in his short life from his first book, *Der Künstler* to *Art and Artist* and *Beyond Psychology*. As time goes on evaluations of Rank will depend almost wholly upon his work without the biographical facts that his reticence concealed. His letters to Jessie Taft and his relation to Anaïs Nin as described in her diary are frankness itself without factual detail and a revelation of an outstanding and unusual quality of this man of genius. Like other men of genius—I think particularly of D. H. Lawrence with whom Rank has been compared—his dynamic personality operated as a magnet to draw others to him. But unlike other men of genius his necessity to express himself creatively was finely balanced by a sensitivity to the other person. The discipline he exercised upon his expression of his own creativity eventuated in an understanding of relationship and of relationship psychology that remains his greatest contribution to psychology and to therapy.

Reprinted from Virginia P. Robinson, The influence of Rank in social work: A journey into a past, *Otto Rank Association Journal* 3 (1968): 5–41. Reprinted by permission.

Notes

1. There is no note of this address among Rank's papers strangely enough since it was his practice to keep some note of every paper he gave.

2. Two chapters from *Genetic Psychology* were published in the last issue of this *Journal* 3 (1) (June 1968). During the 1920s some chapters as articles were published in *Psychoanalytic Review* and *Mental Hygiene*.

3. Published in 1942, in *Training for Skill in Social Case Work*, ed. Virginia P. Robinson (Philadelphia: University of Pennsylvania Press, 1942).

4. Virginia P. Robinson, *The Dynamics of Supervision Under Functional Controls: A Professional Process in Social Case Work* (Philadelphia: University of Pennsylvania Press, 1949), 17–18.

5. Anita J. Faatz, *The Nature of Choice in Casework Processes* (Chapel Hill: University of North Carolina Press, 1953), 17.

6. Ibid., 42–49.

7. Jessie Taft, *Otto Rank: A Biographical Study* (New York: Julian, 1958), 229.

8. Family Service Association of America to Study Basic Concepts in Casework Practice, *A Comparison of Diagnostic and Functional Casework Concepts*, ed. Cora Kasius (New York: Family Service Association, 1950), 7–9.

9. Ibid., 13.

10. Kenneth L. M. Pray, "The Agency's Role in Service," in *Training for Skill in Social Case Work*, 117–26; also in pamphlet, Child Welfare League of America, *Problems of Agency Organization and Administration* (New York: Child Welfare League, 1941).

11. Kenneth L. M. Pray, "A Restatement of the Generic Principles of Social Casework Practice," in Pray, *Social Work in a Revolutionary Age and Other Papers* (Philadelphia: University of Pennsylvania Press for School of Social Work, 1949), 260.

12. See *Journal of the Otto Rank Association* (December 1967) for D. Pearce Bailey's account of this occasion and Rank's paper "Psychology and Social Change."

13. Taken from papers on "Activity and Passivity in Social Work," unpublished.

14. From unpublished papers. For Rank's description and explanation of therapy *Will Therapy* in English translation is available.

Commentary

Kathryn Rossé

Influence: "How does one person influence another or a group . . . can it be carried from its original source in one person to create a movement beyond itself as waves follow the stone thrown in a pond?"

By posing this question, Ms. Robinson introduces the central theme of this essay. From this question flows a description of Rank's influence on the professional and personal development of two women—Virginia Robinson and Jessie Taft—and through them the development of the functional approach to social work, which became the foundation for the University of Pennsylvania School of Social Work's approach to social work education. Over time thousands of social workers have been trained in this approach. And, as one of them (SW'66) I will carry this theme into the present by examining the influence of the functional approach on my own professional development as a social work practitioner, supervisor, and educator.

My introduction to the functional approach to social work was both discomforting and a pleasant surprise. I entered the school of social work three weeks after my twenty-first birthday, having just completed an undergraduate psychology program at a large state university. I had had exposure to some brilliant professors and exciting ideas, but for the most part my education consisted of learning in large lecture classes and successfully regurgitating information on multiple-choice tests. By the time I graduated I was confident in my ability to perform academically and was looking forward to graduate school.

However, at the School of Social Work, in an atmosphere that put significant emphasis on *my* response to the material presented, rather than my ability to parrot back what the instructor had imparted, I felt off balance. Initially I struggled with my first year practice professor, Dr. Herman Levin, to give me more direction. Eventually, as I relinquished that struggle and took charge of my own learning, I discovered the thrill of my own creative potential as a helping professional. In describing this process Ms. Robinson quotes Dr. Anita Faatz, another pioneer in the functional approach,

the important change, above all else, which functional casework embodies, is the shift of the dynamic center of the source of the therapeutic results from the helper to the one being helped. From this all other detail of concept, method, process, and content flows.

With time I understood that I was engaged in an educational process that focused on me as the center of my own learning and that, in doing so, paralleled the helping process that I was learning to use with my clients.

Over the years I have endeavored to create a similar educational experience for my supervisees and students. The following reflects my efforts to create a climate of mutual trust, and intellectual challenge where students are free to explore their own creative response to the challenges posed by their social work experience.

Teaching

September 13, 1994
8:30 a.m.
I open the door to an empty classroom designated A-8. No windows, a supporting post in an awkward place.
I walk around the post, arranging chairs in a U shape to facilitate communication and community.

I wonder what this class will be like?
Will they be bright, idealistic, caring and creative?
Or will they become overwhelmed by poverty, pain, injustice and bureaucracy?

In this basement room with no windows, how do I open their hearts and minds to this profession of helping, healing and justice making?

I teach social work practice.
I teach about personal and community strength.
I teach about vision and empowerment.
I teach theory and help my students put theory into practice.

In this basement room with no windows, how do I help my students create their own vision?
How do I help them discover that power within themselves that *will* make a difference?
In this basement room with no windows how do I model empowerment when I sometimes feel disempowered myself?

9:00. The room is filled with anxious and excited students.
Nineteen pairs of eyes, thirty-eight windows to the heart and soul and mind open to me.
If I open my eyes to them, then together we can begin a journey.
From each other we will learn.
I will help them become competent social workers and they will help me to be a competent teacher.

It has been my experience that in today's educational culture there are certain obstacles to achieving this kind of exchange between student and teacher. I believe that the current letter-grading-system, as opposed to the prior pass/fail system, creates pressure to arrive at the "right answer," rather than allowing room for students to explore their own ideas in collaboration with their professors. Moreover, I find that today's emphasis on grades forces the evaluation process into something that can be easily objectified and quantified, not only for the professor's evaluation of students, but also for the student's evaluation of faculty. It therefore focuses more on the science of helping or teaching and tends to overlook the art of creating helping relationships.

In describing the art versus knowledge dilemma, Dr. Robinson quotes Dr. Taft describing the impact that being in analysis with Dr. Rank had had on social worker colleagues who were trying to translate their own experience into a structure for helping others.

> They had learned that help comes from something more than intellectual knowing, that it goes beyond the facts or even the traumas of a life history, that it is a dynamic, present, swift-moving experience with an ending; . . .

Our need, in truth our necessity, to get hold of something we could use in our understanding of the process of change that we had experienced in ourselves and of its applicability to our efforts to help our clients proved to be a powerful dynamic.

As a social work practitioner, it is the experience of reaching inside myself to pull together what I know and what I am experiencing in that unique moment with that client, supervisee, or student that enables me to respond in a way that keeps the other at the center of the process. This, I believe, is the art of helping, the creative process that for me began in those early days at the University of Pennsylvania School of Social Work and that is the source of my continued professional competence and satisfaction. Cultivating this art requires the stimulus, time, and structure for self-reflection and the ability to receive feedback on that process. In my own educational experience, this occurred primarily in three venues: practice class, patterns and process class (personality dynamics) and supervision. In class it came through lengthy comments on my papers and the dreaded "see me" invitation to continue the discussion with the professor in his or her office. In supervision, it was an uninterrupted hour-and-a-half set aside each week for me to report on the process with my clients and, most important, to reflect on my professional growth as well as the obstacles to that growth.

In the current mental health climate of managed care and billable units, supervision is seen primarily as an administrative responsibility. The teaching aspects of supervision are often undertaken in addition to everything else, instead of as an integral part of the delivery of service. Consequently, adequate time is often not allotted for the reflection and introspection that is at the heart of the development of an effective professional use of self.

I believe that the current challenge to my profession is to graduate social workers who are advocates for social justice, who know how to work within an organization to create change and who, at the same time, also are artful in the professional use of self with all client groups.

Chapter 10
The Cause in Function

Harold Lewis

Dr. Faatz's letter inviting me to speak expressed interest in the questions:—"where, today, does the one-to-one helping process stand in the midst of a wave of mass programs and resources in areas that did not exist years ago? Have we lived through a period of making resources available and may there now be a return to interest in how the individual himself uses these resources, makes them available to himself? Are students becoming interested in practice as helping persons?" As you must expect, Dr. Faatz did not restrict my creativity nor seek to limit my choices, urging instead that I approach the subject in any way that seemed most productive to me. Having graduated from the University of Pennsylvania School of Social Work, it would not have occurred to me to do otherwise.

Dr. Faatz's letter was received on May 7, 1976. On that same day massive cuts were being instituted in welfare, health and educational resources in New York City. In choosing to avoid fiscal bankruptcy, those who manage the affairs of this great city chose moral bankruptcy. Property rights were given precedence over human rights. Imagine, then, my reaction to the question, "Have we lived through a period of making resources available?" I was in fact living in a period where the opposite was taking place. I accepted to speak because I believe the perspective that sequences social provision (i.e.—making resources available) and personal utilization of these resources in a linear or cyclical fashion is misleading and deserves more critical appraisal.

Porter Lee, initially, described what he viewed as a normal social process, the move from a cause sought and won to a function which realized in practice the intentions contained in the cause. He contrasted the zeal that inspired a cause, with the intellect that assured the success of the function. Nevertheless, his analysis of his own hypothesis compelled him to conclude that the time had come when the cause must be incorporated into the function. In those threatening days of 1929, he believed the profession must not respond to the challenges confronting it by going back to a day when social work was exclusively or predominantly a cause. He argued that we must meet (the challenge) with the sober recognition that it is and must be both cause and function. Finally, he noted his belief that the dynamic leader of the cause and the efficient executive in charge of the function . . . do not often appear at their best within one temperament. Thus, while he saw the need for both qualities, he doubted the possibility of both being present in one person.

There are several assumptions contained in this view that have not been substantiated by experience. The sequencing as suggested in the hypothesis "from cause to function" and the separation as suggested by "cause and function," obviously did not satisfy Lee either, hence his seeking biological and personality justifications for the social processes he sought to explain. In entitling this paper "The Cause in Function," I deliberately wish to dissent from both the hypothesis and the rationale proposed by Lee to justify its acceptance.

In a provocative recent essay, Robert Rosen, a leading theoretical biologist, sought to answer a question which most of us accept as fact. Do we really need ends to justify the means? He contends . . . "that in some important sense we *need* to engage in these kinds of activities (i.e. politics, education, planning, economics, etc.) quite apart from attaining the goals we frame to justify them; and that we will go even more seriously astray if we do not recognize the real roots of our indulgence in these activities." Man, he believes ". . . has a biologically-rooted need to engage in complex activities, . . . and it is the activities themselves which are needful, not the ends which are supposed to be attained by them; these ends are the inessentialities and the by-products." Finally, he concludes, "We need to extend this lesson to the whole of our experience; namely, that our happiness—in a real sense, the quality of our lives—lies in the doing and not in the done; in the doing is where our real goals lie. And these goals need require no rationalized ends to justify them."[1]

While I am hardly equipped to affirm or deny Rosen's thesis, or to accept the biological imperative it implies, it seems reasonable to assume that human activity is purposeful, and that experiencing the activity is one of its more significant purposes. There would appear to be ample evidence that thoughtful persons engage in intentional activities and are concerned to evolve satisfying procedures for achieving their ends. One need not attribute to purpose a motivating function, nor deny this function to a biological urge, to observe, as Rosen does, that much of the quality of life lies in the doing and not in the done.

Turning to the experience provided by our profession, one cannot help but wonder how ends and means, intentions and procedures, get expressed in professional helping activities. It is my contention that the Porter Lee hypothesis did not anticipate the Rosen hypothesis. It failed to appreciate the ends in means, the social purpose in individualized helping, and the cause embedded in function. But what is more disconcerting is the experience of the past decade during which divisive formulations that dichotomized the profession, such as practice versus social action, social versus individual change, etc., purchased the same inadequate understanding of the means-ends issue, freezing the cause-function dichotomy into curriculum and separating faculties into ideologically non-productive contending camps. Far from contributing to responsible social change failure to understand the unified character of action has permitted socially irresponsible perspectives on practice to survive.

The helper is the focus of my concern, and his experience in activating both cause and function in his practice will be explored for what it may add to our understanding.

I am not here interested in the nature of the problem being addressed by the helper, whether it be a social policy issue, a troubled personality or a financial deprivation. I believe that whatever the problem, it is in the helper's activity that he confronts the issues posed by the Porter Lee hypothesis. It is in the activity that the evidence of cause in function will appear.

What is the relationship of cause and function in the professional helping act? To begin with, it is a dynamic, growth-producing relationship that gives shape and substance to service. We recognize that the entity we call service does not appear in the helper, in the resources of the agency or in the need for which the clientele seeks to use agency resources. Service is created when agency resource and client need are joined. The relationship that links the two creates an exchange invested with significance for the immediate participants in the relationship and simultaneously contributes to an alteration in the available pool of socially provided resources. Thus, every helping act is both a personal and social act, and carries in its service elements the core of what we recognize to be cause—i.e., thus Porter Lee's definitions—"a movement directed toward the elimination of an entrenched evil," and function . . . "an organized effort incorporated into the machinery of community life in the discharge of which the acquiesence at least, and ultimately the support of the entire community is assumed."

At whatever level of community structure, however simple or complex the client-system addressed, and wherever and under whatever auspices the service is rendered, for the professional helper happiness with what he is about will originate in his activities, or will be denied by them. At a very abstract level one can speak of resources being made available through new programs. Concretely, resources are made available when they are converted into services through the activity of the helper and his client. But, more important, services are created by these activities, and it is service to which we attach the power to eliminate an entrenched evil and through which we discharge a community sanctioned transfer of societal resource. Substitute the word service for programs and resources, and the initial question posed by Dr. Faatz reads as follows: "where, today does the one-to-one helping process stand in the midst of a wave of mass services in areas that did not exist years ago?" In this form, the question is confusing, for if mass services now exist, the one-to-one helping process must also exist, since it is essential for their creation. Or, take the second question: "Have we lived through a period of making *services* available and may there now be a return to interest in how the individual himself uses these services, makes them available to himself?" Again, a confusing statement since services cannot be made available without the active and creative participation of the person for whom they are intended. The deliberate substitution of the term service for the terms programs and resources has the effect of highlighting the empty meaning of a cause that is not imbedded in a function.

When the helper assists a family in public housing to avoid a threatened eviction for poor housekeeping, he must help that family use the resources (material and psychological) that the agency is sanctioned by the community to distribute for this purpose, and in so doing contributes concurrently to the possible success of the public housing experiment, prevents the further destruction of housing stock to which such evicted families usually move, and promotes a stronger family unit able to contribute through its own development to the dignity of its members and the neighborhood of which it is a part. Public housing, like most significant and sustained social reforms, was not granted willingly by those with means to assist the disadvantaged. While it was in part justified as a means of promoting the building trades, public housing was fought for and won with the active participation of all those groups for whom the reform was essential for survival including those who would live in such housing. In assisting the family in public housing, the worker is concurrently helping to sustain the hope and will to struggle among these families, who will ultimately have a major role in assuring the extension of the reform and the success of its implementation. The cause *in* function is here undeniable.

Reforms generally are won through struggle on the part of their beneficiaries, who engage in direct conflict with those who must yield some privilege to pay for the costs involved. One need only witness the demonstrations in New York of day-care mothers and their families; of Hostos and John Jay College students; of City Hospital patients, etc. to appreciate the role of the beneficiaries in making reforms possible, and in sustaining them once they have been won. Reforms, resulting as they must from contending interests, are never given for all time. They must constantly be re-negotiated, they can never cease to be a cause for those who benefit from the resources they make available. I'm reminded of the Director of Catholic Charities in a city in the mid-west, who was presenting his agency's budget to the United Fund Budget Committee. When asked if he had any useful measures whereby the effectiveness of his services might be evaluated, he listed some of those commonly cited, but hastened to add, that as a Catholic, he would deem his agency's services successful if they helped his community to a more Christian, a more caring, a more sharing way of life. Thus, for him, the offer of the resources was itself a major measure of success. As I understood his remarks, he argued that his Church believed that the reformation of the human spirit, through charitable effort, was an ongoing cause, which his agency's services made possible. He could no more separate this cause from the agency function than Rank could separate the will from the creative act.

The helper is always engaged in political, economic, aesthetic, scientific and self-realizing activity when he cooperates with a client in creating a service. When he arranges his own inner resources, as well as those provided by his agency, in some priority order, and allocates them on the basis of his preferences, he is engaging in a political act with serious implications for distributive justice. When he seeks the most efficient and effective utilization of these husbanded resources, he is engaging in a productive act with serious economic implications; when he disciplines his activity to reflect agency, professional and personal style, he is influencing the aesthetic quality of his service and the environment in which it occurs. When he informs his activity with what is known and understood, he both utilizes and provides information for improving on the science of human relationships, and when he engages his whole self in these activities, as Rosen would suggest, he more fully realizes this self, and enhances the possibilities available to him to achieve personal happiness. In brief, the helper imparts to his helping relationship a culturally enriched dimension that marks his activity as civilized. It is for this reason one can speak of our helping profession as a civilizing profession, since its practitioners cannot help but act in a civilizing manner if their efforts are to prove truly helpful.

The view of the helper as a civilizing agent is hardly justified if in fact his activities by plan or oversight fail to address each of these dimensions of a civilized culture. Whether, as Rosen argues, each of us engage in all these activities because of our biological needs, or as others may contend, we do so because we are urged on by intentions which we freely and willfully formulate, when we fail to see the wholeness of the act we ought not construe such failure as proof that it lacks such wholeness. When Porter Lee sequences cause and function, or separates them as cause and function, he in effect destroys the wholeness of the act in order to analyze it. I am reminded of Professor Rabi of Columbia who, upon receiving the Nobel Prize for Physics, was asked to distinguish between his contribution and that of Dr. Lawrence who received the prize earlier. Professor Rabi developed an ingenious technique whereby he could study the atom through the flow of electrons in a vacuum tube with the help of a magnetic field, whereas Professor Lawrence developed the Cyclotron—the atom smasher—which leaked off electrons into a cloud chamber in which their movement could be detected and studied. Professor Rabi offered the following analogy. Suppose you were an architect wishing to study the Taj Mahal. My approach would hold the structure intact and study the relationship and nature of its parts. Dr. Lawrence would smash it into bits and then study its parts. No doubt the latter approach had certain value, witness the Atom Bomb. And analogously, Porter Lee's analysis did contribute to our understanding. But I contend Professor Rabi's approach, particularly in relation to human phenomena, makes eminently more sense. We ought to consider the helper's action whole, not destroy its dynamic core for the sake of formal logical analysis. This requires, as a minimum, that we consider not only propositions of the "if this-then that" variety, but also propositions that allow for time and place to be included in derived generalizations. These take the propositional form "from this through time to that," a form frequently employed by Rank and process-oriented theoreticians. I would add the need to consider propositions of the form "this is to this as that is to that," reasoning by analogy, if we are to manage meaningful units of action in our understanding of practice. Reasoning by analogy is the manner in which imagination enters practice, and is the most frequent source of creativity in practice.

To summarize this part of my presentation (and I have only a relatively brief addendum to be added) I propose we recognize the *cause in function*, the *ends in means*, the unity of action. Further, that we recognize service as that which is created by the helping process, and the only real measure of the actualization of program and resource for social welfare purposes. That service be viewed in a dialectical fashion, as the evolving form and substance of the unity and conflict of cause in function, necessitating the constant addressing of both sides of this conflict if positive social change is to be achieved. I have argued that if the helper fulfills his civilizing function, he must approach his activity with an awareness of all its dimensions lest he fault his contribution through oversight and misunderstanding.

The final question posed by Dr. Faatz, "Are students becoming interested in practice as helping persons?'' will provide the framework for the conclusion of this discussion. If the ten New York State Schools of Social Work are representative, and they do graduate about 10% of all M.S.W.s in the United States each year, there has been a decided leveling off of applicants for community and group work, and an increase in those seeking social casework or some combination of methods, emphasizing the one-to-one or one-to-family helping processes. This may or may not represent an increased interest in the one-to-one; it does reflect a decline in the enthusiasm for methods expected to influence program development, service patterns, and coordination. Many factors may account for these recent changes, but clearly we have no evidence that a desire to work with individual clients in social welfare agencies is a major or even a significant cause. If self-report can be taken as a reliable indication, then more students are seeking social work education in order to become therapists, with the expectation of entering at some point into private practice, than have hitherto openly expressed this intention. Where schools have hinted at their preferences for students seeking to practice in social service agencies, applicants with the therapist's intentions have learned to disguise this interest until after acceptance into school, after which this interest quickly surfaces in electives sought, courses avoided, complaints concerning the focus and emphasis of certain required courses or choices of field placements. We suspect that employment possibilities play some part in the changes noted.

Finally, we cannot dismiss the possibility that the changed atmosphere concerning national intentions to press efforts seeking to eliminate poverty, racism and the stresses of aging and ill health that have typified the Nixon-Ford administration, has not also discouraged interest among those who would pursue a career in community and institutional change. Thus, while our statistics may upon examination suggest a move of applicant interest from problems of policy and program to problems of individual change, to interpret this, as a shift of interest from cause to function, in my judgment would be superficial, and probably inaccurate. Given my prior discussion, what appears to be operating as far as my limited data will permit me to conjecture, is a re-evaluation of the cause in function, and a beginning awareness of the need to keep their interaction intact, whatever the problems addressed. Also, given my prior discussion, I would expect that only as these students become civilizing helpers in the full sense in which I have used the term, and their collective efforts are systematically organized and promoted, will services be realized that meet the needs of those who seek the help of persons holding themselves out to be professional helpers.

Reprinted from Harold Lewis, The cause in function, *Otto Rank Association Journal* 11 (1976–77): 18–25. Reprinted by permission.

Note

1. Robert Rosen, "Do We Really Need Ends to Justify the Means?" *Center Report* (February 1974): 29–30.

Commentary

Beth Lewis

Harold Lewis delivered "The Cause in Function" at the Annual Otto Rank Association Meeting in 1976, seven years after his departure from the School in 1969. The invitation extended by Anita Faatz, a member of the faculty from 1946 to 1954, directed Lewis to "approach the subject in any way that seemed most productive to [him]." In acknowledging this direction, Lewis also recognizes the fundamental contribution of the School's orientation to his own development, and to the profession as a whole. His background and contribution to the School, both leading up to and following the delivery of this paper, is of some interest in the context of the School's centennial celebration.

Lewis was recruited by the School in 1956 to help in the development of "the teaching of research in a functional school."[1] By the time Lewis arrived at Penn, he had already played a significant role in the development of social work research curriculum and in the promotion of research in social service agencies. He had served on the National Advisory Committee of the Social Work Research Group in the early 1950s, on the threshold of the establishment of the Council for Social Work Education (CSWE). As a faculty member at Penn, in the mid-1960s, he went on to Chair the CSWE National Committee on Advanced Education for Social Work.

Lewis benefited from the rich intellectual environment at Penn. While a student in the doctoral program (1956–59), and as professor and chair of research (1959–69) he taught the second research course in the master's program in which students were required to develop a research project outline around a specific question of interest to the student and his or her agency. In 1956, this course had not been taught in the recent past and was being reintroduced and integrated into the curriculum as an elective, rather than required, course—although this was soon to change. In his writing during this time, Lewis argued against a "project orientation" toward research in social agencies, supporting instead a view of research as a professional service offered by the agency, and of the research worker as one with both methodological and helping skill.[2]

He regarded social work as a profession uncompromisingly engaged in the social present, and he devoted his career to shaping social work education to both reflect and realize this view. Illuminating the intellectual process employed by social workers in the provision of service was, for Lewis, one component of the work included in this effort. An equally compelling task involved advancing a view of professional helping as containing at its core the elements of struggle for social reform—no matter the level of activity or the target toward which such activity is directed. "The Cause in Function" is an explicit articulation of this view. In further elaborating the use of analogic reasoning in practice,[3] Lewis here presents an original and stirring perspective on the work we do.

Lewis's insights on the relationship between social conditions and professional practice and education were constantly sought by the Penn School of Social Work and the larger community of educators and practitioners. While serving as dean at Hunter College School of Social Work, he was an invited speaker on several occasions of import to the Penn School throughout the 1970s and 1980s. He received an honorary Doctor of Laws from the University in 1985. The extent of Lewis's ongoing contribution to the intellectual life of the School is suggested in this partial listing of invited speaking engagements in the years following his departure:

- "Social Work Education: Preparation for Practice in 1970," presented at the School's Annual Day Program;
- "Values, Knowledge and Practice—Issues Facing the Profession in the Seventies," presented at the Ruth Smalley colloquium in April 1972;
- Speech given at the Orientation Day for New Workers in Philadelphia Social Agencies in November 1973;
- "Management in the Non-Profit Social Service Organization" presented at the Seminar on Education for Management of Social Services in January 1975[4];
- "Comments on the Occasion of the Dedication of the Research Center on Practice at the University of Pennsylvania, School of Social Work " presented in May 1976;
- Speeches given at the School's 70th anniversary in October 1979 and again at the School's 75th anniversary celebration in April 1985; and
- An address to the School's Board of Overseers in October 1981, in which he underlined the consequences, already apparent, of the policies of the Reagan administration: "Giving to the haves and taking from the have-nots, hoping that good intentions will motivate the former to voluntarily give support to the latter, is gambling with the lives of the most disadvantaged."[5]

The themes contained in "The Cause in Function," as in his writing and presentations throughout his career, compel the profession to confront its relationship to the economic and political realities of the time. The targeting of the social work profession for failures in helping that have their roots in the inadequacy of resource provision and social injustice is a dominant theme in Lewis's work. At the time that this paper was delivered, emerging studies were questioning the "effectiveness" of social work as well as the value of educational preparation for professional practice. In another presentation given in 1975, Lewis accurately lodges such work in its social context, in the midst and wake of the massive cuts in social welfare services to which he also alludes in "The Cause in Function":

If, as is not infrequently the case, the agency resources are such that it is unable to meet the demand for its services and as a result must compromise on the quality and quantity of social work services actually provided, findings that suggest no significant difference in outcome for different levels of educational preparation may be evidence of underutilization of social work skills available, and not evidence that such skills would make little difference in outcome.[6]

"The Cause in Function" exhorts the profession to question a dichotomous view of "cause" and "function," and to embrace, instead, a view of social conscience as embedded in the actual service that social workers provide. In 1976, when this paper was delivered, the separation that we experience today between "macro" and "direct" in the curriculum was beginning to take hold. His work sounds a note of concern regarding the future consequences of this developing schism for the profession.[7] His admonition was prescient; the divisions to which Lewis alludes as characterizing the educational experience of social workers have by now become well established.

The emphasis on client activity in the process of service provision is another hallmark of his work, and is reflective of the influence of the functional school. In this paper, he defines professional "helping" as, in large part, ensuring the continued involvement of beneficiaries of service in maintaining the social reforms that were brought about through their own efforts and struggle. Lewis cautions that reforms once won can be taken away—clarifying that "cause" never goes away for the beneficiary. He warns against the inherent dangers of viewing student interest in one-to-one helping as evidence of a shift away from "cause" toward a narrower conception of "function." Such a view, according to Lewis, discounts the potential for such services to contribute to the "cause." Indeed, he points out that the growth in student interest in one-to-one helping at that time was more likely a reflection of the existing federal administration's move away from efforts to eliminate poverty.

Similarly, as we meet with change in students' preferences today, we might consider the role played by persistent impediments to an emphasis on quality in services for the poor. Student preferences are greatly affected by their perceptions of the devaluation of professional work "in the circles that distribute resources," and of the work they are called upon to do as being "demeaned as are the clients they serve."[8]

Delivered in 1976, "The Cause in Function" speaks to issues encountered in social work education and practice today with the same degree of clarity as it did during the period in which it was written. It remains a timeless classic in the field.

Notes

1. Harold Lewis, "Learning to Teach Research in a Functional School of Social Work," 1957 (unpublished manuscript).

2. Harold Lewis, "The Use and Place of Research in the Administration of the Social Work Agency," *Child Welfare: Journal of the Child Welfare League of America, Inc.* 44 (1) (1965): 21–25.

3. Lewis discusses analogic thinking ("this is to this, as that is to that")—or reasoning by analogy—as the form of reasoning and logic most frequently employed in professional practice, previously characterized as largely "intuitive." According to Lewis, this was the logic of imagination that "frees the practitioner to risk action in uncertain situations, where time and circumstance do not permit all that one would want to know before acting." The "analogic" reasoning process is taken up at greater length in his book, *The Intellectual Base of Social Work Practice* (New York: Haworth Press, 1982).

4. Later published as "Management in the Non-Profit Social Service Organization," *Child Welfare* 54 (9) (1975).

5. Harold Lewis, "Address, Board of Overseers, University of Pennsylvania School of Social Work," October 1981 (unpublished paper).

6. Harold Lewis, "Approaches to the Change Process in Curriculum Development: Dean's Perspective," June 1975 (unpublished paper)

7. Lewis later reviewed the socioeconomic roots of this schism in greater depth in "The Micro-Macro in Social Work Education," Guest lecture, School of Social Work, State University of New York at Buffalo, March 1984 (unpublished paper).

8. Excerpts from Harold Lewis, "The Battered Helper," *Child Welfare* 59 (4) (1980): 195–201.

Chapter 11
The Black Instructor: An Essential Dimension to the Content and Structure of the Social Work Curriculum

Louis H. Carter

As educational institutions search for meaningful ways to introduce racial content into the curriculum at all levels, social work educators must assume responsibility for content that will speak to a multiracial class of students. Perhaps one of the most significant influences today on the social work curriculum is the Black educator who provides a perspective that recognizes institutional racism as a major contributor to social problems.[1]

Development of Course on Institutional Racism

Eight years ago I accepted an invitation to teach a newly instituted course, Racism: Implications for Social Work, at the University of Pennsylvania School of Social Work. The course was an outgrowth of the Black movement and student activism in the late sixties. White social work students—in an effort to find their place in the Black movement and in trying to help their clients—identified the need for Black content in the curriculum as essential to their preparation. Black students rejected traditional theoretical formulations as irrelevant to the Black experience. Both were valuable inputs that received faculty endorsement and support. The course began as an option in 1969 and was made a requirement in 1970. In the present curriculum design it is a core course.

The course developed around three conceptual levels: context of racism, consciousness of racism, and implications and strategies for change. The course objectives were "to help students develop awareness of individual-institutional, attitudinal-behavioral systems of racism . . . to help define the responsibility of social work in relation to these phenomena as they apply to the social worker in a professional role."[2] There were three major characteristics of the course: an extensive bibliography, co-teaching arrangement of Black and white instructors, with the Black instructor having the lead role, and the white instructor's responsibility for an examination of white racism.

The Special Dimension of the Black Instructor

A dilemma for Blacks in becoming absorbed in white institutions is to overcome their suspicion of the delegation of power by whites.[3] Initially, the lead teacher role made me feel that I was having my "place" assigned, when in fact it was a relinquishing of power by the white power structure. "Black power" in the classroom stimulates creative tension, enabling students to derive maximum benefit from this course. One student amplified this point:

I saw the black professor as someone who was there to manipulate me into submission for my whiteness. I didn't see him as a person, a black person whose experience I could not know. I saw him only in terms of what he would do to me. As a person he did not exist. I saw the white woman who was coteaching the course in the role of policewoman. She was there to keep this black man's anger from being too destructive, since he couldn't be trusted to be responsible.

What is the nature of the power that the student perceives and seeks or sometimes fears in a teacher? The power that is feared is easy to identify; it stems from the teacher's right and responsibility to assess the student as learner. This has heightened meaning in a professional school because such assessment may shape the career goals of students and affect their future.[4] The added dimension for the white student is that a Black instructor is assessing the student's capacity to participate in a white institution, and this is truly relinquishing power, especially for students who have not experienced being taught by a Black instructor.

The problem with relinquishing power to a Black instructor was highlighted for me in an early session, and affirmed the concept of the Black instructor as "course content." It was necessary to remind the class of their commitment to time as well as to the purpose of the class, which did not include brunch. An irate white student responded that I did not mind the lateness or coffee, but that I was angry for what the white man had done to me for over 300 years. I acknowledged having lived 42 of those 300 years, but since I had not experienced the other 258, his assumption was grossly inaccurate; his attempt to maintain control and power by keeping me preoccupied with a past that could not change had faltered. It became more than the difference of teacher-student; my Blackness and the students' struggle with their whiteness in relation to it, was clearly the core of contention. It was difficult for students to acknowledge that they could learn from me, or that I had indeed set the tone for self-exploration. "In a society where Black is perceived as submission, Black initiative radiates psychological and intellectual arrogance, for it dares to act without permission or sanction of the white majority."[5]

Equally important is the awareness that Blacks cannot deal with 300 years of oppression except to believe that change is possible in the here and now. This concept embraces a school of thought with tremendous promise for the liberation of oppressed peoples.[6] Recognition that it is difficult to accept that Blacks do expect of whites was also helpful to the class awareness of attitudinal and behavioral patterns reflecting racist overtones. The added dimension for the Black instructor is the responsibility to deal simultaneously with the content, the meaning for the individual, and the class response, since each impacts upon the student's learning.

The projection or displacement about Black anger and the attempt of students to exploit it perpetuates racist ideology. I discovered that the degree to which white students had not found a creative use for their guilt, they projected or displaced about my anger. Through such encounters, the concept of projection and displacement[7] came alive for many students in relation to racism and its implications for practice. Racist attitudes among social work students are deep-rooted, and have become an integral part of their value system. This is in direct conflict with social work values, and hence the struggle to come to terms with these feelings. One student's initial response to the course with great intellectual integrity bore witness to this dilemma:

The director of the department is black as well as my supervisor. This was the first time I had ever worked and had been directly dependent upon a black person. . . . I am a student learning the profession of social work; I am also a human being who has been taught by my family, neighbors, schools, and society to discriminate. Having reconciled this conflict of feeling and claimed what is mine, I am now ready to entertain ways of helping people and institutions to change their racist behavior.

I accepted this student's aspiration with compassion and with an awareness that the gap between the mind and the heart is often wide, which was evidenced by the fact that she did not identify me as the course instructor on her paper, but rather listed the white co-instructor.

The discovery of "white liberalism" as a racist institution by the students was important and furthered the attainment of course goals. The students saw liberalism as an apology for their whiteness, which contributed to their inaction. With this new awareness, they began to see their role as going beyond defending the Blacks' right to be angry, and to become involved in institutional change. One student captured this:

Stereotypes are something I was raised with and they're most difficult to combat. I have found that I devote so much attention and energy to myself and my prejudices that I miss seeing things that occur right in front of me that I am supposed to have seen. I think this is true of the feelings most white liberals have to the extent that it is an institution itself.

On another level I saw students discover significant attitudes and stereotypes contributing to racist attitudes. Our relationship made possible this quality of exploration and projection:

I realized that I had internalized the myth which says that all Negro men have great sexual prowess; that they are powerful, uninhibited lovers and that their secret wish is to have all the white girls they can. Black men were sexual beings first, human beings second. To say I picked up this idea and held fast to it because it was one of the many racist notions which my society floated around, would be only half of the truth. I knew intellectually it was a lie—emotionally, however, it stuck tight because it served to fulfill my own neurotic needs and feelings of inadequacy as a woman.

The two preceding quotations are potential pitfalls for the Black instructor, who must accept these responses in the context in which they are given. Maintaining sufficient distance from the explosiveness implicit in them in order to be helpful to the student and the class requires sensitivity and a high level of integration. Only then can the Black instructor respond to the student's need for objective clarification of their attitudinal discoveries.

From Theory to Practice

In addition to the racism course, I was assigned to teach a social work practice course. A student from the racism course told me of his initial reaction when he learned that I would be his second-year practice teacher and adviser. He had to revisit his racist attitudes, and projected that the school wanted to eliminate him by assigning him to my class. Our subsequent discussions revealed that he really felt the added dimension of my power as a screening agent for the profession. The student knew he had intellectualized his use of the racism course and was left with much anxiety from his unresolved racist attitudes, which were threatening now to his survival as a student. He understood that my purpose was not to take responsibility for his racist attitudes by demanding that he change, but that I would make him aware of and support that which was compatible with the expectations of the profession. He was left to choose his own course of action. A major assignment later in the term asked the students to write about some aspect of practice that raised questions for them and to demonstrate their developing competence in handling it. This student's paper was entitled, "Men in a Woman's Profession." He used this assignment to project his feelings about being a male who was entering social work. Women had become a depository for his inadequate feelings in lieu of Blacks, as was the situation in the racism course:

Social work is a profession of love and compassion, and it follows that these qualities are most inherent in the female, who is more sensitive and responsive. I am reminded of this when in my classes females carry the class. . . . for men, I think nothing is worse than to feel impotent at being felt or heard.

There was much to learn from this student about teaching the racism course and how to make the experience alive and sustaining. "How much of teaching ability is an art which cannot be 'learned,' and how much of the ability to teach is both teachable and learnable is a question which will not be settled through rhetoric. Clarity and conviction will emerge with the accumulation of understanding about the teacher-learner transaction."[8]

The student struggle to make the racism course more than an intellectual exercise was at times painful. A class of predominantly white women from time to time identified sexism as their priority in the early stages of the course, rather than confronting the issue of racism. In reality they were searching desperately for a personal frame of reference for change. The discovery that women and men, Black and white, who come to social work have in common the white, male power structure as an oppressor, went a long way toward the realization of the course goals.

Institutional oppression could be studied and strategies for change developed from several vantage points. To minimize sexism and the masculine mystique—"a conception of manhood so central to the politics and personality of America that it institutionalizes violence and male supremacy as a measure of national pride"[9] agencies, that for several years had resisted student intervention on the question of racism, yielded to looking at oppression in the form of sexism, only to discover racism as its companion. Moreover, a personal frame of reference proved to be the most effective means for dealing with white guilt, which often immobilized white students in their effort to effect change. Altruism gave way to self-interest in change, allowing for a highly creative and productive use of guilt. Power to influence one's own destiny is a strategy in itself.

For Black students, the Black instructor as course content provided a role model and stimulus for professional growth that came with self-affirmation. The discovery of their own perpetuation of racism because of their vulnerability by virtue of their Blackness and their defensiveness about it, was significant. A prerequisite to the acquisition of knowledge for use was a positive feeling about one's own Blackness:

Being Black, I have experienced the classical characteristics; I thought white people were superior; I harbored a low opinion of my abilities and potential, and denied my blackness. I understand the reasons for my behavior and thoughts, and with the surge of proud racial identity of Black people, I am adjusting to being called Black, referring to myself as Black, and becoming proud of my heritage.

With less preoccupation with himself and his past, this Black student conceptualized racism and implications for practice thus:

The racist cannot deal with his own inadequate feelings in relation to his racial counterpart, consequently, he finds comfort in projecting that the hatred exists outside himself. In my field practice, I have experienced the racist use of projection. . . . When a Black patient is committed to the mental institution for showing signs of emotional drain or despair, the white clinician quickly diagnoses him as "paranoid schizophrenic."

Having developed a personal frame of reference for change, student responses to a central aspect of this course—strategies for change—were evidence of the value of this experience for professional use. Assignments were structured to involve field placement agencies in this process. Five years ago the course on racism was made a requirement for field instructors in order to provide them with a conceptual framework to support the practice for social change emphasis. Students were asked to identify written and unwritten practices and policies in the agency, including funding sources, board composition, staffing patterns, and service delivery patterns, that tended to exclude or in any form oppress Blacks and other minorities:

When I first started my field placement at the state hospital, I didn't take notice of the fact that all of the patients in the program where I work are White. I have started to look around me with new awareness. The best jobs that Blacks have around the hospital are as nurses' aides, with the exception of a few Black nurses. Most of the menial jobs, in the kitchens, on the grounds, in the shops, are held by Blacks.

With this awareness, the student was able to engage the agency in an analysis of the situation and assist it in a process of change to remedy its perpetuation of institutional racism. This is no easy task for an agency, because in many situations it may encounter conflict with the community, boards, or funding sources. Racism imbedded in service perhaps is the most difficult to identify and eradicate. On entering first-year field placement in a large community mental health center, one student experienced the invisibility of Blacks even in the formulation of the legislation that created the program for which it was designed:

Implicit in the enabling legislation was the understanding that mental disability is inextricably bound up with physical, psychological, social, and economic factors which either cause, exacerbate, or result from mental problems. Since blacks have been excluded from the political process, the enabling legislation was formulated and implemented by White interests based on White values, and was not addressed to the racial situation.

This student's field placement concentrated on administration in the clinic, and provided an excellent opportunity to learn about the administrative process in relation to service delivery, practices, and policies, through initiating and sustaining the process of change.

The social distance created by racism and presented in the helping situation, if ignored, contributes to the institutional oppression of Blacks. White practitioners must see themselves as part of the Black client's problem, recognizing the demand it makes on the Black client to respond to an offer of help. A skillful application of theory reflecting sensitive analysis and knowledge of this form of institutional racism was demonstrated by one student:

I find it hard to confront black clients with the functional limits of the agency, which is essentially a dehumanizing insult to their ability to grow within their relationship to the hospital. I think this relates to my fear of becoming involved with blacks. . . . Previous workers have described the mother of a recently admitted black boy as a borderline psychotic with little potential for change. I was willing to go along with this charade in the previous sessions, taking the excuse provided by the woman's rambling style of speech. . . . I told her I noticed that she seemed uncomfortable talking about her son, and acknowledged that it would be hard, but necessary. Whereas she had been laughing inappropriately, slurring her words, and looking around the room, she began to speak clearly and looked straight at me.

Social work theory historically does not include consideration of racism and other social pathologies as they have affected and influenced practice. Their formulations, although cornerstones of our theoretical beginnings, do not take into account the meaning to minority populations, and therefore, have not served the needs of inner-city consumers of service. In this context, another student questioned the theoretical formulation applied to Black clients in a psychiatric setting:

Although somewhat aware of the unresponsive nature of the psychoanalytic theory to the understanding and diagnosis of the Black Experience, I did not realize my contribution to the perpetuation of this form of institutional racism until I became absorbed in an intake study of a black family. . . . As we proceeded with the interview, it became increasingly apparent that the established outline assumed that all people experience an adolescence of soul searching, have a courtship with the person they will eventually marry, then have a marital relationship before children are born. I altered the "script" a bit in order to describe her experience in a way that did not point to pathology.

Conclusion

Helping social work students develop a theoretical framework for practice that encompasses the social pathology of institutional racism requires the emotional climate generated by the Black instructor. Unlearning racist attitudes resulting from socialization in an oppressive, racist society calls upon the emotional as well as the intellectual resource of the student. "The component responses of learning include emotional feelings and thoughts as well as physiological and motor reactions. The first two categories are open to subjective observation, they are private events and as such constitute special problems in learning theory."[10]

For both the Black and white student, the process of unlearning requires giving up the security of what has been sustaining in human relationships. In this context, the Black instructor is an added dimension to the content and structure of the social work curriculum. A white student's response illustrated this point:

I saw myself in a class led by a Black instructor for the first time in my life. I realized that this situation had never been a part of my white educational experience. I could accept a white expert on racism, but why could I not accept the natural and right idea that a black man should teach whites about the Black Experience? I now realize that Blacks·usually never come this far in the white man's educational system. In addition, I had never met a black man so intense in his convictions.

Has the emergence of the Black educator spanned the gap between ideal and action and achieved the integration espoused more than twenty years ago by Grace Coyle?[11]

If social work as a profession is to survive with credibility, it must address itself to distributive justice and make a firm commitment at all levels of its enterprise. Social work education has a major responsibility to provide relevant theoretical formulations to insure maximum impact from this profession to counteract oppressive institutions. This may require a revisit to its knowledge and value base!

Reprinted from Louis H. Carter, The Black instructor: An essential dimension to the content and structure of social work curriculum, *Journal of Education for Social Work* 14 (1978): 16–22. Reprinted by permission.

Notes

1. Institutional racism is defined as the systematic exclusion of Blacks from equal access to social institutions. Louis L. Knowles and Kenneth Prewett, *Institutional Racism in America* (Englewood Cliffs, N.J.: Prentice-Hall, 1969), 1, 7.

2. Howard D. Arnold, "American Racism: Implications for Social Work," *Journal of Education for Social Work* 6 (Fall 1970): 8.

3. Power has been used in many contexts. A significant reference here would be Sterling Tucker, who stated that "White Power is not always as blatantly overtly discriminatory. Sometimes it operates quietly and quite respectably. . . . White Power is the system under which we live in America. Whites have pushed black men into leadership positions and have manipulated them ruthlessly over the years to accomplish their own ends." Sterling Tucker, *Black Reflections on White Power* (Grand Rapids, Mich.: Eerdmans, 1969), 70–75.

4. Helen Harris Perlman, "And Gladly Teach," in Joseph Soffen, ed., *The Social Work Educator* (New York: Council on Social Work Education, 1969), 113.

5. Willie V. Small, "A Black Practice in Foster Care Service," paper presented at the Fifth Annual Conference of the National Association of Black Social Workers, New York, 1973, 8.

6. The immediate present, a theoretical formulation by Jessie Taft, stated that "the passing present of relationship, on which every helping process depends is a present of immediate, living experience, which both helper and helped would fain remove a little into the safer past, the remote future or the objectivity of intellectualization, in fact, there must be some kind of content whatever the source, to carry the present meaning." Jessie Taft, "Time as the Medium of the Helping Process," paper delivered at the National Conference of Jewish School Welfare, Cleveland, June 1949, 6.

7. "To live we must put ourselves out into and upon our surroundings; we must if we are to survive find the answers to our needs, in parents, in friends, in being able to conquer the spacial world in which we are placed. Science, even psychological science, is primarily based on projection, a learning to understand and to control as far as possible the outside forces, including social forces." Ibid., 3.

8. Perlman, "And Gladly Teach," 2.

9. Lucy Komisar, "Violence and the Masculine Mystique," in Evelyn Shapiro, ed., *Psycho-Sources: A Psychology Resource Catalog* (New York: Bantam Books, 1972).

10. Derek Jehu, *Learning Theory and Social Work* (London: Routledge, 1967), 24.

11. "Some of us faculty members, as I observe us, are in fact better at one or another of these phases of the profession. Some of us focus more naturally on 'must know,' i.e. on intellectual mastery; some on 'must do,' i.e., professional skills; some on 'must be' and 'must feel.' These differences I think are quite natural and inevitable and in fact represent that variety of emphasis and temperament necessary within any faculty to get the blend and balance for the whole." Grace Coyle, "The Role of the Teacher in the Creation of an Integrated Curriculum," in *A Source Book of Readings on Teaching in Social Work* (New York: Council on Social Work Education, 1965),

Commentary

Nicholas Roush

When Louis Carter wrote "The Black Instructor," I was in my second year of Penn's M.S.W. program in the Justice specialization and a student of Professor Carter in the core course on Racism. In addition, he was my first-year practice teacher. To say that he made me reevaluate my white perspective of the world is to greatly understate the influence he had on the social worker professional I have become.

His article, "The Black Instructor: An Essential Dimension to the Content and Structure of the Social Work Curriculum," clearly describes the emotional and intellectual changes that he was able to guide me through. His presence allowed me to experience the process of "unlearning" and give up "the security of what has been sustaining in human relationships." Like the white student quoted, "I saw myself in a class led by a Black instructor for the first time in my life." For not only was it the first time I had a Black teacher, but Louis Carter had designed the course around "the concept of the Black instructor as 'course content'." The intensity of his convictions and his support were a catalyst to my experiences. When he discusses the Black instructor as the "added dimension," he was right.

Always in his classes, the core of contention was "[his] Blackness and the student's struggle with their whiteness in relation to it." This helped put my field experiences as a "white student in the Black community" in perspective. When I was concerned about how I could connect with one of my Black clients, his comment was "have you asked him how he feels?" These clear and direct responses helped me daily in my placement and allowed me to focus on the client's individuality as well as the issue of the day.

When Professor Carter said the "the social distance created by racism and presented in the helping situation, if ignored, contributes to institutional oppression of the Blacks. White practitioners must see themselves as part of the client's problem recognizing the demand it makes on the Black client to respond to an offer of help," he uses the Black instructor as core content to help the white student risk and give up security in relationships in order to make that human connection. Louis Carter gave me insight into the Black Experience as only a Black instructor could, and enabled me to see the client first and foremost as human before I would attempt to engage the client around any issue.

Not only did Louis Carter's article address the role of the Black Instructor but also in the process, helped the student develop strategies for change. "Women and men, Black and white, who come to social work have in common the white, male power structure as an oppressor" is a very important recognition of the established hierarchy and it priorities. Once this is understood, social workers are able to see all of us, male female, black, white, etc., as being on the same team.

Louis Carter is the "Black Instructor" he writes about. His teacher style, his intellect and his enthusiasm are all part of the descriptions within his article.

It's surprising to read this thirty years later and still be able to feel the excitement of the class. For all of us, Louis Carter is a unique part of our educational and developmental social work experience.

Chapter 12
Institutional Change as a Creative Process: Some Educational and Practice Considerations

Howard Arnold and Tybel Bloom

Introduction

The first three articles in this volume attest to the proposition that professional education for social work is a creative activity on the part of the student engaged in it and on the part of the institution which offers it. In his analysis of the contribution of the University of Pennsylvania School of Social Work,[1] to development of social work theory, Lewis confirms the bold theoretical leaps generated by the School which, over time, have produced a major and progressively significant impact upon professional practice and education. Integral to the theoretical formulation is the concept of agency function which embodies organizational form, structure, and purpose as a central social force. It introduced a catalytic element into the powerful dynamic of the client/worker relationship, which had been identified earlier, anchoring its potency for change in social values and purpose. It provided further definition—boundaries and focus—to the helping process, specifying its distinctiveness from, yet underlying relation to, the larger universal of the life process. The agency, as a responsible and responsive social entity representing community/societal sanction, was regarded as an essential area of knowledge and an action base for practice.

The papers of Krakow and Waddington, each marking an individual area of creative expression, reveal a common thread of experience of self-change through professional education, the understanding and conceptualization of which has been transformed into productive use in professional work. Waddington reflects on its influence on artistic development. Through innovations in practice and teaching, Krakow illuminates the synthesis of the individual (use of self) and the social (inter-professional collaboration) elements.

The papers by Lebovitz and Rehr take the exploration and demonstration of change further into professional realms. Lebovitz dissects the nature of the middle phase of the social work helping process, exposing the essence of the "creative moment" in individual change as a dialectical act growing out of social elements. Rehr examines the challenge of and responsibility for dealing with ethical and value issues, which have become more insistent and complex through new technologies, in the larger sphere of inter-professional (social) arrangements and services. In both articles the relationships between form and substance, the symbolic and the real, and the interplay of inner and outer meanings, whether to the individual or to professional groups, are highlighted.

The historical roots of the School support a change orientation, both in its own theory development over many years and in the contributions of the various academic disciplines from which it has drawn. The interdependence of individual and social components has been a consistent under-girding theme. Further, conflicts generated in the social work profession by the introduction of the School's theoretical innovations in the past produced tensions and struggle, well understood in the process of individual change, in the larger scene of institutional change as it related to modifications in ideological and methodological systems. While only in recent years has the latter issue of institutional change been explicitly articulated as an educational and professional practice goal of the School, the experiential base in the School's own life process provides a vital source of authenticity and strength to current efforts to extend practice knowledge and theory into this area.

In 1972 the School adopted as the primary goal for the Master of Social Work program that of education of social workers committed to individual and social change toward distributive justice in the human services and competent to discharge that commitment in their professional performance. The core of the educational policy is an experience of intentional change in becoming a social worker, both change within the self and within the institutions in which they are learning—the School of Social Work and the social agencies. The organizing principle for actualizing the change goal is working toward the elimination of racism and other oppressive practices and policies in the human services. This article attempts to elucidate some of the assumptions and conceptual underpinnings for institutional change practice that have evolved through the teaching/learning experience in the implementation of the principle, particularly as reflected in the courses on American Racism.[2] It may also have implications for some of the crucial issues and some of the criticism of social work education today, such as the place of the individual, the divisiveness of the micro-macro model, and the dichotomizing of the objectives of breadth and depth as polar emphases.

Conceptual Base

Intentional change, directed by social purpose and values, whether in individuals or institutions, may result not only in the development of new attitudes, forms and behaviors, but may also shed new light on traditional attitudes, structures and behaviors. This reflection may take the form of discovery of new depth of meaning in the known, and/or identification of gaps or biases hitherto unrecognized or unacknowledged. What is commonly referred to as continuity and change seems more accurately to be the achievement of new wholes in which the old is transformed to some degree in the process of integration with the new elements each reciprocally affecting the other. It is this creative process, individually experienced and conceptualized by each student and collectively experienced and converted into new knowledge by the school of social work that engenders fundamental understanding of the nature of change in human systems. This learned insight is essential for under girding and sustaining a viable commitment to individual and institutional (social) change as the central core of professional endeavors.

In her monumental study of the mind, Suzanne Langer explains the phenomenon of experience as a unique trait of the human species.

Human experience is a constant dialectic of sensory and imaginative activity . . . In fact, it is only in human life that I think one can really speak of "experience," and it is experiences that make up human memory, a psychical background of each normal person's consciousness and future envisagement. It is this structure that constitutes what we mean by the "life of the mind." The dialectic that makes up that life is a real and constant cerebral process, the interplay between two fundamental types of feeling, peripheral impact and autonomous action, or objective and subjective feeling. As fast as objective impingements strike our senses they become emotionally tinged and subjectified; and in a symbol-making brain like ours, every internal feeling tends to issue in a symbol which gives it objective status, even if only transiently. (Langer 1972, 342)

Recognition of the integral relation of cognitive and feeling elements in human behavior is basic to understanding change purposes and processes.

The quality of organic learning evoked by the expectation of change as an explicit educational objective for social work contributes to the comprehension of and respect for the wholeness of the subjective and objective aspects of knowledge and behavior. Genuine understanding of the internal dynamics of change processes that is growth oriented requires ordered self-knowledge: specifically, knowledge of one's own self, including one's attitudes, preferences, etc.; of one's way of relating to others; and of one's own learning style. Learning style, in this sense, refers to all forms of taking in of new ideas and behaviors and their effect on what is already known. Bronowski describes two modes of knowledge in distinguishing the identity of man.

To be conscious is both to know and to imagine and our humanity flows from this deep spring. When we imagine nature outside ourselves into the future, we create a mode of knowledge which is science. And when we imagine ourselves alive into the future, we create another mode: knowledge of self. These are inseparable halves of the identity of man? (Bronowski, 1965, 80)

The deliberate inclusion of the dimension of self-knowledge as a legitimate content focus in the education of social workers, leading to the evolvement of professional identity, is one of the major channels through which values and social commitment take on reality and depth. Robert Coles, expressing concern about the education of psychiatrists, defines the need "to unite intimately the rational and the intuitive." He points out "We are educated and prepared, able to see and interpret. But we see, talk, and listen through our minds, our memories, our persons" (Coles 1976, 12).

Self-knowledge enables the social work student to appreciate that "the flame of man's urge to extend his arena of activities and his knowledge" (Von Braun 1976,

108) which leads him or her to undertake a course of study in a school of social work is also the force which prompts persons, groups, or organizations to seek or to use the services of social workers and social-welfare agencies to fulfill some felt need or hope. It is also the stimulus to organize against such institutions when they do not provide access to and/or equitable services.

In his comprehensive schema for categorizing social work values, knowledge, and practice, Harold Lewis asserts: "We must also recognize the importance of personal knowledge in practice and realize it is knowable as fact whenever it enters to affect the helping relationship" (Lewis 1972, 82).

Knowledge of self for professional use in affecting institutional and social as well as individual change needs to be affirmed as a positive educational aim, rather than as a remedial concept or as a by-product of the pursuit of other intellectual content. It should be manifest in all parts of a curriculum, and not confined to the traditional sequence areas of human behavior/social environment and social work practice—class and field. The regular infusion of this dimension as an expectation in all courses in the professional program becomes one measure of intrinsic institutional change in the school itself.

Complementary to and of equal importance with knowledge of change derived from the student's conscious development of professional identity is a climate of innovation in the school. The school needs to be engaged in a purposeful program of change, so that the learning environment generates an atmosphere as well as the opportunity for students to participate meaningfully and creatively with others in initiating and shaping new directions, programs, and policies. In order to comprehend for professional use the nature of institutional change, students need to have an authentic role in bringing about change in a social system of which they are a part and in which they have a stake, as a component of their educational experience. Their input into change is essential to their learning about it and providing for and valuing that in-put as integral to the total change effort is the educational responsibility of the school (Bloom 1976, 2). Along with the expected learning related to the substantive issue or problem under consideration, the use of research method, the development of analytical skill, and the evaluation of alternative strategies is the apprehension of what is actually involved in the course of change in an institution. "The inevitable struggle to sustain a commitment, to deal with the contending forces and ensuing decisions, to live with the tensions inherent in the flux and uncertainties of movement, to resist the pull to return to the safety of the familiar or the impulse to veer off into different directions, and, to bear responsibility for the consequences of decisions taken becomes a professionally actualizing endeavor of significance both to the student and to the school as a whole" (Bloom 1976, 3).

The opportunity for appropriate participation in some aspect of organizational or community change in the field placement agency is a corollary educational requisite. The broad ramifications in time and space, as well as the greater complexity of institutional change processes,[3] afford students a different social perspective when they are actively involved in the effort. It conduces toward the goal of achieving a "balanced synthesis in seeing the individual and society steadily and as a whole" (Bandler 1972, 18).

For faculty, the implications of this educational objective, of an environment in movement, and moreover, movement not completely determined by faculty decisions but, affected in part by student initiatives and participation, present a very different contextual reality for teaching and learning. Change that comes about as a result of these conditions of mutual effort affects the school as a whole, class and field instructors and staff as well as students, permeates all courses, and is often very disquieting. In contrast to a conception of a stable institutional framework within which the student moves and grows, the idea is rather that of an ambiance in continuous change. Thus, not stability but learning and teaching in a creative, responsible relation to the dynamics of change becomes the institutional goal, not merely a present uncertain reality. Relinquishing the vision of a "settled" state as the optimum condition for learning and the anticipation of again achieving that state is one of the major changes required of faculty and staff. The experience of adapting to this existential situation should provide data for the intellectual challenge to develop and further refine theories illuminating the character of change processes that are rooted in social work purpose and values.

In this segment, we have attempted to introduce a concept of a context for adult learning in a professional school, viewing the individual student, the school, and the dynamic of purposeful change as interacting elements. These elements form a whole, in motion and in creative tension that promotes and supports growth in the students and in the school. This whole is both real and symbolic; and both aspects are vital to its existence and on-going efforts. In conceptual terms, this constitutes a framework for a holistic, process-oriented approach to professional education for individual and institutional change. The holistic concept in social work respects the integrity of the individual unit—the person, the family, the group, the community, the institution or organization—and regards its interdependence with the whole as intrinsic to its nature, its humanness. The problem, then, is not that of maintaining a dual focus of "individual" and "social" with which much of the literature is concerned, but rather, of defining boundaries and of establishing and maintaining linkages among wholes.

As those familiar with the theories developed by the School will recognize, the importance of the organization (school or agency) in the ideas presented here flows from a functional base. In fact, functional social work itself emerged out of an effort to respond creatively to social changes of the period. It affirms the social sanction for practice which provides both philosophical and theoretical frameworks. In her groundbreaking book, *Theory for Social Work Practice*, Smalley (1967) defines functional social work as "a form of social work practice which utilizes agency function as an integral aspect of whatever social work process is employed . . . the use of agency function (or purpose in action) by the social worker gives focus, content, and direction to a specific helping process and assures its social responsibility, that is, assures that in the particular instance it is being used, to accomplish the particular social purpose for which it is currently being supported" (104). She further states: "The social worker has the obligation . . . not only to use his knowledge and skill in the administration of the service as it presently exists but also to make his experience, knowledge and skill available in responsible ways toward society's continuous review of (1) its purpose in establishing and maintaining the agency and (2) the effectiveness of program, policy and agency structure for its realization" (118).

The current effort to carry forward, through education and practice, the obligation for contributing to change in the organization in order to realize more fully the social mandate is regarded as an expression of an historical process, both internal in the profession and in the larger society. It constitutes an elaboration of, rather than a departure from, the basic philosophy and functional theory of the School.

The Learning Process in the Racism Sequence

Background

Courses on American Racism have been taught in the School for more than a decade. The evolution of this sequence has been affected by variables too numerous to detail here (see Arnold 1970, 1972; Arnold, Jones, and Sylvester n.d.; Axinn and Sylvester 1980; Bloom 1978; Carter 1978a,b). The important fact is that what began as an elective course has evolved into a required sequence within the Master of Social Work program, with a discrete body of knowledge, an identifiable progression in learning, and a major vehicle through which to teach social change theory and practice.

The inclusion of racism content in professional education makes contemporary and relevant many basic concepts that have been the hallmark of the School's educational heritage. The development of the sequence has utilized and extended the scope and meaning of some of its theoretical constructs, e.g., the concept of service, the concept of agency function, to address current needs and issues. A discussion of these adaptations and their effect upon the educational process will be integrated throughout the balance of the text.

Racism has been defined in the literature by a number of authors. Andrew Billingsley states:

Racism is a social force deeply imbedded in the fabric of the society in which we live. It is the systematic oppression, subjugation, and control of one racial group by another dominant or more powerful racial group, made possible by the manner in which the society is structured. In this society, racism emanates from white institutions, white cultural values, and white people. The victims of racism in this society are Black people and other oppressed racial and ethnic minorities.

Attitudinal racism exists when one racial group thinks or believes that another is inferior. Behavioral racism exists when one group excludes, oppresses, or persecutes another, or serves it less well. Racist attitudes and behaviors may be held and exhibited by individuals, shared in groups, or embodied in the policies and procedures of organizations and institutions. (Billingsley and Giovannoni 1972, 8)[4]

The significance of the issue of racism as a central focus for the teaching/learning of institutional/social change rests on the following assumptions which reflect a synthesis of traditional ideology and more recent trends.

- Continuous change is characteristic of natural phenomena and of societies; institutions can be conscious of and responsible for shaping the direction of their changes which, in turn, affects the larger social fabric;
- Institutions and changes within them are viewed holistically; thus, change or alteration in one part affects all others and the system as a whole;
- Racism is a structural phenomenon of institutions in this society;
- Social workers work with people who live in this society where racism is an ever-present force that impacts on blacks and whites; individuals and groups; communities and major societal institutions that serve communities;
- Racism is a complex and pervasive problem which has an integral relationship to all social work endeavors that affect individual functioning and the quality of life;
- The practices and pernicious effects of racism cannot be ignored by social workers; the very essence of social work demands a knowledge of racism and commitment to change in seeking solutions to social problems;
- Addressing the issue of racism in the helping process is a creative activity to bring about social justice employing professional means, knowledge and values, goals and purposes;
- The uniqueness of black experience can contribute importantly to the enhancement of the values and knowledge of society;
- Professional education for social work is an instrument for individual, institutional, and/or social change;
- Professional education must provide a realistic, in contrast to a simulated, opportunity for learning that includes the application of knowledge, values, and the development of skill;
- The necessity for risk rather than a search for certainty, and a practice theory based in process rather than prediction are creative forces in professional practice and education;
- Awareness of and skill in addressing the issue of racism carries forward the School's historical roots of social reform and prepares social workers for addressing other forms of oppression in society when that thrust is supported by a strong professional identity (e.g. learning acquired from the civil rights movement was useful for the women's movement).

There is no question but that the issue of racism as an organizing principle and an educational sequence of the program presents considerable difficulty to students, faculty, and field. Students struggle with its demands in seeking a clear professional identity that embodies the obligation to address racism and other forms of oppression and to sustain a commitment to social change. Faculty, in viewing social change as a creative process, is obligated to teach as well as to contribute to institutional change, testing out change theory and feeding new knowledge and understanding back into the classroom for further analysis. The field is expected to provide significant opportunities and support for the students' professional practice orientation, which views racism as a force which impacts upon client services. Courses on Supervision for Social Change and on Racism have been developed and are a requirement for field instructors in order to support their effort to help students learn. According to Brager and Holloway, "The single, most useful criterion to assess the significance of change is the interdependence of the changing element with other organizational variables" (Brager and Holloway, 1978, p. 23).

The Racism Sequence

This section will describe general characteristics of students' learning process in the racism sequence. The sequence is defined to encompass the required courses in first and fourth semesters, and the content dealing with racism in other courses throughout the curriculum in the field practice. Structured assignments in the racism and other courses, based upon a variety of sources and including the students' own life experiences and current experience in the program itself, provide focus and impetus for movement in learning. The dynamic quality of class sessions resulting from the interaction among students and between students and instructors affords a unique experiential dimension to their learning, important in the development of awareness of self and other, and of the human elements in this volatile issue.

The Beginning Period: Students' Learning Process in the First Semester

The expected learning for the first semester includes, at the very least, that the students:

- recognize the manifestations of racism in society;
- take into account the role of racism in assessing presenting problems and options;
- understand the function of racism in our society, the reasons it cannot be wiped out readily, and interim coping responses that are available/necessary; work toward achieving a professional identity which incorporates an individual examination of attitudes and participation in racist practices by recognizing the need to oppress, the preservation of privilege, the responses of the oppressed, as they relate to professional practice;
- work to develop skills in engaging racist expressions and behavior of whites;
- develop knowledge of the "black experience" and of other oppressed peoples/groups.

While each student, black and white, learns in his/her own individual style and pace, there are general patterns in the learning process that can be conceptualized.

Phase I: Personal Level of Reaction

This phase, comprising the first few weeks of the semester, consists of several steps. Although throughout the sequence and the entire program, black and white students respond differently, by virtue of their different life experiences in society (an important source of knowledge which they later come to value), it is in the first term that these differences are most marked and are most intensely personal in nature. In later stages, though differences, and some tensions, remain, a growing common professional base supports their understanding and professional use of these differences.

Generally, white students are fearful upon entering a course on American Racism. They fear attacks by black students, faculty, and the exposure of feelings, needs, and fears. Often, this takes the form of complete denial of the existence of racism; at other times, it is confined to denying their own participation in racist behavior. The initial response is one of caution and silent waiting to see what will happen. Through defining the extent of the manifestations of institutional racism, particularly their impact upon all members of society, and through assignments related to encountering racism, experiences with blacks, use of racism to ensure white skin advantages and privilege, potential disadvantages of racism to large groups of white people, students begin to test the waters and share in the discussion of issues. Invariably, these experiences cast the self in a "liberal" light. A typical response is to reveal relationships with blacks in the past, such as boy/friend/girl/friend relationships, which are meant to illustrate that they have already dealt successfully with their feelings and attitudes about race.

The initial response of black students is to some extent dependent upon their numerical representation in the class, for here, as in other aspects of their life, they are in the minority. With some exceptions, the assertiveness of blacks is diminished when their number is small. During the years (early to mid-seventies) when blacks constituted a larger percentage of the student body, they were considerably more active and vocal in this first phase. In general, it is observed that black students seem less certain of their conceptual understanding of the issue but very sure of their knowledge from experience and the impact of racism. It is very clear that blacks do not trust whites, the faculty or the School. They are also ambivalent toward black faculty on two scores: first, they are dubious about blacks who represent a white institution; second, having been socialized in this society, as have whites, they too, question the competence of black instructors.

After several weeks of feeling each other out, the students tend to form separate groups based on race. They identify with their fellow group members and begin sharing and discussing some of their feelings. However, all behavior can still be categorized as cautious. Most expressions of feelings and ideas are directed toward self-protection rather than learning.

In the second step of this phase, students develop an historical perspective from the literature on the history of racism, and relate this knowledge to the definitions and current manifestations of racism which they have been engaged in identifying over these weeks. This order of teaching/learning, namely beginning where the student is in the immediate present, will be recognized as an educational principle of the School. The awareness gained by white students serves as an eye-opening experience. The information gained by black students confirms what they have felt. This discovery is often accompanied by an increase in open expression of anger toward white people.

During this first phase, students and instructors alike become aware of the depth of feeling, misperception, and conflict in human relationships between groups in society, and the need to employ professional means, knowledge, and values to form relationships that will conduce toward mutual acceptance and change. White students begin to struggle with different perceptions of reality, to connect with the irrational fear that white people possess and the instinctive thrust toward protection of power, privilege and position. Black students gain a fresh view of white behavior, now reinforced by objective information, not only personal feelings. For some, it is the first time they see the problem with clarity, and their anger, hostility, and lack of trust intensifies visibly.

It should be noted that students usually react to all areas of the professional program on a personal basis as they begin. This can be documented in their responses to the content in the human behavior/social environment courses, the welfare policy courses, the practice course, and the problems they encounter in the field, and is generally expected and well understood by instructors. That it takes on such an emotion laden and substantive importance in the racism course is evidence of the nature of racism itself. Not least, is the fact that this subject has not usually been part of their formal education in the past.

Phase II: Facing the Reality of Racism

The second phase reflects acknowledgment of the existence of racism. White students suddenly seem to realize that it is difficult to be different. They begin to feel that they are not as free as they assumed themselves to be, nor are they as powerful. They find it difficult to act on their own values and concerns. Black students generally need to acknowledge their anger, its rightfulness based upon experience and understanding, and to begin to focus on a creative and constructive expression of their anger.

White students become aware that they are being grouped by blacks and they become "white people" in much the same connotation as blacks have been traditionally grouped by them. White students become acutely cognizant of this discomfort with which they have had little experience. Their responses are generally reflective of uneasiness and anxiety resulting from sensing a loss of individuality. Reaching out to black students at this point might help relieve the anxiety and create a breakthrough but black students have usually chosen this very time to withdraw more into their own group and they will have little to do with white students. Involuntary separation is experienced by white students, often for the first time. Black students discover the power of separation, some for the first time, also.

In working through this emotionally difficult phase, white students begin to grasp the meaning of some powerlessness. They see and feel the sanctions that are placed on white people by other white people toward those who dare to be different. As they try to bring their own values, feelings and behavior into concert with each other, they often discover some contradiction within the self which becomes an inner source of anxiety and discomfort. They are confronted with negative responses from family and friends when they try to express their new learning. For many white students there is a growing feeling of being caught in the middle, a sense of potential loss of family and friends if they persist in their attempt to be different.

Observation by black students of the white students' difficulties creates a climate in which some interaction is possible. Black students begin to feel some empathy toward white students. They recognize how white students are trapped in behavior patterns, mis-educated, and unclear about developing a solid identity as persons unencumbered by superiority inferiority biases. This produces a new value orientation for development of relationships characterized by equality rather than superiority/inferiority statuses. As one student wrote:

I always associated "power" and "control" with white people. It never occurred to me to think of "poor white" people, except when I thought of whites and blacks receiving public assistance. Only in my assigned readings did I stop to separate the few whites with resources and "power" to control from "poor whites"! At that time it occurred to me that the system perpetuates racism not only against blacks but whites as well.

This phase culminates in a turning point that may be described as the students' beginning to discern the necessity for a professional response to racism. All students, black and white, feel overwhelmed by the magnitude of the problem in this country and its world-wide implications. They have become aware of how human beings relate to each other, their need to project feelings onto others, to oppress, to insure status, position and power, to assume privilege and advantage. They have a deepened understanding of the institutional nature of racism which has developed from systematic oppression. The major learning achievement in this phase is the discovery and acknowledgment that racism conflicts with professional social work values and provision of service.

An excerpt from a student's paper clearly reflects this recognition:

A startling contrast can be seen in the disposition and service to a white, upper middle-class family and a poor, black, economically dependent family in two instances of suspected child abuse. The latter involved two black brothers, ages 8 and 6, in a family of five children born to a young, black, poor couple, living in a low income housing district with inadequate resources. The father was chronically unemployed, alcoholic, and had previous involvement with local police. The children were allegedly struck by their father following a domestic fight; however, there were no physical injuries present and medical treatment was not required.

As a white middle-class, educated professional, I was to evaluate the questionable parental practices of these two individuals. I was to measure them by governmental standards established by white middle-class bureaucrats, in all probability. It seemed like an incredibly powerless situation for the black parents but I thought I could "help." Their suspicion and anger, their lack of cooperation, economic limitations and consequent inability to provide caused my supervisor to institute procedures for emergency protective custody for the boys. This warrants involuntary removal for up to 72 hours. The justification was lack of parental care and control to ensure the safety and well being of the children.

Simultaneously, there had been a report of suspected child abuse involving a 5-year old white male who was hospitalized and received sutures above his eye for a questionable fall. Further medical examination revealed extensive bruising to upper and lower extremities and torso, in different stages of healing which suggested earlier trauma. The child was one of four children from an upper middle-class family whose parents were employed in professional capacities. His parents approached the interview cooperatively, able to articulate their concerns, made a comfortable income, therefore, having many more resources. In that they could provide for this child and despite these obvious physical injuries, the child was not removed. Two subsequent reports of child abuse still did not provoke removal of this child. Why then, one might ask, is this white child's situation seen as more desirable when, in fact, his physical safety and well being appeared to be in considerably more jeopardy?

As may be evident, there is much content that falls within the human behavior/ social environment area being learned during this phase through the focus on the meaning of racism to individuals and groups.

Phase III: Discovering an Individual Relationship to Institutional Racism in Social Welfare Institutions

In the final phase of the first semester the knowledge focus is on the macro level as students examine and analyze manifestations of racism in health, education, and welfare institutions in the United States. As their understanding of the systemic and widespread nature of racism deepens, it is accompanied by an urgency that something be done. White students often vacillate between feeling part of the power groups and feeling powerless to change conditions. Black students typically want to move ahead, impatient that things have continued unchanged for so long.

In dealing with this understandable human desire to plunge precipitously into solutions, emphasis is placed on the students' professional role and purpose. The importance of starting with the self by working toward developing behavior consistent with one's feelings and values, in contrast to projecting the need for change onto others, is highlighted. The realization that this is an area in which the student can be in charge, have the power to change, begins to focus energies and is viewed as a most important achievement for first semester. It also complements students' learning in practice class and field where they often begin by expecting to learn how to change others.

By the end of first semester, students are now ready to begin to develop competencies that will enable them to engage in planning for change. They are helped to view the problem of racism less globally, so as to gain a sense of their own role and responsibility in this area. They come to appreciate that purposeful change requires analysis, planning, identification of goals and targets, development of support, action and stabilization of change and is a demanding and creative experience/process.

The Middle Period: Second and Third Semesters

During second and third semesters, the students make use of the foundational content to connect with the learning in other courses. This linkage is facilitated through course structures and content, bibliographies and other resources, and the reality of the field practice situation. Instructors of the racism courses also teach in other areas of the curriculum and help to facilitate the connection and integration. Understanding of racism is used as an analytical tool in the assessment of research; of psychological, social, and behavioral theory; of social welfare policy development; of agency practice and service delivery. Students have an opportunity through assignments and class discussion to deepen analytic skills, clarify values, and develop competencies in social work processes.

The major themes that are emphasized during this period are

- The centrality of racism in resource distribution, opportunity, and the development of self-esteem in understanding the plight of the poor and disadvantaged;
- A broadened understanding of all forms of oppression as a concern of social work, using the knowledge gained in the racism course as a prototype for the development of awareness and understanding of inequities suffered by other oppressed groups;
- The concept of the social agency as part of the social context, representing one form of societal response to problems and needs. Its function is influenced by legislation, regulation, policy and rules which are not static but can be changed to promote improvement in conditions and service;
- The concept of service provided by competent social workers to individuals, families, groups, and communities and based upon knowledge about the community the agency serves, client culture, institutional supports, gaps in institutional service. The concept of service recognizes the client as a person with strengths and the ability to effect change and find solutions to problems;
- The concept of empowerment[5] which emphasizes the responsibility of the service system to facilitate empowerment; to recognize the rights and entitlements of client systems, to provide information for client systems, to take account of the differential impact of policy and practice on different racial and ethnic groups. Basic to the concept is the conviction that the client is at the center of any change process;
- The concept of professional identity and professional purpose based on a conscious and knowing use of self in a social work process, using structure and method directed toward the provision of service, client empowerment, and institutional change. As one student put it: "The struggle against racism must become as institutionalized as racism itself." Understanding of the social context, level of physical and social functioning, gaps in institutional service, the centrality of racism in the provision of resources and opportunity means change is also directed toward institutions with the recognition that support systems are needed for social functioning and enhancement. Clients are viewed as needing service rather than treatment. The meaning of protecting privilege, power and position requires understanding, as do the ways in which the social work profession is implicated in this process.

During this period of intense learning, students are able to use self-awareness and their understanding of institutional racism to assess their agencies and professional practice. Major indicators of racism encountered by students fall into the following broad areas:

- individual racist attitudes and behavior exhibited by staff and clients of social agencies;
- staffing patterns in organizations and implications for service to minority groups;
- policies and/or practices in the organization which may be considered indicators of racism;

- agency service priorities and implications for minority communities;
- lacks in knowledge and understanding of minority experience;
- quality of services to minority group clients.

The following is an illustration of a student in the middle of the learning process (between first and second year) when so much knowledge has been taken in and yet the struggle for integration is still occurring.

The student was placed in an agency whose effort to decentralize the service had led, in effect, to a black and a white office in the community. The full range of agency services was not equally available to the community, because white workers did not feel comfortable relating to the "Black Office."

This particular student was concerned that a less "racist," "elitist" pattern of regionalization be developed, and requested to be assigned to the "Black Office" to develop more suitable placements for black teenagers. She met with black youth regarding service needs, developed a proposal for a group home, and generally confronted the racism in herself as well as in the agency. This took a great deal of conviction and risk and provided a solid professional experience. She wrote, "At the end of the summer, I felt I had accomplished very little.

"I had learned most painful things about myself, often by working in a team with a black worker and perceiving my own racism. I had not really raised the consciousness at all of the more overtly racist people in the unit. I had not instituted some of the changes well in advance of my own leaving to be sure they could be sustained. I felt alienated from the black workers because I became increasingly aware of how unlikely it is at this point for a white person to feel a sense of 'belonging' in a black community and alienated from white workers in my unit who seemed to regard me as 'something else.' However, I would do it again, because I felt I was just beginning to get some ideas about how to address my own racism and I feel like I have never had a more interesting challenge."

Ending Period: Students' Learning Process in Fourth Semester

Phase I: Reconnecting with the Focus on Racism

In the fourth semester, the specific focus on American Racism is resumed through the structure of a course that is closely correlated with the social work practice course. Students' learning over the two preceding semesters is examined in respect to the professional use of self and the understanding of institutional racism as the behavior and values of white people and as a strategy for preserving white power, privilege and position, although a few students may still cling to the notion of blacks' responsibility for their condition. The knowledge which has become internalized must now be objectified at a more conceptualized level for effective use. Questions from the research conducted among white persons by Wellman (1977, 44) serve as a stimulus for this effort.

The reality of the impending end of the educational program and the imminence of entering full professional status dominates fourth semester learning in all areas. Students' future orientation provokes renewed struggle with the idea that responsibility for contributing to institutional change as integral to professional practice. Students' questions now center on the profession's stance on the issue of racism and their concern that the support they have received for their efforts as students may not be forthcoming from the professional community. Students again become engulfed by a sense of powerlessness and hopelessness related to their projections of what may lie ahead for them. This feeling is not exclusive to the racism sequence, but is felt generally at some point in the fourth term. Many white students want to give up the struggle. Black students may want to, but feel they cannot afford to do so. Relief from the feeling of being overwhelmed by the array of issues often comes from a re-examination of the disadvantages suffered by all people in the perpetuation of racism and the fact that inadequate services affect whites as well as blacks and minorities. It also comes from their findings in practice that confirm the strengths in people to deal with problems and to use their services. Students are helped to reconnect with and reaffirm the professional use of self as an instrument of change.

Phase II: Operationalizing Theory in Practice for Social Change

Students are expected to become immersed in the literature on social change theory which is also being approached in the social work practice class. During this phase, which covers most of the fourth term, concepts and principles in planning for change and the process of engaging in purposeful change within the context of an organization and of professional responsibility are dealt with.

Students submit examples from their own practice efforts to test out their application of theoretical knowledge. In discussion of these materials they pursue such themes as the assessment of strengths, resources and motivation; mutuality of expectations in change relationships; anticipated difficulties; clarification of specific change goals. Also included is an understanding of the various forces against change in systems and of people's inertia and resistance to change. Through this theory/ practice concentration, students achieve greater clarity about themselves as instruments of change-their role, position and potential power in organizations-when they have conviction about their responsibility. They discover that it affords creative opportunities directed toward improvement of client service, and often find that it even affects the way in which current policies may be interpreted. They come to realize that whatever the forces, external or internal to an agency, "Organizational change is executed by people whose action is governed by the meaning these forces have for them, their preferences for one or another outcome, and the intensity with which these preferences are held" (Brager and Holloway, 1978, 80).

A student's use of self, taken from a paper written by the student, illustrates this movement.

Three students in a field placement attempted to initiate a plan for looking into the agency's hiring practices that involved interviewing professional staff. When they originally discussed the idea with the director, they received tentative approval. However, when the plan was formally submitted, it met with consternation as to the students' intent and the potential for disruptive activity. The students' reaction was that the director had not recognized the professional integrity they had already demonstrated during their field placement. They expressed this to the director, saying "It is not our style to function in a destructive, unconcerned manner, not is it the intent of the University for us to do so." This affirmation of professional integrity opened discussion of issues which led not only to the granting of permission to pursue the project, but active cooperation with it.

Another student described her learning this way:

I felt that by using the agency's function and my role as a student in becoming a professional person, I was able to initiate some meaningful change in the eradication of racism. My difference as a student enabled me to use myself differently from the other staff. The agency's purpose and function provided an opening for me to begin to effectuate change efforts. I began to discuss issues as they were related to the nature of services provided to the clientele. Initially, I was operating as a black with a commitment. I was not recognizing the agency and my function in the agency. On an individual basis I thought that I could bring about change.

The tendency for students to relate to those issues of oppression in which they have a vested interest, e.g., racism, sexism, agism, the disabled, reinforces the concept that sensitivity in one area creates sensitivity in others, and is a vital integrating factor in their learning. They come to realize that the force for change does not lie in the nature of the particular cause, per se, of the student or worker but in the professional use of self through which values, knowledge, and consistency of purpose can be acted upon; that the professional intent is not to impose change on others but to demonstrate congruity of one's values and actions as a way to create the climate for change.

By the latter weeks of the semester, students gain a sense of where their own control and/or power lie as they begin to claim and take responsibility for themselves as professional persons.

Social Work Practice for Social Change: A Case Illustration

The following condensation of a case study illustrates the participation of students, field agency and community in promoting social change as envisioned by the School's educational program. The process of change described in the case study covers a period of more than four years and is not yet complete. The basic issue on which change is sought is the non-utilization of homemaking services by the eligible black population of the County, and a recognition that social agencies have a responsibility to offer service in a manner that is inclusive of different populations and groups.

The County Assistance office has been contracting for a number of years with the County Homemakers agency[6] to purchase homemaking services for income eligible families and individuals between the ages of 18 and 59. A first year student was given the monitoring responsibility for this contract as part of her field assignment. The student's design of the data collection instrument reflected her recognition of racism as an issue of service, therefore, racial information was collected.

The monitoring report, instead of yielding data from which the student could evaluate the quality of service to whites and minorities, showed that less than 3% of the population served was black. This information came as a surprise since blacks represented at least 30% of the eligible population. The student made 12 recommendations for improving services; one of these was to suggest that a study be undertaken to find possible explanations for the absence of blacks in the consumer population of the Homemaker agency.

During the summer months, after the student had left the County office, the staff of County office met with the staff of the Homemaker agency to discuss the report. All the recommendations met considerable resistance. The one focusing on services to minorities was not singled out as being particularly disturbing at this time.

In the course of the next academic year, another student became involved in monitoring activities on the Homemaker agency's contract. The existence of the problem was verified again. Within the County office, there was a growing awareness of the problem with some anticipation of the difficulty that might develop with the Homemaker agency if this issue were to be actively pursued. It was resolved that the County office, represented by the student, the contract specialist, and the executive director would focus primarily on this concern at the monitoring meeting.

The Homemaker agency was not in the least concerned by the absence of minority individuals in its service population. The Homemaker agency director maintained that the agency served those persons who re-request the service. Most referrals were initiated by medical sources; perhaps minority persons were under-utilizing these same medical sources also. It was clear to County office staff that the Homemaker agency would not accept any responsibility for this problem but would persist in focusing on elements outside its control as possible reasons for this occurrence.

Engagement on the issue of service to minority groups in the community had to be raised to the board level of both agencies and also involved the regional office of Public Welfare. Numerous meetings were held over a three-year period where agency boards and staff grappled with the issues raised originally by students.

Major issues addressed during the change process were

- The limited concept about how and for whom programs are designed; the board of both agencies were generally satisfied with service to whites. Boards had to be educated about the issue of racism in service delivery to recognize the problem;
- The need to develop an orientation to service that puts the responsibility on the agency to offer service to the total community in ways with which they can connect, i.e., brochures, outreach, use of personnel, etc.;
- Combating stereotypes and a general lack of information about black and minority families.

The Learning Process

Students from the school, in their professional activity, identified indicators of racism in how an agency prioritized and thus limited its services to the community.

The County Board executive and staff embraced a concept of service that was inclusive of people in need. The director of the County agency had taken the seminar on Racism for Field Instructors. All these persons educated themselves to the issue of institutional racism and how it was implicated in the way services were provided throughout the community.

Stereotypes and lack of knowledge about black family life had been used to support a policy of exclusion. Data was gathered to refute stereotypes and educate board members, regional Department of Public Welfare, and policy makers at the highest levels on this issue.

It is important to note that the students identified and persisted with this issue until the agency took it over as a priority concern. One of the reasons students have difficulty understanding the difficulty of initiating change is that they are not in the educational program long enough to see the full process, to know the results of what they have initiated and the value of setting a process in motion. This was evident in the illustration of the student's reactions cited earlier in the case of regionalization of an agency service.

While this process is still going forward in the two organizations, with many problems to be addressed, a climate for change has been created in the community and concerned people are beginning to hold social agencies more accountable for the services they offer.

Seminar for Field Instructors and Other Social Change Efforts by Faculty

Two associated activities mentioned earlier as essential to the School's pursuit of its goal of education for social change are the seminar required of field instructors and the faculty's contribution to the larger University Community's realization of equitable educational opportunity for all students. These are briefly summarized here, primarily to illustrate the ramifications and effect of introducing change in one part of a system upon other parts and upon other institutions with which it has functional relationships.

The Seminar for Field Instructors

The field placement agencies are considered full partners in the educational enterprise of the School, and are expected to provide learning opportunities for students that are consistent with the School's philosophy. The year-long seminar on Supervision for Social Change[7] is designed for social workers serving as field instructors for the first time. "The intent is orientation to the MSW program and to the collaborative educational process in preparing social workers for professional practice for social change. . . . The seminar examines the role and responsibilities of the field instructor in helping the student conceptualize and make use of the learning from class and field, and in evaluation of student performance. The materials are drawn from professional literature and the practice materials of field instructors."[8] The seminar aims to sensitize agency field instructors to this obligation and process as it relates to their instruction of students of the School. The focus is on helping students learn to apply change principles through strategies for action and the professional use of the self to all those situations where oppression of humans occurs. The participants are expected to present materials arising from their agency practice reflecting questions and problems appropriate to the focus of the seminar.

Field instructors approach the seminar with many different perspectives, expectations, and resistances. Because it is a requirement, some feel that the School is attempting to indoctrinate them to another kind of practice and/or is questioning their professional knowledge and competence. It is necessary to establish at the outset the purpose for the requirement. The position is that the basic field placement contract is between the agency and the School of Social Work to provide learning opportunities for students. The School has no wish to impose its view about professional practice on anyone. However, field instructors are expected to support the School's conceptualization of practice to the degree that they can meet their responsibility for enhancing students' learning. In operational terms, this means helping to build a climate in the agency that respects and values change and provides realistic learning opportunities for students. The School of Social Work has struggled internally to create such an atmosphere for students. This achievement has been significant even though many unresolved issues and problems still remain. It might also be noted that this is not the School's first experience of encountering and working through issues of its difference in ideology.

As field instructors have engaged in the seminar, as well as in other courses, projects and institutes, it has been evident that there is an analogy between their experience in dealing with issues of racism and the students' process of learning. Along with gaining an understanding of the supervisory process and method, field instructors need to feel confident about their own progress in overcoming their own feelings and attitudes that stem from their acculturation in a racist society. They go through a process similar to that of students, as many of them come to recognize. However there is a major difference in the two learning processes. Field instructors bring a professional self that is highly developed and intact. Whereas with students, the attempt is to help them build an orientation to change and a concern for racism and other oppressions from the very beginning, with field instructors, as has been true of classroom faculty also, it requires some reorganization and/or infusion of this perspective and commitment into an already structured professional identity. This process is sometimes more difficult and an examination and analysis of this effort in the seminar helps them to connect the new awareness and knowledge with the professional knowledge and skill they already possess.

In the past, the issue of institutional racism bas generally been dealt with or denied through a variety of forms, such as a "Gentleman's Agreement" (Weiner 1970), color blindness, or the setting of service priorities that excluded significant minority populations. Hence, bringing the issue to the fore is a highly threatening and anxiety provoking topic in some organizations and among some social work professionals, though others applaud it. If the field instructor is anxious and defensive, the student will not be able to broach the topic, explore feelings and attitudes, confront the issue, take risks, and make changes in behavior patterns that are important to effective service. It is also recognized that field instructors are often vulnerable to internal organizational pressures affecting their upward mobility which may lead to some hesitancy about working toward institutional changes. The School has begun to engage agencies at the executive and board levels to engender support and mitigate the threat felt by some field instructors.

The School's expectation of a learning climate in agencies that values and encourages change includes the following kinds of activity on the part of field instructors. These are not different, in essence, from sound supervisory practice, but expand the scope to include commitment, knowledge, and skill with respect to dealing with issues of racism and institutional change.

- Openness to questions, concerns, and reactions that students bring from their observations;

- Readiness to discuss racial concerns, racial differences, and evaluate value conflicts between student and agency using the concepts of racism as an analytic tool;
- Assignments that assure continuity of service while focusing upon obstacles affecting service such as students' feelings/attitudes, clients' negative feelings, targets for change related to service, realistic limits of change;
- Teaching that highlights the professional role and conduct in pursuit of change, and the need to engage with others, since the agency function and purpose provides resources over and beyond one's individual efforts;
- Support, in the form of communication with administration. intra and interagency endeavors, for the issues raised by students so as not to expect them to carry their concerns alone. In other words, an advocate role which affirms their own investment in helping the organization become more cognizant of issues of racism.

The efforts by field instructors and agencies has had important meaning in furthering their own professional endeavors in meeting current stresses and problems and in their contribution to the profession through the education of students.

Social Change Efforts by Faculty

The faculty of the School of Social Work not only teach students about social change theory and processes, but feel an obligation to contribute to social change.

The faculty has invested in change efforts within and outside the University, directed at issues of racism, sexism, and other forms of oppression. Individual faculty members have served on agency boards, conducted workshops and seminars, given consultations and engaged many of these issues of oppression directly, through work in the community.

Due to the limitations of space, only the specific contributions of black faculty and their work in creating a climate for change in the University will be highlighted here.

The black faculty's involvement at a University-wide level developed as a result of concerns and issues identified while working for change at the School of Social Work (Arnold 1976). It was recognized as early as 1970 that the School's commitment to a minority program was inextricably bound to the broader University, especially in terms of the programs' need for recognition and financial support. It was also recognized at that time that the issues and problems of racism addressed at the School were but a microcosm of the situation in the University as a whole.

The University administration voiced concern about such issues as the need for increased numbers of black faculty and students; the need to develop a climatic in the University that was inclusive and supportive of black student life. However, there was no clearly defined, organized plan to create programs to respond to the concerns.

The black faculty at the School spearheaded the organization of a small group of Black Faculty and Administrators at the University for the purpose of addressing the problems of racism in the University in a planful and concerted way. This participation by faculty of the School was viewed as a part of the professional commitment to contribute to social change concepts to students. A period of study and discussion led to the development of a Black Presence document which, in 1973, was incorporated into the report of the University Development Commission.[9] This Commission recommended approaches to address the outlined concerns of the Black Presence document. Work continues on these recommendations today, which speaks to the long time process of social change in a major institution.

The climate of the University continues to be resistant to change. The change in the economic picture, inflation, costs of energy, etc. have seriously impacted on this process. And yet, some small progress can be identified, much due to the efforts of Black Faculty and Administrators (BFA) and concerned white faculty and staff who have educated themselves to the complexities of institutional racism. The educational benefit to all students of a diversified faculty and student body is an idea that is gaining further attention.

The Black Faculty and Administrators continues to address a number of crucial concerns that fall within the following broad categories:

- Recruitment and Retention of Faculty
- Student Recruitment and Admissions
- University Life—a broad category that deals with issues of the quality of student life, supportive services, academic advising, College House Programs, sororities and fraternities, etc.

Working for change in the University has had its positive and negative impacts. A few examples should illustrate.

On a positive side, the knowledge and skills develop through the process of engaging the University in a social change process has enriched the teaching of students at the School of Social Work. This activity has authenticated the theory and conceptualization of the possibility for organizational changes that a bureaucracy can be influenced, and a climate created that supports and values change. Secondly, social work with its knowledge about people and organizations, its value base and professional skills, has been interpreted to the University Community. It is much more valued by this Community far its potential contribution within this larger system. Thirdly, black faculty has helped white faculty and the School conceptualize social change for professional practice.

Now the negatives! A major issue far black faculty, still unresolved, is how to sustain work on issues of this magnitude and complexity, and still perform all the tasks expected of a fully affiliated faculty member, i.e., teach, publish, advise students, serve on committees. This issue is clearly sharpened in the promotion and tenure process which places the greatest value on research and publication rather than service.

Black faculty has had to guard against being used to quiet dissatisfied black students or act in ways that provide a buffer between University administration and students.

Finally, a major pitfall that warrants mention here is that old institutional strategy far resisting change that puts the responsibility for implementation of change on the group that raised the issue. In other words, the complainant is asked to came up with ways to deal with the complaint which, over time, guarantees that complaints will diminish far the sheer weight of it all.

Overall, the University Community has begun to value the role that a School of Social Work can play in the larger University. The black faculty has tested, through experience the theory and conceptualization that support social work practice far social change and have through these contributions, enriched the educational program of the school.

Summary and Conclusion: Relating Social Work Practice Knowledge to Institutional Change

The experience of the School's own changes ever the last ten years constitutes a substantive source of knowledge of processes of institutional change. This development has been described elsewhere (Arnold 1970; Axinn and Sylveste 1980; Arnold et al. n.d.; Bloom 1978; Carter 1978a). The main point here is that a value stance, expressed through a commitment to action, both sparked and has sustained the changes that have evolved, many unforeseeable at the start. Institutional change has come to be understood as effecting a structure that supports on-going changes. Thus, the product becomes an institutional climate and a way of life during which goals will change over time as a result of many forces, internal and external.

At the core of the students' learning is a view of professional practice that incorporates into the professional role and function responsibility to contribute to institutional change that is integral to professional performance, not an added or separate task nor allocated only to certain staff. Such a perspective, brought to all one's professional endeavors, itself creates an approach to service that leads to innovations.

Two aspects of practice knowledge emphasized are the understanding of organizational change as a process.

Understanding of organizational structure. Just as students learn to look for certain elements in the service situation, in the client, family, group or community, and for the nature of the agency's function, so, too, is it necessary to search out the structural elements of institutions in terms of their relation to the optimum discharge of the service mandate. Knowledge of the strengths, weaknesses, contradictions and/or omissions in policies and procedures and of ether characteristics of structural components needs to be regarded in terms of the system as a whole as well as far its significance *to* the particular service situation.

Understanding institutional change as a process that involves continuing assessment and engagement. Just as students learn the essentiality of recognizing and understanding the forces and tendencies in individuals and groups for and against making necessary alterations adaptations to resolve problems and to achieve chosen goals so, too, is there the need to comprehend the forces that operate in an organization: historical, structural, power, vested interests, resources. The larger arena of institutional change can be characterized by its greater complexity, larger numbers of actors/participants representing different stakes, interacting relationships, different pace and timing, often diverse accountability relationships, and also, often, as signifying a challenge to the professional social workers' perceived self-interest. An adaptation of traditional professional knowledge and skill is required to encompass this broadened field of action.

Perhaps the most challenging and difficult learning is that of engaging others who are part of the situation and have their own stakes in the organization. The concept advanced here does not minimize the tensions, conflicts, struggles and persistence involved in efforts to bring about institutional change nor expect it to occur without upset or disruption of "business as usual." However, as in working with clients, the purpose is not to overcome the other or to establish an adversary relationship. Rather, it is to build upon an understanding of the human dynamic of self-interest and survival so as to connect with the strengths and positive potentials for improving the situation. Here, as in the delivery of direct service, the professional social worker does not have the solution, does not attempt to change or control others, but rather, engages in a mutual effort to seek a more effective, humanly oriented organization. In her study of hospital-based social work practice, Regensburg suggests that social workers "would be helped greatly by making the dynamic connections that exist between the principles and concepts underlying collaboration and those that are basic to achieving institutional change" (Regensburg 1978, 210).

The same professional concepts and principles are observed by the School in its teaching of field instructor's work with agencies, and within the larger University Community. This coherence of knowledge and doing not only advances the School's own knowledge development in this stressful area, but also conveys to others the seriousness of its conviction in working toward the elimination of institutional racism.

The approach that has been described here in the teaching/learning of practice for social change is based on a professional process model rather than on a political model. It holds that the key to social workers' responsibility for institutional change lies in the use of the profession's values, unique knowledge, and skill.

The "web of institutional racism" (Baron 1969) is deep, intricate and tough. Its roots are embedded in our legal, economic, and social structure (Higginbotham 1978) and its elimination requires nothing less that a re-education of all—whites and blacks. The profession of social work cannot, of course, bring about the necessary changes alone, but it can provide leadership in the institutions of which it is a part, health, education, justice, and welfare. It can impact upon the views of the widely diverse people it serves, to re-think attitudes and beliefs about themselves and others and the kind of society that benefits all of its members.

Reprinted from Howard Arnold and Tybel Bloom, Institutional change as a creative process: Some educational and practice considerations, *Journal of Social Work Process* 13 (1981): 4–24.

Notes

1. Hereafter, the University of Pennsylvania School of Social Work is referred to as the School.

2. The two required courses in the Racism sequence are "American Racism: Knowledge and Analysis for Social Work Practice" (first semester) and "American Racism: Knowledge, Analysis and Strategies for Change for Professional Social Work Practice" (fourth semester).

3. The term "institutional change" is used here since the character of the change relates to institutional attitudes, values, and patterns of behavior that derive from the profession of social work and professional education, and that are reflected in the individual school or agency. This term is regarded as more comprehensive than, though encompassing, reorganization of curriculum structure and content or of agency programs. It envisions a basic conceptualization ultimately to eventuate from the combination of new elements and reordering of the old.

4. Other definitions of racism: "The determining feature of race relations is not prejudice towards blacks, but rather, the superior position of whites and the institutions-ideological as well as structural which maintain it" (Wellman 1977, 36); "The essential feature of racism is not hostility or misperception, but rather the defense of a system from which advantage is derived on the basis of race . . . it insures the continuation of a privileged relationship" (222); "The destructive feature of racism thinking is that it justified policies, and institutional priorities that perpetuate racial inequality" (235); "Racism is a white problem in that its development and perpetuation rest with white people. Whites created racism through the establishment of policies and practices that serve to their advantage and benefit and continues to oppress all minorities in the United States. Racism is perpetuated by whites through their conscious *and/or* unconscious support of a culture and institutions that are founded on racist policies and practices. The racial prejudice of white people coupled with the economic, political and social power to enforce discriminatory practices on every level of life—cultural, institutional and individual—is the gestalt of white racism" (Katz 1978, 10).

5. A definition of empowerment in social work is offered by Barbara Solomon: "The social worker engages in a set of activities with the client system that aim to reduce the powerlessness that has been created by the negative valuation of a stigmatized group" (1976, 29).

6. Hereafter, the County Assistance office is referred to as the County office, and the County Homemaker agency is referred to as the Homemaker agency.

7. A special seminar on "American Racism for Field Instructors" is required of those persons who have supervised students of the School of Social Work.

8. "Statement of Purpose of the Seminar on Supervision for Social Change," University of Pennsylvania School of Social Work, 1978–79.

9. *Pennsylvania, One University*, report of the University Development Commission, January 1973, 117.

References

Arnold, H. D. (1970). American racism: Implications for social work. *Journal of Education for Social Work* 6.

———. (1972). Racism in social work education. Paper delivered at the National Conference on Social Welfare, Chicago, June.

———. (1976). Black faculty in social work: Working for change in the university. Paper delivered at the Council on Social Work Education Annual Program Meeting, Philadelphia.

Arnold, H. D., T. Jones, and S. Sylvester (n.d.). Some thoughts and considerations in teaching a course on American racism in schools of social work. Unpublished paper.

Axinn, J., and S. Sylvester (1980). Micro/mezzo/macro: An integrated approach to teaching racism. Paper delivered at the Council of Social Work Education Meeting, Los Angeles, March 1980.

Bandler, B. (1972). Community mental health professions. *Journal of Education for Social Work*, 8.

Baron, H. M. (1969). The web of urban racism. In L. L. Knowles and K. Prewitt, eds., *Institutional Racism in America*. Englewood Cliffs, N.J.: Prentice-Hall.

Billingsley, A., and J. M. Giovannoni (1972). *Children of the Storm: Black Children and American Child Welfare*. New York: Harcourt, Brace, Jovanovich.

Bloom, T. (1976). Social work education as an instrument for social change: An aspect of one school's experience. Paper delivered at the Council on Social Work Education Annual Program Meeting, Philadelphia, March 2, 1976.

———— (1978). The MSW program: Education for social change. *The Sociolog* (Spring).

Brager, G., and S. Holloway (1978). *Changing Human Service Organizations: Politics and Practice*. New York: Free Press.

Bronowski, J. (1965). *The Identity of Man*. Garden City, N.Y.: Natural History Press.

Carter, L. H. (1978a). How do Black social work students benefit from a course on institutional racism? *Journal of Education for Social Work* 14.

———— (1978b). The Black instructor: An essential dimension to the content and structure of the social work Curriculum. *Journal of Education for Social Work* 14.

Coles, R. (1976). *The Mind's Fate: Ways of Seeing Psychiatry and Psychoanalysis*. Boston: Little, Brown.

Higginbotham, A. L. (1978). *In the Matter of Color: Race and the American Legal Process—The Colonial Period*. New York: Oxford University Press.

Katz, J. H. (1978). *White Awareness: Handbook for Anti-Racism Training*. Norman: University of Oklahoma Press.

Langer, S. K. (1972). *Mind: An Essay on Human Feeling*. Baltimore: Johns Hopkins University Press.

Lewis, H. (1972). A program responsive to new knowledge and values. In Edward J. Mullen, James R. Dumpson, and Associates, eds., *Evaluation of Social Intervention*. San Francisco: Jossey-Bass.

Regensburg, J. (1978). *Toward Education for Health Professions*. New York: Harper & Row.

Smalley, R. E. (1967). *Theory for Social Work Practice*. New York: Columbia University Press.

Solomon, B. B. (1976). *Black Empowerment: Social Work in Oppressed Communities*. New York: Columbia University Press, 1976.

Von Braun, W. (1976). Responsible scientific investigation and application. In James Baldwin, ed., *The Nature of a Humane Society*. Philadelphia: Fortress Press.

Weiner, M. (1970). Gentlemen's agreement: Revisited. *Social Casework*, 51.

Wellman, D. T. (1977). *Portraits of White Racism*. Cambridge: Cambridge University Press.

Commentary

Anthony F. Bruno

In their article, "Institutional Change as a Creative Process: Some Educational and Practice Considerations," Arnold and Bloom address a question long at the center of the School's focus: how to enable students to develop a professional identity and, at the same time, instill an understanding of change as a process inextricably bound up with that identity. Using the racism sequence as an explanatory framework, and deploying constructs well known to Functional school graduates like professional purpose use of self and institutional change, the authors explain that knowledge of self in relation to racism, its urgent need for eradication, and its location within a climate of change engendered by the School and into the agency leads to that identity and understanding of change. They describe the impact upon students in this way:

They come to realize that the force for change does not lie in the nature of the particular cause, per se, of the student or worker but in the professional use of self through which values, knowledge, and consistency of purpose can be acted upon.

The "creative process," then, in which students individually experience and conceptualize change, immerse themselves in a School committed to change, and ultimately, come to understand change in relation to agency function—all of these, the authors explain, are and can be transmitted by an engaged and aware faculty who are themselves change agents.

Echoes of Smalley, Lewis, Moustakas, Arnold, Sylvester, Axiin, and Carter resound throughout the article, reminding us of the rich heritage we carry as the end of the first decade of the twenty-first century nears. That heritage was reflected in a personal meeting with Tybel Bloom shortly before her death. I asked what she most valued about the Functional Approach, first as a student and then as faculty at the School. She replied, "I watched faculty embody in the classroom and in their practice the very principles they were teaching and attempted to do so myself when I taught." May the School's faculty and students attend to her words in this, our hundredth anniversary, and may we aspire to express them at the end of our two-hundredth anniversary.

Chapter 13
Social Work and Social Action

Kenneth L. M. Pray

This article is meant to answer, from one single point of view, certain questions which have long divided the profession of social work, its sponsors and supporters, and which have disturbed and retarded the development of constructive relations between the profession and many other groups in our communities who share many of our objectives and are struggling earnestly and effectively for their attainment. Upon the answers to these questions depend, not only the unity and strength and, therefore, the ultimate status and development of the profession as an instrument of service, not only the scope and nature and quality of that service, but, in truth, the very existence of our right and our opportunity to serve at all.

It is not necessary that we immediately find final answers upon which we can all agree; but it is essential that we shall honestly seek agreement, shall search for sound professional principles by which to measure the discharge of professional responsibilities and to guide all of us in coming to terms with the practical problems of our day-to-day relationship with forces of social change and social planning. It is supremely important that we shall not allow ourselves to divide into warring camps, around differing concepts of our role in the world, and shall not find a kind of exhilarating satisfaction in hurling epithets at each other across the chasm that may temporarily divide us on this issue. Whatever other principles may be at stake, it is surely sound professional practice to recognize, respect, and explore our differences, rather than merely to dogmatize or fight about them.

For the purpose of this discussion we shall define social action as the systematic, conscious effort directly to influence the basic social conditions and policies out of which arise the problems of social adjustment and maladjustment to which our service as social workers is addressed. This definition itself may not satisfy all of us to begin with, for it has at least one debatable limitation. While it does not deny, neither does it specifically acknowledge or emphasize the potential and actual indirect influence upon the total social scene which may emanate from the specific services social workers render to particular individuals and groups, through the traditional primary task of helping people to find and use their own strength and the resources around them for the solution of their own problems and the fulfillment of their own lives. I am inclined to believe that the importance and value of this indirect social action, inherent in our day-to-day service, are often unduly minimized or even forgotten in our discussions of social action. But for the present, it is not really in controversy, and I am quite sure that none among us would want to limit our professional service, either in scope or method, so as to preclude these potential, indirect, social gains. It is in relation to the direct, deliberate application of our effort to general social change that our problems and our' differences principally develop.

With reference to this issue, let us state some of the disturbing questions plainly.

First of all, the basic question: Does social work as a profession bear any specific responsibility to apply its knowledge and skill to the end of adjusting social institutions and arrangements to the needs of human beings, or is its responsibility limited to helping people find the utmost of satisfaction and achievement within the social circumstances that surround them, whatever those circumstances may be?

If the profession does have some responsibility to participate in social change, what are the boundaries of that responsibility? Has it any real boundaries? Can it be defined or measured in such a way as to differentiate the responsibility of social work in social action from that of other groups devoted to other forms of human service? Or is our responsibility unlimited, all-inclusive, subject only to a constantly changing and expanding definition of what constitutes social need and social betterment?

If, as a profession, we have an inherent, definite responsibility for participation in social action, is it a universal, individual responsibility, borne by every one of us, each in his own place and station? Or is it essentially a collective responsibility only, to be discharged primarily by chosen representatives of the whole profession, on behalf of all? Or is it, perhaps, a responsibility to be delegated by all of us to a few especially interested and competent individuals, employed in agencies devoted to this particular purpose?

Under any of these concepts, can the discharge of this responsibility be brought under anything like professional discipline? What is the relation of the performance of these tasks to other aspects of professional performance? How does it affect, for instance, our direct service relationships with clients? Can this primary professional service relationship be used in any way as an avenue for discharge of a professional responsibility for social action?

And how does our professional relation to a particular agency—which is an almost uniquely significant factor in the performance of our professional function—affect the scope or nature of our responsibility for social action? Does it define, control, limit, or modify this responsibility?

What is the place of the professional association in this whole problem? Is there anything in its function or its composition, or in our relation to it, that determines or defines the use we can make of it in discharging our responsibility for social action? And what of the union? Can we use it—how or to what extent can we use it—or this professional purpose?

Finally, what of our professional relation to political action, especially partisan political action? What part, if any, can we play as professional people in this recurring contest between opposing social interests and concepts and those that represent or uphold them? Does such participation necessarily violate professional standards, because it involves the abandonment of our primary obligations or the destruction of essential professional relationships? In this regard, does it make a difference whether we act as individuals, or in groups, or as a total profession? Can we, indeed, act as individuals or as groups, without involving our whole profession or entangling our primary professional services with divisive and extraneous public issues?

The history and the generally accepted basic philosophy of social work point to a definite answer to our first question. Social action, once more commonly called social reform, has always been an integral and often a decisive element in social work practice as a whole. From the early days of the charity organization and settlement movements in England, down to the mental hygiene and public welfare movement of our own time, there has never been a moment when professionally conscious social workers have been content wholly to separate their day-to-day service of particular individuals and groups from some measure of responsibility for controlling or preventing some of the broad social factors that caused, complicated, or intensified the problems with which they dealt. And the reason, I believe, is that there is no possibility of such separation in fact. In accepting responsibility for administering particular services, social workers accept, also, the inherent obligation to see that those services find their mark, so far as possible, in the lives of those that seek and use them. The special knowledge and skill and discipline upon which the professional character of our whole function rests are directed precisely to that end. Otherwise it would be empty pretense. But suppose, in that effort, we discover circumstances beyond the immediate control of ourselves or our clients which frustrate or obstruct the full and fruitful use of our service? That cannot absolve us from our inherent responsibility to make our service available and useful in fact, as well as in theoretical purpose. And how can we discharge that full responsibility without undertaking somehow to help in removing the obstructions that confront us and our clients? And what is this but social action?

In affirming this basic concept that social work, as a profession, necessarily involves and includes social action as a professional function, we are brought close to an answer for our second question, as to the nature and scope of that responsibility. Social work is not the whole of social welfare enterprise. It is not the exclusive custodian or captain of social progress. The social welfare, in a true sense, is the common ultimate objective of every social institution; it is the characteristic aim of many parts of our modern culture. Social work cannot possess, it can only share, that objective. We have learned through experience the essential practical value, as well as the theoretical validity, of a limited and defined function as the basis of our direct professional service to clients. We know that we need that limitation as the focus of our own development in skill and knowledge, and as the solid framework that sustains and sanctions our helping process. We know that the client needs it, too, among other reasons, in order that he may know whether the service we offer meets his need, and whether he can use it with satisfaction and success. The same principle applies with equal force to that secondary aspect of our task which concerns our participation in helping the community effect broad change in itself. We need to know the limits within which we can truly help, as a basis for the development of our own skill and the formulation of our own criteria of the validity of change. The community needs to know the area of our special knowledge and capacity, as the basis of its discriminating acceptance and use of our help.

What, then, defines the province within which, as a profession, we carry responsibility for social action? It cannot be bounded once and for all, by the range of the human problems with which it is concerned, in terms of the aspects of human living with which those problems are identified. One decisive characteristic of social work as a total professional field is the fact that there is no problem of human living in society which is not likely, appropriately, to come within the orbit of some of its professional practitioners. Problems of health, work, play, education, of family life, parenthood, childhood, of every social relationship within which people must find their place, are grist to our mill. Yet, obviously, that cannot mean that our specific professional capacity and responsibility extend to the understanding and treatment of all the infinite ramifications of human life as a whole, or of any of these problems in their entirety.

There is, however, one focal point to which all our professional services do converge, whose specific significance sets off our tasks from every other part of social welfare enterprise. That is our concern with the actual impact of any or all of these problems upon the individual life, and the way in which human beings face and meet these problems, and thus attain, through social relationships, their mastery over them. We do not know, for instance—we have no way to find out through our own professional service or training—what constitutes a good and complete health program in any community, in terms of the technical components of such a program. We do know and we must know, because we are responsibly helping people to face their health problems as factors in their social adjustment, what stands in the way of the maintenance of health and the full use of health resources. We know the effect upon individual people of inadequate or inaccessible health resources, inadequate provision for meeting the economic hazards of illness, inadequate appreciation and, therefore, inadequate provision of integrated treatment, of the interacting physical, social, and emotional factors of illness. We know some of the conditions, mechanisms, and processes that are prerequisite for the attainment of recognized standards of health. With respect to these aspects of the community's health problem we have a clear professional responsibility to make our help available, not only in the realization, but also in the formulation of its own health standards and health program.

Take another example: We do not know, nor can we conceivably learn—as a part of our own professional study and practice—all that must go into the organization and operation of an adequate and satisfying economic system. But we do know the impact of economic factors of life upon individual human beings and groups, and we know the problems that people face in the actual process of adjusting to these fundamental realities of social living, because we have been responsibly and studiously engaged in helping people through that actual process. We do know, therefore, not only the fact, but the meaning to real people of inadequate income, of intermittent employment and unemployment; we know the meaning to the individual of real work, of creative, free, self-respecting participation in the economic process and in the determination of his own working conditions. This does not entitle us to prepare or to endorse a detailed blueprint of a total reform of the economic system. It does obligate us to contribute of our special knowledge and our professional judgment to the formulation of acceptable criteria of the validity of economic arrangements, and to exert our influence toward the introduction into our economic structure of those mechanisms and processes that make it possible for people continuously to find positive satisfactions, through sound relationships, in all their working life.

The province of professional social work, then, either in its direct service or in its social action, does not encompass the total life problem of anybody, not the whole of any problem. We are concerned with social process—the impact of social structure and policy upon individuals, and the process by which people are enabled to meet and master the problems this impact presents.

It is obvious, if this be true, that the responsibility of social work for social action is both an individual and a collective responsibility. It cannot be entirely separated from individual practice; it cannot be wholly entrusted to a special group of workers charged exclusively with the specific set of tasks involved in social action; it cannot be delegated by each of us to a few chosen representatives of all of us. Each of us carries a dual responsibility: first, to perform with all the competence and faithfulness we can muster the particular services which are entrusted to us by the particular agency with which we are identified; second, to contribute steadily of our understanding and skill, derived from this experience, to help the community constructively to relate its institutions and arrangements and services to the fundamental needs of human beings as these are disclosed in our service relationships. No one of us can know all about all these needs; each of us can and must know a part, and each of us must be responsible, therefore, for contributing his own part to the larger whole.

There are four kinds of relationship within which this responsibility must be defined and controlled, if professional standards are to be discovered and upheld. There is the client-worker relationship; the agency relationship; the relationship to the profession as a whole; and the relationship with other organized forces of social change and control in the larger community.

It seems clear that the client-worker relationship must be held clear for service, and for service only. Any use of that relationship for the attainment of any goal other than that to which it is dedicated in advance—the service of a particular need upon which the agency has offered help, through the worker—is a betrayal of the client's confidence, of the agency's purpose, and of the worker's professional obligation. The process of service itself, by helping to discover and release strength and energy in clients, which they may ultimately turn, along with others, if they choose, toward the conscious change of social policies that affect them, may, it is true, indirectly promote social change. But this must always remain one of the incidental, unpredictable, and undesigned outcomes of service—never its goal.

The professional social worker's agency relationship is of another order. Here he is somewhat freed to participate directly in social action affecting the problems encompassed within agency function. As an individual he discharges this aspect of professional responsibility in helping the agency to mold its own part of the total social structure to the needs of those who seek its help. By the consistent and continual registration of the worker's actual experience, and the circumstances surrounding the client's need and his use of agency service, through the established agency channels, the worker contributes responsibly to that alert awareness of, and readiness for, change, which is the hallmark of every effective social agency. By sensitive and discriminating participation, at every appropriate time, in the formulation and expression of progressive agency policy, geared to clients' needs, the individual worker helps to mold this little part of the total organized community. This is no negligible contribution. Given an agency under professional leadership, in which there is a constant two-way flow of creative interest and experience, among board, administration, and professional staff, the habit of sensitive response to the changing needs and new meanings of its own service is bound to grow into an expanding concern for factors beyond agency control that cause or complicate the problems with which agency service is concerned. And that kind of an agency is going to feel an obligation to contribute, as a whole—not only through its professional elements—to the pool of community feeling and understanding out of which new and more serviceable social structure and policy will emerge. I venture to affirm that every social agency expressing, as it must, in its own function, the community's purpose to meet a specific need, is obligated to help the community to fulfill that purpose completely, by removing the obstructions that prevent the service from reaching its mark in the lives of people, and by relieving the conditions that steadily augment or intensify the need.

But it is also true that every agency necessarily carries, in practice if not in theory, a limited function. Its responsibility for social action—and, hence, the opportunity of professional workers to discharge their responsibility through it—is limited to the area of need with which it is functionally involved. Furthermore, the agency is composed of both lay and professional elements. It can only act, as an entity, within the area of its own internal agreement. It may not, at a given time and place, be ready to act, or capable of acting effectively, toward ends that its professional staff, or some of its members, consider to be necessary for the full discharge of their professional responsibilities. Does this circumstance absolve the individual professional worker of all further responsibility? Or, to put it another way, is the professional staff member stopped from further professional social action beyond that which he can discharge through the agency or within it?

On the contrary: Professional responsibility is individual. It cannot be surrendered or evaded. Within the bounds of one's direct functional service, the professional worker is, of course, the representative of the agency and faithfully applies its policy, expressing his own professional self in the process of helping clients use agency function and policy to the utmost for their own good. Beyond those boundaries, one still carries one's own individual professional responsibility to free oneself for professional performance in accordance with one's own professional standards. It is here that the professional association, as an instrument of professional social action, serves an indispensable purpose. Here the limitations of an individual service responsibility, and the limitations of a particular agency function, are erased; here, as a member of the total professional group, the worker finds an avenue through which to bring to expression his whole professional self, in behalf of the highest professional standards.

As a united body, pooling the experiences and the resources of all its members, the profession is free to establish its own criteria of social structure and policy, to articulate its own total contribution to the guidance of social change, and to participate in social action to that end in accordance with its own deliberately accepted standards and methods. The circle of individual responsibility and influence is thus widened; one's own interests and purposes and standards are measured and tested against others. In the end, one can join confidently and helpfully in support of professional interests and aims even far beyond those bounded by one's own specific experience. To help the professional association serve that useful purpose, with courage, with foresight, with consistent determination, in social action, is one of the solemn obligations professional workers accept with their membership in the association.

Here again there are prerequisite conditions that must be observed and maintained. The association unites professional workers around one basic interest-the discovery, progressive development, and consistent use of the highest professional standards of service. It is concerned with the actual performance of social workers, through the acceptance and enforcement of such standards. Its members are not asked to check their religious, their political, even their economic and social convictions and differences at the door. They are asked to join in support of certain common standards of performance, whatever other differences may divide them. The usefulness of the association as an instrument of social action is necessarily limited by that primary functional concern with professional standards. Even within this area of interest, its practical usefulness depends upon the degree of its actual internal agreement. It is foolhardy and dangerous for the association to presume or pretend to speak for the whole profession upon any issue, even those affecting or affected by professional standards, when actually professional agreement does not exist. It is sound principle and serviceable practice that have led the association usually to limit its undertakings in social action to those that, after study and discussion by the whole membership, command the convinced support of a clear majority.

There is, of course, danger in this concept of the limitation of association responsibility. Endless study, aimless talk, may become an easy refuge from the perils involved in clear conviction and decisive action. The boundary between intelligent discretion and unconfessed cowardice is sometimes difficult to draw, but we must depend upon a growing, vital sense of true professional responsibility to protect us against yielding to ignoble fears.

We can also depend upon vigorous individual and group action, supplementing united association effort; for, just as the individual's professional responsibility for social action is not completely absorbed into agency function, so the individual's responsibility is not completely submerged in the professional group. Each of us continues to carry that responsibility for living up to our own standards, and for finding a way to discharge this responsibility, whether or not the whole profession supports and sustains it. It is right here that the union in social work finds a suitable and effective place in the discharge of individual responsibility for social action. The union opens, in a way, a still wider circle of interest and effort and influence than that of the association. As the professional association breaks down the barriers of individual specialization, of experience, and of agency function, in relation to the worker's responsibility for social action, so the union levels the walls enclosing a narrow professionalism. It unites professional workers, not only with other workers in social agencies, but also with the whole wide labor movement. It may thus open avenues for the effectual application of concerted conviction upon matters about which all professional workers are not now and may never be united. It offers, therefore, to groups of professional workers an instrument for effective use on matters beyond the area of association function and association agreement.

Here again there is a true functional limitation. The union in social work, like any other labor union, is united around common economic interests. It is an appropriate and effective instrument for protection or realization of those interests. It is certainly not the most appropriate agency for the determination or formulation of professional standards, nor for the articulation of programs involving the application of professional standards. That is a professional responsibility for which professional workers are accountable to their peers, and which they cannot share with nonprofessional colleagues. As the professional association more and more consistently and courageously represents truly professional interests in social action; as it recognizes the value, even to itself, of freeing groups of its members to unite with other workers in promoting causes, upon which the whole profession is not and probably cannot be united—it is to be hoped that the union need no longer seem to be an intruding competitor in professional circles, but an additional instrument through which individual professional workers may promote some of their legitimate professional interests, in social action.

Upon the same basis rests the validity of individual and group action of professional workers in the political arena, where many social issues come inevitably to final settlement. It is perfectly obvious that a social agency, dedicated to a specific service, about which, alone, its sponsors and its supporters are united, cannot ethically or practically expend its energies or resources to ends not directly related to that service. Its social action must be, confined to the interpretation of its own experience, in terms of chosen objectives, accepted principles and incontestable facts, commended on their merits, as factors in the determination of community policy affecting its service. It cannot take responsibility for measuring the relative importance of this aspect of public policy, as compared with others, as decisive factors in a political contest. It would be wholly inappropriate for an agency, therefore, to espouse a particular party cause or candidate.

The professional association is in a somewhat similar position. It is united upon objectives and principles, on the basis of professional standards. In all but the rarest instances, it cannot command the judgment of its members, or bring them to agreement, as to the relative weight to be assigned to these agreed concepts, as compared with other issues involved in a political campaign, nor as to the relative capacity and determination of opposing candidates to carry these concepts to realization in public policy. It would be utterly inappropriate, it seems to me, for the association, as such, to throw its influence in behalf of one or another party or candidate in a political contest in which other than strictly social issues were at stake.

Does the same set of limitations bind the individual professional worker? To answer that question in the affirmative seems to me to threaten the integrity both of the individual and of the profession as a whole. The individual not only can but must exercise his judgment as to the relative weight of issues at stake; he must make a final choice, as a citizen. If, in his honest and considered judgment, social issues are paramount, and if his choice is made between parties or candidates on the basis of their position on these problems and of their relative capacity and determination to solve those problems by measures that conform with professional principles, must he stifle those convictions, remain silent, and refuse to make his judgment as a social worker available to anybody else? And because the professional group as a whole is prevented by its collective responsibility and function from direct participation on the political level, must social work have no voice at all in the moment of decision? The individual must, if he is true to his own professional responsibility, remain free to act as an individual beyond the level of agreement of all his colleagues. It is that freedom, that personal obligation of the individual to be an independent creative unit, which is the essence of professionalism. It is likewise the source of the progress and achievement of the profession as a collective whole.

It is of special consequence to the profession of social work that this freedom should be conserved and protected. It is of the nature of professional social work practice that the individual practitioner shall not be completely free in the performance of a specific service. He is, and must be, the representative of a social agency, bound to operate within its policies, which cannot always express his own highest ideals of service since they must incorporate, also, the differing viewpoints of nonprofessional sponsors and supporters. He is protected against the loss of professional integrity, in this complete identification with agency, by his active and responsible participation in the development of agency policy, on the one hand, and by his membership in the professional association, where standards are sustained, on the other. If, however, his identification either with agency or with association limits or nullifies his independence as a professional person in the realm of social action in pursuit of professional objectives, then he has no further means of protecting his professional integrity—the fulfillment of his own sense of professional responsibility. His independence even as a citizen is qualified and limited.

There is risk in this individual freedom which we affirm—risk to the individual, to the agency, and to the profession. But that risk is as nothing compared to the danger of placing social workers and their profession under the suspicion that any considerations other than honest conviction and the analyzed outcomes of their study and experience can determine the part they shall play in decisive struggles for the realization of social ideals. The perfect pattern of political action affecting social work would be achieved, I firmly believe, only when every administrator, every board member, every practitioner of every rank, in every social agency, would regard it not only as a privilege, but an obligation, frankly and openly to relate the knowledge and judgment derived from his own social work experience to contested public issues, and thus to make his special sincere contribution to the formulation of enlightened public judgment and decision. I would have no fear of divided counsels in the field. I would welcome them in the open forum, where differences could be defined and tested, and where, in the end, social work would surely find a voice worthy of its own potential role in human affairs.

Reprinted from Kenneth L. M. Pray, Social work and social action, *National Conference on Social Welfare Proceedings* (1945).

Commentary
Carol W. Spigner

Born in the 1880s in Wisconsin, Kenneth L. M. Pray had a career that spanned a formative era for the social work profession. Employed as a political editor for the *Philadelphia Recorder*, Pray was engaged in a number of civic activities related to the charity movement and the social work profession. He served on the boards of the Pennsylvania Prison Society, the State Industrial School, and the Industrial School for Women. He also worked as the executive secretary for the Public Charities Association and served as chief of staff of the Goodrich Commission, which developed Pennsylvania's state plan for public welfare. Described as an "American philosopher of the social service," he became director of the Pennsylvania School of Social Work in 1922 and spearheaded the School's initial affiliation with the University of Pennsylvania and its transition to a full-fledged graduate school of the University in 1945. During this period, he was a frequent speaker at social work meetings and was vice president of the American Association of Social Workers.

His work is characterized by a commitment to professionalizing social work through education, fostering professional identity, and examining the critical philosophical and practice questions related to the function, boundaries, and quality of social work.

In 1945, when the address "Social Work and Social Action" was given to the National Conference on Social Welfare, the United States had recently experienced the Great Depression and World War II. It was a period of transition for the society and the profession. The Depression resulted in the economic dislocation of many Americans and led to the inundation of private charity; and the expansion of federal responsibility for the needy. The development of the national social welfare and social insurance programs provided new public organizations that employed professional social workers and gave legitimacy to their roles. The postwar era would be one of economic growth that would provide increased resources to meet human need.

Prior to the Depression and the war, social work had two very clear streams: casework, the direct service of individuals and families, and social action, directed toward changing social conditions and improving the well-being of vulnerable citizens. The casework tradition emerged in the late nineteenth century and involved helping individuals and families to confront their social problems. Casework focused on helping individuals make the adjustments necessary to manage the issues of poverty, dependency, abandoned and delinquent children, and mental health. The predominant frame work was a psychodynamic approach that placed the source of problems in one's personal history and the responsibility for change on the individual. The social action tradition was anchored in the settlement movement and the advocacy of individuals like Dorothea Dix and Jane Addams, and was directed toward changes in the social policies and practices of the states and the federal government. The focus was on changing the social environment by increasing the role of government in helping to protect and support the development of its citizens. This work resulted in the development of kindergartens, the establishment of women's suffrage and juvenile court, the outlawing of child labor, and the regulation of working conditions. After World War II, the profession was challenged to merge these two traditions, casework and social action, in the context of the emergence of complex public programs that required skilled planning and administration. The integration of these practice traditions needed to be linked to the values of the profession and the emerging knowledge base.

Kenneth Pray engaged these issues. He wrote:

it is essential that we shall honestly seek agreement, shall search for sound professional principles by which to measure the discharge of professional responsibility and to guide all of us in coming to terms with the practical problems of our day-to-day relationship with forces of social change and social planning.

His thinking was anchored in a conceptual framework that included the mission and values of the profession, the importance of human diversity to society, the function of the agency, and the individual's capacity for change and influence. To this was added the importance of social policy as a tool for changing the social environment and integrating social relationships.

Pray understood planning and administration and presented a nuanced discussion of the relationship of social action to direct work. The central premise of this work is that there is a professional obligation to ensure that social work practice meets professional standards consistent with the values of the profession. The discussion underscores the importance of professional standards for practice, and the obligation of every social worker to advance social and organizational conditions that would allow us to meet these standards. The professional obligation is to seek social change and social justice in those circumstances in which conditions impede the ability of individuals and groups to pursue their goals and/or block the profession from effective, ethical helping processes.

Described as an idealist and a pragmatist, Pray directed us to examine multiple opportunities for change and the constraints of each opportunity. Recognizing that direct work must be centered on the client and his or her needs, Pray identified the opportunities for and constraints against social action in the relationships with clients, our employing agencies, the professional organization, and unions. The opportunities and limitations that were identified are as real today as they were in the 1940s.

I first read "Social Work and Social Action" in the 1970s, nearly thirty years after it was penned. It was a clarifying article that made the linkages among the different approaches to social work clear and provided a new social worker with an integrated framework for change at the individual, family, organizational, and societal levels. When I think about the work I do today, which is focused on the education of students and the reform of public child welfare agencies, I recognize that the "Pray principles" were and are core to my approach to linking direct practice to social policy. All of my policy students are exposed to a framework that integrates: social issues, policy and program with direct service, advocacy, planning, administration and evaluation. Consistent with Pray's approach, the work I do in public agencies is guided by the desire for better results for children and their families, and uses many levels of intervention to achieve change.

What is most striking to me is the challenge of holding on to the values of the profession in a time when public agencies are large, complex, and compliance driven, and leadership may come from a variety of disciplines. This challenge is further complicated by a social context in which limited value is placed on the social services; the vulnerable are devalued; and where policy requirements have shaped practice in unanticipated ways.

Pray's perspective is as critical today as it was in 1945. It should be essential reading for every student, as a compliment to the NASW Code of Ethics. Pray's view of the philosophy of the profession is summed up in a presentation made shortly before his death:

The philosophy of social work shines forth in these objectives. It rests in a profound faith in human beings, their inherent and inviolable right to choose and to achieve their own destiny, through social arrangement of their own making, within the essential framework of a progressive society. It rests on a deep appreciation of the validity and value to the society as a whole of these individual differences in human beings . . . and conceives of social unity and progress as the out come of integration not suppression and conquest. Accordingly it tests all social arrangements and institutions by the impact on individual lives, by their capacity to utilize for the common good the unique aspects of individual human beings through relationships that enlist their active and productive participation. It is in short a genuinely and consistently democratic philosophy. (Pray 1948)

Kenneth L. M. Pray will continue to be noted for his unique contribution, which has helped to clarify the nature and boundaries of social work and strengthen the philosophical base of the profession, and his commitment to social work standards and professional education. As professionals we need to hold on to this framework at a time when political and social institutions often challenge the values on which it is based.

References

Pray, K. L. M. (1948). When is community organization social work practice? *Proceedings of the National Conference on Social Work: Selected Papers, Seventy-Fourth Annual Meeting* (New York: Columbia University Press).

——— (1945). Social work and social action. *National Conference of Social Welfare Proceedings.*

——— (1925). Some reasons for the development of the professional school. *Annals of the American Academy of Political and Social Science* 121: 169–71.

Alvarez, A. R. (2003). Articulating the essence: Kenneth L. M. Pray on social work and community organization. *Journal of Community Practice* 11 (3): 87–89.

Part III
Writings on the Influence of the
Functional Approach

Chapter 14
Functional Theory: Its History and Influence on Contemporary Social Work Practice

Martha M. Dore

Introduction

Social work practice, particularly direct practice with individuals, families, and groups, is frequently taught as though it exists in a vacuum, with little or no reference to the threads of the past represented in the fabric of current practice theory. The historical underpinnings of contemporary practice are dismissed as antiquated relics of another era with little relevance for today's social work practitioner. One school of thought seldom referenced in current practice pedagogy is the functional school. Along with the diagnostic school, the functional school is one of the two most dynamic and influential theoretical orientations in the historical development of professional social work.

Despite this current lack of recognition of its influence, an exploration of functional literature, developed primarily in the 1930s when educators in Functional Theory were struggling to define a unique practice theory that the rapidly developing social work profession could call its own, reveals a number of seminal ideas still reflected in the core of social work practice today: "starting where the client is," the client's "right to self-determination," and the concept of assessment as an ongoing process in treatment are but few of the elements of contemporary functional thought.

This article traces the development of functional theory at the Pennsylvania School of Social Work in the 1920s and 1930s against a contextual backdrop of social work's struggle to carve out a professional identity. The evolution of this theory will be discussed, including a look at the sometimes bitter functional-diagnostic debates of the 1930s and 1940s, Finally, the lasting influence of functional theory on current practice theories, including those underlying ecosystems and problem solving approaches, the life model, and the psychosocial model of practice, will be addressed.

The Early Years

Early social work education consisted of training in the model of helping developed in the Charity Organization Society (COS) movement.[1] This model was presented first by Mary Richmond in her book *The Good Neighbor* and later developed more fully in her classic text *Social Diagnosis*.[2] The focus of practice in this model was the family in need; the goal of an intervention was to determine the parameters of this need and obtain the resources with which to fulfill it. While there was much in the COS model that would be considered judgmental by today's standards, it was also consistent with contemporary practice in that it observed the family functioning in its environment.

By the time Richmond's *Social Diagnosis* was published, however, professional training had already begun to move away from the person-family-environment configuration to a psychodynamic practice model influenced by the medical profession's conceptual framework of disease diagnosis-cure and its focus on the individual organism.[3] In its earliest years social work was under great pressure to prove itself as a true profession.[4] Adopting a scientific approach to its work by emulating the medical model was one way in which social work could gain the recognition it sought.

As others have pointed out, the post-World War I era was also a period in which society moved away from emphasis on social reform to a renewed focus on individual achievement and responsibility for self.[5] The Progressive Era's emphasis on communal responsibility gave way to a new social value that frowned on things "socialistic" and praised the rights of the individual as dominant.

Reflecting this social context, social work training increasingly incorporated psychodynamic theory as its foundation theory of human behavior. In 1919, at the National Conference of Social Work in Atlantic City, Jessie Taft, later to be a major figure in the development of functional theory, and Mary Jarrett, director of the newly founded Smith College School for Social Work, create a now-legendary stir among their colleagues by Identifying the psychiatric base for all social work practice an calling for incorporation of material on mental hygiene In a training programs.[6]

For schools of social work like the Pennsylvania School, founded 1908 as a "Course of Training in Child Helping," this meant adding a specialization in psychiatric social work, which appeared in its course catalogue for the first time in 1919.[7] That same catalogue boasted of a program advisory committee of 29 eminent psychiatrists and analysts, including such luminaries as A. A. Brill, William Healy, E. E. Southard, and William A. White.[8]

Field training, too, embraced the new mental hygiene focus. During the 1920s the Commonwealth Fund, in cooperation with the National Committee for Mental Hygiene, established seven demonstration child guidance clinics across the country.[9] The Institute for Child Guidance in New York City and the Philadelphia Child Guidance Clinic both served as training sites for students in schools of social work.[10] The work of these clinics reflected a growing interest in the mental hygiene of the child and recognition of the influence of parent-child relationships on psychological growth and development.

By the end of the 1920s, as Virginia Robinson noted in her 1930 study of the development of social work practice over its first quarter century, Freudian thought permeated casework teaching in most professional schools.[11] In 1929, Porter R. Lee, director of the New York School of Social Work, and his colleague, Dr. Marion E. Kenworthy, published the first social work practice text based on Freudian principles, *Mental*

Hygiene and Social Work, firmly establishing the New York school, along with the Smith College program, as a center for psychoanalytically informed practice.[12]

The Pennsylvania School

At the same time that Freudian thought was taking hold elsewhere, events were occurring at the Pennsylvania School of Social Work that were to have a profound influence on the future direction of practice theory. Early in the 1920s, Taft, then director of the Department of Child Study at the Seybert Institution in Philadelphia, chanced to hear a presentation by Otto Rank at an international conference on psychoanalysis in Atlantic City.[13] She was thoroughly captivated by his ideas and, through her relationship with the Pennsylvania School of Social Work, where she was an adjunct lecturer, arranged for him to give the school's commencement address in June 1924.[14]

This was the beginning of an ongoing series of lectures and courses at the Pennsylvania School by Rank.[15] So convinced was Taft of power of Rank's ideas that she entered analysis with him in New York City in 1926, traveling by train twice a week from her home in Philadelphia.[16] Her colleague, Virginia Robinson, the assistant dean of Pennsylvania School, completed her analysis with Rank a year later.[17]

Another event that strongly influenced the future direction of the Pennsylvania School and hence the direction of its practice theory development was the appointment of Kenneth L. M. Pray as its director in 1922.[18] Pray, who served as director and later dean until his death in 1946, had received his academic training in political science. He worked as a journalist and a community organizer before joining the Pennsylvania School's faculty in 1916 and was deeply committed to social interpretations of individual difficulties.[19]

The year Pray became director, the course in mental hygiene disappeared from the Pennsylvania School of Social Work curriculum.[20] A specialization in psychiatric social work was no longer listed in its 1922 catalogue. In its place was a new philosophy emphasizing the role of environment in problem formation and as a focus for change: "Training and practice in specialized fields, such as family case work, group work, health work, research, or community organization in the narrower sense, must be founded upon, not substituted for, an understanding of the underlying community problems out of which arise the special conditions that confront social and health workers in their daily tasks."[21] Thus, while other social work training programs changed their curricula during the 1920s to incorporate an emphasis on the individual as the locus for change, the Pennsylvania School renewed its earlier emphasis on a sociological approach to human behavior, an emphasis on the individual as influenced by participation in a variety of social groups.[22] In 1926 this philosophy of social work practice was reaffirmed in the school catalogue: "The fundamental point of view [is] of the individual as conditioned by his social environment . . . to be treated through his social relations."[23]

It was against this backdrop of a social interaction perspective on human functioning and a concept of social work practice that encompassed the individual in the social environment that functional theory was developed at the Pennsylvania School of Social Work in the 1930s.

The Development of Functional Theory

The functional model of social work practice was based on the personality theory of Rank, a member of Freud's inner circle in Vienna who began to break away from his mentor in the early, 1920s.[24] *Trauma of Birth* his first published work to depart from traditional psychoanalytic theory, appeared in 1924. In it, Rank rejected the deterministic Freudian concept of the personality as essentially established by events in early childhood.[25] He saw instead that the basic human struggle, and the source of most individual problems, was the ongoing tension between a desire to realize one's separate and distinct individuality—to move toward growth and change—and the competing wish to remain psychologically connected and dependent on others—to retreat from growth and change.[26] This struggle was symbolized by the separation of the infant from its mother at birth. It was, however, a process that continued throughout the life cycle. Rank also differed from Freud in his recognition of individual difference in the developmental process. His academic background in the arts and humanities, as opposed to the medical training of Freud and his other followers, led him to incorporate a broader, more culturally focused perspective on personality development into his theoretical framework.[27]

In Rank's view, the force for change had to come from within the individual, from an active, self-assertive Will.[28] The Will, a central concept in Rank's theoretical formulation, refers to the organized, integrated personality engaged in positive, creative action.[29] The therapeutic task was to strengthen and mobilize the Will. The medium through which this task was accomplished was the helping relationship.

According to Rank, relationship was central to the helping process.[30] Therapist understanding of the patient grew out of "experiencing" the other as he or she presented him- or herself in the treatment relationship, as opposed to "knowing" the patient through a cognitive or intellectual process.[31] Consequently, the emphasis in helping was on the here and now, on what was transpiring between patient and therapist, rather than on events and feelings from the past.[32]

Following from his emphasis on process in the treatment relationship, Rank identified time as an important therapeutic tool and established time limits as crucial components of the therapeutic process.[33] Placing time limits on the helping relationship had the effect of forcing worker and client to focus on separation and termination as an integral component of the treatment process. According to Rank, it was through planned separation, the letting go of the known to venture into the unknown, that true growth and change took place.[34]

As a result of their experiences in analysis with Rank and their growing engagement with the intellectual content of his ideas, Taft and Robinson began seeking ways to incorporate his ideas into a model of social work practice. Taft studied with a group of Rankian analysts in New York and eventually became the English translator of his most important works in German.[35] In 1929, when Rank formally broke with Freud and was subsequently abandoned by most of the American Psychoanalytic community, Taft was one of his few remaining American adherents.[36]

Taking Rank's basic principles of individual psychology and human growth and change, Taft and Robinson applied them in a new theoretical model of social work practice, This new practice theory unfolded slowly during the early 1930s, culminating in Taft's seminal statement of functional practice, which appeared as the lead article in the first issue of the *Journal of Social Work Process*, published by the Pennsylvania School in 1934.[37]

The Contrast Between Diagnostic and Functional Practice

During the period in which functional theory was gradually evolving at the Pennsylvania School, educators and practitioners in other parts of the country, especially along the East Coast, were incorporating Freudian principles into social work practice in a variety of settings with a range of client populations. Widely read journals like *The Family* and *Mental Hygiene* were replete with articles such as "Some Contributions of Therapy to Generalized Case Work Practice," by Florence Hollis, and "Basic Concepts in Social Case Work," by her colleague at the New York School of Social Work, Gordon Hamilton.[38] Articles such as these formed the foundation of the diagnostic approach, a complete explication of which first appeared in Hamilton's *Theory and Practice of Social Case Work*, published in 1940.[39]

The diagnostic approach was named for its emphasis on accurate understanding of problem etiology and client need as the critical element in the treatment process. As in the medical model on which it was based, diagnosis played a central role in the development of an appropriate treatment plan. "The meaning which the practitioner derives from incidents, history and behavior, as these are presented, is called 'diagnostic thinking' or 'impression' and, in its formal recorded version, 'diagnostic summary' or 'diagnostic statement.'"[40] Like the physician treating illness, the social worker diagnosed the problem's causes from the data presented, then designed a course of treatment leading to problem resolution.[41]

Focus on Client Participation

In the diagnostic model, the practitioner carried primary responsibility for the outcome of the intervention; correct interpretation of case material resulted in selection of the right intervention and led to a positive outcome.[42] In contrast, one of the major themes in the social work practice model that evolved at the Pennsylvania School was an emphasis on the central role of the client in her or his own change process. In an *early* explication of the theory she was helping to develop, Taft described the client's active participation in treatment as "an opportunity to experience more completely than is ordinarily possible the direction, depth and ambivalence of the impulses which relate the self to the other, to outer reality, and to discover first hand the possibility of their organization into an autonomous, creative will."[43] Later she wrote of the meaning of the client's participation: "Even the client himself can only discover what his need *really* is *by* finding out what he does in the helping situation."[44]

In functional theory, the client, not the social worker, chose the problem to be addressed.[45] It was through the inherent struggle involved in admitting to a problem and working toward its resolution that client growth and change were thought to occur.[46] "Starting where the client is," was an early functional principle that has been thoroughly subsumed in the rubric of professional social work practice. The phrase referred to the importance of accepting the client's interpretation of the problem and using that interpretation to organize the focus of the interaction.[47] There was no assumption that the presenting problem masked the client's real concerns or covered his or her real need as was a premise of the diagnostically trained worker who emphasized the preconscious or unconscious basis for a client's presenting difficulties.[48] In the diagnostic approach, the task was to explore the symbolic meaning of the underlying, unspoken problem in the client's situation.[49] For the functionally trained worker, the presenting problem was a literal representation of the client's most pressing need. The assumption was that the client, not the worker, knew his or her experience best, and it was his or her desire and motivation that had to be tapped to stimulate change.[50] Similarly, the outcome of treatment was controlled by the client, not the worker. It was the client who made the ultimate choice between growth and change, or stability and, possibly, stagnation.[51]

The Helping Relationship

A second major theme of functional theory was its focus on the interaction between client and worker out of which the movement toward change emerged. The sum of this interaction was designated the "helping process," and it was within and through this process that the client would reveal him- or herself to the worker and change would occur.[52] The functional concept that the practitioner's understanding of a client grew solely out of the events of their relationship, and that worker's knowledge of the client was limited to the self presented in their transactions, placed it squarely in opposition to the diagnostic approach. The latter emphasized the importance of a cognitive understanding of the client and his or her capacities as the basis for engaging in the treatment relationship.[53] While this understanding could be modified as treatment progressed, the treatment itself was designed based on diagnosis established prior to embarking on that treatment.

Pray underscored the differences in the functional concept of process in the helping relationship in his 1947 presidential address to the National Conference of Social Work: "For relationship is itself always a process—a dynamic, fluid, developing process, never static, never finished, always chiefly significant for its inner quality and movement, for its meaning to those it engages, rather than for its form or status or outcome at any instant in time."[54]

Building on Rank's identification of time as a critical variable in the change process, the functional model identified three specific time phases in the development of the helping relationship.[55] Each phase – beginning, middle, and end—contributed its specific characteristics to the totality of the change process.[56]

Use of Agency Function

A third major differentiating theme in the functional model was the use of agency function as an organizing concept. Early in their efforts to incorporate Rank's ideas into a model for social work practice, Taft and Robinson struggled to define the difference between social work and psychoanalysis.[57] The difference as they saw it was in the function of the social agency.[58] "In social work, the limitation with which we operate is necessarily the function . . . it is the known factor, the comparatively stable, fixed point about which client and worker may move without becoming lost in the movement."[59]

Unlike psychoanalysis, in which the analyst alone carries responsibility for the structure and direction of treatment, the function of the social agency is to establish a dynamic within which the helping process evolves.[60] According to Taft, "The worker sets up the conditions as found in his agency function and procedure; the client representing the unknown natural forces, reacts to the limitation as well as to the possible fulfillment inherent in the function, over a period of testing it out. He tries to accept, to reject, to attempt to control, or to modify that function until he finally comes to terms with it enough to define or discover what he wants, if anything, from the situation.[61]

Interaction between social worker and client was thus limited and defined from the beginning by agency purpose and its resulting function. It established the kind of help that could be offered, the terms on which help was given, and what was required of the client in return for taking help.[62] In the functional model, the agency, through social agreement as to its purpose and function, became a symbolic representation of external reality, the reality of life against which the client struggled in the reach toward growth and change.[63] It was believed that, as clients grappled emotionally and psychologically with these externally imposed boundaries on meeting immediate needs, they began to understand and acknowledge their own participation in their current distress and thereby became actively engaged in problem resolution.[64]

The 1940s and Beyond: The Diagnostic Versus Functional Debates

In December 1938 the Pennsylvania School of Social Work published a second volume of the *Journal of Social Work Process*, entitled "Method and Skill in Public Assistance." The seven papers collected in this volume represented the application of functional principles to administration and direct practice in public agencies. Rosa Wessel, editor and assistant professor at the Pennsylvania School, summed up the functional approach to public assistance thus: "The professional public relief worker has found in the necessary administrative and legislative restrictions of the public job, a structure for the process of giving within which it is possible for the client to find again and again, renewed opportunity to exercise decision and control, to organize his own wavering courage, to take hold and use to his best advantage if he will, the resources, meagre as they may be, which society has made available to him on its own often relentless terms."[65]

Unlike the diagnostic approach, which focused on intrapsychic causes of client problems, and whose theory of intervention rested on the medical notion of cure, the functional model was readily adaptable to public agency clientele. Its emphasis on the importance of the relationship between worker and client as the medium through which growth was generated was as applicable to establishing eligibility in public relief as in giving service in a counseling agency. In a paper entitled "Education for Public Social Work," Pray wrote, "It is clear that into the most limited of relationships, once defined and so accepted on both sides, can go as much of understanding and sensitivity to feeling and to the meaning of behavior, as in any other. The helping process is ultimately validated by what happens to the individual persons involved through the means employed and the relationships set up in that process."[66]

In addition to expanding its purview into public social services, adherents of the functional model actively sought to apply its principles to other forms of social work practice. Through journal articles such as Taft's "Function as the Basis for Development in Social Work Processes," which appeared in the *Newsletter of the American Association of Psychiatric Social Workers*, and books such as Robinson's *Training for Skill in Social Case Work*, the functional approach was presented to a wide audience of social work educators and practitioners.[67]

From the beginning, functional theory was controversial. Some of its controversy stemmed from its basis in the personality theory of Rank. He had questioned Freudian theory at a time when doing so was regarded as heresy and was denigrated and ostracized for his efforts. An approach to social work practice based on his ideas would inevitably come under immediate suspicion, if not outright rejection, from those influenced by Freudian thought.[68]

There were also questions raised regarding the scientific validity of the functional approach. In an era when professional social work was struggling to prove its scientific legitimacy, the functional approach, with its lack of reliance on data collection and hypothesis testing and its outright rejection of pre-established outcome goals, appeared thoroughly unscientific to its many critics.[69]

A third aspect of functional theory and its practice approach that caused controversy was its emphasis on agency function rather than client need as central to the helping process. The functional conceptualization of agency function as an immutable given, which clearly defined the role and activities of the worker and sharply limited the range of client needs to which the worker could respond, was anathema to diagnostically trained practitioners. As Hamilton observed, "agency policy and procedures should subserve rather than become the center of the treatment process."[70]

Differences between functional and diagnostic theorists became heated during the 1940s, when a barrage of articles criticizing first one side and then the other appeared almost monthly in professional journals.[71] So acrimonious was the debate that the Family Service Association of America decided in 1947 to appoint a committee to study the two schools of thought in an attempt to find common ground between them.

That committee, whose final report was published as *A Comparison of Diagnostic and Functional Casework Concepts*, could find no real commonalities, only difference.[72] It also found "wide gaps in mutual understanding which interfered with our attempts to arrive at comparisons."[73]

It was not until the 1957 publication of *Social Casework: A Problem Solving Process* by Helen Harris Perlman that synthesis of functional and diagnostic theory began to emerge.[74] Based on new developments in ego psychology as well as learning theory, Perlman's book presented a model for social work practice that incorporated functional as well as diagnostic concepts. Changes in the original Freudian concept of the role and function of the ego in human behavior had brought the concept must closer to that of Rank's Will. Ego psychology's greater recognition of the importance of the cognitive processes in human adaptation suggested to Perlman theoretical support for a more active role for the client in the treatment process, one that recognized and built on client strengths rather than focusing on correcting weakness.[75]

Echoing functional thinking, Perlman saw the client-worker relationship as the medium through which growth and change might occur.[76] She also drew on the functional theorists' notions of time in describing the beginning, middle, and end phases of treatment.[77] However, as in the diagnostic model, Perlman's social worker still carried primary responsibility for structuring the intervention based on her informed assessment of the client's problem-solving capacities and the external resources that could be employed in bringing about change.[78] Thus, using concepts from both diagnostic and functional theory and drawing on new theories of human development to bridge them, Perlman presented a unified model of social work practice in her problem-solving approach.

Functional Theory in Contemporary Social Work Practice

In her article, "Direct Practice in Social Work: An Overview," written for the 1987 edition of the *Encyclopedia of Social Work*, Carol Meyer identified a turning point in the 1960s and 1970s in the development of social work theory and models for practice.[79] Because of challenges to the utility of traditional practice models by nontraditional client groups seeking a role in human services, professional social work was forced to explore new ways of responding to the needs of this previously unserved clientele. New practice models were developed, based not on a specific modality as in the past when interventions with individuals were the preferred form of treatment, but on professional values, sanction, purpose, knowledge, and skills. According to Meyer, this movement away from modality as the defining variable in model development allowed theorists an opportunity to identify generic themes across modalities and models of practice, themes that reflected the mission and purpose of the profession as a whole.

Among these themes are many originally articulated by functional theorists, evidence of the functional model's continued influence on contemporary practice. For example, the client's right to self-determination is a functional principle that has become so ingrained in the fabric of the profession that it is now an article in the National Association of Social Workers' *Code of Ethics*.[80] It is a professional value recognized and embraced by a range of practice models from the psychosocial therapy of Hollis to William Reid and Laura Epstein's task-centered approach.[81]

Crisis intervention theory and research has reaffirmed the functional emphasis on time as a structuring variable in the treatment process.[82] Like functional practice, the crisis intervention model incorporates a notion of growth and change through intrapsychic struggle.[83] It, too, is a practice theory that engages the client as an active partner in the change process, a process that is time limited and structured by the purpose of the intervention.[84]

The functional concept of the use of time as a structuring variable has also gained support through practice research. In 1969, Reid and Ann Shyne published findings from a study carried out at the Community Service Society in New York City.[85] They discovered that most agency clients received the help they sought within the first eight sessions, suggesting a time structure inherent in the helping process as theorized many years earlier by Taft in her paper, "Time as the Medium of the Helping Process."[86]

The functional concept of the importance of time was further recognized in the ecological perspective developed by Carel Germain and others.[87] According to Germain, time is "concerned with cycles and the spiraling accumulations of patterns and processes. It focuses on the manifest and a latent function of what is going on, rather than on the division into effects neatly preceded by causes."[88] In the ecological perspective as in the functional model, efforts to understand the client in his or her problem situation are focused on the here and now, on events in the present.[89] There is also recognition that the process unfolding between client and worker contributes as much to an understanding of client capacity for change as the content of the presenting situation.[90]

The ecological perspective, in turn, provides a theoretical foundation for the life model approach to social work practice developed by Germain and Alex Gitterman.[91] This practice model, like its functional predecessor, sees the human personality as engaged in a continuous process of growth and change.[92] A variety of obstacles may impede this ongoing life process, and it is the role of the social worker to engage with the client in a mutual effort to remove these obstacles and restore the growth process.[93] It is an interactional practice perspective that builds on functional principles with later concepts from systems theory.

Conclusion

In the years since the functional model was developed at the Pennsylvania School of Social Work, its basic concepts have become an integral part of professional social work practice, often without real awareness of their origins. In almost every contemporary social work practice text, a practice approach is described that includes functional principles such as the client's right to self-determination, the understanding of individual difference, starting where the client is, the evolving nature of client assessment, the important role of relationship in the helping process, and a recognition of time as the organizing component of the intervention process. An appreciation for the origins of these aspects of contemporary practice can reinforce a sense of history in developing a professional identity.

Reprinted from Martha M. Dore, Functional theory: Its history and influence on contemporary social work practice, *Social Service Review* 64 (1990): 358–74. Reprinted by permission.

Notes

I wish to express my sincere appreciation to Dean Michael J. Austin of the University of Pennsylvania School of Social Work for his generous support of this work as well as to faculty and alumni of that school for their many helpful suggestions and comments. In addition, particular gratitude is expressed to Harold Lewis, Max Siporin, and Bernece Simon for sharing their wisdom, experiences, and insights in response to earlier drafts of this article.

1. See, e.g., Porter R. Lee, *Social Work with Families and Individuals: A Brief Manual for Investigators* (New York: New York School of Philanthropy, 1915).

2. Mary E. Richmond, *The Good Neighbor in the Modern City* (Philadelphia: Lippincott, 1907), and *Social Diagnosis* (New York: Russell Sage, 1917).

3. Charlotte Towle, "The Individual in Relation to Social Change," in Helen Harris Perlman, ed., *Helping: Charlotte Towle on Social Work and Social Casework* (Chicago: University of Chicago Press, 1969), 209–34.

4. Abraham Flexner, "Is Social Work a Profession?" (576–90), and Felix Frankfurter, "Social Work and Professional Training" (591–96), both in *Proceedings of the National Conference of Charities and Corrections* (Baltimore: Hildemann, 1915).

5. Frank J. Bruno, *Trends in Social Work, 1874–1956* (New York: Columbia University Press, 1957); Shirley Hellenbrand, "Main Currents in Social Casework, 1918–1936" (D.S.W. dissertation, Columbia University, 1965).

6. Jessie Taft, "Qualifications of the Psychiatric Social Worker" (593–99) and Mary C. Jarrett, "The Psychiatric Thread Running Through All Social Work" (587–93), both in *Proceedings of the National Conference of Social Work* (Chicago: Rogers & Hall, 1919) .

7. Letter from Porter R. Lee, general secretary of the Philadelphia Society for Organizing Charity and lecturer at the Philadelphia Training School for Social Work, to J. W. Magruder, general secretary, Federated Charities, Baltimore, Maryland, dated March 13, 1911, describing the founding of the Training School in 1908 as a series of lectures, sponsored by the Philadelphia Children's Bureau, a consortium of child-serving agencies (box 107, University of Pennsylvania Archives). Also, the *Thirty-Second Annual Report* of the Philadelphia Society for Organizing Charity for the year ending September 31, 1910, notes the expansion of the Children's Bureau lecture series into a "definitely organized school with curriculum providing both class work and field work and with definite tests and graduation" (box 107, University of Pennsylvania Archives). The Philadelphia Training School for Social Work held its first commencement on June 1, 1911; 54 graduates were listed in the program of the day's events, "The Class of 1911" (University of Pennsylvania Archives, mimeographed); "Six Month Courses in Social Psychiatry and Medical Social Service," *Bulletin of the Pennsylvania School for Social Service* (Philadelphia, February 1919).

8. Advisory Committee, *Bulletin*, 2.

9. David Levy, "The Beginning of the Child Guidance Clinic Movement," *American Journal of Orthopsychiatry* 38 (October 1968): 41–54.

10. Dorothy Hankins, "An Incomplete History of the Philadelphia Child Guidance Clinic" (Philadelphia Child Guidance Clinic, 1969, typescript).

11. Virginia P. Robinson, *A Changing Psychology in Social Case Work* (Chapel Hill: University of North Carolina Press, 1930), p. 85.

12. Porter R. Lee and Marion E. Kenworthy, *Mental Hygiene and Social Work* (New York: Commonwealth, 1929).

13. Jessie Taft, *Otto Rank* (New York: Julian, 1924), foreword.

14. "Biographical Notes," in a handbill announcing a series of six lectures by Otto Rank entitled "Practical Social Application of Psychoanalytic Viewpoints," Pennsylvania School of Social and Health Work, 1928 (box 107, University of Pennsylvania Archives).

15. Taft, *Otto Rank.*

16. Virginia P. Robinson, ed., *Jessie Taft: Therapist and Social Work Educator* (Philadelphia: University of Pennsylvania Press, 1962).

17. Virginia P. Robinson, "The University of Pennsylvania School of Social Work in Perspective: 1909–1959," *Journal of Social Work Process* 11 (1960): 15.

18. *The Pennsylvania School of Social and Health Work Catalogue, 1922–1923*, vol. 13, no. 1 (Philadelphia: Pennsylvania School of Social and Health Work, 1923), 3.

19. Robinson, "The University of Pennsylvania School of Social Work in Perspective"; Kenneth L. M. Pray, "New Emphases in Education for Public Social Work," in Rosa Wessel, ed., *Method and Skill in Public Assistance, Journal of Social Work Process* 2 (1) (December 1938): 88–100.

20. *Catalogue, 1922–1923.*

21. Ibid., 12.

22. The New York School of Social Work, e.g., introduced a single course in social psychiatry, taught by Dr. Bernard Glueck, in 1919. By 1925 the school's offerings had grown to eight courses in a separate department of mental hygiene, including "Clinical psychiatry," "Psychopathology," and a "Seminar in Psychiatric Social Work" (Catalogues of the New York School of Social Work, 1919–20 and 1925–26, Columbia University School of Social Work Archives).

23. *Pennsylvania School of Social and Health Work Catalogue, 1926–1927*, vol. 17, no. 1 (Philadelphia: Pennsylvania School of Social and Health Work, 1927), 20.

24. Taft, *Otto Rank*, 61–120; see also Esther Menaker, *Otto Rank: A Rediscovered Legacy* (New York: Columbia University Press, 1982); Fay B. Karpf, *The Psychology and Psychotherapy of Otto Rank* (New York: Philosophical Library, 1953); Ernest Jones, *The Life and Work of Sigmund Freud* (New York: Basic, 1955) for perspectives on the relationship between Rank and Freud.

25. Otto Rank, *The Trauma of Birth* (New York: Harper and Row, 1973).

26. Ibid.

27. Menaker, *Otto Rank.*

28. Rank introduced the concept of Will in the second volume of his three-volume work *Technik der Psychoanalyse* (Vienna: Deuticke, 1926). This volume along with the third in the series were combined in an English translation by Jessie Taft entitled *Will Therapy* and published in conjunction with her translation of another of Rank's works, *Truth and Reality* (New York: Knopf, 1936).

29. Otto Rank, *Will Therapy and Truth and Reality*, trans. Jessie Taft, chap. 4, "Past and Present" (New York: Knopf, 1945), 33–45.

30. Ibid., chap. 1, "The Therapeutic Experience," 1–6.

31. Ibid., preface to pt. 2, "The Therapist and the Neurotic as Complementary Types," 98–102.

32. Ibid., chap. 13, "The Role of the Therapist in the Therapeutic Situation," 167–83.

33. Ibid., chap. 14, "The End Phase and the Therapeutic Agent," 184–88.

34. Ibid.

35. Taft, *Otto Rank*, xii.

36. Ibid. In the foreword to her biography of Rank, Taft describes how, when Rank's introduction of the concept of Will in *Technik der Psychoanalyse* became widely known in the United

States, it proved almost impossible to find a psychiatrist to serve as discussant of a paper he was to present at the 1930 International Mental Hygiene Association meetings in Washington. Of the 15–20 Rank analysands, most of them psychiatrists, who met regularly in New York to discuss his analytic theories, only Taft continued to support him publicly after his final split with the Freudian group in 1929.

37. Jessie Taft, "The Relation of Function to Process in Social Case Work," *Journal of Social Work Process* 1 (November 1937): 1–18.

38. Florence Hollis, "Some Contributions of Therapy to Generalized Case Work Practice," *Family* 15 (February 1935): 328–34; Gordon Hamilton, "Basic Concepts in Social Case Work," *Family* 14 (July 1937): 147–56.

39. Gordon Hamilton, *Theory and Practice of Social Case Work* (New York: Columbia University Press, 1940).

40. Ibid., 213.

41. Hollis, "Some Contributions of Therapy."

42. Lucille Nickel Austin, "The Evolution of Our Case Work Concepts," *Family* 19 (April 1939): 48–49.

43. Jessie Taft, *The Dynamics of Therapy in a Controlled Relationship* (New York: Macmillan, 1933).

44. Taft, "Relation of Function to Process," 7.

45. Almena Dawley, "Diagnosis—The Dynamic of Effective Treatment," *Journal of Social Work Process* 1 (November 1937): 19–31. Dawley, who was head social worker at the Philadelphia Child Guidance Clinic for many years, clearly explicates a functional perspective on problem identification and client assessment in this article, despite its title.

46. Taft, "Relation of Function to Process," 7–8.

47. Else Jockel, "Movement Toward Treatment in the Application Interview in a Family Agency," *Journal of Social Work Process* 1 (November 1937): 32–40. In a clear explication of the difference between the functional and diagnostic approaches, Jockel states, "We have confused the problems we saw with those the client presented, and have made an effort to get him to become aware of the former, instead of offering him help with the ones of which he was already conscious" (37).

48. Fern Lowry, "The Client's Needs as the Basis for Differential Approach in Case Work Treatment," in *The Differential Approach in Case Work Treatment* (New York: Family Welfare Association of America, 1936).

49. Gordon Hamilton, "The Underlying Philosophy of Social Case Work, *Family* 22 (July 1941): 139–47.

50. Jessie Taft, "A Conception of the Growth Process Underlying Social Casework Practice," in *Social Work in the Current Scene: Selected Papers, 17th Annual Meeting, National Conference of Social Work* (New York: Columbia University, 1950), 294–306, also published in Virginia Robinson, ed., *Jessie Taft: A Professional Biography* (Philadelphia: University of Pennsylvania Press, 1962), 325–42.

51. Taft, "Relation of Function to Process"; see esp. "Conclusion" for a discussion of the nature of individual growth and change from a functional perspective.

52. Herbert Aptekar, "Meaning and Process in Social Case Work," *Family* 21 (October 1940): 194–201. See also Aptekar's functional practice text, *Basic Concepts in Social Case Work* (Chapel Hill: University of North Carolina Press, 1941), as well as Saul Hofstein's "The Nature of Process: Its Implications for Social Work," *Journal of Social Work Process* 14 (1964): 13–53.

53. Austin, "Evolution of Our Case Work Concepts."

54. Kenneth L. M. Pray, "A Restatement of the Generic Principles of Social Casework Practice," *Journal of Social Casework* 28 (October 1947): 283–90.

55. Jessie Taft, "Time as the Medium of the Helping Process," in Robinson, ed., *Jessie Taft: Therapist*, 305–24.

56. Ibid.

57. Anita Faatz, *The Nature of Choice in Casework Process* (Chapel Hill: University of North Carolina Press, 1953), esp. chap. 4, "The Discovery of Function," 34–43.

58. Ibid.

59. Taft, "Relation of Function to Process," 8.

60. Ibid.

61. Ibid.

62. Grace F. Marcus, "Family Casework in 1948," *Journal of Social Casework* 29 (July 1948): 261–79. Although trained in the diagnostic approach, Marcus came increasingly to integrate functional principles in her writings on social casework in the late 1930s and 1940s. For a fuller discussion of Marcus's role, as well as that of Bertha Reynolds in attempting to mediate the growing functional-diagnostic debates, see Lois Ann Hartman, "Casework in Crisis, 1932–1941" (D.S.W. dissertation, Columbia University, 1972).

63. Kenneth L. M. Pray, "The Agency's Role in Service," in Virginia P. Robinson, ed., *Training for Skill in Social Case Work* (Philadelphia: University of Pennsylvania Press, 1942).

64. Taft, "Relation of Function to Process."

65. Rosa Wessel, ed., "Special Issue: Method and Skill in Public Assistance," *Journal of Social Work Process* 2 (December 1938): 2.

66. Pray, "New Emphases," 98–99.

67. Jessie Taft, "Function as the Basis for Development in Social Work Processes," *Newsletter of the American Association of Psychiatric Social Workers* 9 (June 1939); Robinson, ed., *Training for Skill in Social Case Work.*

68. Austin, "Evolution of Our Case Work Concepts."

69. Helen Ross and Adelaide M. Johnson, "The Growing Science of Casework," *Journal of Social Casework* 27 (November 1946): 273–78.

70. Hamilton, *Theory and Practice,* 128; see also Crystal M. Potter and Lucille N. Austin, "The Use of the Authoritative Approach in Social Case Work," *Family* 19 (March 1938): 19–24.

71. Hartman, "Case Work in Crisis." According to Hartman's extensive analysis of social work literature published between 1932 and 1941, open expression of difference between diagnostic and functional adherents was still the exception in the late 1930s. Until the early 1940s, leading diagnostic theoreticians such as Gordon Hamilton sought areas of agreement between the two schools of thought. Although Lucille Austin had sharply called functional practice into question in the 1938 and 1939 articles in the *Family* references here, according to Hartman, it was not until Gordon Hamilton read a paper entitled "The Underlying Philosophy of Case Work Today" at the National Conference of Social Work in 1941 that irreconcilable differences between the two approaches were publicly recognized.

72. Cora Kasius, ed., *A Comparison of Diagnostic and Functional Casework Concepts* (New York: Family Service Association of America, 1950).

73. Ibid., 5.

74. Helen Harris Perlman, *Social Casework: A Problem-Solving Process* (Chicago: University of Chicago Press, 1957).

75. While Perlman drew from both functional and diagnostic sources in developing her treatment model, the theory of human growth and change undergirding her practice approach reflects post-World War II developments in ego psychology. These developments, first presented in the publications of Franz Alexander, Thomas French, Erik Erikson, and others, moved psychoanalytic theory away from the determinism of Freudian thought to a belief in the human capacity for lifetime growth and change. Like Jessie Taft, who had studied with Dewey at the University of Chicago, Perlman was strongly influenced by John Dewey's theories of learning. While the works of both Taft and Perlman reflect Dewey's emphasis on the experiential process in movement toward change, Perlman, unlike Taft, draws equally on Dewey's theories of the cognitive processes in problem solving, for which she finds support in the new ego psychology.

76. Perlman, *Social Casework,* 65.

77. Ibid.

78. Ibid.

79. Carol H. Meyer, "Direct Practice in Social Work: Overview," in *Encyclopedia of Social Work* (Washington, D.C.: National Association of Social Workers, 1987), 1: 409–22.

80. Code of Ethics of the National Association of Social Workers, adopted by 1979 NASW Delegate Assembly, effective July 1, 1980.

81. Florence Hollis and Mary E. Woods, *Casework: A Psychosocial Therapy*, 3rd ed. (New York: Random House, 1981); William J. Reid and Laura Epstein, *Task-Centered Casework* (New York: Columbia University Press, 1972).

82. In her book on crisis intervention, *Treatment in Crisis Situations* (New York: Free Press, 1978), Naomi Golan credits the functional school as the first "to emphasize the importance of time as a factor in the casework relationship" (43).

83. Ibid., 70; see also Lydia Rapoport, "Crisis Intervention as a Form of Brief Treatment," in Robert W. Roberts and Robert H. Nee, eds., *Theories of Social Casework* (Chicago: University of Chicago Press, 1970); Howard J. Parad, ed., *Crisis Intervention: Selected Readings* (New York: Family Service Association of America, 1965); Sandra Dixon and Roberta Sands, "Identity and the Experience of Crisis," *Social Casework* 64 (April 1983): 223–30.

84. Douglas A. Puryear, *Helping People in Crisis* (San Francisco: Jossey-Bass, 1979).

85. William J. Reid and Ann Shyne, *Brief and Extended Casework* (New York: Columbia University Press, 1969).

86. Taft. "Time as a medium."

87. Carel B. Germain, "Time, an Ecological Variable in Social Work Practice," *Social Casework* 57 (July 1976): 419–26.

88. Ibid., 420.

89. Carel B. Germain and Alex Gitterman, *The Life Model of Social Work Practice* (New York: Columbia University Press, 1980); Geoffrey L. Grief and Arthur A. Lynch, "The Eco-Systems Perspective," in Carol H. Meyer, ed., *Clinical Social Work in the Eco-Systems Perspective* (New York: Columbia University Press, 1983).

90. Germain and Gitterman, *Life Model*, 19

91. Ibid.

92. Ibid., 5.

93. Ibid., 20–21.

Commentary

Martha M. Dore

In 1986, nearing completion of my dissertation and graduation from the doctoral program at the University of Chicago School of Social Service Administration, I cast about for a position as assistant professor in a school of social work. I was then working as a full time lecturer at the Columbia University School of Social Work, teaching four practice courses a semester while finishing my dissertation. At CUSSW I quickly became aware of the passion with which faculty members held their various perspectives: the "diagnostic" faculty warred with the "life modelers," at other times it was the practice faculty against the community organizers, or the empiricists against the experientialists. The experience prepared me well for the journey that was to come.

In the spring of 1986 I accepted an offer to join the faculty at the University of

Pennsylvania School of Social Work as an assistant professor of practice. When I excit-
edly told Carol Meyer, doyenne of the CUSSW practice faculty and daughter of the
diagnostic tradition there, of my great good fortune in securing a terrific job at such
a fine institution as Penn, she looked pityingly at me and said, "Oh, I am so sorry." In
response to my startled look, Carol mumbled something about "those functionalists."
That was my first inkling that I was about to embark on a journey that would lead me
into the darker reaches of social work history, but would eventually broaden my thinking and enable me to integrate various threads of knowledge into a clearer understanding and greater appreciation of the early architects of social work practice.

It is important to this story to know that I was the first person hired to teach in the
practice sequence at Penn in many years, maybe ever, who had not graduated from
the social work program there. Even then, in the mid-1980s, when there were many
fewer doctoral programs in social work, most schools of social work, including my own
alma mater, SSA, would not hire their own graduates for fear of institutionalizing a
narrow perspective on social work practice. Not so with Penn SSW. Indeed, a singular
focus and understanding of practice was what was wanted and those who had a different orientation were quickly brought to heel. It was as though everyone there spoke a
language that was similar to but not quite the same as mine. Form, function, purpose,
process, structure . . . what were they talking about? I was clearly stamped with a large
D for diagnostic and made to understand that the failure to communicate belonged
only to me.

In frustration, I went whining to the Dean, Michael Austin, also an outsider, having
recently come from University of Washington in Seattle—but at least he didn't have
to teach practice! Being wise in the ways of deans and knowing of my earlier training
as a historian, Dr. Austin assigned me the task of writing a paper on the historical
development of functional social work at Penn. As I worked on this paper, reading
Jessie Taft's thoughtful writing as she worked to apply the concepts put forth by Otto
Rank to social work practice, Virginia Robinson's summary of the development of
social work practice that was her doctoral dissertation, and the subsequent writing of
so many of their colleagues and students who explored the application of functional
practice in a variety of venues, I fell in love. Not so much with the theory itself, though
I found myself agreeing more than disagreeing with its ideas and concepts, but with
the women, and a few men, who made it their struggle to bring form and function to
the developing profession of social work.

As an SSA doctoral student, my understanding of practice theory had been greatly
influenced by ego psychology through the teaching and scholarship of Bernece K.
Simon and Helen Harris Perlman, the latter of whom had studied at Columbia with
Gordon Hamilton and Florence Hollis, progenitors of diagnostic theory and its
application in social work practice. I was aware in some vague way of the functional-
diagnostic debates as well as efforts to reconcile the differences between these two
schools of thought. But it wasn't until I was wholly immersed in the scholarship of
functional and diagnostic theory that I came to understand and appreciate their real
differences with regard to social work practice as well as to appreciate the energy and
passion with which each was embraced by its adherents.

Jessie Taft and Virginia Robinson were pioneers in many ways. In 1913 Taft earned a doctorate in psychology studying with George Herbert Mead at the University of Chicago at a time when few women went to college, let alone earned an advanced degree. And Dr. Taft and Miss Robinson, as they were commonly known, despite the fact that Virginia Robinson also had a Ph.D., were partners in life as well as professional colleagues. They adopted two children in an era when same sex relationships were barely acknowledged let alone considered the basis for adoptive parenting. While their portraits hanging in the lobby of the Penn SSW depict two rather formidable middle-aged women, there must have been an intellectual fearlessness and adventuring spirit about these two individuals that allowed them to take on the prevailing diagnostic wisdom of the day and advocate an alternative approach to social work practice that has contributed so much to the thinking and practice in our field.

Chapter 15
The University of Pennsylvania School of Social Work: Reflections of a Graduate

SaraKay Smullens

Preface

It is rare to have the opportunity to be surrounded by both academic and professional genius and passion in a groundbreaking setting while on the cusp of adulthood. The golden opportunity to study at the University of Pennsylvania School of Social Work in 1964–65 afforded me this uncommon experience, one that happened by chance. What follows are some of my remembrances and observations, expanded from a 1990 essay that appeared in our school publication then called *Sociolog*. At that time I was an overseer of our School, a position I was privileged to hold for nine years.

I believe that each who benefited from our Penn School experience found it uniquely personal and took from it different qualities of interpretation and endurance. With this in mind, please know that I share only from the vantage point of what my experiences and observations were and are. I also want to apologize to graduates who may be reading this, who attended our alma mater the same time that I did, but who do not find their favorite professors noted. Since I transferred to Penn for my second year, I only met faculty that shared with the section where I was assigned.

At the Penn School, as it was referred to at the time, I experienced a depth of integrated and cohesive faculty investment that was total, unique, and unselfish. Through a learning experience that was both captivating and controversial, I came to view functional social work as art that grows from intense clinical scrutiny. I learned and saw first hand how this amalgam of art and science grew into a union of hope, insight, and strength that when thoroughly integrated into the professional focus and lens of the clinician can produce positive impetus to grow and change in the lives of those we are privileged to work with.

I view all the vivid, exciting, and energizing new programs now offered at our School as having strong roots in our profession of social work, as do so many other fields, from activism to advocacy to couple, family, and group counseling and therapy, to name only a few. With this in mind, I have long believed that far too little of the profound and unique philosophy of our School and all that it has birthed and inspired has been both documented and passed on to our current students. I have believed it important to try to share, to bring to dimension through the written word, the inimitable life-affirming experience offered at my alma mater and to illustrate how its unique creative genius has become the basis of many professions and outlooks, and has been integrated into many additional and diverse fields, almost always without a footnote.

During my years as an overseer and following, in order to remedy misunderstandings about the Penn approach and what I have come to regard as unintentional perversion of a brave genius, in order to at long last set the record straight, I suggested and continued to urge that our School offer a clinical DSW. In this way our profound influences can be documented, recognized, and acknowledged and our pioneering contributions can be shared in their originality, purity, truth, and passion. In the process of this documentation, I have learned from Dr. Ram Cnaan, who has pioneered this effort, that it has received faculty and overseer approval. To say that I am ecstatic about this extraordinary leadership decision is an understatement.

What follows is a personal statement, one that I hope can illustrate how the lessons of my alma mater have never ceased throughout my life in both direction and depth. It is also an expression of grateful thanks for one life definitively enriched through a unique academic and professional experience that has grown more vivid, more meaningful, and more wise and authentic with every passing year.

One of the first of many startling sentences I heard when I entered the second year of The Penn School's Class of 1965 was "the personal is the professional." This meant that all of us, schooled to keep our personal lives and feelings to ourselves as we studied rational theory and thought, were to learn that the very opposite was expected, required, demanded. We were taught that if we did not face our feelings we could never see and understand ourselves clearly. Without this vision we could never see and understand our clients, and thus we would fail miserably in our professional mission. Though I was not specifically told this, I now see that implicit in our faculty message was that the personal/professional continuum also includes "political" in its range. It is the political climate that offers hope that the futures of all of our citizens can be protected, and in this way "the personal is the professional is the political." And inherent in our education was the understanding that receiving a Penn degree marked a promise that working for social justice and opportunity for growth and change for all, in whatever way we chose, must never stop being an integral part of our lives.

My young adult years was a time marked by the assassination of John F. Kennedy, the young and charismatic President who had implored America, especially her youth, to "ask not what your country can do for you but what you can do for your country." Despite the enormity of this loss the period remained one rich with hope and the determination to address the challenges of the day with unyielding commitment. A Voting Rights Act that the late President had been unable to get through Congress in his lifetime was passed, and the Great Society was birthed. Times were not yet burned by bitter disillusionment or seared with intractable rage. The assassinations of Martin Luther King and Robert Kennedy had not yet occurred. Our Supreme Court seemed determined to secure a legal climate where human lives and choices were far more important than property. Though surely their seeds had been planted, they were in this era invisible, for the tormented and bitter divisions of Viet Nam, Watergate, and abortion were not yet upon us.

During this brief cusp of time there was great optimism that society could and would grow to include opportunities for the disadvantaged and oppressed, and those of us fortunate to live in this rarified time truly believed with all our hearts that we could make the world a better place. We set out to do just that.

Those like me who were raised below the Mason Dixon line were sickened by the horrors of segregation that we were expected to view obliviously. The inequities and indignities imposed on African Americans—riding in the back of buses, not being able to enter stores and restaurants, appalling schools, separate water fountains in public parks, horrific restrooms in public places, to name only a few—created a stain on human consciousness.

While a student at Goucher College, then a women's college, located in Towson, a suburb of Baltimore, I became deeply involved in student activism of the early 1960s. Black students and employees at our college could not get a meal or a cup of coffee in Towson. Nor could they use a beauty salon or bowling alley. A group of us worked tirelessly for two years to reverse Towson's hateful segregation policy, a goal we finally reached peacefully in June 1962. Our activism also moved us to work tirelessly for John Kennedy's presidential candidacy, and I worked for the President and the Democratic National Committee upon my graduation from Goucher.

In our generation the rigidly imposed roles of women also began to be questioned. Many who questioned why women merited a higher education had been calmed when assured that an excellent undergraduate education would be helpful for husbands' well being and advancement. Sadly, many women of my generation believed (and many still believe, though perhaps more quietly), that this is why they were at college and that they were failures if they were not wearing an engagement ring by senior year. Still, thankfully, in the 1960s women began to ask why it was *mandated* that we be at home during the heart of every day. Finally we were asking: "What are *our* needs, *our* choices. Where are *our* voices?"

In this time frame women also began demanding that updated information about birth control be provided on college and university campuses. To quiet critics who were vehemently against providing this information, some institutions stated that it would only be offered to those engaged to be married, with a ring to show it. This led to great popularity of "diamonds" sold in the now defunct "five and dime" Woolworths chain stores. This also led to contradiction: Though we picketed against the policies of discrimination at the Woolworths lunch counters, to learn about updated birth control information, we also went inside to buy "diamonds."

Three of the most challenging professions of the time that attracted liberal arts female graduates were law, medicine and social work. Though there were exceptions, the former two usually attracted students who knew they must put aside desires to marry and have children for a later time, if at all. Social work was a profession that attracted both single women and those who yearned for a dynamic professional world, as well as marriage and children.

It was on November 22, 1964, during my first year of graduate school, that President

Kennedy was assassinated. A few months later I became engaged, and my fiancé was in Philadelphia.

The mid-1960s were years when it was highly unusual for a young married couple to live apart for any part of the week. I loved the graduate school I was attending in Washington, D.C., and felt enormously grateful that all faculty I met were respectful of my ideas, and that I received a full scholarship and stipend. Still, I believed it imperative to leave D.C. and transfer to a Philadelphia based school.

At my previous school, I heard fleetingly about the differences between the diagnostic and functional schools of social work, that the former was Freudian, the latter Rankian, in the minority, and definitely on the weird side. Specifically, though I learned a great deal from my first year field placement at what was then called D.C.'s Department of Welfare, my identity and direction as a social worker was not derived or directed from this experience. I was told that a student in a functional school received identity, direction and purpose from the "function" of the Agency where she or he worked. What was jolting to me, however, was being told that functional students were forced to revisit what was remembered or imagined in their womb experience. I learned, too, that functional schools, of which Penn was the primary one, were referred to as "the pain schools," though no one I asked was able to tell exactly why or what that meant.

Though a strong identification and direction from my professional setting made sense to me, I reasoned that being a newly wed was surely incompatible with examining my womb and being in pain. It seemed a "no brainer": I applied to another local highly regarded diagnostic school. However, when I called for preliminary information I was told that all places in their second year class were filled and was encouraged to apply to transfer the following year, which seemed light years away.

And so with trepidation I telephoned Penn. To my surprise, the Admissions Director, Dr. Margaret Bishop, answered the telephone. She was warm and encouraging, acting as if she had all of the time in the world.

On a warm spring day I boarded a train in D.C., destination Philadelphia, for my admissions interview with Dr. Rosa Wessel. It was not until my arrival to the 30th St. station that I realized that our School was removed from Penn's west Philadelphia campus. I will never forget my awe, as well as my disorientation, as I entered the elegant center city mansion at 2410 Pine St. where social work students learned and studied in splendid isolation from our university campus.

For this interview I wore what every Southern young woman wore for an important interview—white gloves. Dr. Wessel's first words to me were devoid of pleasantries and small talk, and a bit sarcastic: "Now Miss Sherman, if you will take off your little white gloves, we can talk about why you want to be a social worker and why you want to attend The Penn School." Dr. Wessel was warning that Penn students were expected to be involved, to get their hands dirty. What I did not realize was that Dr. Wessel was not merely talking about a social conscience and social action. She was referring to the examination of the unsettling truths in the Self (specifically my Self, the angry, hurt part of us that we keep buried) that The Penn School would require.

Soon after my acceptance I learned that Laura Downes would be my faculty advisor and casework teacher and that The Philadelphia Society to Protect Children, under the leadership of Dr. Julia Ann Bishop,[1] would provide full scholarship and a stipend living allowance. I was to learn in time that Mrs. Downes, Dr. Wessel, Dr. Julia Ann Bishop, and most of our faculty and field supervisors had been inspired students, disciples, and colleagues of my new School's key visionaries Jessie Taft, Virginia Robinson, and Otto Rank, the only member of Freud's initial Viennese circle who was not a physician.

On my first day of class and for weeks to follow I felt as if I were in a foreign country, one where even the alphabet of the language was totally, shockingly unfamiliar. Only a few months earlier I had been studying and discussing Sigmund Freud and his identification of the unconscious, the id, ego, and super ego. Now these words were not mentioned. Instead, I studied Jessie Taft, Virginia Robinson, Anita Faatz, Kenneth Pray, and of course, Otto Rank, and concentrated intently on discussions of the Will, the Self (negative and positive), patterns, process, the importance of defining and focusing work through your Agency's function, and willing your strength and courage to take risks and dare to love, be loved, and stand up for what you believe. Achieving this required balancing your instincts toward freedoms and responsibility, learning to trust your impulses, developing the determination to "put in your difference," and an appreciation that the "truest gifts are the gifts of the Self."

In varying degrees, students at our Penn School knew the details of the Rank/Taft/Robinson union, which some of us referred to as an academic ménage à trois. Otto Rank was born Otto Rosenfeld in Vienna in 1884. His family was poor and while attending trade school reading Sigmund Freud's *The Interpretation of Dreams* inspired Rank to write *The Artist* in 1907, using the pen name he legally adopted a few years later. Rank believed that successful psychotherapy entailed freeing the unique and individual artist within each of us. He explored art through psychoanalytic principles, and his innovative genius brought him to the attention of Freud, who helped arrange his entry into the University of Vienna and invited him to join the initial Viennese circle.

But Rank infuriated Freud with the 1924 publication, *The Trauma of Birth*, and he was thus ostracized by his cherished mentor and his colleagues. His birth trauma theory stressed addressing repetitive separation anxiety first experienced in birth as the key to autonomous living, and Freud found this work to be a betrayal of the central importance of the oedipal conflict in personal development.

In the 1930s Rank developed a concept of the Will as the guiding force in psychological development, and believed that the Will could be used to direct self-discovery and development. Rank's emphasis was on personal growth and self-actualization: the ability to define and live one's unique artistry, and despite life's inevitable pain and tragedy to love well and deeply, but never as a cover-up for the fear of life's aloneness. Unlike Freud, Rank did not see resistance in negative terms, but as the Will trying to assert itself toward development. He believed that healing depended on the deep (often intense) engagement of client and clinician, with agreed upon goals and a defined ending point of work.

Although her translations are stilted and difficult to sift through and have since been improved upon by later translators, Jessie Taft Americanized Rank by translating many of his cumbersome works. Taft offered Rank respite and recognition with an invitation to join The Penn School faculty after his traumatic personal and professional break. It is Taft who translated Rank's piercing and profound words, the soul and ethic of what we were taught: "As a man thinks in his heart, so is he." The essence of functional social work was to work in mutual respect with each client so that the "thinking heart" could be free to guide with purpose and honor. But first we were expected to achieve this ability for ourselves.

Unlike Freud, Carl Jung, and others he studied with in the initial Viennese circle of analysts, Otto Rank never founded a School. Instead his School became Penn, and Jessie Taft and Virginia Robinson integrated Rankian analytic theory and its application into the formulation of functional casework. These ideas, though largely unsung, are everywhere, from humanists like Carl Rogers, to existentialists like Rollo May, to Aaron Beck's Cognitive school, and Sal Minuchin's System theory.

Ironically, it was Freud's rejection of Rank and his subsequent break with members of the Vienna Psychoanalytic Society that caused the despairing sojourn to America which would save him from the threat of Nazi annihilation. As is true of any devoted union, it became difficult to decipher where the theories of Taft and Robinson and other pioneer functional social workers ended and where Rank began, and vice versa. Thus, Rank and functional social work became one in the same to me, and so they remain.

This period predated what would be referred to in the late 1960s and 1970s as the Sexual Revolution. Yet The Penn School foreshadowed this period by teaching a revolutionary concept that continues to be hotly debated in manifest ways to this day. We were taught that there are two ways for couples to express intimate physical and sexual love, one with the opposite sex and one with the same sex, and that both were healthy. We learned that the important challenge was to be able to love, and that the truest gift was the gift of the Self. It was this gift, in the most professional sense, that we were expected to offer our clients.

We were not explicitly told that Taft and Robinson were life partners who adopted two children, but many of us, perhaps most of us, figured that out. Understanding their brave, devoted, and productive union added to the avant garde, revolutionary, and exciting atmosphere of our School. To teach there, to study there necessitated a resolve, a commitment to claim and celebrate your "difference," your innate individual Self, as well as to make a difference by caring deeply about the state of humankind and resolving to improve it. This academic and professional emphasis was for one reason only—to produce social workers who would bring opportunities for hope and justice to our clients and to our world. This mandate was the hallmark of our work, and it both inspired and strengthened our student body.

All faculty members were in agreement that unless the social worker, like the client, was on the road to developing self-awareness, the recognition of each client's unique qualities of strength and growth potential, his or her humanity and dignity, and thus health, would be undermined and compromised. Through an intimate relationship between student and teacher, we experienced the healing potential of a mutually

respectful professional relationship first hand. Fully in concert, faculty created a setting thoroughly invested in no-nonsense responsibility toward others. In turn, we were
expected, in an arena of complete professionalism and appropriate boundaries, to
offer the same straight forward and focused heart to heart, soul to soul rapport to our
clients, inspiring them to value their unique differences as ours were valued. No
cookie-cutter pigeonholing of diagnosis here—of student or client. Far ahead of the
progressive mental health movement that frowns on heartless labeling of psychiatric
illness, The Penn School recognized such delineation as a rude and disrespectful orientation, one with utter disregard of both innate and potential strength and beauty in
difference.

All the professors of each section and concentration met regularly to discuss the
progress of each student in a coordinated and cohesive way. They cared deeply, yet
they never coddled or infantilized, demonstrating the professionalism they expected
us to offer our clients. Though long before the "tough love" movement, in many
respects these two words describe faculty and field instructors' coordinated and
straight forward expectations in work ethic and academic persistence. If a student
demonstrated what faculty agreed was a cavalier or disrespectful attitude in either
direction, or demonstrated rude behavior to a client or fellow student, he or she was
asked to leave the School.

Without exception, this disciplined quality of concern and involvement coupled
with demanding expectation was reflected by every professor and field instructor I
studied with. All wanted to teach and prepare us with all of the wisdom, ability, and
experience in their repertoire. All gave generously of their time and knowledge. And
all expected us to work very hard!

At Penn we studied literature, not pathology, to appreciate the multilayered complexity of the human condition. We learned about "patterns," the consistency with
which one deals with offered love and closeness, as well as injustice and loss, and
"process," the beginnings, middles, and endings of all of life's myriad experiences,
and in a broader sense, one's ethics, the way one approaches relationships with others
and all institutions of community and society.

There was no prolonged analysis of developmental stages in our coursework.
Instead we learned to listen carefully and respectfully to a client's story well before
such ideas became schools of thought. We learned to define goals in concert with our
clients well before the term "client centered" therapy was birthed. We learned about
destructive and depleting attitudes and behaviors before cognitive and systems therapies were birthed. In true Rankian form our work was time limited, with a "beginning" and "ending" determined by client and social worker clearly in focus.

I would learn later, although it was never verbally explained (to my knowledge),
that faculty and field instructors moved in a way, taught in a way, lectured in a way
that would overwhelm us so that we could actually feel and experience the terror faced
by clients who had no choice once they were brave enough to reach out for help but
to take it. In this way we learned profound respect and empathy for clients. In this way
any condescension as defense was blown away. In this way we learned how to invisibly
take the hand of our clients and, using all that we knew, propel them, will them, to

believe in themselves and chart a course toward something better. And in this way we learned how clients could dare to hope, dare to believe in themselves enough to make changes in themselves and their lives. We were able to work in this way because we had experienced the power of the functional approach, with all of its pain and terror and all of its promise and purpose.

It was during the first year that students wrote of their womb experience, and at first I lived in terror that I would be given a makeup assignment. I never was. However, as time passed, and Rankin psychology was understood, I grew to understand the reason for the assignment. Though this highlighting was revolutionary, and misunderstood, as well as ridiculed, in recent years its psychological underpinnings have been given their due as a highly important area of study and surely no laughing matter, although once again without a footnote to The Penn School.

The womb is each child's first home; and each child is deeply affected by the state of being of his or her mother, the state of the mother's relationship with her partner, the state of her relationship with her family, the health and safety conditions in the community and society. Of essential impact on the child is the extent to which he or she has been planned, is wanted and desired (even if not planned), and is cared for protectively during the womb experience. Further, each infant must find the courage to experience the terrifying journey from womb to world, as well as to dare to take a first terrifying breath.

In parallel ways each adult, to have a meaningful life, must learn to endure the aloneness of life, as well as the inevitable suffering. To see this process through, to bear the prerequisites of meeting repetitive birth traumas (successive beginnings and endings framed by birth and death), requires the discipline to face and grow through pain and fear and in this way develop the courage to live, to love, to hope—despite life's inevitable unfairnesses, losses, injustices, and betrayals.

My relationship with my faculty advisor, Mrs. Laura Downes, was difficult and anxiety provoking from our first meeting. I hid events and related feelings (from her and myself and everyone else) that I was terrified to admit—and her thrust was to decrease my hard won and deeply clung to intellectualizations and denial and make me aware of my feelings, and in this way become sensitized to the kind of pain and anxiety each new client coming for help must face. On paper after paper, Mrs. Downes would write in my margins (always in her signature turquoise ink), "What about the ending of the parental marriage?" "What is keeping this mother from beginning a new life?" And the constant: "I know what you think, but how do you *feel?*"[3]

What I resisted learning is common contradiction. I was to see that throughout my life my pattern was to speak up about the pain and injustice that others faced and to do all that I could to alleviate it. Yet, I had not developed the ability to speak up for myself. I would learn that the more one's inner pain, the easier it may be for some to recognize it in others and yearn to be helpful. It is far harder to recognize it in one's Self, and harder still to do something about it.

In conference after conference, Mrs. Downes would stress: "You cannot know a man until you walk in his moccasins," and "If you have blind spots, your clients will sense them and will not bring up materials they feel can hurt, frighten or anger you. Or if they are able to bring up material threatening to you, you will not understand the significance and gloss over it." Mrs. Downes also said, "Kindness, sensitivity and compassion toward others is essential." And she warned, "Intelligent people without these qualities, unless they face why they are devoid of them, can do grave harm. This is especially true if they are intractable and ambitious." And so she counseled her students: "Face your tears. Honor them. Refuse to bury them. And then Will them into the strength to be an agent of hope and change, for yourself first, then for others."

Mrs. Downes and all of our professors implored us to be proud of the uniqueness that was ours. We were taught that a degree from our School was a promise to trust our instincts (which could be relied upon if we knew ourselves), to speak out against duplicity and hypocrisy, and to never to be afraid to stand alone. "The wisest truths often take light years to be discovered," Mrs. Downes told me. "Honor and protect what you know is right, regardless of the consequences."

On a Friday in late November 1964 at my field placement I became inordinately upset following the brutalization of a beaten young child, a five-year-old girl with cigarette burns all over her body, who had been sheltered in our Agency following her hospitalization. Horrified and hysterical, I could not control my shaking as I called Mrs. Downes late on a Friday afternoon from the shared desk and shared phone of an agency co-worker. "I cannot do this. I cannot take this," I repeated again and again. Of course, at that time, I believed I was only crying for the abused child. I had no idea that this child's horror was touching terrifying experiences of my own. My terror was responded to calmly and kindly, "Of course you can. If you could not take this you would not be here." And then Mrs. Downes told me something that was not even hinted at in my letter of acceptance. "You are the first transfer student that The Penn School has accepted. Your School believes deeply in you, and you can and you must and you will do all that is necessary."

Mrs. Downes scheduled an appointment with me for the following Monday morning, and then she said: "Go right home and tell your husband that he should take care of you this weekend." I did go home and sat in a chair crying for several hours, where my husband found me. I did the best I could to describe the horror of the suffering child I had witnessed and then, daring not ask for myself, I quoted Mrs. Downes' request that he take care of me. I am not sure what I expected or hoped for, but I think it was for my husband to hold me tightly, make it safe, and let me cry my heart out. But I was told, "I did not marry you to take care of you—ever." I should have let out my hurt and anger, or I should have left, or I should have done something on my own behalf. But I could not. I moved from the chair to my bed, where I remained the entire weekend, numb and afraid.

At our meeting the following Monday, among many things, Mrs. Downes asked about my weekend. Without censoring to protect what I didn't want seen, but perhaps also reaching out for help it would take me years to accept, I spoke of the episode with my husband. Mrs. Downes, never one to mince words said, "I am concerned about your marriage. Remember that the road ahead may call for changes. You are going to need further help along the way, more than we at the School will be able to give you. Face your fears, and be brave." Her eyes misted when she told me what she would repeat to me on graduation day: "Remember you are not a transfer to this School, your School. You are a transplant, and you and your work will be remembered here by all of us."

Another cherished professor was Dr. Roland Artigues, our section's knowledgeable and street smart social policy professor. The evening before an exam in his class, a week or so after I had become deeply upset by the burned child who was sheltered in my Agency, I had an awful accident at home, one with deep psychological underpinnings and significance. My husband and I had a small stove in our kitchen, and before using the oven the pilot had to be lit with a match. Without consciously realizing that there was grease in the broiling pan (though I was the last one to use the broiler), I lit the oven, which immediately blew up, flames darting in all directions. I was able both to extinguish the flames and to protect myself. How fortunate I was! My right arm had serious burns; I lost eyelashes and eyebrows and received a singed haircut on one side. For days I smelled like a baked chicken, which was the last thing I had broiled before broiling myself. However, I was fine.

I did, however, miss two days of class, and my first stop upon my return was Dr. Antigues' office for a make-up exam. He told me to take the exam home and complete it, and then he asked, his voice showing deep concern, "Are we asking too much of you?" "Is this all too much for you to bear?" "No," I responded and promised without hesitation, claiming every word: "It is not."

This devotion was also demonstrated by our School's indomitable and exacting librarian, Evelyn Butler. This period predated the integration of libraries on campus, as well as the birth of personal computers; and Miss Butler found us each and every reference we requested, no matter how deeply in the stacks of what library it happened to be buried. When necessary she also reminded us of our School receptionist's ever present stock of aspirin!

The prophetic wisdom I experienced in this year continues to both strengthen and amaze. In class and conference Dr. Artigues taught that although the effectiveness of our profession rested on government responsiveness to those in need, there was danger in "hand-out dependency" that impaired growth of Self. He stressed that all welfare programs must also stress proper support, education, training and impetus for uneducated heads of households and their partners.

Further, Dr. Artigues predicted that as America grew all new cultures might have strong differences and that such differences could divide communities, as well as our profession. He spoke of community and societal structures and professional bodies, even those led by our own or related professions, that could be rigid and unfair, even cruel. He predicted times when societal structures may deprive those desperate for help and of difficulties social workers would have staffing offices whose philosophies they did not respect. He said that in such troubled times Agencies would be horrendously weakened by those in leadership and staff positions without knowledge or concern. He explained that our profession could become misunderstood and scapegoated for society's irresponsibility. He implored us to be "messengers" calling attention to the sources of problems. He told us to expect retaliation against unwelcome messages: "Protect your clients and your profession, even if doing so jeopardizes your position. With this strength, if necessary, you will find or create another position. There is no other approach that protects all you care about. There is no only way to maintain self respect and protect community."

Again, his words: "At Penn we are teaching you to see beyond the obvious, to identify sources of problems, and to find creative solutions. Regardless of the difficulties the Penn approach is to persist in furthering the promise of our privileged profession: help and hope to the vulnerable and the attitudes and directions that make this possible."

Dr. Richard Lodge, a brilliant and dynamic teacher, nurtured our Rankian psychological foundation and demonstrated that art, architecture, and literature (today, undoubtedly, he would include film) are richer vehicles for understanding human behavior—patterns and process—than are theoretical texts. In his class we explored the works of writers such as Willa Cather, Katherine Mansfield and D.H. Lawrence, understanding them by exploring their novels, short stories, essays and journals. Dr. Lodge spoke of the difference between being a caseworker (today's term would be clinician) and being a social worker: "The caseworker must use careful timing in order not to alarm the client by addressing and confronting painful and unsettling incidents before the casework/client relationship is strong enough to cushion. Social workers in their advocacy concentration, however, should pull no punches, 'putting in their difference,' and speaking with honor and direction."

Dr. Lodge also stressed that process, while ordered, is neither rigid nor linear. He described process as one's use of relationships and events in the quest of self actualization; as something fluid and creative; as ideas and experiences building on other ideas and experiences; as the ethics with which one lived his or her life. In his class, "Patterns and Process in Psychological Growth," we learned that the only way that one is "out of process" is to act disrespectfully by the use of insults, condescension, lies, manipulation or betrayal.

Dr. Lodge was as intuitive a person as I have ever met. In January, 1965 I wrote a paper in his class on "The Search of Katherine Mansfield," in which I examined the motivations and coping skills of the highly sensitive New Zealand writer, born in 1888, who died of tuberculosis at the age of thirty-five. At Penn we never received grades. Our papers were returned with pages of commentary, all handwritten, never typed. Obviously knowing how afraid I was of anger, and how I was suffering and frightened, Dr. Lodge wrote: "What a fine grained appreciation of KM this is. You capture the essence of her quality—at least, as I understand her—and point it out with much of your fine flavor. I have two questions. You are so constantly and deeply connected with KM—it's really quite a profound union you seem to have with her—is there anyplace for some difference in your view? Is there a spot where she annoys or puzzles you?" Then, knowing that I was internally struggling in direction in my personal world, he tactfully asked: "My second question is in regard to the balance between 'patterns and process'—you discuss the former perceptively and artistically; the later truly is more elusive." And he concludes with enormous support and kindness: "I trust that the questions I have raised do not loom out of proportion with my substantial respect and enjoyment with this paper—and with the use you have made of this course. It has been a privilege to be one of your teachers."

My brilliant research advisor, Dr. Harold Lewis, stressed the importance, as well as the limitations, of our work with the following words: "The challenge of research is in some ways like a bikini. Although much is revealed, important findings remain hidden awaiting discovery." He adamantly believed that, "those who walk the walk" and those who "talk the talk" must work hand-in-hand in constant mutually satisfying dialogue. In his words, "Our research should help you and your colleagues to do a better job helping your clients and showing our government why it makes sense in every way to offer sources of help and initiative."

Under Dr. Lewis's tutelage my second year research project concentrated on why initially interested foster care parents dropped out of the process of consideration. Like all my professors, his notes to me were voluminous. In our discussion of my research focus, Dr. Lewis wrote: "Do you wish to study factors that discourage? Your design would have to allow for evidence that such factors were not present in parents who followed through. Or do you wish to explore factors associated with decisions to withdraw or not follow through. Think about this." I chose the later, and my eyes still mist after months of work and discussion, I read the following sentence following several comments: "Very well done. With minor changes ready for rough draft of total report."

Dr. Lewis applauded social workers' desire to change the world. However, he told us to be kind to ourselves. He said that as we got older we may learn that all we can change is our little piece of the world, but never to stop trying to do that. Dr. Lewis also spoke of those who had what he called "genius sensitivity." The traits he described which marked this quality of understanding and caring, and the ability to use them to find satisfaction and direction in the world, are precisely those described as by Daniel Goleman in his 1995 groundbreaking book, *Emotional Intelligence*, Dr. Lewis and all my professors explained that this kind of direction, which was the essence of successful process, could only be achieved in settings where authentic communication was offered, where there was always a place to address your concerns, which would be responded to with caring and respect. In was the challenge of social work to create and protect such settings for our clients as well as to develop and maintain them for ourselves—personally, professionally, and politically.

The executive director of my field placement, Julia Ann Bishop, had a national reputation for her excellence in the field of protective service. Because of my work with Miss Bishop (this was the era before the use of Ms.), and my supervisors, Mrs. Anne Wise and Mrs. Ruth Scott, as well as the superb and dedicated social work and clerical staff of the Philadelphia Society to Protect Children, the fit between academics and field work was seamless.

In these integrated professional and academic settings I learned to discuss attitudes and behaviors in the here and now and how these mindsets helped or impeded the stated goals of clients. I learned how and why self-defeating attitudes and behaviors developed, and how to work in concert with clients so that they could experience motivation and move forward. This was a far different practice from that in my first year, in which the caseworker, himself or herself, recorded the "background" and "diagnosis" and "treatment plan" for each client, couple, or family, without consultation with them about these goals.

At Penn such approaches were seen as condescending and patronizing. Goals were set by the client, couple, family, or group. They were achieved through respectful, trusting, mutual interaction of client/s and social worker. Students learned always to ask new clients: "Why are YOU here? What do YOU want to achieve? How would you like me to be of help to YOU?" At the Agency, I was shown the importance of drawing up a contract with each client which focused on what goals the client wished to accomplish, as well as the importance of the beginning, middle and ending phases of the relationship, which were fluidly determined and open to reevaluation. In this way I saw first hand how the knowledge of an ending increased client motivation.[2]

As months passed I grew more and more confident in my skills and abilities as a family caseworker to understand my clients and help them to recognize their goals. I also began to see strong similarities between the lives of our sheltered children and their parents and my own family, and in this way understand from the inside out that it was self awareness that would make the quality of learning offered possible to grasp and to integrate. On one occasion I completely forgot that a client whose wife had left him after the birth of seven children, two sheltered in our Agency, was my 1:30 P.M. appointment. I took a leisurely walk after lunch, returning to my Agency to find my client, who had been waiting for one half hour. Though my case recordings were rich with information about my time periods with his children, without realizing it, I avoided every opportunity to talk to him.

My supervisor, Mrs. Anne Wise, and Mrs. Downes slowly helped me to see that something in this father's life terrified me and helped to show me what and why and how very close to home it all was for me. My academic work brought theoretical understanding to this painful difficulty that taught me so much, and my work with this client became the focus of my 1965 thesis, "Learning to Use the Positive Self on Behalf of Parents Who Have Neglected Their Children." In it I describe how "Mr. Lane" and I grew and changed together.

It does not seem strange that during the months of our work together, Mr. Lane has gained self-confidence—He sits a little straighter now; his voice has grown stronger; and sometimes he smiles. . . . My professional growth paralleled his personal growth. What is the true use of the positive self? It is first to feel, understand, and value the anger, fear, guilt, hesitancy, hate and resentment that are part of us all. With this awareness the worker agrees to accept, respect, expect, and care in the helping relationship. At the same time the client . . . (is) freed for growth. No longer need he wallow in self pity, anger, or guilt. [The social worker] . . . learns to value pain, his own and his client's. For it says, "I feel. I care. I understand. There is something more for you, something better. Can I help you to find it?"

There was one area of concentration stressed in my first year but disregarded at Penn that I found very meaningful. In my first year much time was devoted to an understanding of defense mechanisms first identified by Freud. The Penn School viewed such delineations as ones that would undermine the power of the Will, and one's ultimate belief in his/her ability to live and choose, or to "make or break" one's life. While I saw the value and inherent respect in this approach, I found it interesting and helpful to understand how a client's defense system worked in order to achieve the most trusting relationship and determine the wisest, most fulfilling goals. For instance, a client who projected all of his hate and distrust onto the social worker could not tolerate a chair that was too close and needed a large degree of separation and feeling of control before he/she could trust enough to begin to speak. In a group setting this client would be more comfortable not sitting near the social worker. A client who was in denial needed more time to tell his story before any understanding of separation anxiety could be discussed. Thus, it would be productive to establish more time to work together.

Further, I never felt a contradiction between the importance of resolving the oedipal conflict and the importance of addressing the birth trauma in adult development. I did, however, learn it was more productive to discuss separating with one's parents and the fear of one's aloneness and new beginnings (and other necessary subsequent separations, endings, and beginnings, including dramatic shifts of attitudes and behaviors) than it was to disclose conscious or unconscious sexual passions involving parental figures. Also, I began to see that in addressing and resolving separation anxiety, oedipal conflicts were also worked through and resolved, without ever directly discussing the oedipal triangle.

Soon after graduation in May 1965, I would witness the burgeoning field of marital and family and group psychotherapy, and realize that, though again not footnoted, social work was the true and authentic birthplace of the defined fields of couple, family, and group psychotherapy. I realized that social workers did this quality of work before any other field realized its essential value, and functional social workers learned to do it through a time limited agreement between them and their clients, and with precision, focus, and concentration on the here and now.

Upon graduation, I was stunned to see that an inbred and hostile division of the functional and diagnostic approaches played itself out in the marketplace. My first year after graduation was spent at the Society to Protect Children, which had been a condition of my scholarship and stipend. Following that year I wanted to find employment in a psychiatric setting, where I believed I could best pull together what I had learned thus far in a cohesive way as a foundation for further learning. Without knowing anything about the fine work done at our School, there were agencies and settings rejecting of Penn graduates and openly disrespectful and hostile to Rank and functional social work.

A clinical setting that trained and appreciated our students was the Philadelphia Child Guidance Clinic, where in 1966 I received a beautiful letter encouraging me to join the staff to work with Sal Minuchin, who was described as a revolutionary thinker soon to be joining them as Director. At the time I had no idea who Sal Minuchin was, or what systems work was; and I believed that I needed to catch my breath and take a break from another revolutionary center of learning. Little did I know how very Rankian, how very "functional," how very familiar Minuchin would prove himself to be.

In 1965–66, the academic year following mine, the last social work class studied at the Pine Street address in Center City. Dr. Margaret Bishop and Mrs. Laura Downes both died before our School's move to campus, and a beautiful tribute to them was made on campus at the design site of our School's new home.

The same year I was hired by Philadelphia Psychiatric Hospital, a setting where social workers from various schools were welcomed. A Freudian center, they were beginning important work in family and group therapy, and I was deeply involved in both. The director of residency training, Dr. Morris Brody, was most gracious in allowing me to take courses offered to residents. Also, in time I turned to a former director, Dr. Eli Marcovitz, for intensive therapy that would help me make important changes in my personal life.

As my professional life has evolved, I hope the quality of my work has increased in breadth and dimension. The Penn model has remained my structural and philosophical mainstay in my work with individuals, couples, families, and groups. My approach can most accurately be described as Rankian/functional, which can best be explained as understanding suppressed and repressed fears to be separate, to be creative, to chart one's course in love and to work and then do all I can to integrate this knowledge with a cognitive and systems framing and mutual client interaction. I work the best way I know how with each of my clients so that his or her artist is freed to be guide and comfort and what I describe and have written about as "an emotional sense of direction" is achieved.

Perhaps the greatest compliment in my professional life occurred after the publication of my first book, *Whoever Said Life Is Fair?*, in which I discuss the need for a state of dignity to survive life's unfairnesses, injustices, betrayals, and losses. The book carries the message of empowerment, a word that describes all that we were taught to stand for. And of course, dignity, a combination of pride and humility, is what the faculty modeled for all students. It was at Penn that I was introduced to the importance of journaling, and I turned to it to find strength to care for my children and myself during my process of divorce. It was the journal that grew into my book. Soon after its publication in spring 1980, I received a handwritten "enthusiastic invitation" from Anita Faatz, the dearly respected and distinguished former faculty member of our School, to speak at the Annual Meeting of the Otto Rank Association on October 18, 1980.

In a long follow-up letter following the event, again handwritten, and dated October 28, Anita Faatz graciously called my presentation "superb." In the Winter 1980–81 *Journal of Otto Rank* she wrote: "I am about to try to express what I have never been able to express to my own satisfaction: that in writing about feeling, emotion, the quality of the writing or speaking must carry the essence of what the author or speaker is attempting to convey. It must be it. I think we achieved this at our meeting." She complimented my book, saying that it "achieved universal meaning" and concluded: "Any writing . . . cannot lay claim to authenticity unless it touches the inner reaches of . . . deeply felt truth."

At this meeting in a private conversation Dr. Faatz and I discussed the fact that I had broken with traditional functional social work by going into private practice, no longer receiving my purpose and direction from an Agency. Dr. Faatz understood this decision and was completely supportive: "Respect for process and functionalism is inside of you. You took a necessary and successful risk to care for your daughters and claim a new beginning. Achieving creativity by trusting your life instincts is the essence of Rank's work; you have freed the artist who lives in you." And then Dr. Faatz asked a question that was the ultimate gift: "Did you know that Jessie Taft had a private practice?" I had not.

As years have passed I have valued more and more that it was not until my year at Penn that I become consciously aware of how difficult and painful it is for each person to grow up and mature. I learned that in order to pass from childhood to adulthood, each of us must face very difficult internal and external conflicts and that though some childhoods are easier than others, none is without conflict. In order to grow and reach maturity, every person has an inner turmoil to resolve, all part of the developmental process, one which we both learned about and experienced while students at Penn.

The difficult years realistically predicted at Penn have come to pass, for all of the reasons spelled out. Yet, these realities make holding on to our resolve to remain change agents devoted to protecting and inspiring our clients, as well as protecting the true mission of our profession, even more essential. So many continue to work to meet these challenges.

While an overseer of our School, to highlight the groundbreaking contributions of social work and encourage others to join our efforts, I suggested offering the Crystal Stair Award to honor "natural social workers" from every profession who are committed to offering hope to our most vulnerable. My family and close friends began a fund so that this award could be ongoing. Through the years our School has honored many "natural social workers" with our Crystal Stair Award. The name of this award comes from the poetry of Langston Hughes, specifically his poem "Mother to Son," where a mother implores her young one not to give up hope, not to stop trying: "Don't you fall now—For I'se still goin' honey, I'se still climbin', And life for me ain't been no crystal stair." The Langston Hughes website acknowledges this social work honor.

For me personally the promises of a Penn degree have been deeply internalized, and I am profoundly grateful for all that I received and all that I learned. As Mrs. Downes explained, it is often necessary in life to Will one's tears into strength and determination. During my year at the Society to Protect Children on occasion it was necessary to go to court to request that a child be removed from an abusive home. The children we were trying to protect did not have an attorney. They had me and other social workers, but, despite our deep resolve to protect them, we could not. There was not a time when an abusive or neglectful parent appeared with counsel that the judge did not rule in favor of the parent, often sending the child home to die. And so I worked with others to change this law, and now neglected and abused children have their own attorneys to protect them. In similar manner I worked with many to reform Pennsylvania's antiquated and dehumanizing divorce laws, and columns that I wrote for the *Philadelphia Inquirer* during my years as a single parent were used toward this effort.

After my life stabilized, I began a twenty-year quest to determine, since most parents love their children the best way they know how, what impedes the development of dignity. I realized it was emotional abuse, an invisible and virulent malignancy that passes from generation to generation, always present in physical and sexual violence, but existing independently. I was able to codify five cycles of abuse: rage, rejection/abandonment, enmeshment, extreme neglect, and extreme overprotection and overindulgence, and these efforts have been published in article form and it a book entitled, *Setting YourSelf Free*. During this effort and now, my deepest hope is that identification of these cycles can be used in preventive ways, those geared toward early identification of potential problems and appropriate intervention and coordination of professional efforts. The confidence and spirit to persist in this and related work would never have happened without The Penn School, and I am ever grateful.

Notes

1. Julia Bishop was Dean Margaret Bishop's sister. There were many highly regarded sister teams devoted to the Penn School and social work community, including Jean and Isabelle Goddard, Dorthea and Mildred Hankins, and Ruth and Florence Silverblatt. The lives and work of each of these women and many more I was privileged to know merit study and discussion.

2. It is important to identify others I was privileged to work closely with at this extraordinary protective service agency: supervisor Bettie Bassett Roundtree, case workers Harriet Mishkin and Linda Maybon, head of the clerical staff Betty Slavin, record room director Margaret Harvey, and her second in command, Barbara Rabinowitz. The help all colleagues and supervisors at PSPC contributed to my required research project and thesis was invaluable.

3. These papers and related material noted are now with the archives of the University of Pennsylvania.

Commentary

SaraKay Smullens

Through the years I have continually reviewed the notes of the clients I've worked with to see why some people could learn to relate to others personally and professionally, many with relative ease, as well as withstand life's disappointments and injustices—and even grow in facing them—while others could not. My findings continuously confirm what I learned at Penn: the clients who succeeded best in love and work and who felt whole and autonomous had separated from their past sufficiently enough to move on toward mature creativity. For it is individuation that allows mature, creative, and responsible love and work possible. My challenge has been to work effectively with those who had not achieved such gifts. My challenge, through the years, has been to be there for them, in the same ways my Penn professors had been there for me, to use the therapeutic relationship to enable them to stop being immobilized by past terrors, and to help them to face reality, and see themselves as lovable and competent and capable. Through this process they are able to mobilize the positive resources in both their internal and external world. It has been the deepest of privileges to be present as my clients become more resilient, their visions growing in clarity, and their choices leading to enrichment, rather than depletion. It has been the most privileged of gifts to bear witness as clients see themselves in new ways and gain the strength to face and endure the loss of endings in order for there to be new beginnings.

It was at The Penn School of Social Work that I received the gifts that made it possible to begin this process for myself. Such gifts were far beyond professional. They gave me the foundation to journey toward adulthood. They gave me professional tools I would need to care for my daughters and myself during a long and protracted divorce process. They gave me ethical and philosophical guidelines that are the foundation of my work and my life.

The University of Pennsylvania School of Social Work degree required a promise to care about others, and treat them honorably, and to work for the disadvantaged and vulnerable, a promise that I have tried to keep and to pass on to my four children. You can imagine the joy and honor I experienced in May, 1995 when, as a graduate and an overseer of my cherished alma mater, I marched in the processional of my daughter Elisabeth's graduation from our Penn School. And then, to our surprise and amazement, in the same setting where my MSW was given, I was called upon to give my first born, now a glowing and beautiful young woman, the same degree that had been conferred on me thirty years before.

Chapter 16
Jessie Taft and the Functional School: The Impact of Our History

Rich Furman

The functional movement was one of the most influential approaches to social work practice during the first half of this century. Proponents of the functional movement rejected the deterministic Freudian concept that one's personality is essentially established by events in early childhood. The functional school stressed the capacity of people to make changes and grow. The functionalists developed time-limited, stage-based treatment strategies, many of which continue to influence practice today.

Many of the values, ideas, and concepts that are taken for granted as "givens" within social work in North America and Europe, were revolutionary and controversial developments of the functional school of social work (Yelaja 1986). The purpose of this article is to discuss the nature of Jessie Taft's theoretical orientation toward the practice of social work. It will consider historical and epistemological roots of the development of her thinking. In addition, it will place Taft's ideas in the context of contemporary theories of social work and human behavior. Taft's ideas and those of the other functionalists have had considerable influence on social work in Canada and many other countries.

Taft and the Development of a New Paradigm

Jessie Taft, a professor at the School of Social Work at the University of Pennsylvania, was originally trained in, and a proponent of, the diagnostic school of social work (the dominant theoretical orientation of the time). Several key developments led Taft to depart from the Freudian-influenced diagnostic school.

Taft (1958) noted that perhaps her most formative association was with Otto Rank, who was a member of Freud's inner circle of psychoanalysts. In 1927, Taft underwent daily analysis with Rank for 12 weeks, and became his long-time colleague and student. Through this experience she began to see the shortcomings in her own professional practice. In her own analysis, she began to realize that her behavior and emotions were not determined by her past as she had previously believed (Taft 1939). This experience was personally and professionally liberating for Taft, whose very conception of the human condition began to change.

Three central themes in Taft's thinking have their origins in Rankian thought: the importance of client resistance and will; the fact that each client will accept help in his or her own individual way; and the centrality of the helping relationship as a vehicle for change. Through her therapy with Rank, Taft was able to experience the importance of a warm and empathic worker, as opposed to the distant ambiguous posture of the traditional analyst. Rank's focus on the therapeutic relationship as the central vehicle for change was to become an integral component of Taft's writings. Taft's notion of the centrality of the helping relationship in the process of social work is a central feature of most social work theory (Biestek 1957; Payne 1991). Taft frequently noted that human growth only happens in a social context, in relationship to another. While today we take for granted the importance of an empathic and supportive working relationship, this was truly a radical departure from earlier and contemporaneous theories.

Rank's conception of the will greatly influenced Taft's views regarding human nature. Taft (1962) discussed her view of resistance and will eloquently during a 1947 speech given to school counselors. She noted that resistance can be viewed as a healthy expression of an individual's will; their desire to preserve their individuality. To Taft, one of the essential initial goals of therapy was to help clients to direct their will toward the task of change—toward the function of the helping relationships, whether it be the provision of concrete services, therapy, or some other social work service. The will was conceptualized as the part of the self that is both self-protective and self-corrective. The will, if directed toward the work of change, may help people overcome many difficulties and barriers.

The view of people as powerless products of their past, their biology, or their unconscious was replaced by the conception of people as actors in their own futures and fates. Taft eschewed the diagnostic school's pessimistic view of people as being merely capable of adaptation. She saw human beings as being capable of change, growth, and even transformation. Indeed, the very cornerstone of Taft's theory rests upon the premise that within each person exists an impulse toward better self-organization (Yelaja 1986). Rankian psychology and Taft's developing functional school of social work moved from a psychology of illness to a social work of human potential.

Additionally, Taft posited that healthy expressions of will may greatly vary. Clients are to be seen as individuals with various potential options, many of which represent healthy and pro-social behavior. This acceptance of individual differences was an important development in social work theory. Further, Taft understood that clients will accept services each in his or her own manner, as a natural expression of their own individuality. These ideas are the intellectual forerunners of various theories of social work practice, including humanistic, existential, generalist, and culturally sensitive approaches.

Another major influence on the development of Taft's theoretical orientation was a paradigm shift in epistemology, According to Goldstein (1990), social work has traveled down two distinct epistemological tracks: the positivist and the humanistic. The work of Taft, along with that of other functionalist thinkers and practitioners, is firmly rooted in the humanistic tradition. The positivist tradition's hegemony, with its heavy emphasis on determinism for both the physical and psychological world, had begun to yield to another view of knowledge

To Taft, the positivist tradition was not a suitable model for the investigation of the human spirit. She felt the positivist research tradition could not possibly measure the most important ingredient in the success of an intervention: the strength and perseverance of the human will. To Taft (1933), it is the intensely personal, highly individualized and conscious quality of emotions that makes it so unprofitable a field for traditional scientific research and has driven its investigators to psychological interpretations and purely behaviorist descriptions that miss the essence of a human being.

To Taft, the model of the scientist who sought to quantify and classify emotions, and that of the mental hygienist (social worker, psychiatrist, etc.) who sought to alter and change emotions, both stemmed from a fear of emotions; a fear of their inherent mystery and their power.

A New Place for Emotion

The acceptance and tolerance of emotions was the central component to her theory of mental health and human potential. According to Taft, emotions were to be accepted and experienced, not changed or blunted. She referred to this as a great "burden of responsibility"; a mandate that people be responsible for the experience and containment of their feelings. In Taft's conception of maturity and health, the highly functioning individual is able to tolerate a high degree of emotion without the need to "act them out." Ideally, emotions are to be tolerated and processed through our consciousness prior to any action. Acting out behaviors occur when we are not capable of or do not allow, our emotions to be experienced.

Taft developed several other principles pertaining to emotions and emotional life. First she posited that there is no such thing as good or bad emotions. Emotions are good or bad to the degree to which an individual can accept them. Secondly, she defined emotional superiority as the ability to be extra-sensitive, expressive, and spontaneous in the expression of emotion, as well as tolerant of the emotions of oneself and others.

Taft's conception of emotions can be seen as straddling the border of two views of emotions that have been competing throughout the millennium. The first view is that emotions exist in and of themselves, independent of thought. The second view is that emotions stem from cognitions: thoughts, beliefs, and patterns of thinking. These two views have been long debated by philosophers and others concerned with human change. This debate is deeply concerned with the centrality, importance and independence of emotion in the psychological makeup of the person.

In some ways Taft bridges the gap between these two orientations through her recognition that emotions are indices of values. That is, what one believes to be important will be the subject of emotions.

While Taft's conception of human nature has held up well over time, some research would suggest that her theories of emotion are not entirely valid. Research on depression shows that merely accepting one's feelings does not always lead to health (Beck 1976). The acceptance of feelings of worthlessness, hopelessness and apathy, characteristics of depression, will not lead to an abatement of the disorder. Secondly, this and other researches have also demonstrated the central role of cognition in the development of emotions. The core premise of cognitively based theories (Bandura 1977; Ellis 1958) is that cognition (thoughts, beliefs, and values) is the most immediate and direct cause of affective states (i.e., depression and anxiety). This view of emotion is consistent with humanistic and existential approaches to social work practice (Krill 1986; Payne 1991). Arguing from Taft's perspective, it could be said that such research does not enable us to understand the depth and nature of human emotion. Therefore, any findings they present will be of questionable validity. This position has more recently been supported by others (Holland and Kilpatrick 1991).

Taft's Contribution to Social Work Values

Taft has been instrumental in the formulation of enduring social work values, which are widely shared within the profession internationally (Reamer 1994). Taft wrote frequently of the need to respect clients' right to self-determination, the dignity and worth of each individual, and the inherent goodness of man/womankind.

Social workers throughout the world today take as givens many of these values that have their roots in the functional school. However, these values did not prevail during the first half of the century. When Rank developed his conception of will—the notion that the client's own internal resources, conscious desire and ability to work for change was essential for growth—he was shunned by his peers (Rank 1945). While freedom of choice and self-determination are clearly not constructs created by Taft and the other functionalist of the day, they were instrumental in helping these values become enduring features of social work.

The Functional Movement and Contemporary Social Work Theory

While the direct relationship between the functional school and contemporary social work theory is unclear, many leaders in social work education have been trained at the University of Pennsylvania's School of Social Work—a bastion of the functional approach for over half a century (Sheafor, Horejsi, and Horejsi 1997). The social work pioneers who trained in and developed the functional model, such as Kenneth Pray (1949), Virginia Robinson (1949), and Ruth Smalley (1967), have influenced the thinking of countless social work scholars and practitioners. Further, as previously stated, many ideas of the functional school have become core principles of generalist social work practice and theory. Smalley (1967) delineated the core principles of the functionalist approach, most of which have become core principles of generalist and generic social work practice, in her classic text *Theory for Social Work Practice*. The cores of these principles are

1. assessment (diagnosis) should be related to the use of services;
2. treatment should make conscious use of time and phases of treatment as thera-peutic tools;
3. the function of the agency should serve as a guide to the helping process;
4. the structure of the agency should guide the helping relationship between worker and client; and
5. the helping relationship between worker and client, one that respects the deci-sion-making capacity and rights of clients, is essential.

The strengths perspective also shares many key principles with the functional move-ment. The functionalist notion of strengthening a client's will is analogous co Maluc-cio's (1981) emphasis on recognizing and building competence. Weick (1992) noted that two of the most essential principles of the strengths perspective are the inherent power that lies within each individual, and the ability of people to use this power to transform their lives. These two principles are evident throughout the work of Taft (1933, 1939, 1958, 1962).

Closing

In closing, it is lamentable that the work of Jessie Taft is not more widely studied in social work programs. Her insight, clarity, humanity, and theory have had a significant impact on the profession. Reading the works of early social work pioneers gives one an appreciation not only for the development of social work practice and theory, but also for their courage and willingness to change for the betterment of clients. The functionalists would argue that this courage—a sign of healthy and active will—is indeed a necessary component of each of us.

Reprinted from Rich Furman, Jesse Taft and the functional school: The impact of our history, *Canadian Social Work* 4 (2002). Reprinted by permission.

References

Bandura, A. (1977). *Social Learning Theory. Englewood Cliffs, N.J.: Prentice-Hall.*
Beck, A. T. (1976). *Cognitive Therapy and the Emotional Disorders.* New York: Grune and Stratton.
Biestek, F. P. (1957). *The Casework Relationship.* Chicago: Loyola University Press.
Ellis, A. (1991). *Rational-Emotive Therapy with Alcoholics and Substance Abusers.* New York: Oxford University Press.
——— (1958). Rational psychotherapy. *Journal of General Psychology* 59: 37–47.
Goldstein, H. (1990). The knowledge base of social work practice: Theory, wisdom, analogue, or art? *Families in Society: The Journal of Contemporary Human Services* (Winter): 31–42.
Holland, T. P. and A. C. Kilpatrick (1991). Ethical issues in social work: Toward a grounded theory of professional ethics. *Social Work* 36 (2): 138–44.
Krill, D. F. (1986). Existential social work practice. In Francis J. Turner, ed., *Social Work Treat-ment: Interlocking Theoretical Approaches,* 181–217. New York: Free Press.
Levy, C. S. (1973). The value base of social work. *Journal of Education for Social Work* (Winter): 34–42.

Maluccio, A. N. (1981). *Promoting Competence in Clients: A New/Old Approach to Social Work Practice.* New York: Free Press.

Payne, M. (1991), *Modern Social Work Theory: A Critical Introduction.* Chicago: Lyceum.

Pray, K. L. M. (1949). *Social Work in a Revolutionary Age and Other Papers.* Philadelphia: University of Pennsylvania Press.

Rank, O. (1945). *Will Therapy and Truth and Reality.* Trans. Jessie Taft. New York: Knopf.

Reamer, F. G. (1994). The evolution of social work knowledge. In Frederick G. Reamer, ed., *The Foundations of Social Work Knowledge.* New York: Columbia University Press.

Robinson, V. P. (1949). *The Dynamics of Supervision Under Functional Controls.* Philadelphia: University of Pennsylvania Press.

Sheafor, B. W., C. R. Horejsi, and G. A. Horejsi (1997). *Techniques and Guidelines for Social Work Practice.* 5th ed. Boston: Allyn and Bacon.

Smalley, R. E. (1967). *Theory for Social Work Practice.* New York: Columbia University Press.

Taft, J. (1933). Living and feeling. *Child Study* (January): 105–9.

——— (1939). A conception of the growth process underlining social casework practice *Social Casework* (October): 72–80.

——— (1958). *Otto Rank.* New York: Julian Press.

——— (1962). The forces that make for therapy. In V. P. Robinson, ed., *Jessie Taft: Therapist and Social Work Educator,* 178–90. Philadelphia: University of Pennsylvania Press.

Weick, A. (1992). Building a strengths perspective for social work. In D. Saleebey, ed., *The Strengths Perspective in Social Work Practice,* 18–26. New York: Longman.

Yelaja, S. A. (1986). Functional theory for social work practice. In F. J. Turner, ed., *Social Work Treatment: Interlocking Theoretical Approaches,* 46–67. New York: Free Press.

Commentary

Rich Furman

The work of Jessie Taft is perhaps more important today than it has been at any time in the history of social work education. At its core, social work is a profession rooted in humanistic, progressive values. Social work is not a profession that stays mired in "what is"; the mission of social work is social change, and individual and group transformation. Social work has long been, or perhaps *was*, the profession that sought to transform human suffering and pain into human strength and transcendence. Social work is the profession in American society that has historically championed the poor, and has dared to dream of a society in which the "isms" would be a near forgotten historical footnote.

Yet, this is not the social work we find at the beginning of the twenty-first century. Today, social work and social work education has become dominated by amoral (not to be confused with immoral) positivists who seek to be efficient technologists for human change. Advocates of evidence-based practice argue for the training of practitioners who follow clearly indicated treatment protocols, the efficacy of which has been verified through large-sample, controlled, experimental designs. To proponents of evidence-based practice, the self-reported experiences of clients are "anecdotal" and are of less value than "empirically" derived data. While few would argue with the need for quality research that tests the efficacy of the methods of the profession, something about this formulation for practice rings hollow. Should social workers seek only to find the most efficacious means of ameliorating a given symptom? Should methods that meet specified outcome measures be privileged over helping clients build more satisfying and meaningful communities? Imagine a situation where a client is helped to ameliorate the most difficult symptoms of his or her depression, but continues to toil in a job that destroys his or her body, provides no meaning, and will ultimately lead to a future reoccurrence of depression. Should this be counted as a success?

What these formulations are missing is that social work has always been predicated as much on art as it has on science, and that social work is a profession guided by values of a more just and equal society. It is for this reason that the work of Jessie Taft and the other functionalists remain important and vital. Their insights ring as true today as they ever have. The work of Jessie Taft and the other functionalists was values-based work. It was work of the heart, and from the heart. It valued the strength of each individual, and the capacity of the individual to not merely reduce his or her symptoms, but to transcend their historical and socialized impediments. Through her development of Rank's conception of "will," Taft foreshadowed notions of strength-based and empowerment-oriented practice. Her work with individuals and small systems cherished and valued the inherent worth of the individual; she believed fully in human beings' capacity to actualize the best of humanity through their attending to and valuing what they discover about themselves.

Taft was perhaps the first social work theorist/practitioner to truly understand the importance of the helping relationship. Through establishing supportive, engaging, and at times even challenging helping relationships, clients are able to begin to take responsibility for their own lives. It is through the relationship that clients come to change themselves, and change their worlds. Throughout her career, Taft herself engaged in self-reflection, self-analysis, and personal growth. She was a reflective practitioner who recognized the necessity that social workers' most important tool was "the self": a self that must be nurtured, cherished, developed, and challenged.

One of this author's greatest concerns about the evidence-based practice movement is its preoccupation with testing *methods* of practice and neglecting the primary *tool* of practice: the individual social worker. Knowledge has begun to triumph values; and not just any knowledge, but knowledge based on scientific inquiry. Knowledge about the self and knowledge acquired from intuition or social or spiritual insights are devalued. Social work is becoming a modern, technocratic profession. It is unknown what the long-term consequences of reliance on a scientific paradigm will be. Yet, during our experiment with technocratic efficiency, it will be essential for educators and practitioners to remember the social change, humanistic, value-based roots of Jessie Taft and the functionalists. The Penn School of Social Work, throughout its long history, has been a champion of these values; it my hope that during the next hundred years it continues to do so.

Part IV
Representives of the DSW Program

Chapter 17
An Integrative, Intersystemic Approach to Supervision of Couple Therapy

Stephen J. Betchen

In the 1980s, a plethora of supervision models appeared in the marriage and family therapy literature, most of these based primarily on the major models of marriage and family therapy. Intergenerational supervision models (Beck 1984; Braverman 1984; Keller and Protinsky 1984; Munson 1984; Protinsky and Keller 1986) were influenced primarily by the work of Bowen (1978) and Framo (1976); symbolic-experiential models (Connel 1984; Connell and Russel 1986) were influenced by Whitaker and Keith (1981); and structural/strategic models (Nevels and Maar 1985; Pearson 1987) were influenced by Minuchin and Fishman (1981), Haley (1976), and Madanes (1981).

Lebow (1984) extolled the virtues of an integrative model of supervision. He contended that 1) they arm trainees with a wider array of avenues from which to pursue change in their clients; 2) they more easily enable trainees to match intervention strategies with their own individual personalities, resulting in a better practitioner/practice fit; 3) they expose the trainee to many different models of therapy and, thus, increase the ability of the trainee to better communicate with therapists of different theoretical orientations; 4) they encourage a more open attitude about the existing methods of treatment; and 5) they encourage the formation of a more flexible and knowledgeable therapist.

Despite these benefits, however, relatively few integrative models of marriage and family therapy supervision were presented, and those that were seemed to be primarily family therapy oriented (Duhl 1986; Duncan and Fraser 1987; Keller and Protinsky 1984; Lebow 1984) rather than marital or couple therapy oriented.

The purposes of this paper are to present an integrative, intersystemic model of supervision for treating couples and to demonstrate its effectiveness. Detailed supervision of a trainee will be presented for the preceding purposes.

Supervision Model

The model of supervision proposed in this paper is based primarily on the Marriage Council of Philadelphia's integrative approach to the treatment of couples, the Intersystem Model (Weeks 1989). The Intersystem Model integrates various individual, interaction and intergenerational therapies into one treatment approach. The individual perspective helps to explain personality style, which affects how individuals relate to others; the interactional perspective, in part, takes into account how intimacy, feelings, and communication are dealt with; and the interactional perspective allows the therapist to examine or explore the extent to which each partner's family-of-origin may be influencing their current relationship (Hof and Treat 1989). In essence, the Intersystem Model looks to alleviate problems in couples by examining each partner on individual and intergenerational level and holding them responsible for what they bring to their interactional process. When this model of therapy is employed as a supervisory model, a major emphasis upon object relations theory on the intergenerational level (Fairbairn 1952) has been included.

Just as the Marriage Council's model holds each partner responsible for what each brings to the dyadic or couple interactional process, this supervisory model calls for both supervisor and trainee to accept similar responsibility, as though they were a "couple." More specifically, it is expected that both supervisor and trainee will be prepared to examine themselves on an individual and, if need be, an intergenerational level in an effort to better facilitate their supervisory interaction. It is also expected that the supervisor-trainee "couple" accept responsibility for and attempt to remedy any negative influences their interactional process may be having on the trainee's client couple via isomorphic process. Isomorphism occurs when interactions between the trainee and clients resemble those in the trainee's supervisory relationship and vice versa. Although it is similar in definition to "parallel process," this author prefers the term "isomorphism" because, aside from its descriptive nature, it infers the ability of the supervisor to intervene and bring about appropriate change in dysfunctional interactional patterns (Liddle 1988; Liddle and Schwartz 1983).

When first engaging trainees in the supervisory process, the primary focus of the supervisor should be on joining with them (Minuchin and Fishman 1981) and setting the structure for the supervisory process (Hess 1986). Setting the structure includes discussing trainee-supervisor expectations. The trainee is asked to make as clear as possible what he or she desires to change, learn, or improve upon (Kaslow 1986), while the supervisor is to address his or her expectations regarding appointment times, fees, record keeping, case presentation, and videotaping (Piercy and Sprenkle 1986). Both supervisor and trainee enter into an unwritten contract to work toward change and growth.

Following the initial contract phase, the focus is turned to examining the relationship between the supervisor and trainee on the three levels previously mentioned (i.e., individual, interactional, intergenerational). In terms of the individual level, knowledge of adult personality development theory (Berman and Lief 1975), personality style (Shapiro 1965), and psychopathology (American Psychiatric Association 1994) is important because it provides the supervisor with an idea as to how the trainee relates to others and what resistances may lie ahead. For example, in terms of personality style, if the supervisor is able to recognize that he or she has obsessive-compulsive tendencies or traits while the trainee exhibits passive-aggressive tendencies or traits, perhaps both supervisor and trainee can adjust the supervision process appropriately, rather than spend valuable time in conflict with one another.

Liddle and Schwartz (1983) write, "Trainees at different development/skill levels need to be treated differently" (485). Accurately assessing trainee development is particularly vital in terms of knowing where to begin supervision and what to expect realistically from trainees regarding their knowledge base, level of maturity, and degree of skill. Specifically in terms of trainee development, Stoltenberg and Delworth (1987) report three levels. Level 1 trainees are least experienced and although highly motivated to learn, have a strong tendency to rely on their supervisor for guidance and structure. Level 2 trainees are less dependent, but can be more resistant to supervisory suggestions. Level 3 trainees, the most advanced, have increased client and self-awareness, tend to be less resistant yet more independent and confident, and are able to diagnose more accurately and follow through with an appropriate treatment plan. Stoltenberg and Delworth also apply their three-tier developmental approach to supervisors. In tune with their model, it is suggested here that each supervisor recognize his or her own level of development and how it interacts with the trainee's level. For example, Stoltenberg and Delworth contend that Level 1 supervisors generally have a great deal of difficulty in dealing with the conflict and confusion of a Level 2 trainee, but would fit better with a Level 1 trainee, particularly if the supervisors are experienced therapists.

Lastly, at the individual level, just as it is deemed important to take into account the client couple's race (Hunt 1987), sex (Gilligan 1982), sexual orientation (Carl 1990), socioeconomic status (Aponte 1976), and ethnic background (McGoldrick et al. 1982), the same consideration is merited within the supervisor-trainee relationship.

In terms of supervising trainees on the interactional level, careful attention is paid to the following: 1) verbal and nonverbal communication cues, skills, and style differences (Gottman et al. 1976); 2) hierarchies, boundaries, and levels of enmeshment or disengagement (Minuchin and Fishman 1981); 3) power and control struggles (Goldberg 1987); and 4) specific relationship combinations such as "rejecter-intruder" (Napier 1978) or "pursuer-distancer" (Fogarty 1976), or those outlined by Sager (1976) such as the "childlike-childlike" or "parental-childlike" relationship. Given the isomorphic process that exists between the supervisor and trainee as a couple, and the trainee and the client couple, any of the aforementioned issues not adequately dealt with by the supervisor will most likely not be dealt with at the trainee-client level. For example, in terms of communication, if a supervisor fails to confront a trainee about something he or she is doing that is not helpful, it is likely that trainee will not learn to confront clients directly and, thus, will not do so when it is appropriate.

Toman (1976) wrote that the family exerts greater influence on a person's life than any other social environment. In tune with this philosophy, it is believed that the intergenerational level underlies both individual and interactional levels. That is, clients, trainees, and supervisors, and the way they interact with each other and in relationships in general are influenced by their families-of-origin. With the use of the genogram (Bowen 1978; McGoldrick and Gerson 1985), client couples and trainees are aided by examining their families-of-origin from both a Bowenian (1978) and contextual (Boszormenyi-Nagy and Spark 1973) perspective. The objective is to uncover any triangles, patterns, and unbalanced ledgers that may be responsible for replicating current unproductive or dysfunctional, individual or interactional behavior in clients and trainees alike. Bowen (1978) refers to this process as an attempt to achieve a greater level of "differentiation" from one's family-of-origin.

Also on the intergenerational level, object relations theory (Fairbairn 1952), particularly the concept of projective identification (Klein 1946); it has been applied to marital and couple therapy (Dicks 1967; Scharff and Scharff 1991), is utilized in this supervisory model. In Klein's concept of projective identification, Dicks saw the specific process by which lost aspects of one's primary object relations could be projected onto a spouse or mate. Perhaps more clearly stated, Scharff and Scharff (1991) define projective identification as "the process through which a person projects a disclaimed part of the self into the other, and the other person unconsciously takes it in and feels like that projected part through introjective identification and then behaves in such a way as to confirm it or, in more mature states, to modify it" (8). In tune with Framo (1970), the specific focus here is on the identification and eradication of troublesome supervisor and trainee projections onto one another, and the return of these projections to what is believed to be the original source of their conflict—each participant's family-of-origin.

In supervising trainees, as opposed to treating clients, this author advises strict boundaries for exploring their families-of-origin (Beck 1984; Braverman 1984; Munson 1984). Each trainee is requested to prepare and have their own genogram ready for exploration; however, it is only utilized if it becomes clear that something is consistently blocking their present work. If this is the situation, it is vital that an exploration—which is clear and closely linked to problematic case material (Braverman 1984)—take place for the good of both trainee and client. The exploration should exclude the trainee's family-of-procreation and also be time limited so that it does not shift into psychotherapy (Braverman 1984). However, if family-of-origin supervision does not help to improve the trainee's performance or overcome troubling resistances (Protinsky and Keller 1984), personal psychotherapy would most likely be recommended.

Just as it is believed that trainees need to "know themselves" in order to more effectively treat their clients, it is also believed that supervisors need to be aware of the impact their families-of-origin have laid upon them and how it reflects on their supervisory work (Munson, 1984). Although it is not always necessary to share this information directly with trainees, this author believes that at times it is needed because it can serve to highlight a specific isomorphic process, model "use of self" (Baldwin and Satir 1987), and help to create a trusting and warm environment in which the trainee can grow (Luecke 1987).

Supervision Case

A female trainee was supervised at the Marriage Council of Philadelphia over approximately a two-year period. Supervision consisted of weekly two-hour, one-on-one sessions. The trainee was beginning the second year of a three-year training program at the Marriage Council. At the time, this author was a first-year supervisor who was receiving supervision-of-supervision training at the Marriage Council.

In tune with this paper's philosophy of supervision, the focus in the first supervisory session with this trainee was on joining with her (Minuchin and Fishman 1981), and setting the structure for the supervisory process (Hess 1986). This was accomplished by facilitating clarification as to what our expectations were of each other and, in a sense, establishing a supervisory contract (Kaslow 1986). Specifically, it was requested that the trainee prepare and be ready to present her own genogram if need be, keep coherent session-by-session notes on each client seen or contacted in any way, keep client files and records updated and present client genograms, case review records, and a videotape of the client(s) to be discussed. Issues related to setting fees, trainee evaluations, client confidentiality, emergencies, referrals, and consultation were also discussed and agreed upon. It was made clear to the trainee that she could call on the supervisor at anytime to discuss any case-related difficulty. The trainee requested that she learn more about psychodynamic family-of-origin work and be better able to apply the theory to her practice. She asked that the supervisory process include a didactic component (Beck 1984) as well as an experiential one.

After the contract with the trainee, the focus was shifted to examining the supervisory process on the three levels previously mentioned (individual, interactional, intergenerational). In terms of the individual level, she appeared primarily to be a Level 1 trainee (Stoltenberg and Delworth 1987). That is, she was very motivated to learn, but was far too dependent on the supervisor for guidance. At times, her work with clients seemed directionless, as if she lacked a sufficient framework from which to start. Much of this had to do with her admitted difficulty connecting theory to practice. In terms of her personality style, the trainee exhibited obsessive-impulsive tendencies that were considered positive because they matched up well with those of the supervisors. However, for someone at her level of personal and professional development, the trainee showed an overall lack of "personal power." Specifically, she demonstrated problems with confrontation, caring for the self, and general limit setting.

On the interactional level, the trainee looked for the supervisor to play the "engaged, caring, nurturing father" role. At times she tried to provoke anger and later admitted that she was trying to "get a reaction from the supervisor," or, in a sense, engage him. She also had a tendency to overreact to constructive criticism, as if she were being persecuted by an admired loved one. Regarding the latter point, the trainee would to vacillate between playing "the victim" (e.g., crying) and showing anger and outrage toward the supervisor. This type of interaction reflected in her work in that her videotapes showed that she had difficulty confronting male clients. More specifically, she repeatedly allowed the men to disengage (Minuchin and Fishman 1981) and avoid taking responsibility for their distancing behavior; simultaneously, she allowed the females to complain endlessly or portray themselves as victims, as opposed to helping them "own their own power." Initially, nearly all of her couples sessions were unbalanced in this way, and very little therapeutic movement took place. When compelled to intervene, the trainee would do so by joining with the female client to pursue the male client, who in turn would become angry and distance himself from both of them (Fogarty 1976).

Because of the chronicity of the above problem, both supervisor and trainee agreed to examine the trainee's family-of-origin. The trainee's genogram revealed that she was the youngest of five children (two brothers, two sisters) from a traditional family (her father was a physician and her mother was a housewife) in which men were encouraged to become professionals and succeed, while women were to be subservient and nurturing to men. Much of this was cultural in that the trainee's parents were Italian (Rotunno and McGoldrick 1982).

The trainee described her father as a very brilliant but distant or disengaged man who immersed himself in his work. She reported that he had an emotionally distant relationship with his wife and children, and that she would often try and accommodate him in any way she could in order to have more of a relationship with him. The trainee characterized her mother as a lonely, overworked "victim" who had long since given up trying to pursue her distant husband. The trainee reported that she felt sorry for her mother, but admitted frustration with her for giving up on her husband.

After further exploration, both trainee and supervisor agreed that, because of her low level of differentiation she was replicating her family-of-origin in her work and in the supervisory process. She did so by allowing male clients to escape their wives or mates (as her father escaped his wife and family), while simultaneously overidentifying with the victimized, powerless women (as she did with her mother). When the trainee did intervene, her way of "empowering" the female was to join with her to pursue the male (as she did by accommodating her father).

In the supervisory process, the trainee provoked the supervisor to engage her (as she did with her father), but overreacted to his criticism as if it were coming from a disapproving father who might distance himself from her. In terms of object relations theory, the trainee was projecting the disclaimed "rejecter" (Napier 1978) or "distancer" (Fogarty 1976) in herself onto the supervisor/father. Initially, confused and frustrated by the trainee's behavior, this Level 1 supervisor (Stoltenberg and Delworth 1987) questioned himself in terms of whether he was engaged enough in the supervisory process and whether he was too hard on the trainee in terms of his criticisms of her work. In discussing this situation with his own supervisor of supervision, he learned that he wasn't being "tough enough." In aiding him in exploring his own family-of-origin, the supervisor of supervision pointed out that via introjective identification (Klein 1946; Scharff and Scharff 1991), he was unconsciously accepting the trainee's projected rejecter/distancer as well as replicating a pattern from his own past. That is, feeling sorry for his childlike mother, he often protected her from his father. However, it seemed he could never do enough for his mother, who consistently played the victim in her manipulative attempts to ensure that he would continue to serve as her protector. (Like the trainee, she would show anger when challenged in any way—it was as if the supervisor was being disloyal to her.) Therefore, he never learned to trust his own judgment in terms of how much he was supposed to help a woman whom he viewed, or who portrayed herself, as a victim. The supervisor of supervision helped the supervisor to see that his continuing protection of his mother (as a result of his lack of differentiation and need to disclaim the rejecter/distancer in himself) blocked him from challenging the trainee on her manipulative behavior and, in turn contributed to an isomorphic process that enabled the trainee to avoid challenging and giving appropriate responsibility for change to her clients.

Because the trainee contracted to learn family-of-origin work the supervisor decided to discuss the entire isomorphic process with her (including his own family-of-origin contribution). She presented little resistance and, in fact, thanked the supervisor for sharing himself with her (Baldwin and Satir 1987). She said it helped her to trust him (Luecke 1987) because he was being vulnerable and because he was accepting some responsibility for their process. From this point on, both supervisor and trainee "worked together" to point out deleterious replications both in supervision and in her work with clients. By the end of two years, the supervisory relationship was collegial, and the trainee's work was much more balanced and integrated. Specifically, she owned not only her projections but her power as well (no more victim). In turn, she was more confronting, set better limits, and was much more in tune with how the intergenerational level affects the individual and interactional levels. In essence, both trainee and supervisor had evolved to Level 3 trainee-supervisor. That is, both were more self- and other aware, more objective, able to retain more responsibility for decisions, and able to function independently (Stoltenberg and Delworth 1987). By termination, the terms of the initial supervisory contract were met.

Discussion

Although numerous supervision models (Beck 1984; Braverman 1984; Connell 1984; Connell and: Russell 1986; Keller and Protinsky 1984; Munson 1984; Nevels and Maar 1985; Pearson 1987; Protinsky and Keller 1986) have been presented in the marriage and family therapy literature, few of these were truly integrative models. Duhl (1986), Duncan and Fraser (1987), Keller and Protinsky (1984), and Lebow (1984) offer integrative models, but they appear designed more specifically for family therapy supervision than for couple therapy supervision.

In tune with Lebow (1984), this author highly values the integrative approach to supervision. Perhaps its most valuable asset is that it provides the supervisor with a wider variety of techniques from which to supervise. True to the isomorphic process (Liddle 1988; Liddle and Schwartz 1983), the trainee would then be armed with a wider variety of interventions from which to effect change in his or her couples. With such a wide range of theory and technique to choose from, it is less likely that either supervisor or trainee will become stuck in any one place for too long. Also, neither be so easily tempted out of desperation or frustration to fit either trainee or client couple into the "one and only" model of supervision or therapy known. Just as it is taught that no individual is exactly the same as another, it is believed here that no one particular model of supervision will necessarily apply to every trainee, and, in return no one particular model of marital therapy will apply to every couple.

As the numerous models of supervision presented have been based primarily on the major models of marriage and family therapy (Bowen 1978; Framo 1976; Haley 1976; Madanes 1981; Minuchin and Fishman 1981; Whitacker and Keith 1981), the integrative model presented in this paper is based primarily on the integrative, Intersystem Model of couple therapy developed at the Marriage Council of Philadelphia (Weeks 1989). Specifically designed to treat couples, this model, which combines individual, interactional, and intergenerational therapies into one cohesive unit of treatment (Hof and Treat 1989), is best suited to supervise trainees wishing to learn couples work, in part because both supervisor and trainee form a "couple" of their own. It is also considered valuable in working with two trainees. In this case, armed with a couple's model of supervision, the supervisor can more easily sort out the dynamics that so often occur in the trainee "couple."

Integration and specialization notwithstanding, this model does have its limitations. First, because it has been designed more specifically for couple training, it would be less effective in providing supervision of family therapy and in supervising more than two trainees at a given time. The American Association for Marriage and Family Therapy Supervision Committee (1991) defines the latter as "group supervision." Second, because a strong component of this model is intergenerational, it is believed to be much more effective in longer (minimum of one year) rather than short-term supervision. It takes time and the development of a somewhat intimate relationship for both supervisor and trainee to feel comfortable exploring family-of-origin issues and for significant projections to begin to develop (Berman et al. 1981; Scharff and Scharff 1991).

Even with limitations such as these, however, it is hoped that others specializing in couple therapy and supervision will contribute to the literature in terms of integrative models designed specifically for couple supervision, rather than rely on more general or family therapy-based models of supervision. The model presented in this article is offered for consideration to supervisors who seek a couple-based model of supervision, in the hope that it will promote further discussion of the issues raised within.

Reprinted from Stephen J. Betchen, An integrative, intersystemic approach to supervision of couple therapy. *American Journal of Family Therapy* 23 (1995): 48–58. Reprinted by permission.

References

American Association for Marriage and Family Therapy Supervision Committee (1991). *The AAMFT Approved Supervisor Designation: Standards and Responsibilities*. Washington, D.C.: AAMFT.

American Psychiatric Association (1994). *Diagnostic and Statistical Manual of Mental disorders*. 4th ed. Washington, D.C.: APA.

Aponte, H. (1976). Underorganization in the poor family. In Philip J. Guerin, ed., *Family Therapy: Theory and Practice*, 432–48. New York: Gardner Press.

Baldwin, M., and V. Satir, eds. (1987). *The Use of Self in Therapy*. New York: Haworth Press.

Beck, R. (1984). The supervision of family of origin family systems treatment. In Carlton E. Munson, ed., *Family of Origin Applications in Clinical Supervision*, 49–60. New York: Haworth Press.

Berman, E., and H. Lief (1975). Marital therapy from a psychiatric perspective: An overview. *American Journal of Psychiatry* 132: 583–92.

Berman, E., H. Lief, and A. Williams (1981). A model of marital interaction. In G. P. Sholevar, ed., *The Handbook of Marriage and Marital Therapy*, 3–34. New York: Spectrum Medical and Scientific Books.

Boszormenyi-Nagy, I., and G. M. Spark (1973). *Invisible Loyalties: Reciprocity in Intergenerational Family Therapy*. New York: Harper and Row.

Bowen, Murray (1978). *Family Therapy in Clinical Practice.* New York: Jason Aronson.

Braverman, S. (1984). Family of origin as a training resource for family therapists. In C. E. Munson, ed., *Family of Origin Applications in Clinical Supervision,* 37–47. New York: Haworth Press.

Carl, D. (1990). *Counseling Same-Sex Couples.* New York: W.W. Norton.

Connell, G. M. (1984). An approach to supervision of symbolic-experiential psychotherapy. *Journal of Marital and Family Therapy* 10: 273–80.

Connell, G. M., and L. A. Russell (1986). In therapy consultation: A supervision and therapy technique of symbolic-experiential family therapy. *American Journal of Family Therapy* 14: 313–23.

Dicks, H. V. (1967). *Marital Tensions: Clinical Studies Towards a Theory of Psychological Interaction.* New York: Basic Books.

Duhl, B. (1986). Toward cognitive behavioral integration in training systems: therapists: An interactive approach to training in generic systems thinking. In Fred P. Piercy, ed., *Family Therapy Education and Supervision,* 91–108. New York: Haworth Press.

Duncan, B., and J. S. Fraser (1987). Buckley's scheme of schemes as a foundation for teaching family systems theory. *Journal of Marital and Family Therapy* 13: 299–305.

Fairbairn, W. R. D. (1952). *Psychoanalytic Studies of the Personality.* London: Tavistock.

Fogarty, T. (1976). Marital crisis. In Philip J. Guerin, ed., *Family Therapy: Theory and Practice,* 325–34. New York: Gardner Press.

Framo, J. (1970). Symptoms from a family transactional viewpoint. In Nathan W. Ackerman, ed., *Family Therapy in Transition,* 271–308. Boston: Little, Brown.

———— (1976). Family of origin as a therapeutic resource for adults in marital and family therapy: You can and should go home again. *Family Process* 15: 193–210.

Gilligan, C. (1982). *In a Different Voice: Psychological Theory and Women's Development.* Cambridge, Mass.: Harvard University Press.

Goldberg, M. (1987). *Keeping It Together: The Fine Art of Marital Survival.* Philadelphia: Marriage Council of Philadelphia.

Gottman, J., C.Notarius, J. Gonso, and H. Markman (1976). *A Couple's Guide to Communication.* Champaign, Ill.: Research Press.

Haley, J. (1976). *Problem Solving Therapy: New Strategies for Effective Family Therapy.* San Francisco: Jossey-Bass.

Hess, A. K. (1986). Growth in supervision: Stages of supervisee and supervisor development. In Fl. W. Kaslow, ed., *Supervision and Training: Models, Dilemmas, and Challenges,* 51–67. New York: Haworth Press.

Hof, L., and S. R. Treat (1989). Marital assessment: Providing a framework for dyadic therapy.In G. R. Weeks, ed., *Treating Couples: The Intersystem Model of the Marriage Council of Philadelphia,* 3–21. New York: Brunner/Mazel.

Hunt, P. (1987). Black clients: Implications for supervision of trainees. *Psychotherapy* 24: 114–19.

Kaslow, F. W. (1986). Seeking and providing supervision in private practice. In Florence W. Kaslow, ed., *Supervision and Training: Models, Dilemmas, and Challenges,* 143–58. New York: Haworth Press.

Keller, J. F., and H. O. Protinsky (1984). A self-management model for supervision. *Journal of Marital and Family Therapy* 10: 281–88.

————. (1984). Family therapy supervision: An integrative model. In Fred P. Piercy, ed., *Family Therapy Education and Supervision,* 83–90. New York: Haworth Press.

Klein, M. (1946). Notes on some schizoid mechanisms. *International Journal of Psycho-Analysis* 27: 99–110.

Lebow, J. (1984). On the value of integrating approaches to family therapy. *Journal of Marital and Family Therapy* 10: 121–38.

Liddle, H. A. (1988). Systemic supervision: Conceptual overlay and pragmatic guidelines. In Howard A. Liddle, Douglas C. Breunlin, and Richard C. Schwartz, eds., *Handbook of Family Therapy Training and Supervision,* 153–71. New York: Guilford Press.

Liddle, H. A., and Richard C. Schwartz (1983). Life supervision/consultation: Conceptual and pragmatic guidelines for family therapy trainers. *Family Process* 22: 477–90.

Luecke, D. (1987). Counseling with couples. In Barry K Estadt, John R. Compton, and Melvin C. Blanchette, eds., *The Art of Clinical Supervision: A Pastoral Counseling Perspective*, 136–39. New York: Paulist Press.

Madanes, C.. (1981). *Strategic Family Therapy*. San Francisco: Jossey-Bass.

McGoldrick, M., and R. Gerson (1985). *Genograms in Family Assessment*. New York: Norton.

McGoldrick, M., J. K. Pearce, and J. Giordano, eds. (1982). *Ethnicity and Family Therapy*. New York: Guilford Press.

Minuchin, Salvador, and H. Charles Fishman (1981). *Family Therapy Techniques*. Cambridge, Mass.: Harvard University Press.

Munson, C. E., ed. (1984). *Family of Origin Applications in Clinical Supervision*. New York: Haworth Press.

Napier, A. Y. (1978). The rejection-intrusion pattern: A central family dynamic. *Journal of Marriage and Family Counseling* 4: 5–12.

Nevels, R., and J. Maar (1985). A supervision for teaching structural /strategic therapy in a limited setting. *Journal of Psychology* 119: 347–53.

Pearson, D. (1987). The strategic family therapy ritual as a framework for supervision. *Journal of Strategic and Systemic Techniques* 4: 17–28.

Piercy, F. P., and D. Sprenkle (1986). *Family Therapy Sourcebook*. New York: Guilford Press.

Protinsky, H. O., and J. H. Keller (1984). Supervision of marriage and family therapy: A family of origin approach. In Carlton E. Munson, ed., *Family of Origin Implications in Clinical Supervision*, 75–80. New York: Haworth Press.

Rotunno, M., and M. McGoldrick (1982). Italian families. In Monica McGoldrick, John K. Pearce, and Joe Giordano, eds., *Ethnicity and Family Therapy*, 340–63. New York: Guilford Press.

Sager, C. J. (1976). *Marriage Contracts and Couple Therapy: Hidden Forces in Intimate Relationships*. New York: Brunner/Mazel.

Scharff, D. E., and J. S. Scharff (1991). *Object Relations Couple Therapy*. Northvale, N.J.: Jason Aronson.

Shapiro, D. (1965). *Neurotic Styles*. New York: Basic Books.

Stoltenberg, C. D., and U. Delworth (1987). *Supervising Counselors and Therapists: A Developmental Approach*. San Francisco: Jossey-Bass.

Toman, W. (1976). *Family Constellation: Its Effects on Personality and Social Behavior*. New York: Springer.

Weeks, G., ed. (1989). *Treating Couples: The Intersystem Model of the Marriage Council of Philadelphia*. New York: Brunner/Mazel.

Whitaker, C., and D. Keith (1981). Symbolic-experiential family therapy. In Alan S. Gurman and David P. Kniskern, eds., *Handbook of Family Therapy*, 187–225. New York: Brunner-Mazel.

Commentary

Stephen J. Betchen

Family Therapy and Social Work

The 1950s laid the context for a movement away from classical psychoanalysis and its focus on individual psychopathology to the concept of viewing the individual as an integral part of a highly influential, circular, familial system; hence the birth of the family therapy movement as we know it today. Given the movement's origins in working with chaotic families (and in the 1960s, the underclass) and the field of social work's focus on the "individual-in-the-environment," it was inevitable that many social workers would be drawn to family therapy and in fact, become some of its leaders; people such as Virginia Satir, Olga Silverstein, and later, Harry Aponte and Monica McGoldrick, to name a few.

Training and the Development of a Therapeutic Model

Having wanted to study marriage and family therapy from my early days as an undergraduate psychology major, the Penn School of Social Work seemed the appropriate place for me to continue to pursue this objective particularly given its proximity to the former Philadelphia Child Guidance Clinic and its renowned training program the Family Therapy Training Center, as well as the Marriage Council of Philadelphia (renamed the Council for Relationships). The Center focused primarily on family therapy training and treatment and boasted some of the biggest names in family therapy such as Salvador Minuchin, founder of the Center and the Structural Family Therapy model, and Jay Haley of Strategic Family Therapy fame. By contrast, The Marriage Council founded by social worker Emily Mudd, concentrated on couples' and sex therapy training and treatment, and by this time was led by well-respected couples' therapists Harold Lief and Ellen Berman.

Although a graduate student in the joint MSW/DSW program at Penn, I was unable to land a coveted field study at either of the aforementioned institutions. I did, however, secure the next best thing: a placement in my home state of New Jersey at the Drenk Memorial Guidance Center—called by some the "Philadelphia Child Guidance Clinic of New Jersey." It was referred to as such because many of its supervisors had studied at the Philadelphia Child Guidance Clinic under Minuchin and Haley and in turn, championed their models. Drenk also had a one-way-mirror—the hallmark of training and supervision of the Structural and Strategic Family Therapy models.

Following my one-year field study at Drenk, I was fortunate enough to remain there as a part-time employee for the next three years while I continued work on my doctorate. While I found the structural model to be of great value in working with indigent and less educated families, for whom it was originally developed (Minuchin, Montalvo, Guerney, Rosman, & Schumer 1967), the model was less effective for these and other clients who desired a deeper treatment. I never truly felt comfortable with what I perceived to be the more manipulative strategic model.

At Drenk I was also beginning to enjoy my work with couples. Albeit my experience with them was limited, couples seemed much more manageable than families, and I was intrigued by the potential depth and intellectual challenges of the treatment process. I soon came to fervently believe that unless the marriage was successful, family therapy held little value. Despite my emotional and intellectual curiosity, however, I never lost sight of the larger environmental context of the couple. In fact, during my graduate training I became attracted to Carel Germain's Life Model—an "ecological" approach to social work practice which advocated that social workers consider a client's physical and social environment in the treatment process (Germain and Gitterman 1980).

The Supervisory Model and Subsequent Article

With the major models of family therapy already in place by the 1980s (e.g., Bowenian, Contextual, Experiential, Strategic, and Structural), a plethora of supervisory approaches based on these models began to appear in the marriage and family therapy literature (Betchen 1995). I, at this time, was working as a full-time couples therapist for the Marriage Council of Philadelphia where all senior staff clinicians were required to become certified as Approved Supervisors of the American Association for Marriage and Family Therapy (AAMFT). It was during this supervisory training process that I noticed that there were few supervisory models suited to working specifically with couples. This realization, and the AAMFT requirement that supervisory candidates demonstrate their own personal models of supervision, compelled me to study the marriage and family therapy supervision literature and to create a model of supervision tailored for couples therapists.

The model I ultimately developed was significantly influenced by the training I received at the Marriage Council and reflective of their integrative, systemic approach to treatment. A model of this nature was in tune with the professional climate of the late 1980s and 1990s; it was during this time that systems therapists truly seemed to value integrational models of treatment as opposed to fitting all client-couples and families into one neat therapeutic package (Betchen, 1995). It was also a time when some of the leading systems therapists advocated more prominently for the integration of couples and sex therapy (Schnarch 1991; Weeks and Hof 1987).

It is with great pleasure that I submitted the aforementioned article to appear in this commemorative book for the Penn School of Social Work. It is not only an honor for me to be included in this project, but the inclusion of my article also honors the many individuals who have trained and supervised me over the years. It also pays homage to couples therapy and supervision, which are arguably the most challenging of all the psychotherapeutic and supervisory modalities, modalities toward which social workers will no doubt continue to show a natural inclination.

References

Betchen, S. (1995). An integrative, intersystemic approach to supervision of couple therapy. *American Journal of Family Therapy* 23: 48–58.

German, C., and A. Gitterman (1980). *The Life Model of Social Work Practice.* New York: Columbia University Press.

Minuchin, S., B. Montalvo, B. Guerney, B. Rosman, and F. Schumer (1967). *Families Of The Slums: An Exploration of Their Structure and Treatment.* New York: Basic Books.

Schnarch, D. (1991). *Constructing the Sexual Crucible: An Integration of Sexual and Marital Therapy.* New York: Norton.

Weeks, G., and L. Hof, eds. (1987). *Integrating sex and marital therapy: A clinical guide.* New York: Brunner/Mazel.

Chapter 18
Reflections upon University Retirement: With Thanks and Apologies to James Joyce

Gerald L. Euster

In recent years, the transitioning of college and university faculty into retirement has emerged as a topic of great concern, not only to faculty anticipating retirement, but for the institutions of higher education that they represent. College and university faculty are part of a significant demographic change in the United States during recent decades—the decline in labor force participation of older men (Quinn 2001). Even more remarkable, according to Quinn, is that "the era of earlier and earlier retirement seems to have come to an abrupt halt" (69). Clearly, many American workers do not completely withdraw from the labor force. Instead, retirement is best viewed as a "process" rather than single event. The retirement process of many older workers often includes a "bridge job" or, as described by Quinn, a period of "partial employment on the way out" (72).

For many older workers, significant policy initiatives have increased work and even new career options, altering the relative attractiveness of work and retirement. In our advancement toward an era of gradual retirement in America, negative stereotypes about older workers are slowly diminishing (Hillier and Barro 1999). Clearly, we are witnessing a period of phased retirement opportunities, expanded full-time and part-time work options, career development, and retraining initiatives aimed at older adults who possess a strong work ethic.

In the United States, the 1967 federal Age Discrimination in Employment Act (ADEA) (amended in both 1974 and 1978) set in motion the protection of individuals from age discrimination in hiring, discharge, compensation, and other aspects of employment (Schultz 2001). Still, by the 1970s, mandatory retirement had become nearly a universal event in the lives of faculty in colleges and universities (Ashenfelter and Card 2001). Despite a further amendment to the ADEA in 1986, prohibiting mandatory retirement of workers at any age, a special exemption permitted colleges and universities to enforce mandatory retirement of faculty at age 70. On January 1, 1994, following another amendment to the ADEA, American institutions of higher education ended (uncapped) age-based mandatory retirement for tenured professors, allowing them to work indefinitely if they wished (Lane 2003). In a paper delivered at the 2003 Annual Conference of the Association for Gerontology in Higher Education, Lane recognized two emerging themes in the area of faculty retirement research: (1) a focus on retirement as a social process and (2) the impact of the elimination of mandatory retirement on colleges and universities. In response to the uncapping of the mandatory retirement age, Lane concluded that further research would benefit higher education since many universities were witnessing a mass exodus of faculty.

A study of the effect of the elimination of mandatory retirement on faculty retirement patterns in the United States was conducted by Ashenfelter and Card (2001). Using administrative records of 16,000 older faculty members in 104 colleges and universities, their findings projected an increased number of older faculty who will remain employed in future years. Data from their Faculty Retirement Survey (FRS) suggested that about 40% of 60-year old faculty at private research universities would remain employed to age 70, while only 25% of 60-year old faculty at public research universities could be expected to remain until age 70. Faculty in social and physical sciences have significantly lower retirement rates than their counterparts in humanities, life sciences, and professional schools. Economic factors appear to impact on faculty retirement. Faculty are less likely to retire if they anticipate a higher salary; they are more likely to retire if they anticipate a greater pension income during retirement.

Factors Influencing Retirement Decisions

Retirement for older workers in our society represents a critical and, most often, voluntary life transition, impacting upon individuals and families in different ways. In reality, our previously held theory of retirement as a single life transition has evolved as many individuals make additional transitions to "unretirement."

A significant study by Dorfman (2002) focused on "stayers and leavers" in higher education following the lifting of mandatory retirement. Using a case study, interview method, the researcher examined the characteristics of, reasons for continuing to work or to retire, and satisfaction of employed and retired faculty from a single university. Faculty remaining in higher education and those who chose retirement both revealed high levels of life satisfaction. Faculty working past age 70 appeared to have a stronger commitment to professional roles, including teaching, research, creative work, academic administration, consulting, and service to the institution and community. Most professors continued to work beyond age 70 because of the intrinsic rewards of their work, feeling that it was important to continue to remain active, both for themselves and their respective academic disciplines. Those who stayed in higher education did so mainly because they enjoyed their work. Those leaving desired other life options, felt it was time to retire, or expressed various concerns about their workplace. In a recent study of emeritus faculty (Chase, Eklund, and Pearson 2003), the researchers found that more than one half of those studied seemed to have no difficulty in their retirement status. One-third reflected problems associated with feelings of detachment and with difficulty in managing transition.

Adult development and aging literature continues to provide considerable speculation about the multitude of factors affecting the timing and process of retirement

(Hillier and Barrow 1999; Hooyman and Kiyak 2002). Retirement often is described as a critical life transition, impacting upon individuals in various ways. While many persons begin retirement with clear motivation and direction, others are confronted with uncertainties related to health, functional limitations, adequacy of social security and private pension income, spouse's employment, living arrangements, or even prospective, later life employment options. Decisions to continue or restart employment often are enhanced by late-retirement incentive programs (LRIPs), one's organizational status, organizational morale, and perception of the quality of the work environment. This is further reinforced by Schultz and Lindbo (2000), in their study of retirees' interests in working and volunteering at or on behalf of their organization. The researchers concluded that individuals were most likely to engage in these post-retirement activities as a form of "reciprocity" to their respective organizations. Perceived organizational support was strongly correlated with the reciprocity factor.

Gerontologists and social scientists increasingly approach the subject of retirement as a highly anticipated, planned event, linked to such factors as the individual's financial security, an opportunity to begin long-delayed couple activities, intergenerational roles, and community commitments. Hooyman and Kiyak (2002) describe retirement satisfaction as affected by opportunities to learn and feel useful, including activities that provide autonomy and a sense of control. Personal resources, a positive outlook on life, a strong social support system of reciprocal relationships, and good health contribute to a more satisfying retirement.

Method

The author utilizes an interior monologue, stream-of-consciousness approach to reflect thoughts and feelings before and after retirement as a university professor. James Joyce, Irish novelist and poet, is well known for his experimental use of this approach in such books as *Portrait of the Artist as a Young Man* (1928) and *Ulysses* (1934). As one of Joyce's famous literary devices, the interior monologue, stream-of consciousness technique reflects thoughts, feelings, sometimes ungrammatical constructions, and free association of ideas. According to Richard Ellmann (1959), Joyce's development of the interior monologue enabled readers "to enter the mind of the character without the chaperonage of the author . . . Joyce in *Ulysses* boldly eliminated the journal, and lets thoughts hop, step, jump, and glide without the self-consciousness of a journal" (369).

I'm Retired?

12/31/02 . . . end of my status as a full time faculty member . . . 1/1/03 beginning of formal retirement . . . a pensioner? . . . it finally hit me . . . SS . . . wife at work . . . retired? . . . this is all new . . . back to November . . . fancy reception with finger foods, wine, entertainment by a very weird dance group . . . customary laudatory speeches . . . hearty handshakes from colleagues, deans, and students . . . presented two volumes tracing the history of the university and a massive framed picture of the campus . . .

plethora of unexpected hugs and kisses from faculty, staff, invited guests . . . three hours later my wife and I escaped out the door toting my retirement gifts . . . a grand affair . . . pleased so many attended . . . greatly appreciated the recognition . . . retiring faculty recognized by Board of Trustees . . . shook hands with Chairperson, Provost and President . . . applauded for years of continuing service . . . dedication to the University . . . elated, of course, with my new title . . . now a DPE (Distinguished Professor Emeritus) . . . no more t/p meetings . . . publications and conference papers sit in file cabinet all in a row . . . hundreds of courses taught . . . thousands of students . . . so many agency consultations and community service meetings . . . dreadfully long and boring faculty and committee meetings . . . enough . . . no more . . . retirement with apparent ease? . . . professional identity? . . . loss of my professional role? . . . retirement "process" here and now . . . a "stayer" or "leaver"? I stayed . . . a little . . . darnedest thing happened on my road to retirement . . . sounds like a Hope/Crosby movie. . . .

1/15/03 back in classroom . . . taught one of my favorite courses . . . introduced some very new course material . . . needed to spruce up the course . . . tell students each year I go beyond what's shown in the course syllabus . . . a few smirks . . . like what am I getting into with this guy? . . . their final semester . . . maybe mine, too . . . retired and still teaching? . . . already some resistance . . . do we have to buy all the textbooks and a course packet too? what's a genogram? a mid-term exam? . . . weekly journal, too? . . . same questions, new year . . . yes, we will cover all that material . . . this is graduate school . . . this is required, advanced practice course . . . curriculum committee determines content . . . fifteen-week semester . . . student attendance and participation required . . . yes, course flowed nicely . . . but students not as well prepared as in past years . . . some should not be in grad school, our school . . . don't belong here . . . wonder how they got here . . . I knew . . . a few lousy journals . . . really didn't give it much effort . . . last semester and they didn't give a hoot . . . what-can-he-do-to-me attitude by some . . . not many As for this class . . . can't be gatekeeper for the profession . . . more gatekeeping needed . . . still, felt great with a high teaching evaluation . . . important validation . . . needed it . . . perhaps I will teach again . . . still do it well . . . enjoy teaching about family treatment . . . know a lot about how families work, and don't work, why they fail, how they can be helped . . . done this a long time . . . time to let go? . . . not sure . . . ambivalent . . . stay or leave . . . need to be useful, productive, attached . . . no more committees, just teach . . . stay active . . . planned to retire at 65 or thereabouts.

Met my faculty replacement . . . terrific . . . qualified, great experience . . . takes over my college roles . . . they're not mine any more . . .my course for 29 years . . . shucks, I don't own the course . . . I'm retired . . . each Fall semester, 5–8 . . . all those years, all those students . . . I helped write the course . . . it's my baby . . . administered the program . . . let go already . . . all those grads . . . advised most of them . . . approved all those programs of study . . . followed their progress . . . approved their internships . . . cleared them for graduation . . . served on some of their doctoral committees . . . followed their careers . . . even wrote about their successes . . . their contributions . . . damn proud of their progress out there . . . still run into grads at conferences, malls

. . . some come to my continuing education workshops . . . they remember me . . . time to let go . . . the program will be fine . . . help replacement get started . . . replacement is a dumb word in a university . . . it sounds like the military . . . wish I had a better one . . . we can all be replaced . . . my job is to let go . . . transitions are hard work, painful . . . wonderful not to make admissions decisions . . . advisement . . . preparing the course syllabus . . . ordering books . . . course packets . . . already a difficult admissions decision . . . dean said turn it over . . . needs to get feet wet . . . will be fine . . . offer more advice? . . . maybe doesn't want my advice . . . can't throw someone out there right away . . . will be fine . . . told my wife many times that no one is irreplaceable . . . she's a school principal, she knows . . . teachers come and go . . . faculty come and go . . . the new ones know a lot that we don't know . . . schools need new faculty, directors, deans, administrators . . . believe, it gets better after we turn it over.

Back up six months . . . dean appointed new faculty recruitment chair . . . my role for many, many, many, perhaps too many years . . . said I didn't want to interview faculty applicants . . . take them to dinner . . . go to their presentations . . . didn't think faculty wanted my input . . . after all, I had recruited and helped bring most of them onto the faculty . . . let them do it all . . . they need to learn now that I'm retired . . . they want to do it themselves . . . I'm gone . . . like Norma Desmond in Andrew Lloyd Webber's Sunset Boulevard . . . "As If We Never Said Goodbye" . . . but, I said goodbye . . . did I? . . . saw SB at the Adelphi in London . . . lyrics perfect for gerontology students . . . all about stardom, growing older, being needed, forgotten, will the audience want me again, yes they will, comebacks, no, it's over . . . the lyrics tell it all . . . if you believe that nonsense . . . Streisand sings it best of all.

Time to downsize . . . too many books to move into my stinky new office . . . gave hundreds to university libraries . . . this goes in the box . . . no, I'll need it . . . no, it goes in the box . . . 250 more times . . . I'll take it to my new office . . . need it later on . . . no, time to tape up the boxes . . . do it already . . . let go . . . library staff is here to haul it away . . . these boxes to Korea . . . those 15 boxes to USC . . . these go home . . . the rest to my new office . . . down to one book case . . . shredded thousands of pages . . . still too much crap . . . old exams, course materials, assignments, readings, memos . . . last looked at some of this stuff 20 years ago . . . hasn't seen the light of day in all those years . . . out of here . . . will never need it . . . into the shredder but the old shredder broke . . . still have a ton of papers in file cabinets . . . all over my desk . . . in boxes, in piles on the floor, here and there . . . it must go, eventually . . . maybe I'll need it later if I teach that course again . . . maybe.

In the midst of my "retirement crisis" (first time this popped into my head), guess what? Spring vacation . . . not like Chevy Chase's version . . . returned to my place of origin . . . we moved away 61 years ago . . . first time back after 50 years . . . interstate most of the way . . . turned into town . . . greeted by a McDonald's . . . five minutes to find my old street . . . that's new . . . so is that . . . so is that . . . can't believe this . . . our first house, gone . . . now a warehouse . . . grandparents' old home, still standing . . . just as I remembered it, but converted into apartments . . . shabby, what a mess . . . grandparents took pride in their home . . . their garden, all covered with trash . . . I loved that garden . . . connected to our house— . . . my first school, gone . . . my first movie theater, now a Kentucky Fried Chicken . . . the corner drug store, five cent cherry Cokes, now a rehab center . . . walked down to the tree I climbed as a child . . . still there and all grown up . . . looked for my father's store . . . it was long gone . . . now a church . . . dad held me over his shoulder and I cut my finger on a hunting knife . . . still have the scar . . . grandfather's store, now a child welfare agency . . . across the street, a senior center . . . can you believe it? . . . no senior centers back then when I was a kid . . . not many social workers either . . . I'm a gerontologist now and teach about senior centers . . . five rolls of film on my old Kentucky home . . . the mayor remembered my family . . . so did the barber and the museum docent . . . so did the librarian . . . she helped me locate our family history . . . there it was in the county history book . . . needed another day or so to look up official records . . . when was our house sold? . . . what happened to our family stores? . . . all my father's aunts, uncles, cousins deceased . . . I knew that . . . what became of their kids? . . . my search has started . . . want to gather more family history . . . my wife came along for the ride . . . she knew it was important . . . she snapped photos of me and my memories . . . I owe her big time . . . next time to KC, across the wide Missouri . . . still processing my pilgrimage . . . it was important to return . . . is this what retirement is all about? . . . to share with our girls, show them where I came from . . . where we came from . . . I teach about life review and reminiscence . . . Lewis and Butler (1974), Burnside and Haight (1994) . . . I teach their theories . . . their protocols . . . how to.

Three days later, back home again . . . colleagues circled my office like vultures waiting for me to move out . . . wanted my office . . . two windows, corner office . . . goes to a senior member of the faculty . . . 21 May moving day . . . movers came late . . . told then to be careful with my desk and computer . . . onward to my new office . . . took three hours to get to my "retirement office" . . . could be called a Retirement and Geriatric Center . . . they scratched my furniture, big time . . . mildew galore, complained . . . carpet filthy, lousy cooling system, plaster peeling, complained . . . dean approved a dehumidifier . . . retirees go to a stinky old house . . . yuk . . . BSG abstract accepted . . . final touches on paper . . . airline and hotel reservations done online . . . Ph.D. student needs help with dissertation . . . committee, where are you? Please help . . . I'm retired? . . . e-mail and Internet down . . . complained and still waiting . . . nasty virus, wait it out.

Retired? . . . taught two courses during summer school . . . do I want to do this again? . . . can I still contribute? . . . maybe . . . no . . . maybe . . . wait and see . . . no . . . I have choices . . . no one pushing me out the door . . . we want to travel . . . planned that years ago . . . how can I visit major league baseball parks? . . . 50th high school reunion next year . . . will go . . . long list of places to visit . . . we'll have the time if she retires too . . . my . . . our retirement goals . . . perhaps I can do it all . . . no, no . . . why not? . . . maybe . . . wife is school principal . . . she's still working . . . I must hang in there . . . she's off to work each day . . . works late . . . I don't work . . . she works . . . what does that say about me? . . . retired . . . can't stay home with garden and honey-do list . . . will teach one course fall semester . . . next summer . . . no, no . . . retired . . . decide later . . . since 1975 taught every summer except one . . . helped build the summer program . . . helped write doctoral program, too, a long time ago

. . . doctoral course each summer . . . junior faculty will teach my course for the first time . . . heck, I don't own the course.

E-mail dean, yes I will teach a course next spring but only on Wednesday morning . . . want that time slot . . . I do have seniority, choices . . . The State (Marrow 2003), read in newspaper that in Goose Creek, South Carolina, rural mail carrier, age 82, after 40 years, has no plans to slow down. Said patrons are kind, show respect, are appreciative . . . my students and colleagues are so kind . . . respectful.

35 years as a university professor . . . finished doctorate . . . great interview at Jane Addams, they liked me . . . hired . . . first daughter born . . . what an incentive to complete dissertation . . . did it before moon landing . . . baby daughter sat on my lap as astronaut climbed from spacecraft . . . now a Fighting Illini, Big Ten . . . loved football, big time football . . . went to every game rain or snow . . . beat the stuffing out of Iowa in a blizzard and feet nearly froze . . . wife came with me to every game . . . blasted by Penn State and many other teams . . . five great years, world class university . . . learned how to teach . . . publish, publish, publish, publish, so I did . . . second daughter born . . . snow up to our behinds . . . job offer . . . to Gamecock Country, USC . . . wife also taught . . . reminded my friends and colleagues we were the first USC . . . what's a gamecock they all asked . . . some kind of fighting chicken I replied . . . helped write our gerontology education program . . . approved by the Commission on Higher Education . . . part of my life for 25 years . . . it's not really mine, but feel ownership . . . not any more . . . I don't own the program . . . it belongs to the university, to the state . . . let someone else administer the program . . . 21 years later the dean let me award a master's diploma to daughter . . . took photos next to Ben Franklin . . . she's now a geriatric social worker . . . something good rubbed off . . . born in Illinois . . . off to Michigan . . . then Penn, that rhymes . . . that's my school and she went there too . . . so proud . . . married . . . proud of both girls . . . one became a wolverine, another a badger . . . go Big Blue . . . go Big Red . . . then to the other USC (she's a Trojan?) . . . successful . . . neat kids . . . wow, they're all grown up but still our babies . . . isn't email great . . . wireless phones, too . . . home for Thanksgiving . . . they cooked for the first time . . . we're all together . . . we reminisce . . . look at old albums . . . videotapes . . . want to see them more often . . . I'm retired . . . I can.

Late August . . . new gamecocks arriving on campus . . . outside my window they're unloading SUVs next to the dorm . . . parents, some former gamecocks, sweating with flushed faces and ready to drop . . . big, big boxes, trunks, TVs, VCRs, the works . . . all kinds of stuff . . . been there, done that . . . it all fits in those tiny rooms . . . I'm retired and they are beginning . . . university life has been good— . . . uncapped, but I still wear my Cincinnati Reds cap . . . want to visit the Great American Ball Park soon . . . want to visit all the ball parks . . . I'm still here . . . no one is pushing me out, yet . . . gradual, part-time, yes . . . indefinitely, no . . . ambivalent, yes . . . loyal . . . strong work ethic, productive . . . the university has treated me very well . . . is this all about reciprocity?

Students still like my classes . . . must remain active . . . still come in early each day . . . have control of my time, choices . . . Atchley and Barusch (2004) taught me that older adults are predisposed and motivated in the direction of inner psychological continuity, along with outward continuity of social behavior through selected activities . . . Baltes and Baltes (1990) have taught me about adaptive competence in retirement . . . Rowe and Kahn (1998) guide me toward retirement and successful aging . . . I hope . . . for many years I have taught retirement theory . . . yes, I want to continue teaching . . . selectively . . . it's here and now . . . need to remain productive . . . tell neighbors I'm retired, but still working . . . need to stay connected, included . . . don't want them to say he has nothing to do . . . we both have good health . . . eagerly await travel brochures. . . .

Reprinted from Gerald L. Euster, Reflections upon university retirement: With thanks and apologies to James Joyce, *Educational Gerontology* 30 (2004): 119–28. Reprinted by permission.

References

Ashenfelter, O., and D. Card (2001). Did the elimination of mandatory retirement affect faculty retirement flows? Working Paper 8378. Cambridge, Mass.: National Bureau of Economic Research.

Atchley, R. C., and A. S. Barusch (2004). *Social Forces and Aging: An Introduction to Social Gerontology.* Belmont, Calif.: Wadsworth-Thompson Learning.

Baltes, P. B., and M. M. Baltes (1990). *Successful Aging: Perspectives from the Behavioral Sciences.* Cambridge: Cambridge University Press.

Burnside, I., and B. K. Haight (1994). Reminiscence and life review: Therapeutic interventions for older people. *Nurse Practitioner* 19: 55–61.

Chase, C. L., S.J. Eklund, and L. M. Pearson. (2003). Affective responses of faculty emeriti to retirement. *Educational Gerontology* 29: 521–34.

Dorfman, L. T. (2002). Stayers and leavers: Professionals in an era of no mandatory retirement. *Educational Gerontology* 28: 15–33.

Ellmann, R. (1959). *James Joyce.* New York: Oxford University Press.

Hillier, S., and G. M. Barrow (1999). *Aging, the Individual, and Society.* Belmont, Calif.: Wadsworth.

Hooyman, N. R., and H. A.Kiyak (2002). *Social Gerontology: A Multidisciplinary Perspective.* Boston: Allyn and Bacon.

Joyce, J. (1928). *A Portrait of the Artist as a Young Man.* New York: Modern Library.
——— (1934). *Ulysses.* New York: Random House.

Lane, W. C. (2003). Faculty retirement research: Where we have been, where we are today, and where we are going. Paper presented at Annual Meeting of the Association for Gerontology in Higher Education, St. Petersburg, Florida, March.

Lewis, M. I., and R. N. Butler (1974). Life-review therapy: Putting memories to work in individual and group psychotherapy. *Geriatrics* 29: 165–71.

Marrow, D. (2003). No stranger to work. *The State,* July 26, B1.

Quinn, J. F. (2001). Retirement trends and patterns in the 1990s: The end of an era? In K. E. Nazor, and B. Williamson, comps., *Public Policy and Aging,* 69–75. Washington, D.C.: Association for Gerontology in Higher Education.

Rowe, J. W., and R. L.Kahn (1998). *Successful Aging.* New York: Pantheon.

Shultz, K. S., and T. L. Lindbo (2000). Measuring retirees' interests in work and volunteering. Paper presented at the annual meeting of the Gerontological Society of America, Washington, D.C., November.

Schulz, James H. (2001). *The Economics of Aging.* Westport, Conn.: Auburn House.

Commentary: . . . And the Travel Brochures Arrived

Gerald L. Euster

. . . . . they arrive almost daily . . . too many, but still Sandi and I read them . . . we were hooked. . . . Hawaii, Toronto. . . . must sees . . . and we did . . . in the tradition of Captain Cook and Shackleton, on to Antarctica. . . . oh, yes, the expedition of a lifetime . . . 4 days in, out, and through the sounds, straits, channels, bays . . . blocked and turned back by ice. . . . just 88 nautical miles from the Antarctic Circle . . . we loved it. . . . Rio, Montevideo, Buenos Aires, Santiago . . . rich, developing, but so many pockets of poverty! Auckland, Tauranga, Wellington, Christchurch, Dunedin . . . New Zealanders are so kind and resourceful . . . they believe in themselves. . . . across the Tasman to Tasmania. . . . over to Melbourne. . . . . fed eucalyptus leaves to the koalas and petted the kangaroos . . . must return to Sydney someday. . . . needed more time there. . . . need much more time to see Australia.

Back to work . . . one course per semester . . . faculty and staff turnover . . . some have moved on. . . . new dean . . . an evolving university mission . . . new expectations. . . . I always taught that change was good in social systems. . . . now share my stinky office . . . mailbox still fills up with all that stuff. . . . technology allows me to do much of my work from home . . . good health. . . . love my Southern garden. . . .

. . . My wife, Sandi, also retired, but not altogether. . . . school principals don't like to retire . . . still does projects for her school district. . . . supervises student teachers. . . . serves as substitute principal. . . . full retirement. . . . not yet!. . . . aerobics, pilates. . . . treadmill daily. . . . a must.

Back to Philly. . . . 5:30 a.m. phone call that we were about to be grandparents. . . . get up here quick . . . US Airways on time for a change. . . . cab driver raced down Pine Street. . . . got us to Pennsylvania Hospital before our daughter's delivery. . . . new digital camera in hand and still reading the manual. . . . waited for the good word. . . . a beautiful granddaughter . . . the digital photos were super. . . . camera was glued to my chest for the next two weeks . . . even learned how to email photos to family and friends.

Just a few blocks from the hospital was the Rebecca Gratz Club where I completed my doctoral field work more than forty years ago . . . now a private residence. . . . I had to take a look at the old place. . . . gentrification marches on . . . Starbucks, trendy restaurants, new buildings all over Center City. . . . Lord and Taylor now owns the eagle and I still meet my wife and daughters there . . . it's true, *the more things change, the more they stay the same.*

Thirty-seven years after graduation from Penn, and three years following retirement from the University of South Carolina, I am honored to be invited to reflect and reminisce about my years of doctoral study at Penn. As indicated in the accompanying article, I have incorporated reminiscence and life review in my gerontology courses over the past several decades. More recently, I have offered Continuing Education and Lifelong Learning workshops on the topic.

Married in July 1964, my wife and I moved to Philadelphia a few weeks later. She took a teaching job at the Fairhill School in North Philly. I enrolled in the School of Social Work following two years of postgraduate study and practice at the Menninger School of Psychiatry and Menninger Clinic in Topeka, Kansas. I felt well prepared to advance my professional career through doctoral education in social work. Karl Menninger and many world-famous psychiatrists, psychologists, and social workers helped provide a superb foundation for advanced social work studies. At the Menninger Clinic I had the opportunity to practice both in the Adult Hospital and Retirement and Geriatric Center. The RGC was, in 1963, one of the first geropsychiatric facilities in the United States, igniting my continuing interest in gerontological and geriatric social work.

At Penn, Professors Lewis, Lodge, Artigues, and Dean Smalley provided the first year of instruction. Much of my later teaching skill at the University of South Carolina was an outgrowth of Ruth Smalley's human behavior course. Weekly papers pertaining to our life cycle growth and development were required. My classmates and I dreaded notes at the bottom of returned papers for us to schedule appointments to meet with her. She always expected us to feel and express more deeply our experiences of growth and development. She was a creative, demanding teacher, and a significant role model. The social work practice course, taught by Richard Lodge, stressed "process, process, process, feeling, feeling, feeling." My clinical field placement was with the Rebecca Gratz Club, a residential half-way house in Philadelphia offering casework and social group work services for young women with psychiatric disabilities. At the end of Dr. Lodge's first year course we were required to write an extensive paper dealing with our clinical field work practice. My paper, "Communication of Feeling as an Element of Skill in Social Group Work with Returning Mental Hospital Patients," served to integrate the learning experience. The Rebecca Gratz Club, like many privately funded halfway houses at that time, was closed many years ago. The building still stands as a lovely residence in historic Philadelphia.

Three electives were taken outside the School of Social Work, one with the sociologist Otto Pollak, and two with outstanding anthropology faculty members. Toward the end of my doctoral program an informative social work elective in International Social Work was taken. With the globalization of social welfare during the past several years, Dr. Richard Estes has clearly moved Penn into its preeminent leadership position in International Social Work education and research. In addition, I learned a great deal from Lloyd Setleis's terrific course on social work supervision, at that time required of all field work supervisors. I remember well his strong voice and caring attention to each student. He, too, was a marvelous role model.

Max Silverstein guided my dissertation research at Philadelphia State Hospital between 1967 and 1969. Other members of my dissertation committee included Louise Shoemaker, Julius Jahn, and Otto Pollak. The Community Mental Health Centers Act of 1963 (PL 88–164) foreshadowed my employment as a social work training specialist at PSH. My work focused on the training of mental health workers who would be deployed in Pennsylvania state mental hospitals to (1) accelerate the social rehabilitation of severe and persistently mentally ill patients and (2) facilitate the transition of these patients to their respective communities and designated mental health center programs. Indeed, the deinstitutionalization of mental hospital patients in Pennsylvania and throughout the nation took place gradually over the following decades. Several federally funded projects at PSH were innovative at the time and provided impressive models for the humane care, treatment, and social rehabilitation of mentally ill persons in institutions. My first journal publication was based on my doctoral dissertation research at Philadelphia State Hospital (1971). Looking back, I am proud to have been a part of our nation's mental health movement during those years. Like most large state hospitals, PSH has been closed for many years. Surfing the Internet recently, I found many images of the old buildings and grounds, all boarded up with trees and weeds growing out of control. Perhaps one day the state will utilize the property as a park or botanical garden for the betterment of the city of Philadelphia.

For many years much of what I learned and practiced at PSH was infused into my teaching at the University of South Carolina. Hundreds of my students completed field work with the South Carolina Department of Mental Health. Many have remained in that system, practicing in and administering our extensive community mental health center programs. Our large state hospital in Columbia was closed only a few years ago. It, too, is ready for implosion so that the property can be utilized for the enrichment of our citizens in Columbia.

In the twenty-five years prior to retirement I helped conceptualize, strengthen, and administer the Certificate of Graduate Study in Gerontology Program at the University of South Carolina. The interdisciplinary program was aimed at professionals engaged in planning, administration, and provision of services for older adults, as well as master's and doctoral level students from social work, public health, psychology, sociology, nursing, education, and other fields. Enrollment in required and elective courses, across disciplines, allowed students to obtain specialized preparation for new career opportunities or to advance career objectives in the rapidly expanding fields of gerontology and geriatrics. My education and practice at the Menninger Clinic and experience at Philadelphia State Hospital proved to be useful in shaping the first graduate level gerontology curriculum in South Carolina. I am satisfied that the program is in good hands and will be maintained by the university in the years ahead as part of its elaborate health sciences mission.

Reference

Euster, G. L. (1971). Mental health workers: new mental hospital personnel for the seventies. *Mental Hygiene* 55 (3): 283–90.

Chapter 19
Boundary Spanning: An Ecological Reinterpretation of Social Work Practice in Health and Mental Health Systems

Toba S. Kerson

The Development of This Approach to Practice

This addition to the ecological perspective was developed inductively, that is, it comes from the literature overlayed with my own practice experience and 28 years teaching practice, participating on social service organizations' advisory boards and keeping close touch with the work of many former students. As I tried to codify and articulate the perspective, and before I began to write, I gathered approximately 150 examples from social workers in a range of health and mental health settings so that the writing would take the shape of real practice. Examples were requested from the most creative social workers I knew including some who had redefined or stretched the boundaries of health-related activity. Each social worker was asked to provide a practice example involving:

1. relationships with two or more systems
2. managed care
3. the crossing of funding and/or policy boundaries
4. an ethical or another dilemma
5. an innovative assessment
6. creative or unusual intervention strategies
7. creative definition or social work roles, title, department, affiliation, or function, or
8. another dimension that is important for learning to be a social worker.

The simple form that followed asked for: the presenting problem, concern, or need, means of and tools used for assessment (including graphic and mapping devices), strategies and interventions (attach charts, pathways, timelines, or strategic plants), and conclusions. Several people sent examples of the closest they came to traditional social casework because they themselves did not classify what they were doing as social work. For example, one social worker organizes fund-raising events for self-help groups focused on a particular illness. I consider that all her activity (even organizing banquets) is on behalf of her population, and it is all health related. As a representative of an umbrella social services organization, another social workers scouts opportunities for new programming and new facilities in cities other than her own. Another manages all the step-down units in her hospital, while another manages a rehabilitation facility for substance abuse, and one is doing development work for her social work agency. All these activities are health-related and carried out on behalf of social work clientele.

I learned that social workers can be an extraordinarily persistent and patient lot. Many of the programs they describe were created over a long period while they were doing many other kinds of work in an organization. They held onto a vision, nurtured and tended it until it came to fruition. They all reported that managed care and the increasing attention to finances and financial constraints are extraordinarily frustrating and individual clients and consumers are moved too quickly through systems of care. Still, the social workers who remained positive and, indeed, upbeat about their work and their clients' possibilities were adaptive people who could maintain a clear, resolute realistic optimism. Thus, the conceptualization that follows comes from exposure to the writing of many disciplines, my teaching, and from the experiences of present and former students.

The Place of This Approach in an Ecological Perspective

This approach is couched in an ecological perspective that was developed over many decades by Germain and Gitterman but informed by Meyer (1983, 1988) and many others beginning with Richmond in her work on case coordination and social diagnosis. Wakefield (1996a,b), MacNair (1996), Gitterman and Shulman (1994), Allen-Meares and Lane (1987), Meyer (1983, 1988), Siporin (1980), and others have also made important contributions to this approach. For example, Karls and Wandrei (1994a,b) developed the person-in-environment system (PIE) for describing, classifying, and coding adult social functioning problems, a fine contemporary effort to make an ecological perspective practical and systematic.

An ecological perspective is drawn from studies of ecology and general systems theory. General systems theory has been described as a direction or program in the contemporary philosophy of science, an overachieving framework, an abstract metatheory, or a model of relationships between objects rather than theory. The general systems paradigm provides social work with "a way of thinking and a means of organizing our perceptions of relatedness and dynamic processes" (Ell and Northen 1990, 2). The framework purports that any systems—be they biological, social, or psychological—operate according to the same fundamental principles. All systems, for example, are open to influencing activity, are adaptive, incorporate notions of communication and control, have smaller organized activity flows that serve larger activity flows, and define the individual actor through the functional linking of subordinate parts in the operating whole. Systems are organized wholes consisting of elements that are related in varying nonlinear, mutual, or unidirectional and intermittent causal relationships. They are capable of primary and reactive change and evolution, and they maintain differentiation through continuous input from and output to their environment. Thus systems are made up of complexes of interacting components or subsystems. Therefore, action flows within each system and outside of it, linking it to other systems and influencing that system.

The term ecological comes from ecology, the division of biology that studies the relationships between organisms and all the parts of their environment that affect them and that they affect in any way. Ecology views people and their environments as interdependent. Individual components and aspects are separated for study in order to develop strategies for altering the relationships, but all units, dimensions, and aspects must be viewed together to be truly understood. In biological terms, ecology deals with the relations between organisms and their environment. In sociological parlance, ecology is the branch concerned with the spacing of people and institutions and the resultant interdependency. Ecologists study adaptation to changes in the environment. Thus, studies of the relationship of structural, physical, and social stress to illness, life event research, and studies of social support and health are all part of an ecological understanding of the relationship of the individual to the environment. "An ecosystemic perspective enlarges the unit of attention to include the individual, social institutions, culture, and their interactions and transactions among systems and within specific systems" (Ell and Northen 1990, 10). Thus an ecological perspective assumes a specific worldview and view of the individual from which all means of assessment, strategy building, and tools for intervention are drawn. I find an ecological perspective compatible with my own world view and view of the individual but not sufficiently applied or pragmatic for practicing or teaching the practice of social work. Therefore, I have added content from other disciplines and combined parts of social work enterprise that have sometimes been seen as separate.

Like an ecological perspective, this boundary spanning approach is neither a model nor a theory but a useful way of thinking about practice (Meyer 1988). A perspective is defined as the relationship of aspects of a subject to each other and to a whole as well as a mental view or outlook (*American Heritage Dictionary of the English Language* 2000). The term perspective conveys depth and distance, as it does in art, lending added dimensions to understanding. A model is a description or representation of a structure that shows the proportions and arrangements of its component parts. A theory is "a scheme or system of ideas or statements held as an explanation or account for a group of facts or phenomena: a hypothesis that has been confirmed or established by observations or experiment and is propounded or accepted as accounting for the known facts; a statement of what are held to be laws, principles or causes of something known or observed" (*Oxford English Dictionary* 1971).

An ecological perspective presupposes the necessity of thinking systematically and necessarily disallows linearity. Thus, one cannot think in terms of one cause and effect. It also presupposes that all systems have boundaries but that the boundaries are almost all permeable. In the case of social entities, that is, families, groups, organizations, or communities, boundaries can be redrawn or recast to work most effectively for the client. An ecological perspective is all about relationships, especially the relationship between people and their environments. It is particularly suited to social work practice because it is all encompassing and solves the perpetual social work dilemma of how to address the person and the environment in a way that subsumes both. An ecological perspective suggests that clients, projects, programs, communities, and all the salient aspects of environment are parts of an interesting whole. In order to know why, when, and how to intervene, social workers must understand context, the interrelated conditions in which the client, project, program, or community exist.

Many frameworks for business management are derived from ecology and general systems theory as well. These frameworks have much to offer to social work practice. According to Drucker, with the exception of certain public health reforms, no new knowledge has contributed more to productivity and profitability in this century than developments in systems, people, and information management (Drucker 1974, 1999). Specifically, business management frameworks provide pragmatic, clear ways for people to make sense of the structure, organization, and processes of systems. Because they are action-oriented and empowering, focused on the mission and goals of systems and the relationship of the work of all participants to the system, such frameworks undergird social workers' abilities to negotiate systems and advocate effectively for clients.

The ability to work within and manage these systems in highly productive, goal-oriented ways is critical for present and future social work practice. Such information has always been salient for social work practice, but the current environment in health and mental health care makes critical social workers' ability to understand organizations as systems, to speak the language and to maneuver in ways that help clients reach their goals (Levinson 1992). In particular, the work of Peter Senge, Chris Argyris, John Kotter, Henry Mintzberg, and Peter Drucker informs this approach. Each of these people explores different dimensions of management that contribute to social workers' understanding of systems and to their ability to practice in increasingly complex environments. For example, Drucker's "Management by objectives and control," Senge's "learning organizations," and Kotter's particular understanding of leadership can enrich social workers' understanding of systems, ecology, and an ecological perspective (Bailey and Grochau 1993).

Drucker explains that every system that is more complicated than the simplest mechanical assemblage of inanimate matter contains multiple axes. Thus the body of every animal has many systems, including a skeletal-muscular system, a respiratory system, sensory systems, and a reproductive system. While each system is to some degree autonomous, all interact, and each is an axis of organization. Organizations are not, and should not be, as complicated as biological organisms. Still, business and public service organizations must be constructed with several axes, including one for making decisions and distributing authority and information, as well as one for understanding the logic of the task and the dynamics of knowledge. In addition, individuals must have positions within these organizations so that they can understand and manage a number of axes related to task, 527).

Systems thinking is guided by two central principles. First, "structure influences behavior," which means that the ability to influence reality comes from recognizing structures that are controlling behavior and events. The second principle, "policy resistance," refers to the tendency of complex systems to resist efforts to change their behavior. Therefore, efforts to manipulate behavior will generally improve matters only in the short run and often lead to more problems in the long run (Senge 1990, 373–74). Such thinking uses systems archetypes to observe and fathom underlying structures in complex situations. For example, a mastery of systems thinking leads one to understand family problems or organization problems as emanating from underlying structures rather than from individual mistakes or negative intentions. Systems thinking leads to seeing "wholes" instead of "parts" and experiencing the interconnectedness of life. Thus, systems theory contributes to the understanding of organizations and management that has been developed in business, and social workers in health and mental health need this knowledge in order to be effective with and for their clients.

Some Boundaries to Be Spanned

Spanning Health and Mental Health

The first boundary that must be spanned is the one that separates health care from mental health care. New knowledge about the causes, symptoms, and treatment of a range of illnesses indicates that the dichotomy between physical health and mental health is false. While scientific and medical knowledge do not support this split, social responses, including administrative structures and funding streams, continue as if physical health and mental health were separate entities.

Expanding Definitions of Health-Related Settings

The second boundary area that must be redefined is the setting for health-related social work. The field can no longer afford to have factions fight from within about which settings are most prestigious or what are most acceptable. Definition of setting must be wherever populations are located whom we wish to help and where we can employ our knowledge and skills. Since the health-related social work moved public health situations into university-affiliated hospital wards for indigent patients, we have created problems for and between ourselves. Certain historical moves seem overdrawn today, but it would be good if we could learn from them. For example as psychiatry and psychoanalysis developed, social work established new boundaries in terms of setting and discipline, with psychiatric social work splitting off from medical social work. There was a time following that division when social workers set and allowed to be set for them parameters related to the levels of consciousness on which they could work. While psychiatrists could work on all levels, social workers could work only on the conscious and preconscious levels, never the unconscious level. At that time, many social workers worked one-on-one with their clients in fifty-minute increments, thus again setting tight parameters for their work and isolating themselves from the whole of the health-related enterprise. Today, social work practice in health and mental health occurs in schools, work sites, residential facilities, camps, homes, rehabilitation programs, neighborhood health centers, mental health centers, prisons, long-term care settings, advocacy and support groups, and hospitals.

Spanning Levels of Practice

A third boundary exists between levels of practice. For many years, boundaries were drawn between modalities, with social workers calling themselves caseworkers, group workers, or community organizers. There were courses in schools of social work called "Group Work for Caseworkers" and "Community Organizing for Group Workers," but even within such courses, the lines were clear. The lines could sometimes be crossed, but the primary definition of the work was the tightly drawn modality. Now boundaries are drawn between those who are direct practitioners, those who do program development, and those who work in the policy arena. Those equally limiting barriers must be spanned for social work practitioners to act most effectively for and with clients.

Expanding Knowledge Bases

Other boundaries have been drawn through determining what kinds of knowledge bases could inform social work in health and mental health. The field has embraced, rejected, or debated various aspects of psychology, biology, sociology, economics, and political science, but sometimes has difficulty absorbing important knowledge that comes from sources not thought to reflect social work's value base. In the past, feuds erupted about the knowledge base for social work, such as that between the diagnostic and functional schools, or various schools of community action or group work. In the current managed care environment, the field has been loath to embrace the aspects of business management that might be very helpful to the social work enterprise. Many of these debates continue.

Methods for Spanning Boundaries

This article briefly describes methods for social workers to span out-dated and limiting boundaries using: (1) population expertise; (2) mapping devices; (3) legal and ethical knowledge for better advocacy (Bertelli 1998; Dickson 1995; Sunley 1997); (4) similar relationship skills for work with clients, colleagues, and organizations (Abramson 1993; Gitterman and Shulaman 1994; Mulroy and Shay 1997); (5) assessment techniques addressing individual, program, organizational, and community capacities (Griffiths 1997; Kettner, Maroney, and Martin 1999; Menefee 1997; Saltz and Scaefer 1996; (6) business management skills for understanding systems and the relationships within and between them (Drucker 1999; Senge 1990); and (7) multiple modes of intervention and evaluation (Mullen and Magnabasco 1997; Zeira and Rosen 1999).

Be population experts. Because it is not possible to know everything, yet one is measured in terms of knowledge and skill, health-related social workers can become expert only in terms of knowledge and skill necessary to practice in relation to specific populations. That is, if one works with people with a chronic condition such as diabetes or schizophrenia, or a population such as mothers and young children or the very old, one must know the laws that entitle and restrict that population, understand the conditions themselves and possible medical and social interventions, the ways in which these conditions affect significant others, the ways these conditions are handled in different cultures, etc.

Use mapping devices. Graphic representations or aping devices are essential in this approach. Like other kinds of maps, these representations are meant to show social workers and clients/consumers where they are in a situation or in the work process, and to indicate direction for work. Turning something complex and overwhelming into a flat image on one page provides a sense of mastery and control if that image can suggest movement and direction. Varied use of such mapping devices allows social workers to span boundaries of time, place, and system in planning, monitoring, and evaluating their work.

Representations that have been found helpful are organigraphs (Mintzberg 1994; Mintzberg and Lampel 1999); Mintzberg and Van der Heyden 1999), driving forces maps (Christensen 1997), balanced scorecards (Kaplan and Norton 1996), as well as genograms, ecomaps. and systematic planned practice figures (Rosen 1993, 1999). Visualizing complex sets of relationships and activities gives social workers a broader scope that deepens their understanding and helps them to choose points and methods of intervention (Tufte 1997). These devices require that those who use them make their assumptions explicit through diagrams. They support contracting about how to view systems in context. Additionally, they provide ways to intensify moments in helping relationships by creating a concrete focus of attention. In all, such devices help social workers to assess, plan, make concrete, monitor, and compare. These devices can locate and follow social workers in their working systems, help them to visualize services for client systems, contribute to an understanding of organizations and systems and the relationships within and between them, and engage in strategic planning and programming. The organigraph, developed by Mintzberg and Van der Heyden (1999) to depict the workings of organizations, is one very helpful mapping device with which social workers may not yet be familiar. While traditional organizational charts seem to indicate that all units are independent boxes that are connected through chains of authority, the organigraph looks at how people and processes converge and where ideas flow. It maintains the conventional components of an organizational chart: sets of people and machines and chains of command, and it adds two components: hubs and webs. In the hub, the process of managing brings together and coordinates the work of people who are intrinsically empowered. In the web, work is fluid and the facilitation of collaboration energizes the whole network. Social workers' ability to have adequate influence in their workplace and to be able to advocate for clients/consumers depends on their participation in hubs and webs.

Unlike ecomaps, genograms, or organizational charts, organigraphs often look very different from each other. Using the building materials of sets, chains, hubs, and webs, they assume the overall shape that presents the clearest portrait of an organization or system. The organigraph focuses on how processes and people come together and where ideas have to flow. It does not eliminate little boxes from organizational charts, but it introduces new components. The two conventional components in the device are sets of items (machines or people) and chains (assembly lines). The newer components are hubs and webs. In the hub, managing occurs at the center, bringing together and coordinating the work of people who are intrinsically empowered. In the web, the work is fluid so that collaboration is facilitated and the whole network is energized. Because the hub is the center of the organigraph, the graphic may resemble an eco-map. (For discussion and examples, see Hammer and Kerron 1998 and Kerron 2002.)

Understand legal and ethical realms. Understanding the legislation that affects particular populations will enable social workers to help clients use all the entitlements and protections available to them through state and federal government as well as the courts. A prime example in the United States is the Americans with Disabilities Act. The Americans with Disabilities Act (ADA) of 1990 is an important resource for those with physical and mental disabilities because it expands their rights, supports them as they become more fully participating members of society, and, most important, makes society responsible for accommodating the individual (Orlin, 1995). According to Orlin (1995, 233), "The ADA establishes that the nation's goals regarding individuals with disabilities are to ensure equality of opportunity, full participation, independent living, and economic self-sufficiency." The ADA requires public accommodations and services, businesses, transportation, and communications authorities to treat people as if their disabilities do not matter while simultaneously requiring special treatment for them (Feldblum 1991; Kopels 1995). Thus the ADA demands that society accommodate those with disabilities to the degree that will allow them to take their rightful places in society. More boundary-spanning opportunities are afforded by exploring and becoming comfortable with a range of ethical issues that are part of the work. Included here are ethical dilemmas that have no answer but that social workers must work within situations such as abortion, end of life decisions, and other medically and socially complex interventions. Examples of ethical decisions in which social workers might be involved include allocating limited health care resources, beginning or ending aggressive treatment, return to home or nursing home, and clashes between patient, family, and institutional interests.

Understand organizations, systems, linkages, and means of communication. This knowledge allows social workers to move more freely, build professional and interdisciplinary networks, understand patterns of authority and responsibility, and make organizations more responsive to clients and consumers. It reflects an ecological perspective because it assumes a constant interplay between the individual and the environment. Here issues are related to location, access, authority, and change; turf conflicts, teamwork and interdisciplinary, intra- and interagency work have to be managed. An overarching theme is that, although the settings where the work occurs may change, the critical importance of the work and the very high levels of knowledge and skill that social work requires will not. For example, because ill people are now hospitalized for as short a time as possible, work that used to occur in a hospital setting may now have to take place in a rehabilitation center, a nursing home, a senior center, home care, or a support group related to a specific illness or condition. Literature that supports this discussion of "place" is in social work administration, community and organizational development, and business.

Know that relationship skills are the same for everyone with whom you work. In this approach, excellent relationship skills are seen as a conduit for effecting change for the client system in every practice situation. Although both the context and strategies of the social worker in health care have become more extensive over the decades, the importance of the relationship between social worker and client system remains constant. No matter how large the unit of attention—whether it is a community, a large organization, a family, or an individual—the accomplishment of goals depends on the social worker's relationship abilities with individuals as clients or with individuals who represent larger client systems or health care organizations. Communication skills remain critical. The ability of social workers to understand the psychological nuances of relationship and to carry themselves differently in the relationship depending on the needs of the client system and the goals of the service are critical to this endeavor. It is argued that similar relationship skills are necessary for working with clients, colleagues, and those from all related systems. Therefore, traditional social work concepts such as self-awareness, conscious-use-of-self, and the overall capacity to develop and sustain relationships are explored. The overarching tasks of the relationship are to act as a conduit or catalyst for helping the client to reach goals, carry hope, lend a vision, and intervene in varied ways depending on the capacities and needs of the client system, the needs of other systems with whom social workers may be working, and the tasks necessary to meet needs and objectives. Such relationship skills are also critical in working in teams, in negotiating for clients with managed care and insurance company representatives, and with others with whom clients or social workers may have adversarial relationships. The notion of boundary spanning is essential to social workers' building and maintaining such relationships.

Use assessment across context as a continuous decision-making process. All practice concerns gathering information, making judgments and decisions, and acting on those judgments. The relationship of assessment to the development of objectives and outcome measures is critical for evaluation and continued support of individual client systems and programs. Whenever possible, practice must be empirically based, that is, closely linked to the products and processes of research. In relation to assessment, social workers must be able to answer the following questions: Who makes up the client/consumer system? What are the ecological boundaries that must be drawn to make sense of the situation? What are the probable parameters based on access, proximity, entitlement, and need that help the social worker to draw ecological boundaries? What range of services should be viewed as possible in this situation, especially in relation to the needs and capacities of the client system? What are the goals of the client/consumer seeking help? Are they realistic in the face of capacities and access? Are objectives drawn ahead of time by an organization, law, or funding sources? What tools, such as mini mental status exams, activities of daily living scales, functional status, and community assessments, are available for assessment? Is the bio-psychosocial assessment sufficient to help client systems to develop strategies to reach their goals?

Understand two interventional sets. Two sets of interventions are seen as important for all social workers in health and mental health to master. The first set involves the planning process: determination of goals and objectives; uses and varieties of contracts in social work practice in health and mental health; the place, uses, and importance of strategizing; and the overarching importance of teamwork in all of social work practice. Typically, strategies are an amalgam of professional, family and other social supports, governmental, voluntary, self-help, relational, informational, and in-kind interventions. These may not occur at the same time or be carried out by one social worker, but the social worker is part of a large network of helpers moving in and out of work with the client system over time. Particular attention is paid to the relationship between self-help and professional help, as well as to interdisciplinary teamwork.

The second interventional set focuses on traditional direct practice tools. Here, advocacy is seen as an intervention in its own right, as well as part of all other interventions. Universal strategy issues include: the place of relationship techniques in all interventions, problem solving, the ability to partialize (to break down ways to address problems into small, manageable action steps), giving advice, the place of insight, interpretation and reflection, the use of questions designed to refocus the work (Are we working? What are we working on?), issues of timing (including sources of time constraints), court orders, funding sources, and varied models of intervention. Group strategies include work with individuals, families, organizations, and communities, in relating to other social workers, to interdisciplinary teams, and even in adversarial situations. Thus group techniques from problem solving, psychotherapy, and community work are important. In the same way, skills for developing and implementing policy help social workers understand, formulate and implement policies and remain active participants in policy debates. The usual boundaries are spanned in order to extend the panoply of interventions available to all health-related social workers.

Take an active part in all aspects of evaluation. The last part of this approach describes the relationship of the establishment of realistic goals and objectives to concrete measures of outcome to evaluate direct and indirect practice. Much of the discussion relates back to assessment, planning and contracting material, in ways that allow the objectives of the work to be measurable and thus possible to evaluate. Quality assurance and evaluation of social workers and their work are all dimensions of practice.

Conclusions

This discussion of the parts of this approach might suggest to the reader that learning is linear: that is, social workers use relationships to access, then strategize, then intervene, then evaluate, all within a context that comprises history, laws, values, ethics, and organizational constraints. In fact, little learning or intervention is linear, and context is not made up of smaller and smaller concentric circles in which the social worker and client sit. Each element flows into all the other, and learning and intervening are both circular and continuous activities.

Overall, this boundary spanning approach is a next small step in the continued development of an ecological perspective for health-related social work. It combines management and more traditional social work information with a series of mapping devices, calls for social workers to be advocates and case managers, and requires excellent relationship skills and decision-making abilities. The approach is flexible and practical. Every part of the work is related to meeting the needs of clients, consumers, programs, and communities. The work answers these questions: What do clients need from me? What can they expect from me and from my profession here in my organization and in the larger systems to which they and I must relate? The work honors the past, is responsive to the present, and helps the social worker to proceed sensitively, professionally, and efficiently to help clients, consumers, programs, and communities enhance their well-being.

No approach to practice that has been developed so far is without serious flaws, and this reinterpretation is no exception. Overall, this is meant to broaden the scope of the social worker to incorporate more of the dimensions of context that are necessary for helping clients. Second, it encourages and enables social workers to act in powerful ways. It suggests that social workers must obtain and keep sufficient authority to do their work by becoming experts in relation to specific populations. It exhorts social workers to understand the needs and capacities of clients/consumers, programs, and communities, to understand the rich and complex systems in which the work occurs, and to use all possible levels of intervention to forward the work. All told, the purpose of boundary spanning is to enable to social workers to span outmoded barriers to work as deeply and broadly as possible to help their clients reach their goals.

Reprinted from Toba S. Kerson, Boundary spanning: An ecological reinterpretation of social work practice in health and mental health systems. *Social Work in Mental Health* 2 (2004): 39–57. Reprinted by permission.

References

Abramson, J. (1993). Orienting social work employees in interdisciplinary settings: Shaping professional and organizational perspectives. *Social Work* 38 (2): 152–57.

Allen-Meares, P., and B. A. Lane (1987). Grounded social work practice in theory: Eco-systems. *Social Casework* 68 (9): 515–21.

Argyris, C. (1994). Good communication that blocks learning. *Harvard Business Review* (July–August): 77–85.

Bailey, D. and K. E. Gorchau (1993). Aligning leadership needs to the organizational state of development: Applying management theory to organizations. *Administration in Social Work* 17 (1): 23–28.

Bertelli, A. M. (1998). Should social workers engage in the unauthorized practice of law? *Boston Public Interest Law Journal* 8 (15): 1–28.

Bogdan, R., and S. J. Taylor (1998). *Introduction to Qualitative Research methods: A Guidebook and Resources.* New York: John Wiley.

Christensen, C. M. (1997). Making strategy: Learning by doing. *Harvard Business Review* (November–December): 141–56.

Dickson, D. T. (1995). *Law in the Health and Human Services: A Guide for Social Workers, Psychologists, Psychiatrists, and Related Professionals.* New York: Free Press.

Drucker, P. F. (1974). *Management: Tasks, Responsibilities, Practices.* New York: Harper and Row.

——— (1999). *Management Challenges for the 21st Century.* New York: HarperBusiness.

Ell, K. O., W. Obier, and H. Northen (1990). *Families and Health Care: Psychosocial Practice.* New York: Aldine de Gruyter.

Feldblum, C.R. (1991). Employment protections. *Milbank Quarterly* 69 (supp. 1–2): 81–110.

Germain, C. B. (1984). *Social Work Practice in Health Care: An Ecological Perspective.* New York: Free Press.

Gitterman, A., and L. Shulman (1994). *Mutual Aid Groups, Vulnerable Populations, and the Life Cycle.* 2nd ed. New York: Columbia University Press.

Griffiths, L. (1997). Accomplishing team: Teamwork and categorization in two community mental health teams. *Sociological Review* 45 (2): 59–78.

Hammer, D. L. and T. S. Kerson (1998). Reducing the number of days for which insurers deny payment to the hospital: One primary objective for a newly configured department of case management. *Social Work in Health Care* 28 (2): 31.

Kaplan, R. S., and D. P. Norton (1996). *The Balanced Scorecard: Translating Strategy into Action.* Boston: Harvard Business School Press.

Karls, J. M. and K. E. Wandrei, eds. (1994a). *Person-in-Environment System: The PIE Classification System for Social Functioning Problems.* Washington, D.C.: NASW Press.

——— (1994b). *PIE Manual: Person-in-Environment System.* Washington, D.C.: NASW Press.

Kerson, T. S. (2002). *Boundary Spanning: An Ecological Reinterpretation of Social Work Practice in Health and Mental Health Systems.* New York: Columbia University Press.

Kettner, P. M., Moroney, R. M. and L. L. Martin (1999). *Designing and Managing Programs: An Effectiveness-Based Approach.* 2nd ed. Thousand Oaks, Calif.: Sage.

Kopels, S. (1995). The Americans with Disabilities Act: A tool to combat poverty. *Journal of Social Work Education* 31 (3): 337–46.

Levinson, H. (1992). Fads, fantasies, and psychological management. *Psychological Journal* (Winter): 1–12.

MacNair, R. H. (1996). Theory for community practice in social work: The example of ecological community practice. *Journal of Community Practice* 3 (3/4): 181–202.

McGoldrick, M., and R. Gerson (1985). *Genograms in Family Assessment.* New York: Norton.

Menefee, D. (1997). Strategic administration of nonprofit human service organizations: A model for executive success in turbulent times. *Administration in Social Work* 21 (2): 1–19.

Meyer, C. H., ed. (1983). *Clinical Social Work in the Eco-Systems Perspective.* New York: Columbia University Press.

——— (1988). The eco-systems perspective. In Rachelle Dorfman, ed., *Paradigms of Clinical Social Work,* 275–94. New York: Brunner/Mazel.

Mintzberg, H. (1994). *The Rise and Fall of Strategic Planning.* New York: Free Press.

Mintzberg, H., and J. Lempel (1999). Reflecting on the strategy process. *Sloan Management Review* 40 (3): 21–30.

Mintzberg, H., and Ludo Van der Heyden (1999). Organigraphs: Drawing how companies really work. *Harvard Business Review* (September–October): 87–94.

Mullen, E. J. and J. L. Magnabosco, eds. (1997). *Outcome Measurement in the Human Services: Cross-Cutting Issues and Methods,* 3–19. Washington, D.C.: NASW Press.

Mulroy, E. A., and S.Shay (1997). Nonprofit organizations and innovation: A model of neighborhood-based collaboration to prevent child maltreatment. *Social Work* 42 (5): 515–24.

Neugeboren, B. (1996). *Environmental Practice in the Human Services: Integration of Micro and MacroRoles, Skills, and Contexts.* New York: Haworth Press.

Orlin, M. (1995). The Americans with Disabilities Act: Implications for social services. *Social Work* 40 (2): 233–39.

Rosen, A. (1993). Systematic planned practice. *Social Service Review* 67 (1): 84–100.

Rosen, A., E. K. Proctor, and M. M. Staudt (1999). Social work research and the quest for effective practice. *Social Work Research* 23 (1): 4–14.

Saltz, C. C., and T. Schaefer (1996). Interdisciplinary teams in health care: Integration of family caregivers. *Social Work in Health Care* 22 (3): 59–70.

Schatz, M. S., L. E. Jenkins, and B. W. Shaefor (1990). Milford redefined: A model of generalist and advanced generalist social work. *Journal of Social Work Education* 26: 217–31.

Senge, P.M. (1990). *The Fifth Discipline: The Art and Practice of the Learning Organization.* New York: Currency Doubleday.

Siporin, M. (1980). Ecological systems theory in social work. *Journal of Sociology and Social Welfare* 7 (4): 507–32.

Strauss, A. L. and J.M. Corbin (1998). *Basics of Qualitative Research Techniques and Procedures for Developing Grounded Theory.* 2nd ed. Thousand Oaks, Calif.: Sage.

Sunley, R. (1997). Advocacy in the new world of managed care. *Families in Society* 78 (1): 84–94.

Tufte, E. R. (1997). *Visual Explanations: Images and Quantities, Evidence, and Narrative.* Cheshire, Conn.: Graphics Press.

Wakefield, J. (1996a). Does social work need the eco-systems perspective? Pt. 1: Is the perspective clinically useful? *Social Service Review* 70 (1): 1–32.

——— (1996b). Does social work need the eco-systems perspective? Pt 2: Does the perspective save social work from incoherence? *Social Service Review* 70 (2): 183–219.

Zeira, A., and A. Rosen (1999). Intermediate outcomes pursued by practitioners: A Qualitative analysis. *Social Work Research* 23 (2): 79–87.

Commentary

Toba S. Kerson

In many ways, I have been developing a boundary spanning approach to practice for all of my forty-two years as a social worker. I have learned that spanning what appear to be well-established and somewhat insurmountable limits is the work and, in fact, the responsibility of all social work practitioners.

In my first weeks as a twenty-three-year-old, newly minted master's graduate, I began to work as a psychiatric social worker at the Baltimore City Hospitals where I realized that helping individuals to find insights was not really helping anyone very much. In that acute psychiatric unit, I worked with families and groups in order to help individuals who were managing mental illnesses to fulfill their family, workplace and community roles. When organizational rules interfered with the effort, I worked with others to demand systemic changes. I could not accept established definitions of levels of practice and still effectively intervene with and advocate for my clients. This notion was further supported when I left psychiatry to become the Follow-Up Coordinator of the Baltimore City Hospitals. In this position, I was the emergency department social worker and, since most entry to any area of the system was through the emergency room, I was particularly responsible for patients' keeping clinic appointments. Within weeks, I learned that the problems were the result not of poor compliance but of organizational barriers. That is, patients were given appointments to hypertension or medical clinic with no explanation that even though their symptoms were abated, the progress of their disease was not. In addition, they were not offered help in relation to transportation or dealing with straightforward family or employment issues or in navigating the system. So, with the aid of a clerk, I instituted a plan to address simple barriers for patients referred to hypertension clinic. We improved the return rate from less than 20 percent to about 90 percent. The director of the Medical Clinic asked if I could do the same for her. Since she could hardly keep up with her present demand, I asked what she would do if we increased her volume more than four times. She stopped asking. This experience confirmed my understanding that organizational obstacles must be targets of change.

Several themes emerged from those years of practice that became permanent dimensions of my work: an interest in chronic situations, especially health problems; the notion that effective responses to most individual problems are almost always related to social support; and that to advocate for their clients, social workers must be organizational and systems experts. At that point, I was thinking that I would apply to programs either in fine arts with some kind of emphasis on design, in social work or public health. I have always been interested in visual explanations of relationship as a way of seeing beyond immediate problems and situations in order to increase possibilities. I began the Penn doctoral program with an eye to becoming a director of a social work department in a university hospital. What Penn afforded me was the opportunity to work not just in social work but in communications, law, community medicine, education and sociology. I was also taught by professors with backgrounds in economics, anthropology, linguistics, and social psychology. In the end, one doctorate was not enough and after I completed the requirements for the social work degree, I stayed on for a Ph.D. in sociology because I needed several theoretical orientations, modes of thinking, and ways of intervening to address the kinds of chronic social and health problems in which I continue to be interested.

Because of my experience as the follow-up coordinator, when I began to teach practice and health-related courses at Bryn Mawr thirty years ago, I was assigned a course called Social Service Management. This course, which bridges direct practice, program development and management, and advocacy within and between organizations, continues to be an alternative to the clinical and policy/advocacy tracks. It was in developing that course that I refined this boundary-spanning approach.

I was asked to write the book of which this article is a kind of summary because the publishers wanted a volume on health-related ecological practice. They were familiar with my work especially through two of the books that I had written. The first, *Understanding Chronic Illness* (1985), explores the medical and psychosocial dimensions of nine diseases. By looking at constraints and decision-making, the second book, *Social Work in Health Settings: Practice in Context* (1997), begins what I later articulate as boundary spanning. It frames cases from a wide variety of health and mental health settings in relation to political, technological and organizational constraints. For *Boundary Spanning*, I wanted first to describe as deeply as possible ecological elements that are critical for being able to practice social work on any level. Also, with my continuing interest in design and visualization, I wanted to find visual tools in addition to the classic genograms and ecomaps that could inform decisions (Tufte 1997, 2001). Thus, to these traditional social work tools, I added personal balanced scorecards (Kaplan and Norton 1996), and organigraphs (Mintzberg and Heydan 1999) and driving forces maps (Daloisio, Kerson, and McCoyd 2002). These tools are drawn from the business literature on which I rely increasingly to teach students how to understand and manage relationships in complex organizations and to evaluate clients and the work at the onset of a new project, program or intervention. In addition, as I had done in the books that I have mentioned, I wanted to work from real situations in the field rather than write the book and fit examples to my practice wisdom.

To begin this work, I wrote to 120 experienced, respected social work practitioners to submit examples of cases, projects, or programs demonstrating best practice or practice innovations with an emphasis on working across established limits. Using the techniques of grounded theory, I built categories from the data. Identified boundaries included those restricting knowledge bases, setting definitions, and funding, separating health from mental health, and those that isolate systems of service delivery and levels and modalities of practice.

From those categories, I developed this notion of boundary spanning as a more flexible approach to health-related social work that is based in but goes beyond ecological and systems perspectives. This approach challenges social workers to locate boundaries that limit client functioning, to assess the ability to span those boundaries in effective ways and to intervene in order to modify the functioning of the structures surrounding clients as well as to intervene with clients directly. To aid these processes, social workers are introduced to mapping devices and techniques drawn from social work, social science, organizational development and business to assess, plan, make-concrete, monitor, and compare work with particular clients, programs, organizations and larger systems, and to evaluate their clients' and organizations' progress as well as their own development. This approach helps social workers work in large, complex systems of care that demand more creativity and advocacy from practitioners in less time with less support.

In conclusion, when I became a social worker and worked for several years for a Penn trained functionalist, I incorporated the concepts of agency function, use of time, client self-determination, and the power of the relationship between social worker and client into my work. When I was a student at Penn, we were teaching students to be change agents. These concepts are all part of this boundary-spanning approach. I can end with a phrase from the Penn School of Social Policy & Practice Web page: "the social work practitioner engages in a continuous process of planned change to improve the delivery of services and link social resources to the areas of greatest need." A boundary-spanning approach to practice extends across previously drawn barriers in order to afford social workers a greater scope of understanding, greater latitude in interventions, and greater access to organizations and systems. And I continue to cross boundaries in my research and teaching (Kerson and Kerson 2006).

References

Daloisio, F., T. S. Kerson, and J. McCoyd (2002). Driving forces maps: Case studies of a tool for implementing change. *Social Work in Health Care* 36 (2): 1–20.

Kaplan, R.t S., and D. P. Norton (1996). *The Balanced Scorecard: Translating Strategy into Action.* Boston: Harvard Business School Press.

Kerson, T. S. (1997). *Social Work in Health Settings: Practice in Context.* New York: Haworth.

——— (2002). *Boundary Spanning: An Ecological Reinterpretation of Social Work Practice in Health and Mental Health Systems.* New York: Columbia University Press.

Kerson, T. S., and L.e A. Kerson (1985). *Understanding Chronic Illness: The Medical and Psychosocial Dimensions of Nine Diseases.* New York: Free Press.

——— (2006). Implacable images: Why epileptiform events continue to be featured in film and television, *Epileptic Disorders* 8 (2): 1–11.

Mintzberg, H., and L. Van der Heyden (1999). Organigraphs: Drawing how companies really work. *Harvard Business Review* (September–October): 87–94.

Tufte, E. R. (1997). *Visual Explanations: Images and Quantities, Evidence and Narrative.* Cheshire, Conn.: Graphics Press.

——— (2001). *The Visual Display of Quantitative Information.* Cheshire, Conn.: Graphics Press.

Chapter 20
Challenging Injustice and Oppression

David G. Gil

The emotional and intellectual roots of this essay reach back to my own experiences of injustice and oppression, following the German occupation of Austria in 1938. At that time, our family's business was coercively "aryanized"; our livelihood was destroyed; my father was imprisoned in a concentration camp; I was expelled from my school and placed in a segregated school for Jewish children. Eventually, my mother sent me abroad with a "Kinder-transport" of refugee children. Our family was never reunited.

These experiences and the trauma of separation from my family at age fourteen, led me to raise a difficult question, which has become a major focus of my work: "How can we overcome and prevent injustice and oppression, regardless of who the victims are?" My quest has led me gradually to a philosophy of social equality, liberty, real democracy, individuality through community, cooperation, and active non-violence. (Buber 1958; Freire 1970; Gil 1998; King 1992; Kropotkin 1956; Tawney 1964).

The present essay is based on my quest for answers to the above question. It clarifies the meanings of injustice and oppression, sketches their sources and history, and examines their consequences for key institutions of social life. It then discusses strategies to overcome these dehumanizing social conditions.

Meanings of Injustice and Oppression and Their Opposites

Oppression refers to social structures and relations involving domination and exploitation of individuals, classes, and communities within a society, and of peoples beyond a society's territory. Domination serves to institute economic, social, psychological, and cultural exploitation and to establish privileged conditions of living for certain social classes and peoples. The goals of domination and exploitation are implemented by expropriating resources and products of dominated classes and peoples, and by controlling their work and productivity.

Domination and exploitation have usually been initiated by force, followed by socialization and ideological indoctrination. Over time, these processes, backed by systems of social control, resulted in the internalization of the perspectives and culture of dominant classes and peoples, into the consciousness of their victims, and in willing submission of the latter to the expectations of the former.

Injustice refers to the consequences of domination and exploitation: multi-dimensional inequalities and development-inhibiting, discriminatory, and dehumanizing conditions of living. These coercively established and maintained conditions include, but are not limited to: slavery, serfdom, and wage labor; unemployment, poverty, hunger, and homelessness; discrimination by race, ethnicity, age, gender, sexual orientation, disabilities, etc.; inadequate health care and inferior education.

Justice means the absence of domination and exploitation: it implies equal liberty and equal rights, responsibilities, and constraints for all. Domination, exploitation and injustice, on the other hand, involve unequal liberty, rights, responsibilities, and constraints of oppressed individuals, groups, classes, communities, and peoples.

Oppression within and beyond societies, and conditions of injustice have always been results of human choices and actions, rather than inevitable expressions of human nature. Evidence in support of this proposition is provided by the existence, throughout history, of human groups whose ways of life and social relations were shaped by values of equality, liberty, solidarity, and cooperation, rather than by dynamics of domination, exploitation, and competition (Kropotkin 1956).

Being results of human choices and actions, domination, exploitation, and injustice, were, therefore, never, nor are they now, inevitable. People could always have made different choices, and they can now and in the future chose to transcend oppression and injustice. Indeed, people have often challenged such dehumanizing conditions and relations, and are likely to do so again by spreading critical consciousness and organizing liberation movements (Freire 1970).

Societies that evolved internal relations of domination and exploitation tended to extend these relations also beyond their populations and territories. Colonialism, genocide of native peoples, and slavery, as well as contemporary economic and cultural imperialism illustrate this tendency. Such oppressive practices intensified over time as a result of resistance by victims and reactive repression by perpetrators, as well as due to competition for dominance among different colonial and imperialistic powers. By now, relations of domination and exploitation, and conditions of injustice have penetrated most branches of humankind in the name of neo-liberal, globalized "free" market capitalism.

Relations of domination and exploitation from local to global levels came gradually to be reflected not only in social, economic, political, legal, and cultural institutions, but also in the consciousness, values, attitudes, and actions of most people including also victims of oppression. Overcoming oppression and injustice would, therefore, require not only transformations of the institutions which maintain them (liberation of institutions), but also transformations of people's consciousness, values, attitudes, and actions (liberation of consciousness and practice).

Societies whose human relations are shaped by oppressive tendencies are usually not divided simply into oppressors and oppressed people and classes. Rather, people in such societies, regardless of their class position, tend to be oppressed in some contexts and oppressors in others.

Key Institutions of Social Life in Just and Free, and in Unjust and Oppressive Societies

To discern characteristics of just and free, and of unjust and oppressive societies, one needs to examine how individuals and social classes participate in, and are affected by, key institutions of social life, including the following:

- stewardship, ownership, and control of life-sustaining natural and human-created resources
- organization of work and production
- exchange and distribution of concrete and symbolic goods and services and of civil and political rights and responsibilities
- governance and legitimation
- reproduction, socialization, and social control (Gil 1992)

The way these inter-related key institutions function shapes the circumstances of living and relative power of individuals and social classes, the quality of human relations among individuals and classes, and the overall quality of life in society. Characteristics of just and free, and of unjust and oppressive societies are sketched below with reference to these key institutions.

Just and Free Societies

In just and free societies all people are considered to be of equal intrinsic worth, in spite of individual uniqueness and differences, and are, therefore, entitled to equal rights, liberties, and responsibilities concerning participation in the key institutions of social life.

In such societies, exchanges of work and of products do not involve exploitation; everyone's individual needs and potential are considered equally important; and all are treated as equals in the distribution of concrete and symbolic goods and services, and of civil and political rights and responsibilities. Marx's pithy phrase, "to each according to needs, from each according to capacities," seems an apt characterization of just and free societies (Tawney 1964; Tucker 1978).

Unjust and Oppressive Societies

In unjust and oppressive societies, on the other hand, people are not considered to be of equal intrinsic worth, and are, therefore, not entitled to equal rights, liberties, and responsibilities concerning participation in the key institutions of social life.

In such societies, people belonging to different classes are entitled to different rights and are subject to different expectations and conditions of work. Also, exchanges of work and of products involve economic and social exploitation. Furthermore, the needs and potential of members of dominant classes are deemed more important than the needs and potential of members of dominated classes. Hence, the former receives routinely preferential treatment in the organization of work and in the distribution of concrete and symbolic goods and services, and of civil and political rights, liberties, and responsibilities. Establishing and maintaining such inequalities concerning the key institutions of social life, is usually not possible without coercion, i.e., social-structural violence (Gil 1999).

Variability of Oppression and Injustice

Oppression and injustice tend to vary among societies, and over time also in the same society. These variations reflect differences in social values and in degrees of inequality concerning the key institutions of social life in particular societies at particular times. The higher the degrees of inequality, the higher are the levels of coercion necessary to enforce it, as well as the levels of resistance from dominated classes, and the levels of reactive repression by dominant classes.

While variations are possible in degrees of oppression and injustice, variations are logically not possible concerning justice and non-oppressive relations, which are predicated upon equality of rights, liberties, responsibilities, and constraints. Equality, however, is not a continuum, but the zero point on the continuum of inequality, and therefore can not vary by degrees.

It follows that whenever inequalities are present in a society, its ways of life involve oppression and injustice; its people are not free in a meaningful sense; and its political institutions are essentially undemocratic and coercive, in spite of elections and claims, such as "being part of the free world."

Historical Notes

The story of social evolution reveals that oppression and injustice did not become institutionalized until the spread of agriculture and crafts, some ten thousand years ago. These major changes in ways of life resulted gradually in a stable economic surplus which was conducive to the emergence of occupational and social classes, differentiations into rural and urban settlements, and centralized forms of governance over defined territories (Eisler 1987).

Pre-Agricultural, Egalitarian Communities

For several hundred thousand years, prior to the development of agriculture and crafts, people lived in isolated communities that subsisted by hunting, gathering, and fishing. Internal relations in these communities were usually based on egalitarian, cooperative, and communal principles, and did not involve institutionalized domination, exploitation, and injustice.

Stewardship over resources was exercised collectively to meet people's basic needs. Organization of work was based mainly on age, gender, physical conditions, and individual capacities, but not on criteria such as caste and class. Everyone had roughly equal rights and responsibilities to work in order to secure the survival of the community. The exchange and distribution of goods and services did not involve exploitation.

Civil and political rights, liberties, and responsibilities tended to be shared equally, and people were subject to equal constraints. Everyone's needs were deemed equally important, and were met, subject to limits set by natural resources and collective productivity.

The ways of life of early communities were not conducive to economic exploitation such as slavery, for their simple technologies did not enable people to produce more than they consumed. They, therefore, were not able to generate a reliable surplus for appropriation and exploitation by others—the material base and precondition for oppressive systems.

I do not mean to idealize pre-agricultural ways of life, nor to advocate a return to that stage of social evolution, in order to overcome contemporary oppression and injustice. I am also aware that human relations were then not free from oppressive tendencies, especially in relations between men and women, older and younger persons, and community members and strangers. Also relations between different societies were not always peaceful.

However, from what is known from archeology and anthropology about the pre-agricultural period of human evolution, domination and exploitation were not institutionalized policies and practices then. We could, therefore, derive important insights from the values and ways of life of early human communities.

Post-Agricultural Societies

Gradual increases in population, which upset the balance between people and life-sustaining resources, led to the development of agriculture and animal husbandry. This had revolutionary consequences for the ways of life of nomadic communities and for their internal and external relations.

Gradually, people settled into permanent communities which generated a food supply beyond their consumption needs. It was, therefore, no longer necessary for everyone to engage in food production, and many people were able to pursue alternative occupations. This led to the emergence of occupational and social classes, including peasants, artisans, and traders; priests, scholars, professionals, and artists; civilian administrators, soldiers, and ruling elites.

Occupational differentiations led also to spatial differentiations—the emergence of cities and neighborhoods, and to social, economic, political, and cultural differentiations, all of which resulted in differences in ways of life, consciousness, interests, values, and ideologies among subgroups of societies.

The new ways of life evolved tendencies toward expropriation of resources and complex divisions of labor, that yielded an economic surplus—the base for the emergence of domination, exploitation and injustice. These changes led to changes in modes of exchange and distribution, and in overall social organization, values, and ideologies. Illustrations of these developments are the ancient civilizations of Mesopotamia and Egypt (Durant 1935).

To be sure, these developments took centuries and millennia, and involved at any stage many choices, none of which were ever inevitable. Indeed, different societies which developed agriculture and animal husbandry, made different choices and developed different patterns of key institutions, values, and ideologies. Rather than developing patterns of oppression and injustice, they used the economic surplus from their increased productivity toward enhancing the quality of life for all their members, and they continued to manage resources, to organize work and production, and exchange and distribution in accordance with egalitarian, cooperative, and communal values. Illustrations of this tendency have been identified among native peoples in the Americas, Africa and elsewhere. Many of these "native societies" preserved just and non-oppressive ways of life until, and often beyond, the violent conquest of their lands by colonizing European empires (Farb 1968; Zinn 1980).

Types of Societal Oppression and Injustice

The ways by which oppression and injustice were established varied among societies. Two related and interacting types may be distinguished: 1) dominating and exploiting strangers, i.e., other societies and their people; and 2) dominating and exploiting fellow citizens. Societies that practiced domination and exploitation have usually done so at home and abroad, as both types involve similar assumptions, value premises, and ideologies, and as internal and external human relations interact with, and influence, one another. It is nevertheless useful to differentiate conceptually between internal and external oppression, and to analyze their emergence separately.

Dominating and Exploiting Strangers

Crops ripening in the fields of people who had preceded others in developing agriculture, attracted nomadic tribes to invade peasant villages in order to appropriate their products. These invasions were the beginnings of warfare motivated by efforts to achieve control over economic resources. Invasions of ancient European villages by Asian nomadic tribes, the Kurgans, illustrate this process (Eisler 1987).

These violent encounters were not inevitable. The discoverers of agriculture may have been ready to share their knowledge and skills peacefully, as native peoples have actually done in the Americas, when European explorers and conquerors first arrived.

The invasions of peasant communities around harvest time resulted gradually in their enslavement by nomadic tribes, who became accustomed to securing their food supplies by appropriating the fruits of other people's work. With time, the invaders realized the advantage of keeping the peasants alive, rather than killing them, and to coerce them to continue raising crops and to turn over much of the product to the invaders. Eventually, nomadic societies not only coerced conquered communities to continue farming and turn over their surplus products, but they captured men and women from conquered villages, enslaved them, and exploited them sexually.

One can identify the typical elements of oppression and injustice in these early relationships between nomadic peoples and peasant communities over whom they gained dominance coercively, and whom they subsequently enslaved. The motivating factor is exploitation of the victims. This is accomplished by gaining control over their resources—their territories and their knowledge and skills—and forcing them to work and turn over their surplus product.

With time, social, psychological, and ideological dimensions evolved around the economic roots of oppressive relationships: the prestige of work performed by enslaved people declined relative to the activities engaged in by the dominant people, regardless of the objective importance of the work and activities; and the status and prestige of dominated, enslaved workers declined relative to that of members of dominant societies. These perceptions of the relative status and prestige of work and workers were internalized into the consciousness of everyone involved in exploitative relations, and became the core of discriminatory ideologies and practices concerning different social groups, classes, and peoples. Phenomena such as racism, sexism, and classism are contemporary manifestations and expressions of this ancient tendency.

Imposing oppressive relations and unjust conditions on other societies in order to exploit their resources, the potential of their people to work, and their human-created goods and services, as was done on a relatively small scale by nomadic tribes, has gradually become the model for building colonial empires during antiquity, the Middle Ages, and modern times. Historical details have varied from case to case, but institutional practices concerning resources, work and production, and exchange and distribution, have remained essentially the same throughout history, and so have the social, psychological, and ideological dimensions, as well as the secular and religious rationalizations for domination, exploitation, injustice, and discrimination (Frank 1977; Magdoff 1977).

Dominating and Exploiting Fellow Citizens

Oppression and injustice emerged within many but not all societies, as a consequence of occupational, social, and spatial differentiations. Whether or not these differentiations resulted in oppressive relations and unjust conditions seems to have depended largely on the terms of exchange between peasants and people pursuing newly emerging crafts and other occupations.

If exchanges were balanced in terms of work and material resources invested in products, then relations between peasants and groups pursuing other occupations, and living mainly in cities, could evolve along non-oppressive, and synergetic patterns, with everyone benefiting equally (Maslow and Honigman 1970).

If, on the other hand, exchanges were imbalanced, establishment and maintenance of such conditions required physical and ideological coercion. In these situations urban dwellers were bent upon exploiting the peasantry and gradually also each other, as occupational specializations and social differentiations multiplied, and as each occupational group aspired to appropriate as much as possible of the economic surplus by claiming privileged shares of available goods and services.

Unjust and oppressive societies which are based on coercively maintained exploitative exchanges among social classes engaging in different occupations and performing different roles, and enjoying different levels of rights, responsibilities, and liberty, were not as stable as pre-agricultural, egalitarian, and cooperative communities. They were changing continuously due to gradually intensifying competition and conflicts among individuals and social and occupational groups, who gained control over different shares of resources and different roles in the work system, and who consequently were able to command different shares in the distribution of goods and services, and civil and political rights and power.

During early stages of the emergence of unjust and oppressive relations, the egalitarian, cooperative, and communal values, ideology, and consciousness of pre-agricultural societies were gradually transformed into their opposites. These value changes toward inequality, competition, and selfishness were conducive to the ongoing development and reproduction of occupationally, spatially, and socially fragmented and stratified societies.

Perpetuation of Inequality

Once inequalities concerning the key institutions of social life were established in a society, they tended to be perpetuated, since individuals and groups who controlled disproportionally larger shares of resources and access to preferred work, were in advantageous positions to assure continuation of their privileges, and even to increase them. Also emerging legal and political institutions tended to reflect established inequalities and power relations among competing interest groups and classes, and were, therefore, unlikely to upset temporary equilibria among them.

The processes and logic of conflict and competition within societies originated in minor, initial inequalities in exchanges among individuals and occupational and social groups, which barely required coercion. However, the emerging tendency to legitimate, institutionalize, and increase initial minimal inequalities did require coercion. This resulted usually in resistance from victimized groups, to which privileged groups reacted with intensified coercion. The vicious circle of oppression, resistance, and reactive repression intensified with time, as people tended to react to the latest violent stages in the circle, but did not trace the sources of these destructive interactions, and, usually, lacked insights and motivation for reversing their course, and moving in alternative, constructive, non-exploitative directions.

The tendency for inequalities to intensify, once they are initiated on a small scale, has important implications for people who advocate reductions, rather than elimination of inequalities: as long as inequalities, at any level, are considered legitimate, and are being enforced by governments, competitive interactions focused on restructuring inequalities tend to continue among individuals, social groups and classes, and a sense of community and solidarity is unlikely to evolve.

One reason for the constant intensification of coercion in unjust and oppressive societies was that people's motivation to work declined in proportion to the increase in exploitation. Work discipline had, therefore, to be assured by ever more overt and covert coercion. Expectations concerning a "work ethic" became typical elements of socialization, and of religions and ideologies which interpreted and justified established, inegalitarian conditions of life and work. And socialization and indoctrination were routinely backed up by elaborate systems of submission-inducing rewards and sanctions, and by open and secret police and military forces, the instruments of "legitimate violence" within inegalitarian societies, and among societies of unjust and exploitative world systems.

The history of oppression and injustice within and among societies over the past ten thousand years is essentially a series of variations on the theme of coercively initiated and maintained exploitative modes of resource stewardship, work and production, and exchange and distribution. This history is a tragic one indeed. The mere mention of coercive work systems such as ancient and recent slavery, feudal serfdom, and early and contemporary industrial and agricultural wage labor, brings to mind images of toiling people, transformed, not by their own choice, into dehumanized "factors of production," dominated and exploited by tyrants and slave masters, absolute rulers and aristocracies, and individual and corporate, capitalist employers. Such work systems could never have been established and perpetuated without massive coercion and violence in the form of civil and foreign wars, genocide, murder, torture, imprisonment, starvation, destitution, unemployment, and ever-present threats of these and other oppressive measures (Gil 2000; John Paul II 1982; Tucker 1978).

Social-Change Strategies to Overcome Injustice and Oppression

An important insight gained from the history of social change is that activists need to differentiate short-range from long-range goals. Short-range reforms such as transition policies based on President Roosevelt's proposals for a Bill of Economic Rights and on the United Nations Universal Declaration of Human Rights will not be discussed here, as our focus here is on eliminating the roots of oppression and injustice (Gil 1998).

It is important to emphasize, however, that pursuing short-range goals is not only necessary, but is also ethically valid, in order to reduce the intensity of injustice and oppression as far, and as soon, as possible, even before eliminating their institutional sources. Pursuing short-range goals need not be an obstacle to the pursuit of long-range goals and can be connected strategically with the pursuit of fundamental social transformations, as long as activists do not confuse these different sets of goals.

Long-Range Visions

Fundamental social transformations toward just and free societies are unlikely to come about through spontaneous, brief, revolutionary events. Rather, they require lengthy processes, involving counter-cultural education toward critical consciousness, initiated and sustained by social movements seeking to transform development-inhibiting institutions into development-conducive alternatives. Such transformation processes and movements require long-range visions to guide them.

Transformation visions need to identify essential attributes of just and free societies, and of strategies toward their realization. The visions should reflect the common interest of people anywhere to meet their human needs. Accordingly, the visions would have to include the following institutional attributes (Gil 1992; Maslow 1970; Tawney 1931).

Establishing a Public Trust of Productive Resources

Natural and human-created, concrete and non-concrete, productive resources would have to be considered and administered as "public trust," or "commons," available to everyone, on equal terms, for use in productive, life-sustaining and life-enhancing pursuits. Stewardship of the public trust would have to be carried out through decentralized, horizontally coordinated, democratic processes, from local to global levels. While the public trust would replace private and corporate ownership and control of productive resources, consumption goods could be owned by individuals, households, and groups of people.

Redefining Work and Production

Work and production would have to be reorganized, redefined, and redesigned, to meet the actual needs for goods and services of all people, anywhere on earth (Gil 2000). Education for, and participation in, work and production, in accordance with individual capacities, would have to be assured to all throughout life. All people would have the rights, responsibilities, and opportunities to become self-directing "masters of production," who use their faculties in an integrated manner, rather than be forced to labor as "hired hands," or "factors of production," under alienating conditions, in the perceived interest, and at the discretion of, individual or corporate employers.

Furthermore, all people would have equal rights, responsibilities, and constraints, to choose and change their occupations; to design, direct, and carry out their work; and to share by rotation, in socially necessary work, not chosen voluntarily by enough people. Also, work would have to be redefined to include all activities conducive to the maintenance and enrichment of life, and would have to exclude life-impeding activities. Thus, caring for one's children and dependent relatives would have to be considered and rewarded as socially necessary work, while weapons manufacture—to use an extreme example—might have to be considered as "counter-work," and phased out. All socially necessary work would have to be deemed to be of equal worth and rewarded accordingly.

Finally, work would have to be in harmony with nature, with requirements of conservation, and with global demographic developments: it would, therefore, have to produce high-quality, long-lasting goods, use renewable resources where possible, and avoid waste.

Exchanging Goods and Services Nonexploitatively

Goods and services would have to be exchanged and distributed on fair, non-exploitative terms. All people, engaging in socially necessary work, would have to have equal rights to have their needs acknowledged and met by obtaining goods and services in adequate quantity and quality. Also social, civil, cultural, and political rights, responsibilities, and constraints would have to be assured to all on equal terms.

Developing Democratic Structures and Processes of Governance

Structures and processes of governance, on local and trans-local levels, would have to be truly democratic, non-hierarchical, decentralized, horizontally coordinated, and geared to assuring equal rights, responsibilities, and constraints, and serving the real needs and interests of everyone living now and in the future. Government service would not entitle elected and appointed officials to privileged living conditions relative to the conditions of the people whom they represent and serve.

Applying Egalitarian Socialization Processes

Socialization practices, during all stages of life, would have to be shaped by egalitarian and democratic values, so that all children and adults would have equal rights, responsibilities, and opportunities to develop in accordance with their innate potential, with due regard for individual differences in needs, capacities, and limitations.

Feasibility of Realization of Long-Range Visions

When people encounter long-range visions like the one sketched above they tend to doubt that such visions could actually be realized. Such skepticism is understandable, given peoples' lifelong experiences with prevailing social, economic, political, and cultural realities, and their adaptation to, and identification with, these realities.

People living long ago would have been similarly skeptical concerning the possibility of ever realizing long-range visions involving comprehensive transformations toward contemporary ways of life. Yet such transformations did come about, not quickly and spontaneously, but through lengthy processes, involving efforts and struggles by critical thinkers, social activists, and popular movements. By analogy, one may hypothesize, that visions of just and free societies, which seem to most people unrealistic and utopian, could eventually be realized through persistent efforts and struggles, over lengthy periods of time, by contemporary and future thinkers, activists, and social movements.

Theoretical Perspectives on Transformation Strategies

Social transformation toward long-range visions of just and free societies involves discerning, and eventually overcoming, forces and processes which maintain, and reproduce, existing unjust and oppressive societies and cultures. Human societies and their particular institutional systems have always been shaped by the actions and social relations, and by the consciousness of their members. Hence, the forces and processes which liberation movements have to target for transformation include

- patterns of action, interactions, and social relations of the members of societies
- processes of consciousness which underlie, motivate, and facilitate the existing patterns of actions, interactions, and social relations

Transformation of unjust and oppressive societies into just and free ones would require major changes in patterns of people's actions, interactions, and social relations. In turn such changes seem to depend on prior changes of people's consciousness, which would be conducive to alternative patterns of actions and relations. Activists, pursuing long-range visions of social justice and freedom, ought, therefore, to devise and implement strategies aimed at facilitating the emergence of "critical consciousness," in order to induce and sustain appropriate changes in people's actions, interactions, and social relations (Freire 1970).

Critical Consciousness: Key to Fundamental Social Change

To advance visions of just and free societies by non-coercive, voluntary, truly democratic means (the only strategic mode likely to be effective) rather than by coercive, authoritarian, non-democratic ones, seems to require transformation of the status quo-reproducing consciousness of most people, into alternative, status quo-challenging critical consciousness. Accordingly, social movements pursuing the elimination of injustice and oppression would have to make intense efforts to facilitate the spreading of such critical consciousness. These efforts would involve dialogical, educational processes to promote changes concerning:

- images of social reality most people now hold
- ideas, beliefs, and assumptions people tend to take for granted, without critical examination
- perceptions of individual and collective needs and interests which underlie and motivate the actions, thoughts, and social relations of most people
- values and ideologies, which derive form the perceptions of needs and interests, and affect the choices, actions, thoughts, and social relations of individuals, groups, and classes

Images of Social Reality

As for changes in the images of reality, people have to be helped to discover that social realities are results of human actions and thoughts; that people have changed realities in the past and will change them in the future; that by acting together, people have power to influence the directions of future changes, even though as individuals they feel and are powerless to do so.

People also have to be helped to realize that prevailing social inequalities were established, and are being reproduced, by coercion and socialization, rather than by democratic choices; and that "law and order" in the context of "legitimate," social inequalities does not imply justice and freedom, for the existing legal system tends, actually, to uphold injustice and oppression.

Unexamined Assumptions and Beliefs

Ideas, beliefs, and assumptions that people have to be helped to examine include the views that humans are compelled, rather than merely enabled, by nature, to be selfish, greedy, competitive, and violent; and that just, non-oppressive, egalitarian, cooperative, and non-violent societies have, therefore, never existed, nor is it possible to establish such societies in the future.

People would also have to examine the social and individual dimensions of human nature. Once they come to understand these intrinsic aspects of the human condition they are likely to realize that individuality can develop optimally only in the context of communities, but fails to develop adequately in the context of individualistic pursuits, unrelated to, or damaging to, a community (Fromm 1955; National Conference of Catholic Bishops 1986).

Other widely held beliefs to be challenged are that everyone who tries can secure adequate living conditions by working within the established social order; that, therefore, no major structural changes, but only marginal adjustments, may be necessary; and that people who fail to secure adequate conditions may be inherently deficient, and would have to blame themselves (Ryan 1971).

Furthermore, people ought to examine Adam Smith's controversial, yet influential, assumptions (which have not been supported by history), that the public good tends to appear spontaneously, as if created by an "invisible hand," when individuals act selfishly and competitively in pursuit of material gain; and that, therefore, governments should not interfere with supposedly "free markets," nor should they plan for, and attempt to promote the public good (Smith 1961).

Underlying Perceptions of Individual and Collective Needs

As for perceptions of individual and collective interests, people have to be helped to realize that institutionalized inequalities are incompatible with their true interest to satisfy their real human needs. Given the dynamics of contemporary capitalist societies and cultures, many people may be able to satisfy their needs for biological-material necessities, though often under alienating and stigmatizing conditions, and at substandard levels. However, given these dynamics, people are usually unable to meet their social-psychological, productive-creative, security, self-actualization, and spiritual needs at adequate levels (Gil 1992; Maslow 1970). The consistent frustration of human needs due to the dynamics of injustice and oppression of contemporary societies is a constant source of social, emotional, and physical pathology and violence, and of individual and community underdevelopment.

It is important to note that being "successful" in economic terms, under prevailing social and cultural conditions, does not imply that one's nonmaterial needs are being realized adequately, and that one's development is not inhibited. Affluent people are now as unlikely as poor people to fulfill their nonmaterial needs adequately. They, too, would, therefore, have to reexamine the current perceptions of their needs and interests, and they, too, might discover that they would be more likely to meet their real needs in a just and free society shaped by different perceptions of individual and collective needs and interests.

Values and Ideologies

Finally, people would have to be helped to reexamine the dominant values and ideologies of their culture, which they internalized into their consciousness while growing up and interacting with others in everyday life. Once people internalize these values and ideologies, they come to perceive their interests in adapting to the practices and expectations of their society and they are motivated to think and act in ways that continuously reproduce the institutional status quo.

When people are helped to discover that their real needs are being frustrated consistently in the context of established unjust and oppressive institutions, they are also likely to realize that transforming these institutions into just and non-oppressive ones would serve their interest, as it would be conducive to their personal development by enabling them to meet their real needs.

These insights would enable them also to recognize the necessity of shifting currently dominant values and ideologies, which sustain unjust and oppressive ways of life, toward alternative values and ideologies which affirm equality, liberty, individuality, community, cooperation, and harmony with nature.

Strategies to Expand Critical Consciousness

Expanding critical consciousness through everyday social and professional encounters involves initiating political discourse in social gatherings and in places of work. When people interact socially or professionally, in everyday life, their actions and communications can either conform to, or challenge, the social status quo and prevailing patterns of human relations. When people speak and act within the range of "normal" expected behavior, they reinforce the existing social order and its "common-sense" consciousness. On the other hand, when people's words and acts transcend "normal" behavioral ranges by questioning and challenging the status quo, they create opportunities for the emergence of reflection and critical consciousness on the part of others with whom they interact.

Based on these considerations, the strategy suggested here involves efforts by activists to "deviate" in everyday social and professional encounters from system-reinforcing behaviors, to pose challenging questions, and to engage people in reflection and dialogue concerning consequences of prevailing social, economic, political, and cultural realities for the quality of their life.

As dialogues evolve, stimulated by the behavior and questions of activists, they could identify themselves as advocates of social and economic justice and real democracy—feasible alternatives to capitalism and plutocracy. They must not practice self-censorship concerning their political views, as people tend to do in unjust and oppressive realities. One cannot help others to extricate themselves from the dominant ideology and culture, unless one is comfortable to acknowledge one's alternative perspective.

In pursuing this strategy, activists need to be sensitive to the thoughts, feelings, and circumstances of people with whom they engage in dialogue. As the goal of these encounters is to stimulate reflection, one needs to be sure that people are ready to communicate. Also, activists have to be tolerant of positions they reject. For whatever positions people hold, do make sense to them in terms of their life experiences and frames of reference. People have to be respected in these encounters, even when their positions and values conflict with those of the activists.

There are many opportunities to act in accordance with this strategy. Were many activists to use these opportunities routinely, many people might become involved in political discussions, and the taboo against discourse that challenges capitalism might be overcome. Gradually, growing numbers of people might undergo transformations of consciousness, might join transformation movements, and might carry on this strategy.

It is important that people pursuing this strategy do not try to do too much too soon, but develop their skills and sensitivity gradually, in order to avoid "burnout." People using this strategy are likely to benefit by joining support groups whose members can help one another to examine and improve their political practice. Applying this strategy to "radical" practice of social work, and other professions requires a separate essay (Gil 1998).

From Conventional Politics to Politics of Common Human Needs

Conventional politics concerning work place and community issues, the rights of groups subjected to discrimination, protection of the environment, electoral politics, etc. tend to pursue short-term goals rather than long-range visions of fundamental social change. However, radical activists can use participation in conventional politics to help people trace connections between apparently separate issues and discern their common roots in the prevailing social order. When exposed to such insights, people may realize that they would have to confront root causes in order to deal effectively with the separate issues they intend to solve.

Expanding people's consciousness concerning the connections and the common roots of discrete problems, around which interest groups tend to form, could enable them to overcome fragmentation and competition for limited resources. Such fragmentation and competition are politically dysfunctional, for they reinforce the status quo of power by reducing the potential collective strength of separate interest groups. The goal of radical activists in these situations is, therefore, to transform conventional interest group politics into "politics of common human needs."

Beyond Critical Consciousness: Changing Behavior and Institutions

Unless shifts in consciousness cause individuals and groups to evolve new patterns of actions and social relations, the process of social change would stall on the level of ideas. New patterns of action and social relations depend on self-transformation by individuals, as well as on institutional transformations carried out collectively by individuals, groups, and networks among them.

Individual Changes

Changes in the consciousness of individuals could gradually lead to changes in attitudes and relations toward people with whom they live and work, and toward the natural environment on which all life depends. People could try to avoid dominating, exploiting, and competing in relation with others, and to reduce socially structured inequalities and benefits derived from racism, sexism, and other types of discrimination. In their everyday social relations, people could foster cooperation, solidarity, and community as far as possible, in spite of prevailing social structures and dynamics.

People could modify their actions and social relations in accordance with their transformed consciousness, by testing and expanding accepted limits, in settings and situations over which they exercise some influence. They could create in this way "liberated spaces," prefiguring possible futures. People could also reduce their personal involvement in wasteful and destructive consumption of the earth's limited resources, and they could aim to adjust personal life styles to principles of global distributive justice and environmental sustainability. Through such socially less unjust and ecologically less damaging practices, people could reduce somewhat the contradictions between their newly evolving values and everyday realities (Simple Living Collective, American Friends Service Committee 1977).

Collective Changes

The transformation of the oppressive institutions and culture of globalized capitalism could be furthered by gradual emergence of alternative economic practices that transcend the principles of capitalism, and by simultaneous spread of emancipatory philosophical and ideological systems, such as democratic socialism.

A renaissance of cooperative economic enterprises began in the eighteenth and nineteenth centuries, and has become a worldwide phenomenon during the twentieth century (Buber 1958; Thompson 1994). Modern cooperative institutions include consumer cooperatives; cooperative financial services such as credit unions, cooperative banks, and rotating community loan funds; producer cooperatives and networks of producer cooperatives for bartering and marketing; and "total" cooperatives which combine cooperative production and consumption with living cooperatively (Blum 1968; Buber 1958; Gil 1979; Lindenfeld and Rothschild-Whitt 1982; Morrison 1991).

Consumer cooperatives are not as significant a challenge to capitalism as producer cooperatives and total cooperatives. However, consumer cooperatives demonstrate the value and ideology of cooperation, and in this way they challenge the dominant, competitive ideology of the culture of capitalism.

Producer cooperatives and their marketing associations challenge a basic capitalist principle: the separation of ownership and control of enterprises from workers employed by them. In producer cooperatives, workers own the means, skills, and knowledge of production, and they control and design the processes of production and marketing. While capitalism exists, producer cooperatives are forced to function as capitalist units, responsive to dynamics of capitalist markets. However, internally, they are a cooperative alternative to the dominant competitive economic model. Their spread in many parts of the world, could, in theory, replace capitalism gradually from within, and they are, therefore, a significant action strategy toward a just and non-oppressive economy, society, and culture.

Total collectives, like the kibbutz and kibbutz networks in Palestine and Israel, and religious and secular communes in the USA and elsewhere, transcend and challenge capitalism not only as an economic system, but also in social, political, cultural, and philosophical-ideological terms. They are models that pre-figure just and non-oppressive societies, and they demonstrate the feasibility of creating such comprehensive alternatives within prevailing realities. They also reveal the difficulties involved in creating such alternatives. Yet, like producer cooperatives, they are important elements of a comprehensive strategy for social transformation, for they combine into a living reality the transformation of consciousness, actions, and social relations (Buber 1958; Gil 1979; Kanter 1972, 1973; Fellowship of Intentional Community 1990; Spiro 1970).

Violence and Social Change

It is widely assumed that violence and "armed struggle" are necessary to overcome injustice and oppression. It is, therefore, important to examine this assumption when developing strategies for human liberation.

When analyzing the origins and dynamics of injustice and oppression, we concluded that initiating societal violence was used in establishing unjust and oppressive social orders, and that maintaining and reproducing these orders depends on subtly coercive processes of socialization, as well as on overt and covert, coercive social control. Coercion and societal violence are, therefore, constant features of life in unjust and oppressive societies. Poverty, homelessness, exploitative work, unemployment, inadequate health care, poor education, and individual and social underdevelopment are but some of the symptoms of persistent societal violence of established ways of life in unjust and oppressive societies.

Societal violence is also used by dominant social classes to defend the established way of life against challenges from dominated and exploited classes. Social movements struggling against injustice and oppression are, therefore, likely to encounter coercive and violent measures used against them by the legal system and the armed forces of the established order. It follows that when liberation movements engage in armed struggle, in self defense against an unjust and oppressive state, or in order to gain control over centers of state power, they are not initiating violence, but are reacting with "counter-violence" to the initiating societal violence used against them by agents of the state (Gil 1999).

Whether coercion and violence are present in liberation struggles is, therefore, a moot question. They are inevitably present as constant societal violence used by dominant social classes to maintain unjust social orders. The proper questions liberation movements ought to consider when planning their strategies, are, therefore, whether, when, under what conditions, and toward what targets and ends, they should use counter-violence, and whether counter-violence can actually achieve just and non-oppressive social orders.

There are no universally valid answers to some of these questions since the conditions of injustice and oppression vary greatly in different situations, places, and times, and since strategies of liberation movements need always to be designed in relation to specific societal realities and opportunities. Moreover, only people involved in, and affected by particular unjust and oppressive realities, rather than distant supporters and observers, have a moral right to determine what means to use in their struggle. For they alone must live (or die) with the consequences of their strategic choices. To illustrate this point, outsiders could not have determined the mode of struggle of the American colonists against the British, the revolutionaries against the French monarchy, the African National Congress against the apartheid system, the Bolsheviks in Russia, the Maoists in China, and Castro's movement in Cuba.

Students of social change can, and should, however, examine the consequences of the use of counter-violence in armed struggles in various historic situations. They should also compare the consequences of armed struggles with those of active nonviolent struggles, and they should study theoretical and philosophical positions concerning armed and nonviolent struggles.

Such studies suggest that while armed struggle can be effective in dealing with intense injustice and oppression in the short term, it is unlikely to eliminate domination and exploitation, the root causes of injustice and oppression. It has, at times, overpowered dominant classes that oppress people and benefit from coercively maintained injustice, but it has, so far, not eliminated the practice of domination and exploitation, and is unlikely to do so in the future. It has merely changed the agents and victims of oppression.

The implication of such studies is that armed liberation struggles, whatever their apparent achievements, may have to be followed by long-term, non-armed, active nonviolent liberation struggles, aimed at overcoming the root causes of injustice and oppression, rather than merely their most severe manifestations (Bruyn and Rayman 1979; King 1992; Lakey 1987; Sharp 1973, 1979).

Continuing the Conversation

In this essay, I have presented my tentative insights into the nature, dynamics, and perpetuation of injustice and oppression, and into strategies to struggle against these destructive social practices. It is important that readers examine these issues critically for themselves, in order to develop their own perspectives. The following questions, along with others that may occur to readers, should be useful in such an examination:

- Do the concepts and definitions of oppression and injustice in this essay make sense? Would you suggest others?

- Is the concept of key institutions of social life useful in understanding oppression and injustice, and in developing strategies to overcome them?
- Is the sketch of the history of oppression and injustice useful in reflecting about strategies to overcome them?
- Do the strategies suggested in this essay make sense? Would you suggest others?
- Does armed struggle fit into a comprehensive strategy against injustice and oppression, and if so, when and how?

I have referred to my insights as "tentative," because the search for understanding injustice and oppression, and modes of overcoming them, is a life-long process. Certainty will be reached only when social movements succeed, sometime in the future, to create and maintain just societies. Only then will people know what has worked and what insights and strategies were valid. Until then, our views on these matters will be, at best, informed hypotheses.

Reprinted from David G. Gil, Challenging injustice and oppression, in Michael O'Melia and Karla Krogsrud Miley, eds., *Pathways to Power: Readings in Contextual Social Work Practice* (Boston: Allyn and Bacon, 2002), 35–54. Copyright © 2002 Pearson Education. Reprinted by permission of the publisher. The essay is based on the author's book, *Confronting Injustice and Oppression* (New York: Columbia University Press, 1998).

References

Buber, M. (1958). *Paths in Utopia*. Boston: Beacon Press.
Blum, F. H. (1968). *Work and Community: The Scott Bader Commonwealth and the Quest for a New Social Order*. London: Routledge.
Bruyn, S. T. H., and P. M. Rayman (1979). *Nonviolent Action and Social Change*. New York: Irvington.
Durant, W. (1935). *The Story of Civilization*. Vol. 1, *Our Oriental Heritage*. New York: Simon and Schuster.
Eisler, R. T. (1987). *The Chalice and the Blade: Our History, Our Future*. New York: Harper and Row.
Farb, P. (1968). *Man's Rise to Civilization*. New York: Avon.
Fellowship for Intentional Community and Communities Publication Cooperative (1990). *Intentional Communities—1990/1991 Directory*. Evansville, Ind.: Fellowship for Intentional Community; Stelle, Ill.: Communities Publication Cooperative.
Frank, A. G. (1977). *World Accumulation, 1492–1789*. New York: Monthly Review Press.
Freire, P. (1970). *Pedagogy of the Oppressed*. New York: Herder and Herder.
Fromm, E. (1955). *The Sane Society*. Greenwich, Conn.: Fawcett.
Gil, D. G. (1979). *Beyond the jungle*. Cambridge, Mass.: Schenkman.
—— (1992). *Unravelling social policy*. Rochester, Vt.: Schenkman.
—— (1998). *Confronting injustice and oppression*. New York: Columbia University Press.
—— (1999). Understanding and overcoming social structural violence. *Contemporary Justice Review* 2 (1): 23–35.
—— (2000). Rethinking the goals, organization, designs and quality of work in relation to individual and social development. *Contemporary Justice Review* 3 (1): 73–88.
John Paul II (1982). *Encyclical on Human Work*. Boston: Daughters of St. Paul.
Kanter, R. M. (1972). *Commitment and Community*. Cambridge, Mass.: Harvard University Press.
—— (1973). *Communes: Creating and Managing the Collective Life*. New York: Harper and Row.

King, M. L., Jr. (1992). *I Have a Dream: Writings and Speeches That Changed the World.* San Francisco: Harper.

Kropotkin, P. A. (1902). *Mutual Aid, a Factor of Evolution.* Boston: Porter Sargent, 1956.

Lakey, G. (1987). *Powerful Peacemaking: A Strategy for a Living Revolution.* Philadelphia: New Society.

Lindenfeld, F., and J. Rothschild-Whitt, eds. (1982). *Workplace Democracy and Social Change.* Boston: Porter Sargent.

Magdoff, H. (1977). *Imperialism: From the Colonial Age to the Present.* New York: Monthly Review Press.

Maslow, A. H. (1970). *Motivation and Personality.* New York: Harper and Row.

Maslow, A. H., and J. J. Honigman (1970). Synergy: Some notes of Ruth Benedict. *American Anthropologist* 72: 320–33.

Morrison, R. (1991). *We Build the Road as We Travel: Mondragon, a Cooperative Social System.* Philadelphia: New Society Publishers.

National Conference of Catholic Bishops (1986). *Economic Justice for All.* Washington, D.C.: the Conference.

Ryan, W. (1971). *Blaming the Victim.* New York: Pantheon.

Sharp, G. (1973). *The Politics of Nonviolent Action.* Boston: Porter Sargent.

——— (1979). *Gandhi as a Political Strategist.* Boston: Porter Sargent.

Simple Living Collective, American Friends Service Committee, San Francisco (1977). *Taking Charge.* New York: Bantam Books.

Smith, A. (1961). *The Wealth of Nations.* Indianapolis: Bobbs-Merrill.

Spiro, M. E. (1970). *Kibbutz—Venture in Utopia.* New York: Schocken Books.

Tawney, R. H. (1931). *Equality.* London: Allen and Unwin, 1964.

Thompson, D. J. (1994). Co-operation in America. *Cooperative Housing Journal.*

Tucker, R. C., ed. (1978). *The Marx-Engels Reader.* 2nd ed. New York: Norton.

Zinn, H. (1980). *A People's History of the United States.* New York: Harper and Row.

Commentary

David G. Gil

I comment below on two issues dealt with in my essay, "Challenging Injustice and Oppression":

1. Are the tentative answers suggested in the essay concerning ways to overcome injustice and oppression still valid, in spite of the 9/11/01 attacks in New York City and elsewhere in the USA, or do these answers have to be revised?

2. Specifying the meanings of the concept "social justice" more clearly than was done in the essay.

Overcoming Injustice and Oppression in the Context of the "War on Terrorism"

"Challenging Injustice and Oppression" was written years before the tragic events of 9/11/01 in New York City and elsewhere in the U.S., and their aftermath, the global war on "terrorism" and the invasions of Afghanistan and Iraq. This essay was but a stage of my search for answers to key questions implicit in the "Code of Ethics" of NASW: "What is injustice and how can it be overcome?" These questions had gradually become a focus of my work since experiencing injustice and oppression under German occupation prior to and during World War II.

Do the U.S.-declared global war on terrorism, and the events that preceded it, and the invasions of Afghanistan and Iraq, require revisions of the tentative answers developed in my essay? I do not think so for reasons indicated below. Following the events of 9/11, I wrote an essay, "Eliminating Terrorism in a Structurally Violent World: Mission Impossible," for the journal of the Massachusetts Chapter of NASW, *Focus* (Gil 2001). In that essay I argued that the answers sketched in "Challenging Injustice and Oppression" were still valid, rather than invalidated, by the "terrorist attacks" in the United States.

Using public health theory, according to which primary prevention involves identification and eradication of causes of diseases, rather than neutralization of their symptoms, I suggested that prevention of terrorism ought to involve unraveling and eliminating its sources and dynamics. I then traced the sources of terrorism to "structural violence" from local to global levels, that is, systems of domination and exploitation of large segments of the world's people by past and present nations and colonizing empires. These historic and contemporary patterns of domination and exploitation tend to obstruct the satisfaction of the basic, universal human needs of domestic and foreign victims, and consequently to block the realization of their innate developmental potential. The results of these processes are reflected in widespread individual and social underdevelopment all over the world.

Terrorism is revealed as processes and acts of "counter-violence," i.e. manifestations of blocked, constructive human energy transformed into destructive energy, in reaction to coercively established and maintained conditions of injustice and oppression. The logical solution to terrorism would, therefore, be the elimination of its sources, that is, domestic and global injustice and oppression, by fairly sharing the aggregate wealth and knowledge base of humankind among all the people of the globe, rather than employing military measures and ideological coercion to maintain the status quo of domination, exploitation and massive injustice. These are the very same measures suggested in the tentative answers of the essay, "Challenging Injustice and Oppression."

The Meanings of Social Justice

Social workers are expected by their "Code of Ethics" to advance social justice and to act to overcome social injustice. However, the Code does not clarify the meanings of these terms. As a result, while social workers tend to be committed to a vague idea of social justice, they usually lack a clear intellectual position concerning it.

I am sketching here my understanding of social justice on three related levels: individual human relations, social institutions and values, and global human relations. My insights into social justice are, of course, not "correct" in an absolute sense. They are merely the meanings in which I use this concept. I do think, however, that all advocates of social justice and all social workers ought to specify the meaning the concept has for them when they use it in discourse with others. Such specifications seem especially necessary for deliberations on strategies toward the realization of social justice from local to global levels.

On the level of individual relations, social justice means that everyone should acknowledge and treat every individual as an autonomous, authentic subject with equal rights and responsibilities, rather than as an object, as is frequently done in contemporary cultures, especially in economic relations. Gradual expansion of such just individual relations could eventually phase out all kinds of domination and exploitation among individuals, groups, classes and peoples.

On the level of social institutions and values, social justice means ways of life conducive to the fulfillment of everyone's intrinsic needs, and to the realization of everyone's innate potential, and hence to optimal individual and social development and health. Just societies are egalitarian, structurally nonviolent, and genuinely democratic. Egalitarian here means that all people, in spite of their unique individuality and their multidimensional differences, have to have equal rights, responsibilities, and opportunities in all spheres of life, including control of natural and human generated resources; organization of work and production; distribution of goods, services, and rights; governance; and biological and cultural reproduction.

Just societies do not require structural violence by the state as unjust societies do. Structural violence has been used, and is now being used, to establish, maintain, and expand social, economic, and political inequalities among individuals, groups, and classes. Inequalities of rights, responsibilities, and opportunities among people of a society are unlikely to be established and maintained voluntarily. Rather, their establishment always requires coercion in the form of initiating violence that is gradually complemented by a consciousness of submission resulting from ideological indoctrination—the colonization of people's minds.

The social values that shape just institutional orders or structurally just societies include equality, liberty, individuality, community orientation, and cooperation/mutualism, rather than inequality, domination and exploitation, individualism/selfishness, disregard for community, and competition. These latter values shape unjust institutional orders or structurally unjust societies.

Social justice on a global scale requires extending just human relations and the institutional context of social justice and its supporting social values from local to global levels. The institutional requirements of global justice could be met by sharing the aggregate productive resources, knowledge, work, goods, and services of the global community in ways conducive to meeting everyone's intrinsic needs, and realizing everyone's innate capacities. People everywhere would thus have equal social, economic, and political rights, responsibilities, and opportunities and no-one could dominate and exploit others.

Contrary to intuitive assumptions and fears, such global sharing would not cause declines in the quality of life of currently privileged people and nations. Global wealth is not a fixed, zero-sum quantity and quality, but would be enhanced both quantitatively and qualitatively as the productive potential of currently underdeveloped people and countries is liberated.

Quality of life would actually be enriched if people everywhere were free to develop their innate capacities and were entitled to use the necessary resources, knowledge, and skills in productive endeavors. The real wealth of humankind is, after all, not the aggregate of privately controlled wealth, but the aggregate of realized human potential, the globe's natural and human created resources, and the aggregate of knowledge and skills generated since early stages of social evolution.

Social injustice is simply the absence of the requirements of social justice on all three levels: individual human relations, social institutions and values, and global human relations. While social injustice tends to vary by degrees of intensity among different societies and at different times, social justice cannot vary by degrees. For social justice is simply the zero point on a continuum of social injustice. When candidates for political office promise "more social justice" they actually mean lower levels of social injustice. For logically, more or less social justice is not possible. Societies can be either just or unjust, and at present societies tend to be unjust in different degrees. To eventually achieve social justice, societies from local to global levels would have to reduce over time the scope of social injustice.

References

Gil, D. G. (2001). Eliminating terrorism in a structurally violent world: Mission impossible. *Focus* 28 (12).

———— (2004). Perspectives on social justice. *Reflections* 10 (4).

———— (2006). Reflections on health and social justice. *Contemporary Justice Review* 9 (1).

Chapter 21
Partnering with the Jewish Community of Romania and Transitioning from Holocaust and Communism to Modernity

Zvi Feine

The earliest signs of Jewish life in present day Romania probably date back to the second century C.E. As of the twelfth century, Romania became a haven for Jews from the anti-Semitism prevalent throughout Eastern Europe and their numbers slowly grew. The Romanian Jewish community of recent times largely dates back to two large migrations of Jews to the Romanian territories: one from the Ukraine and Southern Poland (Galicia) that began 500–600 years ago and the other from Spain following the expulsion of Jews at the end of the fifteenth century (Rezachevici 37–40; Denize 61–62).

While suffering from economic and social oppression during the nineteenth century, many Jews took part in efforts to emancipate Romania, at first from Turkish, and then from Russian rule. Jews were granted political and civil rights only in 1856, having fought for Romanian independence in 1848 and having contributed significantly to the economy of the country then and in ensuing years (Iancu 112–13).

Rich Orthodox, Neolog, and Chassidic Jewish traditions flourished under the tolerant Turkish Empire, which ruled Romania from the thirteenth to the seventeenth centuries. It was not until the Russian conquest in 1819 that Romanian Jews first felt the sting of anti-Semitism. This escalated during World War I with the institution of anti-Jewish laws, pogroms, expulsions, revocation of citizenship, and a ban on employment in industry and government.

Pogroms intensified during World War I. Due to the war's result, Romania annexed Transylvania, Bukovina, and Bessarabia, greatly increasing the Jewish population. Due in part to their efforts as rank-and-file Romanian soldiers, Jews were granted citizenship and civil rights at the end of the war.

Late in the nineteenth century, Jews contributed immensely to developing the commerce, agriculture, industry, arts, literature, music, and medicine of Romania. For example, they played a major role in establishing Oradea, a flourishing city in North Eastern Transylvania, and represented 30 percent of the population and over 80 percent of the commerce for many decades (Teresa 1–3).

However, many Jewish communities suffered the ravages of World War I, requiring much reconstruction work after it. Many thousands of Jewish families were impoverished through these events—and were in need of help.

The newly founded American Jewish Joint Distribution Committee (AJJDC, also known as AJDC, JDC, or Joint[1]) was established in New York in 1914 in response to urgent Jewish needs in Palestine and in Eastern Europe focusing on rescue relief and reconstruction of Jewish communities (Bauer 5–7). The JDC responded to the devastation of Jewish community institutions and the suffering of large segments of the Romanian Jewish population, with financial support for the Jewish community in Romania beginning in 1915. The JDC, at that time, allocated funds for provisions such as food and clothing to assist thousands of Jewish veterans and refugees. JDC also opened loan kassas (cooperatives) to offer credit and job opportunities to Jews struggling due to the economic depression (14–15).

In order to meet the growing needs of reconstruction after the war, JDC in 1919 installed an American resident country director, Lt. James Becker, who in partnership with the Jewish community initiated the opening of loan and work cooperatives and built and funded orphanages, summer camps, informal Jewish education, and other Jewish community facilities (15).

Difficult economic conditions in postwar Romania led to heightened tension, pogroms, and rioting against Jews when the Fascist Iron Guard began rising to power in 1929. In 1935, Jews were barred from work in all industries and thousands of unskilled Jewish laborers lost their jobs. As anti-Semitism continued to rise, the JDC increased its allocations to Romania and struggled to keep the loan kassas open, enabling many Jews to open and maintain businesses (212–15). By 1932, in accordance with JDC policies of reconstructing and empowering Jewish communities, management of these activities were assumed by the Romanian Jewish community, supported by continued funding from the Joint. Between 1919 and 1938, JDC allocated more than $55 million in support for Romanian Jewry.

In 1940, after King Carol II's abdication, Prime Minister Marshall Ion Antonescu seized power and intensified anti-Jewish laws after forging an alliance with Germany. Pogroms began in Bucharest in January 1941, spread to Dorohoi, Iasi, and other Moldavian cities and included death trains, as of July 1942. Beginning in May 1942, Jews from the Bukovina, Bessarabia, and Transylvanian provinces were deported en masse to the Transnystria detention center, where JDC provided funds for whatever food and medical aid were allowed by Antonescu. At least 15,000 Jews lost their lives in the famous Fascist-led pogrom of Iasi in 1944 as well as in death trains that originated from the region just east of Iasi. Others died in pogroms in Dorohoi and Bucharest and from forced labor (ICHR 381–82). At the same time, the Jewish Community of Bucharest, playing on Antonescu's fears of continued German losses and postwar consequences, was able to save the majority of its members from deportation and to feed and clothe them through unofficial funding from the Joint (Ioanid 118–52).

During the Holocaust, the Jews of Romania suffered from the same atrocities that took place everywhere else in Europe. Overall, an estimated 380,000 Jews lost their lives in Romania and territories under its control, including Jews from Northern Transylvania who lost their lives in Auschwitz, Birkenau, and other Nazi death camps. Other Jews, largely from the Bessarabia region, lost their lives at the hands of rampaging Romanian soldiers. Transnystria served as the final destination for many Jews who died of hunger, illness, and extreme cold during deportation from other parts of Romania, while others were murdered there.

In 1944, King Michael led a successful revolt against Antonescu, severing Romania's alliance with Germany. Russian soldiers liberated Transylvania, and JDC was officially allowed to reenter Romania. The prewar Romanian Jewish population of approximately 800,000–900,000 had been reduced to 450,000, the largest Jewish population remaining in postwar Eastern Europe. JDC began relief work immediately, providing food and clothing to survivors returning from concentration camps. To expedite reconstruction, JDC re-established more than thirty loan kassas that helped to restart businesses and to open twenty-two health clinics to provide survivors with medical attention (Rotman 68–71). These activities continued until March 1949, when the Communist government no longer tolerated the presence of the JDC and other Jewish and Zionist organizations. JDC was expelled along with all other foreign NGOs (33).

As of 1945, immigration of Jews, largely to Israel, proceeded in spurts in accordance with Romanian government policies. Large waves of emigration from Romania occurred in the late 1940s, 1950s, and 1960s and proceeded slowly but surely after that. Dr. Radu Ioanid, director of the International Archival Programs Division, U.S. Holocaust Memorial Museum, tells this story well in his book *The Holocaust in Romania: The Destruction of Jews and Gypsies Under the Antonescu Regime, 1940–1944* (2000).

With the establishment of the Communist government in 1949, the Jewish community increasingly suffered from persecution as a religious minority along with other Romanian citizens. All foreign welfare organizations were requested to cease operations in Romania, including JDC. Jews applying for immigration to Israel summarily lost their jobs. Those with relatives in Israel or the West were barred from holding any positions of responsibility in companies throughout Romania. All Jewish schools were closed down and the Jewish hospitals, orphanages, health clinics, and so on were nationalized. Only synagogues were permitted to function; however, any Jew identifying with or participating in such activities often lost his or her job. In the early 1950s, numerous Jews were jailed for what the Communist government considered political or economic crimes. Yet, immigration to Israel, as noted above, was tolerated and supported by the Communist government at various times and, ultimately, 320,000 Jews of Romanian origin immigrated to Israel, comprising one of the largest immigrant groups in the country. This group achieved unusually high success in the fields of medicine, law, security services, agriculture, commerce and industry, and more and is considered one of the most successful immigrant groups in Israel. At the same time, this process largely depleted the Romanian Jewish community's religious, educational and leadership ranks (Rotman 89–108).

Despite the growing poverty and suffering of the Jewish community, neither the JDC (nor any other welfare organization) was able to assist Romanian Jewry between the years 1949 and 1967, even in the unofficial capacity that it successfully achieved elsewhere in Eastern Europe. As a result, survivors, and particularly the elderly, were forced to live in poverty, unable to subsist on their meager pensions. Some lived in overcrowded tenements, while others were forced to seek shelter in the caves of Moldavia. The Romanian government succeeded in keeping the condition of the Romanian Jewish community secret from the Jewish world and the JDC. During this difficult time, Romanian Jews were sustained and guided by the leadership and faith of Chief Rabbi Dr. Moses Rosen, who served both as the president of the Federation of Jewish Communities of Romania (FEDROM) and its chief rabbi. He, together with covert representatives of the Israel government, was instrumental in the highly successful emigration of Jews from Romania during the Communist period (83–88).

In 1965, President Nicolae Ceausescu led Romania into a new political era by seeking closer ties with the West. Due to his special relations with the U.S. Government and his influence on securing Most-Favored Nation status for Romania, Rabbi Moses Rosen was granted certain concessions including JDC's return in 1967. It bore the distinction of being the only foreign volunteer relief organization invited to enter and remain in an Eastern Bloc country more than two decades before the fall of Communism. The Jewish community was also permitted to establish choirs and Sunday schools for Jewish children and youth in twenty-two localities. The JDC reinstituted financial and professional support for health and welfare programs but was barred from supporting informal Jewish educational, cultural, as well as community and lay leadership development programs (Rosen 242–3).

The Jewish community of Romania numbered over 40,000 in 1967 when the JDC carried out a needs assessment by Cecille Mizrachi, a professional Jewish social worker from Greece and by Moe Levine, a decorated U.S. paratrooper in World War II. The JDC helped FEDROM and its Social and Medical Assistance Department (hereafter SMAD) create a full-scale relief operation providing kosher food packages, clothing, and medical services to the elderly and impoverished. A sociomedical outpatient center was established in Bucharest and, ultimately, in twenty-five other localities throughout the country. The JDC helped FEDROM open eleven subsidized kosher kitchens, called "kosher restaurants" by Rabbi Moses Rosen, in order to add an extra measure of dignity for the patrons, and provided food packages, meals on wheels, cash assistance, winter relief, homecare, and other help to over 2,000 needy Jews. In the early 1970s, JDC and FEDROM built old age homes in Bucharest, Arad, Timisoara, and Dorohoi. Together with World Jewish Relief of Great Britain, they established the Amalya and Rabbi Moses Rosen Home for the Aged in Bucharest, a relatively modern facility that accommodated almost 200 residents. This relief program continues to provide help to needy, elderly Jews of Romania and now assists children as well. This program will be described in more detail below. Unquestionably, by meeting basic needs of mostly Jewish elderly survivors who had little or no family in Romania to help support them, thousands of lives were saved.

The Communist government tolerated the critical financial and professional support of the JDC during the Communist period from 1967 to 1989. This was a result of Rabbi Rosen's political activities on its behalf in the West; the political intervention of major Jewish organizations such as the American Jewish Committee, B'nai Brith, the Appeal to Conscience Foundation, and others; as well as the economic benefit to

Romania of the JDC purchasing all goods and services in Romania with sorely needed U.S. dollars. The JDC had also secured broad recognition in Romania through its significant nonsectarian efforts in famine relief in 1945 and in relief following the disastrous earthquake in Bucharest in 1977. The results were a greater modicum of religious freedom, some limited informal Jewish education for youth, and a far-flung and highly effective health and welfare program administered by FEDROM's SMAD, while supported and supervised by the JDC (Rotman 86–87).

Since JDC and FEDROM had little or no access to resources from other countries or from within Romania, the social and medical service noted above evolved as a completely independent, financially secure, professional, and efficient social service delivery system.

The fall of Communism in December 1989 and the death of Rabbi Rosen in 1994 marked the end of an era and the beginning of a transitional period for Romanian Jewry and for JDC. In 1989, FEDROM reported 14,000 registered Jews and estimated up to 5,000 additional unregistered Jews in Romania. Events during the December 1989 revolution—the only bloody revolution in Eastern Europe during that era—were indicative of the social processes, culture, and leadership issues.

After the revolution, in early 1990, many Jewish community leaders feared there could be an adverse reaction to Chief Rabbi Rosen in particular, and to the Jewish community in general, for having secured special privileges from President Nicolae Ceausescu. The JDC helped bridge those uncertainties and gave a sense of security to the Jewish community by

1. Sponsoring a meeting of the Chief Rabbis of Europe's Jewish communities in Bucharest exhibiting their support and praise for Rabbi Rosen that was covered extensively by the Romanian media—this contributed greatly to Rabbi Rosen's prestige and legitimacy in the eyes of the Romanian public and allayed criticism.
2. An enormous, urgently needed, quantity of emergency medication, medical supplies and equipment, as well as powdered milk, was flown in by JDC and the World Jewish Relief of England under the auspices of FEDROM in early February 1990. Romanian TV coverage of this significant contribution featured Rabbi Rosen, the Deputy Minister of Health, and myself. I emphasized on Romanian national TV that in times of need the JDC and the Jewish community of Romania provide for needs of all the needy in Romania, regardless of religion or ethnicity, as in the famine of 1945 and earthquake of 1977. In addition, visits of Western diplomats (especially the U.S. ambassador) and high-level delegations from abroad to Rabbi Rosen, exhibited the Western world's support for the Jewish community.

All this contributed to both a sense of security on the part of Romanian Jewry and the continued prestige and legitimacy for the Jewish community now under a democracy, which Rabbi Rosen had first earned under Communism.

Within the Jewish community, Chief Rabbi Rosen mirrored the dictatorial style of President Ceausescu. Rabbi Rosen was famous for this and made no apologies for his style, relying on his achievements under Communism. However, the burgeoning democracy and changes in the Romanian government developed very slowly in the Jewish community. Rabbi Rosen continued his austere style, which many in the Jewish community increasingly viewed as inappropriate, until his death in May 1994.

The following vignette exemplified his difficulty with this transition. In early 1988, the JDC and Chief Rabbi Rosen placed a large covering (parochet) overhanging the rostrum (Bimah) area of the Temple Choral (main synagogue) in Bucharest attesting to the major ceremony that took place there in October 1967 marking the return of the JDC to Romania in 1967. The hangings and text were embroidered in Romanian, English, and Hebrew. The wording included "the Social Republic of Romania." After December 1989, it took fifteen months of constant pressure by me to get Rabbi Rosen to replace that wording with "Romania." He had difficulty parting with the previous wording and was not convinced that Communist rule in Romania was finally at an end.

After Rabbi Rosen's death in May 1994, the Council of Leaders of FEDROM pressed Prof. Nicolae Cajal—an eminent physician, virologist, academician, champion of human rights, and a highly popular public figure in Romania—to serve as president. Rabbi Rosen's position was divided into president and chief rabbi. Prof. Nicolae Cajal provided the Jewish community with high profile, esteemed leadership with great tolerance for all minorities and religions. He was a great believer in exhibiting the enormous contribution of Romanian Jewry to the country as his way of combating anti-Semitism rather than momentarily fighting it in the media, as Chief Rabbi Rosen had done. As an example, shortly after his election, he established the Hasefer Publishing Company that published over 150 books in Romanian on Jewish subjects—mostly on the various Jewish contributions to Romanian letters, commerce, the helping professions, and so on. Interim president Adv. Iulian Sorin, who provided the Jewish community and FEDROM with security and continuity, realizing that this was a transitional period, followed him, and served from 2004 until 2006.

A temporary rabbi, Rabbi Yecheskiel Mark, filled the latter position for two years, followed by Rabbi Menachem Hacohen, an orthodox rabbi from Israel enjoying great prestige in Romania, Israel, and elsewhere (AJJDC 35). Currently, a Romanian Jewish educator has finished his training as a rabbi in the USA and will become the first young, indigenous Romanian rabbi to serve the Romanian Jewish community in many decades.

In November 2006, the first democratic elections for a FEDROM leadership were held with ninety Jewish community leaders from throughout Romania acting as electors. The result was the election of Prof. Aurel Vainer as president. He had served as the FEDROM representative as a member of Parliament, a veteran vice-president of the Romanian Chamber of Commerce, and a professor of Economics. In addition, a vice president and secretary-general were elected in the first democratic elections since the 1940s. Prof. Vainer brought with him a commitment to economic self-sufficiency for the Jewish community; managerial, structural change, and transparency; and greater involvement of the Jewish communities themselves in the decision making process of FEDROM. The transition noted above continues as democratization, openness to change, and economic initiatives, which have become central to the current leadership.

During Communist times, a unique social and medical service system was set up to meet the needs of the Jewish community with major support from the JDC. During Communist times, this program was essential for meeting basic needs for elderly Jewish Holocaust survivors—most of whom had no family support. Eighty-five percent of the caseload was one-person households. From 1990 until the present, the Romanian government's social and medical services system has been mostly unable to meet the basic needs of its elderly and needy children, thus necessitating the continued operation of the program to be described below.

Transition of Programs—1990–2006

Social Welfare and Medical Programs

The SMAD assistance programs noted above gradually evolved since 1968 to serve the needs of its clients better. These were funded 80 percent or more by JDC since the late 1990s with significant help from the Conference for Material Claims against Germany (Claims Conference) and 20 percent by FEDROM (FEDROM 2006). The services established by FEDROM and the JDC in 1968 continued as a "well-oiled machine" to meet the basic existential needs of its clients and, since the early 1990s, improved the quality of care of elderly beyond those basic needs. The program was aptly named the "Dignity Program," and all services were delivered in a dignified manner. The services were predicated on the lack of a medical care service of the government capable of supplying minimal quality health care to elderly, lack of available institutional care for elderly and average pensions too low for a minimum level of subsistence. An eligibility system was refined over the years based on membership in the Jewish community and financial need. Social workers investigate each application for assistance carefully, to ensure that there is no other financial support available, thereby leaving the Dignity Program as the "last resort." The fact that the number of clients served decreased only 1 percent annually over the past four years—despite 24 percent mortality for the caseload—illustrates the dire economic realities of Romanian elderly (Jew and non-Jew alike). Many new persons have applied for assistance because the average pension of $80–100 is insufficient to support them in an economy in which the average income is $300 per month.

The basic programs established by the JDC and FEDROM in 1968 at SMAD are as follows:

1. *Medical care* for Jewish elderly throughout Romania is provided by 26 small clinics with part time physicians and nurses, supplementing the limited medical care provided by the Romanian government for elderly. Limited medication (in-kind or cash), medical supplies, and devices are provided free of charge. In Bucharest, a Jewish medical center provides twelve specialty medical services, as well as laboratory analyses and treatment.

2. A basket of *in-kind services* serves almost 1,800 clients in 75 localities throughout Romania and includes food packages, meals on wheels, clothing, homecare, home repairs, and more. Clients with an income under a poverty line set by FEDROM and JDC are provided with monthly financial aid that is periodically recalculated and updated.

3. *Winter relief* is provided in cash to purchase wood, gas, or other kinds of heating covering 60 percent of the average cost.

4. The main *institutional facility* for Jewish aged is the Rosen Home in Bucharest, supplemented by a regional one in Arad, in Western Transylvania. In recent years, Rosen Home staff and consultants have focused on improving quality of care, featuring staff training, a program for ameliorating incontinence, enhancement of nutrition, and more.

Over the past fifteen years, in an era of Jewish community openness to new initiatives and no government restrictions, many new programs have been developed to enhance the quality of care for elderly beyond the programs meeting basic needs, noted above, including

1. *Warm Houses*: An effective program imported from Israel and the Former Soviet Union, it provides lonely elderly with social activities and nutrition, hosted by volunteers in eight residential homes throughout Romania.

2. *Jewish Braille Institute of America for Blind and Visually Impaired Elderly*: This program features visual aids and social activities.

3. *Social day care centers*: These centers are located in three communities, serving lonely and disabled elderly.

4. *Youth volunteer programs for elderly*: Includes "Adopt a Grandparent" combating loneliness of elderly in Bucharest and in five other communities across the country.

5. *Vision treatment*: In hundreds of home visits in the late 1980s and early 1990s, I came across very large numbers of elderly Jews who were visually impaired and, in the Romanian reality, homebound. Most of them suffered from cataract problems and other diseases affecting the elderly—most of which were being successfully treated in Western countries but not in Romania. In 1994 I succeeded in initiating a partnership with FEDROM, JDC, Project Vision, Inc—a nonprofit organization based in Atlanta affiliated with the local Jewish Federation—together with the Harry & Jeanette Weinberg Foundation and Claims Conference, committed to serving Jews in Israel and in other countries with their vision problems. This partnership enabled one of the most successful intervention programs initiated by JDC and FEDROM in Romania. Over thirty volunteer physicians from the USA and Israel visited Romania for diagnostic and treatment purposes. Through an innovative connection with a private clinic in Bucharest with the help of Project Vision's Medical Director, Dr. Steve Kutner, the JDC and FEDROM staff, diagnostic help, ophthalmological equipment, and internal ocular lenses were provided to successfully operate on over 1,000 elderly Romanians

(70% Jewish) suffering from cataracts. This effort not only restored or improved these individuals' vision, but also offered significant help to 250 elderly suffering from other ophthalmological problems. The success was so dramatic that a weekly club in Bucharest sustained by the Jewish Braille Institute of America, Inc. and serving low vision clients became known as the "Formerly Blind Club" instead of the "Blind Club."

6. *Incontinence amelioration*: One of the most difficult problems facing frail elderly and those requiring nursing care is urinary incontinence. ESHEL—the Association for the Planning and Development of the Services for the Elderly in Israel (a partnership of the JDC and the Israel Government)—in conjunction with the Rambam Medical Center and its Center for Amelioration of Incontinency in Haifa, developed a successful program in Israel to train and educate physicians and nurses. This program in Israel helped ameliorate the incontinency of 70 percent of the elderly served through targeting, individualizing diagnostics, and treatment, choosing the best solution for the elderly, and helping to train and equip the medical staff who serve them. The Rambam program and staff have been utilized in Romania (and in other east European countries) and is already showing initially important results such as a 50 percent reduction of those elderly Jews served by FEDROM who required adult diapers in 2005. Based on the Rambam training, FEDROM medical staff are currently implementing a region by region program of training and consultation for ameliorating incontinence.

7. *Children in Need Program*: Since 1968, the entire JDC/FEDROM welfare and medical program concentrated on meeting the needs of the elderly. This emerged from JDC's commitment to serving elderly Holocaust survivors. The assumption was that families with needy children had an option of immigrating to Israel at any time and rehabilitating their lives economically there. However, in the late 1990s JDC staff in the Former Soviet Union realized that there were tens of thousands of nutritionally deprived Jewish children—grandchildren of the elderly who were being served. As a result, various feeding, medical, and other programs were initiated there. This created an opening to consider the need for a Jewish child welfare program in Romania.

The JDC established the European Center for Children in Budapest in 2003 that served to guide, train, and support the development of Jewish child welfare programs throughout Europe to address these issues. In Romania, child welfare needs are barely addressed by the Romanian government. The FEDROM Youth Department together with the Social and Medical Assistance Department, with the professional consultation of the European Center for Children and JDC welfare consultant Rosalba Galata, surveyed the needs of children through the distribution of questionnaires to community leadership throughout the country as well as by visits of staff from Bucharest to those communities. Eligibility criteria were established and a program patterned on the FEDROM program for the elderly was initiated, serving 125 needy children up to age nineteen with monthly food packages, grants for clothing, school supplies, and cash assistance for the neediest cases.

Medical assistance was supplied to thirty of those children, beginning in 2005, providing them with medical attention by a group of pediatricians who visited Romania under the auspices of the Tommy Hofheimer Medical Mission, Physicians for Peace, and the Tidewater Jewish Federation. These physicians helped diagnose the children's problems. This also led to the hiring of an expert pediatrician at FEDROM's Jewish Medical Center in Bucharest, resulting in proper medical treatment and solutions to untreated problems of these children.

Introducing this program was a much lengthier process than expected because the leaders of Jewish communities in Romania had been oriented over many years to serve only the elderly. A good example of this was my visit to a small, remote Jewish community in southeast Romania. This town once had 6,000 Jews and now has fewer than sixty. Prior to the visit, the president of the Jewish community insisted that he had no children in the city who were in need of help. After I established a warm relationship with him and prodded him, he revealed that there was indeed a family with a Jewish mother, married to a Roma, with four children under age eighteen, living in abject poverty. They had only occasional income, experienced difficult living conditions, and had to deal with a child suffering from HIV. They were quickly admitted to the program, ameliorating their situation dramatically. Many "discovery" situations such as this one have stimulated change in the program.

This intervention program is considered highly successful and has done much to ameliorate the day-to-day living situation of these children. However, many of them had little or nothing to do with the Jewish communities of which their parents were members, often because they were embarrassed by their economic situation. Therefore, in 2005, JDC initiated an outreach program to involve them in the Jewish community, with dramatic results, enabling the children to feel welcome and be integrated into community programs. Clearly, the most effective approach is one of family-oriented intervention that recognizes poor families instead of poor children. Parents must be targeted for help to enable them to improve their economic situations, parenting, and other aspects of family life.

8. *Welfare assessment*: In 1992, I was asked to head a team of JDC professionals to "revalidate" the level of welfare assistance being provided by JDC to the various communities of Central and Eastern Europe. Recognizing the huge economic and cultural differences between these Jewish communities as well as the difficult challenge of measuring welfare needs across borders and cultures, I led a JDC staff team that created a system to measure the standard of living and welfare needs of elderly Jews throughout the countries of Eastern Europe (Revalidation Committee). The study introduced concepts such as "total income" (including pensions, cash, in-kind relief, and other income) for those targeted to be served, and a "modest minimum level of income" that we would strive to secure for all eligible elderly being served in the region. These indices reflected both objective and subjective data collected by staff in each country. The establishment of these measurements afforded comparisons between the countries and showed certain inequities. For example, the study indicated that JDC assistance to needy, elderly

Bulgarian Jews allowed them to live at a much lower standard of living compared to other countries. As a result of the study, JDC corrected this and brought Bulgaria's country program into line with those of other countries.

The Romanian data were especially interesting since the relatively large extent of goods and services (food packages, canteen meals, clothing, medication, homecare, etc.) were quantified and included in the "total income" and "modest minimum income" measures. The welfare and medical program for Romania was found to be justified based on these concepts and measures. Subsequently, the professional and lay leadership of the AJJDC approved all of these proposals and utilized them as guidelines for determining welfare programs in all the Central and Eastern European countries, including Romania.

Informal Jewish Education

During the Communist era, it was impossible to engage in informal Jewish education or community development. As of the mid-1990s, Jewish community life and education were still limited to religious services, weekly cultural events, as well as choirs and Talmud Torahs. These veteran programs, as they were, clearly would not keep pace with democracy, cultural and educational opportunities within Romanian society, and modern times. They also did not appropriately involve the middle and younger generation in Jewish communal life. The informal Jewish education programs had teachers in their eighties and textbooks used in the 1940s. FEDROM had no attractive informal Jewish education or cultural programs for its youth or middle generation.

Therefore, JDC and FEDROM introduced numerous programs to develop educational leadership, material, and programs. JDC provided pedagogical consultants and program development experts from Israel and the USA to help guide those programs, to develop the indigenous personnel, and to assist the community in becoming self-sufficient from the staff and leadership perspective. Since 1996, college graduates from the USA and Israel have served as JDC Jewish Service Corps volunteers (JSC) for one year, residing in Romania. They served as role models and helped initiate various new programs and initiatives primarily geared toward informal Jewish education such as "Jewish Education Through the Mail" (JEM) of lessons in Judaism to 400 subscribers, "Jewish Education Network" (JEN) and Internet-based informal Jewish education programs in Romanian, annual national Judaism seminars, regional Jewish seminars, and matchmaking gatherings. Other new programs included

1. *Reinvigorated Talmud Torahs:* Educational staff began to recruit and to train new Talmud Torah teachers, while developing modernized curricula and supervision. This was the key to infusing Jewish knowledge, along with the successful choirs and youth clubs—providing one of the highest levels of informal Jewish education and knowledge in any Eastern European community.
2. *Yosef Hirsh Pedagogical Center:* This pivotal resource was established by FEDROM and the JDC in Bucharest, under the leadership of Yosef Hirsh, a gifted JSC vol-

unteer in 1998/9 spearheading the development of appropriate Jewish curriculum material for all educational facilities of the Jewish community throughout Romania. It also provides guidance and staffing for regional and national informal Jewish educational efforts. An example is the publication of a prayer book (siddur) for Friday evening services in Hebrew, Romanian translation, and transliteration—allowing all youth (and others who had no access to informal Jewish education under Communist rule) to participate appropriately in the service and attracting them to the synagogues. Thanks to the Center's resources, many other Jewish outreach programs, regional meetings, youth leader training, and more occurred.

3. *Jewish Camp at Cristian*: A summer camp at the village of Cristian in the Carpathian Mountains was turned into a center for informal Jewish education with a new Jewish camping facility established by FEDROM and JDC with the support of the Sandler family of Virginia Beach, Virginia. It reaches out to Jewish youth and families especially from small Jewish communities or in isolated villages from throughout Romania. The camp, completed in late 2006, functions year-round and serves as the major center outside of Bucharest for training, leadership development, and national informal Jewish educational programs.

Community Building and Leadership Development

During the Communist era, it was impossible to engage in leadership development for the Jewish community of Romania or to support informal Jewish education. However, until Rabbi Rosen's death in May 1994, any investment in lay or professional leadership development still proved impossible due to his opposition to them and the iron grip that he had on the entire lay and professional leadership. No leadership development was taking place and leadership in Jewish communities was largely "closed" to the middle and younger generations.

To remedy the situation, JDC and FEDROM stimulated many programs to develop leaders and to help them play enhanced roles in their communities for the services that they were delivering. At first, almost all program initiatives came from JDC (via my personal efforts), but, as time progressed and new leaders took their places in the new community structure, many created their own initiatives. They included:

1. *Organization of Jewish Youth in Romania (OTER)*: A network of twelve Jewish youth clubs featuring computer clubs and more were established throughout Romania, serving as a focal group for Jewish youth and empowerment initiated by Yosef Hirsh and supported by FEDROM and JDC.
2. *Buncher Community Leadership Program*: Besides numerous training programs in Romania and abroad for youth leaders, educators, social workers, and physicians, certainly the most meaningful effort was through the Buncher Community Leadership Program established by JDC in partnership with the Buncher Family Foundation and the United Jewish Federation of Pittsburgh. Through this program, beginning in 1998, three cohorts of fifteen lay and professional leaders through-

out Romania were trained in modern management styles. This included mentoring, development and implementation of projects, and so on with the teaching taking place both in Romania and in Israel by qualified professionals. As a result, almost all of these young and middle-aged leaders assumed higher positions of community responsibility and filled senior positions at FEDROM. Furthermore, they have revolutionized many of FEDROM's programs and comprise the only corps of trained leaders in Romania today.

3. *Middle generation*: In 2001, Jodi Guralnick, JDC Ralph Goldman Fellow, carried out a study on the needs and aspirations of Romania's Jewish middle generation. This cohort of thirty-five to sixty-five-year-olds was considered the "lost generation"—having suffered from lack of access to informal Jewish education and Jewish identity programs due to Communism. According to the study, they were hungry for programs, which met their needs and wanted to contribute to the community. This led to the establishment of thirty middle generation clubs throughout Romania with over 1,200 active members today. They also became prime targets for the Buncher leadership development program, noted above and became the leaders of many communities.

4. *Jewish Community Centers (JCCs)*: Over the past few years, JDC and FEDROM initiated a needs assessment and community planning effort as a precursor for establishing a Jewish community center in Bucharest, designed to attract both unaffiliated and affiliated Jews, help meet their needs for enhanced Jewish informal education, and house recreational programs. This new program—currently in the form of a Jewish Community Center (JCC) without walls, but soon to have its own facility in a Jewish communal property recently restituted from the Romanian government—will help further change the image of the Jewish community and its leadership as both modern and appealing.

An example of a Jewish community reviving itself is Oradea in western Romania. The Arnall Family Youth and Middle Generation club in Oradea (700 members), is nearing completion and will help further renew this dynamic and growing Jewish community in western Romania. Indeed, probably the most active and exciting, relatively large Jewish community in Romania today is Oradea. The leadership and programs of this community are so attractive that the census of the Jewish community rose from 525 in 2002 to 700 in 2006. The OTER youth club has fifty-five members and the middle generation club has 150 members. They boast a prize winning Israeli dance troupe (first place in the 2006 Romanian National Folk Dance Competition for Ethnic Minorities) and regularly perform their well-attended Purim Spiel and other programs at the main Oradea Theater. They benefited from the menu of all the programs noted above and have hosted numerous regional seminars for other Jewish communities in the area. Special financial resources from donors allowed them to translate their energy into successful Jewish programs for all ages. The middle generation program is the largest active one in Romania today, and a small day care center for the elderly opened in mid-2006 serving elderly and disabled Holocaust survivors. The modern youth and middle generation club is presently being built in a 120-

year-old Jewish community building in space not utilized in fifty years. Also, their 130-year-old, historic orthodox synagogue is undergoing a major renovation, also thanks to the Arnall family. The youth cry out for more Jewish and religious education—a need JDC and the community are trying to meet.

5. *Fundraising*: As fitting with the transition toward a self-sufficient community, a JSC volunteer joined FEDROM for 2006–7 as a fundraising consultant (with the support of the Meyerhoff Family Foundation) along with two other members of the Romanian Jewish community to create a Fundraising Department. Financial resources are potentially available from Israelis and Jews from abroad doing business in Romania, as well as from some newly wealthy members of the Jewish community in Romania. A fundraising infrastructure and plan need to be created—sixty years after the Holocaust decimated a community that previously largely supported its own extensive community facilities and programs. JDC also initiated two fundraising seminars for fifteen leaders and professionals of the Jewish community in Romania in 2005.

6. *Strategic planning*: In the late 1990s, JDC noticed that FEDROM was doing no strategic planning to identify and deal with the major issues that it faces. These issues included the enhancement of the quality of care for elderly (and not just the material goods being provided); enhancement of meeting community and leadership development needs; enhancing income in Romania from property holdings and other sources, and more. In 1995, JDC initiated an annual strategic planning retreat with the top FEDROM leadership, for this purpose, consisting of a three-day series of presentations and discussions as well as a written summary and conclusions of the proceedings—providing a basis for strategic thinking and a base for making new and innovative programmatic decisions. Almost all new Jewish community initiatives are discussed and decided on at these retreats.

Conclusion

The Jewish community of Romania succeeded well in transitioning from a community controlled by a Communist government to a Jewish community functioning in the context of a democratic and modern state in Eastern Europe. Various social welfare and medical services of the Communist period remained intact but were expanded to serve unmet needs. The Jewish community, with the help of JDC, developed a broad array of informal Jewish educational, community building, innovative health, welfare, and other programs, which positioned the community for the modern and changing realities of a democratic Romania.

Original paper.

Note

1. The American Jewish Joint Distribution Committee (JDC) receives its funds primarily from American Jewry through the United Jewish Communities. It also receives funds from World Jewish Relief (UK), the United States government, and a number of foundations and international organizations.

References

American Jewish Joint Distribution Committee. *2001–2002 Country Progress Report: Romania.* New York: AJJDC, 2002.

Bauer, Yehuda. *My Brother's Keeper: The History of the American Jewish Joint Distribution Committee, 1929–1939.* Philadelphia: Jewish Publication Society, 1974.

Denize, Eugen. "The Sephardic Jews in Wallachia and Moldova, Sixteenth to Nineteenth Centuries." In Paul Cernovodeanu, ed., *The History of the Jews in Romania,* vol. 1, *From Its Beginnings to the Nineteenth Century.* Tel Aviv: Tel Aviv University, 2005. 61–76.

International Commission on the Holocaust in Romania. *Final Report.* Bucharest: Polirom, 2005.

Ioanid, Radu. "The Antonescu Era." In Randolph L. Braham, ed., *The Tragedy of Romanian Jewry.* New York: Columbia University Press, 1994. 117–71.

Revalidation Committee for Individual Welfare Programs for Holocaust Survivors in Central and Eastern Europe. *Final Report.* New York: the Committee, 1992

Rezachevici, Constantin. "The Jews in the Romanian Principalities, Fifteenth to Eighteenth Centuries." In Cernovodeanu, ed., *The History of the Jews in Romania.* 1. 37–60.

Rosen, Rabbi Dr. Moses. *Dangers, Tests and Miracles: The Remarkable Life Story of Chief Rabbi Rosen of Romania as told to Joseph Finkelstone.* London: Weidenfeld and Nicholson, 1990.

Rotman, Liviu, ed. *The History of the Jews in Romania,* vol. 4, *The Communist Era Until 1965.* Tel Aviv: Tel Aviv University, 2005.

Iancu, Carol. "The Struggle for the Emancipation of Romanian Jewry in the Late Nineteenth Century." In Liviu Rotman and Carol Iancu, eds., *The History of the Jews in Romania,* vol. 2, *The Nineteenth Century.* Tel Aviv: Tel Aviv University, 2005. 111–50.

Teresa, Dr. Mozes. *Comunitatea Evreilor Oradea: Monography of the Jewish Community of Oradea.* Oradea: Comunitatea Evreilor Bahor, 2005.

Further Reading

Braham, Randolph L., ed. *The Destruction of Romanian and Ukrainian Jews During the Antenescu Era.* New York: Columbia University Press, 1997.

———. *The Tragedy of Romanian Jewry.* New York: Columbia University Press, 1994.

FEDROM. *Social Assistance and Medical Department Reliefs and Services Provided to Assistees Through JDC and the Federation of the Romanian Jewish Communities.* Bucharest: FEDROM, 2006.

Rotman, Liviu, and Raphael Vago, eds. *The History of the Jews in Romania,* vol. 3, *Between the Two World Wars.* Tel Aviv: Tel Aviv University, 2005.

Commentary

Zvi Feine

I was born in New York, USA, and made my Aliyah—that is, Jewish immigration to Israel—in 1960. I completed my undergraduate social work education in Israel and then returned to the United States to pursue my doctorate at the University of Pennsylvania, earning my DSW from the School of Social Work in 1974. I have served as director of the Hebrew University's Schwartz program, a postgraduate program for directors and senior personnel for community centers in Israel. At the time of this writing, I am serving as director of Africa and Asia for the American Jewish Joint Distribution Committee (AJJDC or JDC) and deputy director of JDC-Israel. Previously, I served the JDC as country director for Poland, and consultant on social services for many countries, including Morocco, France, Romania, and the transmigrant programs in Vienna and Rome. I have also served as chief program officer for JDC-New York, which included serving as area director for Central and Eastern Europe, Africa, and Asia.

The paper presented above on the Jewish community of Romania includes events during the Holocaust and Communism. My work in Romania, on behalf of the JDC, began in Communist times in 1986. Since then, the Jewish community of Romania, with the help of the JDC, transitioned in its social welfare and medical programs, maintaining services that met basic needs but also quality of life services. Following the Communist era, it was possible to engage in informal Jewish education, community building and leadership development—making a better functioning and renewed Romanian Jewish community.

My activities in Romania began during my tenure as the International Social Welfare Consultant for JDC based in Paris in 1986. I carried out a renewed needs assessment for the aged and review of the social welfare programs serving them. In 1988, I was appointed country director for Romania on behalf of JDC, based in Jerusalem, serving concurrently as deputy director of JDC-Israel. I replaced Leon Leiberg, who had been Harvey Steinberg's successor after Ted Feder (JDC director of European operations) had replaced Moe Levine. All my predecessors had been based in Europe, and with the consent of the Romanian Communist Government, I was the first JDC country director based in Israel.

Until the fall of Communism in 1989, my primary roles were to oversee the Federation of Jewish Communities of Romania (FEDROM) social welfare medical service delivery system and, most important—periodically negotiate the price of food purchased from the Romanian government for food packages and various feeding programs. While given free latitude by the Romanian Communist government to make hundreds of home and community visits throughout Romania to ascertain the needs of the elderly and help continually refine FEDROM's welfare programs, purchasing the food from TERRA, the government agency charged with this, was the most sensitive and important of my roles. It provided the vulnerable members of the Jewish community with sustenance in the countrywide context of very limited food supplies and allowed for JDC's carefully supervised system of importing foreign currency to Romania to purchase those items and to fund FEDROM's Social and Medical Assistance Department (SMAD) activities.

In December 1989, I was officially "uninvited" by Rabbi Rosen, the chief rabbi of Romania, on behalf of the Communist government to attend the traditional eight-day celebration of Hanukkah in Jewish communities throughout the country. The government considered my presence "inconvenient" at the time. During the revolution, there were fears for Rabbi Rosen's life based on unconfirmed information. He was secretly put in hiding through the efforts of one of the top leaders of the revolution, who had served as an assistant to Rabbi Rosen until then. Ultimately, there were three Jewish deaths directly attributed to the revolution. A seventy-five-year-old destitute Jewish assistee was found dead in her apartment with a bullet hole through her head from one of the many tens of thousands of rounds fired in "Victory Square" (the site of the bloodiest battles fought during the revolution). She was found by deliverers of the kosher meals on wheels program, which functioned smoothly throughout the revolution. The second casualty was of a young man in his thirties who demonstrated in the streets of Bucharest and had planned to immigrate shortly to Canada under the auspices of HIAS. The third was a seventeen-year-old protestor, a member of the Jewish choir and Sunday school of Bucharest.

The transition from Communism to democracy was not easy for the Jewish community of Romania, and it was my role, on behalf of the AJJDC, to consult and guide the community and its leadership through the process of inevitable change. The first event permitting change was the December 1989 revolution; the second was Rabbi Rosen's death in March 1994.

In 2002, I was asked once again to lead a staff group to assess the situation in a larger area—the Former Soviet Union (FSU), Central and Eastern Europe, and North Africa. Since JDC was now serving a much larger number of Jews in need—especially in the FSU—and since ten years had passed, this necessitated a fresh look at the level of care JDC was providing (see Global Task Force). The purpose was to ensure that there were no glaring inequities in the level of goods, services, and cash being provided by JDC to needy, elderly Jews in the geographic areas noted above. This was done with extensive help from the Claims Conference and the Harry & Jeanette Weinberg Foundation and North American Jewish Federations through United Jewish Communities, Inc., in partnership with Jewish community organizations. The task was daunting since the economic and cultural differences were more heterogeneous than in the previous study. However, we were able to produce a series of measurements based on objective and subjective data to compare the level of support provided to meet the actual needs of elderly in their respective countries. These measurements were presented to the JDC in order to improve future policy planning and implementation.

Since the fall of Communism in December 1999, it has been possible for the Jewish community to engage in informal Jewish educational programs as well as community building and leadership development programs to ensure its viability. This necessitated a major shift in goals and programs of the Jewish community as well as programs that I was able to facilitate and develop as a legitimate change agent on behalf of the JDC in partnership with FEDROM. The paper I wrote especially for this volume summarizes a long-term macro-practice social work intervention designed to alleviate suffering for a disadvantaged community amid a changing environment. It is a testimony to the skills and concepts that social work education equipped me with and the doctoral program at Penn solidified.

Reference

Global Task Force for the Rationalization of Welfare Programs Supported by JDC, American Jewish Joint Distribution Committee. *Report*, 2002.

Chapter 22
Introduction to a Dissertation: Posing Questions on Perceived Empowerment and Community Problem Solving

Jacqueline B. Mondros

The first purpose of this study was to develop and test a tool for analyzing neighborhood organizations, a tool which could be used to categorize and describe neighborhood organizations. The second purpose of this study was to use the descriptions of neighborhood to look at the relationships between these descriptions and certain specific consequences of neighborhood organizations, particularly those consequences related to perception of empowerment, and the ability to resolve neighborhood issues.

The intent of the study, then, was to describe the ways in which neighborhood organizations differ as regards a number of variables which seem to denote essentially different organizations. The descriptions were then used to investigate the relationships and interrelationships among 1) organizational descriptions, 2) issue resolution, and 3) perceptions of empowerment.

[This chapter introduces the questions studied; the author addresses some of the findings from the dissertation in her commentary.]

Neighborhood Organizations

Neighborhood organizations constituted the first major area of inquiry in this study. In most of the social work literature, neighborhood organizations had not been considered separately, but have subsumed under the more comprehensive heading of community organizations. This literature was applicable to a discussion of neighborhood organizations. This study focused on two important issues which had been discussed throughout the community organization literature, but about which no conclusions had been reached. The first issue dealt with the combination of variables which could be used to describe community organizations and which, if used, could categorize organizations. The second issue dealt with the uniqueness of neighborhood organizations and the importance of the type of organization.

While the subject of community organizations had been debated throughout the history of social work, no one single definition of what a community organization is had been agreed upon, nor had a conclusion been reached regarding the combination of variables which would be used to describe community organizations. During the course of social work history, community organizations, their intent and goals, had continually been redefined.[1] Community organizations had been alternately defined as entities established for community chest fundraising,[2] social education,[3] community development,[4] community planning,[5] for community psychotherapy,[6] as a form of colonialism.[7] In such famous works as Pray's "When Is Community Organization Social Work Practice?"[8] Seider's "What Is Community Organization Practice in Social Work?" [9] Rothman's "Three Models of Community Organization Practice,"[10] and Cox, Erlich, Rothman, and Tropman's *Strategies of Community Organization*,[11] strenuous efforts had been made to define community organizations. Nevertheless, there was no single accepted definition but, rather, a wide range of activities that could be called community organization.[12]

Furthermore, in the literature there was much debate and little agreement about the variables which define community organizations. Social work research on community organizations had focused on four major areas: community organizer practitioner styles, structure of the community organization, goals of the community organization, and attitudes of the participants of community organizations. In many cases these four areas had been studies independently of one another; correlations among these variables had been infrequently drawn.

Some authors had described differences in the styles of community organizations' strategies[13] and some had described the activities of community organizations.[14] Styles included community participation, advocacy, campaigning, confrontation, collaboration and social upheaval. Activities of community organizations included developing community resources, working on governmental advisory boards, providing neighborhood based services, and resisting change enforced from outside the community, for example, urban renewal. Other authors had described community organizations using variables which were just as applicable to other groupings, such as social service organizations.[15]

At the same time, community organizations had flourished outside of the field of social work. The Alinsky approach, developed in the 1940s, had spawned a number of training institutes, neighborhood organizations, and community organizations which functioned outside of and, many times, in opposition to the service delivery system.[16] Because of their emphasis on confrontation tactics and taking action, however, these organizations spent little time researching their own activities, and thus far, very few studies had been made of them.[17] Thus a major community organization style had been left largely uninvestigated.

What the literature presented, therefore, is a variety of styles and activities which did not construct a clear framework for analyzing community organizations, nor was there a great deal of discussion regarding a categorization which could permeate and transcend all styles and all activities. This lack of formulation constituted a serious problem.

A second problem derived from the fact that the literature seldom made a clear distinction between community organizations related to a small physical locale and community organizations related to larger physical entities. Within most of the community organization literature, all neighborhood organizations were seen as similar due to their base in physical community and differences among neighborhood organizations were largely unstudied. While neighborhood organizations may have in common their relatedness to a physical space, their researcher points out that differences may have created essentially different neighborhood organizations and that these differences may have transcended the one similarity of physical space.

For purposes of this study, a neighborhood[18] was defined as a physical locale smaller than the recognized government subdivision and which had been designated by a name and boundaries which are mutually accepted by external and internal institutions. A neighborhood organization[19] was defined as a voluntary association of residents where the activities and attention of the association were directed to the wants and needs of people living within the neighborhood. While neighborhood organizations may have been involved in diverse tasks such as community planning, community service, the establishment of local development corporations, and social action, the key distinctions were the voluntary nature of the neighborhood organizations, the governance of the organization by neighborhood residents, and the organization's relationship to a spatial unit known as a neighborhood. The study's intent, then, was to design and apply a tool which analyzed neighborhood organizations using a number of variables suggested by the wider community organization literature.

Resolution of Neighborhood Issues

The resolution of neighborhood issues is the second major area of inquiry in this study. A limited amount of research had been done on community and neighborhood organizations' abilities to resolve specific neighborhood issues. Few major authors had considered resolution of specific issues as being a primary goal of community organizations.[20] Some of the literature suggested that neighborhood organizations act more often as a reference group, a bonding, than a decision making body.[21] Yet, if neighborhood organizations were to impact on their environment, the objective resolution of specific neighborhood issues becomes an important function. However, the literature on neighborhoods suggested that although socioeconomic indicators related to neighborhoods remained unchanged despite needed improvement, people living in neighborhoods where there is an established neighborhood organization may have felt better about their neighborhood.[22] That is, the neighborhood organization may not have resolved specific neighborhood issues, but neighborhood residents may have felt better for having made the effort. Therefore, both objective and subjective indicators of resolution of issues must have been evaluated.

This study investigated the resolution of neighborhood issues, specifically in relation to the descriptions of neighborhood organizations. Resolution of neighborhood issues included both objective and subjective indicators.

Empowerment

The third major area of inquiry in this study was the empowerment of the participants in neighborhood organizations. A frequently stated consequence of community organizations in general, and neighborhood organizations specifically, was the empowerment of powerless people.[23] Community organizations were often seen as a means of acting collectively either in resistance to or in support of some change that was imposed from outside or inside of the neighborhood.

The bonding together of persons with mutual interest was seen as a method of controlling the destiny of a community. Empowerment goals included community control, resistance, revolution, and people's democracy.[24]

Not only did the goals vary, but the way people felt about the potential for the goals varied as well. Neighborhood organizations saw themselves as everything from participating in the democratic process to being "a power to be reckoned with" in the larger governmental context.

Contribution to the Literature

It was intended that this dissertation would make a contribution to the current social work literature on community organization.

First and most obviously, the study focused on neighborhood organizations as a subset of community organizations. The distinction used in this study allowed for a more careful investigation of neighborhood organizations and of those variables which made neighborhood organizations different from one another. The substantial differences found among neighborhood organizations suggested that these organizations were essentially different, despite their relatedness to physical space.

Secondly, the study intended to broaden the current understanding of neighborhood organizations in a way that further explicated and analyzed the similarities and differences among neighborhood organizations. The study developed a tool which when applied, can be used to describe individual neighborhood organizations. These descriptions suggested a beginning categorization of neighborhood organizations. The results of the study could indicate that a descriptive characterization of organizations may have transcended current methods of describing neighborhood organizations. It was also suggested that this tool could be extended to apply to all community organizations to allow for distinguishing descriptions.

Thirdly, the study attempted to substantiate largely untested consequences of neighborhood organizations, particularly their ability to resolve neighborhood issues, and to empower people. In this way, the study offered the direction for further research regarding the effectiveness of neighborhood organizations in relation to issue resolution and empowerment.

Lastly, the study seemed to have implications for community organization practice. The study suggested the type of organization to be used when a community organizer and community residents have particular results in mind. The study clarified some of the impact of neighborhood organizational efforts, what kind of results they could expect, and implied which type of organization increases the chance for the organization to reach specified objectives. The study, then, added to the body of knowledge and skill needed to educate community organization students.

The Organization of the Study Plan

The general plan of the study and the way it is reported here included six stages of inquiry which were 1) the development of a tool to analyze neighborhood organizations; 2) the application of the tool to categorize differences and similarities in the neighborhood organizations; 3) drawing a sample of organizational participants; 4) the development and administering of an instrument to measure the resolution of neighborhood issues; 5) the development and administering of a questionnaire to test participants' perception of empowerment; and 6) an analysis of the results obtained from the instruments which measured issue resolution, and empowerment, and the description of organizations all of which allow for a discussion of interrelationships. These six stages of inquiry related to the chapters of this study, and will now be briefly described.

1. A tool was developed which measured neighborhood organizations in respect to four dimensions: organizational approach to change, structure and goals of the organization, relationships among participants, and leadership and staff arrangements. These dimensions, gleaned from the literature, were further clarified by thirty variables selected from a variety of sources. In addition, identifying information related to the organizations were included as part of the tool. The development of the tool for analyzing neighborhood organizations, the literature which led to its formulation, and the hypotheses and research questions related to the tool's use were fully described in Chapter Two of this study, entitled "Neighborhood Organizations."[25]

2. Two Philadelphia neighborhoods (Kensington and Fishtown) which were matched for a number of demographic indicators were chosen for the study. From these neighborhoods, two neighborhood organizations (Kensington Action Now (KAN) and Fishtown Civic Association (FCA)) which were also matched for a number of variables were chosen. The tool was then used to analyze the two neighborhood organizations during a five month period. The application of the tool and the use of appropriate statistics allowed for the categorization of discernable differences between the organizations along the four dimensions and the thirty variables. The computation of these differences allowed for a description of the organizations of Kensington Action Now and Fishtown Civic Association. The method used, the descriptions of the neighborhoods and organizations, the results of the application of the tool, and the discussion of the organizations can be found in Chapter Two, entitled "Neighborhood Organizations."

3. A sample of those participants who attended 50% of the meetings of either Fishtown Civic Association or Kensington Action Now was drawn. This sample of par-

ticipants was used for the investigation of the resolution of neighborhood issues, and empowerment. Demographic data on each participant in the sample was also collected. A description of the method of sampling used and a report on the demographic characteristics of the sample is included in Chapter Three, entitled "The Sample of Participants."

4. Issue resolution was measured by using three sources; researcher observations recorded during meetings of each organization, media reports about each organization collected throughout the five-month period of the study, and by asking the sample of organizational participants an open ended question related to their perception of their organization's ability to resolve issues. These three sources of information about issue resolution allowed for a discussion of the relationship between the ability to resolve specific neighborhood issues and the descriptions of Kensington Action Now and Fishtown Civic Association. A discussion of the literature, hypotheses and research questions, research methodology, results and analysis related to the resolution of specific neighborhood issues, and a discussion of the relationship between the descriptions of the organizations and issue resolution can be found in Chapter Four, entitled "Resolution of Neighborhood Issues."

5. A questionnaire was developed to study perception of empowerment and was administered to the sample of participants from each organization. The questionnaire measured perception of empowerment along four dimensions: critical thinking, rationally motivated action, commitment, and opposition. These dimensions were further defined by eighteen variables gleaned from the literature on empowerment. Appropriate statistics were used to measure perception of empowerment for the sample of participants and allowed for a discussion of the relationship between participants' perception of empowerment and the descriptions of Kensington Action Now and Fishtown Civic Assocation. The literature, hypotheses and research questions, methodology, results and analysis related to perception of empowerment, and the discussion of the relationships between the descriptions of the organizations and perception of empowerment is included in Chapter Five, entitled "Perception of Empowerment."

6. The results obtained from the instruments which measured issue resolution, and empowerment, and the tool which allowed for the description of Kensington Action Now and Fishtown Civic Association were then used to discuss the relationships among issue resolution, empowerment, and neighborhood organizational approach. This discussion can be found in the final chapter, entitled, "Discussion and Conclusions," which also includes perspectives for further research.

A diagram of the organizational of the study and the relationship to the chapters of this dissertation is shown in Table 1.

TABLE 1. Organization of the Study and Relationships to Dissertation Chapters

Steps of the study	Sample used	Chapter relationship	Chapter topics
1. Development of the tool to analyze Neighborhood Organizations		Chapter 2—Neighborhood Organizations	Literature Review Research Questions & Hypotheses Compositions of the Tool
2. Application of the tool to two Neighborhood Organizations	*Neighborhood Sample*—Kensington & Fishtown *Organization Sample*—Kensington Action Now & Fishtown Civic Association	Chapter 2—Neighborhood Organizations	Description of neighborhoods & organizations Methodology for use of the tool Results and Analysis Discussion of Organizational Approaches
3. Sample drawn of Organizational Participants	*Participants* who attended 50% of the meetings of Fishtown Civic Association or Kensington Action Now	Chapter 3—Sample of Participants	Sampling Method Report on demographics of participant sample
4. Investigation of Resolution of Neighborhood Issues a. Researcher's Observations b. Media Reports c. Open ended question to participant sample	*Organizational Sample*— Kensington Action Now & Fishtown Civic Association *Participant Sample*— participants of Kensington Action Now & Fishtown Civic Association	Chapter 4—Resolution of Neighborhood Issues	Literature Review Research Questions & Hypotheses Methodology Results & Analysis Discussion of Issues Resolution and Organizational Descriptions
5. Investigation of Perception of Empowerment	*Participant Sample*—Participants of Kensington Action Now & Fishtown Civic Association	Chapter 5—Perception of Empowerment	Literature Review Research Questions & Hypotheses Methodology Results & Analysis Discussion of Organizational Descriptions and perception of empowerment
6. Investigation of Relationships among Issue Resolution, Perception of Empowerment, and Organizational Descriptions	*Neighborhood Sample*—Kensington & Fishtown *Organization Sample*—Kensington Action Now & Fishtown Civic Association *Participant Sample*— Participants of Kensington Action Now & Fishtown Civic Association	Chapter 6—Discussion & Conclusions	Relationships between issue resolution, perception of empowerment, and organizational descriptions Perspectives for further research

From Jacqueline B. Mondros, "A Study in Neighborhood Organization: Issue Resolution and Empowerment," Ph.D. Dissertation, University of Pennsylvania, 1981 (Ann Arbor, Mich.: University Microfilms).

Notes

1. See Mona Heath and Arthur Dunham, *Trends in Community Organization: A Study of the Papers on Community Organization, Published by the National Conference on Social Welfare, 1874–1960* (Chicago: School of Social Service Administration, 1963); Robert Perlman and Arnold Gurin, *Community Organization and Social Planning* (New York: Wiley, 1972).

2. Mary P. Follet, *The New State: Group Organization the Solution of Popular Government* (New York: Columbia University, 1918).

3. Edward Lindeman, *The Community* (New York: Association Press, 1921).

4. See Ward Goodenough, *Cooperation in Change* (New York: Sage, 1963); William Biddle and Loureide Biddle, *The Community Development Process: The Rediscovery of Local Initiative* (New York: Holt, Rinehart, and Winston, 1965).

5. See Peter Maris and Martin Rein, *Dilemmas of a Social Reform* (New York: Atherton Press, 1967); Jack Rothman, "An Analysis of Goals & Roles in Community Organization Practice," in Ralph Kramer and Harry Specht, eds., *Readings in Community Organization Practice* (Englewood Cliffs, N.J.: Prentice-Hall, 1969), 260–68.

6. Martin Rein, "Social Work in Search of a Radical Profession," in Neil Gilbert and Harry Specht, eds., *The Emergence of Social Welfare and Social Work* (Berkeley: University of California Press, 1976).

7. Marjorie Mayo, "Community Development: A Radical Alternative?" in Roy Bailey and Michael Brake, eds., *Radical Social Work* (New York: Pantheon, 1975), 129–43.

8. Kenneth Pray, "When Is Community Organization Social Work Practice?" *Proceedings of the National Conference of Social Work, San Francisco, 1947* (New York: Columbia University Press, 1948).

9. Violet Seider, "What Is Community Organization Practice in Social Work?" *Social Welfare Forum, Proceedings, National Conference in Social Work, St. Louis, 1956* (New York: Columbia University Press, 1956).

10. Jack Rothman, "Three Models of Community Organization Practice, Their Mixing & Phasing" in Fred Cox et al., eds., *Strategies of Community Organization*, 3rd ed. (Itasca, Ill.: Peacock, 1979), 25–45.

11. Fred Cox et al., eds., *Strategies of Community Organization*, 3rd ed. (Itasca. Ill.: Peacock, 1979).

12. For a broad historical perspective on the various definitions of community organizations see Follet, *The New State*; Lindeman, *The Community*; Walter Petel, "Some Prognostications in the Field of Community Work," *Proceedings of National Conference of Social Work, Denver, 1925* (Chicago: University of Chicago Press, 1925); Robert P. Lane, "Reports of Groups Studying the Community Organization Process," *Proceedings of the National Conference of Social Work, 1939* (New York: Columbia University Press, 1939); Leonard Mayo, "Community Organization Method and Philosophy in 1946," *Proceedings of the National Conference of Social Work, Buffalo, 1946* (New York: Columbia University Press, 1947); Pray, "When Is Community Organization Social Work Practice?"; Clarence King, *Organizing for Community Action* (New York: Harper and Row, 1948); Arthur Dunham, "What Is the Job of the Community Organization Worker?" *Proceedings of the National Conference of Social Work* (New York: Columbia University Press, 1949); Wilber Newsletter, "The Social Intergroup Work Process," *Proceedings of the National Conference of Social Work, San Francisco, 1947* (New York: Columbia University Press, 1948); Ernest Harper and Arthur Dunham, *Community Organization in Action* (New York : Association Press, 1959); Heath and Dunham, *Trends in Community Organization*; Goodenough, *Cooperation in Change*; Rothman,

"Three Models"; Saul Alinsky, *Rules for Radicals* (New York : Vintage, 1969); Michael Austin and Neil Betten, "Intellectual Origins of Community Organizing, 1920–1939," *Social Service Review* 51 (1) (March 1977): 155–70; Cox et al., eds., *Strategies of Community Organization.*

13. See Rothman, "Three Models"; George Brager and Harry Specht, *Community Organizing* (New York: Columbia University Press, 1973).

14. Sherry Arnstein, "Eight Rungs on the Ladder of Citizen Partcipation," in Edgar Cahn and Barry Passet, eds., *Citizen Participation: Expecting Community Change* (New York: Praeger, 1971), 69–91.

15. See Rothman, "Three Modelse"; Roland Warren, *Social Change and Human Purposes: Toward Understanding and Action* (Chicago: Rand McNally, 1977).

16. Alinsky, *Rules for Radicals.*

17. Robery Bailey, *Radicals in Urban Politics: The Alinsky Approach* (Chicago: University of Chicago Press, 1974).

18. Neighborhood is a physical locale, smaller than a recognized government subdivision, designated by a name and boundaries mutually accepted by external and internal institutions.

19. Neighborhood organization is a voluntary association of residents with activities and attention are directed to the wants and needs of the people living in the neighborhood. Neighborhood organizations may be involved in diverse tasks such as community planning, community service, establishment of local development corporations, and social action, but the key distinctions are its voluntary nature, governance by neighborhood residents, and relationships to a spatial unit known as a neighborhood.

20. Jack Rothman, John Erlich, and Joseph Teresa, *Promoting Innovation & Change in Organizations & Communities: A Planning Manual* (New York: Wiley, 1976).

21. See Murray Ross, *Community Organization* (New York: Harper and Row, 1967); Richard Sennet, *The Uses of Disorder* (New York: Knopf, 1970).

22. For a discussion of the resurgence of a sense of neighborhood despite a decreased use of neighborhood facilities see Albert Hunter, "Loss of Community: An Empirical Test Through Application," *America Sociological Review* 40 (October 1975): 540–43. For a discussion of members of neighborhood organizations feeling safer despite a continued crime problem see Ellen Cohn, "Fear of Crime & Feelings of Control: The Effect of Age & Family Composition" (Ph.D. dissertation, Temple University, 1978).

23. Frances Piven and Richard Cloward, *Poor People's Movements* (New York: Pantheon, 1977).

24. Alinsky, *Rules for Radicals.*

25. These chapters of the author's dissertation are not included here.

Commentary: If I Had Known Then What I Know Now

Jacqueline B. Montros

At the time of my dissertation study (1978–1989), Philadelphia was still a series of small segregated ethnic neighborhoods, many of which had active community groups. In those years both Kensington and Fishtown were primarily white working-class neighborhoods comprised of large Irish, Italian, and Polish families. The Roman Catholic Church and the unions (mostly Teamsters) were the most influential institutions in these communities. While the neighborhoods were similar, the organizations differed significantly. Kensington Action Now (KAN) was an Alinsky style organization using what now might be called a "conflict approach." It was established as a federation of member groups, many of which were churches, what now would be called "faith-based organizations." A professional organizing staff was central to its leadership development, issue identification, and strategy. Fishtown Civic Association, on the other hand, did what today would be called "consensus organizing," cooperating and planning with City officials, was based on individual memberships, and was run by a few active residents.

Much has changed since the data were originally collected more than twenty years ago. Kensington is now a largely Latino low-income neighborhood. Though Kensington Action Now eventually disbanded, Kensington Welfare Rights Union, an organization focused on issues of poverty and employment, was active in the same neighborhood for a time. Fishtown has experienced some gentrification, with "yuppies" moving north from the Northern Liberties neighborhood. The Civic Association remains, though, largely inactive.

My dissertation asked the questions: Do community organizations identify neighborhood issues and solve them? Is there a relationship between differences in neighborhood organizations and participants' perceptions of empowerment? Is there a more significant relationship between a neighborhood organization which uses a conflict approach and participants' perceptions of empowerment, as opposed to an organization that uses a consensus approach and participants' perceived empowerment? To measure empowerment, I created an empowerment instrument. It included many Freirian principles such as "increasing commitment of individuals to persons perceived as similar and to an ideology which supports those similarities," an ability to identify with others on the basis of common interests, and to act with others on those mutual interests; and increasing commitment to the nurturance of in-group ties. My findings suggested that KAN was more likely to identify and solve community issues. There was no difference between participants in the two organizations in perceived empowerment, but participants in the organization using the conflict approach did have a more clearly defined sense of common interests. KAN participants showed a small but insignificant difference in attachment to ideology, but there was no difference on increasing commitment to in-group ties.

At the time the study was conducted, while there was an identifiable community organization skill set, there was very little sociological theory or social psychological theory that informed it. Both Solomon's (1976) seminal work on empowerment and Gerlach and Hine's (1970) understanding of group action were newly published, both focused on how collectives were effective in opposing vested power interests and mitigating the effects of discrimination and oppression. Freire's (1970) work on popular education had become known in the United States. I relied heavily on these insights in my work, but an understanding of how groups developed and gained power, and the utility of that understanding in community organization had not yet been established.

Since my dissertation, I have continued to be preoccupied with questions about social action and community organization. It seems appropriate to ask what I might do differently, if I were studying these community organizations today.

Certainly, I would place much more emphasis on neighborhood context as a variable. Just as Piven and Cloward (1977) suggested, it was naïve to assume that one could attribute neighborhood change to the actions of a community organization. External political and economic forces have proven themselves to be much more powerful factors in community transition, and organizational power much more ephemeral, especially given the disappearance, variability, and accountability issues inherent in funding for community groups.

Nevertheless, there is new technology that might help study how community organizations pursue problem-solving. Geographic Information Systems (GIS) is used to map risk factors and assets of a designated neighborhood. For example, one can map not only numbers of cases of childhood asthma and hospital admissions for it, but also health centers which treat the disease. Neighborhood residents can elaborate the GIS by adding their own personal knowledge to the map, for example, which doctors are known to effectively treat the disease, and the homes of parents and teens who can share their experiences. Were I to study neighborhood problem solving now, I would ask the neighborhood leaders to identify the issues the organizations are working on, use GIS to map related aspects of the problems, and ask leaders to elaborate the map with personal knowledge. Then I would ask the leaders to identify the risks and assets on which they feel the organization is most likely to be able to affect change, what other factors are likely to affect change, and then track whether change occurred or not and what was most likely to be the major instigator of the change. Obviously, such a study would best be done longitudinally, to truly account for economic and political influences. For example, KAN was working on affordable housing which could have been mapped using GIS, then elaborated by leaders with information about apartments and realtors. Then KAN participants might have been asked what they felt the organization could influence, what other influences existed, and the results analyzed over subsequent years.

Second, my own subsequent work and the work of many others (Mondros and Wilson 1994; Fisher and Shragge 2000) suggests that community organizations should not be characterized as either conflict or consensus, but arrayed along some continuum of use of conflict and consensus building strategies. Most organizations shift their strategies in response to opposition. Even KAN, a classic Alinsky style organization, developed alliances with former opponents once a problem was solved. Aetna Life and Casualty, the central "target" in the redlining campaign, became a strong supporter of the organization's first foray into low-income housing by establishing a $2.5-million revolving loan fund for the organization.

I thought that participants' perception of empowerment would be correlated with the use of conflict strategies. In fact, it is more likely true that perceived empowerment is correlated with issue resolution. On the other hand, maybe it isn't. The most important insight I gained from my dissertation study is that organizing victories, that is, solving a problem, was *less* likely to make people feel satisfied. KAN solved more issues, but its leaders were more dissatisfied with the neighborhood. Solving one problem seemed to result in leaders worrying about myriad other neighborhood difficulties they faced and how much more needed to be solved. Successful activism, in fact, seemed to breed dissatisfaction. Such pessimism then had to be countered with celebrations to instill a sense of pride and well-being among leaders.

Additionally, the new social psychological theories about why people protest today would necessarily influence the study of empowerment. Using sophisticated quantitative and qualitative data, researchers have posited a number of important theories about why and when people become "protest ready" or what we might call empowered. Three distinct sets of factors have been identified: societal opportunities and constraints that shaped political protest, such as sudden deprivation or rising expectations following deprivation (Morrison, 1978); the mobilization of formal and informal organizational resources that enabled collective action (Tilly 1978; McCarthy and Zald 1977; Gamson 1975; Oberschall 1973); and the processes by which movement participants framed perceptions of injustice and developed a sense of shared identity (Meyer et al. 2002; Mansbridge and Morris 2001; Gamson 1992). These factors are frequently combined to provide a fuller picture of the onset of protest (Ryan and Gamson 2006; Morris and Mueller 1992).

Consequently, a new study might look at the degree to which the neighborhood was showing signs of deterioration or improvement, and the number of formal and informal organizations that encouraged collective action in each community. Interestingly, my original study did analyze participants' perceptions of injustice and shared identity. However, there is new evidence that joint action can emerge from either a shared sense of confidence or a collective sense of stigma (Owens and Aronson 2000). It would be interesting to include questions in the empowerment instrument that attempted to distinguish between empowerment based on perceptions of strength and empowerment based on a sense of deficits.

Perhaps the most important innovation in studying communities since my dissertation is the advancement of the concepts of social networks and social capital. No study of community organization today could ignore this new and significant body of knowledge. The study of social networks and social capital has enhanced both Gerlach and Hine's (1970) and Solomon's (1976) understanding of the significance of collective bonds in instigating community change.

Social network theory describes the structural aspects of an individual's support system, that is, the connections among people who are related by kinship, friendship, employment, or community ties. An understanding of social networks allows us to analyze the structure of the community organization's participation, that is, who is connected to whom, and how; how many connections people have (through church, through familial ties, through the neighborhood organization), and whether the networks are facilitated, enhanced, or intervened in by joining the community organization (Cox 2005). In my dissertation, as in much of the early work in community organization, "strategic interconnectedness" among members was assumed. Today, an analysis of the social networks of organizational participants would help us to explore whether or not participants were connected, the quality and quantity of the connections, and how those connections influenced organizational commitment and activity.

Social capital refers to the ability to leverage social networks as a resource. Robert

Putnam (2000) encouraged researchers to demonstrate the usefulness of social capital in different domains, and Loeffler et al. (2004) argues that social capital is at the core of community organizing because of its ability to generate opportunity for collective action.

Both Loeffler et al. (2004) and Saegart and Thompson (2002) describe the use of social capital in community work. They discuss how social capital creates bonds among people within communities, bridges people across communities, and links communities to financial and public institutions. Therefore, today an analysis of the bonds, bridges, and links emerging from the social capital of organizational participants would be possible, and these aspects of social capital could be examined for their influence on the organizations' capacity to solve identified problems. Of particular interest would be an examination of the links to financial and public institutions achieved by organizations along the conflict to consensus continuum. It would be important to know which organizations managed to develop better linkages that led to problem solving.

In summary, while the essential questions I asked in the dissertation would be similar today, we have many new tools and concepts which could be useful in providing better answers. Paying attention to context, new understandings of the array of organizational strategies, and utilizing the new social and social psychological theories would certainly strengthen the evidence about organizational efficacy and perceived empowerment.

References

Cox, K. F. (2005) Examining the role of social network intervention as an integral component of community-based family-focused practice. *Journal of Child and Family Studies* 14 (3) (September): 443–54.

Fisher, R., and E. Shragge (2000). Challenging community organizing: Facing the twenty-first century. *Journal of Community Practice* 8 (3): 1–19.

Freire, P. (1970). *Pedagogy of the Oppressed.* New York: Seabury Press.

Gamson, W. A. (1975). *The Strategy of Social Protest.* Homewood, Ill.: Dorsey Press.

———. (1992). The social psychology of collective action. In A. D. Morris and C. M. Mueller, eds., *Frontiers in Social Movement Theory.* New Haven, Conn.: Yale University Press. 53–76.

Gerlach, L. P., and V. H. Hine_(1970). *People, Power, Change: Movements of Social Transformation.* New York: Bobbs-Merrill.

Loeffler, D. N. et al. (2004). Social capital for social work: Toward a definition and conceptual framework. *Social Development Issues* 26 (2/3): 22–38.

Mansbridge, J. J., and A. D. Morris, eds. (2001). *Oppositional Consciousness: The Subjective Roots of Social Protest.* Chicago: University of Chicago Press.

McCarthy, J., and M. Zald (1977). Resource mobilization and social movements. *American Journal of Sociology* 82: 1212–42.

Meyer, D. S., N. Whittier, and B. Robnett, eds. (2002). *Social Movements: Identity, Culture and the State.* New York: Oxford University Press.

Mondros, J. B. and S. Wilson (1994). *Organizing for Power and Empowerment.* New York: Columbia University Press.

Morris, A. D., and C. M. Mueller, eds. *Frontiers in Social Movement Theory.* New Haven, Conn.: Yale University Press

Morrison, D. E. (1978). Some notes toward theory on relative deprivation, social movements, and social change. In L. E. Genevie, ed., *Collective Behavior and Social Movements*. Itasca, Ill.: Peacock. 202–9.

Oberschall, A. (1973). *Social Conflict and Social Movements*. Englewood Cliffs, N.J.: Prentice-Hall.

Owens, T. J., and P. J. Aronson (2000). Self-concept as a force in social movement involvement. In S. Stryker, T. J. Owens, and R. W. White, eds., *Self, Identity, and Social Movements*. Minneapolis: University of Minnesota Press. 191–214.

Piven, F. F., and R. J. Cloward (1977). *Poor People's Movements: Why They Succeed, How They Fail*. New York: Pantheon.

Putnam, R. (2000). *Bowling Alone: The Collapse and Revival of the American Community*. New York: Simon and Schuster.

Ryan, C., and W. A. Gamson (2006). The art of reframing political debates. *Contexts* 5 (1): 13–18.

Saegert, S., J. P. Thompson, and M. R. Warren (2001). *Social Capital and Poor Communities*. New York: Sage.

Solomon, B. B. (1976). *Black Empowerment: Social Work in Oppressed Communities*. New York: Columbia University Press.

Tilly, C. (1978). *From Mobilization to Revolution*. Reading, Mass.: Addison-Wesley.

Part V
Contemporaries: Recent Ph.D.s and Faculty

Chapter 23
The Role of Social Disadvantage in Crime, Joblessness, and Homelessness Among Persons with Serious Mental Illness

Jeffrey Draine, Mark S. Salzer, Dennis P. Culhane, and Trevor R. Hadley

Social problems among persons with mental illness, such as involvement with the criminal justice system, unemployment, and homelessness, are receiving heightened attention in the media and the psychiatric literature. It would surprise many service providers and advocates to learn that mental illness is not as potent an explanatory factor for these problems as the psychiatric literature might lead us to believe. Researchers have sought to improve services that address these problems among persons with mental illness but have frequently failed to recognize that the experience of people with mental illness is often contextualized in disadvantaged social settings.

In other words, persons with mental illness experience social problems more frequently because they live in a world in which these problems are endemic, not just because they are mentally ill. Thus social problems become erroneously simplified as psychiatric problems, resulting in the creation of overly simple interventions and policies to address a complex phenomenon.

Much of the psychiatric services research is based on samples of participants who meet criteria for mental illness. Using data from these samples, researchers frequently make inferences about the social problems of individuals who have mental illness. According to these data, problems such as unemployment, crime, and homelessness are pervasive among people with mental illness. Thus it is inferred that mental illness itself is a prime explanatory factor for these social problems among these individuals.

However, in most cases these inferences are not valid, essentially because of failure to compare the experience of persons who have serious mental illness with that of persons in similar socioeconomic situations who are not ill. In the few studies in which such comparisons have been made, the impact of mental illness was much smaller than that implied in most of the psychiatric literature. In arguing for this perspective, we do not want to exchange biological reductionism for social reductionism. Cohen (1) recently warned of the dangers of too great a focus on biomedical reductionism in examining treatment and services for persons with serious mental illness. One aspect of this reduc-tionism is a "social amnesia" when it comes to understanding the broader social con-text for the difficulties encountered by persons with mental illness. At the same time, we do not want to lose the benefit of gains we have made in biological explanations of psychiatric illness. The question is one of achieving a balance that best informs policy and practice toward a better community life for people with mental illness.

In addressing social problems among persons with mental illness, researchers need to give more consideration to social factors that overlap the boundaries of mental ill-ness and mental health. These factors have links to psychiatric illness but are also closely linked to the social and economic characteristics of the communities in which people with mental illness live.

Our position is that poverty is an important moderator of the relationship between serious mental illness and social problems and that this moderating role is not suffi-ciently accounted for in research, service planning, and policy. Poverty and its associ-ated social disadvantage can also be linked to important mediating factors, such as decreased self-efficacy and coping. If persons with mental illness are not poor to begin with, they are likely to become poor, and poverty factors become salient in explaining common outcomes, such as quality of life, social and occupational functioning, gen-eral health, and psychiatric symptoms.

To discuss the refocusing of research on social problems and mental illness, we use three social problems by way of illustration: crime, unemployment, and homelessness. In this article we suggest ways in which research on each of these problems may have suffered from inattentiveness to the general knowledge base—that is, outside of psy-chiatry—in these areas. We present selected evidence in each of these areas as a way of illustrating our point.

Crime

The prevalence of mental disorders detected in jail populations gives rise to rhetoric about jails replacing hospitals for the mentally ill. The metaphor of the "largest men-tal hospital" (2) has been used in the media to refer to the jails of Los Angeles, Chi-cago, and New York. Among mental health advocates, this phenomenon is routinely attributed to the failures of the mental health system. However, such an explanation ignores the increasing incarceration rates in the general U.S. population.

The number of prison inmates in the United States quadrupled between 1970 and 1999 and could double again by 2005 (2). There have been similar increases in the number of individuals in jails or on probation and parole.

An alternative explanation for the increase in the number of people in jail with a mental illness over this period is that individuals with mental illness are also members of other groups with a high risk of being arrested. Persons who are substance users, are unemployed, have fewer years of formal education, and have low incomes have a greater risk of incarceration. It would follow from the general increase in incarcera-tion rates that persons with mental illness are disproportionately caught up in the criminal justice system because of their greater risk of arrest as a result of these other factors, independent of mental illness.

This phenomenon was documented in a recent study in Australia showing that an increase in the numbers of persons with schizophrenia who were arrested after deinstitutionalization was accounted for by an increase in arrest rates in the general population, not by psychiatric status (3). This finding confounds the conclusion that mental illness has been criminalized or that the institutionalization of persons with mental illness has shifted from state hospitals to jails (4).

Studies of persons with serious mental illness who are living in the community have consistently found lifetime arrest rates in the range of 42 to 50 percent (5–7). Although these rates initially appear remarkable, they are similar to rates observed in general community samples. Studies of crime indicate that 25 to 45 percent of urban males have been arrested by the age of 18 years, and about half of those who are ever arrested during their lifetime are arrested before the age of 18 (8). African Americans are almost twice as likely as whites to have been arrested (8). The lifetime arrest rates we have noted above were taken from adult populations with an average age well beyond 18 years. Two of the three samples were from communities in which African Americans predominated. Thus when the demographic and community contexts are considered, the apparent disparity in arrest rates for persons with mental illness is no longer so obvious.

Some research has linked symptomatic behavior to a greater likelihood of arrest (9,10), but even this research has not indicated that a substantial portion of persons who show evidence of mental illness are arrested (8, 9). Thus an empirical link between the extent of symptomatic behavior encountered by police and the bulk of the jailed population with mental illness is tenuous. It is likely that the majority of the persons in jail who have a diagnosis of a psychiatric disorder have risk factors other than their psychiatric symptoms. However, the empirical weakness of the criminalization argument has not prevented some advocates from using indirect evidence to support such a conclusion.

For example, a recent study by the National Institute of Justice estimated that 16 percent of persons in jails and prisons had a mental illness (11). Mental illness was defined as a self-reported "mental or emotional condition" or any overnight stay in a "mental hospital, unit, or treatment program." For most mental health researchers, this definition is far from sufficient as a valid operationalization of mental illness status. However, even if this operationalization were valid, the study found no data that make a case for a link between change over time and mental illness or psychiatric hospitalization patterns.

Nevertheless, the results of the study were used extensively by advocates and by federal agencies to support the proposition that persons with mental illness are being "criminalized." Multiple studies have shown a disproportionately large number of persons with mental illness in jails and prisons, but few studies are designed to allow investigators to attribute this incarceration to mental illness (12) rather than to other risk factors or to the historical increase in incarceration generally.

As the idea of the criminalization of the mentally ill has become part of the policy context, advocates have pushed for more mental health treatment resources as a means of preventing the incarceration of persons with mental illness. Model mental health interventions are being funded and implemented more extensively as a way of addressing this problem. However, few of these interventions use crime theory and research to conceptualize criminal behavior among persons with mental illness. Instead, their conceptualization tends to focus on shifting people out of the criminal justice system and into the mental health system.

Few mental health interventions are conceptualized around the idea that many individuals could reasonably be treated as both criminal offenders and recipients of mental health services. Such a conceptualization would seem to tolerate the criminalization of mental illness. However, regarding an individual as both an offender and a service recipient has important implications for the treatment of the individual as a citizen, not just as a psychiatric patient. When a person is shifted from the criminal justice system to the mental health system, there is also a significant shift in due process procedures, which the individual may not perceive as being in his or her best interests.

Behavior that is linked to acute symptoms could be addressed by increasing police access to effective crisis services (13). There is no evidence that exempting persons who are not acutely symptomatic at the time of arrest from accountability to the criminal justice system is beneficial to the individuals or to the community (14). This group of individuals probably constitutes the bulk of persons with mental illness in jails.

Thus it could be more beneficial to develop a range of interventions that integrate mental health services throughout the criminal justice system. Individuals could maintain their rights as criminal defendants while receiving effective mental health treatment.

Research has shown that psychiatric status is a poor predictor of criminal recidivism (15) and may not be a strong factor in explaining involvement with the criminal justice system (3) when other factors strongly associated with crime are also considered (15). This does not mean that mental illness among persons who are involved with the criminal justice system should be ignored. Interventions that integrate criminal justice services and mental health services may be more effective for many individuals than a shift "back" to the mental health system. Such interventions would consider the complicated context of criminal behavior, including risk factors common to both mental health and criminal behavior—for example, substance abuse, problems with employment and housing, and a low likelihood of having prosocial attachments (15, 16).

Thus research and intervention could more realistically accept the overlap between mental health and criminal justice populations as an expected and unsurprising phenomenon. Such acceptance may provide a foundation for a greater understanding of criminal behavior among persons with mental illness and for more services that are effective in the criminal justice system.

Employment

Employment of persons with severe mental illness has historically been related to prognosis (17). Various explanations have been postulated of the impact of mental illness on work, including inability to cope with the stresses of work, poor social skills, and diminished cognitive abilities. One result of these perceived deficits is that persons with serious mental illness may not know how to apply for jobs and may do poorly in job interviews (18).

The data pertaining to the work lives of persons with serious mental illness are grim. Among persons with a disability due to mental illness, the labor force participation rate—that is, whether a person has a job, is on temporary layoff, or is actively looking for work—ranged from a low of 21.5 percent in 1985 to 27.2 percent in 1994 (19). This rate has been relatively stable and is similar to the 25 percent employment rate for persons with serious mental illness computed from surveys conducted in the early 1980s among participants in community support programs (20).

Research on the lifetime work experiences of persons with serious mental illnesses is limited, possibly because of the expectation that the work experiences of persons with mental illnesses are restricted. In a study of 100 young adults with a diagnosis of schizophrenia, 85 had maintained a competitive job for more than three months during their lives (21). In a study involving almost 300 people with a wide range of diagnoses, nearly all had been competitively employed at some point (22).

A small study of persons with serious mental illness who were seeking vocational rehabilitation services showed that the mean ± SD number of full-time jobs held was 2.70 ± 2.38 and the mean number of part-time jobs held was 1.89 ±1 .79 (23). The median employment tenure among employed persons with a psychiatric diagnosis was seven months (22), and the mean ± SD employment tenure across all jobs held was 18.57 ± 26.81 months (23). The temptation to conclude that mental illness is the primary factor in shaping vocational careers is strong.

However, a more complicated picture of the relationship between mental illness and employment status emerges when these data are considered in the context of various sociodemographic factors. For example, there is a strong link between educational level and mental illness, and educational level is also an important factor in employment. Data from the national comorbidity study (24) indicate that the early onset of a psychiatric disorder may have an adverse impact on a person's educational attainment.

Similar observations can be made from data obtained as part of the Epidemiologic Catchment Area study. For example, although 57.4 percent of persons with a diagnosis of schizophrenia graduated from high school—a rate that is slightly, but not significantly, lower than that of the general U.S. population (65.7 percent)—only 4.8 percent were college graduates, compared with 17.2 percent of the U.S. population (25). Thus there is some complexity in the relationship between mental illness and employment. It appears that symptoms over the course of a person's life may have an impact on educational attainment, which also affects employment.

In 1992 the employment rate for persons with a college degree was 2.7 times higher than the rate for those with only a high school diploma (26). High school graduates worked 8 percent fewer weeks from 1991 through 1995 than college graduates and experienced significantly more episodes of unemployment than college graduates (27). Education also dictates the types of jobs a person can seek. Lower educational attainment is associated with entry-level jobs known for rapid turnover—the same types of jobs that persons with serious mental illness frequently take.

For example, McCrohan and associates (22) interviewed 279 persons with schizophrenia (68 percent), affective disorder (21 percent), or another mental disorder (11 percent). The current or last job for 51 percent of respondents was in the service industry—for example, food service, janitorial work, and personal services, such as child care worker or nurse's aide. Thirty-one percent of respondents held benchwork jobs, such as light assembly or employment in a sheltered workshop. Fewer than 5 percent held clerical jobs or sales positions. These types of positions are generally associated with a short job tenure—for example, 1.8 years for retail trade positions, 1.2 years for sales positions, 1.3 years for food service, 1.6 years for construction laborers, and 1.9 years for equipment cleaners, helpers, or laborers (28). Not surprisingly, education also significantly influences earnings and wages (26).

There has been a promising shift in orientation from work—or lack thereof—as a prognostic indicator of illness toward rehabilitation and recovery models that emphasize ameliorative approaches to overcoming the impairment and disability associated with mental illness. Tremendous strides have been made in the development of effective vocational rehabilitation programs. For example, the individual placement and support model has been found to dramatically increase the total numbers of persons with serious mental illness who obtain employment in competitive work settings (29).

However, vocational rehabilitation providers and researchers have been somewhat stymied in the degree to which they can bring about more satisfying and stable employment for persons with serious mental illness. One study found that the maximum employment rate of persons receiving individual placement and support was only 34 percent over an 18-month period, with an average job tenure of 16.5 weeks (29). Other studies have found similar employment rates for other vocational rehabilitation programs (30–32).

Race, sex, age, presence of a disability, and residence in a metropolitan area also play important roles in employment status, independent of mental illness. Results from one analysis found that sociodemographic factors play a significantly larger role in the employment of persons with a disability due to a mental illness than the mental disability itself (33). In fact, these data suggest that the impact of programs aimed at addressing the mental illness and resulting disability pales in comparison with what might be achieved if factors associated with various sociodemographic characteristics that limit employment opportunities could be adequately addressed.

For example, expanding supported education programs would go a long way toward improving the work lives of persons with serious mental illness. Other factors that limit employment opportunities include racial factors, such as prejudice in hiring, and factors related to a person's place of residence—for example, the fact that fewer jobs are available in poorer neighborhoods. Addressing such factors could maximize the potential of mental health interventions such as individual placement and support to improve vocational outcomes for persons with mental illness.

Homelessness

The casting of homelessness as "primarily a mental health problem" began during the early 1980s, when a resurgence in homelessness was identified by advocates, the news media, and researchers. Mental health researchers were among the first to study the problem (34, 35). The apparent "disturbed" nature of the street homeless population created an expectation that the public mental health system would assume responsibility for this vulnerable group.

The first set of studies argued that as many as 90 percent of homeless persons had a "mental disorder" (34, 35), and such estimates were widely reported in the national news media. Rates for more serious mental disorders, such as schizophrenia, were reported to be around 30 percent. Nevertheless, the early research confirmed and even promoted the view that homelessness was a problem that stemmed from the deinstitutionalization of persons with mental illness (36).

Reviews of this research have not been favorable. The many shortcomings to which critics have pointed in questioning the generalizability of research findings include single shelter sites, in one case a shelter attached to a state-owned hospital; screening criteria for admission to shelters; and unsystematic diagnostic procedures (37). Nevertheless, the dictum that "one-third of the homeless have a severe mental illness" can ultimately be traced to this relatively minimal body of evidence (37).

Research conducted in the latter half of the 1980s was based on larger, more representative samples (38, 39). These studies also involved structured, standardized diagnostic interviews. Not surprisingly, they yielded far more convergent results (40). In a meta-analysis, Lehman and Cordray (41) reported that the rate of severe mental disorders among the homeless samples in these more rigorous studies was about 18 to 22 percent, or about a third less than that reported in the earlier literature. However, even these larger studies could not be fairly generalized to "the homeless," because they excluded homeless families, a population that has lower rates of mental illness. In some cities, the number of people in homeless families has outpaced the number of homeless adults. Thus generalizations of research findings to "the homeless" need to be qualified.

A study of the rates of severe mental disorders among homeless persons in Philadelphia, which used longitudinal administrative treatment and shelter records, found that 18 percent of homeless adults without accompanying children had received services for a severe mental disorder (42). However, the estimate dropped to a range of 12 to 15 percent when mothers of the children were included. Furthermore, when the children were included, the rate of treatment for severe mental disorders among the homeless population dropped to a range of 7 to 9 percent. In this context, it is clear that mental illness is not the primary cause of homelessness. Excluding data on families has inflated the estimated rate of mental disorders among homeless persons.

Administrative data on use of homeless shelters have provided an opportunity to assess population-adjusted risks of homelessness among persons with mental illness and in other groups. This research has shown that while the annual rate of shelter admission in the general population was about 1 percent in New York and Philadelphia throughout the 1990s (43), the annual rate among persons with serious mental illness in the Medicaid population, at least in Philadelphia, was about 3.6 percent (44).

It is surely significant that the shelter admission rate of persons with serious mental illness is more than three times that of the general population. However, the rate appears to be no lower than that for other poor people. In Philadelphia, about 6 percent of the poor population stays in a shelter each year, including about 9 percent of poor children and 12 percent of poor adults in their 30s and 40s, the primary age groups of homeless adults.

The annual rate of shelter admission among poor black children in New York City was 16 percent in 1995, and the rate among poor black men in their 30s and 40s is as high as 20 percent per year. Given that the comparable rate among persons with serious mental illness is 3.6 percent (43), is it possible that severe mental illness actually confers some protection against homelessness?

More carefully controlled studies that compared the housed and homeless poor populations have found that although serious mental illness might not offer protection from homelessness, it does not represent a distinguishing risk factor for becoming homeless. Multivariate studies of families in New York City (45) and Worcester, Massachusetts (46), showed no effect of mental illness or substance use disorders on the risk of shelter use.

Multivariate studies among single adults in Chicago (47) and Buffalo (48) likewise found no effect of mental illness or substance abuse on becoming homeless or on having been homeless in the past. The evidence more strongly suggests that, among persons with mental disorders, substance abuse is a common risk factor for homelessness (49, 50), but, again, mental illness per se does not distinguish between the vulnerable poor population who remain housed and those who become homeless.

Furthermore, and perhaps most interestingly, study results show that although substance abuse does consistently predict long-term homelessness or difficulty in exiting homelessness, no such consistent evidence exists of an association between homelessness and mental illness. In some cities, such as New York and Buffalo, people with mental disorders have been found to stay homeless (48, 51); in others, mental illness has no effect (52, 47), and in still others it actually appears to have a mitigating effect on the duration of homelessness (51).

It is likely that differences in the local treatment system explain why the findings of these studies have been so disparate. In cities that are better organized to conduct outreach and move people with serious mental illness into housing, mental illness may indeed be a protective factor against long-term homelessness. Availability of Supplemental Security Income, greater access to inpatient services, access to a public system of outpatient and rehabilitation programs, and even special housing outreach programs specifically for persons with mental illness who are homeless should, if developed appropriately and expanded sufficiently, act to reduce the risk of long-term homelessness among persons with mental illness relative to the risk for poor persons in general.

Clearly, homelessness is more than a mental health problem. That homeless persons have much higher rates of mental disorders, including severe mental disorders, than the general population may seem shocking. However, in the context of the poor populations from which they come, such rates are not as noteworthy. When dramatically adverse shifts in housing affordability and crowding occurred during the 1980s and 1990s, people with mental illness were among those who suffered their effects. They may even have been the first to make the problem visible. However, homelessness affects a much broader segment of the poor in general and is not unique to people with severe mental illness.

From a mental health policy perspective, what is disturbing is that severe mental disorders are so prevalent among the poor in general and that having a mental disorder does not convey adequate social protection from impoverishment. Such protection should include effective outreach to improve access to treatment, housing combined with services to prevent homelessness, and adequate income. Thus the problem is one of relating social forces to treatment effectiveness in explaining outcome.

Implications

It has long been understood that persons with mental illness are largely among society's poor (1). The precipitating factors of many socially adverse events are strongly associated with complicated issues such as crime policy, the war on drugs, race, poverty, and economic development—not with psychiatric symptoms. Acknowledging this reality should help keep these social problems among persons with mental illness in perspective.

This is not to imply that having a psychiatric disorder is not a risk factor for social problems or for exacerbation of the problems. It is important to note that much of the current mental health services literature leaves an impression of a greater impact of mental illness in explaining individuals' experience of these problems than is probably warranted. Our understanding of social problems among persons with mental illness could be more effectively anchored by theoretically valid comparisons with persons from the general population who are in similar socioeconomic strata.

Implications for Services

Mental illness is nevertheless an important variable to consider in addressing these social problems. In fact, using the proper comparisons to contextualize social problems among persons with mental illness is a step toward providing more effective services. Such an approach may provide data to enable more thorough integration of effective mental health services with the service systems that address these problems in the general population. It also may provide an additional social benefit for people with mental illness. When we conceptualize the problems these individuals face in the appropriate social context, our policy ideas begin with the premise of integration with society.

Specialized services for persons with mental illness may produce additional layers of stigma. This potential should not be treated lightly. It is possible to develop more effective policies and programs to address social problems among persons with mental illness that integrate these individuals into service systems that address such problems. If we view each of these social problems solely as a mental health treatment problem, we may further stigmatize persons with mental illness while providing insufficient interventions.

Implications for Research

Current thinking holds that the etiology of major mental illnesses is largely biological. In light of the impact of past thinking, this is fortunate in many ways. The development of scientific knowledge used in the treatment of these disorders has improved the lives of many people. It has also provided ammunition to advocates as they fight the stigma associated with mental illness and mental health treatment. Thus the medical treatment of serious mental disorders is widely accepted and has provided progressively greater advantages to many individuals who experience such disorders. This acceptance has influenced social research on serious mental illness, and many social scientists now focus on the study of service delivery and the development of social interventions.

Mental health services research has necessarily focused on diagnostically homogeneous groups. Designs of the most influential research include controls that heighten internal validity to establish the efficacy of interventions. These studies will affect policy as "best practices" become established on the basis of this research, which in turn will leverage reimbursement mechanisms from care organizations. Thus the prestige of the mental health professions will be enhanced by a process that focuses on discrete diagnostic categories.

Over the past 30 years, a meta-diagnostic category—serious and persistent mental illness—has dominated much of public mental health services research. This designation is based on a three-pronged definition that includes diagnosis (generally schizophrenia and major affective disorders), disability, and duration of the disorder. Studies have used this designation to link mental illness to broader social problems and costs. Certainly this effort is well intentioned. It seeks to call attention to the need to develop effective intervention strategies and public health policy for the people most seriously affected by psychiatric illness. However, by isolating this population for study, we subvert our capacity to accurately assess the relative risk mental illness poses for other problems.

In addition to comparing individuals on the basis of their current status—for example, homeless, employed, or incarcerated—examining the role of these states during the life course of individuals with and without mental illness can be informative. Longitudinal research on the relative risk of multiple experiences and their relation to mental illness may increase our understanding of social forces and of treatment effectiveness.

We should expect researchers to do more work that compares the experiences of persons with serious mental illness with the experiences of persons who live in similar circumstances but who do not have mental illness. Theoretically, this work should be conducted among persons who are at risk of homelessness, involvement with the criminal justice system, and unemployment. The impact of this strategy is highlighted in the homelessness research example above. When use of homeless shelters by persons with mental illness was compared with use in the general population, mental illness appeared to be a strong factor in explaining homelessness. However, when use of shelters by persons with mental illness was compared with use in the population of persons living in poverty, the implications were nearly the opposite—mental illness could possibly be seen as a protective factor against homelessness, particularly long-term homelessness. Here we have provided similar examples for employment and involvement with the criminal justice system. Other factors that might be shown to mediate the impact of mental illness include substance abuse, physical health, educational attainment, child abuse and neglect, and juvenile delinquency.

Making comparisons of this sort will require specialized sampling strategies, which need to be both targeted on serious mental illness and generalizable to larger populations. Much of the epidemiological research that has focused on mental illness and social status has used samples from the general population. As a result it has focused on a much broader conception of mental illness and thus a broader range of illness than the serious mental illness designation (24, 53, 54). Because persons with serious mental illness account for less than 5 percent of the general population, generalizations of this research to the population of individuals with serious mental illness are tenuous. For example, in an analysis that linked poverty indicators to development of a mental disorder by using data from the Epidemiologic Catchment Area study, only four new cases of schizophrenia were found during the longitudinal follow-up period (53).

Although it initially appears that a great deal of research has been conducted on social mobility, social problems, and mental illness, it quickly becomes apparent that this research is not readily applicable to populations of individuals with serious mental illness. In future studies linking serious mental illness to social problems, sampling designs could include stratified sampling to ensure sufficient numbers of persons with serious mental illness as well as a generalizable comparison with persons who do not have serious mental illness in the same sociodemographic contexts.

Implications for Policy

A greater focus on social context has mixed policy implications for mental health service advocacy. The use of "disease" as the explanation for social problems has permitted advocates to acquire additional resources for treatment and to create primary mental health services for people who are homeless, involved with the criminal justice system, or unemployed. Disease-based interventions can be more focused, and outcomes can be expressed more readily on an individual level. Because it is easier to generate interest and support for such interventions than for broader social welfare–oriented interventions, it is easier to fund these interventions as medical interventions.

However, because the interventions are based on the disease, their effectiveness is theoretically limited to the extent to which the disease affects the problem. If psychiatric disease is only a small part of the problem, services focused on psychiatric treatment are limited in the extent to which they can illuminate effects for social outcomes. Such limitations do not suggest that the role of mental illness in these problems should be neglected, only that policies aimed at mental illness will be only partially effective.

If explanatory frameworks highlight a smaller role for mental illness, mental health professionals—and policy makers in general—gain information from the overall framework to develop appropriate interventions. Grounding intervention research further in the existing research from a greater variety of theoretical frameworks will expand the range of intervention activities. This approach should provoke greater innovation in practice and policy, including innovations that are not necessarily linked to the conventional roles of mental health professionals. Such roles may include community level interventions, social welfare programs, conventional and alternative law-enforcement programs, and development of greater infrastructure for supporting self-help and mutual-aid associations among persons whose lives are affected by mental illness.

In considering a role for more broad-based policies, two sets of goals might be considered. First, public policies could reduce the risk of social problems in general: joblessness, poverty, undereducation, housing crowding, and lack of access to adequate, affordable housing. Interventions focused on these problems will benefit persons with serious mental illness insomuch as these individuals themselves are disproportionately affected by them.

Alternatively, policies could focus on reducing the prevalence of these risk factors among persons with serious mental illness. These persons should be more adequately protected through social insurance programs so that they do not become poor, destitute, and homeless. They should be provided with more employment accommodations to enable them to work and with the services and supports that would help them avoid the risks of crime and incarceration.

Reprinted from Jeffrey N. Draine, Mark S. Salzer, Dennis P. Culhane, and Trevor R. Hadley, Role of social disadvantage in crime, joblessness, and homelessness among persons with serious mental illness, *Psychiatric Services* 53 (2002): 565–73. Reprinted by permission.

Notes

1. Cohen CI: Overcoming social amnesia: the role for a social perspective in psychiatric research and practice. *Psychiatric Services* 51:72–78, 2000.

2. Blumstein A, Beck AJ: Population growth in US prisons, 1980–1996, in *Crime and Justice: A Review of Research*, 26. Edited by Tonry M, Persilia J. Chicago, University of Chicago Press, 1999.

3. Mullen PE, Burgess P, Wallace C, et al: Community care and criminal offending in schizophrenia. *Lancet* 355:614–617, 2000.

4. Whitmer GE: From hospitals to jails: the fate of California's deinstitutionalized mentally ill. *American Journal of Orthopsychiatry* 50:65–75, 1980.

5. Draine J, Solomon P: Comparison of seriously mentally ill clients with and without arrest histories. *Journal of Psychiatry and Law* 20:335–349, 1992.

6. McFarland BH, Faulkner LR, Bloom JD, et al: Chronic mental illness and the criminal justice system. *Hospital and Community Psychiatry* 40:718–723, 1989.

7. Solomon P, Draine J: Issues in serving the forensic client. Social Work 40:25–33, 1995.

8. Blumstein A, Cohen J, Roth JA, et al.: *Criminal Careers and "Career Criminals,"* vol 1. Washington, DC, National Academy Press, 1986.

9. Teplin LA: Criminalizing mental disorder: the comparative arrest rate of the mentally ill. *American Psychologist* 39:794–803, 1984.

10. Teplin LA: The criminalization hypothesis: myth, misnomer, or management strategy? in *Law and Mental Health: Major Developments and Research Needs.* Edited by Shah SA, Sales BD. Rockville, MD, National Institute of Mental Health, 1991.

11. Ditton PM: *Mental Health and Treatment of Inmates and Probationers.* Washington, DC, US Bureau of Justice Statistics, 1999.

12. Teplin LA, Voit ES: Criminalizing the seriously mentally ill: putting the problem in perspective, in *Mental Health and Law: Research, Policy, and Services.* Edited by Sales BD, Shah SA. Durham, NC, Carolina Academic Publishers, 1996.

13. Steadman HJ, Stainbrook KA, Griffin P, et al: The Need for a Specialized Crisis Response Location for Effective Police-Based Diversion Programs. Delmar, NY, Policy Research Associates, 2000.

14. Draine J, Solomon P: Describing and evaluating jail diversion services for persons with serious mental illness. *Psychiatric Services* 50:56–61, 1999.

15. Bonta J, Law M, Hanson K: The prediction of criminal and violent recidivism among mentally disordered offenders: a metaanalysis. *Psychology Bulletin* 123:123–142, 1998.

16. Benda BB: Undomiciled: a study of drifters, other homeless persons, their problems, and service utilization. *Psychosocial Rehabilitation Journal* 14:40–67, 1991.

17. Strauss JS, Carpenter WT: *Schizophrenia.* New York, Plenum, 1981.

18. Liberman RP, Jacobs HE, Blackwell GA: Overcoming psychiatric disability through skills training, in *Psychiatric Disability: Clinical, Legal, and Administrative Dimensions.* Edited by Meyerson AT, Fine TF. Washington DC, American Psychiatric Press, 1987.

19. Trupin L, Sebesta DS, Yelin E, et al.: Trends in Labor Force Participation Among Persons With Disabilities, 1983–1994. Disability Statistics Report 10. Washington, DC, US Department of Education, National Institute on Disability and Rehabilitation Research, 1997.

20. Mulkern VM, Manderscheid RW: Characteristics of community support program clients in 1980 and 1984. *Hospital and Community Psychiatry* 40:165–172, 1989.

21. Test MA, Knoedler WH, Allness DJ, et al: Characteristics of young adults with schizophrenic disorders treated in the community. *Hospital and Community Psychiatry* 36: 853–858, 1985.

22. McCrohan NM, Mowbray CT, Bybee D, et al: Employment histories and expectations of persons with psychiatric disorders. Rehabilitation Counseling Bulletin 38:59–71, 1994.

23. Baron RC, Salzer MS: Career patterns of persons with serious mental illness: generating a new vision of lifetime careers for those in recovery. *Psychiatric Rehabilitation Skills* 4:136–156, 2000.

24. Kessler RC, Foster CL, Saunders WB, et al.: Social consequences of psychiatric disorders: I. educational attainment. American Journal of Psychiatry 152:1026–1032, 1995.

25. Keith SJ, Regier DA, Rae DS: Schizophrenic disorders, in *Psychiatric Disorders in America: The Epidemiologic Catchment Area Study.* Edited by Robins LN, Regier DA. New York, Free Press, 1991.

26. Blank RM: Outlook for the US labor market and prospects for low-wage entry jobs, in *The Work Alternative: Welfare Reform and the Realities of the Job Market.* Edited by Nightingale DS, Haveman RH. Washington, DC, Urban Institute Press, 1995.

27. Bureau of Labor Statistics, 1998, ftp://146. 142.4.23/pub/news.release/nlsoy.txt.

28. Bureau of Labor Statistics, 1998, ftp://146. 142.4.23/pub/news.release/tenure.txt.

29. Drake RE, Becker DR, Clark RE, et al: Research on the individual placement and support model of supported employment. *Psychiatric Quarterly* 70:289–301, 1999.

30. Fabien ES, Wiedefeld MF: Supported employment for severely psychiatrically disabled persons: a descriptive study. *Psychosocial Rehabilitation Journal* 13:53–60, 1989.

31. MacDonald-Wilson KL, Revell WG, Nguyen NH, et al: Supported employment outcomes for people with psychiatric disabilities: a comparative analysis. *Journal of Vocational Rehabilitation* 1:30–44, 1991.

32. Shafer MS, Huang HW: The utilization of survival analysis to evaluate supported employment services. *Journal of Vocational Rehabilitation* 5:103–113, 1995.

33. Yelin EH, Cisternas MG: Employment patterns among persons with and without mental conditions, in *Mental Disorder, Work Disability, and the Law.* Edited by Bonnie RJ, Monahan J. Chicago, University of Chicago Press, 1997.

34. Bassuk EL, Rubin L, Lauriat A: Is homelessness a mental health problem? *American Journal of Psychiatry* 141:1546–1550, 1984.

35. Arce AA, Tadlock M, Vergare M, et al: A psychiatric profile of street people admitted to an emergency shelter. *Hospital and Community Psychiatry* 34:812–817, 1983.

36. Bassuk EL: The homelessness problem. *Scientific American* 251:40–45, 1984.

37. Ropers R: *The Invisible Homeless: A New Urban Ecology.* New York, Human Sciences Press, 1988.

38. Fischer PJ, Breakey WR: The epidemiology of alcohol, drug, and mental disorders among homeless persons. *American Psychologist* 46:1115–1128, 1991.

39. Koegel P, Burnam MA, Farr RK: The prevalence of specific psychiatric disorders among homeless individuals in the inner city of Los Angeles. *Archives of General Psychiatry* 45:1085–1093, 1988.

40. Tessler RC, Dennis D: Mental illness among homeless adults: a synthesis of recent NIMH-funded research. *Community and Mental Health* 7:3–53, 1992.

41. Lehman AF, Cordray DS: Prevalence of alcohol, drug, and mental disorders among the homeless: one more time. *Contemporary Drug Problems* 20:355–383, 1993.

42. Culhane DP, Averyt J, Hadley TR: The prevalence of treated behavioral disorders among adult shelter users. *American Journal of Orthopsychiatry* 26:207–232, 1998.

43. Culhane DP, Metraux SM: One-year rates of public shelter utilization in New York City (1990, 1995) and Philadelphia (1995). *Population Research and Policy Review* 18: 219–236, 1999.

44. Culhane DP, Averyt J, Hadley TR: The rate of public shelter admission among Medicaid-reimbursed users of behavioral health services. Psychiatric Services 48:390–392, 1997.

45. Shinn M, Weitzman BC, Stojanovic D, et al.: Predictors of homelessness among families in New York City: from shelter request to housing stability. *American Journal of Public Health* 88:1651–1657, 1998.

46. Bassuk EL, Buckner JC, Weinreb LF, et al.: Homelessness in female-headed families: childhood and adult risk and protective factors. *American Journal of Public Health* 87:241–248, 1997.

47. Sosin MR: Homeless and vulnerable meal program users: a comparison study. *Social Problems* 39:170–188, 1992.

48. Toro PA, Bellavia CW, Daeschler CV, et al: Distinguishing homelessness from poverty: a comparative study. *Journal of Consulting and Clinical Psychology* 63:280–289, 1995.

49. Caton CLM, Shrout PE, Eagle PF, et al.,: Risk factors for homelessness among schizophrenic men: a case control study. *American Journal of Public Health* 84: 265–270, 1994.

50. Caton CLM, Shrout PE, Dominguez B, et al: Risk factors for homelessness among women with schizophrenia. *American Journal of Public Health* 85:1153–1156, 1995.

51. Culhane DP, Kuhn R: Patterns and determinants of public shelter utilization among single adults in New York City and Philadelphia: a longitudinal analysis of homelessness. *Journal of Policy Analysis and Management* 17:23–43, 1998.

52. Wong I: Patterns of homelessness: a review of longitudinal studies, in *Understanding Homelessness: New Policy and Research Perspectives.* Edited by Culhane D, Horburg S. Washington, DC, Fannie Mae Foundation, 1997.

53. Bruce ML, Takeuchi DT, Leaf PJ: Poverty and psychiatric status: longitudinal evidence from the New Haven Epidemiologic Catchment Area study. *Archives of General Psychiatry* 48:470–474, 1991.

54. Dohrenwend BP, Levav I, Shrout PE, et al: Socioeconomic status and psychiatric disorders: the causation-selection issue. *Science* 255:946–952, 1992.

Commentary

Jeffrey Draine

During the time that the Social Work Mental Health Research Center was active at the school, Phyllis Solomon and Trevor Hadley (director of the Center for Mental Health Policy and Services Research in the Department of Psychiatry and a member of the social welfare graduate group) co-led a doctoral level seminar in mental health services. It alternated course titles year to year to cover both policy and research methods. On several occasions, I led a session on the interaction of mental illness in the criminal justice system. It was during one of these sessions that the germ of the idea for this paper sprouted.

I was giving what is (and remains) the conventional line of reasoning for explaining the rise in the numbers of people with mental illness in the criminal justice system since 1970. As described in the paper, this is the "criminalization hypothesis." The argument goes that in the era of deinstitutionalization of the treatment of people with mental illness, jails and prisons have become the more accessible alternative social control institution. As part of presenting the data I had to bring to this argument, I was presenting data from research among people with mental illness in West Philadelphia, using a sample of general community mental health service consumers (i.e., not sampled for involvement in the justice system). These data showed about a 40 percent lifetime arrest rate among these consumers. I thought this seemed high, and I thought it most certainly supported the criminalization of mental illness idea right in our back yard.

Trevor Hadley interrupted me. He asked if I knew the arrest rate generally for West Philadelphia. I had to say I didn't. He challenged the assumption that 40 percent was unusually high for West Philadelphia. I checked it out later. It wasn't.

In addition to reshaping our conversation that day, this interjection began a larger conversation about how we think of social problems among people with mental illness. Following from a paternalistic framework of caring for people with mental illness, it is easy to conclude that the challenges in their life emanate from the mistreatment of the illness. This would be a perspective derived from the motivation of most people entering social work and other helping professions: to be helpers. We will have a tendency to reduce social problems to their smallest solvable unit. Often, this unit is a weakness in the person we identify as a client. From that, we follow a logical path of finding a way to blame society for the unfair treatment of this vulnerability. Then we can not only help "them" with their weakness, we can also "save" them from society. The criminalization argument falls into this line of logic. It is easy then the rally our professional comrades to be champions for our clients or patients.

This works well for our professional identity as healers, soul savers, and change agents. However, it essentially blinds us from our own culpability for this problem. The real underlying issue in the criminalization of mental illness is the criminalization of lots of things, not just mental illness. The rising use of arrest and incarceration as a social policy instrument is something that we accede to as citizens. Because it is often a hidden process, it is something to which we can easily be blind as social observers.

What I received that day in the seminar was some correction in my vision. I allowed myself to change the depth of field in my focus on mental illness in the criminal justice system. I could see more of the context for the involvement of people with mental illness in the criminal justice system. As a result, I could also see the limits to our imagination in creating policy responses to the issues of mental illness in the criminal justice system.

At the Center for Mental Health Policy and Services Research, the conversation continued. We could see the same process in other areas where policy discussions had focused too quickly on treatment of mental illness as the policy solution for a social problem that was more complex than the side effects of a diagnosis. Thus, we began to talk about writing this paper. I could write about criminal involvement. Mark Salzer (a member of the Center Faculty and an adjunct faculty member of the school and a graduate group member in social welfare) could contribute his observation of the same dynamic in employment interventions. Dennis Culhane (also SP2 faculty) could contribute from his work on homelessness.

We considered including substance abuse as an additional topic area of focus. Substance use is often framed as a problem associated with mental illness. However, we know that substance abuse is also contextualized in terms of the availability of substances, changes and differences in social prohibitions regarding substance abuse, and differences in treatment access, prosecution, and sentencing. Since the plan for the paper was already relatively long and involved for the publication venues we had in mind (*American Journal of Public Health* or *Psychiatric Services*), we decided to not include substance abuse in the topics covered.

We initially pitched the paper to *American Journal of Public Health* as a special review. The journal's editorial policy was to accept proposals for such papers. There was initial interest from the editor, and we submitted the paper there, but it was ultimately rejected. We then submitted it to *Psychiatric Services*. It was accepted there without a request for revision. However, upon publication, we found that the paper had a "second opinion" attached from Scott Nelson, a well-known psychiatrist with a long career in public mental health services. While he agreed with some of our assertions, he strongly took issue with our approach. He asserted that the issue was and remains treatment of the mental illness.

The regular "Taking Issue" editorial at the front of the issue was also focused on our article. It was written by Margaret Severson and Alice Lieberman from the University of Kansas School of Social Welfare. They asserted that our perspective was so commonly accepted and understood that it was almost a waste of time and energy to be studying it—that we were "reinventing the wheel" and that what was needed was more action on this view, and less focus on research and more research. There is a hint in their critique that they, as social workers, had been part of this movement for some time. Since our affiliation in the journal was identified with a center in a department of psychiatry, the fact that all four of us were associated with a social work school and the first author was a social worker was obscured. I wonder if they would have seen us more as allies continuing and expanding the conversations of social work if that had been more clearly understood.

We could not have been better set up to respond to these public criticisms of our article. Both responses criticized our paper from different, somewhat opposed perspectives, both saying that the valid view point (theirs) was self-evident, and that we need not distract ourselves with any more such idle talk. Thus, we had the opportunity to reinforce the idea that we need to continue to both act and think (not one or the other) critically about the issues we address. We need to be skeptical of received wisdom, and constantly open to different or new perspectives. If there is anything that the practice of research as a domain of social work practice offers, is the insistence on this skepticism. Even those things that are most self-evident should be open to question.

What is important about maintaining that vigilance is not our identity as social workers, but our effectiveness in seeking to bolster the social inclusion of those we might consider clients. Since being interrupted by Trevor in that seminar, I have used my corrected vision in a number of projects, to reshape how we see the social forces that impinge on the lives of people with mental illness, among others. My personal hope is that we become less focused on our role as helpers, and more focused on building policy and practice generally that takes pleasure in a critical skepticism, an openness to different ways of seeing an issue, and differing voices in the conversation.

Chapter 24
Social Services of African American Congregations in the Welfare Reform Era

Stephanie C. Boddie

From slavery to the present, African-American congregations have provided for both the spiritual and social welfare of their members and communities. With public policy initiatives such as Charitable Choice[1] and the White House Faith-Based Initiative, policymakers are expecting African-American congregations to play an even greater social service role in many urban communities. Some scholars have suggested that African-American congregations respond differently and more comprehensively than non-African-American congregations to the needs of their communities (Lincoln and Mamiya 1990; Billingsley 1999)—a response largely due to their distinct evolution within a racially segregated society and a reluctant welfare state (Quadagno 1994). This comparative study of African-American, interracial, and white congregations explores the extent to which African-American congregations have a unique niche as social service providers. Findings of this study will help us better understand the service delivery role of African-American congregations in the welfare reform era.

Over the last thirty years, scholars have called into question the continued centrality of congregations in the African-American community, given the increasing availability of secular organizations such as the Urban League, the NAACP, and government agencies (Frazier 1963; Mukenge 1983; Nelsen 1988). African Americans who moved to urban areas at the beginning of the 20th century during the Great Migration were among the first to experience the diminished role and capacity of African-American congregations as they entered a new geographic and economic environment (Frazier 1963; Mukenge 1983; Nelsen 1988). Nelsen (1988) concluded that: "With the urbanization of the African-American church caused by the migration of African-Americans to the urban South and North the church could not meet all the functions required in the complex urban environment, and it [the church] had no monopoly to do so" (407). Nelsen suggested that new social and economic conditions that resulted from the migration and urbanization of African Americans required new methods and strategies to support and improve conditions for African Americans—strategies and methods that could not be fully achieved through the limited resources of African-American congregations. Mukenge (1983) speculated that African-American congregations would become overwhelmed by needs, much like white congregations had been during the Great Depression, and hence recede into a niche focused on the spiritual needs of their members.

Frazier (1963), Mukenge (1983), and Nelsen (1988) hypothesized that, over time, the function of African-American congregations would become only religious, and thus completely differentiated from its historical overlap with the roles of government and the market in providing services and financial resources for African Americans. Their assertions also implied that African-American congregations provided services less efficiently than their secular counterparts. African-American congregations, therefore, would become more like White congregations that accepted the government as having the primary responsibility for providing social services (Harris 1987). This being the case, as organizations set within similar environments, African-American congregations would demonstrate institutional isomorphism (DiMaggio and Powel, 1983) rather than a process of differentiation. That is, a particular congregational service profile would become the dominant and legitimate institutional form for all congregations. In addition, this theory of complete differentiation rests on the assumption that religion must be coupled with secular issues to maintain a public role. Lincoln and Mamiya (1990) challenged the notion of complete differentiation and isomorphism by offering a principle of partial differentiation. Rather than completely receding into a religious niche, Lincoln and Mamiya argued that African Americans began to have more interactions within the mainstream sectors of society as a result of the Great Migration and the Civil Rights movement. Lincoln and Mamiya (1990) frame their hypothesis with the following argument:

First, white churches do not have the kind of institutional centrality in their communities that black churches have; second, there are far more competing secular institutions among whites. Probably the only time when white churches and pastors in the United States experienced a similar kind of centrality in their communities occurred in the colonial period when churches were at the center of social life and pastors were considered the major community leaders. Lastly, black churches have a greater range of social problems to contend with. Since close to 35 percent of the black population is mired in an economic underclass. (188)

African-American congregations have continued to maintain involvement in some social and community areas while leaving other service areas to the government and market sector. In their study of 1,894 urban ministers representing 1,531 African-American churches, Lincoln and Mamiya (1990) found that 71% of the churches provided community services while 29% focused exclusively on religious services.

In more recent studies, scholars have compared the level of social service of African-American congregations with other congregations (Chaves and Higgins 1992; Cavendish 2000; Cnaan and Boddie 2001; Tsitsos 2003). These studies concluded that African-American congregations were not more involved in all types of social and community services, and highlighted the value of considering specific social services provided by African-American congregations as compared to other congregations. Using a sample of larger congregations, Chaves and Higgins (1992) found that African-American congregations were more likely than white congregations to offer support services to help the underprivileged in the local community. Using a nationally representative sample of Roman Catholic congregations, Cavendish (2000) reported similar findings. Based on an analysis of 1,044 Philadelphia congregations, Cnaan and Boddie (2001) found a different pattern. For instance, African-American congregations were more likely to provide summer day camp, clothing closets, programs for gang members, prison ministry, health education, mentoring, computer training for youth, street outreach to the homeless, neighborhood cleanup, and drug and alcohol prevention than non-black congregations (i.e., white, Latino, Asian congregations). Further, Tsitsos (2003) found that African-American congregations were more likely than white congregations to provide a limited range of services: education, job-related, substance abuse, and mentoring. These comparative studies primarily focused on the percent of congregations providing particular types of social services and used the number of social services as the measure of social service involvement (Chaves and Higgins 1992; Cavendish 2000; Cnaan and Boddie 2001; Tsitsos 2003). This measure of social service involvement is limited. It does not consider other ways in which congregations may demonstrate their level of social service involvement, namely the level of informal services or the percentage of financial resources allocated.

Methods

This study uses a multi-dimensional measure of social service involvement, which is expected to present a different picture of the level of social service involvement of African-American congregations compared to white and interracial congregations. Given that limited resources have been suggested as one reason African-American congregations have a diminished role as a community social service provider, this study also examined the provision of informal services and the allocation of financial resources for social service provision. By presenting the profile of formal services as well as identifying the informal services and financial investment, these findings shed light on how public and private sector partners can support the social service investment of African-American congregations. The data used for this analysis were drawn from two waves of a cross-sectional survey of congregations from seven cities—Chicago, Indianapolis, New York, Mobile, Philadelphia, San Francisco, and Houston (Cnaan, Boddie, Handy, Yancey, Schneider 2002). The original sample of 111 congregations housed in historic properties was randomly selected in Chicago (16), Indianapolis (25), New York (15), Mobile (15), Philadelphia (24), and San Francisco (16). To offset the bias toward selecting congregations founded before 1940, congregations established after 1940 were targeted in Chicago (5), Houston (24), Indianapolis (29), Mobile (25), Philadelphia (39), and San Francisco (11).

The unit of analysis for this study was 228 congregations with 75% or more African-American members ($n = 70$, 31%) or 75% or more white members ($n = 122$, 54%). Congregations without a predominant racial or ethnic group were classified as interracial ($n = 36$, 16%). Due to the low number of cases, 16 congregations that were predominately Latino and Asian were excluded from this study. Thus, this study's sample of 228 congregations reflects the diversity of the estimated 350,000 U.S. congregations from seven cities, each region of the U.S., different religious traditions, various congregational sizes, different political orientations, theological orientations and socioeconomic status.

Trained interviewers conducted in-depth, face-to-face interviews with clergy, administrators, and program leaders. A three-part survey instrument was administered to more than one person in each congregation. Congregation leaders were asked questions about the congregation's history and membership profile; the congregation's governance and resources; the nature and scope of social and community services; and up to five specific services and their resources as well as staffing patterns. The social services were identified from a list of 190 services. This recognition method was preferred over asking respondents to recall the services provided in the last 12 months.

Using a social service inventory of 190 services, respondents were asked if within the last 12 months the congregation had provided a specific service upon request or when needed, run a formal program on their own property, run a program administered by the congregation elsewhere, or referred congregants to a program run by someone else. Respondents were also asked what percentage of the church's annual budget was designated for outreach, social action, social ministry, and social programs. Bases on these items, the congregations' level of social services activity was measured by (a) the total number and percentage of congregations providing formal services, (b) the total number and percentage of congregations providing informal services, and (c) the percentage of the annual budget allocated to provide social services. The percentage of the annual budget allocated was used rather than the absolute number allocated (in dollars) so that the size of financial contribution was independent of the size of the membership and the resource base of the congregation. Calculating various descriptive statistics using the items described above provided indicators for the three measures of the congregations' social service activity.

Results

When examining the formal social service provision of the African-American, interracial, and white congregations, approximately 40–50% of all three congregations provided music performance, hospital visitation, recreation for teens, choral groups, summer programs for teens, holiday celebrations, services for the sick and homebound, and visitation buddy programs. A similar pattern emerged for informal social services. Approximately 70% of all three congregations provided bereavement counseling, couple counseling, and family counseling when a request is brought to the clergy or another congregation leader. However, a distinct profile for formal services emerged for African-American congregations as compared to interracial and white congregations. Of the social and community-oriented services identified in **Table 1**, African-American congregations were more likely to provide all of these services than interracial congregations and white congregations.

When social service activity is measured as financial investment, the results are mixed. The mean scores for the percentage of the overall budget allocated for social

TABLE 1. Social Services: Comparing African-American, Interracial, and White Congregations

Services Sponsored by Congregations	African-American Congregations N = 70	Interracial Congregations N = 36	White Congregations N = 122	Total N = 228
Food pantries	35 (50.0%)	13 (36.1%)	36 (29.5%)	84 (36.8%)
Clothing closet	32 (45.7%)	12 (33.3%)	19 (15.6%)	63 (27.6%)
Summer day camp	29 (41.4%)	13 (36.1%)	31 (25.4%)	73 (32.0%)
Voter registration	29 (41.4%)	9 (25.0%)	18 (14.8%)	56 (24.6%)
Tutoring	28 (40.0%)	9 (25.0%)	21 (17.2%)	58 (25.4%)
Sports activities	26 (37.1%)	11 (30.6%)	28 (23.0%)	65 (28.5%)
Cooperationwith police	23 (32.9%)	9 (25.0%)	14 (11.5%)	46 (20.2%)
Neighborhood Association	22 (31.4%)	8 (22.2%)	26 (21.3%)	56 (24.6%)
Space for police/community meetings	22 (31.4%)	4 (11.1%)	15 (12.3%)	41 (18.0%)
Street outreach to homeless	21 (30.0%)	7 (19.4%)	24 (19.7%)	52 (22.8%)
Single parents	20 (28.65)	6 (16.7%)	16 (13.1%)	42 (18.4%)
Health education	19 (27.1%)	5 (13.9%)	15 (12.3%)	39 (17.1%)
Drug & alcohol prevention	19 (27.1%)	8 (22.2%)	14 (11.5%)	41 (18.0%)

services for the three groups of congregations were African-American (M = 25.8, SD = 21.7), interracial (M = 24.3, SD = 19.2), and white (M = 19.9, SD = 16.7). Differences in mean scores were not statistically significant (F = 2.25, p = .11). However, it is important to note that overall African-American congregations had lower annual budgets (36.2% under $100,000) and more members with lower incomes (35.1% with incomes less than $25,000 per year) as compared to interracial congregations (34.3% with budgets under $100,000 and 38.1% members with incomes $25,001-$50,000 per year) and white congregations (21.4% with budgets under $100,000 and 30.5% members with incomes $25,001–$50,000 per year).

Discussion

Although this study is not based on a representative sample, it builds upon the findings of past research to document differences and similarities in the social service patterns of African-American congregations compared with interracial and white congregations.

These findings provide evidence to support Lincoln and Mamiya's (1990) partial differentiation hypothesis by documenting a unique profile for the social service provision of African-American congregations. While these results do not support the opinion that African-American congregations are more involved in all services or only services for underprivileged populations, they suggest that African-American congregations are engaged in a broad range of services, often at much higher levels than interracial and white congregations. Further, the levels of social service provision by African-American congregations are also higher than those reported in previous studies (with the exception of food programs) (Tsitsos 2003). This broader range of services may be explained by the fact that African-American congregations are responding to the needs of the underprivileged, the working poor, and the middle class represented within their congregations and local communities.

African-American congregations give a significant portion of their annual budget to provide social services while balancing their need to maintain the congregation's facility and membership concerns. Relative to their resource base and financial capacity, African-American congregations appear to dig deep into their reservoir of resources to serve those in need. With such a picture, it may not be possible for African-American congregations to increase their social service provision without threatening their own survival. The expansion of social services by African-American congregations should be accompanied by the assessment and development of their institutional assets. The present forms of fundraising and the limited grant making to congregations may not achieve the institutional capacity needed to support expanded social services.

The differences in this study's findings and previous studies may be accounted for by the difference in data collection method, measurement of social service activity, and number of African-American congregations in the sample. Unlike previous studies that used a recall method to identify only formal services, this study used a recognition method to identify formal and informal services. It was expected that the recognition method would ensure consistency and reliability of the measures across all of the congregations studied. Future study is needed using a more representative sample to test this hypothesis. In addition, the demand for services relative to the supply of services should be further explored as well as the capacity of these congregations to respond to the demand for services in their communities.

In conclusion, this study moves the present discussion of African-American congregations forward by using a comprehensive face-to-face interview that includes additional measures of social service activity. This study also included a larger and more diverse sample of black churches. It also examined the extent to which African-American congregations have maintained their unique difference from white and interracial congregations as a more public religion that is less differentiated from the market and government spheres.

Reprinted from Stephanie C. Boddie, The social services of African-American congregations in the welfare reform era, *African American Research Perspectives* 10 (2004): 36–43. Reprinted by permission. *African American Research Perspectives* is an occasional report published by the Program for Research on Black Americans (PRBA), Institute for Social Research, University of Michigan. PRBA was founded by Dr. James S. Jackson; the current director is Dr. Harold W. Neighbors. *African American Research Perspectives* began under the direction of Dr. Robert Joseph Taylor. Dr. Letha Chadiha is currently executive editor.

Note

1. The Charitable Choice provision of the 1996 welfare reform legislation is a policy that encourages states and local governments to contract with faith-based and community- based

organizations to deliver social welfare and related services while preserving the religious identity of the service providers and upholding the religious freedom of the clients.

References

Billingsley, A. (1999). *Mighty like a River: The Black Church and Social Reform.* New York: Oxford University Press.

Cavendish, J. C. (2000). Church-based community activism: A comparison of black and white Catholic congregations. *Journal for the Scientific Study of Religion* 39: 371–84.

Chaves, M. and L. M. Higgins (1992). Comparing the community involvement of black and white congregations. *Journal for the Scientific Study of Religion* 31 (4): 425–40.

Cnaan, R. A., and S.C. Boddie. (2001). *Black Church Outreach: Comparing How Black and Other Congregations Serve Their Needy Neighbors.* Philadelphia: University of Pennsylvania Center for Research on Religion and Urban Civil Society.

Cnaan, R., S. C. Boddie, F. Handy, G. Yancey, and R. Schneider, R. (2002). *The Invisible Caring Hand: American Congregations and the Provision of Welfare.* New York: New York University Press.

DiMaggio, P. J., and W. W. Powell (1983). The iron cage revisited: Institutional isomorphism and collective rationality in organizational fields. *American Sociological Review* 28 (2): 147–60.

Frazier, E. F. (1963). *The Negro Church in America.* Liverpool: Liverpool University Press.

Harris, J. H. (1987). *Black Ministers and Laity in the Urban Church: An analysis of political and social expectations.* Lanham, Md.: University Press of America.

Lincoln, C. E., and L. H. Mamiya (1990). *The Black Church in the African-American Experience.* Durham, N.C.: Duke University Press.

Mukenge, I. R. (1983). *The Black Church in Urban America: A Case Study in Political Economy.* Lanham, Md.: University Press of America.

Nelsen, H. M. (1988). Unchurched black Americans: Patterns of religiosity and affiliation. *Review of Religious Research* 29 (4): 398–412.

Quadagno, J. (1994). *The Color of Welfare: How Racism Undermined the War on Poverty.* New York: Oxford University Press.

Tsitsos, W. (2003). Race differences in congregational social service activity. *Journal for the Scientific Study of Religion* 42 (2): 205–16.

Commentary: The Black Church from a Functional Perspective

Stephanie C. Boddie

A distinguishing feature of the University of Pennsylvania School of Social Policy & Practice is its functional approach, which calls for a dynamic interplay between the individual and society, "difference and likeness," and "freedom and community" (Kramer 1995a, 222). Instead of institutionalized help that only social workers can provide, the functional approach acknowledges natural sources of help, such as family, friends, neighbors, and communities of faith (Taft 1937, 1944). I find this approach attractive because it takes the focus off of the worker and places it on the relationships between the worker and the client and client systems. From the functional perspective, social work is about helping people to become more accepting of their *difference* from and relatedness to others (Rank 1958, 1994). The primary goal of social work practice from this perspective emphasizes client empowerment and recognizes the client's capacity to change, grow, and choose (Faatz 1953). As opposed to psycho-analytic-based models, this perspective seems more relevant and meaningful for those pushed or pulled by social and economic forces. The Penn approach offers a professionally and personally challenging perspective!

My biotechnology background predisposed me to appreciate connections between biology and social work, such as those highlighted by Penn School of Social Work pioneer Ruth Smalley (1953, 1971). Drawing from the thesis of embryologist Dr. George Corner (1944), Ruth Smalley recognized the resourceful nature of the individual that contends with its intrauterine environment and survives a "biological struggle" to embrace life (Smalley 1953, 300–301). Smalley asserted that all resources should be marshaled for the purpose of helping the client or client system (e.g., family, community) just as the client is mobilizing his or her own resources and purposes. According to the functional approach, the provision of resources for meeting basic needs is a birthright. The fight for life engages the mind and spirit as well as the body. Dr. Edmund Sinnot (1950) writes about this synthesis as biology of purpose and a progressive development that is rooted in protoplasmic activity. Through this first developmental process, the functional social worker recognizes that the client that comes for help has survived struggle and experienced the need to use outside resources to achieve its development, growth, and full functioning. The mother's womb is the first outside resource. For me and many Americans, another primary outside resource is the Black church.

Black congregations are an important outside resource and lifeline, particularly for the marginalized and oppressed. They are a catalyst to stir the spirit and will of the client. *But are they all that they can be?* Coming to Penn, I was excited to learn that just before the doors of the Penn School of Social Work opened in 1908, W. E. B. Du Bois documented the assets of 55 Philadelphia congregations in his seminal book, *The Philadelphia Negro*. A graduate of Harvard University, sociologist Du Bois was brought to the University of Pennsylvania to conduct one of the first extensive neighborhood surveys. With respect to the function of the Negro Church in Philadelphia, he provided evidence suggesting that these churches represented the best organized efforts of the race. Du Bois documented 55 congregations with 12,845 members owning $907,729 worth of property with an annual income of at least $94,968 (Du Bois 1899). These Black churches were regarded as a frontline resource for social care and mutual aid, supplying everything from food pantries meeting basic needs to loan associations promoting home ownership. These Black congregations provided significant institutional support, given the fact that during this time, Negroes were largely closed off from the emerging social work profession. Du Bois believed that Black churches should exchange their spiritual and otherworldly fervor for a more pragmatic social and economic agenda. He challenged the Negro churches of his day to a religious rebirth that would have expressed the power of religion as a "mighty social power" and the "most powerful agency in the moral development and social reform of 9,000,000 Americans of Negro blood" (Du Bois 1903, 208). Like Du Bois, I have serious doubts that Black congregations have reached their full potential to serve the community.

I arrived at Penn to pursue my graduate studies seemingly just at the right time—ideas about Black congregations were coming full circle. There was new interest, by both scholars and policy-makers, in studying congregations. It was 1996 and I was an MSW student recruited to assist Dr. Virginia Smith of Lincoln University (MSW'72, FA'90) to study 100 Black churches and perceptions of Black lawyers. This study of Black congregations helped me discover new connections between those congregations and the functional approach. In accordance with the functional approach, Black congregations "contain the dynamic and attraction best suited to work with oppressed peoples, for it seeks to free the individual will of external and internal forces and strengthen it to work for its own survival" (Small 1973, 17). Black congregations can provide a space "to acquire a new sense of assertiveness—expectations of self and others" (Carter 1978, 33).

In 1997, I continued my interest in Black congregations and studied with Dr. Ram Cnaan. This was an exciting and productive time. From 1997 to 2002, the national and local policy scene quickly changed, stimulating scholarly interest in faith-based social services. The expectation for Black congregations to serve the community now extended beyond local interests to the establishment of a National Faith-based and Community agenda under the George W. Bush administration. The Penn context provided significant motivation to extend my involvement in the work with Dr. Cnaan beyond what was required as a doctoral student. This extension included work on three major research projects and co-authorship of several publications.

Infected with Rankian ideas,[1] I set out to explore my own research questions, expecting to find empirical evidence supporting the claims of the unique difference of Black congregations (as compared to interracial and white congregations). Experientially, I understood the self-directing nature and creative will of Black congregations. I valued the unique history and expression of African spirituality and American striving for democracy and freedom. Like many people, I regarded the Civil Rights Movement as the best social change effort of Black congregations. However, I remained cautious about expecting too much of Black congregations and the directions of policy and research.

Over the last ten years, I have attempted to maintain a balanced approach to my intellectual journey as I remain open to learning more about Black congregations—the social and community services they provide, how they provide these services, whom they serve, the resources they generate to sustain service delivery, and their potential to do more with the finite resources they have. This work has ultimately generated questions as well as answers (Boddie 2002, 2003, 2004, 2005). For example: What will be the appropriate role for Black congregations in the twenty-first century in light of their legacy, limited organizational resources, and persistent wealth and health disparities? What can Black congregations contribute to the social, civic, and economic life of the community? What will those who come to them for help require of them? How will social workers help their clients make use of this important resource? What can social work do to recognize and support the needs of Black congregations sharing a great portion of the burden for social care in many disadvantaged communities? I continue to explore some of these questions as I revisit Du Bois's "Philadelphia Negro" with my Penn colleague, Dr. Amy Hillier.[2]

The functional approach will continue to shape my thinking and experiences as well as clarify my *purpose* and illuminate the *difference* we all must accept!

Notes

1. Robert Kramer (1995b) speaks of being "infected by Rankian ideas."
2. See the development of Du Bois's Philadelphia Negro project at http://www.mappingdu bois.com/index.php.

References

Boddie, S. C. (2002). Fruitful partnerships in a rural African-American community: Important lessons for faith-based initiatives. *Journal of Applied Behavioral Science* 38 (3): 317–33.

——— (2003). Faith-based Organizations and the Sharing of Social Responsibility: Comparing the community programs of black, interracial, and white congregations. *Social Development Issues* 25 (1/2): 205–18.

——— (2004). The Social Services of African-American Congregations in the Welfare Reform Era. *African American Research Perspectives* 10 (1): 36–43.

——— (2005). *Way to Give: Tithing Practices That Benefit Families, Congregations, and Communities.* St. Louis: Washington University, Center for Social Development.

Carter, L. H. (1978). How do Black graduate social work students benefit from a course on institutional racism? *Journal of Education for Social Work* 14 (3): 27–33.

Corner, G. W. (1944). *Ourselves Unborn: An Embryologist's Essay on Man.* New Haven: Yale University Press.

Du Bois, W. E. B. (1995/1899). *The Philadelphia Negro: A Social Study.* Anniversary edition with introduction by Elijah Anderson. Philadelphia: University of Pennsylvania Press. Original 1899.

——— (2003/1903). *The Negro Church: Report of a Social Study Made Under the Direction of Atlanta University; Together with Proceedings of the Eighth Conference for the Study of the Negro Problem.* Anniversary edition with introduction by Phil Zuckerman, Sandra L. Barnes, and Daniel Cady. Walnut Creek. Calif.: Alta Mira Press.

Faatz, A. J. (1953). *The Nature of Choice in Casework Process.* Chapel Hill: University of North Carolina Press.

Kramer, R. (1995a). The birth of client-centered therapy: Carl Rogers, Otto Rank, and the beyond. *Journal of Humanistic Psychology* 35 (4): 54–110.

———. 1995b. *Search for Meaning: Managing for the Health, Our Organizations, Our Communities, and the Natural World.* San Francisco: Jossey-Bass.

Rank, O. (1958/1941). *Beyond Psychology.* New York: Dover.

——— (1945/1936). *Will Therapy: An Analysis of the Therapeutic Process in Terms of Relationship.* New York: Norton).

——— (1924/1994). *The Trauma of Birth.* New York: Dover.

Sinnot, E. W. (1950). *Cell and Psyche: The Biology of Purpose.* Chapel Hill: University of North Carolina Press.

Small, W. V. (1973). New dimensions in functional social work education: Implications for the Black social worker. Paper presented at the Fourth Annual Career Day, Alliance of Black Social Work Students and The University of Pennsylvania School of Social Work. January

Smalley, R. E. (1953). Mobilization of resources within the individual. *Social Service Review* 27 (3): 300–307.

——— (1971). *Theory for Social Work Practice.* New York: Columbia University Press.

Taft, J. (1937). The relation of function to process in social case work. *Journal of Social Work Process* 1: 1–18.

——— (1944). *A Functional Approach to Family Casework.* Philadelphia: University of Pennsylvania Press.

Chapter 25
Education for Social Development: Curricular Issues and Models

Richard J. Estes

Introduction

Renewed emphasis is being placed in social work on the need to sensitize students and practitioners to the international dimensions of practice in their own countries (Healy 1992; Kendall 1990; Midgley 1990; Stein 1976; Van Soest 1992). Attention is also being given to preparing students for professional careers in international social work (Estes 1992; Jones 1981; Sanders and Pedersen 1984; Walz 1984), but especially in the thousands of non-governmental and quasi-governmental organizations that contribute to social development in all regions of the world (Burek 1991). In support of both initiatives, various approaches to international social work education have emerged that integrate the theory base and rich practice tradi-tions of social work with those of social development (Estes 1992; Healy 1992; Hollister 1977; Spergel 1977).

This paper identifies and discusses a broad range of educational issues related to the introduction of social development content into social work educational programs. The paper is divided into three parts. Part I defines what is meant by "social development" and identifies the operating assumptions, knowledge base, and goals of social development practice. Part I also identifies eight levels of social development practice and the dominant sectors of development activity within which each level of practice occurs. Part II of the paper identifies four models of social development practice and, hence, of education for social development. Part III of the paper discusses various contextual issues associated with the introduction of social development content into programs of professional education in social work.

Part I: Social Development, Social Work, and Social Change

Social development is a multi-disciplinary and cross-sectoral field of practice that seeks to improve the social and material well-being of people everywhere (Estes 1990 1993a; Jones and Pandey 1981; Meinert and Kohn 1987; Paiva 1977). Social development is practiced across all geo-political borders and at all levels of social, political, and economic organization (Jones and Pandey 1981; Estes 1993b; Freire 1985; Korten 1990; Midgley 1984). In social work, social development generally is practiced within the context of the emerging field of international social work (Billups 1990; Estes 1994; Healy 1992; Rosenthal 1991; Wolk 1992), albeit much of development-oriented social work practice also occurs at the local, state, and national levels (Bolan 1991; David 1991 1993; Hollister 1982; Kendall 1990; Lee 1988; Price 1987).

According to the late Daniel Sanders, development practice in social work can be viewed as *a movement, a perspective,* and *a practice mode* (Sanders 1982). As the "means" of "developmental social work" (Stein 1976), social development refers to the processes through which people are helped to realize the fullness of the social, political, and economic potentials *that already exist within them.* As the "goal" of developmental social work, social development refers to the realization of new, but sustainable, systems of "inter-personal" and "inter-national" relationships that are guided by a quest for peace, increased social justice, and the satisfaction of basic human needs.

The Goals of Social Development

Wide agreement exists among development specialists concerning the goals of social development practice:

1. the realization of more balanced approaches to social and economic development (Billups 1990; Estes 1992, 1993b, 1994; United Nations/ESCAP 1992a,b);
2. the assignment of the highest priority to the fullest possible *human* development (UNDP 1994);
3. the fullest possible participation of people everywhere in determining both the means and outcomes of development (Nayak and Siddiqui 1989; Sanders 1982; Twelvetrees 1994);
4. the elimination of absolute poverty everywhere in the world (Bolan 1987; World Bank 1990; UN1990a, b; UNDP 1994);
5. the elimination of barriers to development which, in every society, have been used to oppress historically disadvantaged population groups, but especially women, the aged, the poor, children and youth, disabled persons, political and economic refugees, the mentally ill as well as persons who have been disadvantaged on the basis of race, religion, ethnicity, social class, caste, and sexual orientation (Campfens 1990; Nayak and Siddiqui 1989; Meinert and Kohn 1987);
6. the realization of new social arrangements that accelerate the pace of development and assure the satisfaction of basic needs of people everywhere (Paiva 1977; Estes 1988); and,
7. the transformation of societies toward more humanistic values based on social justice, the promotion of peace, and the attainment of the fullest possible human development (Khinduka 1987; Sanders and Matsuoka 1989).

The Assumptions of Social Development Practice

Agreement also exists among development specialists concerning the "orienting values" and practice assumptions of social development (Bargal 1981; Bolan 1987; Cummings 1983; Gil 1981; Lee 1988; Meinert and Kohn 1987; Van Soest 1992; Vershelden 1993):

1. that social, political, and economic events occurring in other regions of the world have direct, often immediate, sometimes lasting consequences on the quality of life in all other regions of the world;
2. that the underlying dynamics of human degradation and social injustice found in local communities often emanate from social, political, and economic forces that are international in character;
3. that international social forces both contribute to and sustain social inequalities in particular locales (e.g., the international dimensions of global poverty and discrimination on the basis of race, class and caste);
4. that international social forces often contribute to and sustain patterns of interpersonal violence between people (e.g., racial, ethnic, and cultural intolerance);
5. that many of the social problems confronting social workers are rooted in national and international dynamics that transcend local boundaries;
6. that only under conditions of peaceful co-existence can local, national and international social development and, in turn, human development be accelerated;
7. that human survival to the year 2000 and beyond requires a fundamental restructuring of the relationships between peoples, communities, and nations;
8. that a restructuring of the national and international social orders is particularly urgent in reducing the profound, largely unnecessary, levels of human misery, degradation, and interpersonal violence that persist in many countries and regions of the world;
9. that social development specialists possesses a unique body of knowledge and skills that can positively impact upon the national and international social situation, especially in helping to find sustainable solutions to recurrent local, state, national and international social problems; and,
10. that acting individually and collectively, substantial numbers of social development specialists, including social workers, are continuing the national and international social movements begun by their forbearers toward the establishment of a more peaceful and socially just world order.

These assumptions are far-reaching and provide a framework for integrating the diverse social change activities of the various disciplines and professions that contribute to social development. These assumptions also bear directly on the purpose, goals, and structure of professional programs of development education (Estes 1992; Healy 1992; Rosenthal 1988; Van Soest 1992).

The Social Development Knowledge Base

Social development specialists draw substantially for their knowledge from *sociology* (esp. stratification theory, the sociology of mass movements, processes of regional

CHART 1. Levels and Definitions of SED Practice in Social Work

Levels of SED practice	*Major purposes, outcomes, or processes associated with levels of international social work practice*
Individual and Group Empowerment	Through "self help," "mutual aid," and "conscientization" strategies, individuals and groups learn how to perceive and *act upon* the contradictions that exist in the social, political, and economic structures intrinsic to all societies.
Conflict Resolution	Efforts directed at reducing: (1) grievances between persons or groups; or, (2) asymmetric power relationships between members of more powerful and less powerful groups.
Institution-Building	Refers both to the process of "humanizing" existing social institutions and that of establishing new institutions that respond more effectively to new or emerging social needs.
Community-Building	Through increased participation and "social animation" of the populace, the process through which communities realize the fullness of their social, political, and economic potential; the process through which communities respond more equitably to the social and material needs of their populations.
Nation-Building	The process of working toward the integration of a nation's social, political, economic, and cultural institutions at all levels of political organization.
Region-Building	The process of working toward the integration of a geo-political region's social, political, economic, and cultural institutions at all levels of social organization.
World-Building	The process of working toward the establishment of a new system of international relationships guided by the quest for world peace, increased social justice, the universal satisfaction of basic human needs, and for the protection of the planet's fragile eco-system.

development), *political science* (esp. power domains, political influence, and structures of political parties), *economics* (esp. theories of economic production, distribution, and consumption), *education* (esp. theories of adult learning), *philosophy* (esp. theories of justice and social ethics) and, in some cases, from *religion* (e.g., the "liberation theology" of Gutierrez et al. 1973).

Developmental social workers also draw heavily from *group work, social planning*, and *community organization* practice for much of their skill base.

Levels of Social Development Practice

Chart 1 identifies the primary processes and major outcomes associated with eight "levels" of social development practice: individual empowerment; group empowerment; conflict resolution; institution-building; community-building; nation-building; region-building; and world-building.[1]

In addition to these eight levels of social development practice, developmental social work practice also includes

1. *the provision of personal social services* to people in distress, e.g., war victims, refugees, orphaned children (Breton 1988; Estes 1993b, 1994b; Humble and Unell 1989; Kahn and Bender 1985);

2. *organizational efforts directed at helping poor and other powerless people* remove the sources of their oppression, e.g., corrupt landlords, unjust employers, colonial administrators, racism, etc. (Alger 1990; Campfens 1990; Cnaan 1991; Freire 1971, 1973; Gutierrez 1973; Lusk 1981);

3. *the establishment of new social institutions*, e.g., for credit unions, mutual aid societies, community welfare centers, seed banks, social security schemes, etc. (Liyang 1988; Omer 1989; Turner 1993; Umana and Brandon 1992; Wilson 1992);

4. *the reform of existing institutions* so as to make them more responsive to the needs of those for whom the institutions were designed (Jones and Pandey 1981; Korten 1990; Lusk 1981; Paiva 1981);

5. *efforts that seek to accelerate the pace of social development in local communities, states and provinces, nations, regions and, ultimately, the world itself* (Benjamin and Freedman 1989; David 1991 1993; Rotberg 1992; Seidman and Anang 1992; UN 1990a);

6. *the promotion of internationally guaranteed human rights* (UN/Center for Human Rights 1992);

7. *peace promotion* (David 1993; Khinduka 1987; Sanders and Matsuoka 1989; Van Soest 1992; Verschelden 1993); and,

8. *protection of the planet's fragile eco-systems* (Estes 1993b; WCED 1987; WRI 1993).

Hence, social development specialists can be found in every country and region of the world and in all areas of professional practice. Within social work, development specialists function as caseworkers and group workers, community organizers, administrators, social planners, researchers, consultants, educators, and members of boards of directors (Estes 1988; Rosenthal 1991). They also serve in the councils of governments and are members of national parliaments. Developmental social workers also are employed by or serve as consultants to the United Nations and other quasi-governmental bodies. And, developmental social workers provide professional leadership to the tens of thousands of non-governmental organizations that operate throughout the world (Burek 1991).

Sectors of Social Development Practice

Social development is practiced across of broad range of sectors, i.e., public and private institutions and organizations that seek to promote "the common good" through the provision of highly specialized services and other activities (e.g., health, education, transportation, communications, finance, etc.). Chart 2 identifies the major sectors in which social development is practiced, albeit a larger number of sectors in which development specialists work can be identified.[2]

Part II: Models of Education for Social Development in Social Work

The vast majority of social development specialists function within one of four basic models of practice: the Personal Social Services Model (PSSM); the Social Welfare

CHART 2. Major Sectors of SED Activity

Agriculture	Energy	Religion & Religious
Communications	Environment	Organizations
Consumer Security	Food	Rural Development
Criminal & Juvenile Justice	Health	Social Services
Culture	Housing	Sports
Defense	Human Rights	Technology
Economic Development	Income Support	Transportation
Education	Leisure Time & Recreation	Urban Development
Employment	Population	

Model (SWM), the Social Development Model (SDM), and the New World Order Model (NWOM) (Estes 1992, 1994; Meinert and Kohn 1987; Rosenthal 1991; Sanders 1982). Each model of practice reflects a different ideological orientation with respect to its formulation of the causes of national and international "mal-development." Each model also prescribes a different set of solutions for advancing more balanced approaches to social and economic development and for helping historically disadvantaged population groups and others achieve increased political equality.[3] These models also inform the specialized educational goals, substantive content, and programmatic structure of different programs of development education, including those that seek to prepare social workers for leadership roles in social development (Estes 1992; Healy 1992; Van Soest 1992).

The Personal Social Services Model

The Personal Social Services Model (PSSM) of social development practice seeks to extend to people everywhere a range of basic social services that are needed to either restore or enhance their capacity for social functioning. The model's primary goals are: 1) to provide *remedial* and *preventive* services to individuals, families, and groups whose optimal social functioning is either temporarily impaired or interrupted; and 2) to extend *social protection* to population groups that are threatened by exploitation or degradation. The PSSM also seeks to ensure increased sensitivity and responsiveness on the part of human service providers to the special service needs of culturally diverse population groups (Chu 1990; Maxwell 1990).

The Social Welfare Model

The Social Welfare Model (SWM) of social development practice is rooted in comparative social policy and comparative social research. The goals associated with the SWM include: 1) self help; 2) mutual aid; 3) humanitarianism; and 4) the establishment of effective, preferably universal, systems of formal social provision (Evers and Wintersberger 1988; Kamerman and Kahn 1989; Rein et al. 1987; Rose and Shiratori 1986). The SWM also views developmental social welfare practice as part of the worldwide movement that seek to promote social security and social justice for people everywhere (Elliott 1990; Friedman et al. 1987; USDHHS 1994).

The Social Development Model

The Social Development Model (SDM) has its origins in community organization and community development practice and does, therefore, promote the fullest possible participation of people in deter-mining both the means and goals of social development. In doing so, the model seeks to provide a frame-work for understanding the underlying causes of human degradation, powerlessness, and social inequality every-where in the world. The ultimate goal of the SDM, however, is to guide collective action toward the elimination of all forms of violence and social oppression (Billups 1990; Bolan 1987; Campfens 1990; David 1993; Estes 1993a; Hollister 1982; Khinduka 1987; Lee 1988; Meinert and Kohn 1987; Paiva 1977; Wolk 1992).

The New World Order Model

The New World Order Model (NWOM) of social development practice is closely associated with the writings of "visionary" economists, political scientists, legal scholars, and environmentalists (Brandt Commission 1981; Coates and Jarratt 1989; Falk 1992; Falk 1972 1992; Henderson 1992; Korten 1990; WCED 1987; WRI 1993). Major components of the NWOM are reflected in the fundamental social, political, and economic reforms in the existing international "order" that are being sought by the United Nations (UN 1990a 1990b; UN/ESCAP 1992b), the United Nations Development Programme (UNDP 1993 1994), the World Bank (World Bank 1990 1993) and other leading international develop-ment assistance organizations. Elements of the NWOM also have been described by social work theoreticians (Estes 1992; Healy 1992; Van Soest 1992).

The NWOM asserts that the most serious problems confronting humanity are rooted in the fundamental inequalities that exist in the present world "order," i.e., in the system of international social, political, and economic institutions that govern relationships between nations and, within nations, between groups of people. In promoting its social change objectives, the NWOM calls for the creation of a "new world order" based on: 1) recognition of and respect for the unity of life on earth; 2) the minimization of violence; 3) the satisfaction of basic human needs; 4) the primacy of human dignity; 5) the retention of diversity and pluralism; and 6) the need for universal participation in the process of attaining worldwide social transformation.

The Models Contrasted

Chart 3 reports a formal analysis of the major features of the four models of social development practice. The chart contrasts, for example, each model's: ideological orientation; dominant values; social change goals; dominant change strategies; "targets" of intervention; and pressures for change. The resulting analysis also suggests the broad parameters within which formal programs of development education should be structured.

CHART 3. Models of International Social Work Practice

	Personal Social Services Model	Social Welfare Model	Social Development Model	New World Order Model
Basic assumptions regarding the contemporary human condition	At various times in their lives people require limited assistance in coping with problems of daily living (e.g., serious illness, disability, family dysfunction, income insecurity, etc.). Others, owing to more serious problems, are unable to function independently and require more intensive assistance over the long-term. The personal social services seek to restore or enhance the social functioning of people to an optimal level of self-sufficiency.	Owing to the interdependent nature of contemporary society, all people confront predictable social "risks" for which formally organized programs of social protection are needed (e.g., loss of income, serious illness, old age, solitary survivorship, etc.) Other groups of people—owing to factors that are largely beyond their control—are disadvantaged by stratification norms that reward some, but penalize many. Social welfare is viewed as the primary mechanism through which societies respond to the legitimate needs of socially dependent population groups.	Dominant national and international systems frustrate the efforts of disenfranchised people (and countries) in their efforts to achieve parity with "social haves." Persistent social, political, and economic inequalities in developing countries result from: 1) a legacy of colonialism; 2) "victimization" by international systems that better serve the interests of rich and powerful countries; 3) internal corruption; and 4) "accidents" of geography that trap resource poor countries in conditions of perpetual deprivation. Within rich countries, persistent inequalities and poverty mirror patterns that exist in the global system.	Existing social, political, and economic "world order systems" are controlled by a minority of rich and powerful countries that have a vested interest in maintaining the economic and political dependency of poorer, less powerful, countries. Persistent inequalities between rich and poor nations contribute directly to recurrent wars, civil strife, and increasingly to more serious problems of global poverty and social injustice.

Social Change Goals	The protection of socially vulnerable population groups from exploitation and human degradation. The provision of a range of services that restore and, as possible, enhance the capacity of people to meet their social obligations.	The establishment of effective and cost-efficient systems of social provision that benefit the largest possible number of people. Access to a basic standard of social and economic well-being viewed as a basic "right" of citizenship or residency.	The redistribution of power and material resources to historically disadvantaged population groups, but especially to the poor, landless persons, women, minorities, and others. Fuller participation of people at all levels of social organization in the dominant political and economic systems of their countries.	Transformation of existing world order systems to systems that reflect active participation of all people and all relevant sectors in the transformation process; the alleviation of human suffering everywhere; increased social and distributive justice; and the attainment of world peace and war prevention.
Change targets	Individuals, families, and small groups	The broader society with special emphasis on the social and economic well-being of individuals and family groups.	Groups, formal and informal organizations, communities, national sub-regions and nations.	People at all levels of social organization including people's movements, nations, world sub-regions and regions, and various international cooperative movements.
Special international emphasis	Increased sensitivity and responsiveness to the special service needs of culturally diverse population groups.	Social work and social welfare are viewed as worldwide social movements that seek to promote peace, social justice, and social security for people everywhere.	Through a sense of identification with oppressed people everywhere, local groups are assisted in undertaking change efforts that benefit themselves and others.	The model emphasizes the need for new international systems based on: global sharing rather than squandering global cooperation rather than competition; and global conservation rather than exploitation.

CHART 3. (Continued)

	Personal Social Services Model	Social Welfare Model	Social Development Model	New World Order Model
Basic change strategies	The provision of various forms of psycho-social treatment and rehabilitation. Limited financial assistance and other economic services to the poor based on eligibility and established need.	The extension of basic social guarantees and protections to people everywhere, i.e., to minimal standards of living and assured access to at least basic health, education, and other essential social services.	A broad range of group- and community-building mehods are employed: conscientization (i.e., social animation), self-help, mutual aid, conflict resolution, institution-building, etc.	Change activities are multifaceted and draw from the full spectrum of governmental and non-governmental actors, practice methods, and organizational skills.
Primary agents of social change	Professionals and non-professionals employed by public or private human service organizations.	Interdisciplinary teams of human service professionals working in various welfare-related sectors (e.g., housing, health care, education, income security, etc.).	Teams of trained professionals and community development specialists in cooperation with governmental entities, people's organizations, social movements, and other social collecivities.	People and governments working cooperatively in creating new social systems that reflect dramatically altered international realities.
Pressures for social change	Increasing numbers of "dysfunctional" or socially dependent people. Deteriorating social conditions that threaten the life style or economic security of more advantaged population groups.	Recognition of new or emerging social needs coupled with a political willingness to respond to those needs. Social conflicts arising from a growing "under class" of people who are unable to participate meaningfully in existing social order.	The social "animation" of previously oppressed peoples. International pressures to respond more equitably to the legitimate needs and rights of disenfranchised populations.	Recurrent crises brought on by: 1) the inability of existing world order systems to cope with mounting pressures for change; or 2) the occurrence of global catastrophes of such seriousness that fundamental changes to existing world systems cannot be avoided.

Part III: Education for Social Development: Issues of Curricular Intensity

Social development content can be introduced into programs of professional education at one of three levels of curricular "intensity," i.e., on a "selective" or "concentrated" or "integrated" basis (Estes 1992, 38–49). Each level of curricular intensity imposes different demands on the resource base of individual programs and does, therefore, result in graduates with varying degrees of preparation for work in social development.

In general, program's should be guided in their choice of level of curricular intensity by: 1) the degree of faculty commitment to preparing specialists for practice in social development; 2) the adequacy of available financial, library, field practica, and other resources; 3) the need to balance the requirements of education for social development with those of other educational priorities; and, 4) the sometimes contradictory expectations imposed on programs by other educational "stakeholders," including students and their families, alumni, funding sources, boards of directors, accreditation bodies, prospective employers, and so on. Experience has also taught me that resolution of the curricular intensity issue also is influenced by institutional history, organizational climate, and departmental or school "politics."

The general educational purposes, learning objectives, and programmatic requirements associated with each level of curricular intensity in development education are described below. Chart 4 identifies more specific requirements associated with each approach to education for social development.

The "Selective" Approach

In the "selective" approach to development education, social development is studied primarily for the purpose of helping students gain a fuller understanding of the international dimensions of domestic social problems (e.g., the impact on domestic social services of the growing numbers of political and economic refugees, of other economic migrants, of AIDS, of international drug trafficking, etc.). The "selective" approach includes both limited course work and opportunities for limited field practice. In general, the "selective" approach to development education can succeed in reaching a large number of students, but the level of preparation of these students for work in social development tends to be less than adequate. The primary advantage of the selective approach to curriculum-building for programs is two-fold: 1) it does allow for the inclusion of at least some development education content in the curriculum; and 2) the resource demands of the approach tend to be rather modest.

The "Concentrated" Approach

In the "concentrated" approach to education, social development is identified as a discrete field of professional practice. The goals of the concentrated approach to development education include helping students acquire a deep understanding of the international forces that influence the development dilemmas that exist in their country and elsewhere (e.g., the international dimensions of racism and poverty, the feminization of poverty, minority/majority group conflicts, etc.). In general, programs that choose a concentrated approach to development education offer a wide array of specialized courses and field practica; students, in turn, may elect social development as their "major" or field of "specialized" study.[4] Hence, the "concentrated" approach to development education makes demands on the resources of educational programs comparable to those required by other areas of specialized study.

The "Integrated" Approach

The "integrated" approach to development education requires the creation of highly specialized programs that seek to prepare students for leadership roles in national and international development. The faculty of these programs tend to be drawn from all areas of the social sciences and, often, from the humanities and physical sciences as well. Integrated programs of development education also tend to reflect a cross-sectoral perspective on development practice.

The resource demands of integrated programs of development education are considerable. However, the need for such programs is justified on the basis of: 1) the transnational and cross-sectoral nature of many of the most urgent social, political, and economic problems that confront the world today; and 2) the many national and international career opportunities that exist for highly educated specialists in social and economic development (Burek 1991; ICC 1990) (Chart 4).

Conclusions

Recent events occurring in all regions of the world offer compelling evidence of the need for new approaches to the education of human service workers (e.g., the dramatic rise in global poverty in Asia and Latin America; repeated famines in Sub-Sahara Africa; the growing numbers of political and economic refugees in Asia, Africa, and the Caribbean; the AIDS pandemic; growing problems of homelessness combined with un- and under-employment in Europe, North America, and Oceania, and elsewhere, etc.). Indeed, many of the most difficult "domestic" social problems confronting contemporary human service workers are rooted in transnational forces that originate in other regions of the world.

Human service workers require new models of practice if they are to contribute effectively toward the resolution of social problems that are rooted in worldwide social, political, and economic realities. At a minimum, these new models of practice must reflect an understanding of the transnational nature of the social problems that bring clients, client groups, and other constituencies to the attention of human service workers. They also must be grounded on empirical evidence and must offer positive guidance concerning a range of social development solutions that can be applied to discrete social needs.

In this paper, I have sought to introduce the reader to the emerging field of social development practice and to the advantages that a "developmental perspective" can

CHART 4. General Curricular Structure of Three Approaches to Education for Social Development

	Intensity level I: the "selective" approach	Intensity level II: the "concentrated" approach	Intensity level III: the "integrated" approach
General structure	Social development content is "infused" selectively into existing course and field practica offerings; coverage of social development content competes with other curricular issues for attention.	Students may declare a "major," or "concentration" in social and economic development, the concentration is supported by both required and elective courses and appropriate opportunities for field practica.	Social development content is central to all major learning experiences; in some cases, dual degree programs related to international development may be initiated with other units of the university.
Required courses	Selected social development content is incorporated into relevant social policy, human behavior, research, and practice courses (e.g., ethnic-sensitive practice; comparative social policy).	Substantial social development content is incorporated into all required social policy, human behavior, research and practice courses, as needed, new required courses are added.	A rich variety of required courses are offered in both the foundation and advanced curricula.
Elective courses	Students are encouraged to take one or more development-related electives relevant, however, such courses succeed in reaching only small numbers of students.	New electives are developed to support more specialized social development interests of students; students are encouraged to matriculate in relevant electives in other units of the university as well.	A rich variety of electives are offered both within the program and through other units of the university, opportunities also exist for transferring credits from other universities, including those outside the U.S.
Field practice	Students work with clients representing diverse social and cultural backgrounds.	Students work with culturally diverse groups of "clients" and other social development "constituencies" located locally, in the U.S., and in other countries.	Students work with culturally diverse groups of "clients" and "client systems" located locally and elsewhere in the U.S. and other countries.

CHART 4. (Continued)

	Intensity level I: the "selective" approach	Intensity level II: the "concentrated" approach	Intensity level III: the "integrated" approach
Thesis options	Students may choose to undertake original research on a broad range of practice issues related to social development.	Students document their professional involvement in a significant internaional practice activity; alternatively, students undertake a small-scale comparative analysis of a welfare-relevant issue of interest to the student.	Students document their involvement in a significant international practice activity, alternatively, students conduct a small-scale comparative analysis on some aspect of social work, social welfare, or social development in a variety of countries.
Foreign language requirements	Optional; required when needed to work with clients speaking languages other than English.	Optional; required when needed to work with non-English speaking populations.	Required, especially one major international language other than English.
Other avenues for student learning	Agency-based in-service education; attendance at university and agency fora, colloquia, and other internationally-focused programs; participation in international student and professional groups.	Participation in university and agency seminars on various aspects of national and international development, conference attendance; provide leadership to international student groups and professional organizations.	Participation in university and agency seminars on various aspects of development; national and international conference attendance; join and give leadership to international student groups and professional organizations.

offer in helping to solve social problems that are rooted in international social forces. Various models and levels of social development practice and have been identified; the dominant institutional sectors within which social development is practiced also have been identified. The paper also offers some general guidance concerning the range of issues that affect the extent to which social development content may be included in individual programs of human service education.

Reprinted from Richard J. Estes, Education for social development: Curricular issues and models. *Social Development Issues* 16 (1994): 68–90. Reprinted by permission.

Notes

1. For a partial listing of authors whose work is most closely associated with each level of social development practice see Estes (1992, 1993b)

2. For a discussion of the various sectors and other "stakeholders" that contribute to social development in the Asia and Pacific region see UNESCAP (1992a,b).

3. Differences in practice orientation stem from the varied social science disciplines and intellectual traditions that inform the social work knowledge base (e.g., economics, political science, sociology, psychology, adult education, etc.). These differences also reflect the multiple levels of intervention in which social workers are involved, i.e., ranging from addressing the psychosocial needs of individuals and families to cooperative activities with other development "stakeholders" in transnational social movements.

4. Schools of social work that are known to offer graduate concentrations in social and economic development (SED) include Washington University (St. Louis) and the University of Pennsylvania (Philadelphia).

References

Alger, C. F. (1990). Grass-roots perspectives on global policies for development. *Journal of Peace Research* 27 (2): 155–68.

Bargal, D. (1981). Social values in social work: A developmental model. *Journal of Sociology and Social Welfare* 8 (1): 45–61.

Benjamin, M., and A. Freedman (1989). *Bridging the Global Gap: A Handbook to Linking Citizens of the First and Third Worlds.* Cabin John, Md.: Seven Locks.

Billups, J. O. (1990). Toward social development as an organizing concept for social work and related social professions and movements. *Social Development Issues* 12 (3): 14–26.

Bolan, R. S. (1987). Social welfare, dependency and social development. *Social Development Issues* 11 (1): 3–20.

Bolan, R. (1991). The state and social development in Poland: Responding to new realities. *Social Development Issues* 14 (1): 37–55.

Brandt Commission (1980). *North-South: A Programme for Survival.* London: Pan Books.

Breton, M. (1988). The need for mutual aid groups in a drop-in for homeless women: The "sistering" case. *Social Work with Groups* 11 (4): 47–72.

Burek, D., ed. (1991). *Encyclopedia of Associations: International Organizations.* New York: Gale Research, Inc.

Campfens, H. (1990). Issues in organizing impoverished women in Latin America. *Social Development Issues* 13 (1): 20–43.

Chu, K. F. Y., and J. Carew (1990). Confucianism: Its relevance to social work with Chinese people. *Australian Social Work* 43 (3): 3–9.

Cnaan, R. (1991). Neighborhood organization and social development in Israel. *Social Development Issues* 13 (2): 44–53.

Coates, J., and J. Jarratt (1989). *What Futurists Believe.* Bethesda, Md.: World Futurist Society.

Cummings, R. E. (1983). Social development: The economic, political, and the normative emphasis. *International Social Work* 26 (1): 13–25.

David, G. (1991). Participation in social development for the 1990s: Yes, but how? *Social Development Issues* 13 (3): 14–28.

——— (1993). Strategies for grass roots human development. *Social Development Issues* 15 (2): 1–13.

Elliott, D., N. S. Mayadas, and T. D. Watts, eds. (1990). *The World of Social Welfare: Social Welfare and Social Services in International Context.* Springfield, Ill.: Charles Thomas.

Estes, R. J. (1988). International experiences of American social work educators. *Journal of International and Comparative Social Welfare* 4 (2): 1–17.

——— (1990). Development under different political and economic systems. *Social Development Issues* 13 (1): 5–19.

———— (1992). *Internationalizing Social Work Education: A Guide to Resources for a New Century.* Philadelphia: University of Pennsylvania School of Social Work.

———— (1993a). Group work in international perspective. In D. Fike and B. Rittner, eds., *Working from Strengths: The Essence of Group Work.* Miami: Barry University Center for Group Work Studies. 122–47.

———— (1993b). Toward sustainable development: From theory to praxis. *Social Development Issues* 15 (3): 1–29.

———— (1994). Community welfare centers in international perspective: Past accomplishments and future promises. *Social Welfare: Journal of the Korea National Council on Social Welfare.*

Evers, A., and H. Wintersberger, eds. (1988). *Shifts in the Welfare Mix: Their Impact on Work, Social Services and Welfare Policies.* Vienna: European Centre for Social Welfare Training and Research.

Falk, R. (1972). *This Endangered Planet: Prospects and Proposals for Human Survival.* New York: Vintage Books.

———— (1992). *Global Civilization.* New York: World Order Models Project.

Friedman, R., N. Gilbert, and M. Shere, eds. (1987). *Modern Welfare States: A Comparative View of Trends and Prospects.* New York: New York University Press.

Freire, P. (1971). *Pedagogy of the Oppressed.* New York: Seabury Press.

———— (1973). *Education For Critical Consciousness.* New York: Seabury Press.

———— (1985). *The Politics of Education: Culture, Power, and Liberation.* South Hadley, Mass.: Bergin and Garvey.

Gil, D. (1981). Social policies and social development: A humanistic-egalitarian perspective. In J. Jones and R. Pandey, eds., *Social Development.* Delhi: Macmillan India. 61–80.

Gutierrez, G. (1973). *A Theology of Liberation.* Maryknoll, N.Y.: Orbis.

Healy, L. M. (1992). *Introducing International Development Content in the Social Work Curriculum.* Washington, D.C.: National Association of Social Workers.

Henderson, H. (1992). *Paradigms in Progress: Life Beyond Economics.* Indianapolis: Knowledge Systems.

Hollister, D. (1977). Social work skills and social development. *Social Development Issues* 1 (1): 9–20.

———— (1982). The knowledge and skill bases of social development. In D. S. Sanders, ed., *The Developmental Perspective in Social Work.* Honolulu: University of Hawaii School of Social Work. 31–42.

Humble, S., and J. Unell (1989). *Self Help in Health and Social Welfare: England and West Germany.* London: Routledge.

International Chamber of Commerce (1990). *Yearbook Of International Organizations.* Brussels: Union of International Associations.

Jones, J. (1981). Can we teach social development in a social work curriculum? *International Social Work* 24 (4): 29–31.

Jones, J., and R. Pandey, eds. (1981). *Social Development Conceptual, Methodological, and Policy Issues.* New York: St. Martin's Press.

Kahn, A., and E. Bender (1985). Self-help groups as a crucible for people empowerment in the context of social development. *Social Development Issues* 9 (2): 4–13.

Kamerman, S. B., and A. J. Kahn (1989). *Privatization and the Welfare State.* Princeton, N.J.: Princeton University Press.

Kendall, K. A., ed. (1990). *The International in American Education.* New York: Hunter College School of Social Work.

Khinduka, S. K. (1987). Development and peace: The complex nexus. *Social Development Issues* 10 (3): 19–30.

Korten, D. C. (1990). *Getting to the 21st Century: Voluntary Action and the Global Agenda.* West Hartford, Conn.: Kumarian Press.

Lee, J. A., ed. (1988). Group work with the poor and oppressed (Special issue). *Social Work with Groups* 11 (4).

Liyang, G. (1988). *Revolution Under the Breadfruit Tree: The Story of the Sarvodaya Shramadana Movement and Its Founder, A. T. Ariyaratne.* Nugegoda, Sri Lanka: Sinha Publishers.

Lusk, M. (1981). Philosophical changes in Latin American social work. *International Social Work* 24 (2): 14–21.

Maxwell, J. A. (1990). Cultural values as determinants of service integration: Some examples in international perspective. *International Social Work* 33 (2) 175–84.

Meinert, R., and J. Kohn (1987). Toward operationalization of social development concepts. *Social Development Issues* 10 (3): 4–18.

Midgley, J. (1984). Social welfare implications of development paradigms. *Social Service Review* 58 (2) 181–98.

——— (1990). International social work: Learning from the Third World. *Social Work* 35 (4): 295–301.

Nayak, R. K., and H. Y. Siddiqui, eds. (1989). *Social Work and Social Development.* New Delhi: Gitanjali Publishing.

Omer, S. (1989). Institution building. In J. Jones and R. Pandey, eds., *Social Development.* Delhi: Macmillan India. 95–107.

Paiva, J. F. X. (1977). A conception of social development. *Social Service Review* (June): 327–36.

——— (1981). Program planning. In J. Jones and R. Pandey, eds., *Social Development.* Delhi: Macmillan India. 81–94.

Price, L. D. (1987). Global neighborhoods. *Social Development Issues* 11 (1): 49–55.

Rein, M., G. Epsing-Anderson, and L. Rainwater (1987). *Stagnation and Renewal in Social Policy: The Rise and Fall of Social Regimes.* Armonk, N.Y.: M.E. Sharpe.

Rose, R., and R. Shiratori, eds. (1986). *The Welfare State East and West.* New York: Oxford University Press.

Rosenthal, B. S. (1988). *Development Education: Making It Work in and for Your Organization.* New York: CARE.

——— (1991). Social workers' interest in international practice in the developing world: A multivariate analysis. *Social Work* 36 (3): 248–52.

Rotberg, R. I. (1993). Nation-building in Black Africa. In F. J. Ramsay, ed., *Africa.* 5th ed. Guilford Conn.: Dushkin Publishing Group. 180–85.

Sanders, D. S., ed. (1982). *The Developmental Perspective in Social Work.* Honolulu: University of Hawaii School of Social Work.

Sanders, D. S., and J. K. Matsuoka (1989). *Peace and Development: An Interdisciplinary Perspective.* Honolulu: University of Hawaii School of Social Work.

Sanders, D. S., and P. Pedersen, eds. (1984). *Education for International Social Welfare.* Honolulu: University of Hawaii School of Social Work.

Seidman, A., and F. Anang, eds. (1992). *21st Century Africa: Toward a New Vvision of Self-Sustainable Development.* Atlanta: African Studies Association Press.

Spergel, I. (1977). Social development and social work. *Administration in Social Work* 1 (3): 221–33.

Stein, H. (1976). Social work's developmental change perspective: Their roots in practice. *Social Service Review* 50 (1): 1–10.

Turner, J. E. (1993). *Villages Astir: Community Development, Tradition and Change in Korea.* Westport Conn.: Praeger.

Twelvetrees, A., ed. (1994). *Community Economic Development in the UK and the USA.* London: Pluto Press.

Umana, A., and K. Brandon (1992). Inventing institutions for conservation: Lessons from Costa Rica. In S. Annis, ed., *Poverty, Natural Resources, and Public Policy in Central America.* New Brunswick, N.J.: Transaction Publishers. 85–107.

United Nations (1990a). The Fourth United Nations Development Decade (Resolution 45/199 of 21 December 1990. New York: UN.

——— (1990b). The Paris Declaration and Programme of Action for the Least Developed Countries for the 1990s (Resolution 45/206 of 21 December 1990]). New York: UN.

United Nations Center for Human Rights (1992). *Teaching and Learning About Human Rights..* New York: United Nations.

United Nations Development Programme (1993). *Human Development Report 1993.* New York: Oxford University Press.

——— (1994). *Human Development Report 1994.* New York: Oxford University Press.

United Nations Economic and Social Commission for Asia and the Pacific (1992a). *Proceedings of the Fourth Asian and Pacific Ministerial Conference on Welfare and Social Development* (ST/ESCAP/1070). Bangkok: UNESCAP.

——— (1992b). *A Social Development Strategy for Asia and the Pacific: Toward the Year 2000 and Beyond* (ST/ESCAP/1170). Bangkok: UNESCAP.

United States Department of Health and Human Services (1994). *Social Security Programs Throughout the World 1993.* Washington, D.C.: Social Security Administration.

Van Soest, D. (1992). *Incorporating Peace and Social Justice into the Social Work Curriculum.* Washington, D.C.: National Association of Social Workers.

Verschelden, C. (1993). Social work values and pacifism: Opposition to war as a professional responsibility. *Social Work* 38 (6): 765–69.

Walz, T. (1984). Field learning and experiences in international social work. In D. S. Sanders and P. Pedersen, eds., *Education for International Social Welfare.* Honolulu: University of Hawaii School of Social Work. 109–13.

Wilson, L. S. (1992). The Harambee movement and efficient public good provision in Kenya. *Journal of Public Economics* 48: 1–19.

Wolk, J. L. (1992). A cross-national perspective on social workers in the political arena. *Social Development Issues* 14 (2/3): 50–59.

World Bank (1990). *World Development Report 1990: Global Poverty.* New York: Oxford University Press.

——— (1993). *World Development Report 1993: Investing in Health.* New York: Oxford University Press.

World Commission on Environment and Development (1987). *Our Common Future.* New York: Oxford University Press.

World Resources Institute (1993). *World Resources 1992–93.* New York: Oxford University Press.

Commentary

Richard J. Estes

Since joining the Penn faculty in 1973 nearly all of my professional work has focused on the international dimensions of social work theory and practice. During the early years I was mostly concerned with conceptualizing the nature of social work in international settings (e.g., Estes 1976, 1983, 1984a,b) and, subsequently, those efforts led me to concentrate on the development of empirical approaches for measuring not only the international components of social work but those of social development and social policy as well (e.g., Estes 1990a, 1990b, 1992c, 1993a). Many publications have resulted from these efforts, including some 10 books (e.g., Estes 1988a, 2005a, 2006b),

6 monographs (e.g., Estes 1992a,b, 1998b) and nearly 80 articles and book chapters——all focused on different aspects of social work practice in the international community (e.g., Estes 1988c, 1989, 1993b, 1997a, b, 1998a, 2001, 2002, 2005c). Some innovations in social indicators research also resulted from this work and, today, I continue to track the changing capacity of countries in providing for at least the basic social and material needs of their populations using a rather complex index that I developed at Penn in the mid-1970s (e.g., Estes 1987, 1995, 1996, 2000, 2004, 2007a,b). During the past five years I also have devoted considerable attention to the needs of vulnerable children, especially those of children exposed to various forms of commercial sexual exploitation, i.e., child pornography, juvenile prostitution, and tracking of both domestic and foreign children across international borders (e.g., Estes 2003, 2005b, 2006a).

The chapter preceding initially was published in *Social Development Issues* in 1994 (Estes 1994). The chapter suggests a different paradigm for the practice of international social work and discusses the goals values and both the theory and skill base on which a "development-focused" approach to social work practice is premised. More specifically "Education For Social Development: Curricular Issues and Models" identifies a new paradigm for international social work with an emphasis on *political* and *economic* change of national and international systems rather than the more individually-focused *psychosocial* approaches to practice that predominate in the United States and other economically advanced countries. The chapter compares and contrasts four models of distinctive models for international practice and also briefly refers to the major sectors in which development-focused social work practice occurs. The second half of the chapter focuses on the sometimes complex curricular changes that are required to prepare practitioners for various levels of work in the international community . . . ranging from a more generalist approach to international practice to highly specialized practice focused on broad-based social, economic and political development.

None of this work, I believe, would have been possible without the rich interdisciplinary and international environment that characterizes Penn and the School of Social Policy & Practice. We have a truly international mix of faculty and students and many share a commitment to spending at least a portion of their professional activities working on international issues that deal directly with a wide range of social welfare concerns. We also have a substantial number of international students in the School and, now, each year approximately 6–14 master's degree students spend a substantial portion of their work engaged in international/comparative studies in other countries. All these activities have been made possible by supportive administrative personnel in both the School and the University. These activities also speak to the increasing recognition on the part of the all involved in the interdependence that exists between social concerns within the United States and those affecting other nations. Increasingly, the School, the University, and our students are positioning themselves to assume major leadership positions in helping to resolve major social problems that transcend national borders (e.g., HIV/AIDS, unemployment, domestic violence, serious mental illness, and poverty among many others).

Selected International References

Estes, Richard J. (2007a). Asia and the new century: Challenges and opportunities. *Social Indicators Research.*

———— (2007b). Development challenges and opportunities confronting economies in transition. *Social Indicators Research.*

———— (2006a). (with Cooper, Sharon W., Angelo P. Giardino, Nancy D. Kellogg, and Victor I. Vieth) *Child Sexual Exploitation: Quick Reference for Healthcare, Social Services, and Law Enforcement Professionals.* St. Louis: GW Medical Publishing.

———— (2006b). *Advancing Quality of Life in a Turbulent World.* Social Indicators Research Series 29. Dordrecht: Springer.

———— (2005a). *Social Development in Hong Kong: The Unfinished Agenda.* London: Oxford University Press.

———— (2005b). *Medical, Legal & Social Science Aspects of Child Sexual Exploitation: A Comprehensive Review of Child Pornography, Child Prostitution, and Internet Crimes Against Children* (with Cooper, Sharon W., Richard J. Estes, Angelo P. Giardino, Nancy D. Kellogg, and Victor I. Vieth (Editors).

———— (2005c). Global change and indicators of social development. Chapter 28 in Marie Weil, ed., *The Handbook of Community Practice.*Thousand Oaks Calif.: Sage.

———— 2004. Development challenges of the "New" Europe. *Social Indicators Research* 69 (2): 123–66.

———— (2003). *La infancia como mercancía sexual: México, Canadá, Estados Unidos (The Commercial Sexual Exploitation of Children in Mexico, Canada and the United States)*, with Elena Azaola. (Mexico City: CIEASAS & Siglo XXI Veintiuno Editores).

———— (2002). Rich and poor: competing definitions and alternative approaches to measurement. In Wolfgang Glatzer, ed.; *Rich and Poor.* Dordrecht: Kluwer. 9–32.

———— (2001). Charitable foundations in East Asia: Tax shelters for the well-off or partners in developSocial development trends in the Middle East, 1970–1995: Implications for social policy reform. In Belkacem Labbas, ed., *Building and Sustaining the Capacity for Social Policy Reforms.* Aldershot: Ashgate. 17–46.

————(1998a). Trends in world social development, 1970–95: Development prospects for a new century. *Journal of Developing Societies* 14 (1): 11–39.

———— (1998b). *Resources for Social and Economic Development: A Guide to the Scholarly Literature* Philadelphia: University of Pennsylvania School of Social Work.

———— (1997a). Social work, social development and community welfare centers in international perspective. *International Social Work* 40 (1): 43–55.

———— (1997b). The world social situation: Social work's contribution to international development. In Richard Edwards, ed., *Encyclopedia of Social Work.* Supplement to the 19th Edition. Washington, D.C.: National Association of Social Workers. 343–59.

———— (1996). Social Development Trends in Latin America, 1970–1994: In the Shadows of the 21st Century.

———— (1995). Social development trends in Africa: The need for a new development paradigm. *Social Development Issues* 17 (1): 18–47.

———— (1994). Education for social development: Curricular issues and models. *Social Development Issues* 16 (3): 68–90.

———— (1993a). Toward Sustainable Development: From Theory to Praxis. *Social Development Issues* 15 (3): 1–29.

———— (1993b). Hacia un indice de "calidad de vida." In Bernardo Kliksberg, ed., *Pobreza: Un tema impostergable—nuevas respuestas a nivel mundial.* Caracas: Programma de las Naciones Unidas para el Desarrollo. 131–48.

———— (1992a). *Towards a Social Development Strategy for the ESCAP Region* (with Edward Van Roy). Bangkok: UNESCAP.

———— (1992b). *Internationalizing Social Work Education: A Guide to Resources for a New Century.* Philadelphia: University of Pennsylvania School of Social Work.

———— (1992c). The International Index of Social Progress. *Encyclopedia of Social Inventions.* London: Institute for Social Inventions.

———— (1990a). The International Index of Social Progress. *Encyclopedia of Social Inventions.* London: Institute for Social Inventions. 186–88.

———— (1990b). Social development under different political and economic systems. *Social Development Issues* 13 (1): 5–19.

———— 1990c. Development trends in the Asian and Pacific region: Assessing the adequacy of social provision, 1970–1987. In *Guidelines oOn Methodological Approaches to the Conduct of a Regional Survey on the Quality of Life as an Aspect of Human Resources Development.* Bangkok: UNESCAP. 32–59.

———— (1989). International experiences of American social work educators. *Journal of International and Comparative Social Welfare* (Spring).

———— (1988a). *Trends in World Social Development: The Social Progress of Nations, 1970–1987.* New York: Praeger.

———— (1988b). World social rankings. In George Kurrian, ed., *Encyclopedia of the Third World.* New York: Facts on File.

———— (1988c). Toward a Quality of Life Index. In James Norwine and Alfonso Gonzalez, eds., *The Third World: States of Mind and Meaning.* London: Unwin and Hyman. 23–36.

———— (1987). Beyond famine relief: the continuing crisis in development. *International Journal of Contemporary Sociology* 3/4: 27–41.

———— (1984a). *The Social Progress of Nations.* New York: Praeger.

———— (1984b). World social vulnerability: 1968–1978. *Social Development Issues* 8 (1–2): 8–28.

———— (1983). Adequacy of world social provision." In George Kurrian, ed., *Book of World Rankings.* New York: Facts on File.

———— 1976). World social welfare analysis: A theoretical model (with John S. Morgan). *International Social Work* 19 (2): 29–41.

Chapter 26
The New African American Inequality

Michael B. Katz, Mark J. Stern, and Jamie J. Fader

The interpretation of twentieth-century African American inequality remains fraught with controversy. Have barriers to African American economic progress crumbled or remained stubbornly resistant to fundamental change? Has the story been similar for women and men? What mechanisms have fostered or retarded change? Those questions matter not only because they cut so close to the heart of twentieth-century American history but also because they bear on important public-policy choices in the present. In this article, we rely primarily on census data assembled in the University of Minnesota's Integrated Public Use Microdata Series (IPUMS) to examine the controversial topic of black inequality. Our answer to the questions the data pose does not support either the optimistic or the pessimistic version of African American history. But it does not come down in an illusory middle, either. Rather, it recasts the issue by arguing that after World War II the nature of black inequality altered fundamentally. Inequality, we contend, worked differently at the end of the twentieth century than at its start or midpoint. At the start of the twentieth century, pervasive, overt racial discrimination barred blacks from most jobs, denied them equal education, and disenfranchised them politically. During the second half of the twentieth century, slowly and sometimes in the face of violent opposition, the situation of African Americans changed dramatically. Courts and Congress—prodded by a massive social movement, national embarrassment on the world stage during the Cold War, and the electoral concerns of urban politicians—extended political and civil rights. Affirmative action and new "welfare rights" contributed to the extension of social citizenship—guarantees of food, shelter, medical care, and education. By the end of the century, legal and formal barriers that had excluded blacks from most institutions and from the most favorable labor market positions had largely disappeared. Black poverty had plummeted, and black political and economic achievements were undeniable.[1]

Yet, for many people—both white and black—the sense remained that racism still pervaded American society, operating in both old and new ways, removing some barriers but erecting others. Observers found discrimination in racial profiling by police; in verbal slips by members of Congress; in disproportionate poverty, incarceration, and capital punishment; and in institutional and public policies that disadvantaged blacks. Racism, they maintained, kept African Americans residentially segregated and clustered disproportionately in the least desirable jobs, if not out of the work force altogether, and circumscribed their opportunities for education, high incomes, and the accumulation of wealth. Far more often than whites, African Americans lived in poverty. Most black children were born out of wedlock, and a very large fraction ot them grew up poor. And in the 1980s and 1990s, some indices of black economic progress began to reverse direction.

Two books captured the debate over black progress. In *Two Nations: Black and White, Separate, Hostile, Unequal,* the political scientist Andrew Hacker stressed the continued force of racism in American life. In *America in Black and White: One Nation, Indivisible,* written partly in response to Hacker, the historian Stephan Thernstrom and the political scientist Abigail Thernstrom emphasized its attenuation. Hacker highlighted the continuing obstacles confronting blacks; the Thernstroms focused on black progress. Hacker intended his analysis to buttress affirmative action; the Thernstroms wanted to undercut its legitimacy. Economic inequality was only one among several topics considered in each book. But it was crucial—fundamental to the story of progress or of its absence. Was the glass half empty or half full? Could past black achievement be projected into the future, or had it stalled, leaving an enduring categorical inequality etched deeply into the substrate of American life?[2]

In this article we argue that trying to understand black inequality in the terms posed by the Hacker-Thernstrom debate takes us in the wrong direction. The problem of black economic inequality should not be framed in either/or terms or assessed on a single scale of progress. Rather, we hope to redirect analysis by arguing that the historic pattern of black inequality based on social, economic, and political exclusion largely shattered in the course of the century—replaced by 2000 by a new configuration of inequality with rearranged features. In the early twentieth century, the sources and results of America's black/white divide overlapped with and reinforced one another. What stands out about the new pattern of inequality is the cumulative process that produces it and the internal differentiation that is its product. The inequality of African Americans with whites no longer grows out of a massive and mutually reinforcing legal and extralegal, public and private system of racial oppression.[3] Rather, a subtler series of screens filters African Americans into more or less promising statuses, progressively dividing them along lines full of implications for their economic futures. Thus, the first goal of this article is to re-frame the debate over black economic progress by historicizing inequality as a process working in ways that vary with time and place.

Our second goal is to highlight one of the principal ways inequality has worked throughout American history. Despite repeated contractions and expansions in the degree of economic inequality in the United States, the income and wealth pyramid has remained durable and steep, with continuities in the distribution of rewards by work, ethnicity, and gender. Yet immense individual and group mobility has accompanied the structural durability. The coexistence of structural rigidity with individual and group fluidity we call the paradox of inequality. We argue that the process of internal group differentiation demonstrated in the recent experience of African Americans resolves the paradox. Differentiation is one of the principal and continuing mechanisms reproducing inequality in modern American history.

The third goal of this article is to elevate gender to a central place in the history of African American inequality. For the history of black economic inequality is very much a story about gender—although gender has not received nearly as much systematic analysis as it deserves. The tendency is for historians to write about either black men or black women, paying only incidental attention to comparing their experiences over time. Inequality, however, has proceeded differently for African American women and men. African American women, who at midcentury fared much worse than African American men or white women, have vaulted ahead of African American men in educational and occupational achievement. They have closed the gap between themselves and white women more successfully than African American men have closed the gap with white men. This story of African American inequality is thus not only about the relation between blacks and whites. It also traces the emergence of a gender gap between black men and women.[4]

Our fourth goal is to emphasize the role of public and quasi-public (privately controlled but government-funded) employment in African American history. Public employment, we argue, has been the principal source of black mobility, especially for women, and one of the most important mechanisms reducing black poverty. It has not received anything like the attention it deserves from historians or social scientists. Its erosion in recent decades is a primary force undermining black economic progress. We also—this is the fifth goal—want to challenge the common argument that the problems of black men in the labor market result from deindustrialization. Midcentury discrimination denied most African American workers access to steady work in the manufacturing economy. Thus, their disadvantage was evident much earlier than often assumed, and the timing of the collapse of agricultural employment played a much larger role in their subsequent labor market difficulties than historians have appreciated. Finally, another of our goals is to complicate the role of education. Here is another paradox. Contrary to much common wisdom, education has served as a powerful source of upward mobility for African Americans, although they have simultaneously suffered, and continue to suffer, from structural inequalities that leave them educationally disadvantaged. In making these arguments we do not intend to ignore or deny the force of racism. Our intent is to shift the focus away from individualist interpretations and toward structures and processes that result from racism but, once set in motion, operate with a logic of their own.

In the rest of this article, we make the case for the late twentieth-century change in the form of African American inequality by examining inequality through five lenses. Our data come primarily from decennial censuses.[5] The lenses are (1) participation—the share of African Americans who worked for pay; (2) distribution—the kinds of jobs they held; (3) rewards—the relative income they received; (4) differentiation—the variation among them on scales of occupation and earnings; and (5) geography—where they lived. Because it underlies the other forms of inequality, we discuss geography first.

Geography

Throughout American history, African Americans have clustered disproportionately in the nation's most unpromising places. Because the sources and features of inequality have always been tied so closely to where they have lived, changes in the spatial distribution of African Americans have mapped the reconfiguration of inequality among them. The consequences of African American migration have been immense as blacks, at the start of the twentieth century primarily a southern and rural people, became at its end an urban population distributed far more equally throughout the nation. Movement off southern farms resulted in a mixed legacy for black inequality. It brought African Americans closer to more rewarding sources of work, but in the end it left them isolated in America's new islands of poverty. Because the story of black migration from the South is so well known, we will not dwell on its details. Rather, we emphasize a few of its aspects that bear on the history of inequality.

Black migration from the South to the Northeast and Midwest represented a shift from rural to urban living. In 1900 only 16 percent of adult blacks, compared to 35 percent of whites, lived in a metropolitan area, as defined by the Census Bureau. But by 1960 blacks had become more urbanized than whites—a distinction they retained: in 2000, 86 percent of blacks and 78 percent of whites lived in metropolitan areas. Not only did blacks become more urban: over the course of the century, they concentrated in central cities more than whites did. In 1900, 26 percent of white and 12 percent of black adults lived in central cities. The situation reversed between 1940 and 1950. By 2000 the African American fraction had climbed to 52 percent while the white had dropped to 21 percent.[6]

In the decades after World War II, with whites leaving and blacks entering central cities, de facto racial segregation increased, reaching historic highs by late in the twentieth century. Such segregation was much higher in 2000 than it had been in 1860, 1910, or 1930, when in northern cities other than Chicago and Cleveland whites still predominated in the neighborhoods in which the average African American lived. This situation reversed by 1970: between 1930 and 1970, the neighborhood in which the average African American lived went from 31.7 to 73.5 percent black. Affluent as well as poor African Americans lived in segregated neighborhoods. In 1980, Douglas S. Massey and Nancy A. Denton found that blacks with incomes of less than $2,500 and those with incomes of $50,000 or more experienced the same degree of segregation. One of every three African Americans in sixteen metropolitan areas, they showed, lived in a condition of extreme racial isolation that they called "hypersegregation." The segregation index went down after 1980 but still remained high. At the end of the twentieth century, the typical African American still lived in a neighborhood where two-thirds of the other residents were blacks.[7]

In the century's last decade, black suburbanization increased modestly: the percentage of blacks living in suburbs rose from 34 to 39 percent. But most black suburbanization was movement to inner-ring suburbs, themselves segregated and developing the problems of inner cities. Between 1990 and 2000, there was no change in the segregation of blacks within suburbs; in both years the average African American suburbanite lived in a neighborhood that was 46 percent black.[8] Overall, post-World War 11 configurations of spatial segregation and inequality remained mostly in place.

Racial segregation did not happen as a result simply of individual preferences, the racism of homeowners, or the venality of realtors who practiced blockbusting—although all those influences were at work. It resulted just as much from government policy and action. All levels of government share the responsibility. The underwriting practices of federal agencies that insured mortgages introduced redlining, that is, the refusal to lend to buyers in certain neighborhoods, which virtually destroyed central-city housing markets, froze blacks out of mortgages, and encouraged white flight to suburbs. Governments also sited interstate highways and other roads to manipulate racial concentration by confining African Americans to inaccessible, segregated parts of cities. In the 1930s, when the federal government initiated public housing, its regulations forbade projects to disturb the "neighborhood composition guideline"—the racial status quo. Thus, even before World War II, two-thirds of blacks in public housing lived in wholly segregated projects. After the war local governments found ways to use public housing to increase black segregation even further.[9]

The spatial redistribution of America's black population in the twentieth century matters because it intersects with their history of economic inequality. Spatial segregation, Massey and Denton showed, itself initiates a vicious cycle that concentrates poverty and magnifies its impact.[10] The bulk of African Americans started the twentieth century clustered in Americas poorest spaces, rural southern farms; they ended it again concentrated disproportionately in the nations least promising spaces—now, central cities where only 21 percent of whites remained.

Participation

The geographic redistribution of African Americans offers one lens on the reconfiguration of black inequality in the twentieth century; the altered relation of black men to the labor market another. For it is among black men, more than among black women, that the trends have created a new form of disadvantage.[11]

The meaning of black women's work in the paid labor force has varied over the century in ways that limit the usefulness of statistics of labor-force participation by themselves as indicators of improvement or deterioration in their situation. (Here the labor force is defined as those for whom census records list an occupation.) For much of American history, black women worked out of necessity. As slaves, they were forced to labor; after slavery and in the North, they worked to supplement men's meager wages or because they were more often widowed than white women were. In post-World War II cities, disincentives built into public assistance kept many of them from employment until after 1996, when new welfare legislation forced them into the labor force—for some a welcome opportunity, for others a chance to join the ranks of the working poor. In the late twentieth century, better education, the impact of the civil rights movement, and the expansion of government and health care employment opened more attractive jobs to black women. By contrast, for many black men jobs in the regular labor market were then proving elusive, a situation highlighted by social scientists who lamented black men's chronic detachment from the labor force.[12]

Between 1900 and 1920, black women of all ages listed an occupation much more often than white women. White women were not only less likely to work; their labor-force participation, unlike that of blacks, declined with age. Until 1960 black women continued to work more than white women. Then the labor-force participation of both began to increase with the white rate growing faster than the black. The result narrowed and .sometimes reversed the gap between them. But the most striking feature became the similarity of their rates of labor-force participation. By the end of the century, at all ages, only one-fifth to one-quarter of adult women from either group remained outside the labor force. That similarity of course reflected the swift and revolutionary rise in the labor-force participation of all married women in the late twentieth century.[13]

Very few adult black men were outside the labor force before 1940, and their participation paralleled that of white men. After 1940 a stunning disparity in labor-force participation opened between them and white men of all ages. In the late twentieth century, black men remained outside the labor force much more often than white men. Among black men aged 21–25, the proportion not in the labor force rose from 9 percent in 1940 to 27 percent in 1990 and 34 percent in 2000. Between 1990 and 2000, nonparticipation increased for black men of other ages as well. In 2000, for instance, more than 25 percent of black men aged 41–50 remained out of the labor force.[14] The rates of nonparticipation were much higher for black men than for white men. And they increased even though official black unemployment went down. Despite this decline, the unemployment rate for black men remained about twice the rate for white men, testimony to the durability of inequality. Official unemployment figures count only individuals actively seeking work, not those discouraged, ineligible to register for unemployment benefits, or otherwise out of the labor market. That is why it is important to focus on nonparticipation in the labor force instead of unemployment. Our analysis of census data suggests that in 1940 the ratio of black to white nonparticipation (black/white x 100) already showed an alarming disproportion, especially for men over the age of 25. Among 26- to 30-year-olds, it was 185, and among 41- to 50-year-olds, 168. In the decades that followed, the situation worsened. By 2000 more than twice as many black as white men in their prime earning years, 31–40 and 41–50, were not in the labor force. This increasing absence of black men from the labor force coincided with a stunning rise in their rates of incarceration. Between 1990 and 2000, as labor-force detachment spiked, the fraction of 26- to 30-year-old African American men living in institutions—mainly prisons—increased by one-third. In 2000 nearly 12 percent of black men in that age group resided in an institution.[15]

The institutionalization of black men reflected the national explosion of incarceration. On June 30, 2002, 1,355,748 inmates filled federal and state correctional facilities. The number represented an 82 percent increase since 1990. Another 665,475 inmates resided in local jails, representing a 64 percent increase since 1990. The federal prison system, which grew 153 percent between 1990 and 2002, had become the largest in the nation. Most of the increase reflected mandatory sentences for drug

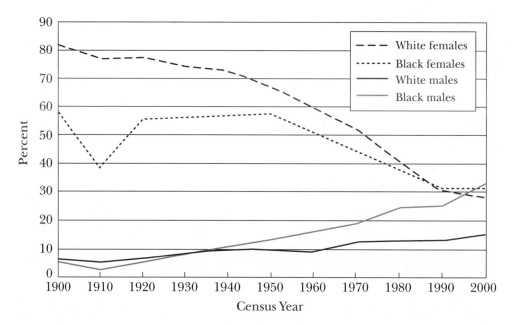

Figure 1. Percent of persons 18 years of age and older not participating in the labor force, by race and gender, 1900–2000. Authors' calculation from Steven Ruggles et al., *Integrated Public Use Microdata Series: Version 3.0* (Minneapolis: Historical Census Case Projects, University of Minnesota, 2003), http://www.ipums.org.

offenders, who constituted 57 percent of federal prisoners. As a result of this increase in the prison population, the United States could boast the highest race of incarceration in the world—702 persons per 100,000 in the population. America surpassed Russia, whose incarceration rate had fallen to 628 per 100,000 and was still headed downward. America's incarceration rate was five to eight times the rates in western Europe and Canada.[16]

Black men bore the brunt of America's rise in incarceration. Nationally, 49 percent of prisoners, but only 13 percent of the overall population, are African American. On any given day in the late twentieth century, nearly one in three black males aged 20–29, according to the Sentencing Project, was "under some form of criminal justice supervision . . . either in prison or jail, or on probation or parole." The rate of adult black men incarcerated on a given day doubled between 1985 and 1995, when it reached one in fourteen. Those rates do not reflect increased convictions for crimes against persons or property. Rather, they result from the "war on drugs" under way since 1980, which has exacerbated racial disparities by "increasing [those convicted of] drug offences as a proportion of the criminal justice population" and pushing up the proportion of African Americans among drug offenders.[17] The explosive growth of African American men's incarceration fuels inequality. For one thing, since 1994 Congress has prohibited inmates from receiving Pell Grants with which to continue their education, and many states have cut back on education for inmates, who leave

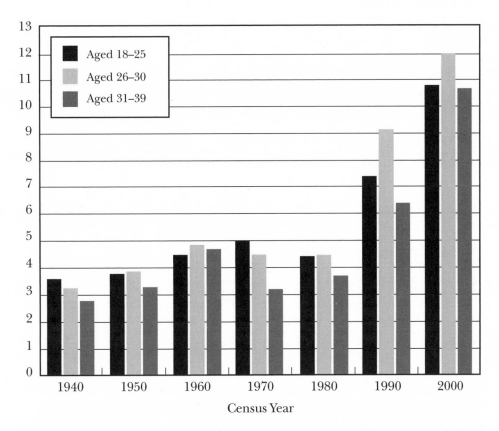

Figure 2. Percentage of black men living in institutions by age, 1940–2000. Authors' calculation from Steven Ruggles et al., *Integrated Public Use Microdata Series: Version 3.0* (Minneapolis: Historical Census Case Projects, University of Minnesota, 2003), http://www.ipums.org.

TABLE 1. Ratios of Black to White Nonparticipation in the Labor Force, Persons Ages 26–36, by Gender, 1900–2000

	1900	1910	1920	1930	1940	1950	1960	1970	1980	1990	2000
Male	127.7	120.1	131.4	—	185.1	182.8	249.8	227.4	275.0	272.6	257.0
Female	73.1	50.9	72.8	—	77.4	79.4	78.6	72.6	82.5	106.4	98.2

For example, in 2000 26–30-year-old black men were more than 2.5 times as likely to be out of the labor force as white men of the same age.
Source: Authors' calculations from Steven Ruggles et al., *Integrated Public Use Microdata Series: Version 3.00.* Minneapolis: Historical Census Projects, University of Minnesota, 2003, http://www.ipams.org

prison without the skills essential for finding employment. Indeed, recent research shows, not surprisingly, that former inmates, who encounter employers reluctant to hire ex-convicts and who lack job skills, have great difficulty finding work.[18] One consequence is the high rate of black men who remain outside the regular labor force.

Two important conclusions derived from the rates of labor-force detachment need emphasis. First, black men have been much more likely than their white counterparts to be outside the labor force. For various reasons—lack of skills, incarceration, racial discrimination—they remained over time and throughout their life course much less able than white men to find market work.[19] Second, their labor-force disadvantage started earlier than most commentators assume. Present already in 1940, it did not result initially from deindustrialization in the 1960s and 1970s, although rates of non-participation increased in those years, and it was not solely the consequence of incarceration. Thus black men's inability to find work in the regular labor market is not the residue of a golden age when many worked at well-paying industrial jobs. Its origins lie in the shift of black men out of agriculture and their relative inability to move—as had white men—into other kinds of work. It remains a structural aspect of the inequality present in American labor markets at least since the 1940s. On account of discrimination and bad luck with timing—a labor market with a decreasing number of semi-skilled manufacturing jobs—black men displaced from agriculture often found themselves on the margins of the economy. The enormous scope of the changes in work that underlie these trends is revealed by the distribution of black men and women among industries.

Distribution

At the start of the twentieth century, the structure of black inequality emerged from the powerful convergence of geography and work. Clustered in the rural South, African Americans worked mainly in agriculture and household service. Only a small minority escaped the simultaneous forces of racism and of the demand for cheap labor to enter the skilled crafts or white-collar and professional jobs. The transformation of blacks' truncated occupational structure depended on their movement off southern farms to cities and to the Northeast and Midwest. Thus, only with the second Great Migration after World War II did black occupational mobility accelerate. Although African Americans ended the century in a far wider array of industries and jobs than they began it, theirs was a distinctive and fragile progress. Women outpaced men. Parity in the best jobs remained elusive. Upward mobility depended heavily on the public sector, and black gains were reversible, vulnerable to shifting political and economic tides.

Industry

A comparison of the industries that employed black women and men at the beginning and end of the twentieth century highlights the reconfiguration of work among African Americans. In 1910 agriculture employed nearly half of the black women in the paid labor force while most of the rest worked in private households. By 1940 agricultural employment had plummeted; in 1970 it was only 1 percent. By contrast, the fraction of black women working in private households rose to 58 percent in 1940 before falling to 15 percent in 1970.[20] Thus, black women's industrial history passed through two phases: movement out of agriculture and into household service—the first major employer of black women who moved north—and, after 1940, movement out of household service into other industries. Theirs is a story of astonishing change. By 2000 the transition out of domestic service was nearly complete, facilitated by work opportunities in the service sector and in government or government-related jobs.

The twentieth-century history of occupational structure—notably the rise and feminization of clerical work early in the century and the explosion of service-related employment later—expanded work possibilities for women, including black women.[21] Black men, by contrast, even during the high point of America's manufacturing era, often found themselves excluded from the best industrial jobs and facing a declining job market for industrial work.

Although black men also moved out of agriculture, the timing of their transition differed from black women's. As late as 1940, 36 percent of employed black men (compared to 16 percent of employed black women) still worked in agriculture. By 1970 agriculture employed only 5 percent, and the largest employer had become the construction industry at 9 percent. By 2000 agricultural work had dwindled to 1.5 percent. Unlike black women, relatively few black men worked in private households at any time. Instead, construction and transportation provided many with jobs.[22]

The collapse of agricultural employment was a more important source of joblessness among black men than the decline in manufacturing opportunities, and it deserves far more attention from historians. In 1970, when black employment in manufacturing peaked, only about 12 percent of employed black men did blue-collar work in manufacturing industries. By 2000 the percentage had fallen to approximately 8.[23] To take a local example, the historian Robert Self explained that in Oakland, California, although the decline in manufacturing in and after the 1960s "hit black workers hard," much "worse was the decline of employment in West Oakland, where the rail yards, docks, and warehouses once provided thousands of jobs for the community." For decades, moreover, young African American men had been excluded from apprenticeship programs, "the principal gateway to well-paying blue collar jobs." They were also denied service-sector jobs, "especially in retail and wholesale trades, restaurant and hotel work, banks and insurance companies." They gained significant jobs only "in government service, where fair hiring" had made most progress.[24]

Many black men moved into state-related industries, such as education, health care, social service, and public employment. For them federal and local public administration—employing about 8 percent—was more important than health or educational services. In 2000, 19 percent of employed black men worked in state-related industries—that is, in public agencies or publicly funded private agencies—while 35 percent (compared to 39 percent of employed black women) worked in retail and service industries.[25] Public and quasi-public employment proved even more important for black women. At the end of the century, nearly half of employed black women (43 percent) worked in state or state-related industries, including 18 percent in health and hospitals, 14 percent in education, 7 percent in federal and local public administration, and 2 percent in welfare and religious services. Clearly, the expansion of government, education, and health care in late twentieth-century America opened a plethora of new opportunities seized by African American women. Another 39 percent found work in expanding retail and service industries. For black women, America's economic transition from manufacturing to service was a source of opportunities gained, not lost.

"The prewar black middle class," notes *A Common Destiny*, a major examination of the state of black America, "was drawn heavily from the salaried managerial private sector; the post-1960s black middle class is much more rooted in public service."[26] Public employment, in fact, became African Americans' distinctive occupational niche. The Brown V. Board of Education U.S. Supreme Court decision (1954), which declared school segregation unconstitutional, the Civil Rights Act (1964), the Voting Rights Act (1965), and affirmative action policies in the 1960s and 1970s—all built pressure to desegregate work and expand opportunities for African Americans. In some places the federal government had begun hiring African Americans during World War II, but racial barriers to employment crumbled most quickly and widely in public and publicly funded jobs when their number exploded in the 1960s and early 1970s. During those years—the time of the War on Poverty and the Great Society— public spending on social programs escalated at an unprecedented pace. Between 1965 and 1972, federal social spending increased from $75 billion to $183 billion. In constant dollars, the rate of increase between 1950 and 1965 averaged 4.6 percent annually; between 1965 and 1976 it leaped to 7.2 percent. It accounted for 7.7 percent of gross domestic product (GDP) in 1960, 10.6 percent in 1965, and 16 percent in 1974.[27] This spending translated into the creation of jobs in government and in government-financed private programs. In the public sector African Americans, assisted by affirmative action, gained a disproportionate share of the new jobs. Critics often chide the War on Poverty and the Great Society for lacking a jobs program. That criticism is only partly valid: the expansion of public and quasi-public employment was their hidden labor market policy.[28]

Consider a statistic called the index of representation, which we calculate using census data. A score of 100 on this index indicates that the representation of a group is equal to its representation in the population. A score greater than 100 indicates a disproportionately high representation. In 1960, among adult male workers, the score for both native white and African American men for public-sector employment was close to 100. By 1970 the white score had dropped a little, while the black score rose to 138. From there it grew to 176 in 1980 and 1990, and 182 in 2000. Among women the story was similar: in 1960 the score was a little over 100 for white women and 89 for black women. A decade later the black score had risen to 180 and the white fallen to 91. The score for black women continued to increase to 211 in 1980 before dropping to 209 in 1990, and 200 in 2000, by which time the score for white women had declined to 85.

Public-sector jobs generally paid more than private employment. In 2000 the median income of black men who worked full time in the public sector was 15 percent higher than that of those who worked full time in the private sector. Among black women the differences were even wider: in 2000, 19 percent between median full-time private- and public-sector earnings. Public and publicly funded employment, these figures suggest, has been a powerful vehicle for African American economic mobility and the most effective antipoverty legacy of the War on Poverty and the Great Society.

The statistics of African American employment in different industries tell an important story. Black women negotiated a series of transitions—first from agriculture to private household service, then from private household service to expanding opportunities in state-related industries and in retail and business services. Black men took longer to leave agriculture. When they finally made the last transition, industrial opportunities had dried up, and they found themselves less able than black women to enter state-related industries or even to find work at all.

Occupation

Trends in occupational statistics reinforce the industrial story of black employment. For most of the twentieth century, the majority of both blacks and whites held agricultural or blue-collar jobs. As black men left agriculture, they moved into the manual working class. By 1960 the proportion of employed black men in that class was 61 percent—exceeding the 48 percent of employed white men in it—before declining to 44 percent in 2000. More important is the racial division of occupations within the manual working class: black men were much less likely to be in skilled craft occupations and more likely to work as laborers. Black women never had much presence in the crafts or among laborers, but a substantial number moved into semiskilled work as operatives after World War II. The proportion more than doubled during the 1940s and reached its high point, 18 percent, in 1970, before declining to 9 percent in 2000.[29]

For black women, as agricultural, domestic-service, and blue-collar work declined, white-collar employment increased. Indeed, the movement of black women into white-collar jobs was stunning. In clerical work the gains between 1940 and 2000 were 908 percent for black men and 2,297 percent for black women. In professional/technical jobs the increase was 718 percent for black men and 1,394 percent for black women. "Once consigned to mostly menial work," as the reporters Ellis Cose and Allison Samuels observed, "black women (24 percent of them, compared with 17 percent of black men) have ascended to the professional-managerial class."[30] In percentage terms, African Americans, led by black women, outpaced whites in their movement into white-collar work by a wide margin. The changes were not simply products of population growth or shifts in the occupational composition of the work force. In 1900 employed white men held white-collar jobs almost 7 times more often than employed black men (20 percent compared to 3 percent); by 2000 the white lead had dropped to about 1.5 times (52 percent compared to 39 percent). Among employed black women, the share doing white-collar work increased from only 2 percent in 1900 and 7 percent in 1940 to about 63 percent in 2000—an astonishing record of change.

As a result, blacks began to close the occupational distance between themselves and whites. Larger proportions of whites than blacks still held the most desirable jobs, but by 2000 the gap was much narrower than it had been at the start of the twentieth century or at its midpoint. In 1900 employed white males were more than 3 times as

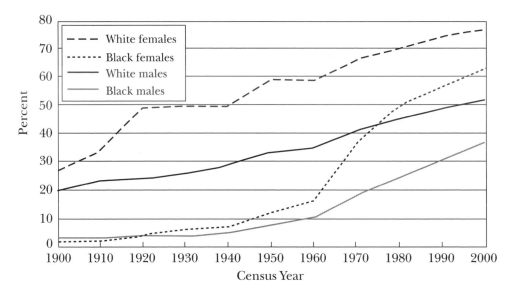

Figure 3. Percentage of employed persons 18 years of age and and older in white-collar occupations, by race and gender, 1900–2000. Authors' calculation from Steven Ruggles et al., *Integrated Public Use Microdata Series: Version 3.0* (Minneapolis: Historical Census Case Projects, University of Minnesota, 2003), http://www.ipums.org.

likely as blacks to hold professional/technical jobs. In 1940 the distance had widened slightly; by 2000 it had narrowed to about 1.3 times. In 1940 white males were about 12 times as likely as black men to be managers, officials, or proprietors. In 2000 they were just over twice as likely. This decrease in the white lead did not result from a greater share of black men in the most prestigious professions, however, for a disproportionate share of the professional and managerial jobs they held were in the public sector.[31] Similar patterns marked the experience of women. In 1900 white women were 6 times as likely as black women to work in clerical jobs; in 1940 the distance had increased to more than 20 times. By 2000 the percentages were nearly identical. In 1940 white women were about 6 times as likely to work in professional/technical jobs as black women. By 2000 their advantage had shrunk to about 1.2 times.

Broad occupational categories, however, mask important differences based on sex and race. For instance, a growing number of black women—a fivefold increase between 1940 and 2000—worked as technicians, the lowest rung on the professional/technical ladder. Only a small fraction of women professionals, either black or white, worked in law and medicine at any time in the twentieth century. Instead, for the most part women professionals worked in human services, such as social work and nursing: 81 percent in 1900, 89 percent in 1940, and 70 percent in 2000. Those fractions remained similar among white and black women professionals, although they were slightly higher for blacks—in 2000, 69 percent for white and 72 percent for black women. They reflected the importance of teaching as a woman's occupation and, later in the century, of social work and nursing.[32]

TABLE 2. Changes in Occupational Categories of Persons in the Labor Force, by Race and Gender, 1940–2000

| Occupational category | Percent change in percentage of group in occupation | | | |
| | Male | | Female | |
	White	Black	White	Black
Professional/technical worker	290	718	232	1394
Teacher	205	481	10	56
Manager, official, proprietor	53	490	146	564
Clerical worker	9	908	19	2297
Salesperson	11	374	−19	674
Crafts person	17	203	12	290
Operative	−26	70	−74	11
Household service worker	−34	−79	−88	−95
Other service worker	64	49	18	125
Laborer	−54	−69	−30	2
Farm owner/tenant	−93	−100	−84	−100
Farm laborer	−89	−98	−83	−99

Source: See Table 1.

By 2000 the differences between the fractions of black and white women in professional and technical occupations were minor. That was not the case with men. Whites remained much better represented in law and in scientific and technical work and less common in human services. In 1940 white men with professional and technical occupations were 13 times as likely as black men to be lawyers or judges; in 2000 the odds had fallen to just under 3 times. By contrast, in the years since 1940, black professional men have been a great deal more likely than white men to work in human services (in 2000, 29 percent of white and 47 percent of black male professionals did so).

Three points about this record of black industrial and occupational change require emphasis. First, improved occupations meant higher incomes. In 2000 the median income of black women professionals and managers was more than 1.5 times that of black women clerical workers and 1.9 times that of black women service workers. For black men upward occupational mobility also brought economic rewards, although the income differences among occupations were not quite as large as for women. Second, the dependence of their occupational mobility on government left African Americans vulnerable. Reductions in public employment and spending struck them with special ferocity and undermined their often fragile achievements.[33] Third, occupational change worked through differentiation, sorting African Americans into the familiar ranks of America's class structure. As a result, the reconfiguration of black inequality produced a new pattern of stratification among African Americans—a point to which we turn shortly.

Within this story of occupational transformation, the comparative experiences of women and men remain especially puzzling and consequential. Why did black women enjoy more occupational mobility than black men? The answer lies partly in history— the kinds of work available and open to blacks when their employment in southern agriculture collapsed. The answer also lies partly in incarceration, which leaves huge numbers of black men unemployable or employable only in low-wage, often temporary work. Another part of the answer is the preferences of employers, who, surveys and interviews demonstrate, prefer to hire black women over men.[34] Not only do black women appear less threatening, they seem to have more of the "soft skills" required by work in an economy based on service and information. Still another component to the puzzle's answer lies in school. One major source of black progress has been education. Without more education, black women and men would not have been able to enter the white-collar jobs that a transformed labor market, civil rights legislation, and affirmative action had made available. While African Americans of both sexes gained more education, black women's achievements outpaced black men's.

Educational Attainment

In the last half of the twentieth century, African Americans made stunning educational progress. Among both black men and women, educational attainment began to reach white levels, although women moved forward more quickly. It has been customary to argue that education did not deliver on its promises to blacks because racism blocked them from the jobs for which they were qualified. That undoubtedly happened often. But education also made possible the mass movement of blacks, especially black women, into the world of white-collar work. Nonetheless, despite this increase in educational attainment, inequality in the kind of education that mattered most did not disappear, and education continued to stratify, as well as help, black Americans.[35]

In 1940 more than 4 of 5 blacks had at best an elementary education, compared to about 1 of 2 white men and women. Those figures did not reflect lack of commitment to education among African Americans, who showed an intense interest in their children's schooling. Rather, it resulted from their poverty and from the dreadful underfunding of black schools in the South, which received only a small fraction of the money allotted to white schools. In the next sixty years, with the expansion of educational facilities and the movement of blacks to the urban North where they attended better-funded schools, the numbers with such minimal schooling fell precipitously. By 2000 they were tiny. In the same years, among both blacks and whites, high school graduation increased dramatically. In 1940 only about 10 percent of blacks aged 26–30 had completed high school, compared to 40 percent of whites. Although the fraction rose for both groups, the pace of change for blacks accelerated after 1960. At the end of the twentieth century, about 90 percent of 26- to 30-year-old blacks and whites had at least twelve years of schooling. That percentage overstates black progress, however, because it equates the general equivalency diploma (GED), a high school-equivalency diploma earned more often by blacks, with high school graduation, which leads more frequently to higher education and income.[36]

College graduation is another story. "The first pattern has been persistent white advantage. In fact, the difference between blacks and whites in college graduation rates was greater in 2000 than in 1940. Among whites the relative position of women

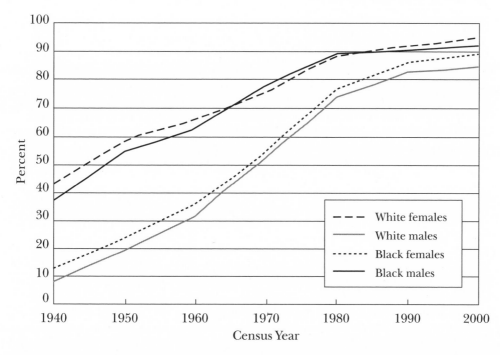

Figure 4. High school completion rate of persons 26–30 years of age, by race and gender, 1940–2000. Authors' calculation from Steven Ruggles et al., *Integrated Public Use Microdata Series: Version 3.0* (Minneapolis: Historical Census Case Projects, University of Minnesota, 2003), http://www.ipums.org.

and men reversed after 1980. Until 1980 white men graduated more often than women. In 1990 graduation rates converged, and then women pulled ahead. Even though the fraction of white men graduating from college picked up in the 1990s, white women's graduation rate accelerated faster, leaving them substantially ahead of men. Black women began to graduate from college more than black men in the 1950s, and their lead gradually widened until the 1980s, when they began to pull more sharply away from black men. In 2000, 25 percent of black men aged 18–24 were in college, compared to 35 percent of black women; of those in college, 35 percent of black men and 45 percent of black women graduated.[37] Still, in 2000, 15 percent of 26- to 30-year-old African American women had graduated from college, compared to about 33 percent of white women of the same age. For men 26–30, the spread was proportionally larger: college graduates were about 29 percent of white men and a very low 12 percent of black men.

Why do black men acquire less education than black women? There are undoubtedly a variety of reasons. Black women can see jobs at the end of the school tunnel more readily than can black men—at least that was so in the past, and expectations formed over decades die slowly. Peer-group influence, socialization patterns, and teachers' expectations certainly play a major role. Researchers, the *New York Times* has

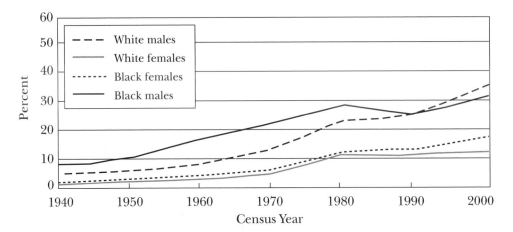

Figure 5. College graduation rate of persons 26–30 years of age, by race and gender, 1940–2000. Authors' calculation from Steven Ruggles et al., *Integrated Public Use Microdata Series: Version 3.0* (Minneapolis: Historical Census Case Projects, University of Minnesota, 2003), http://www.ipums.org.

reported, list as obstacles preventing "black men from earning college degrees . . . poor education before college, the low expectations that teachers and others have for them, a lack of black men as role models, their dropout rate from high school and their own low aspirations." Those influences, "common to disadvantaged minority students regardless of their sex," strike black men especially hard because they "have the special burden of being pigeonholed early in a way that black female students do not."[38]

Two points about educational attainment need emphasis. First, the timing of black and white progress in educational attainment differed. Whites, responding to economic change and expanded school facilities, increased their educational attainment first. Blacks lagged, needing the intervention of the state to help them over the hurdles that blocked their access to high school graduation and then to college. The first white cohort where a majority completed twelve years of schooling was born in 1926–1935; the first black cohort to pass the same milestone was born a decade later, in 1936–1945, and entered high school in the 1950s. The initial African American cohort to send at least a third of its members to college for a year or more was born in the next decade, 1946–1955. It was among African Americans who benefited from the civil rights movement, affirmative action, increased funding for historically black colleges after 1954, and the expansion of community colleges that educational attainment moved sharply upward.[39]

Second, despite great progress, blacks still remained well behind whites where it counted most. That has always been the case. Earlier in the century, only when elementary and, later, high school education had ceased to be of much use in landing a good job did blacks reach parity with whites in acquiring such schooling. In the late twentieth century, when a college degree had replaced a high school diploma as the key to the best jobs, blacks lagged well behind. Thus educational progress failed to erase the durable inequality that marked the history of race in America.[40]

Rewards

By themselves trends in occupation and education do not show that income inequality between blacks and whites lessened. Large income differences might have separated blacks and whites with similar jobs and educations. As it happened, blacks generally did reduce the income gap with whites. But women were more successful than men, and the pace of improvement was uneven. Nor could blacks' rising individual incomes erase black-white disparities in family income and wealth. In the end, economic inequality proved a cumulative process that left African Americans closer to whites, but still at a distance that showed no sign of diminishing any time soon.[41]

Earnings

We begin by looking at earnings trends from 1940 to 2000. The first question is whether groups were under- or overrepresented at different points on the earnings scale. A useful summary measure is the ratio of the proportion of blacks to whites within each income quintile. There are three principal conclusions to be drawn from the data. First, blacks were overrepresented among the lowest (poorest) quintile and underrepresented in the highest. Second, the degree of over- and underrepresentation changed notably between 1940 and 2000. In other words, blacks closed a substantial part of the earnings gap that separated them from whites. Third, black women closed more of the earnings gap than did black men.[42]

Here are some examples. Between 1940 and 2000, in the poorest quintile, the overrepresentation of black men fell from from 2.5 to 1.5 times (from 255 to 147), and in the highest quintile underrepresentation went down, as the ratio increased from 9 to 51. For women, the overrepresenration dropped from 251 to parity (102) in the lowest quintile and rose from 12 to 74 in the top quintile.

There are two ways to look at these trends: by 2000 black men were only 51 percent and black women only 74 percent as likely to be in the top economic quintile as white men and women. Or, in the sixty years since 1940, the likelihood that black men and women would be in the top quintile had risen 6 times while the probability that they would be found among the poorest had dropped by more than half. Nonetheless, sociologist Reynolds Fatley has reminded us, "*Never in our history has there been a time when the majority of blacks were members of the middle economic class.* The majority of blacks remains poor or near poor."[43] But the share in poverty has varied over time. In fact, trends in poverty among African Americans also allow multiple interpretations. Although poverty rates plummeted for all groups, including African Americans, the disparities—the degree of difference between blacks and whites—remained surprisingly durable. The proportion of blacks living in poverty plummeted from 75 percent in 1939 to 24 percent in 1999. Nonetheless, it was about twice the white rate (39 percent) in the first year and triple (8 percent) in the second.[44] Poverty, like earnings, highlights the coexistence of progress with durable inequality.

Two other related points about black poverty are very important. First, high black poverty rates did not result from deindustrialization. Except in Detroit and Chicago, in major cities African Americans did not find extensive work in manufacturing and were denied the best industrial jobs. Even where black industrial work was common, the core of black urban employment remained service jobs. Black industrial workers, moreover, did not earn higher wages or work more steadily than African Americans employed in other sorts of work. In a sample of fifteen representative cities in 1949, Buffalo, New York, had the second-largest fraction of black industrial workers, after Detroit, but its black poverty rate was among the highest. In cities with the lowest black poverty rates, relatively few African Americans worked in industrial jobs. Second, government employment reduced poverty and proved the best predictor of African American poverty rates. It accounted for 60 percent of the variance in black poverty rates across the fifteen cities. Public employment reduced poverty by providing steady, well-paid employment. African American access to public employment also signaled increasing black political influence, which encouraged local welfare bureaucracies to respond more generously to black need. Thus, in cities with the highest levels of black public employment, more blacks escaped poverty through public transfer programs—the size of black public employment explained 33 percent of the effectiveness of cities' public assistance programs in reducing poverty. Overall, the correlation between African Americans' poverty rate and African Americans' employment in government was strikingly negative ($-.7$).[45]

Another way to measure black progress is to look at black median earnings in relation to white.[46] Trends show remarkable progress in reducing the earnings gap between blacks and whites, with women leading the way. For men aged 40–49, the ratio of black to white earnings increased from about 41 percent to 69 percent between 1940 and 2000; in those years, it rose from just under 40 percent to 96 percent—near parity—for black women of the same age. The earnings gap that separated black and white women fell first among women who came of working age in the prosperous post-World War II years, the cohort born in 1926–1935. It dropped further for black women who joined the work force in the 1960s, very often children of migrants to the North who had experienced improved education and other advantages while growing up or the children of African Americans who had moved to southern cities, where education and opportunities were also improving. Those earnings gains began to erode in the 1980s and 1990s, not because the absolute earnings of black women dropped, but because the earnings of white women rose faster. Still, black women's relative earnings remained far higher than they had been in 1940. Among men, the black-white earnings ratio increased at a steadier pace, without dramatic leaps until it reversed direction and actually declined slightly between the cohorts born in 1946–1955 and 1956–1965. The latter cohort came of age amid the economic hard times of the 1980s, when most workers' incomes—regardless of race or ethnicity—went down.[47]

Despite progress in closing the black/white earnings gap, black men's earnings generally declined between pre- and post-World War II birth cohorts. Although they usually earned more than women, they were not as capable of sustaining earnings gains across cohorts when the economy soured. With their hold on jobs less solid than white workers', blacks proved especially vulnerable to the forces that were eroding wages, job stability, and upward mobility.[48] Earnings went down especially steeply for black men born after 1945. Median earnings, in 1990 dollars, for 30- to 39-year-old men born in 1926–1935 were $15,975. They increased to $20,510 for men born in 1936–1945 when that cohort reached the same age. Then they started to go down: for men born in 1956–1965, who came of working age in the late 1970s and the 1980s, the median earnings when they were in their thirties were $18,500.

Measures of economic well-being need to distinguish between *individual* and *family* earnings. The resources available to individuals result in part from the total earnings of family members who live together. Our examination of census data indicates that family earnings modify the trends in individual earnings: they reduce the earnings gap between black and white men and increase it between black and white women. By the end of the twentieth century, the earnings of families headed by black men were about three-quarters of those headed by white men—a higher ratio than for men considered individually. The same distinction held true in earlier years and reflects the greater participation of married black than white women in the labor force. Prior to 1960 black women household heads appeared to be earning more than white, probably because they worked more. By 2000, however, the trend had reversed: the earnings of families headed by black women had dropped to 74 percent of the earnings of families headed by white women, as married and divorced white women increasingly entered the labor force.

Overall, black women made stunning economic progress. In most occupations, they earned as much, or nearly as much, as white women. By 2000 there were essentially no differences in individual earnings between black and white women in the same occupational categories. Black men fared much less well. Although they reduced the earnings gap with whites, sharp differences in earnings between black and white men in the same occupational categories remained. Between 1940 and 2000, for instance, for men the increase in the earnings ratio went from 45 to 73 in professional/technical occupations and 30 to 76 for managers, officials, and proprietors. (The earnings gaps reflect the differences in the kinds of jobs black and white men held in the same broad occupational category. The professional/technical category, for instance, includes both physicians and lawyers and social workers in public human-service agencies. White men, as noted earlier, disproportionately held the better jobs.) Within the blue-collar world, the earnings of black men grew still closer to those of white men: in crafts from 52 to 86 percent. But no group erased the advantages of white men. This white male advantage was not the result of differences in education; it persisted across all groups, regardless of the level of education that they had reached.

Whether African American men experienced economic mobility during their prime working years depended in part on when they were born. Men born earlier in the century made the most dramatic gains. The post-World War II economic boom combined with migration from southern farms to boost the earnings of African American

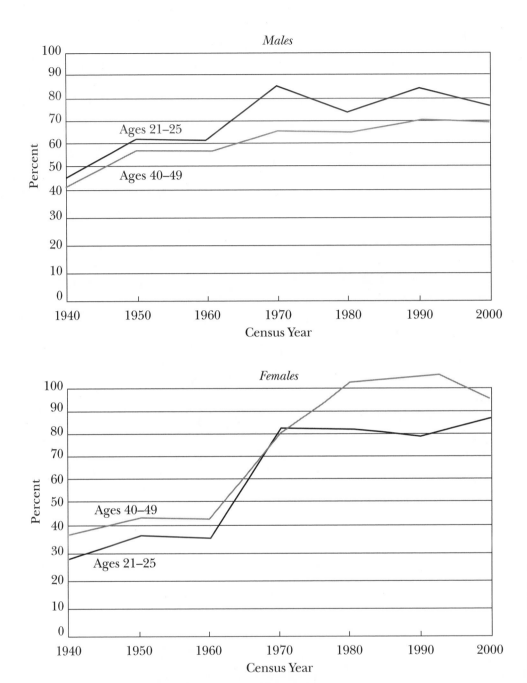

Figure 6. Black wages as a percentage of white wages for selected ages, by sex, 1940–2000. Authors' calculation from Steven Ruggles et al., *Integrated Public Use Microdata Series: Version 3.0* (Minneapolis: Historical Census Case Projects, University of Minnesota, 2003), http:// www.ipums.org.

TABLE 3. Ratios of Median Earnings of Employed Persons of Different Races and Genders, by Years of Schooling, 1940–2000 (%)

Years of schooling	Year	Black/white earnings ratios		Female/male earnings ratios	
		Males	Females	White	Blacks
9–11 years	1940	50	45	55	50
	1970	65	80	36	45
	2000	78	108	52	71
12 years	1940	60	48	63	50
	1970	70	94	43	58
	2000	74	94	59	75
1–3 years college	1940	48	47	57	55
	1970	78	115	41	61
	2000	81	104	62	80
4+ years college	1940	49	55	59	66
	1970	73	108	55	81
	2000	80	106	64	85

Source: See Table 1.

men throughout their working lives. The median earnings of black men born in 1906–1915 more than doubled in the twenty years between 1936–1945 and 1956–1965. Men born ten years later benefited from the same influences, although their earnings did not spike as sharply. Men who entered their prime working years during the difficult years from the mid-1970s to the mid-1980s did not experience the same economic mobility. Their adult earnings hardly budged over time.

Earnings depended on age, sex, race, and education, as well as historical events and the economic climate. Five important observations emerge from an analysis that shows the relative influence of these factors more exactly.[49] First, because education mediated their influence, the impact of sex and race varied substantially with educational attainment. In both 1940 and 2000, earnings increased with education within each group defined by both sex and race. Nonetheless, in 1940 the influence of race was so strong that it trumped education and gender. Black male college graduates earned only 11 percent more than black male high school graduates and less than either white males who had not finished high school or black female college graduates. In 2000 education overrode the influence of race. Indeed, the influence of education grew remarkably during the sixty years. For instance, the earnings difference between a black male high school graduate and a black male college graduate increased from 11 percent in 1940 to 71 percent in 2000. The gap between a white male high school graduate and a white male college graduate rose in the same period from 33 percent to 100 percent. Black female college graduates, in contrast, consistently earned dramatically more than less-educated black women: In 1940 black female high school graduates earned (in 1990 dollars) an estimated $5,222 and black female college graduates $ 10,049; in 2000 their earnings had increased, respectively, to $14,733 and $26,734.

Second, race mattered, but more in 1940 than in 2000.[50] Earnings of the best-

TABLE 4. Ratios of Earnings of Employed Persons by Occupational Category, by Race and Gender 1940–2000 (%)

Occupational Category	Year	Black/white earnings ratios		Female/male earnings ratios	
		Males	Females	Whites	Blacks
Professional/technical worker	1940	45	58	52	66
	1970	70	93	54	72
	2000	73	100	63	86
Manager, official, proprietor	1940	30	30	50	50
	1970	68	113	48	81
	2000	76	94	63	77
Clerical worker	1940	79	57	68	49
	1970	83	98	57	67
	2000	88	100	80	91
Crafts person	1940	52	40	64	50
	1970	75	98	52	67
	2000	86	108	73	92
Operative	1940	60	71	52	62
	1970	73	86	50	59
	2000	91	98	63	68
Laborer	1940	80	54	91	62
	1970	79	90	59	68
	2000	84	107	70	90

For example, black male professional or technical workers earned 45 % as much as white male professional or technical workers in 1940. By 2000 the percentage had improved to 73 %.
Source: See Table 1.

educated blacks and whites grew closer to each other over time, even though blacks generally still earned less. In 1940 blacks with college degrees, both men and women, earned substantially less than white high school graduates. In 2000 they earned a lot more. (The following figures are in 1990 dollars.) In 1940 black men who had graduated from college earned $3,681 *less* than white high school graduates; in 2000 they earned $7,723 *more*. In 1940 black women college graduates earned $1,918 *less* than white men who had graduated from high school; in 2000 they earned $3,208 *more*. The ratio of black to white median earnings increased over time among individuals who had stayed in school for the same number of years. The increase, however, was much steeper among women than men. After 1980 black women generally earned the same as, or more than, white women with comparable educations. In contrast, the racial gap between male college graduates increased after 1980. African American male college graduates' earnings rose from 52 percent of white male college graduates' earnings in 1940 to 75 percent in 1980, but then fell to 67 percent in 2000.

Third, in 1940 racial discrimination prevented blacks with a college education from earning as much as whites with a high school education. By 2000 this anomaly had disappeared. But the earnings of white men, more than of any other group, benefited from college graduation. No other group even came close. In 1940 white men who had graduated from college earned $3,998 more than white male high school graduates. By 2000 their advantage had risen to $23,119. The earnings advantage for black

TABLE 5a. Estimated Mean Personal Earnings of Men, by Educational Attainment and Ethnicity, 1940–2000 (general linear model, 1990 dollars)

Census year	Ethnicity	Less than high school graduate	High school graduate	College graduate	College/high school graduate ratio[a]
			Educational attainment		
1940	Non-Hispanic white	8,025	11,966	15,964	133
	African American	6,018	7,463	8,285	111
1950	Non-Hispanic white	10,380	13,717	16,620	121
	African American	7,902	10,487	11,099	106
1960	Non-Hispanic white	14,818	19,645	27,493	140
	African American	10,095	13,860	16,372	118
1970	Non-Hispanic white	22,195	28,141	41,690	148
	African American	16,787	22,825	29,941	131
1980	Non-Hispanic white	18,212	23,165	33,207	143
	African American	13,997	18,267	24,859	136
1990	Non-Hispanic white	16,169	21,302	37,858	178
	African American	12,814	16,373	25,949	158
2000	Non-Hispanic white	18,283	23,166	46,285	200
	African American	15,480	18,088	30,890	371

Results based on a general linear analysis split by gender and year, controlled for metropolitan status, age, full-time, full-year status, and residence in the South or elsewhere. * = mean earnings of college graduates as percentage of those of high school graduates.
Source: See Table 1.

male, black female, and white female college graduates trailed well behind. No matter how long they had stayed in school, no group matched the earnings of white men. White men had successfully parlayed college education into a strategy for retaining and advancing their historic spot at the top of the earnings ladder.

Fourth, the increased importance of education heightened the internal differences among blacks. It sharpened the dividing lines within black social structure, whose organizing principles came increasingly to resemble those among whites—a point to which we return.

Fifth, education did not erase the cumulative economic disadvantages of African Americans, who remained unable to combine individual earnings within families as successfully as whites. This resulted partly from lower male wages and partly from the higher proportion of single-earner, female-headed households among blacks. At work a black woman earned as much as the white woman with a similar education who sat next to her. But she more often went home to a husband who earned less than the white woman's or to no husband at all. She also lived in a household that had fewer assets.[51] That is the message underlined by trends in home ownership and value.

Earnings are only one basis of family economic well-being. Others are real property, savings, and securities—assets held much less often by blacks than whites, as the research of Melvin L. Oliver and Thomas M. Shapiro and of Dalton Conley has shown.[52] Using the census, only one measure of assets—home ownership—is consistently available across the century. Fortunately, it is a useful measure because their

TABLE 5b. Estimated Mean Personal Earnings of Women, by Educational Attainment and Ethnicity, 1940–2000 (general linear model, 1990 dollars)

| Census year | Ethnicity | Educational attainment | | | College/high school graduate ratio[a] |
		Less than high school graduate	High school graduate	College graduate	
1940	Non-Hispanic white	5,267	7,190	12,485	174
	African American	3,354	5,222	10,049	192
1950	Non-Hispanic white	7,053	8,730	12,235	140
	African American	5,652	7,130	12,386	174
1960	Non-Hispanic white	8,180	10,558	16,949	161
	African American	5,912	8,214	15,855	193
1970	Non-Hispanic white	12,966	15,377	23,878	155
	African American	11,179	15,386	25,915	168
1980	Non-Hispanic white	9,900	11,969	18,354	153
	African American	8,976	11,918	20,759	174
1990	Non-Hispanic white	9,723	12,770	22,005	172
	African American	8,952	12,195	22,572	185
2000	Non-Hispanic white	12,242	15,524	27,390	176
	African American	12,043	14,733	26,374	179

See Table 5.1 for notes and source.

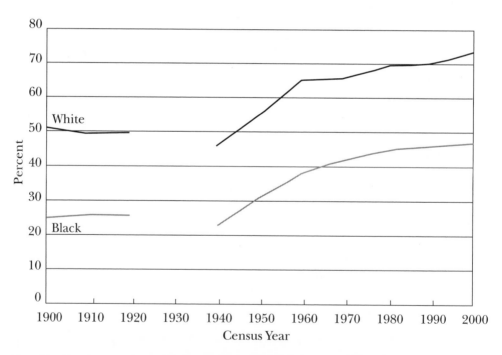

Figure 7. Percentage of household heads owning homes, by race, 1900–2000. Authors' calculation from Steven Ruggles et al., *Integrated Public Use Microdata Series: Version 3.0* (Minneapolis: Historical Census Case Projects, University of Minnesota, 2003), http://www.ipums.org.

homes constitute such a large share of most families' wealth. For 1940 and subsequent census years, it is also possible to examine the value of the homes that families owned.

Throughout the twentieth century, blacks owned homes much less often than whites. Among both white and black households, home ownership rose after 1940—for whites from 45 percent in 1940 to 72 percent in 2000 and among blacks from 23 percent to 47 percent in the same years. Thus, in 2000 the ratio of black to white home ownership was 66, down from a high point of 67 in 1980. Certainly, this ratio represented an advance since 1940, but it still underlined a major disparity.

The homes that blacks did own were worth less than those owned by whites, although their relative value increased over time. In 1940 the median value of blacks' homes was only 20 percent of the value of whites' homes. It rose quickly to 56 percent by 1960 and ended the century at 67 percent. Blacks thus had substantially less wealth than whites. With assets as the measure, the economic gap between whites and blacks appears greater than with earnings. In fact, a view that combines earnings, education, and property qualifies the record of black economic progress. Blacks less often acquired a four-year college education—the key to the highest earnings; men (but not women) who did enter the most remunerative jobs earned less than whites; whatever their jobs or educations, they could not bundle individual into family earnings as large as those of whites; more of them were poor; they owned homes less frequently; and the homes they did own were not worth as much. Economic inequality was a cumulative process. It did not result from a single form of inequity or discrimination but from a series of screens that filtered blacks into less favored compartments whose cumulative result was a new configuration of inequality.[53]

Differentiation

Patterns of economic inequality separating blacks and whites shattered and then recomposed between the end of World War II and the turn of the century. While blacks did not reach economic equality with whites, the configuration of black inequality had been irrevocably transformed. A differentiation within African American social structure was one result. Differentiation is a more precise and objective way to talk about the change than to cast it as the emergence of a black middle class—a common trope in discussions of recent trends in black social structure but one lacking precise features and difficult to track over time.[54] Differentiation underscores the importance of disaggregating blacks' experience by gender and class. Only through disaggregation is it possible to pinpoint what has persisted and what has changed in African Americans' history of work, income, education, poverty, and mobility. Here we review some of the data already presented to illustrate how the process works.

The first measure is geographic. From a population three-quarters concentrated in the South, blacks spread throughout the other regions of the nation. By the end of the century, they had become far more geographically diversified than at its start or even at its midpoint. Blacks also replaced their rural concentration in 1900 with metropolitan residence. As blacks moved to cities and then to suburbs, segregation put a brake on their differentiation by residence and helped concentrate blacks in central cities and inner suburbs.

Differentiation also marked the history of black labor-force participation, but mainly in one respect. For most of the twentieth century, married black women worked for wages far more often than married white women, who caught up with them toward the century's end. It was male labor-force participation that bifurcated most dramatically with the emergence of a large fraction of jobless adult black men in the 1970s and 1980s. Black men had divided into those in and those out of the regular labor market.

Differentiation also proved the hallmark of black industrial and occupational history in the twentieth century. Census data indicate that in 1910 just 2 industries—agriculture and private household service—employed nearly 90 of 100 black working women. In 1940 the same 2 industries still accounted for 75 of 100. By 1970, however, it took 17 industries to encompass the same share of black working women—a number that remained approximately steady for the rest of the century. Among black men, 8 industries accounted for three-quarters of employment in 1910, a number that grew to 16 in 1940, and 32 in 2000. Clearly, here too differentiation was a major theme.

The same held true for occupations. As black women left agriculture and domestic service, their occupational structure bifurcated, with nearly 2 of 3 in white-collar jobs in 2000 but a third still employed in manual work and lower-level services. Among men the occupational story was also one of dramatic differentiation. In 1900 nearly 80 of 100 black men were laborers, farm owners or tenants, or farm laborers. By 2000 black men had entered a variety of other occupations as their occupational structure differentiated. At the end of the century about 39 of 100 held white-collar jobs.

Manufacturing played a relatively minor role in the differentiation of African Americans among industries and occupations. When their agricultural employment disappeared, not even 1 of 5 black men found alternative employment in manufacturing. With limited education, lacking the skills necessary for government-related or other white-collar jobs, without a clear new economic niche, disadvantaged by a prison record, many remained—and remain—chronically detached from the labor market. Black women, by contrast, found in domestic work an alternative to agricultural employment that tided them over until, helped by their educational advance, they began to find white-collar and government-related jobs.

Our analysis of census data shows that in 1900 African Americans clustered in the lowest levels of educational attainment. By 2000, as a substantial fraction graduated from college, the share of the black population with and without some college experience had become about equal. Earnings repeat the by-now-familiar tale. In 1940 black women and men clustered in the two lowest economic quintiles. By 2000, 36 percent of employed African American men and 24 percent of employed African American women had reached the top two. In the same years, as poverty rates plunged, African Americans were no longer a people almost universally poor, and race by itself influenced earnings much less in 2000 than it had in 1940. Instead, education was now the major source of economic differentiation. Again, the evidence points to a population divided, this time by economic rewards. The same trend, finally, was evident in the differentiation of blacks by home ownership, an important achievement in its own right and a surrogate for the accumulation of total assets.

It was through such differentiation—the accumulation of many small and not-so-small distinctions—that black social structure came increasingly to resemble that found among whites and that black inequality endured despite individual and group mobility. Differentiation constitutes a powerful analytic tool for understanding stratification because it addresses the paradox of inequality: the coexistence of durable inequalities with individual and group mobility. It show how social mobility reinforces, rather than challenges, economic inequalities. And it highlights the limitations of policies that focus only on access to jobs or education without addressing the factors that structure and reproduce inequality.

Inequality is historically contingent; the way it works varies with time and place. Either/or interpretations of racial progress run the risk of turning a very complicated history into a scorecard that diverts attention from the most important issues. The question is not whether Hacker or the Thernstroms win a debate but how and why the characteristics of black inequality have changed during the twentieth century and what those changes imply. One implication points to the limits of individualist solutions to group problems. Solutions that promote individual social mobility without attending to the processes that reproduce inequality lead to differentiation—the mobility of a fortunate minority who pull away from the rest. They are supply-side solutions to demand-side problems. And they are the way American public policy usually works.

One demand-side problem very clearly is work for black men. The history recounted in this article points out that the trouble African American men face finding work cannot be understood wholly, or even largely, as a result of deindustrialization. It needs to be cast, first, as a result of the conjunction of the disappearance of agricultural work with a changing opportunity structure for which black men's education had prepared them poorly. Persistent racial discrimination, draconian drug laws, extraordinary rates of incarceration, and other influences compounded the circumstances that resulted in the stubbornly high fraction of black men outside the regular labor market. The flip side of demand, this history shows, has been the role of public and quasi-public employment. Such employment provided African Americans with a distinctive occupational niche, served as their primary escalator into the middle class, and reduced poverty among them. But it was an escalator ridden more easily by women than men, and it reinforced the growing gender gap that the data so clearly reveal. It was also an escalator that more or less stopped, and even reversed, in the last decade of the century. More than African American women, African American men were buffeted by the declining wages and weak labor market that undercut most American workers. The growing importance of education, it might be thought, contradicts this demand-side interpretation. For among African Americans, as among whites, the links between education and income grew tighter in the late twentieth century. Education facilitated the social mobility of a great many African Americans, but it also left many behind. It was, that is, a powerful engine of differentiation. And the fraction of blacks that reached the highest levels remained quite small. Opportunity had opened, but whites held onto their lead. Individualist solutions to black inequality that relied solely on education were very likely to fail. But the role of education suggests an advantage to understanding inequality as a process—a series of screens sifting girls and boys, women and men into more or less promising economic and social positions. Interpreted this way, the analysis of inequality highlights the need for multifaceted policy and the points where policy interventions are most needed, and most likely to be successful.

The new black inequality that emerged in the last decades of the twentieth century resulted from powerful technological, demographic, economic, and political forces. It was facilitated by massive social movements and abetted and shaped in everyway by the state. And it left African Americans divided among themselves. A disproportionately high fraction lived in poverty; large numbers were peculiarly vulnerable to political retrenchment and economic reversal because they were employed in public or publicly funded jobs; and many others enjoyed the benefits of upward mobility. While race remained a live force in American life, it worked in some new ways, sifting African Americans through a series of screens—residential, penal, occupational, educational, economic—that advantaged some and left others progressively behind.[55] Certainly, familiar forms of inequality remained, and an alarming gender gap had opened between black women and men. Large differences in labor-force participation and earnings separated black and white men; blacks were poor about three times more often than whites; neither black women nor men finished college as often as whites; and a much higher fraction of whites owned property. Nonetheless, inequality had been transformed. Earlier the embodiment of ubiquitous, converging forces of oppression, late twentieth-century black inequality was the product of a sequence of differentiating experiences. The new inequality was harder to pinpoint or characterize, more diverse, easier for an outsider to miss—but no less real.

Reprinted from Michael B. Katz, Mark J. Stern, and Jamie J. Fader, The new African American inequality, *Journal of American History* (2005): 75–108. Reprinted by permission.

Notes

1. Frances Fox Piven and Richard Cloward, *Poor People's Movements: Why They Succeed, How They Fail* (New York: Pantheon, 1977); Mary L. Dudziak, *Cold War Civil Rights: Race and the Image of American Democracy* (Princeton, N.J.: Princeton University Press, 2000). See also Martha F. Davis, *Brutal Need: Lawyers and the Welfare Rights Movement* (New Haven, Conn.: Yale University Press, 1993); and John David Skrentny, *The Ironies of Affirmative Action: Politics, Culture, and Justice in America* (Chicago: University of Chicago Press, 1996). On black wage growth by 1940, see Robert Higgs, "Black Progress and the Persistence of Racial Economic Inequalities," in Steven Shulman and William Darity, eds., *The Question of Discrimination: Racial Inequality in the U.S. Labor Market* (Middletown, Conn.: Wesleyan University Press, 1989), 9–31.

2. Andrew Hacker, *Two Nations: Black and White, Separate, Hostile, Unequal* (New York: Scribner's, 1992); Stephan Thernstrom and Abigail Thernstrom, *America in Black and White: One Nation, Indivisible* (New York: Simon and Schuster, 1997). For an extended criticism of the latter work and others written by authors the critics term "racial realists," see Michael K. Brown et al.,

Whitewashing Race: The Myth of a Color-Blind Society (Berkeley: University of California Press, 2003). On black progress as of 1990, see Reynolds Farley, *The New American Reality: Who We Are, How We Got Here, Where We Are Going* (New York: Scribner's, 1996), 248–53. See also Shulman and Darity, eds., *Question of Discrimination*; and James Smith and Finis Welch, Black economic progress after Myrdal, *Journal of Economic Literature* 27 (June 1989): 519–64.

3. For the best book-length account of current racial inequality, which stresses its cumulative nature, see Brown et al., *Whitewashing Race*, esp. 21–25. It draws, as does this article, on Charles Tilly, *Durable Inequality* (Berkeley: University of California Press, 1998).

4. African American women's economic experience has received surprisingly little analysis, a point made in Mary Corcoran, "The Economic Progress of African American Women," in Irene Browne, *Latinas and African American Women at Work: Race, Gender, and Economic Inequality* (New York: Sage, 1999), 35–60.

5. Unless otherwise indicated, data are taken or calculated from the remarkable census samples developed by Steven Ruggles et al., *Integrated Public Use Microdata Series: Version 3.0* (Minneapolis: Historical Census Case Projects, University of Minnesota, 2003), http://www.ipums.org. Here we present only a sample of the data on which the analysis is based in order to highlight major trends. Full tables are available on the America at the Millennium Project Web site, http://www.ssw.upenn.edu/america 2000 (December 12, 2004).

6. Statistics on blacks in metropolitan areas come from Frank Hobbs and Nicole Stoops, *Demographic Trends in the Twentieth Century* (Washington, D.C.: U.S. Census Bureau, 2002), 206, table 16. Data on their concentration in central cities are our own analysis of census data provided in Ruggles et al., *Integrated Public Use Microdata Series*.

7. Douglas S. Massey and Nancy A. Denton, *American Apartheid: Segregation and the Making of the Underclass* (Cambridge, Mass.: Harvard University Press, 1993). On the origins of black ghettos, see James Grossman, *Land of Hope: Chicago, Black Southerners, and the Great Migration* (Chicago: University of Chicago Press, 1989); and Arnold R. Hirsch, *Making the Second Ghetto: Race and Housing in Chicago, 1940–1960* (New York: Cambridge University Press, 1983). Lewis Mumford Center, "Ethnic Diversity Grows, Neighborhood Integration Lags Behind," 2001, http://mumfordl.dyndns.org/cen2000/WholePop/WReport/pagel.html (December 13, 2004). The Web site of the Lewis Mumford Center for Comparative Urban and Regional Research is an excellent source of data on segregation, http://www.albany.edu/mumford (December 12, 2004).

8. John Logan, "The New Ethnic Enclaves in America's Suburbs," 2001, 2, 6, 10, *Lewis Mumford Center for Comparative Urban and Regional Research*, http://mumford1.dyndns.org/cen2000/suburban/SuburbanReport/pagel.html (March 9, 2005).

9. John F. Bauman, *Public Housing, Race, and Renewal: Urban Planning in Philadelphia, 1920–1974* (Philadelphia: Temple University Press, 1987); Hirsch, *Making the Second Ghetto*; Raymond A. Mohl, "Race and Space in the Modern Ccity: Interstate-95 and the Black Community in Miami," in Arnold R. Hirsch and Raymond A. Mohl, eds., *Urban Policy in Twentieth-Century America* (New Brunswick, N.J.: Rutgers University Press, 1993), 100–158; Thomas J. Sugrue, *The Origins of the Urban Crisis: Race and Inequality in Postwar Detroit* (Princeton, N.J.: Princeton University Press, 1996).

10. On concentration as itself a source of inequality, see John J. Beggs, Wayne J. Villemez, and Ruth Arnold, "Black Population Concentration and Black-White Inequality: Expanding the Consideration of Place and Space Effects," *Social Forces* 76 (September 1997): 65–91. On the impact of concentration on inequality, see Samuel Cohn and Mark Fossett, "Why Racial Employment Inequality Is Greater in Northern Labor Markets: Regional Differences in White-Black Employment Differentials," *Social Forces* 74 (December 1995): 511–42; Massey and Denton, *American Apartheid*, 179–81.

11. On labor-force attachment, including its measurement, see Monica D. Castillo, "Persons Outside the Labor Force Who Want a Job," *Monthly Labor Review* 121 (July 1998): 34–42. See also John P. Blair and Rudy H. Fichtenbaum, "Changing Black Employment Patterns," in

George Galster and Edward Hill, eds., *The Metropolis in Black and White: Place, Power, and Polarization* (New Brunswick, N.J.: Rutgers University Press, 1992), 72–92.

12. On the history of black women's work, see Jacqueline Jones, *Labor of Love, Labor of Sorrow: Black Women, Work, and the Family from Slavery to the Present* (New York: Basic Books, 1985). See also Alice Kessler-Harris, *Out to Work: A History of Wage-Earning Women in the United States* (New York: Oxford University Press, 1982). For trends in women's work and income, see Michael B. Katz, Mark J. Stern, and Jamie J. Fader, "Women and the Paradox of Economic Inequality in Twentieth Century America," *Journal of Social History* (forthcoming); and Michael B. Katz and Mark J. Stern, *One Nation Divisible; What America Was and What It Was Becoming* (forthcoming), chap. 3. The question of public assistance raises the issue of the impact of changes in family structure on the economic situation of black women. On family structure, see chaps. 7 and 8. Lawrence M. Mead, *The New Politics of Poverty: The Nonworking Poor in America* (New York: Basic Books, 1992); William Julius Wilson, *The Truly Disadvantaged: The Inner City, the Underclass, and Public Policy* (Chicago: University of Chicago Press, 1987); William Julius Wilson, *When Work Disappears: The World of the New Urban Poor* (New York: Knopf, 1996).

13. From 1900 to 1920 black women listed an occupation one-fifth to one-third again as often than white women. Among black women, there were virtually no trends and, in a given year, only small differences by age. Generally, almost half of black women engaged in market work. (The 1910 census figures, which show greater labor-force participation, do not indicate an actual increase. In that year only, the census counted work on a family farm as a formal occupation. Since most blacks worked in agriculture, that designation boosted labor-force participation among them more than among whites.) The difference between black and white 26- to 30-year-old women reflected family work in agriculture among blacks, not market labor. On the relative decline in black women's labor-force participation, see Karen Christopher, "Explaining the Recent Employment Gap Between Black and White Women," *Sociological Focus* 29 (August 1996): 263–80. Many writers have commented on that trend, including Daphne Spain and Suzanne M. Bianchi. *Balancing Act: Motherhood, Marriage, and Employment Smong American Women* (New York: Sage, 1996).

14. On the emergence of an unemployment gap between black and white men, sec Edna Bonacich, "Advanced Capitalism and Black/White Race Relations in the United States: A Split Labor Market Interpretation," *American Sociological Review* 41 (February 1976): 34–51. Our interpretation differs from hers both because unemployment is different from labor force nonparticipation and because we have reservations about her interpretive framework. On black men's nonparticipation in the labor force, see James J. Heckman, "The Impact of Government on the Economic Status of Black Americans," in Shulman and Darity, eds., *Question of Discrimination*, 50–80.

15. Chinhui Juhn, "Black-White Employment Differential in a Tight Labor Market," in Robert Cherry and William M. Rodgers, eds., *Prosperity for All? The Economic Boom and African Americans* (New York: Sage, 2000), 88–109. See also William E. Spriggs and Rhonda M. Williams, "What Do We Need to Explain about African American Unemployment?" ibid., 188–207: "The fact that African American unemployment rates are consistently twice as high as white rates should be one of the greatest mysteries in labor economics, yet is among the least-researched dimensions of racial economic inequality'" (203). On the rise in incarceration, see Christian Parenti, *Lockdown America: Police and Prisons in an Age of Crisis* (New York: Verso, 1999). Labor-force nonparticipation should not be confounded with official unemployment. Unemployment rates have shown little relation to incarceration: the economic boom of the 1990s did not reduce the imprisonment of black men, which had other sources, particularly state policy. See William A. Darity, Jr., and Samuel L. Myers, Jr., "The Impact of Labor Market Prospects on Incarceration Rates," in Cherry and Rodgers, *Prosperity for All?*, 279–307. On the labor market impact of incarceration, see Bruce Western, Jeffrey R. Kling, and David F. Weiman, "The Labor Market Consequences of Incarceration," *Crime and Delinquency* 47 (July 2001): 410–27; and

Devah Pager, "The Mark of a Criminal Record," *American Journal of Sociology* 108 (Match 2003): 937–73.

16. Sentencing Project, "New Incarceration Figures: Rising Population despite Falling Crime Rates," Sentencing Project, http://www.sentencingproject.org/pdfs/1044.pdf (March 9, 2005).

17. Marc Mauer, "The Crisis of the Young African American Male and the Criminal Justice System," April 1999, Sentencing Project, http://www.sencencingprotect.org/pdrs/S022.pdf (March 9, 2005), 8.

18. Pager, "Mark of a Criminal Record." Incarceration also affects inequality by reducing the number of marriageable men—a topic treated in Katz and Stern, *One Nation Divisible*, chap. 5.

19. Jacqueline Jones. "Southern Diaspora: Origins of the Northern 'Underclass'," in Michael B. Katz, *The "Underclass" Debate: Views from History*, ed. Michael B. Katz (Princeton, N.J.: Princeton University Press, 1993), 27–54.

20. The industry analysis uses the industrial classifications developed for the 1950 census. In 2000 only 0.2% of black working women had agricultural employment: 1.3% were in private household service.

21. David Gerald Jaynes and Robin M. Williams, Jr., eds., *A Common Destiny: Blacks and American Society* (Washington, D.C.: National Academy Press, 1989), 169. See Katz, Stern, and Fader, "Women and the Paradox of Economic Inequality"; and Katz and Stern, *One Nation Divisible*, chap. 3.

22. Throughout the century 5–6% of black men worked in construction; in 1910, 6% worked on railroads; later other forms of transportation provided many jobs.

23. The percentages are calculated from the occupational categories for men in manufacturing industries. The numerator is the number of black men in blue-collar occupations in manufacturing, the denominator all employed black men.

24. Robert Self, *American Babylon: Race and the Struggle for Postwar Oakland* (Princeton, N.J.: Princeton University Press1996), 173.

25. The tenuous presence of blacks in public employment before World War II contrasts with the situation after 1960. Gunnar Myrdal, *An American Dilemma: The Negro Problem and Modern Democracy*, vol. 1 (1944; New Brunswick, N.J.: Rutgers University Press, 2002), 327–29. On the crucial role of public employment, see Brown et al., *Whitewashing Race*, 73. The role of public employment in African American history deserves historians' attention. Useful social science articles about it are Peter K. Eisinger, "The Economic Conditions of Black Employment in Municipal Bureaucracies," *American Journal of Political Science* 26 (November 1982): 754–71; Marlese Durr and John R. Logan, "Racial Submarkets in Government Employment: African American Managers in New York State," *Sociological Forum* 12 (September 1997): 353–70; Joshua G. Behr, "Black and Female Municipal Employment: A Substantive Benefit of Minority Political Incorporation?," *Journal of Urban Affairs* 22 (3) (2000): 243–64; and Kevin M. O'Brien, "The Determinants of Minority Employment in Police and Fire Departments," *Journal of Socio-Economics* 32 (2) (2003): 183–95. On black public employment in a large city in 1940, see St. Clair Drake and Horace Clayton, *Black Metropolis: A Study of Negro Life in a Northern City* (1945; Chicago: University of Chicago Press, 1993), 254–57; Robert L. Boyd, "Differences in the Earnings of Black Workers in the Private and Public Sectors," *Social Science Journal* 30 (2) (1993): 133–42; Martin Carnoy, *Faded Dreams: The Politics and Economics of Race in America* (New York: Cambridge University Press, 1994), 161–65.

26. Jaynes and Williams, eds., *Common Destiny*, 169.

27. Self, *American Babylon*, 57. On federal spending, see Michael B. Katz, *In the Shadow of the Poorhouse: A Social History of Welfare in America* (1986; New York: Basic Books, 1996), 266. On the history of federal labor market policy, see Philip Harvey, *Securing the Right to Employment; Social Welfare Policy and the Unemployed in the United States* (Princeton, N.J.: Princeton University Press, 1989); and Margaret Weir, *Politics and Jobs: The Boundaries of Employment Policy in the United States* (Princeton, N.J.: Princeton University Press, 1992).

28. Robert Weisbrot, *Freedom Bound: A History of America's Civil Rights Movement* (New York, 1990); Suzanne Model, "The Ethnic Niche and the Structure of Opportunity: Immigrants and Minorities in New York City," in Katz, ed., *"Underclass" Debate*, 161–93; Skrentny, *Ironies of Affirmative Action*; Roger Waldinger, *Still the Promised City? African-Americans and New Immigrants in Post-Industrial New York* (Cambridge, Mass. Harvard University Press, 1996).

29. Manual working class (here a synonym of blue-collar) is a broader category than manufacturing. Census data show that in 1960, for instance, 10% of black men, compared to 21% of white men, worked in crafts; 28% of black men and 19% of white men were employed as semi-skilled operatives; 20% of black men and only 4% of white men worked as laborers. White women rarely worked in crafts, but many more of them than of black women worked as operatives earlier in the century—operatives constituted 28% of employed white women in 1900, but only 15% by 1940. By 2000 the figure was 6%, lower than the percentage among black women. This essay does not discuss black self-employment, which has remained relatively low. On trends and reasons, see Robert L. Boyd, "A Contextual Analysis of Black Self-Employment in Large Metropolitan Areas, 1970–1980," *Social Forces* 70 (December 1991): 409–29; and Robert W. Fairlie and Bruce D. Meyer, "Trends in Self-Employment Among White and Black Men During the Twentieth Century," *Journal of Human Resources* 35 (Autumn 2000): 643–69.

30. Ellis Cose and Allison Samuels, "The Black Gender Cap," *Newsweek*, March 3, 2003, 46.

31. John F. Zipp, "Government Employment and Black-White Earnings Inequality, 1980–1990," *Social Problems*, 41 (August 1994), 363–82.

32. Among black women, technician jobs became important. In 1940 technicians were 1.8% of white women employed in professional and technical work and 0.0% of black women so employed; in 2000 they were 9.9% of white and 13.4% of black women. What is the most striking, though, is the convergence of black and white women in professional and technical occupations. The increasing sex differentiation in municipal employment is shown for New Orleans in Behr, "Black and Female Municipal Employment," 243–64.

33. Eisinger, "Economic Conditions of Black Employment in Municipal Bureaucracies." A study based on 1980 data found that African Americans were more protected and earned higher incomes in the public sector than in the private. Boyd, "Differences in the Earnings of Black Workers." Declining black incomes in the 1980s resulted in part from reductions in government employment. See Carnoy, *Faded Dreams*, 161–65. Peter Eisinger, "Local Civil Service Employment and Black Socioeconomic Mobility," *Social Science Quarterly* 67 (March 1986): 169–85; M. V. Lee Badgett, "The Impact of Affirmative Action on Public-Sector Employment in California, 1970–1990," in Paul Ong, ed., *Impacts of Affirmative Action: Policies and Consequences in California* (Walnut Creek, Calif.: AltaMira, 1999), 83–102.

34. On employer preferences, see Philip Moss and Chris Tilly Moss, "How Labor-Market Tightness Affects Employer Attitudes and Actions Toward Black Job Applicants: Evidence from Employer Surveys," in Cherry and Rodgers, eds., *Prosperity for All?*, 129–59.

35. On African Americans' commitment to education in the early twentieth century, see Grossman, *Land of Hope*, 246–58; and Timothy L. Smith, "Native Blacks and Foreign Whites: Varying Responses to Educational Opportunity in America, 1880–1950," *Perspectives in American History* 6 (1972): 309–35. On educational attainment among African Americans, 1940–1990, see Farley, *New American Reality*, 228–38.

36. Louis Harlan, *Separate and Unequal: Public School Campaigns and Racism in the Southern Seaboard States, 1901–1915* (Chapel Hill: University of North Carolina Press, 1958). See James L. Leloudis, *Schooling the New South: Pedagogy, Self and Society in North Carolina, 1880–1920* (Chapel Hill: University of North Carolina Press, 1996); and James D. Anderson, *The Education of Blacks in the South, 1860–1935* (Chapel Hill: University of North Carolina Press, 1988); Education Trust, "Telling the Whole Truth (or Not) About High School Graduation Rates: New State Data," December 2003, http://www2.edtrust.org/nr/rdonlyres/4DE8F2E0 = 4D08 = 4600 = B3B0 = 013F6DC3865D/0/tellingthetruthgradrates.pdf (April 13, 2005); Office of the Assistant Secretary for Planning and Development, U.S. Department of Health and Human Services,

"Trends in the Well-Being of America's Children and Youth, 1997 Edition," subsection EA1.3, http://aspe.05/dhhs.gov/hsp/97trends/intro=web.htm (March 9, 2005); David Boesel, Nabeel Alsalam, and Thomas M. Smith, "Educational and Labor Market Performance of GED Recipients," part of a report for U.S. Department of Education, Office of Educational Research and Improvement, February 1998, http://www.ed.gov/pubs/GED/apendb5a.html (Decmber 12, 2004); Jay Greene, "The GED Myth," hitp://www.educationreview.homestead.com/2002 GreeneGEDMytb.html (December 12, 2004).

37. Race and gender trends for individuals with 1–3 years of college differed from those for college graduates. In 2000 adult black women had attended college for 1–3 years slightly more often that white women. On the declining economic prospects of young white men, see Annette Bernhardt et al., *Divergent Paths: Economic Mobility in the New American Labor Market* (New York: Sage, 2001).

38. *New York Times*, December 30, 2003, A1. On how socialization and peer group influence affect Mexican American young people in New York City, a case with parallels to the black experience, see Robert C. Smith, "Mexicans: Social, Educational, Economic, and Political Problems and Prospects in New York," in Nancy Foner, *New Immigrants in New York* (New York: Columbia University Press, 2001), 275–300. See also John U. Ogbu, *Minority Education and Caste: The American System in Cross-Cultural Perspective* (New York: Academic Press, 1978).

39. On the expansion of high school enrollment, see Claudia Goldin and Lawrence F. Katz, "Human and Social Capital: The Rise of Secondary Schooling in the United States, 1890 to 1940," *Journal of Economic Perspectives* 13 (Winter 1999): 37–62. There is much research to he done on the precise links between civil rights measures, affirmative action, and the increase of African Americans in higher education. We hypothesize links working in two ways: by improving access and making facilities more appealing or less threatening; and by giving African Americans access to jobs that require advanced education, that is, by increasing the economic payoff of higher education. The reasons for the increase in higher education among white Americans were also operative among blacks, but African Americans needed something more than occupational change and increasing returns to human capital. On the impact of government antidiscrimination and affirmative action programs on African Americans, see Heckman, "Impact of Government on the Economic Status of Black Americans." See also Badgett, "Impact of Affirmative Action."

40. The concept of durable inequality is borrowed from Tilly, *Durable Inequality.*

41. On African American income trends, see Farley, *New American Reality,* 248–53.

42. The first year in which income was reported on the census was 1940. We analyze *earnings* rather than *income* because the latter includes items other than wages or salary, such as investment results, rent, or public transfers. Thus it is a less exact measure of earning capacity, the thing at issue here. On income trends by gender, see Mary Bowler, "Women's Earnings: An Overview," *Monthly Labor Review* 122 (December 1999): 13–21.

43. Farley, *New American Reality,* 253.

44. For an overview of black poverty, see ibid., 253–59.

45. For more detail, see Michael B. Katz and Mark J. Stern, "1940s to the Present," in Gwendolyn Mink and Alice O'Connor, eds., *Poverty in the United States: An Encyclopedia of History, Politics, and Poverty,* 2 vols. (Santa Barbara, Calif.: ABC-CLIO, 2004), 1: 33–47.

46. The earliest cohort identifiable in the data is the one born in 1876–1885, the youngest the one born in 1976–1985. The income of the latter is not a good measure of economic achievement because many in the cohort had only recently entered the labor market. Therefore, that cohort will not be used as the standard against which to measure black income gains. The denominator here is all individuals who report some income. For 1940, income includes only wages and salaries.

47. John Bound and Laura Dresser Bound, "Losing Ground: The Erosion of the Relative Earnings of African American Women During the 1980s," in Browne, ed., *Latinas and African American Women at Work,* 61–104. Relative incomes of black and white women differed by region.

See Corcoran, "Economic Progress of African American Women." On the decline in black men's incomes and labor market position in the 1980s, see John Bound and Richard B. Freeman, "What Went Wrong? The Erosion of the Relative Earnings, and Employment of Young Black Men in the 1980s," *Quarterly Journal of Economics* 107 (February 1992):, 201–32; Carnoy, *Faded Dreams*; and Richard B. Freeman, "Black Economic Progress Aafter 1964: Who Has Gained and Why?," in Sumner Rosen, ed., *Studies in Labor Markets* (Chicago: University of Chicago Press, 1981). In the 1990s boom, the income of blacks started to rise again—the decline in unemployment had more impact on their prospects than on those of whites. Cordelia W. Reimers, "The Effect of Tighter Labor Markets on Unemployment of Hispanics and African Americans: The 1990s Experience," in Cherry and Rodgers, eds., *Prosperity for All?*, 3–49. For non-college-educated African Americans, the impact of the boom was greatest on young men. Richard B. Freeman and William M. Rodgers III, "Area Economic Conditions and the Libor Market Outcomes of Young Men in the 1990s Expansion," ibid., 50–87.

48. Bernhardt et al., *Divergent Paths*; Bennett Harrison and Lucy Gorham Harrison, "What Happened to African-American Wages in the 1980s?," in Galster and Hill, eds., *Metropolis in Black and White*, 56–71.

49. Educational attainment is only a rough proxy for the acquisition of skills. Some social scientists that black/white income gaps reflect differences in skills measured by standardized tests more than years of schooling or discrimination. See Derek A. Neal and William R. Johnson Neal, "The Role of Pre-Market Forces in Black-White Wage Differences," *Journal of Political Economy* 104 (5) (1996): 869–95. The results in the text are based on two general linear-model analyses that include age, full-time, full-year employment, southern and metropolitan residence, year, ethnicity, and educational attainment as independent variables and real personal earnings (in 1990 dollars) as the dependent variable. The summary statistics cited (partial eta coefficients) are from an analysis in which separate runs were completed for each year and gender. Estimated mean earnings arc based on separate analyses for each gender. In addition to the main effects of each variable, the model included two-way effects for education and ethnicity, ethnicity and year, and educational attainment and year. It also included a three-way interaction effect for educational attainment, ethnicity, and year. Residence in the South or in a nonmetropolitan area depressed earnings; working full time for the full year increased them. But here the question is the relation between race and earnings as mediated by sex and education. The population is divided into three groups: those with less than a high school diploma, high school graduates (including those with some college), and college graduates. Income data collected in each census year referred to the earnings in the previous year; in other words, 1940 earnings were those reported for 1939.

50. The partial eta coefficients for ethnicity fell from .08 to .06 for men and from .10 to .01 for women, and the amount of variation accounted for by the entire analysis (multiple R-square) fell from .40 to .23 for men and from .36 to .24 for women. The argument that the influence of race on inequality increased between 1976 and 1983 does not contradict the argument here, which uses a much longer time frame. See A. Silvia Cancio, T. David Evans, and David J. Maume, Jr., "The Declining Significance of Race Reconsidered: Racial Differences in Early Career Wages," *American Sociological Review* 61 (August 1996): 541–56.

51. On the different pathways from marriage and employment to economic security for black and white women, see Andrea E. Willson, "Race and Women's Income Trajectories: Employment, Marriage, and Income Security over the Life Course," *Social Problems* 50 (February 2003): 87–110.

52. Melvin L. Oliver and Thomas M. Shapiro, *Black Wealth/White Wealth: A New Perspective on Racial Inequality* (New York: Routledge, 1997); Dalton Conley, *Being Black, Living in the Red: Race, Wealth, and Social Policy in America* (Berkeley: University of California Press, 1999). See also Francine D. Blau and John W. Graham, "Black-White Differences in Wealth and Asset Composition," *Quarterly Journal of Economics* 105 (May 1990): 321–39.

53. A further screen was incarceration, which lowers the subsequent earnings opportunities

of black men. Pager, "Mark of a Criminal Record." On the cumulative deficits acquired by young black men as A result of job instability, see Marta Tienda and Haya Stier, "Generating Labor Market Inequality: Employment Opportunities and the Accumulation of Disadvantage," *Social Problems* 43 (May 1996): 147–65.

54. For a similar argument about black social structure in Los Angeles, see David M. Grant, Melvin L. Oliver, and Angela D. James, "African Americans: Social and Economic Bifurcation," in Roger Waldinger and Mehdi Bozorgmehr, eds., *Ethnic Los Angeles* (New York: Sage, 1996), 379–411. Bifurcation is also discussed in Heckman, "Impact of Government on the Economic Status of Black Americans." On the black middle class, see Thomas J. Durant, Jr., and Joyce S. Louden, "The Black Middle Class in America: Historical and Contemporary Perspectives," *Phylon* 47 (4) (1986): 253–63. See also Harrison and Harrison, "What Happened to African-American Wages in the 1980s?"; Bart Landry, *The New Black Middle Class* (Berkeley: University of California Press, 1987); William Julius Wilson, *The Declining Significance of Race: Blacks and Changing American Institutions* (Chicago: University of Chicago Press, 1978); and Wilson, *Truly Disadvantaged*.

55. Another screen, hard to see and not visible from census data alone, consists of "glass ceilings" in occupations. See Heather Boushey and Robert Cherry, "Exclusionary Practices and Glass-Ceiling Effects Across Regions: What Does the Current Expansion Tell Us?," in Cherry and Rodgers, *Prosperity for All?*, 160–87.

Commentary

Mark J. Stern

W. E. B. Du Bois certainly was correct when he predicted that race would be the defining issue of the twentieth century. For Penn's School of Social Work, the issue of race cast a long shadow. In the wake of the civil rights movement, the School made racism a central element of its mission and curriculum.

Yet, in the three decades since the School's original commitment to addressing racism, the social realities that gave rise to that commitment changed substantially. On the one hand, the civil right movement and federal court and legislative action did change elements of the American system of racial exclusion. Legal barriers to African American participation in the labor market, the educational system, and other elements of American life fell. For the first time, substantial numbers of African Americans were able to enter the professions and management, mainstream institutions of higher education, and predominantly white neighborhoods. On the other hand, mechanisms of racial exclusion proved to be resilient. Sometimes racism became more subtle while in other ways, most notably the American system of mass incarceration, it became more obvious.

The paper included in this volume, coauthored with Michael Katz and Jamie Fader, attempts to make sense of this new reality, one marked by both change and continuity. Using a detailed analysis of census data, the paper documents how a system of racial exclusion, truly an American apartheid, slowly shifted to a system of racial inequality based on a set of filters that progressively reduced the odds that African Americans could fully participate in American life. Growing up in neighborhoods of concentrated poverty, educated in underfunded systems of public education, denied the social networks that benefit other groups, African Americans typically experience racism not as a cataclysmic event like beating or hanging but as the slow, steady outcomes of a system of racial disparity. For us, this is the "new" African American inequality.

Immigration and the changing nature of social relations also complicated the issue of racism. When the School of Social Work first addressed the issue, we typically framed the issue as one of "black and white." But the mass immigration of the late twentieth century changed the composition of the population as Latin Americans and Asian Americans became its fastest growing elements. The breakdown of legal restrictions on interracial marriage brought new attention to those who had more than one racial identity, a fact recognized for the first time by the census of 2000. Where white supremacists had historically held to a "one-drop" rule in defining the color line, by the end of the century it was more frequently black activists than white supremacists who argued that position.

As racism changed, the way the School of Social Work thought about racism also went through change. While the emphasis on racism remained, increasingly members of the faculty saw racism as one of a number of "isms" that undermine people's full participation in American society. As in the broader society, this effort to broaden our perspective had an uncertain effect on the battle against racial inequality. Did seeing racism as part of a broader set of social exclusions strengthen the case against oppression generally? Or did the multiplicity of oppressions mean that attention formerly directed at racism was diverted to other causes? As the School enters its second century, the role of race in American society and in the School's sense of mission remained very much in the air.

Chapter 27
How Evaluation Research Can Help Reform and Improve the Child Welfare System

Richard J. Gelles

The child welfare system in the United States is in crisis. The media are quick to report the repeated failures of the child welfare system to protect children; and, they have many opportunities to report on such failures. As many as half of the children who are killed by parents or caretakers are killed after the children and their families have come to the attention of the child welfare system (Gelles 1996). Children are also killed in foster care, again while supposedly under the protection and supervision of the child welfare system. As many as 600,000 children, One percent of the population of children under the age of 18 years old, are in foster care on any given day (Tatara 1993); and of the children in foster care, the majority are placed there because of allegations of abuse and neglect. The average age of children entering the foster care system is younger than a decade ago, and younger children remain in the system longer than do older children (Barth, Courtney, Berrick, and Albert 1994). Critics of the child welfare system also claim that too many children are removed from their caretakers and placed into out-of-home care (Guggenheim 1999; Wexler 1990). Not only are many children removed inappropriately, but these children are also disproportionately African-American or minority children. Thus many critics of the child welfare system view the system as oppressive and destructive to minority families (Roberts 1999).

A sign of the crisis of child welfare in the United States is that at least 25 state child welfare agencies are presently operating under a court order as a result of lawsuits arising out the various failings of the agencies (Schwartz and Fishman 1999).

Perhaps the most stinging criticism of the child welfare system was contained in the initial report prepared by the U.S. Advisory Board on Child Abuse and Neglect. The Board declared that child abuse and neglect represented a national emergency. In the Board's words:

The system the nation has developed to respond to child abuse and neglect is failing. It is not a question of acute failure of a single element of the system; there is a chronic and critical multiple organ failure. (U.S. Advisory Board 1990, x)

If this medical metaphor was insufficient to make the case, the Board concluded that the child protective system in the United States is so inadequate that the safety of the nation's children cannot be assured (U.S. Advisory Board 1990, x).

If newspaper reports, legal action, and official board reports are no enough evidence, there is one important statistical fact. In the last five years, virtually all forms of violence, homicide, and abuse have declined in the United States. The Uniform Crime Reports indicate that the national rates of homicide and violent crime have decreased (U.S Department of Justice 1998). Even the rate of youth violence and youth homicide has decreased. Self-report data collected as part of the National Crime Victims Survey (U.S. Department of Justice 1998) also show a decrease in rates of violent crime victimization. Domestic violence rates and intimate homicide rates have also decreased nationally since 1994 (Greenfield et al. 1998). Part of the explanation for these decreases may be more effective crime control and interventions. Part of the reason may be that the five years between 1993 an 1998 have been a period of economic advantage, with rising stock market values, low unemployment rates, and low inflation.

The booming economy and apparent effective strategies to control crime and domestic violence have had less of an effect on child maltreatment. Child abuse and neglect reports, approximately 3,000,000 per year, have leveled off (U.S. Department of Health and Human Services 1996). Reports of sexual abuse have declined; however, there has been no overall decline in the rates of maltreatment comparable to decreases of rates of violent crime. Child fatality numbers have remained steady at around 1,200 per year (National Committee to Prevent Child Abuse 1998).

By any indicator, as the century closes, the United States child welfare system continues to be unable to assure the safety of children.

Why the Crisis? The Usual Suspects

The crisis of child welfare is not new. Child welfare agencies have been under siege for the last three decades. The implementation of mandatory child abuse reporting in the mid- to late 1960s resulted in an increase of reports submitted to agencies that were not staffed to handle the increased number of allegations of child maltreatment. In the years after the institution of mandatory reporting, definitions of child abuse and neglect were broadened, resulting in even more reports. Public awareness campaigns generated more reports, and technology, such as toll free telephone lines, made it easier to file reports. Agencies were expected to respond to maltreatment reports quickly. Here again technology, such as pagers and cell phones, created the possibility that reports could be responded to rapidly.

Of course, child welfare agency staffing never kept pace with either the number of reports or the expectation that reports would be investigated quickly. Not only were there too few child welfare workers, in absolute numbers, but the training of the staff was far below the level needed to respond to the complex and difficult nature of child maltreatment reports.

When a tragedy or crisis hits a local, county, or state child welfare agency, the response typically falls under one or more of the "round up the usual suspects" explanations and proposed solutions:

- *More Money.* We have too little money; we need more. Funding for child welfare never kept pace with the rising number of reports and the complexity of child abuse and neglect cases. Thus, child welfare agency administrators are constantly trying to secure sufficient budget allocations to hire and train staff and develop and implement appropriate policies and interventions. To a certain extent, broadened definitions, technology, and public awareness campaigns bolstered the case for more funds by generating more reports, but there has always been a significant gap between resources and caseloads.
- *More Staff.* As funds were always short, so, too, agency administrators argued that they had too few workers to meet the demands of child welfare. When a crisis or tragedy became public, the nearly automatic response was to request an increase in child protective staff. While agencies rarely received what they believed to be adequate staffing, staffing tended to increase following a tragedy or crisis.
- *More Training.* More staff would allow caseloads to be decreased, so that child welfare staff did not have to carry 40 to 60 cases each. In the unusual event that caseloads would meet the desired level of about 15 to 20 cases per worker (Child Welfare League of America 1993), the child welfare problem was not resolved. New and old child welfare workers often receive only the most minimal pre-service training before they are assigned a caseload. It is not unusual for a child welfare worker to get 20 hours of training before being assigned a full caseload. In-service training is also minimal. Thus, agency workers and director would often respond to a crisis with a call for new and more training for workers.
- *Blame the Judges and/or the Laws.* The final "usual suspect" is the legal system, or "the judges." Child welfare workers and administrators frequently identify their core constraint as the legal system and action or inaction of the judges. Workers claim the law requires them to make "every possible effort" to keep families together. They also claim that judges ignore caseworkers' recommendations. Legal reform and judicial training is the solution, many child welfare critics claim.

A case can be made for each and all of the above arguments. The child welfare system is understaffed, under-funded, under-trained, and limited by legal constraints and judicial decisions. Yet, each of the above problems has been addressed over the past three decades with little measurable impact. As important as the "usual suspects" are they do not constitute the real "offender" that causes the child welfare crisis.

The Real Failures

Clearly, rounding up the usual suspects—funding, staffing, training, the legal system—has not eased the crisis of child welfare. The national emergency and the "multiple organ failure" described nearly a decade ago still exist.

I would propose that the child welfare system's problems arise less from money, staff, and management and more from lack of rigorously evaluated services and interventions. This section examines the "standard" interventions and programs that make up the child welfare system. The following section summarizes what evidence exists for the effectiveness of the standard interventions.

The Standard Interventions

Mandatory Reporting. When Kempe, Silverman, Steele, Droegmueller, and Silver (1962) wrote about what they called the "battered child syndrome," a key problem with protecting children was the fact that severe child abuse was either unrecognized or not responded to by the key sentinels—physicians, nurses, and hospital personnel. Kempe himself championed the development of mandatory reporting laws that would require key medical, school, criminal justice, and social service personnel to report suspected cases of child maltreatment to a central authority. In order to encourage reporting, the central authority was to be child welfare agencies. While the police could have been the agency to receive reports, Kempe and others felt that making child abuse a crime would deter mandatory reporters from filing reports, especially reports where there was no clear evidence of an intentional inflicted injury.

The United States Children's Bureau played a pivotal role in developing model child abuse reporting laws (Nelson 1984). The federal Child Abuse Prevention and Treatment Act of 1974 required states to conform to federal standards, including standards for reporting, in order to receive funds from the newly created National Center for Child Abuse and Neglect. In the space of ten years, mandatory reporting became the cornerstone of the nation's child welfare system.

Investigation. Once a report was received by a state, county, or local child welfare agency, the report would be screened and if the allegation met the screening standards (i.e., the suspected abuse met the state's legal criteria for maltreatment and there was sufficient evidence to initiate an investigation-names, address, etc.), the report would be assigned for investigation.

According to the National Child Abuse and Neglect Data System (U.S. Department of Health and Human Services 1997), states received 2,025,956 reports of child maltreatment, representing just over 3 million individual child victims. Of the 970,000 child victims for whom maltreatment was indicated or substantiated and for whom there were data on type of maltreatment, 229,332 experienced physical abuse, 500,032 experienced neglect, and 119,397 experienced sexual abuse. From the reports, about 1,625,000 investigations were conducted. A main focus of the investigations was to determine whether the reports were substantiated and required an intervention. Thirty-four percent of the more than one and one-half million investigations resulted in the report being substantiated or indicated (U.S. Department of Health and Human Services 1998).

Responses. In theory, at least, the child welfare system has a varied toolbox with which to respond to confirmed or substantiated cases of child maltreatment. In terms of child protection, child welfare agencies have the ability to obtain ex parte orders allowing the child welfare department to take the custody and control of endangered children. Child welfare agencies can also petition to have a child's control and custody for a longer period of time. Title IVE of the Social Security Act of 1935 created an open-ended entitlement that provides federal matching funds to states to pay for out-of-home care for dependent children. States are required to match the federal share. In 1996 the federal share of Title IVE was $3 billion (Green Book 1996).

For nearly the last twenty years, The Adoption Assistance and Child Welfare Act of 1980 (PL 96-272) required states, as a condition of receiving Title IVE funding, to make "reasonable efforts" to keep children with their families, or return them if they have been removed. This law enforces a long tradition of the child welfare system focusing its resources and responses at supporting and preserving families. The resources include hard and soft services. Hard services include house-keeping assistance, parenting classes, medical help, day care, and even housing. Soft services include case management, advocacy, therapy, and counseling.

Sensitive about the number of children in out-of-home care and the cost, many states implemented Intensive Family Preservation Services in the late 1970s and through the 1980s and 1990s.

Intensive Family Preservation Services were designed to be an alternative to the "business as usual" attempts at providing families resources and services. In the Intensive Family Preservation Services model, the essential service is short-term crisis intervention designed to prevent the placement of a child outside of the home. The core goal is to maintain the child safely in the home or facilitate a safe and lasting reunification. Services are meant to be provided in the client's home. The number of sessions is variable, but unlike traditional services, intensive services are available seven days a week, 24 hours a day. The length of the service is brief, typically fixed at a certain number of weeks. Caseworkers are able to deliver intensive services because they carry small caseloads, often as few as two or three cases. The actual services delivered may be the same as the traditional child welfare services, but their delivery and intensity is different.

Of note is how few families who come to the attention of the child welfare system actually receive any services. One study of 169 investigations found that 59.7 percent of substantiated cases were offered no services other than placement (Meddin and Hansen 1985). For those cases that were offered some kind of services, 13 percent received placement and 11 percent counseling (Meddin and Hansen 1985). A second study found that 56 percent of all indicated cases were closed on the same day they were officially substantiated (Salovitz and Keys 1988). While closing a case on the same day it is substantiated does not necessarily mean no services were offered or delivered, it does mean that no follow-up or monitoring took place after the case was substantiated and services were offered and/or provided.

Summary. In summary, the standard interventions or the typical "tool box" of the child welfare system consist of: (1) An investigation; (2) Some form of counseling or tangible services; and, (3) Placement of a child with monitoring and services.

This seems like a relatively limited toolbox, but the range and depth of the standard intervention is of less concern than how well the existing tools work to protect children and assist families.

The Evaluation Data

It is not a surprise that efforts to respond to, prevent, and treat child maltreatment advanced at a much faster pace than efforts to evaluate the positive and negative effects of both the standard and innovative responses to the problems of child maltreatment. Once it was clear that the abuse and neglect of children were far more extensive than commonly believed, activities to treat and prevent the problem expanded rapidly. In addition, newly implemented, innovative interventions are not good candidates for scientific evaluations (National Research Council, 1998). Innovative programs often begin with a common sense or discipline-based notion of how to respond, and the response changes and is modified based on the experience and feedback of those involved in delivering and managing the intervention. Some times a single approach is changed, modified, and altered; other times a multi-pronged effort may add or delete components. Programs and interventions require an opportunity to evolve and mature before they can be properly evaluated. Maturity is important for three reasons. First, the often-amorphous nature of an innovative treatment may result in a "black box" evaluation, whereby the so-called "treatment" cannot be defined or categorized. Thus, even if the evaluation demonstrates that the "treatment works," it may not be clear what exactly the "treatment" was. Second, the time needed to "ramp up" the program may mean that in the early stages, the program offers a smaller "dose" of the ideal intervention and/or the program may not be delivering the actual intervention as planned to all clients. An evaluation in an early stage may fail to find effectiveness of the new program, not because the program is ineffective, but because the program is not yet being delivered as designed. Finally, innovative programs often begin with small staffs and small caseloads. The initial dose of the treatment may be quite minimal. Small sample sizes and low dosages may result in falsely accepting the null hypothesis (that the program has no significant effects).

Evaluation Studies

Notwithstanding all of the above caveats, it is surprising that almost forty years after the modern discovery of the problem of child maltreatment there are so few sound studies of the effectiveness of efforts to prevent and treat child maltreatment.

In 1994, the National Academy of Sciences established the Committee on the Assessment of Family Violence Interventions. One of the five charges to the Committee was to:

Characterize what is known about both prevention efforts and specific interventions dealing with family violence, including an assessment of what has been learned about the strengths and limitations of each approach. (National Research Council 1998, 17)

After many debates, the Committee chose the following criteria to use when selecting evaluation studies for detailed analysis to meet the above charge:

1. The evaluation involved a program intervention that was designed to treat or prevent some aspect of child maltreatment, domestic violence, or elder abuse.

2. The evaluation was conducted between 1980 and 1996.
3. The evaluation used an experimental design or quasi-experimental design and included measurement tools and outcomes related to family violence; and
4. The evaluation included a comparison group as part of the study design (National Research Council 1998, 21).

While appropriate standards of evidence for evaluation research, these criteria, especially criteria 2 and 4, were far below the "Gold Standard" for evaluation research, in that the criteria did not require that groups be randomly assigned.

For the period 1980 to 1996, the Committee's staff was able to identify a total of 114 evaluation studies that met the above four criteria. The search included published and unpublished studies, although the majority of the 114 studies had been published.

Of the 114 studies, 78 evaluated some aspect of the prevention and treatment of child maltreatment. Fifty studies evaluated social service interventions, four studies evaluated legal interventions, and 24 studies evaluated health care interventions.

While obvious, it is worth noting that the forty-year effort to prevent and treat the maltreatment of children yields only 78 studies that met rather minimum design standards for evaluation research.

The explanation for the paucity of evaluation research can no longer be blamed on the newness of the enterprise, as efforts to prevent and treat child abuse are at least 40, if not 200, years old. The justification is not lack of funds, given that in 1996 the federal and state governments spent nearly $10 billion on efforts to treat child maltreatment (Child Welfare League of America 1999).

The Interventions Evaluated

In the "social service category" the programs evaluated included child-parent enrichment programs, parent training, network support services, home helpers, school-based sexual abuse prevention, intensive family preservation services, child placement services, and home health visitors. "Legal interventions" evaluated included: court-mandated treatment for child abuse offenders, court mandated treatment emphasizing child management skills, and in-patient treatment for sex offenders. Evaluations of "health care interventions" included: an identification protocol for high-risk mothers, mental health services for child victims; and home health visitor/family support programs. The largest number of evaluations was of school-based sexual abuse prevention programs and intensive family preservation programs.

Noteworthy in this summary is that almost all of the interventions or programs that were evaluated were innovative programs that were alternatives to the standard package of interventions and programs offered by child welfare systems. Interventions that were not evaluated using scientifically appropriate designs included mandatory reporting, investigations, and foster care, kinship care and other out-of-home placements. In short, not a single one of the main components of the child welfare system had been subjected to a scientific evaluation between 1980 and 1996; this, despite the fact that billions of dollars are spent each year on these interventions and despite the continued and mounting criticisms of the failings of the system.

The Findings

The one commonality of the 78 evaluations of child abuse and neglect prevention and treatment programs was, in scientific terms, a failure to reject the null hypothesis. While it may be too harsh a judgment to say these programs have not and do not work as intended, the National Research Council report did come to the following conclusion regarding social service interventions:

Social service interventions designed to improve parenting practices and provide family support have not yet demonstrated that they have the capacity to reduce or prevent abusive or neglectful behaviors significantly over time for the majority of families who have been reported for child maltreatment. (National Research Council 1998, 118)

With regard to intensive family preservation services, here, too, there was little evidence that such services resolve the underlying dysfunction that precipitated the crisis. Nor was there evidence that such services improve child well-being or family functioning.

What little research there was on out-of-home placement found that children who reside in foster care fare neither better nor worse than those who remain in homes in which maltreatment occurred.

While some programs and interventions show promise, the promise is not yet evident in empirical data that confirm that the programs actually attain their goals and objectives.

In the legal area, the main child maltreatment legal intervention, mandatory reporting, has yet to be evaluated.

Finally, there was positive and promising data from evaluations of health care interventions. Home visitation represents one of the most carefully evaluated and promising opportunities for the prevention of child maltreatment. Research reported subsequent to the National Research Council report confirmed the Committee's assessment-home visitation has demonstrated long-term effectiveness (Kitzman et al., 1997; Olds et al. 1997). Subsequent to the National Research Council's review, a review of more recent evaluations of home visitation programs concluded with a more modest and less sanguine finding. The evaluations conducted by Olds and his colleagues of their original intervention in Elmira, New York, found clear and consistent evidence of fewer substantiated child maltreatment reports among those receiving the full complement of home health visits. However, evaluations of the Hawaii Healthy Start Program and Healthy Families America found no differences in the rates of reported child abuse and neglect (Gomby, Culross, and Behrman 1999).

Why So Little Evidence of Program Effectiveness?

There are a number of reasons why research on child maltreatment prevention and treatment programs is generally unable to find evidence for program effectiveness.

First and most pessimistically, it is possible that the programs and services, while well-intended, are, in and of themselves, not effective. It is possible that the theories (mostly informal and untested) behind the programs and services may be inaccurate or inadequate and the programs themselves, therefore, may not be addressing the key causal mechanisms that cause child maltreatment. Second, the programs or services may be effective, but they may not be implemented properly by the agencies and workers that are using the programs. For example, when the evaluation data for the Illinois Family First program were made public (Schuerman, Rzepnicki, and Littell 1994), the data failed to support the hypotheses that the program reduced out-of-home placement, costs, and/or improved family functioning. An initial reaction was that there was considerable variation in how intensive family preservation was being implemented at the different sites in Illinois. The overall implementation was also not true to the "Homebuilders" model of intensive family preservation. Thus, the lack of support for the effectiveness of the services was blamed on the programs not being properly implemented. A third plausible explanation may be that the theory behind the program may be accurate and the program itself may be appropriate, but the "dose" may be too small. This applies to many interventions designed to prevent and treat all forms of family and intimate violence and is not unique to child maltreatment services. The National Academy of Sciences (National Research Council 1998) concluded that the duration and intensity of the mental health and social support service needed to influence behaviors that result from or contribute to family violence may be greater than initially estimated. With regard to social service interventions, the Committee opined that:

The intensity of the parenting, mental health, and social support services required may be greater than initially estimated in order to address the fundamental sources of instability, conflict, stress, and violence that occur repeatedly over time in the family environment, especially in disadvantaged communities. (National Research Council 1998, 118)

Thus, it is likely that more services are necessary or the length of the interventions should be increased.

With regard to theory, there are other plausible explanations for the apparent ineffectiveness of child maltreatment interventions. Many current child welfare programs assume that abuse and maltreatment are at one end of a continuum of parenting behavior. However, it is possible that this model of abusive behavior is inaccurate. It may be that there are distinct types of abusers (Gelles 1991, 1996). Abuse may not arise out of a surplus of risk factors and a deficit of resources, but rather, there may be distinct psychological and social attributes of those caretakers who inflict serious and/or fatal injuries compared to caretakers who commit less severe acts of maltreatment. If there are different types of offenders and different underlying causes for different types of abuse, it is reasonable to assume that a "one size fits all" intervention or policy will not be effective across the board. Irrespective of the model of abuse, to date evaluations of interventions demonstrate little impact. Thus, the problem is not trying to make "one size fit all" but finding any size that fits.

Another problem with the child welfare system is the crude way behavior change is conceptualized and measured. Behavior change is thought to be a one-step process; one simply changes from one form of behavior to another. For example, if one is an alcohol or substance abuser, then change involves stopping the use of alcohol or drugs. If one stops, but then begins again, then the change has not successfully occurred. A second assumption is that maltreating parents or caretakers all want to change-either to avoid legal and social sanctions or because they have an intrinsic motivation to be caring parents. As a result, those who design and implement child abuse and neglect interventions assume that all, or at least most, parents, caretakers and families are ready and able to change their maltreating behavior. Of course, the reverse may also be true-that abusive and neglectful parents do not want to change and/or cannot change, and this explains the negative results of evaluation research.

However, research on behavior change clearly demonstrates that change is not a one-step process (Prochaska and DiClemente 1982, 1983, 1984; Prochaska, Norcross, and DiClemente 1994). Rather, changing behavior is a dynamic process and one progresses through a number of stages, including relapse, in trying to modify behavior. There are also cognitive aspects to behavior change that can be measured.

One of the reasons why child welfare interventions may have such modest success rates is that most interventions are "action" programs. These programs are often provided to individuals and families in what Prochaska and his colleagues call the pre-contemplator or contemplation stage of change (Prochaska DiClemente 1982, 1983, 1984). This is what others may refer to as denial or ambivalence about the need for change. For interventions to be more successful, there is the need to balance readiness for change with the immediate risk in a particular family (Gelles, 1996).

Why So Few Interventions?

Before turning to the issue of how to move ahead and use evaluation research to help improve the child welfare system, it is important to consider why there has been so little evaluation research on child welfare interventions and, equally important, why there has been so little emphasis on carrying out evaluation research. Obviously, the first answer to this question is money. Although public and private expenditures for child welfare in the United States is in the $10 billion to $15 billion dollar range, comparatively speaking, this is not much money. Michael Petit, Deputy Director of the Child Welfare League of America, points out that $15 billion dollars per year for child welfare is half of what the nation spends on pizza (Petit 1999). Given the chronic gap between the demands on the child welfare system and the system's resources, it is not surprising that funds for research are minimal. Federal and foundation funds for child maltreatment are also relatively small, and those funds that are available are allocated for programs rather than research. With 3 million reports, 1.5 million investigations, 600,000 children in out-of-home care, and 1,200 child abuse and neglect fatalities annually, it seems obvious that scarce resources would be allocated toward "doing something," rather than "studying something."

But, when nearly forty years of "doing something" has not yielded much in the way of evidence that the "something" does any good, the answer to the question of "why so little research?" must be more than just limited funds.

An alternative answer to "lack of funds," is that those who work and administer the child welfare system are reluctant to evaluate what they do and equally reluctant to take heed of what evaluations have been carried out. In the latter case, Senator Daniel Moynihan proves the point of reluctance to take heed of results. Moynihan (1996) describes his experience chairing the Senate Finance Committee when the committee was, in 1993, considering an administration proposal to spend $930 million on family preservation. This program was proposed during a time when the Finance Committee was charged with reducing federal spending by $500 billion. Moynihan recounts that he wrote to Dr. Laura D'Andrea Tyson, then chair of the President's Council of Economic Advisors, saying that after hearings on family preservation, he had followed up on administration claims that data existed that showed that family preservation was effective. Moynihan checked out two citations offered by the administration that supposedly demonstrated the effectiveness of family preservation. The citation Moynihan obtained stated that "solid proof that family preservation services can effect a state's overall placement rate is still lacking" (Moynihan 1996, 48). Despite finding no data to support the claim for the effectiveness of family preservation services, the bill passed with Moynihan's support. Nearly $1 billion was spent on family preservation services in the next four years, and the program was re-authorized with more funding in 1997. Interestingly, between 1993 and 1997 when the legislation was re-authorized, the published results of evaluations of intensive family preservations programs also failed to find evidence of the effectiveness of this service (Heneghan, Horwitz, and Leventhal 1996).

Part of the reason for the rejection or ignoring of data or findings that fail to support the hypothesis that a program or service is effective, is that caseworkers and administrators work in an ideographic world. By this I mean that the worldview of the child welfare system is through the lens of individual cases. Based on 30 years of personal experience, in both the field and classroom, it is my impression that caseworkers and administrators do not use a nomothetic paradigm (paradigm that looks for patterns across cases) and seek patterns. Their world is made up of individual cases and the failures and successes of those cases. Thus, effectiveness of a program is not to be found in aggregate evaluation data, but in individual case records and experiences. Thus, in many ways, the child welfare system operates on the basis of "intervention by anecdote," both good and bad anecdotes. In response to research that fails to support a claim for program or service effectiveness, workers and administrators can and do summon up a case or many cases where the service was effective. In response to media accounts of failures, caseworkers and administrators know that there are many unreported cases of program or service effectiveness.

Intervention by anecdote is bound to fail. To put much too fine a point on this issue, a blind squirrel will eventually find an acorn. That a single case or a number of cases are helped by a service proves nothing, and is not justification for continued support for and funding of a service.

The larger problem is that evaluation research on child welfare interventions fails to find effects for most programs and interventions that have been evaluated. As Moynihan pointed out in his discussion of data on family preservation, the consistent pattern since the mid-1960s is that evaluation studies find no effects, few effects, or negative effects (Moynihan 1996, 49). This he called "Rossi's Iron Law." The law is: "If there is any empirical law that is emerging from the past decade of widespread evaluation research activities, it is that the expected value for any measured effect of a social program is zero" (Moynihan 1996, 49).

Whether they know about Rossi's Iron Law or not, agency directors and administrators must be concerned that an evaluation will conform to Rossi's law and their program will be found wanting in terms of scientific data. Rather than take a chance that a program that helps some people (policy by anecdote) will lose its funding, administrators resist having programs evaluated. If a program is evaluated, the evaluation is typically poorly funded and inadequately designed and implemented. Poor funding and an inadequate design actually enhance the likelihood of proving Rossi's Iron Law, thus creating a vicious circle that leads to no evaluations or even more poorly funded and poorly designed evaluations.

Another reason why some interventions are not evaluated is that many components of the "standard intervention," such as mandatory reporting and appointing a guardian ad litem, are mandated by law. It would be somewhat pointless to evaluate a program or intervention component that could not be changed or even modified.

Another explanation for the lack of evaluation research is that what is considered the "gold standard" for evaluation research, a randomized experiment, is often considered impractical, impossible, or unethical by agency and program directors. The notion that one group will be randomly deprived of a service, even a service with no proven value, is considered completely unethical and inappropriate. Even when an agency agrees to random assignment, they may fail to understand exactly what random assignment means. In such cases, workers may violate the random assignment protocol in order to assure that certain clients get what the workers think are effective services (see Schuerman et al. 1994, for an example of this in the Illinois Family First evaluation).

Sometimes the "gold standard" simply cannot be used. For example, in an attempt to evaluate a Children's Advocacy Center in Rhode Island we found that the program had achieved statewide status and a comparison or control group simply did not exist (Youngblood and Gelles 1997). Moreover, the essential aspect of the intervention, keeping interviews with children to a minimum, constrained our ability to collect pre- and post-test measures from the children. Any interviews that we would conduct with the children would have contaminated the actual intervention. To resolve this problem, we relied on administrative data from the agencies involved in the cases as well as reports from parents and guardians of the children.

Finally, the innovations in the prevention and treatment of child maltreatment move much faster than evaluation research. Thus, for example, by the time a sufficient body of evaluation research on intensive family preservation services had been accumulated, intensive family preservation services were no longer the new innovative intervention. Researchers presenting their data on intensive family preservation services were told this was no longer important, as child welfare had discovered and was implementing "family conferencing."

To a certain extent, foundations are partially culpable for the pattern of limited evaluations because their priorities are typically to fund promising new programs. While foundations do often require evaluation research of their funded programs, they often promote promising results prior to the completion of the evaluation research. Some foundations rapidly move from one "cure du jour" to the next, without properly evaluating any new program.

Conclusion: The Solution

To a certain extent, the solution is rather simple—do more evaluation research and do it better. The crisis of the child welfare system will not and cannot be resolved until such time as we have some idea of what interventions work for what children and families, and under what conditions. Forty years of intervention by anecdote and the resistance to research and evaluation research have yielded an expensive and complex system that fails to provide basic protection to America's vulnerable and dependent children.

There are three basic steps that need to be accomplished in order to allow for better evaluation research. (1) The first step was articulated by the National Research Council's Committee on Assessing Family Violence Interventions. The Committee pleaded for *more collaborations between researchers and programs* (National Research Council 1998). Collaboration does not mean that program administrator throw open their doors and allow researchers to implement "gold standard" randomized field experiments. It means a genuine collaboration where both researchers and program operators understand the benefits and risks of evaluation research and both endeavor to design appropriate scientific evaluations. Such collaborations are not forged by having both groups work as partners for only 14 days in responding to requests for proposals. Sound collaborations require both groups learning about one another's language, assumptions, and paradigms. Such interactions are needed to establish the basic trust that must exist before a sound evaluation project can be put into place. (2) A second recommendation is that *funding—government, corporate and foundation—should eventually be based on accountability of a program.* In order to accomplish this, government agencies and foundations must set aside funds for evaluation research. Funding should be available at the outset of a program so that appropriate baseline data can be obtained. Funding needs to be adequate to allow for a proper design sample. It is a relatively easy task for government agencies to include set-asides equal to 10 percent of program costs for evaluation research and it is also relatively easy to include prescriptions for acceptable designs to be used to evaluate programs and interventions. (3) Finally, *evaluation researchers must be flexible in their designs to accommodate and accept the realities of implementing and operating prevention and treatment programs for child maltreatment.* There will be many instances where practical and ethical issues constrain the ability to field a "gold standard" evaluation. These situations call for creative and innovative evaluation designs. For example, we could not use a "gold standard" design to evaluate Child

Advocacy Centers. Yet, such centers need to be evaluated, as they have become a well-established and well-funded component of the child welfare system. It is not yet known whether Child Advocacy Centers actually produce the desired results of reducing trauma for children and increasing successful persecutions. Our approach in this one case was to use a dose response design, whereby we assessed outcome in terms of the "dose" of the intervention and the goodness of fit of the actual intervention to the theoretical model (Youngblood and Gelles 1997).

The crisis of the child welfare system will have to be addressed. We cannot continue to have 1 percent of America's children in foster care, 3 million reports of maltreatment each year, 1,000 homicides, and countless lawsuits, tragedies, and controversies plaguing the system. Rounding up the "usual suspects" as an attempt to fix the system has not worked. No amount of funding can rescue a system that cannot answer the basic question of whether anything it does is effective. It is time to find out what works, for whom, and under what conditions.

Reprinted from Richard J. Gelles, How evaluation research can help reform and improve the child welfare system. *Journal of Aggression, Maltreatment & Trauma* 4 (2000): 7–28. Reprinted by permission.

References

Barth, R. P., M. Courtney, J. D. Berrick, and V. Albert (1994). *From Child Abuse to Permanency Planning: Child Welfare Services Pathways and Placements.* New York: Aldine de Gruyter.

Child Welfare League of America (1993). *Recommended Caseload/Workload Standards: Excerpted from CWLA Standards for Child Welfare Practice.* Washington, D.C.: Child Welfare League of America.

——— (1999). *Child Abuse and Neglect: A Look at the States.* 1998 CWLA state book. Washington, D.C.: CWLA Press.

Gelles, R. J. (1991). Physical violence, child abuse, and child homicide: A continuum of violence, or distinct behaviors? *Human Nature* 2: 59–72.

——— (1996). *The Book of David: How Preserving Families Can Cost Children's Lives.* New York: Basic Books.

Gomby, D. S., P. L. Culross, and R. E. Behrman (1999). Home visiting: Recent program evaluations—analysis and recommendations. The Future of Children, 9, 4–26. Green Book (1996). *Background material and data on major programs in the jurisdiction of the Committee on Ways and Means.* Washington, D.C.: U.S. Government Printing Office.

Greenfield, L. A., M. R. Rand, D. Craven, P. A. Klaus, C. A. Perkins, C. Ringel, G. Warchol, C. Maston, and J. A. Fox (1998). *Violence by Intimates: Analysis of Data, Crimes by Current or Former Spouses, Boyfriends, and Girlfriends.* Washington, D.C.: U.S. Department of Justice, Office of Justice Programs.

Guggenheim, M. (1999). Established and emerging rights: Exploring juvenile rights under the Constitution. Discussion at University of Pennsylvania Journal of Constitutional Law, Second Annual Symposium, Philadelphia.

Heneghan, A. M., S. M. Horwitz, and J. M. Leventhal (1996). Evaluating intensive family preservation programs: A methodological review. *Pediatrics* 97: 535–42.

Kempe, C. H., F. N. Silverman, B. E. Steele, W. Droegmueller, and H. K. Silver (1962). The battered child syndrome. *Journal of the American Medical Association* 282: 107–12.

Kitzman, H., D. L. Olds, C. N. Henderson, R. Cole, R. Tatelbaum, K. M. McConnodiie, K. Sidora,

D. W. Luckey, D. Shaver, K. Engelhardt, D. James, and K. Barnard (1997). Effect of prenatal and infancy home visitation by nurses on pregnancy outcomes, childhood injuries, and repeated childbearing. *Journal of the American Medical Association* 276: 644–52.

Meddin, D., and I. Hansen (1985). The services provided during a child abuse and/or neglect case investigation and the barriers that exist to service provision. *Child Abuse and Neglect* 9: 175–82.

Moynihan, D. P. (1996). *Miles to Go: A Personal History of Social Policy*. Cambridge, Mass.: Harvard University Press.

National Committee to Prevent Child Abuse (1998). *Current Trends in Child Abuse Reporting and Fatalities: The Results of the 1997 Annual Survey*. Chicago: National Committee to Prevent Child Abuse.

National Research Council (1998). *Violence in Families: Assessing Prevention and Treatment Programs*. Washington, D.C.: National Academy Press.

Nelson, R. J. (1984). *Making an Issue of Child Abuse: Political Agenda Setting for Social Problems*. Chicago: University of Chicago Press.

Olds, D., J. Eckenrode, C. R. Henderson, H. Kitzman, J. Powers, R. Cole, K. Sidora, P. Morris, L. Pettit, and D. Luckey (1997). Long-term effects of home visitation on maternal life course and child abuse and neglect: Fifteen-year follow-up of a randomized trial. *Journal of the American Medical Association* 278: 637–48.

Petit, M. (1999). Comments at the National Institute of Justice Law Enforcement Response to Child Maltreatment Strategic Planning Meeting, Washington, D.C., March 15.

Prochaska, J. O., and C. C. DiClemente (1982). Toward a more integrative model of change. *Psychotherapy: Theory, Research and Practice* 19: 276–88.

——— (1983). Stages and processes of self-change in smoking: Toward an integrative model of change. *Journal of Consulting Clinical Psychology* 5: 390–95.

——— (1984). *The Transtheoretical Approach: Crossing Traditional Boundaries of Change*. Homewood: Dow Jones/Irwin.

Prochaska, J. O., J. C. Norcross, and C. C. DiClemente (1994). *Changing for Good*. New York: Morrow.

Roberts, D. (1999). Is there justice in children s rights? The critique of federal family preservation policy. Paper presented at the University of Pennsylvania Journal of Constitutional Law, Second Annual Symposium, Established and Emerging Rights: Exploring Juvenile Rights Under the Constitution, Philadelphia.

Salovitz, R., and D. Keys (1988). Is child protective service still a service? *Protecting Children* 5: 17–23.

Schuerman, J., T. L. Rzepnicki, and J. H. Littell (1994). *Putting families first: An Experiment in Family Preservation*. New York: Aldine de Gruyter.

Schwartz, I. M., and G. Fishman (1999). *Kids Raised by the Government*. Westport, Conn.: Praeger.

Tatara, T. (1993). U.S. child substitute care flow data for FY 1992 and current trends in the state child substitute care populations. VCIS Research Notes, 9, 1–11. Washington DC: American Public Welfare Association.

U.S. Advisory Board on Child Abuse and Neglect (1990). *Child Abuse and Neglect: Critical First Steps in Response to a National Emergency*. Washington, D.C.: U.S. Government Printing Office.

U.S. Department of Health and Human Services (1996). *Study Findings: Study of the national Incidence and Prevalence of Child Abuse and Neglect: 1993*. Washington, D.C.: U.S. Government Printing Office.

U.S. Department of Health and Human Services (1997). *Child Maltreatment 1996: Reports from the States to the National Center on Child Abuse*. Washington, D.C.: U.S. Government Printing Office.

——— (1998). *Child Maltreatment 1997: Reports from the States to the National Center on Child Abuse*. Washington, D.C.: U.S. Government Printing Office.

U.S. Department of Justice (1998). *Uniform Crime Reports for the United States, 1997*. Washington, D.C.: U.S. Department of Justice, Federal Bureau of Investigation.

Wexler, R. (1990). *Wounded Innocents: The Real Victims of the War Against Children*. Buffalo, N.Y.: Prometheus Press.

Youngblood, J., and R. J. Gelles (1997). Measuring the impact of all intervention on tire well-being of victims of sexual abuse. Paper presented at the Fifth International Family Violence Research Conference, Durham, N.H.

Commentary

Richard J. Gelles

At the time I published my first article on child abuse and neglect (Gelles 1973), it seemed unlikely that my career would eventually lead to a position in a school of social work. My doctorate is in sociology and my training and mentoring put me on an academic path as a logical positivist who believed in theory-driven research. My initial publication, "Child Abuse as Psychopathology: A Sociological Critique and Reformulation," critiqued the existing psychopathological theoretical framework used to explain and treat child maltreatment, and, using the same data presented in the published work at the time, argued that the existing data were much more supportive of a sociological, rather than a psychopathological explanation for child abuse and neglect.

Ironically, and perhaps foreshadowing my future career path, the scholar whose work was most consistent with my theoretical framework was David Gil, a MSW ('58) and DSW ('63) from the School of Social Work at the University of Pennsylvania. Although David and I would have our professional differences of opinion, David has been one of my role models for more than thirty years.

The role of a logical positivist is to develop theory that is the most parsimonious with the available data, and then test the theory through new empirical research. The first decade of my career was spent developing and testing theories. While I kept my focus on my research and theory construction, a new noise was infiltrating my thinking. Whenever I presented at a professional meeting or conference, most of the questions that followed my presentations came from clinicians—mostly social workers. Their basic question was, based on my research, "what do I think is the most effective means of intervening and helping families and protecting children?"

I was, by training and inclination, quite unable to answer this question. My assumption, which I now know was entirely naïve, was that clinicians and practitioners would, on their own, be able to apply the results of research to clinical practice.

After many years of being unable to answer clinically related questions, I thought perhaps the best thing to do was to try to apply the results of research to clinical practice on my own. Toward that end, I sought and received a fellowship with the Family Development Study at Children's Hospital of Boston. The fellowship was designed to recruit researchers and provide them supervised clinical training. The goal of the fellowship would be for researchers to develop more clinically relevant research. The head of the fellowship program was pediatrician Eli Newberger. In the 1970s Eli emerged as one of the leading hospital-based scholar/clinicians in the field of child abuse and neglect. My clinical duties involved carrying out clinical assessments for children and parents as well as carrying a modest clinical caseload. I also worked with the Family Development Study's multidisciplinary outpatient assessment team and the child abuse team. My clinical activities were supervised by psychiatrist and social worker Betty Singer. True to form, I published the results of my one-year fellowship in the clinical trenches (Gelles 1982).

In the next decade, logical positivism took a back seat to clinically-relevant questions. I even changed my academic appointment at the University of Rhode Island and took a joint appointment in the Department of Psychology working with doctoral students and faculty in clinical psychology.

In keeping with the Socratic Method, answers to questions generated more questions. As I struggled to link research to practice, I became more aware of how little link there was between research and social policy. The crucible from which my new interest would be developed was participating in the review of a child death. The fatality review was led by the Rhode Island Office of the Child Advocate. My initial assumption when beginning the review was that the caseworkers had failed to use the existing knowledge base in their casework with a mother and father who had severely abused their newborn daughter. In the end, I found that casework, whether good or bad, was heavily influenced by social policy, which itself was not informed by research.

That experience led to another publication (Gelles 1996) and another fellowship— this one as an American Sociological Association Congressional Fellow. During my fellowship, I had the opportunity to work on a number of key federal legislative initiatives, including the welfare reform legislation of 1996, the amendment to the Multi-Ethnic Placement Act of 1994, and finally the development of what would become the Adoption and Safe Families Act of 1997.

About halfway through my fellowship, I met Ira Schwartz, then Dean of the School of Social Work at the University of Pennsylvania. Somehow, this meeting became an epiphany for me. After visiting the University of Pennsylvania and meeting a handful of faculty, and then spending more time with Dean Schwartz, I came to understand that the academic entity that best integrated my interests in applying theory and research to practice and policy was a school of social work.

By 1997 I had set out to try to find an academic position in a school of social work. This was not as easy a task as it seemed. A number of prestigious schools of social work wanted only to hire faculty with an MSW degree. While I had courses and experience that approximated an MSW, I did not hold the degree. Many schools I visited paid mere lip-service to applying research to practice and policy and the fit would have been poor for both me and the schools.

Finally, I focused back on the University of Pennsylvania. The School of Social Work had the intellectual and academic tradition that forged one of my academic heros, David Gil. The school also had the faculty, leadership, and academic mission that best captured where I wanted to spend my academic career.

The article above was my first Pennsylvania School approach to child maltreatment and child welfare. Obviously, my thinking and work have evolved, but the article itself captures the ideas and spirit that drew me to the University of Pennsylvania School of Social Work.

References

Gelles, R. J. (1973). Child abuse as psychopathology: A sociological critique and reformulation. *American Journal of Orthopsychiatry* 43: 611–21.

———— (1982). Applying research on family violence to clinical practice. *Journal of Marriage and the Family* 44 (February): 9–20.

———— (1996). *The Book of David: How Preserving Families Can Cost Children's Lives.* New York: Basic Books.

Chapter 28
On Becoming a Scholar-Practitioner

Kenwyn K. Smith

Preamble

For me, the search for an integrated professional persona has been long, arduous and rewarding. Today I see my work as a researcher, my role as an educator, my actions as a community builder, and my contributions to the academy, as highly interwoven. When functioning as an educator, be it in the classroom or the field, I am engaged in research, reconfiguring community dynamics, and service; when intervening in fragmented and fragmenting community relations, I am serving as a scholar-educator, contributing to our School's and Penn's overall mission, etc. I am an organizational psychologist, operating in the action science, ethnographic, appreciative inquiry paradigm, and am engaged in the hands-on work at every point of the research cycle, the educational process, and the communitarian enterprise. As a member of the scholar-practitioner tradition, I am involved primarily in theory building that has direct applications and applied work that contributes to the development of theory.

On Becoming a Researcher

My contributions to social and behavioral science knowledge, best captured in my books, address three interlinked domains: (1) group and intergroup relations, (2) conflict in human systems, and (3) organizational change. In each of these arenas I have added to established theories, developed new theoretical breakthroughs, laid the philosophical-epistemological-methodological foundations for more sophisticated theory to be developed over time, demonstrated the robustness of my conceptualizations, and shown their applicability to organizations of all kinds.

Group and Intergroup Relations

1. *Power and Group Relations.* As I began my scholarly life, research on group and intergroup relations (done in the Tavistock, the National Training Laboratories, the social psychological, the therapeutic, the managerial, and the sociological traditions) had built a theoretical and empirical base for understanding individual functioning within

groups, group-as-a-whole behavior, group evolution and interactions among groups. However, the impact of power relations and context on group and intergroup behavior had yet to be adequately explored. I was eager to grasp the influence of power. Building on the work of Barry Oshry, I launched my research program and made a key "discovery," which is fully elaborated in *Groups in Conflict: Prisons in Disguise* (1982).

Classic hierarchal authority in human systems that make possible organizational processes such as strategy formulation, division of labor, responsibility mapping, etc., generate a number of "structural encasements," each linked to the relative power of organizational groups. These "structural encasements" help in the development of important internal group dynamics such as creativity, cohesion, and efficacy. However, they also impact the intergroup relations within which each group exists, resulting in system-wide dynamics such as (a) groups with power have minimal insight into the impact of their actions, (b) groups with little power get imprisoned by the self-protective barriers they erect to deal with their vulnerability, and (c) those caught in the middle between the powerful and the powerless are dependent on preserving the very relations they are trying to change, creating for themselves energy-draining and stress-filled conundrums. Equally important was the discovery that every group in an organization can be caught up in multiple structural encasements simultaneously, because in regular organizations, any group is usually powerful in one configuration of relations, powerless in another and caught in the middle in yet a third. For example, a group of principals in a school is in a position of power when making decisions about internal school organization, assigning of teachings, etc.; it is in a position of powerlessness when required to implement unfunded mandates like "no child left behind;" it is in a position of middleness when negotiating with the superintendent's office over resources and staffing for the school. My first major ethnographic study of intergroup relations was undertaken in a school district in New England.

In the two decades since formulating the concept of intergroup structural encasements, along with the intra- and intergroup processes these encasements spawn, my conceptualizations, in tandem with Oshry's work, have become infused into the literature on groups. However my early writing on intergroup relations left unaddressed two troubling issues, how to harness the constructive energy latent in conflict-laden intergroup relations and how to change the problematic processes triggered by hierarchical intergroup relationships that exist in organizations. These seemingly unresolved and unresolvable issues continued to drive my work until the 2003 publication of *Yearning for Home in Troubled Times* (discussed later).

2. *A New Theory of Group and Intergroup Relations.* Within a few years of becoming a researcher I was perturbed by several things, in addition to those identified above. First, prevailing group theories provided post-hoc explanations for group behavior but were hard to translate into action-useable knowledge. Meaningful bridges between group theory and group action had yet to be formulated. Second, there were inadequate links between the actions or inactions of a group and its impact on other groups because the unintended effects were likely to overwhelm the intended ones, which meant a different kind of theory was required. Third, most of group development theories at that time alluded to the presence of conflict in groups but did not address the persistence, character and evolution of conflict in intra- and inter-group life, even

though an earlier generation of researchers (e.g., Bion, Simmel, Coser) had demonstrated conflict was central to group functioning.

As I and my colleague, David Berg, began our collaborative writing on group theory we recognized that "left brain," digital, or so called "rational" thinking, by itself, was not an adequate logical system for understanding these and numerous other theoretical complexities. When we included insights that came from "right brain," analogical, or so called "paradoxical" thinking, we could create a truly robust theory of group and intergroup relations that generated action-useable knowledge. Our formulation of a new theory of group and intergroup relations, published in 1987, was titled *Paradoxes of Group Life: Understanding Conflict, Paralysis, and Movement in Group Dynamics*. This book was reviewed favorably at the time, but it took a while before the ideas began to reach the thinking of other scholars. This work provided a new epistemological platform for the study of group and intergroup relations. What was once deemed intuitive was henceforth recognized as being a highly reasoned process, but within a system of logic quite different from, but as sophisticated as, rationalism. Although we did not, and would not even now, use any of this kind of language, David Berg and I had formulated for group relations, the equivalent of what is currently referred to at the individual level as "emotional intelligence." Our book provided a way to integrate right and left brain reasoning about group and intergroup dynamics, built an action-useable theory of group functioning, and established the essential bridges between the co-evolutionary processes of groups and the systems within which they are embedded.

Both *Groups in Conflict* and *Paradoxes of Group Life* broke new ground and only with the passage of time did the ideas in these books take root. However they have stood the test of time. *Groups in Conflict* is in its eleventh printing and *Paradoxes of Group Life* its fifteenth printing. In the 1990s, as chaos theory and the principles of quantum began to be addressed by organizational thinkers, it was evident our paradoxical theory had uncovered the group-based equivalents of the strange attractor, holism, part-whole parallelisms (fractals) well before the principles of chaos theory were part of social-science vocabulary. In the mid-1990s the publishers included *Paradoxes of Group Life* in their classic series, a great honor to have occurred mid-career. However, by the time this book became recognized, from my perspective the world had evolved at such a pace a whole new body of group-based research and conceptualization was beckoning, which I later set out to explore.

Conflict in Human Systems

There is a vast literature on conflict of all kinds, from face-to-face relations to international conflagrations, covering activities such as bargaining, negotiation, and deal-making through to curbing conflict-escalation such as nuclear proliferation. For decades "conflict resolution" was the approach favored by theoreticians eager to repair fragmenting groups, reign in combative inter-group interactions, and arrest deteriorating organizational relations. The search for compromise, the wish for conflict to disappear so "normalcy" could be restored, and the imposition of regulations to limit conflict, is understandable. However, most theories of conflict resolution have limited utility when human institutions are unstable, when contexts are turbulent, when foundations are shaking. I operate out of a "conflict-release" rather than a "conflict resolution" paradigm. I begin with three premises (Berg and I laid out the underlying theory in *Paradoxes of Group Life*). (1) Conflict is inherent in all human interactions and is not an aberration of any kind. (2) Conflict conveys a message that current arrangements are on the cusp of being altered, refined or falling apart. (3) If the conflict can be released instead of repressed, displaced, or dismantled, it contains enormous, long-gestating, creative energy waiting to be birthed.

I have made several theoretical contributions to the literature on intra-group, inter-group, intra-organizational, and inter-organizational conflict. The essence of it is expressed, using non-technical language, under three broad umbrellas. (1) Conflict is rarely expressed at its source and invariably migrates to another set of relationships, often picking up extra ballast along the way by fusing with other conflicts similarly seeking an outlet; hence when it is expressed it cannot be understood in terms of its manifest form, or as an attribute of the location where it erupts. (My writings, along with Alderfer's, on parallel processes provide theory, data, and discussion on this issue.) (2) Working from first principles, as laid out by the early balance theorists, and augmented by the writings of Murray Bowen in the family therapy tradition, I have constructed a robust way of tracking the pathways by which conflict moves, the mechanisms by which it gets amplified, the processes through which it gets reshaped or eviscerated, and the location towards which it cascades. This offers opportunity to reverse the flow so it can be addressed at its source as opposed to in its symptomatic form, to channel it into either "acceptable garbage dumps" or more productive outlets, and to fuse it with other constructive energies so that it has creative rather than deleterious outcomes. (3) To operate in a "conflict-release" paradigm requires change agents to make use of numerous naturally existing containers in organizations, to create new temporary containers so that the conflict can be "held" until it has been rechanneled or reshaped, and to dismantle unneeded containers so they do not become part of the institutional clutter.

Virtually all my research has been done in settings where significant conflict already exists or is the product of organizations striving to change (to grow, to overcome some destructive pattern of functioning, to innovate, to adapt to or seek a new strategic direction). This means that as action researchers I and my associates are always creating hypotheses, gathering data, intervening, generating collective reflection devices, doing analyses and making meaning, in conflict-filled settings. Hence our theories, methodologies and data-gathering instruments have to be extra robust, because in addition to analyzing conflictual dynamics, they must serve as a container of conflicts.

I have been involved in action-science research on human-system conflicts of every conceivable kind. By way of illustration here are a few: a multi-year project addressing race and gender relations in a Philadelphia bank whose decisions and oversights were profoundly impacting the local economy and the welfare of the urban communities; an intense intervention in an agency in a war-torn nation whose senior leadership was in constant conflict due to different ethnic/cultural assumptions about authority relations; multiple interventions into conflict-filled relationships within the HIV/AIDS community in Philadelphia. My theories about conflict have been tested in different national contexts, in multicultural settings, across racial, gender, sexual orientation divides, on different continents, in stable and chaotic systems, in both aging and young institutions, in the nonprofit, governmental, and private sectors, with service deliverers, with workers, with managers, with senior leadership, and across every possible configuration of hierarchical arrangements.

Organizational Change

The term "organizational change" is a huge canopy under which many complex processes and different logical types have been both coherently clustered and meaninglessly dumped. I have argued that we need "to change the organization of our thinking in order to think about how we change our organizing." The categorization system I laid out for conceptualizing *change* (morpho-genesis, morpho-stasis, development and adaptation) and my decision to think of *organization*, not as an entity or a tangible object, but as "the relations among the elements of a system and the relations among the relations," provided an important base for my research, interventions and writing in this arena. My work has provided a seamless way to make translations between all forms of system thinking, cybernetics and chaos theory and ultimately led to my current theoretical formulation of organizing as "the structuring of chaos for purposeful action."

My theoretical and applied work on organizational change is based on four key principles.

(1) All stability is predicated on change and all change is predicated on stability; since change and stasis co-define each other, neither can exist without the other. The logical consequence of this is a set of paradoxical imperatives, such as "to promote change, preserve the status quo," and "to increase stability, embrace change." Hence, "change programs" and "status-quo programs" are most viable when cast in change-stasis terms reasoned in a both/and logic as opposed to an either/or logic), as in "this change is dedicated to preserving X; this investment in stability is in the service of enabling Y to change."

(2) Beneath all organization is a bedrock of chaos. However there is order in that chaos which can be identified and understood but is also evolving in tandem with the structures by which it is contained. Hence organizational arrangements are in constant need of restructuring to harness the energy that emerges from the chaos upon which it depends. However, chaos is usually seen as threatening the structure and not as structure's valued partner. Such reasoning prompts leaders and managers to try to suppress or remove chaos because of its structure-threatening quality, which in turn leads change agents to restructure for the purpose of getting rid of the chaos. The result? Structures grow more fragile and less able to manage the chaos they are designed to contain and mobilize in the service of their primary purpose. A more productive path is to focus restructuring efforts on mobilizing the vibrant energies coming from its bed-rock chaos.

(3) Developmental change, a natural part of all human systems, occurs within a web of relationships that can enhance or strangle growth. It is well documented that the things assisting development at certain stages hinder it at other times, and that today's successes often ensure tomorrow's failures. The question is how to conceptualize the tipping points before they occur. I argue that understanding when to grow and when to cut back, when to diversify and when to consolidate, when to innovate and when to stick with core practices, requires thinking within multiple logics. This is greatly enhanced by going beyond standard statistical reasoning. For example knowing when continuous consequences of continuous processes are about to be replaced by discontinuous consequences of continuous processes is greatly helped by using alternative mathematical logics like catastrophe theory.

(4) The most potent way to change the internal dynamics of any human organization is to alter the character and form of the external relationships within which it is embedded.

The tapestry created out of these above conceptualizations, interlinked with my group relations and conflict theory, for the past two decades has defined my theory of practice in the domain of organizational change and is found infused into my published works.

A Significant Turning Point

Upon joining the School of Social Policy & Practice (formerly the School of Social Work) I immersed myself in research on several issues at the heart of this profession, and the non-profit sector in general. I focused my energies on five domains: (1) assisting local businesses to engage in culture change programs designed to make their workplace more hospitable and career enriching for African American, Latino, and Asian graduates of Philadelphia high schools; (2) trying to discern which organizational dynamics enhanced versus threatened the physical and emotional health of employees; (3) understanding societal intractables such as homelessness; (4) helping to make HIV/AIDS center stage in the social sciences when this epidemic was still being glossed over by large segments of the academy; (5) exploring how to assist incarcerated fathers find their way back into the main stream of family and societal life.

I built a research center, hired a staff and got launched. From the outset two things happened. (1) I recognized how encased I was in epistemologies that were reparative in nature. I decided to refocus my energies. Rather than work to fix what was already broken, could we, without being trapped by utopian logic, create organizational thinking to assist in the formation, nurturance, maturation and functioning of human systems so they did not need as much fixing? And when repair was necessary could we develop early detection devices, so organizational maintenance could be done before the system became non-functional? (2) I began taking seriously a question I had been asked repeatedly over the previous decade by managers and executives in the non-profit, governmental, and private sectors: "have you ever tried to implement any of your ideas in a real-life organization, in real-time, dealing with real, time-sensitive processes?"

MANNA in the Wilderness of AIDS: Ten Lessons in Abundance. This self-redefining confrontation, identified above, occurred at the time a small group of us, during the early days of the AIDS pandemic, were forming MANNA (Metropolitan Aids Neighborhood Nutrition Alliance). This started for me as a nonacademic enterprise but once I embraced my leadership role within this organization, I realized it was to be one of the most academic things I would ever do. Helping to create and run MANNA, along with the attendant community building activities, was a huge experiment that went way beyond the scope of what most consider as social science research. It became the testing ground of all my theories to date, except they were all being applied in unison and not serially. This work spawned a body of theorizing I had not previously considered. My book, *MANNA in the Wilderness of AIDS: Ten Lessons in Abundance*, although written in nonacademic language is filled with these lessons I garnered during my seven year intense engagement with the Philadelphia AIDS community. It provides robust evidence about which theories of mine work and which need refinement.Due to its narrative form, which includes voices from all parts of the MANNA community, the following claim might surprise some people: in my view it is the most scholarly document I have written to date, and is filled with more academic/applied/creative theory than my previous work combined. However, the theory is latent in the stories recounted, is not bundled in academic-speak, and comes into focus only as the reader engages the emotional and intellectual struggles the text demands.

Most critically my MANNA work, as recounted in this book, demonstrated the transformative possibilities created by exiting the paradigm of scarcity and operating out of the paradigm of abundance. I now realize "abundance" and "scarcity" are ways of thinking with their own inherent logics. I am captivated by the idea of constructing an epistemology based on the principles of abundance as opposed to those of scarcity (upon which all modern economic theory is predicated) and expect to dedicate a large portion of my remaining days to this theme.

Yearning for Home in Troubled Times. My foray into understanding homelessness in the United States led me to a stunning discovery, that all human beings feel homeless in some critical domain in their lives. Hence when society mounts programs to deal with the problems of those with no habitat, important though that is, it is treating only a symptom of a larger societal phenomenon. This treatise, I believe, unlocks the mystery of what, in my view, has wrongly come to be labeled the problem of "homelessness." In this book, I take all my prior work on group and intergroup relations, conflict, paradox, parallel processes, human change processes, etc., and provide my best understanding, at this point of my life, of human functioning. As the investigator, I also include myself among the investigated. I use the motif of power, powerlessness, and caught in the middle, formulated in my earlier work, and show its relevance to every facet of human organizations, at the system-as-a-whole level, in the relationships among groups, in the dynamics within groups and in the inner landscape of each person. This book makes a fully-integrated statement of what I have to offer as a scholar, a practitioner, and interventionist, as of 2002.

Freed to be Fathers: Lessons from Men Doing Time. Triggered by an MSW student project we began a prison-based project in the tradition of "what makes a difference in restoring a life gone wrong?" Our initial findings quickly morphed this into a study on incarcerated fathers. This book, while explicitly addressing fathers in prison, is about the plight of American fathers in general. It is my most significant contribution to the "Men's Movement." Like the books on AIDS and homelessness, it is presented in narrative form, giving voice to untold stories that deserve to be in the public domain.

On Social Work and Spirituality. While writing the above three books I chose to also explore the relationship between organizational phenomena and spirituality. This was personally challenging because I was determined not to use language and concepts aligned with one spiritual tradition and alienating to another. For this aspect of these books, I placed over every phrase I used, the following filter: "will it equally nourish, educate and support people in all three mono-theistic faith-traditions, Judaism, Christianity and Islam?" I also asked myself at each point, if it could be said in a way that is embracing of teachings in faiths such as Buddhism and Hinduism? I was pleased with what this discipline fostered, both in terms of what is on the written page and what it did for me as a human being.

Research Methods. Although I received signification education in mathematics, I use statistics based on least squared analysis only in highly circumscribed settings. My first Master's degree (University of Queensland, Australia) was research-based and required a dissertation the equivalent in scope and size of an American Ph.D. For that degree I redid the classic experiments in social psychology, analyzing the findings using non-Euclidean assumptions (e.g., instead of doing only "least squared analyses," I also did "least cubed analyses," "least quadrupled analyses" through to analyses based on $(n\ (1)$-dimensional space, where n was the number of verifiable dimensions underlying the operationalization of the variables). I discovered what had come to be reified as knowledge in social psychology, conducted using the rigors of the experimental paradigm and analyzed according to the "least squared" statistical conventions of the time, was quite different from what would have been concluded if analyzed according to a mathematics based on $(n-1)$-dimensional space. I did not have the mathematical skill or predisposition to define my career in terms of solving the statistical problem I had stumbled into; but more importantly I felt convinced there were other valid ways of knowing than those defined by the positivist and predictive paradigm and was determined to plumb these, which is where my career took me as a methodologist. My thinking and contributions to the action science, ethnographic, qualitative research methods I most commonly use are explicated in my 1988 edited volume with David Berg, *The Self in Social Inquiry: Researching Methods.*

A Research Project in the Making

As previously mentioned, I am convinced there is a need for a next evolutionary leap in the nature of group and intergroup theory. This is the product of several forces:

(1) social evolution has made the character of the contexts within which groups come into being and develop more complex than the last half of the twentieth century; (2) the purposes and functions of groups has altered; (3) the theories given academic credence in the past were developed primarily within Euro/American-centric epistemologies and organizations.

I am currently exploring relationships with organizations in India to undertake a set of studies, which I imagine will go on for more than a decade. This research enterprise is designed to address three things. (1) The group dynamics in women's self help groups (SHGs) in rural India, which have become the center-piece of many innovative micro-financing practices taking place in Asia. For example, in the State of Andhra Pradesh (AP) there are 25 million people struggling to create sustainable livelihoods while remaining in their rural villages. At this point 500,000 SHGs (all women who have spouses and several children) have been formed and are at different points of their evolution, making approximately 25 million rural poor in AP currently linked in a networked set of evolving relations. There are many NGOs working with such self-help groups across India and several have signaled their willingness to be research collaborators with Penn. (2) There are a number of innovative partnerships being built between the public, private and governmental organizations in India dedicated to creating new forms of sustainable livelihoods in these rural areas. However, to deliver on the dreamt-about collaborations, the established organizations have yet to create many new village and region based organizations, making this a fertile natural experiment in intra, inter-group, intra- and inter-organizational relations. (3) Several organizations are dedicated to educating people at the village level about how to construct never before imagined jobs and to offer institutional development support in the building of sustainable livelihoods. Since this research project will be done in partnership with Indian colleagues it is critical that I learn about and join with an Indian-centered research paradigm befitting the complexities of the Indian setting. However it is already evident that the insights coming from Indian innovations are highly applicable to the social innovations needed to enhance impoverished urban American communities.

On Becoming an Educator

My most unique course is "Group Dynamics and Organizational Politics," the only course of its kind offered anywhere in the world in any educational setting. Entirely of my own creation, it enables students to learn the theoretical knowledge I developed on group relations and power dynamics in human systems, explores its relationships with other group relations theories, shows how this body of knowledge can be meaningfully applied in all kinds of human systems and uses a pedagogical methodology that is a direct product of my scholarly work, documented in three of my books (*Paradoxes of Group Life*, *Groups in Conflict*, and *Yearning for Home in Troubled Times*). This intensely experiential course is extremely demanding, personally and intellectually. It is designed for those who facilitate groups in agencies, educate in classroom settings, direct executive groups, conduct support groups, manage work teams, serve on task forces, chair committees, run organizations, etc. The lessons learned in this course are relevant to workers in all settings, to members of families, to communities large and small, to managers in the non-profit/NGO, government, and profit-making sectors, and those aspiring to be leaders in any sphere.

This course consists of two modules. The first addresses group dynamic theory and practice, which melds the contrasting and complementary insights derived from both the digital and analogic brains, often referred to as left and right brains. The second module focuses on the systemic relationships between the "haves," the "have-nots" and those "caught in the middle" in any human system, along with the transforming potential latent in three distinctly different forms of power, the power to create, the power to block (negate or destroy) and the power to mediate.

The pedagogy of the first module, built on the intellectual foundation laid out in *Paradoxes of Group Life*, was published in *Journal of Applied Behavioral Science* (1995), and represents a new approach to learning about group relations. It delineates the sensory, cognitive and emotional work required to understand the relationship between normally "out of awareness" processes and the overt behavior of groups. This module simultaneously focuses on group-as-a-whole behaviors, the actions of individuals within a group, and the dynamics at play in the context within which the group is embedded. It addresses directly the complex interplay between group actions and race, gender, national identification, sexual-orientation etc. The second module is a "Power Laboratory" as described in Section I of *Groups in Conflict* and Chapters 2 and 3 of *Yearning for Home in Troubled Times*. In the Lab participants explore how creative power, negating power and mediating power play out simultaneously in three different levels of the system, at the level of the experiential mini-society they co-create, within the groups to which they belong, and within their own individual inner landscapes.

This course is unique in that it builds upon both the most recent approaches to group dynamics along with theory about the power dynamics between groups with differential power and access to resources. The course is designed anew on every occasion it is offered and is especially tailored to fit the educational needs of those enrolled, which invariably includes students from multiple graduate programs. The learning is co-created by the instructor and the students as per the documented evidence offered by the students in Chapters 5–9 of *Yearning for Home*.

One way to illustrate how I function as an educator in this course is to quote some of the evaluative comments of recent participants:

This is the most challenging, stimulating, and rigorous course I have experienced at Penn . . . (it) will affect me, in a positive way, for the rest of my life. This course is why I came to graduate school. Professor Smith . . . ingeniously provides the necessary tools for each individual student to travel down her/his own path and on her/his own journey.

Every class I have taken to date has focused on filling my brain. This class actually seemed to expand my brain such that it can be filled throughout the course of my life . . . Kenwyn seeks to engage the groups and individuals in the class in the deepest ways possible in order to maximize the benefit of the experience. This behavior requires the amazing capacity to love each person "where" they are in their life without stopping them from the pain/conflict required to grow. [His] example is personally inspiring to me as a [Wharton] student, Naval Officer, friend, son, husband and father.

Kenwyn guided us through the activities, allowing us the space to come to our own understandings and conclusions. He didn't lecture . . . [but] instead offered us the time to process together all that was happening in our group interactions. After completing the course, reading the various books, and writing the assignments, I felt as if I had come to a good understanding of how group theory actually works in real life situations.

. . . this has been the most influential course I have ever taken. It has also been the source of more learning than I ever expected. The texts are difficult and wonderful at the same time. I do not doubt that I will read them several more times.

I have never met a professor who put forth the time, energy, caring, and commitment as he put into this course . . . his capacity to be nonjudgmental is comparable to no one I have ever met.

What I appreciated most about the class was the extensive feedback on the 2 assignments. Prof. Smith typed a total of 2.5 single spaced pages of feedback which is more feedback than I received in my previous 9 classes combined. . . . he understands well what students are looking to get out of classes.

Kenwyn has an incredible ability to guide students to their own learnings. It is a teaching style best represented by the metaphor of a duck. On the top, he appears calm and at rest. Underneath the water, his legs are ferociously beating . . . Kenwyn seems to have a very passive teaching style that allows the students to arrive freely at their own learnings. However it is a very "Active" passivity—that enables and energizes the class to move . . . [This class] contains lessons in leadership, in society, in human interaction and so many other topics. It is a class that anyone who is ready to do the learning would benefit from no matter what their future path in life.

I plan to keep (the professor's comments on my papers) and pull them out from time to time to help remind myself of the valuable lessons I have learned. . . . This class helped me to address the most important areas for success in business, personal relationships and life in general: empathy, communication and leadership, areas in which I need the most work . . . my model of leadership is quite backward . . . it was really all about me, me, me. I now want to be a leader who is dedicated to serving others . . . I know that it is going to continue to take a lot of hard, painful work to become this kind of leader. I will not quit however.

This is by far the most valuable course I have taken while getting my MBA at Wharton . . . Kenwyn Smith is a professor of the utmost integrity and caring. He allowed us to enter into a true interaction and meaningful exchange with him—something rarely found in the harried and fleeting typical classroom experience.

Each time I teach this course, I organize it around a theme that is at the center of some social crisis. One example is "homelessness," which is the heart of the two Power Labs discussed in *Yearning for Home*. Another was immigration and refugees. Yet a third was taking over a turbulent system from an "interim authority." In each case the participants are co-creators of their own knowledge.

As an educator, no matter what kind of course I teach, I am mindful of four key functions I must fulfill: (1) to create a context in which students with a wide range of learning styles can discover their self-educating capacities; (2) to build, with the students' help, a psychologically safe container, so they can readily push themselves to the cusp of their ignorance (for it is on the boundary of knowing and unknowing that genuine learning occurs); (3) to impart, in an engaging way, established knowledge developed by former scholars so students can use conventional nomenclature, think using established concepts, and embrace the intellectual heritages upon which they depend; and (4) to appreciate that the most significant learning will occur months or even years later, when some of the seeds I am attempting to plant, will have taken root and ultimately sprung into full bloom.

On occasion I have taken a class into the field with me, and educated the students on how to participate in my research. The most significant example was the 250 hours of data-gathering done by a 1996 class of mine that I took into MANNA. This contributed significantly to my book *MANNA in the Wilderness of AIDS*. I wrote the MANNA book for several reasons, but one was I wanted a book I could use with students that documented the conception, infancy and early developmental years of a non-profit organization. At that time, I could not find such a book.

On another occasion, Ann Rogerson, an MSW student, whose husband had died, leaving her a single parent of four adolescent boys, proposed, as part of a course, doing research on the kinds of fathers boys who lose their father early, become. Her course paper was so insightful she convinced me to partner with her in launching a project to explore this theme with incarcerated fathers. This eventually resulted in the publication *Freed to be Fathers, Lessons from Men Doing Time*. I appointed Ann a part-time researcher in my research center, educated her on the research methods for a study of this kind and personally mentored her throughout. This was a role in which Ms. Rogerson functioned extremely well, even while working full time upon graduation, as a hospice social worker. I dedicated this book to Ann Rogerson, my former MSW student, in gratitude for all she prompted me to grapple with in the process of this research.

Serving the Whole of Penn as an Educator

My role as an educator has stretched beyond the bounds of the School of Social Policy & Practice. When the Provost decided to re-invent the Fels Master of Government Administration in the late 1990s, I served on the curriculum committee that redesigned the MGA program, constructed one of the Fels core courses, "Leadership in the Public Domain," which I taught in 1998–2005. I have also taught consistently at Aresty, in Wharton's senior executive education programs (Advanced Management Program and Executive Development Program). In the executive class room every idea I express is scrutinized and passed through three filters: (a) its immediate relevance to the actions being taken by leaders concerned with efficacy, global dynamics, short and long-term organizational and economic viability; (b) how it stands up to the intellectual critique espoused by other scholars and practitioners; and (c) does it add value to the other disciplines such as finance, marketing etc. Every minute I spend in the classroom in these programs, no matter what the topic I am teaching or the people I am engaged with has infused into it, one way or another, the following themes: what reflective devices must be built into regular organizational processes so that the organization-as-a-whole and groups with decision-making responsibilities can learn from their experience and not repeat the same mistakes over and over, and so that new learning can be stored and made accessible when needed; how to ensure that those with the knowledge are empowered to make the relevant decisions; how to access right brain thinking to augment the insights that come from classic rational deliberations; how to make decisions that address the well-being of the whole, (the community and the environment included and not just the business enterprise); how to construct human organizational environments so that the creative contributions of all employees can be tapped; how to address the "isms" that debilitate, such as racism, sexism, heterosexism, etc; how to think in abundance terms and not just within the scarcity paradigm.

On Becoming a Community Builder

Director of the Center for Workplace Studies

When I joined the School I took on the task of breathing life into a moribund, unfunded, un-staffed research center on "Workplace Studies" designed to achieve three purposes: to improve the quality of work-life for employees, to offer organizational assistance to non-profit social service agencies, and to bring in corporate dollars to underwrite the research costs of the center. The Dean at the time was eager to diversify the potential funding pool for the School's research. I got this center off the ground, defined its agenda, crafted a set of research projects, hired a staff, created a business plan, built relationships with an array of local organizations, and covered all the center's costs. Within three years a newly appointed Dean made it clear that this research Center was not compatible with his agenda and asked me to move it off campus. Accepting the political realities of the situation, I continued running this center from an off-campus site until all the center's research commitments were fulfilled, all its financial obligations were met, and all the students and employees under my charge could move on seamlessly to the next stage of their lives. The attendant transitions (building, relocating, and dismantling the research center) were extremely taxing. I, as director, had little discretionary time to write up the research we were doing but contented myself with the knowledge that in a few years I would have a full sabbatical. I immersed myself in the drafting of five books over the last half of the 1990s and setting in place my next research agenda, quietly accepting that one of the political costs I would pay for this huge perturbation in my career, was my research productivity would appear to be minimal for a substantial period and henceforth, I would be seen as not contributing enough to the finances of the school. (Three of these books were completed and published as a result of my 2000–2001 sabbatical at Oxford University.)

Faculty Master of Ware College House

In 1988 I accepted the position as faculty master of Ware College House, moving my family (including three pre-teen children) onto campus for this 24/7, nine months a year, job. I am grateful to the University and my family for this opportunity to serve the undergraduate population in this capacity. Even though this was a wonderful experience for my family, by the time my children became teens they made it clear they needed more of our parental attention than this job permitted. While I was only in this role for two years, I was pleased with what I achieved, but in that time, my physical and emotional reserves became totally depleted. Blessedly, after a year's sabbatical they were restored.

School Transformation Committee

In the spring of 2003 Dean Gelles constituted a committee consisting of a substantial number of faculty and staff with the charge to report by the end of the semester on whether to initiate a major transformation of the school, and if so what shapes might it take. I chaired this committee, which proved to be one of the most collegial, satisfying, and efficiently executed tasks I have been part of at Penn. It was this group that formulated the new direction for the school, unanimously proposing a set of recommendations that subsequently led to the renaming of the school and the decision to introduce two new graduate programs, one in Non-profit/NGO Leadership and one in Social Policy.

Designing and Operationalizing the Non-Profit/NGO Leadership Program

During 2003–2004 I chaired the group consisting of six faculty members, representing our School, Arts & Sciences and Wharton, asked to discern if a graduate program focused on the non-profit/NGO sector should be created by Penn, and if so its structure, design, educational pedagogy, the appropriate market, and the resources that would be needed. This was a huge task but was extremely rewarding as the members of the three schools forged a joint path that would represent a genuine collaboration among the three schools if appropriately implemented. In April of 2004 this committee made its recommendation to the deans of the three schools. In October of 2004 a small group was charged with the task of creating a one year master's program in Non-profit/NGO Leadership (NPL). Again I chaired the oversight group planning this program and took on the task of bringing it to life. In the fall of 2005 the University admitted the first class of students for this program. It is fortuitous that these plans were made as Professor Gutmann was being appointed President of Penn, because this program's agenda is a bold enactment of every aspect of the President's compact. In a way, being asked to bring these three schools into partnership was a task that fit perfectly my skill set, since I am, at present, the only person at Penn who has held teaching responsibilities in all three schools.

The Professional World

I have regularly done reviews for the journals in my field, served on the editorial board of the *Organizational Behavior Teaching Review/Journal of Management Education* for many years and was an associate editor for the *Journal of Applied Behavioral Science* from 1990 to 2003. I have worked on six continents, delivering a large number of seminars (from Oxford University to the State University of Mongolia in Ulaanbaatar), workshops, paper presentations, lectures (to as few as five people in a round table exchange to several thousand in a huge auditorium), conducting research (such as the emerging project in India), being involved in the education of approximately 5,000 international executives in the private, civil society and public sectors, and intervening in organizations (from Australia to Belgium).

Since joining the School of Social Policy & Practice I have helped birth three non-profit organizations in Philadelphia.

MANNA. This has already been discussed. However I want to highlight MANNA's long-term economic contributions. Over the first 15 years of its existence MANNA prepared and delivered, without charge, 5 million meals tailored to the specific nutritional needs of the recipients. This represents a $50 million direct contribution to the HIV/AIDS community. In total, it has cost $25–30 million to run MANNA during these years, thanks to the volunteer labor of 1,000 people per year. The reduction in number of days spent in the hospital by people with AIDS, which can be attributed directly to MANNA's services, has saved the medical system, at minimum, $100 million.

West Philadelphia Alliance for Children (WePAC). In 2004 I co-founded this volunteer-based, non-profit organization to enhance the learning environment in educationally under-resourced neighborhoods and to bridge the racial, economic, geographic and cultural divides between West Philadelphia and its surrounding neighboring communities. Currently serving Carroll Park, Mill Creek and East Parkside, WePAC (a) places volunteers in elementary grades to assist classroom teachers, (b) runs an all-day job and skill-development program for teens who have dropped out of high school, (c) conducts a youth club for street-corner males, (d) provides, with the assistance of Wharton undergraduates, basic business acumen to middle school children who run their own thrift store, (e) works to ensure adequate after-school and early childhood development programs in these neighborhoods, (f) advocates for children and teens having difficulty at home and school, and (g) conducts parenting skills workshops for teens. Presently I chair the board of WePAC.

The Other Carpenter (TOC). This is a volunteer-based housing repair organization, operating on a habitat for humanity model, serving under-resourced home owners in East Parkside. I have no current role in TOC, but along with the current executive director, I drew together the relevant parties, catalyzed the process of bringing this organization into being, and chaired the planning group until the first Board of Directors was appointed.

On Developing an Integrated Persona

It has been important for me to develop an integrated professional persona, which I feel is well illustrated by my role in Penn's support of those striving to end apartheid in South Africa. In the mid-1980s, when students were calling on Universities to terminate their investments in this Afrikaner-ruled nation, Dr. Bowen, President of Princeton, sought the counsel of black South African leaders, who said, "Our people will be badly hurt by this, but we support divesture. This is a price we are willing to pay because the Apartheid rulers will not change until the economy is about to collapse. However we fear once foreign investments end, no one will care what happens to us. Please help create a new communication pipeline so we remain connected to the USA." Dr. Bowen and Penn's President Dr. Hackney organized for Wharton, under the guise of offering a special executive education program for black South Africans, to function as an invisible conduit for the desired communication system. Offering executive education to blacks in companies with a social responsibility agenda (known as the Sullivan Principles—negotiated by the Philadelphian African American leader, Rev. Leon Sullivan) was acceptable to the Afrikaner regime. Wharton and the University of Pennsylvania began bringing cohorts of black and so-called "colored" South African leaders to Penn. I was one of the faculty members who designed and ran this program. It started four years before Nelson Mandela was released from prison, and continued until well into the Mandela presidency. Upon moving from Wharton, where I served in 1985–1990, I transferred this project into the research center I directed on behalf of the School.

When we began, none of us at Penn knew what it was like to be a black leader in an organization under the apartheid regime. So we had to build a set of sustained relationships and create a collective process by which "we" (they and us) could construct an appropriate learning environment and agenda befitting their context and their needs. I was the faculty member assigned this task. The first thing we discovered was the Afrikaner divide-and-conquer strategy had created such intractable divisions among South Africans of color they were unable to speak with a common voice. The second was that these extreme divisions within the oppressed peoples of South Africa meant that post-apartheid, this nation would be in a protracted struggle to avoid a civil war. A large part of our agenda hence had to be knitting a fabric of relations among these many factions. Some of the work we did with black South African leaders occurred at Penn and some took place on the ground in South Africa. Always it was done without fanfare and was kept out of sight, because we never wanted to endanger the covert communication channel we were creating as Penn's contribution to the anti-apartheid struggle. At the peak of this project a wonderful set of partnerships was forged; within Penn it was Social Work with Wharton; externally it was with Howard University and the Martin Luther King Center in Atlanta; internationally it was the USA with a potentially post-apartheid South Africa. Over 250 South African leaders of all races and "color designations" were involved in the Penn-based executive seminars, many of whom moved immediately into senior business, government, and NGO positions upon Mandela's election. A comparable number were involved in the work we did on South African soil, from community building in the black townships surrounding Johannesburg, to addressing race-relations among executive leadership groups of business enterprises. Throughout, the central theme was "what can be done, as the new South Africa comes into being and crafts a new place for itself in the international world, to ensure that it does not tumble into a civil war?"

In the larger political scheme of things, Penn's contribution to the South African struggle to dismantle apartheid and build a nation based on nonracialism was minuscule. However, to this day Penn is a much appreciated and respected institution in the minds of many South African leaders.

This project, with all its nuisances, illustrates how I weave into one fabric my work as a researcher, educator, intervener, and community builder. Given the complex set of dynamics entailed in such work, my writings usually have a long gestation period and are often published well after the work is completed. I have an early draft of a book-length manuscript on the scholarly work undertaken in this ten-year engagement. My experiences with black South Africans catapulted my thinking about the role of conflict in human systems to a level yet to be fully articulated.

An original paper.

References

Smith, Kenwyn K. *Freed to be Fathers: Lessons from Men Doing Time.* Cleveland: Pilgrim Press, 2002.
———. *Groups in Conflict: Prisons in Disguise.* Dubuque, Io: Kendall/Hunt, 1982.
———. *MANNA in the Wilderness of AIDS: Ten Lessons in Abundance.* Cleveland: Pilgrim Press, 2002.
———. *Yearning for Home in Troubled Times.* Cleveland: Pilgrim Press, 2003.
Smith, Kenwyn K., and David N. Berg. *Paradoxes of Group Life: Understanding Conflict, Paralysis, and Movement in Group Dynamics.* San Francisco: Jossey-Bass, 1987.
———. "A Paradoxical Approach to Teaching Group Dynamics: First Thoughts, First Findings." *Journal of Applied Behavioral Science* 31 (1995): 398–414.
———. *The Self in Social Inquiry: Researching Methods.* Newbury Park: Calif.: Sage, 1988.

Commentary

Kenwyn K. Smith

I can still recall the calming effect of Carl Rogers's elegant 1961 treatise *On Becoming a Person.*[1] I was a graduate student at Yale who could not imagine finding a path that could lead to a desirable destination. The pages of Rogers's book were prodding me to accept an important lesson, that it was not essential to get it all figured out while still in my twenties; ahead of me were a host of experiences waiting to embrace me and to be embraced by me. I had already been a high school teacher of mathematics and science, had completed a graduate degree and served as a clinical psychologist for five years in my homeland; and here I was on the cusp of another huge life change. It was into this setting that the words of the old master, Carl Rogers, spoke to me:

"Kenwyn, go towards whatever you wish to avoid (uncertainty, ambiguity, chaos); for the issue is not so much what you are to do with your days, but what kind of a person are you to become?"

The biography of my birth made the question of my "becoming" exceedingly bountiful. And, now, as I enter my senior years, the on-going character of my "becoming" and the "becomingness" of all the people around me is still at the center of my life and work. This is how I expressed it in *Yearning for Home in Troubled Times*.

By the time I had become conscious of myself as a person I felt betwixt and between and wanted solid ground upon which to stand. . . . I felt lost and wanted to find the way. . . . I had no words to capture my yearning, so I carried silently the ache that accompanied my dislocation. I was also too restless to stay still, so, at some point, I cannot recall exactly when, I set off on a journey.

At first I was hungry for knowledge about an age-old question, *Who am I?* Philosophy, psychology, anthropology and sociology became my passions. The more I read, the more lost I became. Everything was so vast, so magnificent, so interrelated. My academic quest produced emotional paralysis as I pondered if it was possible to grasp life's simultaneous complexity and simplicity!

An alternative beckoned: travel the world. Surely, somewhere in this vastness there was a little corner where I would not feel lost. Visiting unfamiliar territories was glorious. I delighted in the various and colorful ways people lived, such a contrast to my own drabness. Of course, it did not matter what locale I visited or what body of literature I embraced, I did not find calm, for I kept taking my inner restlessness with me.

Failing in my search increased my despair. I gave up hope, until the pain of not looking grew larger than the pain of not finding. A quiet voice from somewhere inside me said, "to understand your predicament look in your own back yard." That proved useful.

My first port of call was my accent. Everywhere I have gone people have asked me a perfectly innocent question, "Where do you come from?" Rarely can anyone guess my nationality given how I sound. That did not trouble me in the international arena, for it was understandable. However, all my days I have been asked this same question, even in the country of my birth, in the place where I grew up. As far back as I can recall, my accent prompted every new acquaintance to quiz me about where I was from. I was asked this so often it led me to believe *I must not belong here,* otherwise they would not say this. Each time I faced this, my spirit shrank a little.

I was born to an Australian father and an English mother. I spent the first year of my life in Australia and the second in England. From age two to five I lived in China, and Mandarin became my first language. The only English I ever spoke between the ages of two and five was occasionally in my home and with the Canadian children who lived in our compound in Chengdu, capital of Szechwan province. For the remainder of my childhood and youth I lived in Australia. In my mid twenties I went to the U.S. to complete my graduate schooling.

My dilemma was I never really sounded like an Aussie, but I didn't sound like anything else either, not an Englishman, not an American, not a Welshman. Hence, each time I was asked, "Where are you from?" the juvenile logic of my heart said, "If I do not come from here I must be from somewhere else!" No one thought I came from *here* so I must come from some yet-to-be-discovered *there*. Yet every *there* I went, I faced the same question, which convinced me that no *there* existed to claim me as one of its own. This accentuated my feeling that *I must come from NOwhere,* an awful and awe-filled thought!

Today questions about my accent produce no pain but invite me to celebrate my uniqueness, something I have in common with every person. After all, those who feel they don't belong, all belong to the class of people who don't belong.[2]

When I was five, we narrowly escaped the communist revolution of 1949, a truly traumatic event which, for emotional reasons I could never grasp, was undiscussable in my family. But I became tenacious in my determination to decipher how those China experiences had shaped my essence, and to find a place I could call home. Decades later, I came to discover that *home is a condition of the spirit,* and that it is possible to *feel at home* in the most *foreign of places.*

Once upon a time had anyone suggested I would spend a single day in Philadelphia I would have laughed. And yet this is where I have raised my family and have worked for more than two decades. I have come to love this place. "How come?" ask friends from far away. The answer is simple: "I have given my heart to Philadelphia; and I now know that what you give your heart to is what you come to love." That is why I cherish my professional life so fully; why the insights I gained from people living with, and dying from, AIDS far exceeded the aggregated impact of all my formal education, why my sabbatical in England was so restorative, why I am now directing Penn's Nonprofit/ NGO Leadership program, why I am drawn at this late stage to turn my eyes toward Asia, why parenting with a beloved spouse has been *the* event of my life, and why, if blessed with the gift of years, I may well see out my final days in Australia.

Looking back, my academic questing has been highly linked to my yearning to know myself as well as the people around me, and to grasp the forces propelling us all to act the ways we do on the path to becoming the people we are.

Notes

1. Carl Rogers, *On Becoming a Person: A Therapist's View of Psychotherapy* (Boston: Houghton Mifflin).

2. Kenwyn K Smith, *Yearning for Home in Troubled Times* (Cleveland: Pilgrim Press, 2003), 67–69. Reprinted by permission of Pilgrim Press. Otto Rank has a wonderful discussion about how uniqueness and commonness, while being each other's opposites, are also each other's complement. See Rank, *Will Therapy and Truth and Reality* (New York: Knopf, 1945), 46–59.

Chapter 29
Neighborhood-Representing Organizations: How Democratic Are They?

Ram A. Cnaan

Neighborhood-representing organizations (NROs) serve as a bridge between the individual in private life and the large institutions of public life. They mediate between the local residents and formal government and large service institutions.[1] The goal of an NRO is to empower neighborhood residents, counteracting their feelings of powerlessness and lack of representation.[2] As such, NROs are viewed primarily as a means of representation that increases residents' awareness and responds to their needs and priorities by allocating services and goods. Emile Durkheim notes, "A nation can be maintained only if, between the state and the individual, there is intercalated a whole series of secondary groups near enough to the individuals to attract them strongly in their sphere of action and drag them, in this way, into the general torrent of social life."[3]

The tradition of emphasizing the role of the citizen as an active member of his or her community was introduced into social work in the beginning of this century as part of the settlement house movement and by the Charity Organization Societies' emphasis on neighborhood work.[4] According to this tradition, a key component of community organization, neighborhood organizations of all kinds serve to prevent governmental control and to promote local empowerment.[5]

According to Anthony Downs, there are two types of neighborhood based organizations whose purpose it is to improve the quality of life for residents.[6] The first type is any group, whether voluntary, public, or for profit, that operates within a neighborhood and serves any number of subgroups and their interests. This type may include civic associations, community housing development corporations, co-ops, and local alternative schools.[7] Traditionally, these groups focus on a single issue, and their constituency is limited to active members or users, such as parents of children in an alternative school. In single purpose organizations, formal membership is often required, and at times, active membership is required to be able to benefit from the collective goods.

The second type of neighborhood organization is an NRO. An NRO is a local voluntary group managed by local residents that seeks to represent all residents, regardless of their personal involvement. Neighborhood-representative organizations pressure government agencies to be more accessible and more responsive to residents. Furthermore, NROs traditionally become involved in a variety of communal issues. Mancur Olson described the function of voluntary organizations as the provision of collective goods.[8] In NROs, those who are not official members and who may not contribute toward the collective goods are nevertheless viewed as a constituency and are free to benefit from these collective goods.

While the boundaries between these two forms of neighborhood organizations are often blurred, there are major differences between the two groups. For example, public access to the collective goods and the community's ability to influence the organization may apply to one but not to the other.[9] In this article, I concentrate only on NROs.

There are no reliable data available on the total number of NROs in the United States or abroad. Nevertheless, it can be assumed that the number runs into the hundreds of thousands. Janice Perlman for example, reports some 10,000 block associations in New York City alone, while the National Commission on Neighborhoods lists over 8,000 large neighborhood organizations of all types in the United States.[10] Carl Milofsky, in a survey of neighborhood organizations, found that 35 percent were advocacy oriented rather than service or single-subject oriented, which indicates that about one-third of all neighborhood organizations are NROs.[11] In Scotland, there bas been a coordinated campaign at the national level to establish NROs, while, in Israel, local neighborhood committees (a type of NRO) have sprung up in almost every urban neighborhood.[12]There are two popular stances concerning the level of democracy in NROs. Those taking the first stance believe that NROs are an ideal example of democracy in action. Most proponents of neighborhood based organizations maintain that these organizations are the core of democratic society.[13] Those taking the second stance believe, based on Robert Michels's famous "iron law of oligarchy," that even NROs are, by nature, oligarchic. A third possible stance is that representation in NROs is high while participation is low, or vice versa. This third stance is a mix of the two extreme stances presented above. In this article, I do not take the democratic basis of NROs as a given but, rather, as a basis for inquiry. My purpose is not to challenge the importance of democracy in NROs but, rather, to assess the extent to which NROs are democratic.

A review of the literature on NROs shows that any mention of democracy is usually confined to the overall description of the organizations. Those studies that did focus on the democratic functioning of NROs had a narrow perspective and concentrated largely on a limited number of organizations in one locale. Nowhere in the literature is there a broad analysis of all the components conducive to the democratic functioning of a wide range of NROs. A substantial portion of the literature on NROs is normative in nature, that is, what is ideally expected, and there is little empirical data analyzing the level of democracy in NROs.

In this article I aim (1) to develop a model to define levels of democracy, including both representative and participatory elements of democracy; (2) to review case studies and research findings in the literature on NROs and, based on the proposed model, assess their level of both representative and participatory democracy; and (3) to assess the overall level of democracy in NROs.

Defining Democracy in NROs

Many political and social scientists regard NROs as contributing to a more democratic society. John L. McKnight claims that "the vital center of democracy is the community of associations. Any person without access to that forum is effectively denied citizenship."[14] This value-laden approach has led to increased calk for greater citizen participation and decentralization.[15] Neighborhood-representative organizations are seen as one way to achieve this participatory democracy. Participatory democracy focuses on the extent to which an organization is open to and incorporates all residents. This view applied to NROs would focus on the organization's internal structure and relationships with its constituencies.[16]

Many modern political scientists, disillusioned by the concept of participatory democracy, have found this form of democracy not only impractical but also debilitating. Joseph Schumpeter and Robert Dahl, for example, define democracy, not as a process involving as many people as possible, but as a way to arrive at political decisions by means of a competitive struggle for the people's vote.[17] The ordinary citizen, then, is involved in the democratic process by determining who will make decisions for him or her (representative democracy).

Thus far, I have described democracy as a two-dimensional concept composed of participation and representation. In this article I propose 10 criteria, based in part on Hanna Pitkin, and Carl Milofsky and Joyce Rothschild, by which to assess both the participatory and representative levels of democracy in NROs.[18] Pitkin proposes a more detailed model of democracy that focuses solely on representative democracy. Her model distinguishes among four aspects of representative democracy: formal, descriptive, substantive, and actual representation. Although these categories are important and add to the basic dichotomy mentioned above, Pitkin's model does not fully address the broad aspects of democracy in neighborhood-based organizations because it does not take into account participatory democracy.

Another attempt to measure democracy in neighborhood-based organizations, and one that can be also applied to NROs, was proposed by Milofsky and Rothschild. They focused almost exclusively on issues of participatory democracy. The key components of their model include participation as democracy, voluntarism as democracy, donated resources as democracy, public meeting as democracy, and member activism as democracy.

These two approaches, in combination, provide the following 10 criteria for democracy in NROs.

1. *Free, open elections.* This criterion, which Pitkin labels "formal representation," is the hallmark of all democratic societies and organizations. Without the open and honest election of officials, the power in NROs will be held by those who appoint themselves and who care only for their own interest. This criterion,

which tests the level of representative democracy in an NRO, overlaps with some aspects of participatory democracy because it calls for active member participation. It is important, therefore, to determine to what extent elections are held and how many members participate.

2. *Members' participation.* Another criterion of democracy in NROs is the extent to which the general members are involved in planning and policy-making.[19] Organizations with an active membership are characterized by open meetings, consensus decision making, and members' participation in regular activities and decision-making bodies. This criterion tests the level of participatory democracy.

3. *Informed membership.* A third criterion to assess the level of democracy is the availability of information. It is imperative that officials of any democratic organization keep their members well informed, especially on a local level where most people may know one another and rumors are frequent.[20] This is important for both representative and participatory democracy. Residents cannot be involved in or demand action from elected members of an NRO if they are not aware of what the organization is doing.

4. *Accountability to constituents.* A fourth criterion of democracy is a high level of visibility and accountability of the organization. Democratic organizations and their officials must not only open their records to the public, but they must also permit internal and external examinations of accountability, planning, and accomplishments, including independent investigations and audits.

5. *Due process.* A criterion of participatory democracy is due process, which protects members against nepotism, injustices, and harassment. Due process assures fair treatment and limits the power of authorities in dealing with individuals. Accordingly, a democratic NRO must establish and publish clear procedures for action that citizens may follow.[21] Examples include bylaws and protective procedures, such as grievance procedures. In contrast, an NRO that has no written guidelines and takes action arbitrarily based on the officials' interests can still function, but it cannot be considered a participatory or representative democratic organization. Rothschild and J. Allen Whitt note that alternative organizations, such as community health clinics or parent-run schools, are characterized by minimally stipulated rules and primacy of ad hoc individual decisions.[22] However, in alternative organizations, due process is manifested by lengthy discussions in which all members are actively participating and in which all members are protected.

6. *Level of similarity.* A sixth criterion of representative democracy is the level of similarity between elected officials and the constituency, which Pitkin labels as "descriptive representation." Those who hold office in NROs should resemble those whom they represent because common characteristics often translate into equal interests.[23] This assumption of equal interests may have originated, in part, from the Marxist theory of class consciousness. If leaders and constituencies belong to the same group, then it is likely that they share the same problems and seek the same communal services and goods. If leaders belong to a

different group, then they will likely pursue services and goods in their own self-interest and not those preferred by the majority of residents.

7. *Similarity in perceived needs.* This criterion of representative democracy was categorized by Pitkin as "substantive representation." She argues that good representation entails not only similarity in background but, most important, also a common perception by both leaders and constituents of problems and their urgency. According to this criterion, elected leaders are not to pursue their own private agenda but to represent the interests of all residents. This is especially important in NROs where there is no real competition for office and incumbents can easily become entrenched.

8. *Cui bono?* This eighth criterion of democracy, based on Peter Blau and Richard Scott's typology of organizations, asks who actually benefits from the activity of the NRO.[24] This criterion focuses on those who derive a practical benefit (leaders alone or the whole community). Cui bono is a more direct indicator of democratic representation than the leaders' perceptions of problems or similarity in characteristics, although it is more difficult to measure. According to Richard Rich, it is hard to attract leaders without incentives, yet such incentives increase the potential for conflict between members' interests in collective goods and leaders' interests in maximizing the rewards of their roles.[25] Robert Rosenbloom believes that because neighborhood organizations are local and usually do not focus on social reform, leaders and active members are largely motivated by the desire to preserve their own property value and to improve their quality of life.[26] Thus, a careful analysis is required as to whose interests are being served and to what extent leaders are self-serving.

9. *Successful advocacy.* A ninth criterion of democratic NROs is effectiveness in representing the needs and preferences of residents vis-à-vis formal institutions. This criterion is, to some extent, parallel to what is labeled by Pitkin as "actual representation." I distinguish between the personal benefits of leaders (cui bono) and effective representation, although both are grouped by Pitkin as actual representation. The reason for this distinction is that, although some leaders might not work for their own interests, there is also the possibility that they might not work for the collective good but would give preference to the interests of government and other external public authorities.[27] These governmental organizations could assimilate these leaders and use them as a means of social control to prevent change.

10. *Competition among NROs.* A final criterion of the level of democracy in NROs is competition. Competition by various NROs may in itself be a positive process; however, it can weaken other democratic processes. For example, if several NROs within one neighborhood organize to carry out a particular mission, then they may impede one another's progress compete for the same resources, and unintentionally weaken the neighborhood. Another example would be when representatives of different organizations compete for the same resources for different causes and attempt to influence the same formal organization in their own favor. In the latter case, representatives of upper-middle-class NROs

are likely to be more effective because of their stronger political ties, greater experience in lobbying, and greater resources, thus reversing the representative democratic effect of NROs in low-income neighborhoods.[28] One can argue that such a network of NROs is the ideal form of democracy. However, competitive NROs are likely to have a harmful effect and serve as a means for preventing change and for perpetuating the current social order in the neighborhood.

In the remainder of this article, I will review data from various studies that are relevant to these 10 criteria of democratic functioning. Findings related to single-purpose organizations are excluded. A few methodological limitations should be acknowledged. First, numerous studies are used for this examination, some of which were conducted outside the United States. The meaning and cultural contexts of NROs in different countries may differ. Second, a neighborhood may have more than one NRO; thus, some may represent the whole neighborhood while others serve a certain subpopulation. Both types are included in this study. Third, the NROs studied varied in size, scope of activities, and history. Finally, the decision as to whether a certain local group is an NRO is seldom clear. However, my findings are consistent across this methodological variation and thus indicate strong validity.

Free, Open Elections

Free, open elections are the most common symbol of democracy and thus are an important criterion in testing the level of democracy in NROs. In Dayton, Ohio, even though the city mandated and supported formal elections for NROs and mailed out ballots with stamped return envelopes, only a small percentage of residents bothered to vote.[29] In a study of 11 NROs in Indianapolis, Rich determined that only a small percentage of members had actually voted in the elections and that officeholders in the NROs ran virtually uncontested in the elections.[30] From a study of 20 NROs in Israel, Joseph Katan and I conclude that most officials are either self-appointed or appointed by interested city officials.[31] Ruth Liron and Shimon Spiro, in a study of project renewal in Israel, found that approximately 40 percent of the officials had been appointed and that another third had volunteered.[32] Although it is often difficult for NROs to find residents who are willing to run for office, those who do agree are almost invariably elected, and there seldom is a real threat of being voted out of office.

Ibrahim Regab, Arthur Blum, and Michael Murphy report that in Cleveland, Ohio, all the organizations they studied had been started by a small group of residents who, upset by a critical incident in the neighborhood, had decided to do something about it, which reflects self-appointment.[33] A similar phenomenon of self-appointment is reported by Terry Cooper in a case study in Los Angeles.[34] Cooper notes that, when the NRO became involved in a major planning effort, only members who had the required skills remained active. Michael Masterson reports that, in a government-proposed plan to establish neighborhood councils in Scotland, only 28 percent of the councils held a contested election and that, overall, only about 15 percent of council residents bothered to vote.[35] As a result, councilors, to a large extent, selected one another.

The overall trend from these studies is that the election of many neighborhood officials is not entirely democratic. It may be the voluntary nature of these offices and the attendant costs that make them unattractive to many residents. The lack of competition may contribute to Pamela Oliver's findings that active participation is also based on the belief that there is no one else to do the job.[36] While such a motive ensures some citizen involvement, it is insufficient to generate the competition required for a true democratic election process.

Member Participation

In his Indianapolis study, Rich found that officers and a few activists did almost all the work in NROs. Similarly, Katan and I report that, in Israel, residents are rarely involved in NROs.[37] Paul King and Orly Hacohen discovered that, in Israel, even some officials took no active part in the organization.[38] To a great extent, the few officials who did serve preferred not to be bothered by the dictates of the other residents.

Cooper reports that, the more successful an NRO becomes, the more it tends to deemphasize resident participation.[39] He also notes that, as issues become more technical and professional, the likelihood of organizational stagnation and oligarchic decision making increases. Curtis Ventriss and Robert Pecorella document the case of one organization that was able to avoid professionalization and maintain close contacts with many residents.[40] Nevertheless, it seems that in the life cycle of NROs, professionalization and detachment from residents is more the norm than the exception. Stephen McNamee and Kimberly Swisher report that "the incomplete records and our own observations at meetings indicate generally poor attendance at most priority board meetings."[41] Vincent Bolduc notes that, in most board meetings that were open to all, only the board members participated and that, on average, one new person attended every other meeting.[42] Similarly, Howard Hallman describes a case study in Columbus, Ohio, in which attendance by residents gradually diminished and the executive council became the dominant body.[43] Michael Lipsky and Margaret Levi studied several NROs in poor communities and found that, because the leaders had difficulty in defining what the rewards of membership might be, local residents were not receptive to the organization, even though it might serve them.[44]

The findings from these studies indicate a trend of minimal resident participation. It may be that many officials in NROs recognize the importance of residents' involvement but also view it as costly and as an unwelcome and added burden. This is especially true of older NROs, in which the zeal of the start-up stage has passed.[45]

Keeping Members Informed

In a nationwide study, Curt Lamb discovered that nearly two-thirds of the residents in black neighborhoods could not name even one important local group.[46] In his study, Rich found only very limited contact between officers and members of the organizations.[47] Even when they could expect positive rewards from such contacts, leaders failed to develop adequate networks with residents. Bolduc reports that most of the residents surveyed in Hartford, Connecticut, could not accurately describe any neighborhood association activities, even though the association published a monthly neighborhood newspaper. [48] According to Katan and me, and King and Hacohen, NROs in Israel are not required to communicate with or report to local residents.[49] They report that some organizations used one-to-one communication as a method of reporting and very few mailed out reports or made formal reports in a local newspaper, and then only on an irregular basis. In all cases, the information was filtered by the leaders. Liron and Spiro reveal that only 30 percent of the neighborhood residents studied viewed the organization as representative and only 12 percent knew an organization official by name.[50] Finally, Matthew Crenson studied the level of awareness of NROs by residents in six Baltimore neighborhoods.[51] He determined that only 40 percent knew of such an organization in their neighborhood and were able to name it. This study clearly indicates a level of detachment between NROs and residents, but further study is necessary to validate the findings.

This review of the literature suggests that the means used by NROs to communicate with residents are varied, inadequate, and not entirely democratic in nature. First, there are no clear guidelines as to what information should be made public. Second, most of the methods used by NROs to communicate with residents are informal and on an ad hoc basis. Finally, for the most part, all information they provide is censored and approved by the officials beforehand.

Accountability

Very few of the studies reviewed in this article mention any formal internal or external form of evaluation or auditing. None of the studies report employing a certified public accountant or other qualified professionals as an independent auditor, and none use an external means of evaluation. Furthermore, the studies did not report any attempt at systematic evaluation from within. Interestingly, most studies reviewed, were initiated by the researchers, and officials of the NROs granted permission to the researcher to participate and record. Thus, the officials, once ejected or appointed, apparently had little or no accountability to their constituencies.

One study explicitly deals with accountability. Patrick Sills, Hugh Butcher, Patricia Collis, and Andrew Glen, in a study of five NROs in their formative stage in England, note that those who initiated the new NROs maintained leadership roles and were not accountable to members and residents.[52]

In contrast, most studies of single-purpose organizations find high levels of evaluation and auditing. For example, in a detailed analysis of a civic organization in South Africa, Patricia Wheeldon reports the use of auditing, and Milofsky and Sandra EIion cite the use of evaluation in a local alternative school.[53] It may be that organizations with specific, service-oriented missions encourage careful review, while organizations that are broadly representative tend not to emphasize accountability.

Due Process

McKnight, a strong proponent of NROs, asserts that such organizations can respond quickly to residents' complaints because NROs are not overly complex.[54] There are no formal procedures in selecting an issue and no institutional barriers to planning and taking action. Regardless of the benefits, the literature indicates that due process is seldom found in NROs.

According to Rich, the "leadership cadre" of the NRO makes most of the decisions regarding what projects to implement, how funds should be raised, and what position to take on issues affecting the community.[55] This finding is supported also by Sills, Butcher, Collis, and Glen's study of five NROs in England.[56] Steven Haeberle studied 93 NROs in Birmingham, Alabama, over a 1-year period and found that the number of meetings per association ranged from 0 to 16, with a median of 7, although each association was required to meet once each month.[57] The leaders appeared to make most of the decisions and plans in private with minimal regard for written procedures. Bolduc notes that NRO leaders recognize their uncontested power but do very little to change the situation.[58] Katan and I indicate that none of the NROs in Israel have bylaws that clearly state the rules on public scrutiny or on the appeals process.[59] King and Hacohen also disclose that none of the NROs in their sample have grievance procedures.[60]

These findings indicate that NROs operate with little concern for due process. Most NROs act according to the current leader or activist's preferences and rarely commit to written bylaws. At times they reflect the interests of a small cadre of leaders and active members at the expense of other residents who have no established means to claim their case.

Similarity Between Leaders and Members

Of all types of political participation, community leadership is strongly and positively related to socioeconomic status.[61] This may be because community leadership requires a high degree of professional skill and communication capabilities.[62] Downs finds that residents with the greatest financial or emotional investment in the status quo are the most active in NROs.[63] Because those in power in many NROs prefer only minimal change and strongly support conservative measures to maintain the status quo, many of those who are extremely dissatisfied with the current situation opt to move away from the neighborhood.

Sue Ann Allen found that, while 63 percent of the homes in East Lansing. Michigan, were renter occupied, only 7 percent of the members and 14 percent of the leaders in the NRO were renters, which reflects a clear bias toward homeowners.[64] This does not imply that affluent neighborhoods necessarily have more active NROs; rather, the leaders in each neighborhood, regardless of its relative socioeconomic status, tend to be those whose income and status is higher than that of other residents. Abraham Wandenman, Paul Florin, Robert Friedmann, and Ron Meier observe that, in both Israel and Nashville, Tennessee, "rootedness" in the community is related to active participation in NROs.[65] "Rootedness" means living for a long period of time in the area, intending to stay longer, having children, and owning a home. Regab, Blum, and Murphy report that leaders have higher incomes than members and other residents and are more likely to work in processional or managerial occupations.[66] This trend is borne out by Bolduc's study in Hartford, Connecticut, Masterson's study in Scotland, Sills and colleagues' study in England, and Yasumasa Kuroda's study in Japan.[67] This trend, with minimal variations, has held constant since the early studies on personal characteristics of NRO leaders.[68] Thus, leaders in NROs can be clearly characterized as the neighborhood elite.

The overall findings from the literature indicate that the leaders of NROs are not democratically elected by the residents, operate in seclusion from other residents, are not accountable to residents, operate according to their own interests and style rather than by due process, and are not typical community members but the local elite. This profile raises questions as to the match between the community needs of leaders and residents. It also raises questions as to whom the leaders are serving—themselves, their subgroup within the neighborhood, or the neighborhood as a whole.

Similarity in Perceived Needs

Regab, Blum, and Murphy studied neighborhood needs as perceived by leaders, members, and residents and found that leaders rated problems as more severe than did members and residents.[69] They found a correlation between leaders and residents in the perception of problem urgency of .42. They indicate that this correlation is high but fail to account for chance agreement. If these considerations were taken into account, the correlation would be quite low and would indicate differences in perception between activists and residents. Regab, Blum, and Murphy also note that residents and leaders significantly disagree on 40 percent of the issues, mostly in the area of housing and city services. In a later paper on the same sample, Blum and Regab report that, after a few years in office, leaders became more interested in citywide issues than those of the neighborhood and residents lost interest in the NROs.[70]

Crenson found a similar gap between residents and organizational activists in six Baltimore neighborhoods.[71] In Japan, Kuroda found significant differences between leaders and residents with regard to international attitudes, economic liberalism, taxes, and authoritarianism.[72] Cooper shows how an NRO, involved in carrying out a complex mission of developing, obtaining formal approval, and carrying out a large-scale housing project in the neighborhood, slowly divorces itself from the perceived needs of many residents.[73] According to Cooper, dealing with complex formal organizations shifts the focus of NRO officials from the needs of the residents to those of a technically oriented group of professionals with whom they frequently interact. Thus, officials gradually find it difficult to attend to the needs of the "uneducated" residents. Sills, Butcher, Collis, and Glen and Ventriss and Pecorella show that the act of being attentive to residents' needs and interests is slow, frustrating, and often discordant and can lead to burnout for its unpaid, unrewarded workers.[74]

The overall trend that emerges from the studies reviewed is that, over time, NROs become more professional and bureaucratic while neglecting residents' concerns. Furthermore, long-term leaders become impatient with residents and tend to prefer to work on what they perceive as good for the residents rather than work with the residents, which further widens the gap between the two groups' perceived needs.

Cui Bono

Theoretical literature like that of Rich and Olson assumes that personal gains motivate some or all people who volunteer to be NRO leaders.[75] With some exceptions, the literature does not seem to support a hypothesis that NRO leaders serve solely to bene-fit themselves; they often function to serve the subgroup to which they belong. Robert Whelman and Robert Dupont show how appointment of the local elite to a task force to revive the New Orleans Zoo helped protect the interests of affluent subgroups in the area.[76] Allen found that in East Lansing, Michigan, the positions taken by the asso-ciation were largely those of homeowners (the majority in the association) and not those of renters (the majority in the neighborhood).[77] Bolduc's findings in Hartford, Connecticut, reveal that most residents were unaware of the two programs the NRO offered, which indicates a division between leaders-beneficiaries and general resi-dents.[78]

Rich and Katan and I argue that material rewards gained by leaders in NROs are minimal.[79] Similarly Wandersman, Florin, Friedmann, and Meier find that the cost of participation—that is, donations, time from work or family and neighborhood requests—far exceeds any available material rewards.[80] These studies indicate that the major rewards for leaders are the satisfaction generated by their activities and accom-plishment within the NRO and that most leaders do not use their position to improve their material status or to abuse their office. It may be that these findings are biased by the limited accountability of and challenge to leaders, and abuse of office may be more prevalent than reported. The overall reported trend in the literature, however, is that NRO leaders have more potential for benefiting neighborhood subgroups than for personal gain.

Successful Advocacy

Regab, Blum, and Murphy report limited congruence between the problems per-ceived as most urgent by the residents and those on which NROs actually concen-trate.[81] They explain this gap by noting that residents stressed problems that had direct impact on the quality of their daily life, while leaders sought a balance between imme-diate and long-range problems. However, this gap may also indicate that leaders adopt perspectives that are comparable to those of city officials.

Many studies of NROs indicate that after a stage of reform and activism, both lead-ers and members co-opt into the formal organizations. Instead of representing the interest of local residents, they begin to assist external authorities in delivering services or in obtaining relevant data.[82] These studies reveal that even the most contentious NROs, those that manage to survive for more than a decade, eventually become community service providers and neglect their earlier advocacy function.[83] Katan and I found that very few NROs in Israel were involved in advocacy or reform and that the majority either served formal organizations or were inactive.[84] Similarly, McNamee and Swisher note that NROs in Dayton, Ohio, spend only 4 percent of their time on planning or policy-making at the city or county level.[85] Their main interest is serving the city and county's need for local information and preserving the NRO.

Again, the overall trend indicated in the literature is that, over time, NRO leaders often disassociate themselves from local residents and ally themselves with the formal institutions with which they communicate. Once NROs become institutionalized, they either become co-producers of services for the local government or become inactive. Thus, they abandon the reformist zeal and participatory spirit that led to and characterize their establishment and the representative role for which they continue to exist.[86]

Competition Among Organizations

The existence of several NROs, contrary to single-function organizations, tends to weaken their individual power of representation.[87] A few researchers report hostility and a loss of power among some competing groups whose members are often from different ethnic, racial, or social groups.[88] The existence of NROs in every neighborhood perpetuates class differences and serves to better the interests of the upper middle class. Michael Williams notes several instances in which NROs, claiming to represent residents, managed to keep blacks out of all-white areas and to oppose orders to integrate schools.[89] McNamee and Swisher reveal that the formation of NROs in upper-middle-class neighborhoods results in loss of power and resources in the nearly all black, inner-city neighborhoods.[90] Poor neighborhoods cannot generate resources and will often rely on funds from authorities or be co-opted in other ways.[91] Due to problems in raising funds and hiring professional staff, it seems evident that the poorer the neighborhood, the less powerful the organization will be.

The above findings indicate that NROs, like any other social structure, often serve to undermine their own positive intentions. When a number of neighborhoods have NROs, the relative advantage for low socio-economic neighborhoods disappears. Furthermore, competition among local groups reduces their effectiveness as they fight over narrow interests. Competition also enables public officials to recruit these organizations for their own purposes.

Discussion

Leaders of NROs are usually well-intentioned residents who, concerned by conditions in their neighborhood, decide to organize to improve things. These leaders select methods in line with their experience and values. In many instances, residents become leaders in a non-democratic manner, such as appointment by external organizations or self-appointment. Even those who are elected are elected by a few residents and often face no real competition.

Because rewards for leadership are meager, few people wish to become leaders, a fact that renders officers less vulnerable to the sanctions of impeachment by residents.[92] Furthermore, as is the case with most leaders, these officials are usually at a higher socio-economic level than are their constituencies. Uri Bronfenbrenner sees this as an indication of representative democracy, in which the best and most able represent the interests of all residents.[93] However, it is also a sign of a low-level participatory democracy in which full citizenship is limited to the elite.

Rich uses the exchange theory from a materialist perspective to argue that leaders of NROs very seldom receive material rewards for their efforts on behalf of the neighborhood.[94] Because their rewards are intrinsic, they do not need the other residents to be active in the NRO. The leadership group establishes its own system of social exchanges, such as their periodic meetings over refreshments, that generates benefits that offset the cost of running the organization. This increases the leaders' detachment from their constituencies.

Officials in NROs tend to create a small cadre of activists and to exchange information within this select circle. As a result, most residents are unaware of what is going on, except during the development and conflict phases of the organization. In this respect, NROs, like many other organizations, subscribe to Michels's "iron law of oligarchy"—that is, all organizations develop small but highly centralized and bureaucratic bodies of leaders—the elite—who will necessarily compromise democratic principles and keep most residents from participating and electing new leaders.[95]

Some cities and national organizations have developed bylaws and democratic procedures that NROs are expected to observe in their day-to-day operation.[96] Yet NROs are characterized by a high level of flexibility and informality, which allows leaders to do as they wish. There are very few, if any, mechanisms for control or accountability to hinder officials of NROs.

Marlyn Gittle suggests that democratic citizen participation organizations may initially promote social change and adhere to participatory democratic processes but that they tend to be absorbed by the very institutional structures they had set out to change.[97] Along the same lines, Cooper argues that leadership demands technical and bureaucratic skills that alienate the constituencies—a principal characteristic of the "iron law of oligarchy."[98] Thus, many NROs, which at the outset involved residents in a democratic process, accommodate public authorities once they mature. When the social reform drive wanes, these organizations become less active, more self-preserving, more controlled by outside authorities, and less concerned with their democratic base. John McCarthy and Mayer Zald, in an analysis of social movement organizations, note that, to obtain needed external resources, organizations must meet the idiosyncratic preferences of those providing the resources, the democratic nature of the organization is compromised, and the survival of the organization becomes primary.[99]

Ventriss and Pecorella found one exception: a neighborhood organization that managed to remain accountable and close to its residents.[100] They note that this effort was at the expense of attaining goals and required patient, dedicated leaders who wanted to educate rather than achieve. The fact that this is the only exception reported in the literature indicates that both participatory and representative democ-racies are often compromised in NROs.

Conclusion

The major function of NROs is to moderate the power of complex organizations that influence the local scene and to represent the needs and preferences of local resi-dents. However, a review of the literature indicates a low level of both participatory and representative democracy in NROs. From the representative point of view, NROs appear to be a mechanism of social control used by local government and other authorities. From the participatory point of view, NROs appear to be potentially regressive and elitist groups. Thus, I raise the question as to the overall desirability of NROs.

My analysis in this study focused on the actual functioning of NROs from an atomis-tic framework. One may also view NROs from a holistic perspective. In this respect, Williams notes that NROs can be, and often are, reactionary, racist, and anti-progressive while, paradoxically, serving other important functions in the neighbor-hoods.[101] For example, NROs may assist in the individual and collective process of empowering residents or changing attitudes. Such contributions are essential elements in the democratic structure of any given society, and, though difficult to measure, they should not be ignored. Furthermore, the NROs may have an impact on how city plan-ners and politicians regard the autonomy and self-determination of the residents. Without NROs, apathy and hopelessness might prevail on the neighborhood level, and city and other authorities would be free to do as they pleased, without regard to resi-dents' needs and priorities. Neighborhood-representing organizations may have potentially decreased officials' paternalism. Finally, the mere existence of a local NRO may add to the pride of residents and their feeling of belonging even if they themselves are totally alienated from the organization.[102] The level of democracy should not be the only criterion by which NROs are measured. Indirect evidence as to the impor-tance of NROs is provided by Harry Boyte.[103] Based on a survey by the *Christian Science Monitor* in 1977, he reports that most interviewees believed voluntary organizations were more active in helping cities and neighborhoods than was government or big business. These findings are in line with Constance Smith and Anne Freeman's plural-istic thesis that voluntary organizations of all types contribute to democracy in society as a whole, even if they themselves are not necessarily democratic.[104]

It is quite possible that NROs are worthwhile and democratic only when there is a real threat or common problem strong enough to unite and excite the residents. In such cases, NROs serve the majority, are open to residents' input and participation, and are less subject to the influence of the authorities. However, as time passes and the common cause that united residents fades, NROs tend to become more closed, less democratic, and weaker. As such, it is questionable whether the existence of NROs is justified in the postreform stage. A better alternative may be for residents and com-munity organizers alike to develop lively "ad hoc" NROs and to dismantle them once the goal has been achieved. In this respect, enthusiasm and a higher level of democracy will compensate for lack of experience and established structures. However, like all organizations, survival may become the primary goal in times of peace, and NROs do serve several positive functions that would not be performed were they to be dismantled. These include providing authorities with relevant information in the interest of better services and assisting individual residents with problems.

My thesis in this article is that there is a discrepancy between the potential and actual level of democracy in NROs. Before more conclusive assertions can be made, research is required to assess the level of democracy in NROs. These studies should also focus on practices that increase levels of democracy in NROs. Finally, policymakers, neighborhood activists, and local officials should be more aware of these issues and work in ways that will enable NROs to represent the neighborhood rather than the authorities or the leaders. The problem of rewards for leaders is a crucial one.[105] Because the rewards of leadership are minimal, very few wish to compete for office, and without the fear of being unseated, leaders have no incentive for democratic performance and need not be accountable. A more attractive reward system would increase competition and increase the level of democracy in NROs.

Notes

Earlier versions were presented at the international conference on "Voluntarism, Non-Governmental Voluntary Organizations (NGOs), and Public Policy," May 22–24, 1989, in Jerusalem, Israel, and at the annual meeting of the Inter-University Consortium on International Social Development, August 12–15, 1990, in San Jose, Costa Rica. I wish to thank Benjamin Gidron, Carl Milofsky, Shimon Spiro, and Antonin Wagner.

1. Peter L. Berger and Richard J. Neuhaus, *To Empower People: The Role of Mediating Structures in Public Policy* (Washington, D.C.: American Enterprise Institute for Public Policy Research, 1977).

2. Michael Lipsky and Margaret Levi, "Community Organization as a Political Resource," in Harlan Hann, ed., *People and Politics in Urban Society*n (Beverly Hills, Calif.: Sage, 1972), 175–99; Richard C. Rich, "A Political-Economy Approach to the Study of Neighborhood Organizations," *American Journal of Political Science* 24 (4) (November 1980): 559–92; Ibrahim A. Regab, Arthur Blum, and Michael J. Murphy, "Representation in Neighborhood Organizations," *Social Development Issues* 5 (2–3) (1981): 62–73.

3. Emile Durkheim, *The Division of Labor in Society* (Glencoe, Ill.: Free Press, 1964), 28.

4. Roy Lubove, *The Professional Altruist* (New York: Atheneum, 1975), 22–54.

5. George Brager, Harry Specht, and James L Torczyner, *Community Organizing*, 2nd ed. (New York: Columbia University Press, 1987), 1–31.

6. Anthony Downs, *Neighborhoods and Urban Development* (Washington, D.C.: Brookings Institution, 1981), 19–21.

7. Robert Whelman and Robert Dupont, "Some Political Costs of Coprovision: The Case of the New Orleans Zoo, *Public Productivity Review* 40 (Winter 1986): 69–75; William Dennis Keating, K. P. Rasey, and N. Krumholtz. "Community Development Corporations in the United States: Their Role in Housing and Urban Redevelopment," in Willem van-Vliet and J. van-Weesep, eds., *Government and Housing* (Newbury Park, Calif.: Sage, 1990); John Case and Rose-

mary C. R. Taylor, *Co-ops, Communes, and Collectives* (New York: Pantheon, 1979); and Carl Milofsky and Sandra H. Elion, "The Love Life of an Alternative School: The Oligarchy Problem in Democratic Organizations," paper presented at the meeting of the Association of Voluntary Action Scholars, Kansas City, October 1988.

8. Mancur Olson, *The Logic of the Collective Action* (Cambridge. Mass.: Harvard University Press, 1965), 5–52.

9. Carl Milofsky and Joyce Rothschild, "Are Democracy and Bureaucracy Compatible?" paper presented at the Association of Voluntary Action Scholars, Harrisburg, Pennsylvania, October 1986; Joyce Rothschild and J. Allen Whitt, *The Cooperative Workplace* (New York: Cambridge University Press, 1986).

10. Janice E. Perlman. "Grassrooting the System," *Social Policy* 7 (2) (September–October 1976): 4–20; Harry C. Boyte, *The Backyard Revolution: Understanding the New Citizen Movement* (Philadelphia: Temple University Press, 1980).

11. Carl Milofsky, *Community Organizations: Studies in Resource Mobilization and Exchange* (New York: Oxford University Press, 1988).

12. Michael P. Masterson. "The Creation of Scotland's National System of Official Voluntarism," *Journal of Voluntary Action Research* 8 (1) (January–March 1979): 102–12; Ram A. Cnaan and Joseph Katan, "Local Neighborhood Committees in Israel: Potentials for Self-Help Group Activity," *Journal of Voluntary Action Research* 15 (2) (April–June 1986): 33–46; and Paul King and Orly Hacohen, *Neighborhood Organizations in Israel: Final Report* (Jerusalem: Jerusalem Institute for Public Affairs, 1986).

13. John L McKnight, "Regenerating Community," *Social Policy* 17, no. 3 (Winter 1987): 54–58; Carole Pateman, *Participation and Democratic Theory* (Oxford: Cambridge University Press, 1970).

14. McKnight, "Regenerating Community," 57.

15. See, e.g., Matthew A. Crenson, *Neighborhood Politics* (Cambridge, Mass.: Harvard University Press, 1983); Fremont J. Lyden and Jerry V. Thomas, "Citizen Participation in Policy-Making: A Study of a Community Action Program," *Social Science Quarterly* 50 (3) (December 1969): 631–42; Douglas Yates, *Neighborhood Democracy: The Politics and Impact of Decentralization* (Lexington, Mass.: Heath, 1973); Yates, "Service Delivery and the Urban Political Order," in Willis D. Hawley and David Rogers, eds. *Improving the Quality of Urban Management* (Beverly Hills, Calif.: Sage, 1974), 213–40.

16. Pateman, *Participation and Democratic Theory*, 103–11.

17. Joseph A. Schumpeter, *Capitalism, Socialism and Democracy* (London: Allen & Unwin, 1943); Robert A. Dahl, *Preface to Democratic Theory* (Chicago: University of Chicago Press, 1956).

18. Hanna K. Pitkin, *Representation* (New York: Atherton Press, 1969); Milofsky and Rothschild, "Democracy and Bureaucracy."

19. See, e.g., Richard C. Rich, "The Dynamics of Leadership in Neighborhood Organizations," *Social Science Quarterly* 60 (5) (March 1980): 570–87; Leslie H. Brown, "Democracy in Organizations: Membership Participation and Organizational Characteristics in U.S. Retail Food Co-Operatives," *Organizational Studies* 6 (4) (1985): 313–31.

20. Patricia D. Wheeldon, "The Operation of Voluntary Associations and Personal Networks in the Political Processes of an Interethnic Community," in J. C. Mitchell, *Social Networks in Urban Situations* (Manchester: University of Manchester Press, 1969), 128–80.

21. Raymond R. Albert, *Law and Social Work Practice* (New York: Springer, 1986), 226–32.

22. Rothschild and Whitt, *The Cooperative Workplace*.

23. See, e.g., Ruth Liron and Shimon Spiro, "Citizen Participation in Planning and Management: Criteria for Planning and Implementation in Project Renewal, *Welfare and Society* 9 (1) (September 1988): 36–52; Pitkin, *Representation*.

24. Peter M. Blau and W. R. Scott, *Formal Organizations* (San Francisco: Chandler, 1962).

25. Rich, "Dynamics of Leadership in Neighborhood Organizations."

26. Robert A. Rosenbloom, "The Politics of the Neighborhood Movement," *South Atlantic Urban Studies* 4 (2) (1979): 103–20.

27. Ray H. MacNair, Russell Caldwell, and Leonard Pollane, "Citizen Participants in Public Bureaucracies: Foul-Weather Friends," *Administration and Society* 14 (4) (1983): 507–24.

28. Jeffrey L. Brudney, "Coproduction: Issues in Implementation." *Administration and Society* 17 (3) (November 1985): 243–56.

29. Stephen J. McNamee and Kimberly Swisher, "Neighborhood Decentralization and Organized Citizen Participation," *Sociological Focus* 18 (4) (October 1985): 301–12.

30. Rich, "Dynamics of Leadership in Neighborhood Organizations."

31. Cnaan and Katan, "Local Neighborhood Committees in Israel."

32. Liron and Spiro, "Citizen Participation in Planning and Management."

33. Regab, Blum, and Murphy, "Representation in Neighborhood Organizations."

34. M. Terry L Cooper, "Bureaucracy and Community Organization: The Metamorphosis of a Relationship," *Administration and Society* 11 (4) (February 1980): 411–43.

35. Masterson, "Creation of Scotland's National System."

36. Pamela Oliver, "If You Don't Do It, Nobody Else Will: Active and Token Contributors to Local Collective Action," *American Sociological Review* 49 (5) (October 1984): 601–10.

37. See Cnaan and Katan, "Local Neighborhood Committees in Israel"; Ram A. Cnaan, "Neighborhood Organizations and Social Development in Israel," paper presented at the Inter-University Consortium on International Social Development, fifth symposium, Aland, Finland, August 1988.

38. King and Hacohen, *Neighborhood Organizations in Israel*, 20–46.

39. Cooper, "Bureaucracy and Community Organization."

40. Curtis Ventriss and Robert Pecorella, "Community Participation and Modernization: A Reexamination of Political Choices," *Public Administration Review* 44 (3) (May–June 1984): 224–31.

41. McNamee and Swisher, "Neighborhood Decentralization," 305.

42. Vincent L. Bolduc, "Representation and Legitimacy in Neighborhood Organizations: A Case Study," *Journal of Voluntary Action Research* 9 (1–4) (1980): 165–78.

43. Howard W. Hallman, *Neighborhood Government in a Metropolitan Setting* (Beverly Hills, Calif.: Sage, 1974).

44. Lipsky and Levi, "Community Organization as a Political Resource."

45. See Cooper, "Bureaucracy and Community Organization"; Marlyn Gittle, *Limits in Citizen Participation: The Decline of Community Organizations* (Beverly Hills, Calif.: Sage, 1980); Perlman, "Grassrooting the System."

46. Curt Lamb, *Political Power in Poor Neighborhoods* (New York: Wiley, 1975).

47. Rich, "Dynamics of Leadership in Neighborhood Organizations."

48. Bolduc, "Representation and Legitimacy in Neighborhood Organizations."

49. Cnaan and Katan, "Local Neighborhood Committees in Israel"; King and Hacohen, *Neighborhood Organizations in Israel*.

50. Liron and Spiro, "Citizen Participation in Planning and Management."

51. Matthew A. Crenson, "Social Networks and Political Processes in Urban Neighborhoods," *American Journal of Political Science* 22 (3) (August 1978): 578–94.

52. Patrick Sills, Hugh Butcher, Patricia Collis, and Andrew Glen, "The Formation and Forms of Community Groups," *Journal of Voluntary Action Research* 9 (1–4) (1980): 189–202.

53. Wheeldon, "Operation of Voluntary Associations and Personal Networks"; Milofsky and Elion, "Love Life of an Alternative School."

54. McKnight, "Regenerating Community," 54–58.

55. Rich, "Dynamics of Leadership in Neighborhood Organizations."

56. Sills, Butcher, Collis, and Glen, "Formation and Forms of Community Groups."

57. Steven H. Haeberle, "Neighborhood Identity and Citizen Participation," *Administration and Society* 19 (2) (August 1987): 178–95.

58. Bolduc, "Representation and Legitimacy in Neighborhood Organizations."

59. Cnaan and Katan, "Local Neighborhood Committees in Israel"; Cnaan, "Neighborhood Organizations and Social Development."

60. King and Hacohen, *Neighborhood Organizations in Israel*, 20–46.

61. See, e.g., William Erbe, "Social Involvement and Political Activity: A Replication and Elaboration," *American Sociological Review* 29 (2) (April 1964): 198–215; David Knoke and Randall Thompson, "Voluntary Association Membership Trends and the Family Life Cycle," *Social Forces* 56 (1) (September 1977): 48–65; Perlman "Grassrooting the System"; and Aida K. Tomeh, "Formal Voluntary Organization: Participation, Correlates, and Interrelationship," *Sociological Inquiry* 43 (3–4) (1974): 89–122.

62. Uri Bronfenbrenner, "Personality and Participation: The Case of the Vanishing Variables, *Journal of Social Issues* 16 (4) (1960): 54–63: Sidney Verba and Norman H. Nie, *Participation in America* (New York: Harper and Row, 1972).

63. Downs, *Neighborhoods and Urban Development*, 172–84.

64. Sue Ann Allen, "An Analysis: Community Association Issue Involvement," *Journal of the Community Development Society* 8 (1) (Spring 1977): 98–105.

65. Abraham Wandersman, Paul Florin, Roben Friedmann, and Ron Meier, "Who Participates, Who Does Not, and Why? An Analysis of Voluntary Neighborhood Organizations in the United States and Israel," *Sociological Forum* 2 (3) (September 1987); 534–55; see also K. Cox, "Housing Tenure and Neighborhood Activism," *Urban Affairs Quarterly* 18 (1) (1982): 107–29.

66. Regab, Blum, and Murphy, "Representation in Neighborhood Organizations."

67. Bolduc, "Representation and Legitimacy in Neighborhood Organizations"; Masterson, "Creation of Scotland's National System"; Sills, Butcher, Collis, and Glen, "Formation and Forms of Community Groups"; and Yasumasa Kuroda, "Psychological Aspects of Community Power Structure: Leaders and Rank-and-File Citizens in Reed Town, Japan," *Social Science Quarterly* 48 (3) (December 1967): 433–42.

68. Bronfenbrenner, "Personality and Participation," 54–63.

69. Regab, Blum, and Murphy, "Representation in Neighborhood Organizations."

70. Arthur Blum and Ibrahim I. Regab, "Developmental Stages or Neighborhood Organizations," *Social Policy* 15 (4) (Spring 1985): 21–28.

71. Crenson, "Social Networks and Political Processes."

72. Kuroda, "Psychological Aspects of Community Power Structure."

73. Cooper, "Bureaucracy and Community Organization."

74. Sills, Butcher, Collis, and Glen, "Formation and Forms of Community Groups"; Ventriss and Pecorella, "Community Participation and Modernization."

75. Rich, "Dynamics of Leadership in Neighborhood Organizations"; Olson, *Logic of the Collective Action.*

76. Whelman and Dupont, "Some Political Costs of Coprovision."

77. Allen, "An Analysis: Community Association Issue Involvement."

78. Bolduc, "Representation and Legitimacy in Neighborhood Organizations."

79. Rich, "Dynamics of Leadership in Neighborhood Organizations"; Cnaan and Katan, "Local Neighborhood Committees in Israel."

80. Wandersman, Florin, Friedmann, and Meier, "Who Participates, Who Does Not, and Why?"

81. Regab, Blum, and Murphy, "Representation in Neighborhood Organizations."

82. See, e.g., Cooper, "Bureaucracy and Community Organization"; Gittle, *Limits in Citizen Participation*; Lyden and Thomas, "Citizen Participation in Policy-Making "; and McNamee and Swisher, "Neighborhood Decentralization."

83. Jean Panet-Raymond, "Community Groups in Quebec: From Radical Action to Voluntarism for the State?" *Community Development Journal* 22 (4) (1987): 281–86; Robert A. Rosenbloom, *Pressuring Policy Making from the Grassroots: The Evolution of Alinsky-Style Community Organization* (Ph.D. dissertation, Stanford University, 1979).

84. Cnaan and Katan, "Local Neighborhood Committees in Israel."

85. McNamee and Swisher, "Neighborhood Decentralization." See also Rich, "Dynamics of Leadership in Neighborhood Organizations."

86. Gittle, *Limits in Citizen Participation*; McNamee and Swisher, "Neighborhood Decentralization."

87. Cnaan, "Neighborhood Organizations and Social Development."

88. See. e.g., Hallman, *Neighborhood Government in a Metropolitan Setting*; Ventriss and Pecorella, "Community Participation and Modernization"; and Whelman and Dupont, "Some Political Costs of Coprovision."

89. Michael R. Williams, *Neighborhood Organizations: Seeds of a New Urban Life* (Westford, Conn.: Greenwood Press, 1985), 72–82.

90. See. e.g., McNamee and Swisher, "Neighborhood Decentralization"; and Robert L. Lineberry and Ira Sharkansky, *Urban Politics and Public Policy* (New York: Harper and Row, 1971).

91. Lipsky and Levi, "Community Organization as a Political Resource."

92. See Masterson, "Creation of Scotland's National System"; Rich, "Dynamics of Leadership in Neighborhood Organizations."

93. Bronfenbrenner, "Personality and Participation."

94. Rich, "Dynamics of Leadership in Neighborhood Organizations."

95. Robert Michels, *Political Parties* (New York: Free Press, 1962).

96. See Boyte, *Backyard Revolution*; King and Hacohen, *Neighborhood Organizations in Israel.*

97. Gittle, *Limits in Citizen Participation.*

98. Cooper, "Bureaucracy and Community Organization."

99. John D. McCarthy and Mayer N. Zald, "Resource Mobilization and Social Movement: A Partial Theory." *American Journal of Sociology* 82 (6) (May 1977): 1212–41.

100. Ventriss and Pecorella, "Community Participation and Modernization."

101. Williams, *Neighborhood Organizations*, 55–56.

102. Bolduc, "Representation and Legitimacy in Neighborhood Organizations."

103. Boyte, *Backyard Revolution.*

104. Constance Smith and Anne Freeman, *Voluntary Associations: Perspectives on the Literature* (Cambridge, Mass.: Harvard University Press, 1972).

105. See Olson, *Logic of the Collective Action*; Rich, "Dynamics of Leadership in Neighborhood Organizations."

Commentary

Ram A. Cnaan

In 1978, I left Israel for the first time. It was not a regular tourist trip to experience a new place and come back home shortly thereafter. It was a family trip to Pittsburgh where I was to start a doctoral program in social work. At that time, I served as a social planner and was scheduled to be the Director of Social Planning upon my return from the United States. Being trained as a social worker (both B.S.W. and M.S.W.), I was eager yet terrified of the experience awaiting me: pursuing a Ph.D. in a foreign language, in which I was not fluent. As it turned out, the experience was exhilarating.

The doctoral experience was a unique one. I can claim that my cohort holds the world record for fast completion of the Ph.D. requirements. Three of us did so under

24 months and the other two within 30 months. Indeed, we worked hard, but what was more important was that we collaborated and helped each other. It was a process of offering your strengths and finding support where you least expected it. I offered methodological knowhow and was assisted by my colleagues with English and theory.

My focus was on practical solutions to social problems and learning to do research seemed a necessary tool to help with planning of social services. When I left the doctoral program in Pittsburgh I saw the merit of social science research and enjoyed the process, yet I was destined to be a civil servant leading the front of social services planning. Upon returning to my home country, Israel, I was appointed director of social planning for the State of Israel. I had 40 social planners reporting to me and felt that my efforts and knowledge made a difference. However, soon after, a political change in the Israeli government brought about a political regime that did not put any importance on social services or social planning. My professional desperation was evident when one of my former professors called me and offered me a teaching position at Tel Aviv University School of Social Work, and I accepted it. I was first appointed an adjunct professor, keeping my government position; later I joined the university full-time and kept a partial appointment with the government. In 1982, I started my academic career uncertain of my ability to be full-time researcher. I guess no one knows ahead of time if he or she will succeed in his or her chosen career path.

In the four years that followed, I embarked on a few research projects, some self-supported and some with modest research funds. I attached myself and my projects to every willing senior faculty member and visiting scholar. In doing so, I learned how to become a scholar. I had to learn how to transform lengthy and often tedious research reports into publishable manuscripts. It was this process, a voluntary apprenticeship, that was the basis for my first set of academic articles and research career.

My focus then, and for many years to come, was on how best to meet the needs of needy people. As a social planner, I wanted to understand how best to design a social service system that would meet the needs of the indigent and oppressed. As a community practitioner and researcher, given Israel's welfare system, I focused my research activity on local public welfare offices and professionals who met the needs of local residents. I was also concerned with how residents governed their daily lives, assured quality of services, and communicated with public agencies and private corporations that affected their lives. My interests covered small informal groups that existed on the local scene, such as the Neighborhood Representing Organizations, the Parents of Students Committees, and the Synagogue Leadership Groups. I am amazed by the many ordinary people who assume leadership roles; they fascinated and puzzled me as they voluntarily took on demanding roles with little reward. Yet my experience with them always supported Michels's Iron Law of Oligarchy.

The literature on social movements suggests that these movements will become dominated by their leadership. This phenomenon, known as the Iron Law of Oligarchy, was proposed by Robert Michels in 1915. The idea behind his work is that leaders will want to hold onto their leadership position, which provides them with economic rewards as well as social status, and that they will not wish to return to the rank of membership. Consequently, these leaders create bureaucratic machinery that reinforces their grip on power. These leaders enhance their skills and do not provide such opportunities to other members. A byproduct of this process is known as "becalming." Becalming refers to the stage in which members lose faith in the organization and do not expect it to achieve its original goals. Leaders become self-interested and hence oligarchic, and members tend to be apathetic. I was aware of this stream of literature while in Israel but did little to apply it to my own academic work.

In 1986, I took a sabbatical from Tel Aviv University and came for a one-year visiting post at the University of Pennsylvania School of Social Work. I had applied to over 30 schools for a sabbatical place and Penn was one of two that accepted me. I knew little of Philadelphia, Penn, or the school. The first year was followed by an invitation to stay another year and then another, and later an offer to stay long-term. For the first three years at Penn, I commuted from Boston, where my family resided. Only when I was offered a more permanent position did my family join me in Philadelphia.

In the first year or two I worked on writing and publishing papers based on data I brought with me from Israel. I had quite a few datasets, and I was successful in transforming them into a series of articles. The problem, however, was that I did not plan on staying in the United States and hence did not have a solid research agenda to follow.

In 1987, at my first academic conference after joining the School of Social Work, I met my colleague and friend Carl Milofsky. Carl is a professor of sociology at Bucknell University and I collaborated with him on several articles; we recently published *Handbook of Community Movements and Local Organizations* (New York: Springer, 2006). Carl suggested that informal and grassroots organizations could easily avoid the iron law of oligarchy.

Milosky's 1987 paper dealt with how an alternative school managed to maintain the participatory spirit and avoid the iron law of oligarchy. This did not resonate with my experience in community practice. In my experience, even grassroots organizations formed an oligarchy even if there were no economic rewards. Leaders enjoy being leaders and rarely are willing to transfer leadership. Furthermore, even though the social status rewards of serving on a Neighborhood Representing Organization (NRO) were few and the tasks and aggravations endless, leaders did not want to yield power. But I was not sure whether this was an Israeli phenomenon or a universal one. So I started to research the literature on the democratization and member participation in NROs. I found that leaders of these grassroots organizations became experts in what they did (talking to city officials, reading expert reports, calling for hearings, etc.) and that this expertise allowed them to hold on to leadership and slowly become less open to member participation and more elitist. The results of this study, my first paper conceptualized and written in the U.S., were published in 1991 in *Social Service Review* and are reproduced here as my contribution to the Centennial volume.

Other scholars, equipped with a socialist and democratic worldview, published numerous articles on grassroots organizations that maintained member involvement and where leaders were replaced regularly. Clearly, such cases exist, and they are heartwarming. It was, and still is, my stance that the majority of grassroots organizations will follow the iron law of oligarchy. But, unlike social movements, the leaders' methods of holding to power are through developing expertise that makes their replacement difficult. And, in most cases "becalming" takes effect and members are informed rather than involved.

My research at Penn shifted later to include issues of community mental health (using psychosocial rehabilitation) and information technology in social work. But in all these areas my focus was the means by which we can improve the quality of services provided to the poor and needy. Indeed, it is our duty as social workers to constantly struggle to find means to enhance the quality of life of the "have-nots."

In the early 1990s, I observed two issues. First, in the United States welfare services were very limited and the role of government in meeting human needs was marginal when compared to any other Western democracy. Second, undocumented in the academic social work literature, many welfare services in the United States were provided under religious auspices and were often sponsored through private funds. I also realized that there was, and still is to a large extent, a serious gap between social work and organized religion; while religious groups meet many human needs, both social work education and literature ignore these services. I therefore presented a call for a limited partnership between organized religion and social work which became the focus of many papers and presentations in the past sixteen years. The rift between the two U.S. communities that care for the poor—social work and religion—intrigued me and led to the publication of my book, *The Newer Deal: Social Work and Religion in Partnership* (New York: Columbia University Press, 1999).

This academic interest led to a series of grants from various foundations and organizations. Funded by a local nonprofit organization, I started the study of the role of religious congregations in providing social services. The bulk of the findings from this extensive study and their conceptual and policy implications for America at the dawn of the twenty-first century were published in a book entitled *The Invisible Caring Hand: American Congregations and the Provision of Welfare* (New York: New York University Press, 2002).

While I was completing the study discussed above, I started an ambitious project: a census of Philadelphia congregations and their involvement in social service provision. No census of congregations existed in any city in the U.S., and I wanted to fill this gap. I received a generous foundation grant to conduct this research. After three years of merging lists, asking experts, and canvassing the streets of Philadelphia, we came up with a list of close to 2,100 congregations. We completed 1,400 face-to-face in-depth interviews (three to five hours each) with local clergy. The study culminated with several academic articles and the book *The Other Philadelphia Story: How Local Congregations Support Quality of Life in Urban America* (University of Pennsylvania Press, 2006).

At the time this book is published, I continue to research the role of the faith-based community in meeting human needs. I am also interested in people's self-organizing to meet their needs. The paper I selected for this volume is one written at Penn that represents my transition from being an Israeli scholar to a scholar of U.S. issues.

Chapter 30
Moving from Psychoeducation to Family Education for Families of Adults with Serious Mental Illness

Phyllis Solomon

Over the past two decades, interventions for families of adults with serious and persistent mental illness, particularly schizophrenia, have proliferated. Factors that have stimulated development of these interventions include concerns about patients' lack of compliance with prescribed medication and about the minimal effect of psychotropic medication on negative symptoms and social functioning (1). A particularly important factor was research evidence that patients' social environment influenced the course of schizophrenia. This evidence supported vulnerability-stress models of schizophrenia, which integrated biological and environmental factors to explain relapse (2, 3). But the most important factor was that families became the de facto caregivers for adults with major psychiatric disorders but lacked the requisite knowledge, skills, or resources for this task (4).

This paper reviews the conceptual and empirical base for family psychoeducational interventions. The more recent development of family education approaches is also reviewed, and the distinctions between psychoeducation and family education are delineated. The paper concludes with recommendations for program, policy, and research development in the area of family interventions.

Psychoeducation

Family psychoeducational interventions include both educational and therapeutic components. These programs typically offer didactic material on the etiology, diagnosis, symptoms, course, and treatment of the ill relative's disorder and use therapeutic strategies to enhance families' problem solving, communication, and management skills, with the goal of reducing stress and improving families' coping abilities and ultimately reducing the ill relative's rate of relapse (1,3). Thus the educational component is frequently an introduction to more intensive family treatment. Professionals generally define the problem to be addressed, develop the solutions, and evaluate the outcomes (5).

These approaches have been used most extensively with families of patients with schizophrenia (4). Generally the programs are part of a comprehensive treatment package for the patient that includes medication and outpatient clinical management or in some cases social skills training. Therefore, these interventions are adjunctive to the patient's treatment.

Families are generally asked to be involved in psychoeducational interventions for a minimum of nine months, with some approaches asking as much as a two-year commitment. The interventions are typically initiated at a point of crisis for the patient and family, for example, during the patient's hospital stay or at discharge. These interventions may vary in implementation strategies, such as group versus individual approaches; setting, such as home versus clinic; intensity and duration of the educational component; extent of involvement of the ill relative; credentials and qualifications of the providers; and whether the focus is on problem solving skills, communication, or behavioral management (6, 7).

The predominant conceptual basis for these programs is derived from research on expressed emotion, the family's attitudinal affect toward the ill relative. Expressed emotion has been operationally defined as the family's degree of criticism, hostility or rejection, and over-involvement, as measured by the Camberwell Family Interview (8, 9).

Investigators have found that high ratings on measures of expressed emotion in the family predicted psychotic relapse of recently discharged patients who interacted with the family (9–11). This finding has been replicated in several studies, and observation of families' behavior has provided some validation of the construct (12). However; expressed emotion is a controversial concept, and its measurement validity has been questioned (8). Nevertheless, findings on expressed emotion have supplied direction for the development of family interventions targeted to reduce elements of the construct that are associated with patients' relapse.

Although expressed emotion is the most common conceptual basis for psychoeducational interventions, other theoretical frameworks have been used. Goldstein and colleagues (13) investigated an intervention based on crisis theory. McFarlane's multiple family group approach (4) combined elements from research on expressed emotion and on social support.

Irrespective of variation between psychoeducational interventions in conceptual basis and service delivery substantial evidence supports their effectiveness in reducing relapse (14). They have generally been found to be more effective than "routine care" involving medication management and availability of crisis services (1). However, because positive outcomes may dissipate over time, these programs may be most effective in delaying rather than preventing relapse (15, 16). There is also some evidence that patients' compliance with medication proves when families participate in these interventions; thus improved compliance may be the crucial element in reducing relapse (17). Limited data suggest that the interventions associated with improved family well-being and improved social functioning of the ill relative (14).

Family psychoeducational interventions have several positive aspects, including a strong conceptual base, efficacy established by rigorous investigations, cost-effectiveness attributed to a reduction in hospitalization, and a tendency to foster collaborative and supportive relationships between families and professionals.

However, psychoeducational interventions have several limitations, many of which are due to links between program design and design of the research studies in which the interventions were investigated. Most psychoeducational interventions were designed to fit the requirements of random clinical trials, which had stringent eligibility criteria that limited the range of families who participated. Given the heterogeneity of families with an adult relative with a major psychiatric disorder, the findings of these studies have limited generalizability.

Families in these studies were required to have high ratings in expressed emotion based on the Camberwell Family Interview, to have an ill relative with a diagnosis of schizophrenia or schizoaffective disorder, and to have relatively frequent and extensive contact with the relative (18). Subjects tended to be white and middle-class and to be parents of the ill relative. The ill relative was required to be in treatment, or at least to be receiving medication management services. Because families typically entered these programs during their relative's hospital stay or at discharge, they were likely to be highly motivated, given the recency of an acute episode. The dominant outcome measure was psychiatric relapse, and few studies examined other outcomes for either the patient or the family.

Besides limitations related to selection of participants, psychoeducational interventions are often costly, due to intensive investment of professional resources over an extended period.

Family Education

Despite the positive aspects of psychoeducational interventions, they have had limited acceptance among advocacy groups for families of mentally ill persons. This lack of acceptance may be partly attributed to the association between psychoeducation and the concept of expressed emotion, which implies blame to families for the ill relative's relapses; other reasons include the extensive investment of time required by psychoeducational programs and the programs' failure to address the needs and concerns of families (19).

Unlike psychoeducation, which was developed to meet the needs of the ill relative, family education interventions have been designed primarily with the needs of families in mind. Family education emphasizes "the competencies, not the deficits, of the families" and does "not assume a medical therapy model, in which the presumption of pathology in the family being treated is implicit" (14).

Hatfield (19) distinguished among family interventions, all of which had indiscriminately been labeled as psychoeducation irrespective of their roots and orientation. She suggested that the label "psychoeducation" should be reserved for interventions associated with expressed emotion and a medical orientation. In contrast, family education programs are independent from treatment for either the family or the ill relative. Consequently, they tend to be freestanding rather than part of a comprehensive service package.

Conceptual base

The inspiration for family education programs is found in health education, parent education for those with disabled children, and adult education, rather than in family therapy (19). The conceptual framework for family education programs is based on findings about stress, coping and adaptation, and support (5, 20, 21). Research on the family burden of mental illness has shown that severe psychiatric disorders cause enormous stresses and disruptions in the lives of families (22, 23).

The theory of coping and adaptation assumes that "all living systems strive to maintain themselves in their environment, to overcome obstacles, and to achieve autonomy and self-determination" (5). For families of severely mentally ill persons, coping involves continual adjustments to frequent crises and disruptions in daily life. Education to increase family members' coping skills is likely to increase their confidence or self-efficacy in managing their relative's illness and in reducing their own stress and burden. Supportive relationships with professional providers and members of other families who share similar experiences can buffer stress (24, 25). These processes and supports help the family to adapt to their relative's mental illness.

Solomon and Draine (22) found that family members' levels of social support and coping capabilities contributed more to explaining their feeling of burden than did stressors associated with their relative's illness. In another analysis they found that "more extensive adaptive coping was associated with increased social support as measured by the density of the social network, the extent of affirming social support, and participation in a support group for families" (26). They also found that families with better coping had a greater sense of self-efficacy in dealing with the relative's mental illness.

Program Formats

The goals of family education programs are to reduce the stress and burden of families, to increase their coping skills, and to improve the quality of life for themselves and their ill relative. Such programs may be primarily didactic or may combine didactic and experiential elements, offering participants the opportunity to practice the skills they are learning.

Like psychoeducational interventions, family education programs provide information on diagnosis, etiology, symptoms, course, and treatment. In addition, they provide supportive relationships that communicate acceptance, understanding, and confidence in family members' ability to cope. Some currently operating programs were developed by families and are delivered by families, and others have been developed by professionals. Still others are joint endeavors by professionals and families. Many of these programs originated with grassroots efforts by family members (27).

Family education interventions typically use a group format, which helps to reduce the isolation and loneliness often felt by family members (28). Many programs are designed on the self-help model and offer support from other family participants as well as from the professional or family member who leads the group. The ill relative is frequently not a participant, which encourages family members to freely discuss issues of primary concern to them. Programs are generally short, usually lasting no more than three months or ten or twelve weekly sessions, and some may be as short as one session of a few hours. Programs also vary in the types of educational techniques they use, such as written or audiovisual materials.

An alternative to the group format is the family consultation model of family education, which uses a one-to-one format in which a consultant meets with a family member or the family unit without the ill relative present. In this model education is adjunctive to advice, support, and guidance. The consultant, usually a professional but in some instances a family member, gives advice and information tailored to the specific needs of the family and suggests strategies for addressing objectives established in collaboration with the family (5). The frequency and length of participation are open ended, and the family members themselves determine the intensity and duration of the intervention. As new issues arise during the course of their relative's disorder family members may return to seek additional advice from the consultant.

The consultative function of this approach is primary and the educational function secondary. Before obtaining family consultation, families may benefit from participation in a group educational program (5). An assumption of the consultative model is that families who develop the appropriate knowledge and skills will be able to devise their own solutions to problems with minimal direction from the consultant. Families are seen as the experts on the problems they face. The consultant provides a supportive relationship and helps families obtain the information they need to define their objectives and develop strategies to meet them. Written materials, such as articles about mental illness or a directory of local mental health services may be shared with the family.

Family education, including group programs and individual consultation, is generally open to all families regardless of the ill relative's diagnosis, the recency of the diagnosis or an acute illness episode, whether the ill relative is in treatment, the family members' relationship with ill relative, and the amount or frequency of contact.

Program Evaluation

Unfortunately, controlled research on family education programs is limited (19). A search of the literature revealed four rigorously designed evaluations of self-contained family education programs, plus one recently completed study by the author and her colleagues.

Reilly and his colleagues (29) compared effects of pre-discharge educational workshops for families, conducted with and without the ill relative's presence, with those of a hospital tour and a control condition in which families had no educational contacts or other services. The ill relatives had weekly contact with the family and at least two previous hospitalizations and were expected to be discharged within the month. The workshops consisted of one two-hour session that included a presentation and discussion.

Although participants evaluated the workshops positively, there were no differences between the conditions in the relapse rate of the relatives or in families' involvement in treatment within three to four months after discharge. The groups also did not differ on measures of families' beliefs about the causes of the illness or of criticism or rejection of the ill relative. This study remains in the psychoeducation framework because the outcome indicators were focused on the ill relatives rather than on the family members.

Smith and Birchwood (30) randomly assigned families to participate in four weekly group sessions or to receive an information booklet by mail every week for four weeks. Ill relatives resided with their families or were in close contact had a diagnosis of schizophrenia, and were stabilized on medication. After the intervention, families in the group sessions tended to be more optimistic about their role in treatment. Both groups had significant gains in knowledge from baseline, although families in the groups had a greater increase in knowledge. At six-month follow-up, knowledge gains were maintained, and families in both groups perceived significant reductions in their burden. A weakness in this study was the lack of a no-treatment control group.

Posner and colleagues (31) randomly assigned families in regular contact with a relative with a diagnosis of schizophrenia and at least two hospitalizations to an educational support group of eight 90-minute sessions or to a control group. The support group was led by a professional in a clinic setting. Compared with the control group, educational group members had more knowledge about schizophrenia at termination of the program and six-month follow-up. They had greater satisfaction with mental health services, but only at termination of the program. However, the two groups showed no differences in psychological distress, coping behavior, satisfaction with the cohesion and adaptability of the family, and rehospitalization. This study was well designed and maintained the family focus.

Abramowitz and Coursey (32) compared a group of families who attended six two-hour weekly education sessions with a matched comparison group who were unable to attend the educational groups scheduled for their location. Families who were the primary caregiver of a relative with schizophrenia residing in their home were recruited from four community mental health centers. At termination of the group program group participants reported significantly reduced anxiety and personal distress and improved coping behaviors. However there were no changes in negative attitude toward the ill relative or in participants' sense of self-efficacy. This program was specifically designed with a stress-coping framework and maintained a family focus. The use of an experimental design would have enhanced this investigation.

Solomon and colleagues (33, unpublished data) recently conducted a randomized field trial comparing participants in two models of family education-individual consultation and a group workshop consisting of ten weekly two-hour sessions with a wait-list control group. Family members whose relative had schizophrenia or major affective disorder and who had regular contact with and major responsibility for the ill relative were recruited from the community. Outcomes of burden, grief, social support, self-efficacy, coping behaviors, and stress were assessed at termination of the workshop and six-month follow-up.

Individual consultation significantly increased family members' sense of self-efficacy.

Group education significantly increased self-efficacy for families who had never participated in a support or advocacy group for families of psychiatrically disabled persons. The initial effect for self-efficacy did not significantly attenuate during the six-month follow-up period. However, at six months there was no difference between the two experimental groups and the wait-list control group due to the maturation of the control group over the nine-month study period.

This study used a coping-adaptation framework and maintained a focus on outcomes for the families. The group intervention was collaboratively designed by a family member and professionals and was delivered jointly by professionals and trained family members.

Outcomes for the ill relative, including quality of life level of psychiatric symptoms, rehospitalization, medication compliance, and attitudes toward medication compliance, were assessed as a secondary benefit of the interventions, although the ill relative did not participate in either program. Group family education was associated with improved attitudes toward medication compliance (34).

To summarize, although no consistent outcomes have been reported in studies of brief family education, limited evidence suggests that interventions of more than one session are effective, particularly when they remain focused on family outcomes. Unlike research on psychoeducation, studies of family education have not found an effect on ill relatives' rate of relapse. However they have found that families who participated in the interventions gained knowledge and felt greater satisfaction with mental health treatment; experienced a reduction in burden, distress, and anxiety; and improved self-efficacy and coping behaviors, all outcomes consistent with the objectives of the interventions. There is some evidence of retention of gains for up to six months, although maintenance of gains beyond six months has not yet been addressed. Some data, particularly those from the investigation of Solomon and colleagues (34), suggest that these interventions may produce some secondary benefit for the ill relative, such as improved attitudes toward medication compliance.

A noncontrolled study of an educational and support group for spouses similarly found significant improvement in well spouses' knowledge about the illness and coping strategies as well as in personal distress and negative attitudes toward the ill spouse over the three-month intervention and at one-year follow-up (35). Similarly, a few studies that assessed the educational components of psychoeducational family interventions found that those components did not affect relapse but that they did provide some benefit to families by increasing their sense of support from the treatment team and by decreasing their self-blame (36, 37).

Future Directions

The empirical evidence for the efficacy of psychoeducational interventions and the promising results of effectiveness research on family education provide a strong foundation for efforts to expand the scope of these interventions. It is an opportune time to translate the positive findings from the clinical research setting to agency or nonclinical settings and to move from efficacy research conducted under rigorously controlled "ideal" conditions to effectiveness research conducted under natural service circumstances.

Reforms in behavioral health care require time-limited, efficient, and cost-effective interventions (5). Family education interventions have the potential to meet these criteria, but a host of unanswered questions remain. For example, what is the optimal length of these programs? Does it matter who delivers these services? Is education alone effective, or does it need to be coupled with more intensive support to be effective?

Furthermore, research findings suggest an increased need for readily available and accessible interventions given that 30 to 65 percent of adults with severe psychiatric disorders either reside with their families or receive primary care from their families (38–40). Families' desire for information and training that are not related to treatment is demonstrated by the rapid expansion of a recently developed self-help family education program entitled Journey of Hope (41), which is sponsored and endorsed by the National Alliance for the Mentally Ill (NAMI). The 12-week program was developed by family members and is delivered by trained family members in tandem with regularly scheduled support group meetings. A process evaluation of this program is being conducted.

Family education programs are a relatively recent development, and they require further refinement to increase their effectiveness and make them more attractive to the diversity of families in need (19). Researchers must collaborate with providers and family members in refining and evaluating these interventions to ensure productive research and translation of research findings into practice.

For example, research by Solomon and colleagues (33) suggested that individualized consultation may be more immediately effective than a group intervention in bolstering self-efficacy among families who have already participated in support groups. Based on these findings, providers replaced a predetermined curriculum for family education groups with elements from individual consultation that were adapted to a group context. Group meetings were used to help participants develop their own objectives and then work collectively to develop strategies for addressing these objectives. This approach is similar to that used by McFarlane (4).

Given the heterogeneity of families that could potentially benefit from these interventions, specialized programs may be needed for particular ethnic and minority groups, for families whose ill relative has a particular diagnosis, and for family members with a particular relationship with the ill relative—for example, spouse or sibling. Other characteristics that suggest the need for specialized groups include variation in the amount of time since the ill relative received a diagnosis and whether the ill relative is in treatment.

Guarnaccia and Parra (42) have identified a particularly pressing need for interventions for ethnic and minority groups that are sensitive to social and cultural diversity. Considerations in developing such interventions include the participation of extended or fictive family members, provision of transportation, flexibility in scheduling meetings, and use of languages other than English (43). Interventions for aging family members may address issues in planning for the time when program participants are unable to care for their ill relative.

Variations in program format may be crucial in attracting and providing an effective intervention for particular families. For example, Solomon and colleagues (33) found that the group format was not effective in improving the self-efficacy of family members who had previously participated in support or advocacy groups. This finding suggests that program design should consider the family's educational experiences and level of understanding of their relative's illness. A related issue is dosage, or the optimal number of sessions.

Program planners must consider the limited time and energy that families may have. Home-based programs may be attractive for some families, particularly low-income families. Family education could be linked to case management services and could be delivered by case managers or by professional family educators or trained family members in cooperation with case managers. For families whose ill relative does not receive case management services, local NAMI affiliates could train volunteers who would offer family education, consultation, or support in families' homes in the manner of home visitors. Individualized models may be more attractive to families who are uncomfortable with a group format and may be more responsive to the changing needs of families as they and their ill relative age.

Further evaluation will identify program elements that contribute to long-term retention of information. For example, use of audiovisual aids and easily understood written materials that can be taken home and studied may enhance the learning process (30, 36). A program that families may attend as needed, particularly at points of crisis, may increase long-term retention because families may be more receptive to information they can use immediately.

Flexibility and continuity over time may be important elements in the effectiveness of family education interventions. In the study by Solomon and colleagues (33, unpublished data) comparing individual consultation and group workshop models of family, education consultation was limited to 15 hours for purposes of research. However, providers noted that family members involved in the study often asked at the end of sessions, "How many hours do I have left?"

The providers realized that family members who were not involved in the study typically used consultation as needed, in a series of brief contacts over a period of years as crises or questions about their relative's illness arose. Typical service recipients often commented on the support they felt they received because the service continued to be available as their needs changed over time. Just knowing that consultation was available may have reduced stress and anxiety for these families (Solomon, Draine, Mannion, unpublished data). Had the providers conceptualized this aspect of the intervention as crucial, their search might have been designed differently to incorporate this element, and subjects might have demonstrated greater improvement.

Similarly, for purposes of the controlled research, informal one-to-one support typically provided by group leaders at the conclusion of the group workshop was eliminated. One of the leaders, who had conducted workshops before the research project began, noted that the absence of this informal advice and discussion constituted a loss for research subjects. Again, inclusion of this program element in the research design might have resulted in more beneficial outcomes.

Continuing support may be essential to produce a lasting positive effect. It may be unrealistic to expect that a few sessions can make a measurable difference in preparing families to address the complex problems they face (44). Periodic booster sessions that offer new information or repeat previously presented material may enhance learning retention.

The expected outcomes of an intervention are contingent on how the intervention is conceptualized. For example, the objective of a one- or two-session didactic presentation is likely to be increased knowledge. For a program of ten or twelve sessions involving didactic presentations and training in coping skills, the objectives are likely to be improved coping skills as well as increased knowledge. Objectives of family education programs must be clearly articulated so that evaluations can use appropriate outcome measures.

The major indicator of the effectiveness of psychoeducational interventions—relapse of the ill relative—may not be appropriate for time-limited family education interventions. However, investigators continue to evaluate these interventions based on psychoeducational criteria. These outcome measures may well do a disservice to family education, particularly if the interventions encourage families to take care of themselves and set limits for their ill relative, and their ill relative reacts by decompensating and requires hospitalization.

Although psychiatric relapse has clearer empirical referents and is easier to measure than family-focused concepts such as family burden, coping, and self-efficacy (45), it is not theoretically or clinically linked to family education interventions. Unfortunately, there are no psychometrically established instruments for measuring coping behaviors and self-efficacy among families. What constitutes family burden needs additional conceptual work and refinement (46). Further work on the measurement of these concepts is needed before the effectiveness of family education interventions can be determined.

Psychometrically sound outcome measures are also needed to determine the cost-effectiveness of these interventions. Without established cost-effectiveness, these interventions are unlikely to become self-sustaining components of the mental health service system. Whether these programs are delivered by family members or professionals, they need financial independence to become established services.

Currently, family education programs such as Journey of Hope are funded by the Community Support Program of the Substance Abuse and Mental Health Services Administration, state departments of mental health, and NAMI affiliates. These funding sources are not secure long-term arrangements Evidence of the cost-effectiveness of family education may encourage managed behavioral health care companies to financially support it, but outcomes that are both important to these companies and appropriate to these interventions must be identified and evaluated. For example, if an increase in coping resources and coping behavior of family members is related to decreased use of health services, managed care companies might be persuaded to financially support family education.

Evaluation of outcomes must be complemented by assessment of the implementation of family education interventions, including the actual process of service delivery and the fidelity of programs to particular intervention models. Service delivery elements that are particularly effective should be distinguished to improve existing programs. Identification of other elements that may potentially be effective is also critical.

Research is also needed to assess whether programs allow participants to achieve learning goals such as high motivation, long-term retention, and the ability to transfer information from the learning setting to future situations. The use of scripted material, an approach employed by Journey of Hope, is one method for standardizing programs to ensure fidelity (44). Trained observers or videotaping of sessions can be used in assessing program fidelity (47).

An important future direction for researchers is experimentation to enhance development of family education programs in cooperation with professionals and service providers and family members. Mental health service providers should be trained to conduct family education as a service of their agency or to incorporate the principles of family education into their routine practice. Training in providing family education should be included in the curricula in social work, nursing, psychiatry, and family therapy. Such training would ensure that health care providers in these fields have accurate and current information about serious mental disorders, which may encourage more respectful attitudes toward patients' families.

Conclusions

The transitions from psychoeducation to family education acknowledges the strengths and capacity of families rather than their deficits. A result of this movement is that families have more control in defining their problems, determining the solution, and evaluating the outcomes. Family education approaches recognize the difficulties that confront families with a relative with a severe psychiatric disorder and view these families as facing problems rather than as a "problem family in need of treatment" (20).

Family education holds promise to meet the support and educational needs of families. Further development, refinement, and scientific examination of family, education programs are needed. These programs need to be focused on realistic goals, and to be evaluated within the parameters of those goals. They are not a substitute for treatment of the ill relative. Their primary objective is to meet the needs of families and secondarily to benefit the ill relative.

Dixon and Lehman (14) concluded in their review of psychoeducational interventions that future research must integrate family interventions into routine clinical settings with diverse patient populations, identify program components that are particularly effective for specific patient groups, measure effects of programs on families and patients, develop interventions for other members of the patient's support system besides family members, and examine effects for program participants from a range of cultural backgrounds. Ruther research is essential if independent financial support for family education programs is to be achieved. One cautionary note raised by Hatfield (19) is that the development of these programs should not imply that families are to be responsible for the care of mentally ill relatives. These programs should maintain their focus on improving the quality of life of families who face a difficult situation. Responsibility for the care of families' ill relatives should remain with the mental health system.

From Phyllis Solomon, Moving from psychoeducation to family education for families of adults with serious mental illness, *Psychiatric Services* 47 (1996): 1364–70. Copyright 1996 American Psychiatric Association; reprinted by permission.

Notes

1. Goldstein M: Psychoeducation and relapse prevention. *International Clinical Psychopharmacology* 9(suppl5):59–60, 1995.

2. Anthony W, Liberman R: The practice of psychiatric rehabilitation. *Schizophrenia Bulletin* 12:542–558, 1986.

3. Mintz L, Liberman R, Mildowitz D, et al.: Expressed emotion: a call for partnership among relatives, patients, and professionals. *Schizophrenia Bulletin* 13:227–235, 1987.

4. Mcfarlene W: Family, psychoeducation treatment, in *Handbook of Family Therapy*, vol. 2. Edited by Gurman A, Kinisken D. New York, Brunner/Mazel, 1991.

5. Hatfield A: *Family Education in Mental Illness*. New York, Guilford, 1990.

6. Hatfield A, Spaniol L, Zipple A: Expressed emotion: a family perspective. *Schizophrenia Bulletin* 13:221–226, 1987.

7. Moeser K, Bellak A, Wade J, et al.: An assessment of the educational needs of chronic psychiatric patients and their relatives. *British Journal of Psychiatry* 160:674–680, 1992.

8. Lefley H: Expressed emotion: conceptual, clinical, and social policy issues. Hospital and *Community Psychiatry* 43:591–598. 1992.

9. Vaugh C, Snyder K, Jones S, et al.: Family factors in schizophrenia disorders: a replication. *British Journal of Psychiatry* 121:241–258, 1972.

10. Brown G, Birley J, Wing J: Influence of family life on the course of schizophrenia disorders: a replication. *British Journal of Psychiatry* 121:241–258, 1972.

11. Vaughn C, Snyder K, Jones S, et al.: Family factors in schizophrenic relapse. *Archives of General Psychiatry* 41:1169–1177, 1984.

12. Bellack A, Mueser K: Psychosocial treatment for schizophrenia. *Schizophrenia Bulletin* 19:311–326, 1993.

13. Goldstein M, Rodnick E, Evans J, et al: Drug and family therapy in the aftercare of acute schizophrenics. *Archives of General Psychiatry* 35:1169–1177, 1978.

14. Dixon L, Lehman A: Family interventions for schizophrenia. *Schizophrenia Bulletin* 21:631–643, 1995.

15. Lam D: Psychosocial family intervention in schizophrenia: a review of empirical studies. *Psychological Medicine* 31:423–441, 1991.

16. Mari JDJ, Stiener D: An overview of family interventions and relapse in schizophrenia: meta-analysis of research findings. *Psychological Medicine* 24:565–578, 1994.

17. Strachan A: Family intervention for the rehabilitation of schizophrenia: toward protection and coping. Schizophrenia Bulletin 12:678–698, 1987.

18. Hogarty G, Anderson C, Reiss D: Family psychoeducation, social skills training and medication in schizophrenia: the long and short of it. *Psychopharmacology Bulletin* 23:12–12, 1987.

19. Hatfield A: Family education: theory and practice. *New Directions for Mental Health Services* 62:3–12, 1994.

20. Hatfield A: Coping and adaptation: a conceptual framework for understanding families, in *Families of the Mentally Ill*. Edited by Hatfield A, Lefley H. New York, Guilford, 1987.

21. Marsh D: *Families and Mental Illness: New Directions in Professional Practice.* New York, Praeger 1992.

22. Solomon P, Draine J: Subjective burden among family members of mentally ill adults: relation to stress, coping, and adaptation. *American Journal of Orthopsychiatry* 65:419–427, 1995.

23. Noh S, Turner R: Living with psychiatric patients: implications for the mental health of family members. *Social Science and Medicine* 25:263–271, 1987.

24. Potasznik FL, Nelson G: Stress and social support: the burden experienced by the family of a mentally ill person. *American Journal of Community Psychology* 12:589–607, 1994.

25. Crotty P, Kulys R: Are schizophrenics a burden to their families? Significant others' views. *Health and Social Work* 11:173–188, 1986.

26. Solomon P, Draine J: Adaptive coping among family members of persons with serious mental illness. *Psychiatric Services* 46:1156–1160, 1995.

27. Smith J Birchwood M: Relatives and patients as partners in the management of schizophrenia. *British Journal of Psychiatry* 156:654–660, 1990.

28. Cazzullo C, Bertrando P, Clerici C, et al.: The efficacy of an information group intervention for relatives of schizophrenics. *International Journal of Social Psychiatry* 35:313–323, 1989.

29. Rielly J, Rohrbaugh M, Lackner J: A controlled evaluation of psychoeducation workshops for relatives of state hospital patients. *Journal of Marital and Family Therapy* 14:429–432, 1988.

30. Smith J, Birchwood M: Specific and non-specific educational intervention with families living with a schizophrenis relative. *British Journal of Psychiatry* 150:645–652, 1987.

31. Posner C, Wilson K, Kral M, et al: Family psychoeducation support groups in schizophrenia. *American Journal of Orthopsychiatry* 62:206–218, 1992.

32. Abramowitz I, Coursey R: Impact of an educational support group on family participants who take care of their schizophrenic relatives. *Journal of Consulting and Clinical Psychology* 57:632–636, 1989.

33. Solomon P, Draine j, Mannion E, et al: Impact of brief Family psycboeducation on self-efficacy. *Schizophrenia Bulletin* 22:41–50, 1996.

34. Solomon P: Draine J, Mannion E, et al.: The impact of individualized consultation and group workshop family education interventions on ill relative outcomes. *Journal of Nervous and Mental Disease* 184:252, 1990.

35. Mannion E, Mueser K, Solomon P: Designing psychoeducational services for spouses of persons with serious mental illness. *Community Mental Health Journal* 30:177–190, 1994.

36. Cozolino Goldstein K, Nuerchterlein K, et al.: The impact of education about schizophrenia on relatives varying in expressed emotion. *Schizophrenia Bulletin* 14:675–687, 1988.

37. Tarrier N, Barrowclough C, Vaughn C, et al.: The community management of schizophrenia: a controlled trial of a behavioral intervention with families to reduce relapse. *British Journal of Psychology* 153:532–542, 1988.

38. Carpentier N, Lesage A, Goulet J, et al.: Burden of care of families not living with young schizophrenic relatives. Hospital and Community Psychiatry 43:38–43, 1992.

39. Goldman H. Gattozzi A, Taube C: Defining and counting the chronically mentally ill *Hospital and Community Psychiatry* 32:21–21, 1981.

40. Goldman H: Mental illness and family burden: a public health perspective. *Hospital and Community Psychiatry* 33:557–560, 1982.

41. Lefley H: *Family Caregiving in Mental Illness.* Thousand Oaks, Calif, Sage, 1996.

42. Guarnaccia P, Parra P: Ethnicity, social status, and families' experiences of caring for mentally ill family members. *Community Mental Health Journal* 32:243–260, 1996.

43. Jordan C, Lewellen A, Vandiver V: Psychoeducation for minority families: a social work perspective. *International Journal of Mental Health* 23:27–43, 1995.

44. Hatfield A: New directions in research on families with mentally ill relatives. *American Journal of Orthopsychiatry*, in press.

45. Solomon P, Doll W: The Varieties of readmissions: the case against the use of recidivism rates as a measure of program effectiveness. *American Journal of Orthopsychiatry* 49:230–239, 1939.

46. Maurin J, Boyd C: Burden of mental illness on the family: a critical review. *Archives of Psychiatric Nursing* 4:99–107, 1990.

47. Solomon P: Issues in designing and conducting randomized human service field trials. *Journal of Social Service Research*, in press.

Commentary

Phyllis Solomon

Ever since 1971 when I was hired as an evaluator for an experimental program for what were then called "intractable patients" in the state psychiatric hospital system, my research has focused on improving mental health services for adults with severe mental illness. Initially, this meant assessing the effectiveness of hospital-based interventions. However, by the mid 1970s when the deinstitutionalization movement really took hold, the focus of my research efforts was redirected to the effectiveness of community-based services for this highly vulnerable population, as the locus of care had begun to shift. Through the 1980s my research examined issues of access to and utilizations of mental health service delivery systems and their impact on rehospitalization. The results of these efforts continually reinforced the need for psychiatric rehabilitation services in order for these clients to get off the conveyer belt of continually returning to the hospital.

Consequently, by the 1990s my research became more circumscribed. I began examining the effectiveness of rehabilitative service interventions that had the potential to improve the psychosocial functioning and, ultimately, the quality of life for these clients and their families. At this time my research was a bit more cutting edge, researching specialized populations and interventions that were not accepted by the mainstream mental health system. One study examined whether an effective comprehensive self-contained program, Assertive Community Treatment (ACT), might be beneficial for a highly specialized subpopulation of adults with severe mental illness, those who were homeless and being released from jail. At the time few mental health services researchers were examining issues related to the intersection of mental health services and criminal justice. Another study assessed the effectiveness of mental health consumers delivering case management services to other consumers. At the time the mainstream mental health community did not accept the idea of consumers as providers. A third study, for which this article is a conceptual culmination of this research, was determining the effectiveness of an individual consultation model and a group family educational workshop for families of a relative with severe mental illness. My research continues to the present to examine the effectiveness of psychiatric rehabilitative interventions, investigating whether a workbook for enhancing social participation increases community integration and whether an HIV prevention educational intervention by case managers decreases risk factors for adults with cooccurring substance abuse and mental illness.

From publishing and presenting on the aforementioned family education study, it became apparent to me that many mental health professionals were not making conceptual distinctions between family psychoeducation and education interventions. Consequently, they were judging these family education interventions as ineffective and therefore, as less valued, based on the fact that they did not reduce rehospitalizations. But since the patient was not the primary target of these interventions, this was an inappropriate criterion on which to evaluate these educational interventions.

The article had two primary goals. One objective was to demonstrate the advantages of family education and how they served somewhat different purposes than psychoeducation. The second was to advocate for more research on family education that was more rigorous than in the past and that was consistent with the nature and intention of the intervention rather than evaluating them on the same criteria as psychoeducation.

On reflecting on this article from a ten-year vantage point, it is disheartening in some regards, while personally rewarding in other regards. Disheartening in that it is now a decade later and the research on family education has increased, but still remains quite limited. There is some momentum to improve this situation with two large-scale randomized studies, one recently completed (found positive outcomes) and one currently just beginning, which, assuming positive results as in past research, will help move these family education interventions to greater prominence as an essential element in the service and support systems for adults with severe mental illness. Furthermore, during this decade, mental health providers have increasingly recognized the importance of collaborating with families, and consequently the necessity of providing them with skills, supports, and information. Also, Evidence Based Practice (EBP) has moved from its original scope of physical medicine into mental health and into every practice arena, including social work. With behavioral health managed care now having a strong hold on most public mental health service delivery systems, cost-effective services have become the standard of care. Given the strong research base of psychoeducational interventions, these have achieved the status of EBPs and are now being promoted as one of six EBPs that all public mental health systems should provide. However, there has been difficulty in implementing family psychoeducation for many of the reasons I delineated in this article as problematic. These implementation problems are likely the precipitant needed to promote the research agenda for family education that I laid out in this article. Currently, I view family education as what is called an emerging best practice, one that has promise but not enough evidence to achieve the stature of an EBP. It is disheartening that in the intervening years since this article was published family education did not accumulate enough evidence to be an EBP. However, I am hopeful that within the next decade the agenda from this article will be accomplished and family education will be accepted as an EBP. Finally, this article is personally rewarding, as my foresight regarding these interventions outlined in this article are now being validated as others begin to express these same issues.

My affinity for family education as opposed to psychoeducation is very much in line with social work practice (Sands and Solomon 2003), whereas psychoeducation is more consistent with psychiatry and psychology. It is therefore not surprising that this article was based on a presentation for a psychiatric association annual conference where I was asked to do a presentation on the topic of families of adults with severe mental illness from a social work perspective. The program had speakers representing psychiatry and psychology as well. Family education is very much indicative of the strengths of social work as it acknowledges the person in environment and the importance of supporting families coping with a relative with a psychiatric disability.

This article also demonstrates a common theme of my work, the importance of research to practice. Social work, consistent with the Penn Approach, has promoted empirically based practice for years, but now, as with all practice professions, social work is promoting the use of evidence based practice. The language of EBPs was not being used at the time of this publication. However, if it were written today, the article would have used this terminology.

In conclusion, I want to thank the editor for judging my article as worthy of commemorating the 100th anniversary of the school. It is an honor to be included in this volume.

References

Sands, R., and P. Solomon (2003). Developing educational groups in social work, *Social Work with Groups* 26: 5–21.

Chapter 31
Postmodern Feminist Theory and Social Work

Roberta G. Sands and Kathleen Nuccio

In the past 15 years, an explosion of feminist scholarship has sparked numerous "revisions" of social work knowledge. Feminist writings across disciplines have illuminated an understanding of the status of women in a patriarchal society, sexist biases in social and behavioral theories, and the feminization of poverty. In social work, a number of scholars have explored the striking compatibility between feminist theory and social work (Collins 1986; Gould 1987; Nes and Iadicola 1989; Van Den Bergh and Cooper 1986).

Although social work theories gained many benefits from the earlier wave of feminist theory, the profession has been much slower to confront the opportunities and challenges offered by the more recent postmodern feminist theory. Postmodernism, a cultural phenomenon that sprang to life in architecture and spread rapidly into literature, art, and other areas, together with deconstructionism and French feminism, has stimulated and transformed feminist thinking and practices. The social work literature is only beginning to touch on postmodern feminist themes and methods (Berlin 1990; Jones 1990; Tice 1990), which are on the cutting edge of knowledge in other fields.

This article provides an intellectual background to understanding postmodern feminism and its potential contributions and challenges to social work. This is an ambitious project because the body of works from which postmodern feminists draw is immense and complex. The inaccessibility of postmodern feminist writings, which has been one of the grounds on which postmodern feminism has been criticized, increases the importance of this article. The obtuse nature of the writing, as well as the highly specialized vocabulary, tends to discourage even the most intellectually curious. As the profession prepares for the 21st century, social workers will find that the contributions of postmodern feminism provoke reconceptualizations of many of social work's basic assumptions. Emerging postmodern feminist theory challenges accepted ideas about race, gender and class, as well as political rights, equality, and difference, which are basic to the values of both the women's movement and the social work profession.

Feminist Theory and Social Work

Although issues pertaining to women are discussed widely in the social work literature, feminist theory informs a limited number of these writings. The social work literature that has incorporated or drawn on feminism has taken three directions, the first two of which appear to contradict each other. The first direction recommends eliminating false dichotomies or categories, whereas the second promotes the use of categories. The third direction entails applying ideas about "differences" that have been articulated in feminist psychological literature to social work theory and practice.

Eliminating and Establishing Categories

A popular focus among feminist social workers has been eliminating false dichotomies that emerge from American capitalistic, patriarchal, hierarchical society. Hierarchical dichotomous thinking creates oppositional and zero-sum relationships between areas of knowledge, such as the distinction between policy and practice, which are better represented by a continuous or holistic relationship. A sampling of the writings in this vein insists on eradicating false distinctions and artificial separations (Britker-Jenkins and Hooyman 1986; Collins 1986; Gould 1987; Van Den Bergh and Cooper 1986) and discarding the dichotomy between personal service and social action (Morell 1987). To avoid false dichotomies, an affirmation of the unity of all living things (Wetzel 1986) and the achievement of synthesis (Bricker-Jenkins and Hooyman 1986) have been proposed. Avoiding false dichotomies is particularly compatible with the ecological perspective in social work (Collins 1986), with its focus on wholeness.

Paradoxically, feminist social work literature also often emphasizes the establishment of categories, which are used as an organizing framework for analyzing social work theory and practice. Categories of feminism, such as radical and Marxist, have been described extensively in feminist writings across disciplines (for example, Ferree and Hess 1985; Lengermann and Wallace 1985; Tong 1989). Several social work writers have categorized social work knowledge and practice using three philosophical and political feminist political orientations—liberal, socialist, and radical feminisms (Bricker-Jenkins and Hooyman 1986; Nes and Iadicola 1989). *Liberal feminism* emphasizes the attainment of political rights, opportunities, and equality within the existing political system. *Socialist feminism* attributes women's oppression to the interaction among sexism, racism, and class divisions, which are produced by patriarchal capitalism. *Radical feminism* finds patriarchy an omnipresent influence that needs to be dismantled. Although Nes and Iadicola (1989) noted that feminist social work in itself is "outside of the dominant perspective" (20), they also observed that mainstream social work thinking is most closely allied with liberal feminism. This orientation of social work thinking is reinforced by a recent study by Freeman (1990), which found that most social workers identify with liberal feminism.

Celebration of Differences

A theme within feminist theory that has been adopted by social work writers is the "celebration of differences." Unlike liberal feminism, which emphasizes sameness and equality, this perspective calls attention to and at times applauds the world views of women and describes the divergent developmental paths of women and men. Social work writers Bricker-Jenkins and Hooyman (1986) argued that diversity is a resource that can be used to advance the interests of the women's movement. Furthermore, they found value in the nonrational and emotional, stereotypical characteristics of women that have been used as justifications for the exclusion of women from the "public" sphere, where men claim hegemony.

A number of social work scholars develop the theme of differences from the psychological writings of Chodorow (1978), Gilligan (1982), and Kaplan and Surrey (1984). Rhodes (1985), for example, showed how the different "voices" described by Gilligan are manifested in social work. The responsibility mode is consistent with the emphasis on compassion, nonjudgmental acceptance, and relationship in social work, whereas the individual rights mode is reflected in social work ethics. Similarly, Davis (1985) identified "female and male voices in social work," both of which are needed and desirable. Male social work academics and those researchers who use a positivistic approach to research represent the male voice. In contrast, practitioners represent the female voice, which tends to be suppressed in schools of social work. Reimer (1984) recommended that clinical social workers become aware of their own conceptions of differences so that their biases will not contaminate their therapeutic relationships.

Differences are celebrated in two additional articles in social work journals. Berzoff (1989) viewed connectedness as a theme that is a characteristic of women's development. In a research study of women executives in human services agencies, Chernesky and Bombyk (1988) found that women administrators bring to their positions qualities such as concern, sensitivity, nurturing, mentoring, recognition of dual roles of women workers, and a commitment to staff participation in decision making.

The themes evident in these social work feminist writings anticipate (but do not incorporate) issues that have been developed by postmodern feminist theorists. More recently, Tice (1990) discussed how new feminist scholarship that challenges assumptions of universality and objectivity can be used to transform social work education in the 1990s. Berlin (1990) questioned the value of polarized thinking but did not identify her perspective as either postmodern or feminist. Jones (1990) used deconstruction and feminist theory to interpret a research interview.

Postmodern feminism challenges the validity of categories and promotes the recognition of differences. At times, however, postmodern feminism finds categories to be useful.

The Roots of Postmodern Feminist Theory

Postmodern feminism is rooted in poststructuralism, postmodern philosophy, and French feminist theory, all of which emerged spontaneously around the same time. The boundaries among these schools and the classification of a particular theorist among these and previous traditions are problematic, because themes overlap and philosophies are contradictory, even within a school. Furthermore, the relationship among schools and the progression of ideas are nonlinear. American postmodern feminist theory both adopts and criticizes themes that have been developed in these discourses and introduces perspectives of its own.

Structuralism and Poststructuralism

Structuralism is an analytic method used by scholars within anthropology, linguistics, psychoanalysis, and other human studies. The method is characterized by a search for underlying organizing structures or relations among empirical events in cultures, personality, politics, and other areas (de George and de George 1972; Grosz 1989). Structuralist scholars share the conviction that "surface events and phenomena are to be explained by structures, data, and phenomena below the surface" (de George and de George 1972, xii). Structuralists such as Marx, de Saussure, Freud, Lévi-Strauss, Piaget, and Lacan developed systems of thought in which lawful, explanatory deep structures are proposed. Many of these theorists emphasized the importance of language in shaping power relationships.

Poststructuralism both incorporates and transforms structuralism. Whereas structuralists view meaning that is produced within language as fixed, poststructuralists see meaning as multiple, unstable, and open to interpretation (Weedon 1987).

Poststructuralists look at meaning in relation to the particular social, political, and historical contexts in which language is spoken or written. They view discourses (bodies of language or "texts") and "readers" as situated, rather than neutral. Accordingly, poststructuralists move away from "grand theory," which purports to assert universal truth. Theorists associated with this movement are Derrida (1978), Foucault (1965), and the French feminist Kristeva (1982).

The poststructural theorists whose works interest both the French feminists and postmodern feminists have developed several themes. Among these are (1) criticism of "logocentrism," (2) the nature of "difference," (3) deconstruction of texts, (4) multiple discourses, and (5) the nature of subjectivity.

Criticism of Logocentrism. Poststructuralist writers have identified an assumption in Western metaphysics (post-Enlightenment philosophy) that they find problematic. They call this *logocentrism,* the belief that there is a fixed, singular, logical order (Derrida 1976) that can be found in the immediate presence in "real," "true," and "unmediated" forms (Grosz 1989). Logocentrism is open to challenge for two reasons. One, it assumes that there are "essential" qualities inherent in categories of thinking. According to Derrida (1978), categories, definitions, and constructs vary in relation to their particular social, historical, and political milieus. There are no inherent "essential" meanings; definitions are historically contingent and context bound. Another problem with logocentrism is that it relies on binary categories (polar opposites) for the production of knowledge. This problem is related to the nature of "difference" and the role of language in the production of meaning.

Differences. Derrida (1978) drew a distinction between *différance* and "difference" that affects the reading of texts. Western logocentric thought promotes thinking of differences in terms of binary opposites, such as identity difference, male-female, and reason-emotion, which are perceived as mutually exclusive, oppositional, and hierarchical instead of interdependent. Derrida suggested that, although one may be propelled to think dichotomously, there is a residue of meaning that does not fit into these categories. He used the term *différance* to describe meaning that is both-and (identity *and* difference); neither; or alternative (Grosz 1989).

A major source of categorical thinking is language, which is infused with meanings deriving from the logocentric culture. Language embodies and maintains the perspective of the "Symbolic Order" (Lacan 1977), which is patriarchal ("phallocentric"; Cixous 1981; Derrida 1978). In this respect, the terms within binary categories are valued differently. One of the terms (for example, "male") is "privileged" or dominant, resulting in the relegation of the second term to a negative state (for example, whatever is *not male* is female; Grosz 1989). The privileging (or "valorizing") of one term results in the suppression, marginalization, or devaluation of the other.

Deconstruction. One way to recover suppressed meanings is through *deconstruction.* Deconstruction is a way of analyzing texts that is sensitive to contextual dimensions and marginalized voices. When one deconstructs a text, one does not accept the constructs used as given; instead, one looks at them in relation to social, historical, and political contexts. The deconstructionist identifies the biases in the text, views them as problematic, and "decenters" them. Meanwhile, the perspectives that are treated as marginal are "centered," and meaning in excess of (not accounted for by) the polarities is identified. Through deconstruction, the presumed fixity of the existing social order is "destabilized" and the perspectives of the marginalized can be articulated (Grosz 1989). This process interrupts the hegemony of the dominant order (Hutcheon 1988) and gives prominence to suppressed voices.

Multiple Discourses. Deconstruction has revealed that history obfuscates the perspectives of those who are missing from the text. Foucault (1978) pointed out that at any time; multiple perspectives or discourses are present, but only a few are heard:

> To be more precise, we must not imagine a world of discourse divided between accepted discourse and excluded discourse, or between the dominant discourse and the dominated one; but as a multiplicity of discursive elements that can come into play in various strategies. It is this distribution that we must reconstruct, with the things said and those concealed, the enunciations required and those forbidden, that it comprises. (100)

The discourses that are heard are tied in with power and strategies to maintain power (Foucault 1978). Those concurrent discourses that are silenced, however, are also meaningful.

Subjectivity. Subjectivity refers to "the conscious and unconscious thoughts and emotions of the individual, her sense of herself and her ways of understanding her relation to the world" (Weedon 1987, 32). Within the logocentric tradition, the individual is autonomous and has an "essential" subjectivity, identity, or personality that is stable, unique, and (if healthy) integrated. From a poststructuralist perspective, however, subjectivity is "precarious, contradictory and in process, constantly being reconstituted in discourse each time we think or speak" (Weedon 1987, 33). Accordingly, the subject is multifaceted and speaks in many voices, depending on the context. Contradictions and changes over time are to be expected. Furthermore, subjectivity is the site in which others socially construct one's identity. Thus, subjectivity is connected with the sociocultural, historical, and interpersonal context in which one is situated.

French Feminism

The philosophical perspectives of the French feminists, such as Cixous (1981), Irigaray (1985), and Kristeva (1982), share some common ground with poststructuralist writers such as Derrida (1978) and Foucault (1965), as well as Lacan (1977), who is considered a structuralist. These French feminists are, like Derrida, deconstructionists. Although Foucault was remiss in his exclusion of women, French feminists find his reconstruction of history and his view of the relationship among language, power, and knowledge stimulating.

French feminists share with Lacan an interest in the reinterpretation of traditional Freudian psychoanalytic theory and practice (Tong 1989). French feminists are particularly interested in the relation of psychoanalytic theory to subjectivity and the "gendering" of the body. Using Lacan's (1977) vision of a phallocentric Symbolic Order, they reconstruct the missing female voice in psychoanalytic theory.

Postmodern Philosophy

The emphasis on differences, criticism of logocentrism, and the use of deconstruction are apparent in the writings of contemporary postmodern philosophers (for example, Lyotard 1984; Rorty 1979). These (predominantly male) writers describe their work as a departure from the search for universals that has been the project of "liberal humanism," which characterized the modern era that began in the 18th century (Hutcheon 1988). The postmodernists view their humanist predecessors as "essentialists" who assumed that there were innate rather than historically contingent meanings. Furthermore, they criticize the pursuit of science to provide "objective" knowledge of the world. Postmodernists devalue the search for universal laws and theories and focus on local meanings that are socially constructed.

Postmodern philosophers reject perspectives that have come down to them from their predecessors as *the* "legitimate" narratives (Fraser and Nicholson 1990). Critical of their own discipline, they view what is considered "legitimate" philosophy as one of many possible discourses, all of which should be seen in political, historical, and social contexts. Postmodern philosophers object to binary categories and emphasize diversity, multiplicity, and pluralism. They view categories such as gender, race, and class as too reductive (Fraser and Nicholson 1990). Consideration of these categories as multiple, diverse, and irreducible has been both a contribution and a source of conflict to postmodern feminist theorists.

Postmodern Feminism

Although postmodern feminism is related to poststructuralist theory, postmodern philosophy, and French feminist theory, it bears an uneasy relationship to both feminism and postmodernism. Postmodern philosophers do not recognize the significance of gender, race, and class because these are categories that must be viewed as diverse. Even though this omission is a source of concern for postmodern feminists, they recognize, with postmodern philosophers, the problems that develop when categories become fixed universal explanations of reality. Indeed, diversity is a special concern of postmodern feminists, who highlight/foreground/emphasize/insist on differences. The use of a single label itself—"postmodern feminism"—contradicts the spirit of a movement that emphasizes multiple meanings.

Postmodern feminism also shares with postmodernism a critique of essentialism and a desire to identify the diverse character of categorical knowledge. Accordingly, postmodern feminists have deconstructed the category "woman," recognizing that woman is a cultural construct with which only some women identify. Furthermore, postmodern feminists recognize that feminists of the past (largely middle-class, white, and heterosexual) mistakenly assumed that when they used the term "woman" they were speaking for all women, including women of color, Third World women, and lesbians. To avoid making such assumptions, postmodern feminists have found it necessary to be specific about the women about whom they are speaking (for example, working-class white women, African American professional women). In this way, one can speak about particular "women" rather than of a universal "woman."

Postmodern feminism shares with American feminism a political agenda. Regardless of whether a feminist has a liberal, socialist, radical, or other perspective, she has a desire to change the social and political order so that women will no longer be oppressed. Thus, organizing and taking political action to redress injustices are significant dimensions of postmodern feminism. Indeed, the linkage between theory and practice (or "praxis"), with the demands of practice (everyday considerations) predominating over theory (Fraser and Nicholson 1990), distinguishes postmodern feminism from postmodernism.

Moi (1985) termed postmodernism and feminism "strange bedfellows" (4). The emphasis on differences that is characteristic of postmodern thought creates dilemmas for feminists. Postmodern feminism acknowledges that there is a multiplicity of women and women's movements representing diverse and divergent interests. Nevertheless, the postmodernist emphasis on different and multiple voices conflicts with the pursuit of feminist political activities. Feminist politics requires unity and action on defined women's issues. The emphasis on diversity in postmodernism, however, ignores the need for political entities (predicated on categories and "essences") that can pursue collective political action on women's issues. If one calls for unity among women, one assumes that women are an entity that has "essentially" the same interests. An emphasis on sameness promotes thinking about "essential" womanhood in which the interests of women of a higher status can become dominant. Thus, the marriage between postmodernism and feminism poses a threat to the political agenda of feminists.

Some writers who are grappling with this dilemma have suggested that postmodern feminists adopt a position of "positionality" or "both-and" (Haraway 1989; Nicholson 1990). Accordingly, one need not choose between the postmodern emphasis on multiplicity and feminist politics. When one is engaged in politics, one can act as if women (or African Americans or poor people) are a group that is united around a cause. On other occasions, however, one recognizes and celebrates women's (and other groups') diversity. Not hampered with the need to be "rational" or consistent, one allows the context to influence one's ideology and politics.

Implications for Social Work

Like preceding feminist movements, postmodern feminism is highly compatible with social work. With its emphasis on differences, it recognizes the diverse constitution of client populations and their unique needs. Furthermore, the focus on context in postmodern feminism is in keeping with the person-in-environment perspective in social work. The use of deconstruction to uncover the suppressed voices of marginalized populations provides a means through which social workers can work in concert with client groups to promote social change.

Nevertheless, postmodern feminist thought raises challenging issues for social work. First, the field is permeated with binary categories that influence theory, practice, research, and education. For example, social workers polarize the generalist and the specialist, micro and macro, research and practice, and policy and practice. Social work researchers have held a vigorous debate about quantitative versus qualitative approaches to research, as if these endeavors were mutually exclusive. Social workers can learn from postmodern feminists that categories can coexist and overlap. Where research design decisions historically demanded a choice of either qualitative or quantitative research methods, social work scholars are beginning to develop models that combine these methodologies (Allen-Meares and Lane 1990; Tice 1990).

Social work's use of categories also comes into question when reevaluated through a different theoretical perspective. Overall, social workers find the categories of gender, race, ethnicity, and class extremely useful to understanding and fulfilling the professional mission of overcoming oppression. The Council on Social Work Education prides itself in requiring that content on women, people of color, and other groups be infused throughout educational curricula. Yet, as Tice (1990) noted, the very categories promulgated to stem oppression are themselves oppressive in their superficiality. In much the same way that traditional history courses become the history of "great white men," course content within the social work curriculum on women can too easily fall into the trap of becoming courses about the concerns of white, middle-class women (as is the criticism of Gilligan's work).

But "problematizing" the use of categories (for example, "women," "African Americans") creates a political dilemma. With marginalized populations as a central professional concern, social workers take hold of the "essences" of clients (for example, race, sex, disability) to advocate policies and programs that target special populations. Without these categories and commonly held definitions, social workers will have difficulty communicating with and organizing on behalf of oppressed populations.

On the other hand, categories pose problems for social workers. Social workers object to labeling clients on the basis of a diagnostic category (Sands 1983). Research by Kutchins and Kirk (1988) demonstrated that, although social workers use categories of mental disorders described in the *Diagnostic and Statistical Manual of Mental Dis-*

orders, Third Edition Revised (American Psychiatric Association 1987) to meet administrative requirements of their agencies and to receive third-party payments, they do not rely on it for its alleged purpose—to guide treatment. Usually, social workers use less serious diagnoses (for example, adjustment disorders) so that clients can avoid being labeled with more serious ones (for example, major depression), or they use more serious diagnoses so that clients will be eligible for services (Kirk and Kutchins 1988). Clearly, social workers have been assuming a position of both-and in their objection to, use of, and circumventing of categories.

Postmodern feminism poses unique challenges to feminist social workers. If there is no commonly held definition of "woman," how are women's psychological issues, special needs, and vulnerabilities to be located? If feminist social workers give up their advocacy for special programs adapted to the needs of women (for example, women-centered substance abuse programs), will women clients find themselves in "humanist" programs that are adapted to the needs of men? How can diversity and specificity be preserved simultaneously?

Like postmodern feminists, social workers can resolve these dilemmas by considering the diverse nature of the client population, the particular contexts in which problems are present, and the political exigencies of the moment. Thus, one can be concerned with and act in concert with an individual, a special population, and the person-environment interface simultaneously. By avoiding polarization in practice but assuming an ideological position when it comes to politics—when these positions are called for—social workers can fulfill the mission of social work and the feminist agenda at the same time.

Reprinted from Roberta G. Sands and Kathleen Nuccio, Postmodern feminism and social work, *Social Work* 37 (1992): 489–94. Reprinted by permission.

References

Allen-Meares, P., and B. A. Lane (1990). Social work practice: Integrating qualitative and quantitative data collection techniques. *Social Work* 35: 452–58.

American Psychiatric Association (1987). *Diagnostic and Statistical Manual of Mental Disorders.* 3rd ed., rev.. Washington, D.C.: APA.

Berlin, S. B. (1990). Dichotomous and complex thinking. *Social Service Review* 64: 46–59.

Berzoff, J. (1989). From separation to connection: Shifts in understanding women's development. *Affilia* 4: 45–58.

Bricker-Jenkins. M., and N. R. Hooyman, eds. (1986). *Not for Women only: Social Work Practice for a Feminist Future.* Silver Spring, Md.: National Association of Social Workers.

Chernesky, R. H., and M. J. C. Bombyk (1988). Women's ways and effective management. *Affilia* 3: 48–61.

Chodorow, N. (1978). *The Reproduction of Mothering: Psychoanalysis and the Sociology of Gender.* Berkeley: University of California Press.

Cixous, H. (1981). The laugh of the Medusa. In E. Marks and I. de Courtivron, eds, *New French Feminisms.* New York: Schocken. 245–64.

Collins, B. G. (1986). Defining feminist social work. *Social Work* 31: 214–19.

Davis, L. V. (1985). Female and male voices in social work. *Social Work* 30: 106–13.

de George, R., and F. de George, eds. (1972). *The Structuralists from Marx to Lévi-Strauss*. Garden City, N.Y.: Anchor Books.

Derrida, J. (1976). *Of Grammatology*. Trans. G. C. Spivak. Baltimore: Johns Hopkins University Press.

———— (1978). *Writing and Difference*. Trans. A. Bass. Chicago: University of Chicago Press.

Ferree, M. M., and B. B. Hess (1985). *Controversy and Coalition: The New Feminist Movement*. Boston: Twayne.

Foucault, M. (1965). *Madness and Civilization*. New York: Vintage.

———— (1978). *The History of Sexuality*. Vol. 1, *An Introduction*. New York: Vintage.

Fraser, N., and L. J. Nicholson (1990). Social criticism without philosophy: An encounter between feminism and postmodernism. In L. J. Nicholson, ed., *Feminism/Postmodernism* New York: Routledge. 19–38.

Freeman, M. (1990). Beyond women's issues: Feminism and social work. *Affilia* 5: 72–89.

Gilligan, C. (1982). *In a Different Voice: Psychological Theory and Women's Development*. Cambridge, Mass.: Harvard University Press.

Gould, K. H. (1987). Feminist principles and minority concerns: Contributions, problems, and solutions. *Affilia* 2: 6–19.

Grosz, E. (1989). *Sexual Subversions: Three French Feminists*. Sydney: Allen and Unwin.

Haraway, D. (1989). Situated knowledges: The science question in feminism and the privilege of partial perspective. *Feminist Studies* 14: 575–99.

Hutcheon, L. (1988). A *Poetics of Postmodernism: History, Theory, Fiction*. New York: Routledge.

Irigaray, L. (1985). *Speculum of the Other Woman*. Trans. G. C. Gill,. Ithaca, N.Y.: Cornell University Press

Jones, M. (1990). Understanding social work: A matter of interpretation? *British Journal of Social Work* 20: 181–96.

Kaplan. A. G., and J. L. Surrey (1984). The relational self in women: Developmental theory and public policy. In L. E. Walker, ed., *Women and Mental Health Policy*. Beverly Hills, Calif.: Sage. 79–94.

Kirk, S. A., and H. Kutchins (1988). Deliberate misdiagnosis in mental health practice. *Social Service Review* 62: 225–37.

Kristeva, J. (1982). *Desire in Language*. Trans. L. Roudiez. New York: Columbia University Press.

Kutchins, H., and S. A. Kirk (1988). The business of diagnosis: DSM-III and clinical social work. *Social Work* 33: 215–20.

Lacan, J. (1977). *Écrits: A Selection*. Trans. I. A. Sheridan. New York: Norton.

Lengermann, P. M., and R. A. Wallace (1985). *Gender in America*. Englewood Cliffs, N.J.: Prentice-Hall.

Lyotard, J-F. (1984). *The Post-Modern Condition: A Report on Knowledge*. Minneapolis: University of Minnesota Press.

Moi, T. (1985). *Sexual/Textual Politics*. London: Methuen.

Morell, C. (1987). Cause *is* function: Toward a feminist model of integration for social work. *Social Service Review* 61: 144–55.

Nes, J. A., and P. Iadicola (1989). Toward a definition of feminist social work: A comparison of liberal, radical, and socialist models. *Social Work* 34: 12–21.

Nicholson, L. J., ed. (1990). *Feminism/Postmodernism*. New York: Routledge.

Reimer, M. S. (1984). Gender differences in moral judgment: Implications for clinical practice. *Clinical Social Work Journal* 12: 198–208.

Rhodes, M. L. (1985). Gilligan's theory of moral development as applied to social work. *Social Work* 30: 101–5.

Rorty, R. (1979). *Philosophy and the Mirror of Nature*. Princeton, N.J.: Princeton University Press.

Sands, R. G. (1983). The DSM-III and psychiatric nosology: A critique from the labeling perspective. *California Sociologist* 6: 77–87.

Tice, K. (1990). Gender and social work education: Directions for the 1990s. *Journal of Social Work Education* 26: 134–44.

Tong, R. (1989). *Feminist Thought: A Comprehensive Introduction.* Boulder, Colo.: Westview Press.

Van Den Bergh, N., and L. B. Cooper (1986). *Feminist Visions for Social Work.* Silver Spring, Md.: National Association of Social Workers.

Weedon, C. (1987). *Feminist Practice and Poststructuralist Theory.* Oxford: Blackwell.

Wetzel, J. (1986). A feminist world view conceptual framework. *Social Casework* 67: 166–73.

Commentary: Afterthoughts

Roberta G. Sands

I arrived at Penn in 1990, excited about postmodernism and its potential to enlighten the social work profession and practice. I had begun writing "Postmodern Feminism and Social Work" when I was a faculty member at Ohio State University, where my coauthor and I were members of an interdisciplinary postmodern feminism study group and completed the article while listening to Anita Hill's presentation at the Clarence Thomas hearing. My coauthor and I had the goal of making dense postmodern feminist theory accessible to social workers. We were among the first to bring postmodern feminism to the attention of the profession and, since the article's publication, have been gratified by its numerous citations in the Social Science Citation Index.

Soon after settling here, I learned that functionalism was still embraced by some senior faculty here and that, although many students and faculty were feminists, postmodernism was seen as an obscure notion that was preoccupying European theorists. A fish out of water, I immersed myself in functionalist and Rankian writings to help understand my new environment. At first I was bewildered at how a school of social work could have adopted an ideology that was so identified with the system (the agency). A child of the 1960s, I was suspicious of the establishment. As I delved more deeply into functionalism, however, I discovered some ideas with which I was comfortable. I appreciated the value for students of clarifying the purpose of their interactions with clients and their understanding the function of the agency in which they had their field placement. This was a much more effective approach for social workers than fishing for psychopathology, which I had observed in various practice settings. I also recognized that the focus on "choice" in functionalism was similar to the concept of "self-determination," which is integral to social work practice (Dore 1990).

I also found some aspects of functionalism that were compatible with postmodernism. Functionalism is oriented toward the process, which is dynamic and unfolds over time. Similarly, postmodernism recognizes that nothing is static, there are no "essences," and knowledge is context-related. Postmodernism goes further in viewing knowledge as socially constructed and affected by power relations; postmodern feminism takes these ideas to the next step with its commitment to changing power inequities. The version of functionalism that the School adopted in the 1960s acknowledged power differentials based on race, gender, class, and other characteristics and embraced social change.

By the late 1990s, functionalism was losing its luster as the School's ideology. New faculty had no historical memory of what it was and how it operated. The School's focus now was on research. With this shift in orientation, space opened up for alternative perspectives. Those of us who taught direct (now called clinical) practice began to incorporate postmodernism, social constructionism, and narrative therapy into our courses. I included these perspectives in courses on Women's Voices in Social Work and Social Welfare and Qualitative Research. With more faculty and students energized about these approaches, I no longer was a fish out of water.

Postmodernism and postmodern feminism have been travel companions to me during my career at Penn. I have written other articles (e.g., Nuccio and Sands 1992; Sands 1996; Sands and Krumer-Nevo, in press) and a book (Sands 2001) that used these themes as a lens. Most of my research has been about women as mothers, daughters, and grandmothers (e.g., Sands and Goldberg-Glen 1998; Sands, Koppelman, and Solomon 2004; Sands and Roer-Strier 2000, 2004; Song, Sands, and Wong 2004). Postmodernism has open up space for me to explore women's construction of relationships whether they are affected by poverty, serious mental illness, or religious diversity in their families. Along the way, I have had the good fortune of developing fruitful collaborations with colleagues and doctoral students at Penn.

References

Dore, M. (1990). Functional theory: Its history and influence on contemporary social work practice. *Social Service Review* 64: 358–74.

Nuccio, K., and R. G. Sands (1992). Using postmodern feminist theory to deconstruct "phallacies" of poverty. *Affilia* 7: 26–48.

Sands, R. G. (1996). The elusiveness of identity in social work practice with women: A postmodern feminist perspective. *Clinical Social Work Journal* 24 (2), 167–86.

——— (1998). Gender and the perception of diversity and intimidation among university students. *Sex Roles* 39 (9/10): 801–15.

Sands, R. G. (2001). *Clinical Social Work Practice in Behavioral Mental Health: A Postmodern Approach to Practice with Adults.* 2nd ed. of *Clinical Social Work Practice in Community Mental Health.* Boston: Allyn and Bacon.

Sands, R. G., and R. Goldberg-Glen (1998). The impact of employment and serious illness on grandmothers who are raising their grandchildren. *Journal of Women & Aging* 10 (3): 41–58.

Sands, R. G., Koppelman, N., and P. Solomon (2004). Maternal custody status and living arrangements of children of women with severe mental illness. *Health and Social Work* 29 (4): 317–25.

Sands, R. G., and M. Krumer-Nevo. (in press). Interview shocks and shockwaves. *Qualitative Inquiry.*

Sands, R. G., and D. Roer-Strier (2000). *Ba'alot teshuvah* daughters and their mothers: A view from South Africa. *Contemporary Jewry* 21: 55–77.

——— (2004). Divided families: Impact of religious difference and geographic distance on intergenerational family continuity. *Family Relations* 53 (1): 102–10.

Song, D., R. G. Sands, and I. Wong (2004). Utilization of mental health services by low-income pregnant and postpartum women on medical assistance. *Women and Health* 39 (1): 1–24.

Chapter 32
A Cross-National Study of Adolescent Peer Concordance on Issues of the Future

Vivian C. Seltzer and Richard P. Waterman

The purpose for this study was to examine how the perceived attitudes of peers, on issues about their futures, may be evidenced in how adolescents think about their own futures. The objective was to determine whether adolescent self-perceptions would be in concordance with those they perceived their peers to hold and if not, whether the difference in the perceptions about self and peer would be nation specific or universal.

Some theorists consider adolescence a discrete stage in development (Bios 1962, 1979; Freud 1936); others regard it as a normative transitional stage unlike any other period of development (Masterson 1968; Offer and Offer 1975). Most agree, however, that adolescence is a preparatory period for adulthood: a time when past, present, and future all are alive cognitively (Josselyn 1952); a time when young people begin to think about their future (Nurmi 1991).

Erikson (1950, 1963) introduced the adolescent age-mate—the peer—as a major player in the task of identity achievement. Like Freud, Bios, and others, he subscribed to the psychoanalytic view of adolescent development that young people seek relief from unconscious conflict and attendant anxiety caused by strong sexual feelings toward the parent of the opposite sex. Erikson further argued that this libido was unconsciously transferred to neutral environmental figures: peers. He also theorized that peer groups serve as a forum for experimentation in which adolescents can try out adult behaviors; reflect on their past, present, and future; and work out identity—who I am—in gender and in life direction. Peers and peer groups also play key functions in fostering intellectual growth. Decentering, the cognitive task of adolescence, requires constant cognitive refocusing of perspective and openness to multiple views. Feedback that adolescents receive by talking with many age-mates helps move them away from egocentric thought of childhood into mature thinking of adulthood (Inhelder and Piaget 1958; Piaget 1952).

From the 1950s through the 1970s, the peer rather than the parent was prominent in the adolescent literature because of societal changes caused by rapid industrial change, which some felt put parents out of touch with their adolescents (Friedenberg

1959; Goodman 1956). According to Coleman (1961), peer influence was sufficiently strong to inspire an "adolescent society": a subculture of values and activities distinct and separate from the adult world. The prominence of peers reflected an increasingly complex society with adolescents increasingly left to their own inclinations (Bandura 1964; Keniston 1965). Adolescent literature of the 1970s emphasized the relevance of peers in the educational system (Bronfenbrenner 1970) in problem behaviors such as drug use/abuse (Kandel 1973), promiscuity and pregnancy (Furstenberg 1976) and alcohol use (Jessor and Jesser 1977), and as a force in social maladaptation (Offer and Offer 1975). The Erikson concept of peer groups as settings for experimentation crystallized into a concept of peer groups as psychological islands away from the parental satellite where adolescents could desatellize, that is, reorganize and individuate en route to *resatellization* as mature individuals (Ausubel, Montemayer, and Savjian 1977). Although the literature described in detail the scope of the peer phenomenon, little attention was paid to either peer influence on adolescent thinking about the future or to national variations among peer groups.

In the 1980s, a new model of adolescent psychological growth—Dynamic Functional Interaction (DPI; Seltzer 1982)—introduced the concepts of frameworklessness (temporary condition of insufficient guidelines, direction, limits), peership (a type of friendship unique to adolescents), peer arena (aggregate of existing and psychological reference groups), and comparative acts (series of comparisons that are characteristic of adolescent interactions) that elevated the peer to the most relevant and important figure in adolescence, particularly in planning for the future (Seltzer 1982).[1] This model drew on materials from social psychology about attraction (Cartwright and Zander 1968); affiliation (Schachter 1959); social communication, social comparison, and dissonance (Festinger 1950, 1954, 1957). Moreover, DPI holds that a biologically based predisposition (affiliation readiness), similar to the infant-to-mother attachment instinct described by Bowlby (1969), surfaces in early puberty but as an adolescent-to-peer attachment. It is the adolescents' psychological need to separate, from parents, in their quest for individuation that triggers this attachment (or reattachment) drive. Actual and/or psychological affiliation with peers reduces the insecurities that accompany the changing balance of family bonds and resultant frameworklessness (Seltzer 1982). Emotionally neutral age-mates, facing identical albeit parallel growth tasks, appear as similar others.

The physical attributes, style, social skills, appearance, and abilities that peers model and the topics of present and future that they discuss are functional to psychosocial growth. Comparison with peers enables adolescents to assess their own progress. Being with peers enables the adolescents to evaluate themselves along a continuum, a condition essential to accurate ranking of self in relation to others (Hakmiller 1966; Radloff 1966). Together, adolescent peers observe, listen, and strategize for today and tomorrow. Although observed differences may offer challenge, similarities bring comfort (Suls and Miller 1977).

Comparisons and the search for concordance—that is, agreeing in sentiment or opinion, being in harmony—not only occur with small groups of age-mates but also within a broader framework of peers, the peer arena (Seltzer 1982, 1989). The concept of peer arena is more applicable to adolescent development than that of the peer group because it encompasses, any and all psychological and/or physical interactions with any and all peers. Even characters from books, articles, movies, TV shows, memories, or personal fantasies may serve as psychological peers with whom adolescents compare themselves. Because these comparisons primarily serve to establish the self in adolescence rather than improve the self as they do in later life, they are high in both number and intensity. Paradoxically, peer affiliations that initially reduce adolescent tension later may increase tension as young people compare/rank themselves with others (Brown and Lohr 1987). To reduce this tension, it may be that adolescents perceive that peers think as they do themselves. It may be ironic that the adolescent who seeks independence from family is caught in a new dependence on peers. Thus the need for comparison and concordance with peers remains active during adolescence, declining only as the individual approaches psychological maturity and self-identity.

Literature on the Future and Adolescents

A recent comprehensive literature review (Nurmi 1991) of adolescent future orientation and planning found that adolescent goals and interests focused sequentially on (a) future education, (b) occupation, (c) family life, and (d) material aspects of life—a sequence that follows in life-span development. Adolescents' thinking about today, as well as about when they will be adults, reflects how serious adolescents are about the future. The literature also indicated that perceptions of normative life-span development and related cultural patterns differ according to gender, socioeconomic status, and subculture. Although most studies have attributed those differences to interactions with parents, teachers, and peers, the focus has been on parent/child interaction and family context, not peers. Given the Nurmi awareness of peers as contemporaries who provide incentives for thinking about current life tasks and offer each other the opportunity to compare their own behavior with that of contemporaries who also think about the future, the lack of emphasis on peers in the Nurmi review may reflect the scarcity of empirical studies on peer impact.

It is important to note that an early 1980s literature review (Trommsdorff 1983) on future orientation and socialization had little or no mention of peers. As Trommsdorff noted, "It may well be assumed that parents and teachers influence the process of socialization and the future orientation of the child on account of their own future orientation" (396). Since the Nurmi (1991) review, studies of peers and future have been increasing (Dane 1993; Hendry, Roberts, Glendinning, and Coleman 1992; Nurmi 1992, 1993). There also is interest in other future orientation and socialization issues, such as gender differences, in anticipating the future (Greene and Wheatley 1992; Lennings 1992), the impact of age difference (Seginer 1992), and personal control (Pulkkinen and Ronka 1994). What has not been addressed is the area of adolescent uncertainty about adulthood and the association with peer dynamics. Further, studies have not examined peer perceptions to ascertain whether they are associated with nationality. The current study was the first to address these issues.

Research Issues

The adolescent's route to adulthood is characterized by a new body sense (Blyth, Simmons, and Zakin 1985; Peterson 1985; Tanner 1972, 1974), increased intellectual scope (Piaget 1972), and strong emotions (Freud 1966), as well as changing social relationships and uncertainty about the future (Hartrup 1989). Festinger (1950, 1954) found that people who are uncertain about a situation tend to communicate and compare to establish a new social reality. Schachter (1959) found that people who are anxious about a situation will affiliate with others in a similar condition to evaluate the correctness of their own response. Radloff (1961) found that true also for opinions as well as for emotions. However, comparing opinions or emotions with a few people is insufficient; many comparisons are necessary to provide a range of behaviors (Radloff 1966). Because the adolescent peer arena incorporates age-mates from many peer groups, it does provide the necessary comparison numbers for the adolescent.

In the current study, how and if adolescents use peers to think about future-related issues was examined. It generally has been accepted that adolescents tend to turn to parents and school personnel for advice on career and educational decisions. Yet little is known about the role of the peer with regard to many issues of the future and the passage to adulthood. To determine whether the peer role was to offer reassurance as to the validity of the individual's own position, adolescents in four countries were asked about their views on adulthood and what responses they assumed their peers to hold.

Research Questions

The research focused on two main areas: (a) the amount of concordance according to age, gender, and country; and (b) differences in the amount of concordance between each country, gender, and each age. Inasmuch as adolescence is a period of uncertainty about opinions, aspirations, plans, and behaviors, it may be particularly important to be in concert with counterparts. The search for concordance represents the desire to know that one is in harmony with relevant others about pertinent issues.

The first research question was whether perceptions that adolescents have of their own readiness for adulthood were in concordance with perceptions they believed their peers to hold. The purpose was to examine the degree of perceived concordance between self and peer in each subpopulation, that is, to see if concordance existed and, if so, in what amount. It appears that the literature does not contain information as to the amount of concordance concerning views of the future or, indeed if concordance exists at all. The second research question concerned differences in concordance among subpopulations.[2]

Age differences. Because adolescence involves sequential development tasks over a period of years (Erikson 1950; Havighurst 1972), it was important to determine whether concordance with peers existed at all stages of adolescence. Stated in the two-stage DFI model (Seltzer 1982) is that concordance should be strongest in early adolescence. That is the time when young people begin their psychological separation from parents and when they most need to find, and be in concert with, similar others. Thus the peer arena can be a refuge. It therefore would be expected that, over time, as the maturing self develops, the need for concordance with peers would lessen with age.

Gender differences. Socialization studies of females in Western societies (Jordan, Kaplan, Miller, Striver, and Surrey 1991) have indicated that relationships are essential to females. In that study, females appeared to strive for smooth relationships throughout their lives. In a study of more than 1,100 male and female adolescents, loyalty, trustworthiness, and sensitivity to others were among the 10 most important attributes females look for in other people; they were not in the Top 10 for males (Seltzer 1989). This finding supported results from earlier studies concerning the importance of relationships for women (Gilligan 1982). Therefore, gender differences were predicted.

Cross-national dimensions. Questions still arise as to whether adolescents differ from nationality to nationality or whether adolescent behaviors transcend nations (Davis and Davis 1989; Erikson 1963; Holtzman 1975). As the first in a series of studies that will compare adolescents across four nations, nature and nurture will be considered. It is anticipated that significant concordance would be found in each nationality but would be expressed differentially according to nation.

Hypotheses

Given adolescents' own uncertainties about the future, the following hypotheses were presented:

HI. Adolescents would perceive the views of similar others—peers—about their futures to be in harmony with their own: (a) Significant amounts of concordance would be present for each gender, at all ages, in each country.

H2. The amount of perceived concordance would differ according to subpopulation: (a) The association of gender and age with concordance would vary in pattern from nation to nation.

H3. The amount of perceived concordance (a) would reduce at each older age level, reflecting the increased stability and self-confidence a more advanced definition of an individual's own self brings and (b) would be greater for females than for males.

Method

Participants

The participants in this cross-sectional study were 3,502 adolescents in Grades 7 through 12 in four countries: (a) the United States (a North American nation), (b) Scotland (a Western European nation), (c) Costa Rica (a Central American nation), and (d) the Philippines (an Asian nation). The countries were selected for their location; economic, political, and social condition; as well as type of culture and variations in size and geography. The majority of respondents were 12 through 17 years of age: 1,609 males and 1,893 females, reflecting the goal of balancing the sample with regard to gender. (The small group size of Philippine males ($n = 4$) between 11 and 13 years of age was unfortunate, but this subpopulation was left in the analysis for the sake of completeness). Of the United States group ($n = 1,447$), 68% were Caucasian; 31% were African American; 1% were Asian, Hispanic, and American Indian. Participants from Scotland ($n = 839$) were Caucasian primarily (95%) and had a small representation of Pakistani (5%) students. The Philippine participants ($n = 743$) were native Filipino; the Costa Rican participants ($n = 429$) were Caucasian and of color.

Students in the United States were from the city and suburbs of Philadelphia (Pennsylvania) and Providence (Rhode Island). Participants from Scotland were from suburban Edinburgh and Glasgow. Those from Costa Rica were from San José, and those in the Philippines were from the Manila area. The entire sample included both public and private school students. The majority were considered to be middle-class, relative to the socioeconomic groups within each country.

Measure

The measure used for the four-country study was the Adolescent Future Perception Index (AFPI; Seltzer 1990), a self-administered questionnaire appropriate for group settings. In 1984, Seltzer and Rapoport developed the original AFPI in a series of pilot tests with male and female students of the same age as the respondents in the current study. The development stage of the AFPI was conducted in the United States, Canada, and Israel between 1986 and 1988.

The revised AFPI contains more than 40 items concerning issues of importance to adolescents regarding their future. The items include perceptions of present level of maturity, clarity of plans, distance from goals, need for additional experiences, clarity of adulthood, and desire to be adult. The current report presents findings from the analysis of 12 questions in six related pairs. One question in each pair asked adolescents to state their own position; the other asked them to indicate what they believed the position of their peers to be. The response format was a continuum of six response choices. Participants were asked to place an "x" in the square that best represented their self-perceptions. The first square represented the lowest end of the response scale and the last represented the high end. (For example, Question 1 was "The line to the right represents the distance between childhood and adulthood. Place an "x" in the square in which you see yourself today"). The remaining five questions were the following:

2. How clear are your plans for the way you wish to live your life?
3. How far are you from reaching the goals you wish to achieve in life?
4. How clear is it to you what being an adult means?
5. Would you like to be an adult already?
6. Do you feel that you need to gather additional experiences so that you will be prepared to assume adult roles?

Each of the previous questions was followed by six response choices.

Permissions were received from the principals at each school in each country. Human subjects clearance was obtained through the Office of Research Administration at the University of Pennsylvania The questionnaires were distributed and administered in school classrooms by either the principal researcher, research collaborators, or teachers in each nation. Written instructions were explained to participants. This self-report instrument took approximately 15 minutes to complete. Participants in all nations were surveyed between the years 1991 and 1993. Data collected outside of the United States were entered according to a common code book, transferred to computer disk and mailed to the authors in the United States. The analysis was carried out by the authors at the University of Pennsylvania in the United States.

Statistical Method

Overall levels of concordance.[3] The process for the first stage of the analysis involved constructing the six by six contingency tables for each question pair for each country, gender, and age. Those tables were then aggregated over the six question pairs. The data were reduced to 24 overall tables (4 countries, 2 genders, and 3 age categories). An example of one of these tables is presented in the appendix. Note the clustering of the frequencies about the concordant diagonal.

For each of these tables, Cohen's kappa was calculated to measure the strength of the clustering (Agresti 1990). This is a measure of concordance for each subpopulation that quantifies the excess agreement over that which would be expected to occur by chance. Whereas kappa is used frequently as a measure of inter-rater reliability where high kappas are expected in this study of perceptions, kappa is used to measure the degree of concordance between perceptions of the future for self and peer. A kappa equal to 1 would indicate perfect concordance from everyone in the subpopulation on all question pairs; a kappa of 0 would indicate no more concordance than could be expected by chance alone. Conversely, a negative value would indicate less concordance than would happen by chance.

Differences in concordance score. To perform a more detailed analysis of the differences between the subpopulations, it was necessary to define a score for each individual's perception of concordance with his or her peers. Questions related in pairs were scored as 1 if individuals perceived their peers to answer the question in the same manner as themselves and 0 if not. In the course of the analysis, both a repeated measure logistic regression model (Liang and Zeger. 1986) and a linear regression model for concordance were carried out. These models incorporated the nation and gender variables by treating them as dummy variables (Kerlinger 1986). The results were essentially identical. Results from the linear regression model are reported because of simplicity of interpretation. The concordance score that was used in the linear regression model was defined as the proportion of perceived perfect concordances for each individual in the six paired questions. Although it was possible to lose information through this stringent dichotomization of the data, it was considered necessary because it is possible that participants of differing nationalities have systematic biases in filling out ordinal response scales (Kerlinger 1986).

Both linear and quadratic effects were used to investigate the relationship between age and perceived concordance (Neter, Wasserman, and Kutner 1985; Pedhazur 1982). The more complicated model afforded no additional explanatory power over the simpler linear effect. Again, results are reported from the simpler age effects model. Finally, another linear regression analysis was carried out that excluded the nation in which adolescents displayed markedly different Perceptions. This was undertaken to determine how sensitive the results were to the inclusion of the differing nation.

The regression analysis involved two stages: Stage 1 looked at the contributions at the most discrete level possible (interaction effects); Stage 2 looked at aggregated data (main effects). This approach of first examining interaction effects guards against improper interpretations of main effects.

Results

Presence of Concordance

Table 1 shows the values of the concordance measure (kappa), their estimated standard errors, and the group sizes. Note that the kappas are uniformly positive and significantly greater than 0. (The only exception is the Philippine male group 11 through 13 years of age, which had a group size of 4.)

The estimated concordances displayed in Table 1 indicate consistently higher amounts than would be expected by chance alone. The findings supported first Hypothesis 1a, that significant amounts of concordance would be present for each gender, at all ages, in each country.

Differences in Amount of Concordance

The nature of the national, age, and gender effects for Hypotheses 2a, 3a, 3b were tested by using a linear regression model. Table 2 is the analysis of variance (ANOVA) table and Table 3 displays the output of the regression model. Table 4 presents least square mean concordance scores that are derived from the regression model and calculated for each age, nation, and gender.

Interaction effects. Findings displayed in Table 2 reveal statistically significant interactions between nation and gender ($p < .01$) and nation and age ($p < .001$). They lend support to Hypothesis 2a that the association of gender and age with concordance would vary in pattern from nation to nation. These interactions appeared attributable largely to responses of the Philippine group.

The difference between the genders in the Philippines was greater than the differences observed in the other three countries. The decreasing amount of concordances according to age level in Costa Rica, Scotland, and the United States also was the opposite to those of the Philippines in which an interesting pattern was observed. Note that in Table 3 the only significant interactions are those associated with the Philippines: (a) Philippines x Gender ($p < .01$), (b) Philippines x Age ($p < .05$), (c) Philippines x Gender x Age ($p < .01$)

TABLE 1. Concordance Estimates (Kappa) for Each Age, Gender, and Nation

Nation	Age in years			$\overline{X}$
	12–13	*14–15*	*16–18*	
Males				
United States				
χ	.223	.248	.168	.205
	(.021)	(.017)	(.014)	
n	131	222	296	
Philippines				
χ	.007	.188	.233	.211
	(.131)	(.021)	(.019)	
n	4	133	175	
Costa Rica				
χ	.233	.220	.211	.219
	(.043)	(.025)	(.029)	
n	37	96	79	
Scotland				
χ	.422	.326	.357	.368
	(.023)	(.023)	(.022)	
n	136	127	144	
Females				
United States				
χ	.318	.199	.179	.222
	(.017)	(.014)	(.014)	
n	212	291	295	
Philippines				
χ	.230	.245	.386	.304
	(.041)	(.018)	(.019)	
n	41	195	195	
Costa Rica				
χ	.243	.249	.210	.235
	(.033)	(.026)	(.030)	
n	51	91	69	
Scotland				
χ	.401	.379	.378	.386
	(.022)	(.023)	(.022)	
n	147	139	146	

Standard errors of the kappa statistics are in parentheses.

TABLE 2. ANOVA[a] for Nation, Gender, and Age on Concordance Scores

Variable	df	SS	F
Nation	3	78.739	70.781**
Gender	1	5.196	14.012**
Age	1	3.764	10.152*
Nation × Gender	3	4.463	4.021*
Nation × Age	3	13.735	12.347**
Gender × Age	1	0.020	0.054
Nation × Gender × Age	3	2.380	2.122
Error	3,466	1,285.221	

Age is treated as a continuous variable in this analysis. ANOVA = analysis of variance.
*$p < .01$. **$p < .001$.

TABLE 3. Linear Regression Model Using Nation, Gender, and Age for the Concordance Score

Variable	B	t
Constant	0.365	37.200***
Philippines	−0.005	0.243
Costa Rica	0.027	1.392
Scotland	0.140	8.633***
Gender	0.002	0.185
Age	−0.015	−2.546*
Philippines × Gender	0.080	3.324**
Costa Rica × Gender	0.010	0.356
Scotland × Gender	0.030	1.326
Philippines × Age	0.024	1.971*
Costa Rica × Age	0.016	1.328
Scotland × Age	0.005	0.529
Gender × Age	−0.012	−1.525
Philippines × Gender × Age	0.038	2.390**
Costa Rica × Gender × Age	0.003	0.183
Scotland × Gender × Age	0.017	1.328

United States males are the baseline for dummy variable codes. Age variable is centered at 15 years.
*$p < .01$. **$p < .01$. ***$p < .001$.

TABLE 4. Least Square Mean Concordance Scores and Standard Deviations for Each Age, Nation, and Gender

	Age in years						
	12	13	14	15	16	17	18
Males							
United States							
$\overline{X}$	.410	.395	.380	.365	.350	.335	.320
SD	.021	.016	.012	.010	.011	.015	.019
Philippines							
$\overline{X}$	.332	.342	.351	.360	.370	.379	.388
SD	.043	.032	.023	.016	.014	.020	.029
Costa Rica							
$\overline{X}$	.388	.389	.391	.392	.393	.395	.396
SD	.038	.028	.021	.017	.020	.021	.036
Scotland							
$\overline{X}$	.535	.525	.515	.505	.495	.485	.474
SD	.022	.017	.013	.013	.016	.022	.028
Females							
United States							
$\overline{X}$	.449	.422	.394	.367	.340	.313	.286
SD	.017	.013	.010	.009	.011	.015	.019
Philippines							
$\overline{X}$	.336	.371	.407	.443	.478	.514	.549
SD	.031	.023	.017	.012	.013	.019	.026
Costa Rica							
$\overline{X}$	.427	.419	.412	.404	.397	.389	.382
SD	.036	.026	.019	.017	.022	.031	.041
Scotland							
$\overline{X}$	.552	.547	.542	.537	.532	.527	.521
SD	.022	.016	.013	.013	.016	.021	

Figures 1 and 2 graphically display the information presented in Table 3. Figure 1 illustrates the differing amounts of concordance for each gender in each nation. Figure 2 illustrates amounts of concordance at each age level for each nation. The uniqueness of the Philippine pattern is evident in both figures.

Main effects. Table 2 displays significant main effects for nation, gender, and age. The nation main effect appears largely attribute to Scotland; indeed, Scottish youths showed concordance scores when averaged over age and gender, almost 50% higher than those of their American counterparts. This outcome is clearly visible in Figure 2 and is reinforced by Table 3 where the Scotland effect has $p < .001$.

Hypothesis 3a, that concordance scores would decrease with age, and Hypothesis 3b, which predicted females would have higher concordance scores than males, were supported at this high level of aggregation. However, if the data are partitioned more discretely over the levels of the other independent variable, these effects cannot be assumed to hold true because of interaction between the independent variables (Milliken and Johnson 1984).

Figure 1 offers a graphic display of the gender differences. In each of the four nations the average concordance score was higher for females than for males. In 19 of the 26 possible subpopulation comparisons females had higher concordance scores than males ($p < .05$) (covering seven ages in each of the four nations minus two for which there were no data).

Supplementary analyses. In light of the dramatic interaction of age and country revealed in Figure 2 and to avoid possible misinterpretation of the age main effect, a supplementary analysis was carried out in which the age effect was tested in each country separately. Significantly lower amounts of concordance at older age levels than at younger ages were disclosed in Scotland and United States ($p < .001$) in the ($p < .0001$); there was no evidence for an age relation in Costa Rica. Contrary to the patterns of adolescence in the other three countries, in the Philippines concordance became greater with age level. The significant levels reported here were derived from a test for linear combinations of the regression coefficients (Neter et al. 1985).

Analyses Excluding the Philippines

Because the inclusion of data from the Philippines appeared to influence heavily the findings from aggregated data, an analysis was performed excluding the Philippines to ascertain the sensitivity of the findings to their inclusion. The major findings were twofold. First, findings of statistically significant differences remained; second, no interaction was found between country, age, and gender. A much simpler picture emerged in which the three other countries appeared similar with respect to the relation of age and gender on amount of perceived concordance. The analysis further disclosed that the average concordance score between 12 and 18 years of age could be expected to drop between 20% and 30%.[4] This finding lends support to a major premise of the theory of DPI (from which Hypothesis 3a is derived). Third, the difference between females arid males as to the amount of perceived concordance was no longer statistically significant. Finally, statistically significant differences between nations remained; these were attributable to high amounts of concordance in Scotland.

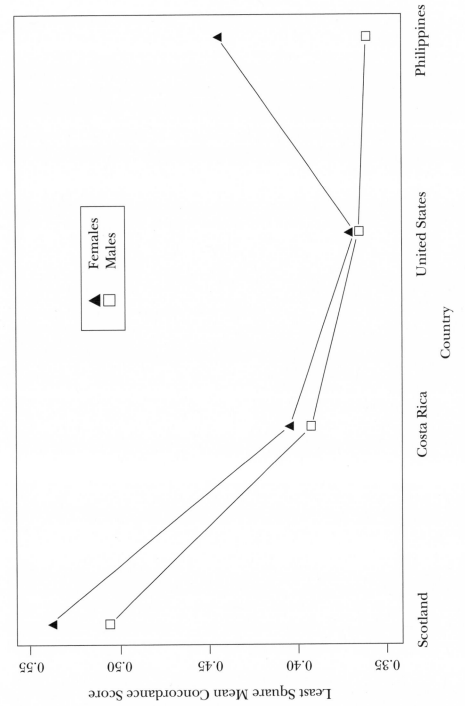

Figure 1. Least square mean concordance score for gender and country (means adjusted for age).

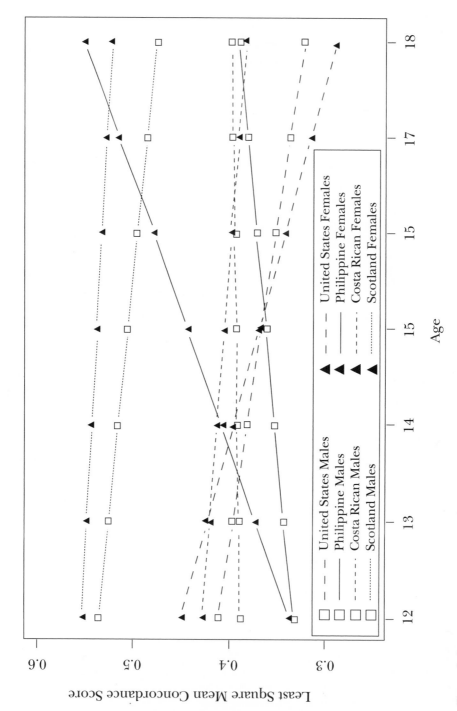

Figure 2. Least square mean concordance score for gender, country, and age.

Discussion

Findings from the study disclosed that adolescents, male and female 12 through 18 years of age in four countries (Costa Rica, Philippines, Scotland, and the United States) perceive themselves in sync with peers on issues of their futures. This perception of similarity occurred at all the ages examined for both genders across all countries. These universal findings are in accord with a theoretical position that nature may predominate over nurture in development. The findings lend support to the notions that (a) adolescents turn to those perceived as similar as a way to reduce the dissonance of uncertainty and (b) the attachment instinct identified by Bowlby (1969) as seen in infancy may be reinvigorated in adolescence (Seltzer 1982). Furthermore, that this perceived similarity is active at all the ages studied fortified current positions that view adolescence as a rather lengthy period of uncertainty.

Several interesting questions concerning national differences were raised. First, the markedly high amounts of perceived concordance observed in Scotland for each age and for each gender bring into question whether this phenomenon may be distinctly national and related to factors like living in a small country, sensitivity to limits of a class system milieu, or a tight economy (Davis and Valsiner 1989). Second, do generally lower amounts of concordance at higher ages found in the United States reflect a national emphasis on independence? If so, is it possible that this emphasis may constrain full expression of powerful internal needs to connect, which are active during periods of stress and uncertainty such as adolescence (Seiffge-Krenke 1995)? Third the pronounced gender differences in the Philippines, as well as their highly interesting opposite age-related pattern in which perceptions of concordance rise in upper age brackets stimulate queries about norms and values that differ from those in the other three countries (Eshelman 1978; Ramirez 1984). Explanations of biological factors such as an older average age for pubescence can be offered; an alternate view might attribute perceptions to traditional role modeling and/or over protectiveness by Philippine parents and an extended group of interested relatives referred to as compound families (Castillo 1979; Murdock 1949), which may delay onset of behaviors associated with adolescent development, particularly individuation/separation behavior (Medina 1991).

Summary

The design of this study was exploratory and was a first in a number of ways: (a) It is cross-national and explored questions of universal and/or nation-specific adolescent psychological perceptions functional to maturational issues concerning their futures; (b) it offered baseline information on similarities and differences between adolescents of both genders 12 through 18 years of age, in four locations of the globe on the relationship between peer self perceptions, adding new insights into developmental needs of adolescents; and (c) it tested fundamental premises of a theory of adolescent psychological development, Dynamic Functional Interaction, which argues specific developmentally stimulated age-related perceptions.

There are several limitations to this study: (a) It is not a random sample and limits the analysis to noncausal inference; (b) it is cross-sectional rather than longitudinal;

(c) there are potential confounding variables that have not been controlled for such as rural/urban location, ethnicity, and social class.

An important outcome of this exploratory study is that it is now reasonable to continue to explore the perceptions of concordance together with taking note of the limitations of this study. Studies that specifically link adolescent dynamics with theories in developmental psychology as well as a variety of research paradigms addressing the contributions of nature and nurture in adolescent development might add important information and insights to this still current debate.

Future research should be carried out in all continents and in clusters of countries in each continent. First, it then might be possible to distinguish between continental and nation-specific components of the adolescent perceptions studied. Second, studies that encompass a wider age range, perhaps even reaching into early adulthood, would provide a more appropriate time span in which to monitor the relationship between age and the amount of perceived concordance with peers. Third, notwithstanding the literature that already has identified the need for connectedness among Western women (O'Connor 1992; Smith-Rosenberg 1985), striking findings in this study of significant overall concordance coupled with findings of no difference between the genders in three of four countries convincingly calls for continuing to examine needs both of males and females for alliance not only in adolescence but continuing into adulthood (West and Sheldon-Keller 1994). Fourth, control group designs, as well as analyses both of main and interaction effects, would reduce the risk of overgeneralization.

Certainly rapid social change, cultural discontinuities, and the impact of cultural compression (Spindler 1974) are evident in modern societies. Studies that deal with adolescents and perceptions of their futures may be increasingly pertinent as a point of reference for investigation into dynamics used by older age groups to deal with uncertain futures—unfortunately, a condition no longer attributed primarily to adolescents.

Appendix

Frequency of Responses for Self and Peer of Costa Rican Females 14 through 15 Years of Age

	Perceived peer response choice					
Self-response choice	1	2	3	4	5	6
1	9	14	9	4	1	2
2	3	14	6	2	3	1
3	2	13	59	20	4	2
4	2	9	63	94	16	2
5	3	1	27	54	41	8
6	0	2	6	14	24	12

Reprinted from Vivian C. Seltzer and Richard P. Waterman, A cross-national study of adolescent peer concordance on issues of the future, *Journal of Adolescent Research* 11 (1966): 461–82. Reprinted by permission.

Notes

1. For more complete descriptions and explanations of these concepts, see Seltzer (1989, 17–24, 37–29, or Part 2).

2. Subpopulation is used in this study to denote the cross-classification of subjects according to country, age, and gender.

3. Concordance at any point in the article should be interpreted as perceived concordance.

4. More detailed findings can be obtained from the authors.

References

Agresti, A. (1990). *Categorical Data Analysis.* New York: John Wiley.

Ausubel, D., R. Montemayer, and P. Savjian, P. (1977). *Theory and Problems of Adolescent Development.* 2nd ed. New York: Grone and Stratton.

Bandura, A. (1964). The stormy decade: Fact or fiction? *Psychology in the Schools* 1: 224–31.

Bios, P. (1962). *On Adolescence: A Psychoanalytic Interpretation.* New York: Free Press.

——— (1979). *The Adolescent Passage.* New York: International Universities Press.

Blyth, D., R. Simmons, and D. Zakin (1985). Satisfaction with body image for early adolescent females: The impact of pubertal timing within different school environments. *Journal of Youth and Adolescence* 14: 207–25.

Bowlby, J. (1969). *Attachment and Loss,* vol. 1, *Attachment.* New York: Basic Books.

Bronfenbrenner, U. (1970). *Two Worlds of Childhood: U.S. and U.S.S.R.* New York: Sage.

Brown. B., and M. Lohr (1987). Peer-group affiliation and adolescent self-esteem: An integration of ego-identity and symbolic interaction theories. *Journal of Personality and Social Psychology* 52: 47–54.

Cartwright, D., and A. Zander; A. (1968). *Group Dynamics: Research and Theory.* 3rd ed. New York: Harper and Row.

Castillo, G. (1979). *Beyond Manila: Philippine Rural Problems in Perspective.* Ottawa: International Development Research Center.

Coleman. J. (1961). *The Adolescent Society.* New York: Free Press.

Dane, E. (1993). Family fantasies and adolescent aspirations: A social work perspective on a critical transition. *Family and Community Health* 12: 34–45.

Davis, D., and J. Valsiner, eds. (1989). *Child Development in Cultural Context.* Toronto: Hogrefe and Huber.

Davis, S., and D. Davis (1989) *Adolescence in a Moroccan Town: Making Social Sense.* New Brunswick, N.J.: Rutgers University Press.

Erikson, E. (1950). *Childhood and Society.* New York: Norton.

——— (1963). *Childhood and Society.* 2nd ed. New York: Norton.

Eshelman, J. (1978). *The Family: An Introduction.* 2nd ed. Boston: Allyn and Bacon.

Festinger, L. (1950). Informal social communication. *Psychological Review* 57: 271–82.

——— (1954). A theory of social comparison processes. *Human Relations* 7: 117–39.

——— (1957). *A Theory of Cognitive Dissonance.* Stanford, Calif.: Stanford University Press.

Freud, A. (1936). *The Ego and the Mechanisms of Defense.* New York: International Universities Press.

Freud, A. (1958). *Adolescence: Psychoanalytic Study of the Child. Writings of Anna Freud* 13. New York: International Universities Press. 255–78.

——— (1966). Instinctual anxiety during puberty. In *Writings of Anna Freud* 13 (rev.) New York: International Universities Press. 152–73.

Friedenberg, E. (1959). *The Vanishing Adolescent.* Boston: Beacon.

Furstenberg, R (1976). *Unplanned Parenthood: The Social Consequences of Teenage Childbearing.* New York: Free Press.

Gilligan, C. (1982). *In a Different Voice.* Cambridge, Mass.: Harvard University Press.

Goodman, P. (1956). *Growing Up Absurd.* New York: Random House.

Greene, A., and S. Wheatley (1992). I've got a lotto do and don't think I'll have the time: Gender differences in late adolescents narratives of the future. *Journal of Youth and Adolescence* 21: 667–86.

Hakmiller, K. (1966). Need for self-evaluation, perceived similarity, and comparison choice. *Journal of Experimental Social Psychology* (Suppl. 1): 49–55.

Hartrup, W. (1989). Social relationships and their developmental significance. *American Psychologist* 44: 120–26.

Havighurst, R. (1972). *Developmental Tasks and Education.* New York: McKay.

Hendry L., W. Roberts, A. Glendinning, and J. Coleman (1992). Adolescents' perceptions of significant individuals in their lives. *Journal of Adolescence* 15: 255–70.

Holtzman, W. (1975). *Personality Development in Two Cultures.* Austin: University of Austin Press.

Inhelder, B., and J. Piaget (1958). *The Growth of Logical Thinking from Childhood to Adolescence: Essay on the Construction of Formal Operational Structures.* New York: Basic Books.

Jesser, R., and J. Jessor (1977). *Problem Behavior and Psychological Development.* New York: Academic Press.

Jordan, J., A. Kaplan, J. Miller, P. Striver, and I. Surrey (1991). *Women's Growth in Connection: Readings from the Stone Center.* New York: Guilford.

Josselyn, I. (1952). *The Adolescent and His World.* New York: Family Service Association of America.

Kandel, D. (1973). Adolescent marijuana use: Role of parents and peers. *Science* 181: 1067–70.

Keniston, K. (1965). *The Uncommitted: Alienated Youth in American Society.* New York: Harcourt, Brace and World.

Kerlinger, F. (1986). *Foundations of Behavioral Research.* 2nd ed. New York: Holt, Rinehart and Winston.

Lennings, C. (1992). Adolescents' time perspective. *Perceptual and Motor Skills* 74: 424–26.

Liang, K., and S. Zeger (1986). Longitudinal data analysis using generalized linear models. *Biometrika* 73: 13–22.

Masterson, J. (1968). The psychiatric significance of adolescent turmoil. *American Journal of Psychiatry* 124: 1549–54.

Medina, B. (1991). *The Filipino Family.* Diliman, Quezon City: University of the Philippines Press.

Milliken, G., and D. Johnson (1984). *Analysis of Messy Data,* vol. 1, *Designed experiments.* Belmont, Calif.: Lifetime Learning Publications.

Murdock. G. (1949). *Social Structure.* New York: Macmillan.

Neter, J., W. Wasserman, and M. Kutner (1985). *Applied Linear Statistical Models.* 2nd ed. Homewood, Ill.: Irwin.

Nurmi, J. (1991). How do adolescents see their future: A review of the development of future orientation and plannings. *Developmental Review* 11: 1–59.

———— (1992). Age differences in adult life goals, concerns. and their temporal extension: A life course approach to future-oriented motivation. *International Journal of Behavioral Development* 15: 487–508.

———— (1993). Adolescent development in an age-graded context: The role of personal beliefs. goals. and strategies in the tackling of developmental tasks and standards. *International Journal of Behavioral Development* 16: 169–89.

O'Connor, P. (1992). *Friendships Between Women: A Critical Review.* New York: Guilford.

Offer, D., and J. Offer (1975). *From Teenage to Manhood.* New York: Basic Books.

Pedhazur, E, (1982). *Multiple Regression in Behavioral Research.* New York: Holt, Rinehart and Winston.

Peterson, A. (1985). Pubertal development as a cause of disturbance: Myths, realities, and unanswered questions. *Genetic, Social and General Psychology Monographs* 2: 205–32.

Peterson, A., and B. Taylor (1980). The biological approach to adolescence. In J. Adelson, ed., *Handbook of Adolescent Psychology*. New York: John Wiley. 117–55.

Piaget, J. (1952). *The Origin of Intelligence in Children*. New York: International Universities Press.

——— (1972). Intellectual evolution from adolescence to adulthood. *Human Development* 15: 1–2.

Pulkkinen, L., and A. Ronka (1994). Personal control over development, identity formation, and future orientation as components of life orientation: A developmental approach. *Developmental Psychology* 30: 260–71.

Radloff, R. (1961). Opinion evaluation and affiliation. *Journal of Abnormal and Social Psychology* 62: 578–85.

——— (1966). Social comparison and ability evaluation. *Journal of Abnormal and Social Psychology* (Supp. 1): 6–26.

Ramirez, M. (1984). *Understanding Philippine Social Realities Through the Filipino Family: A Phenomenological Approach*. Manila: Asian Social Institute Communication Center.

Schachter. S. (1959). *The Psychology of Affiliation: Experimental Studies of the Source of Gregariousness*. Stanford, Calif.: Stanford University Press.

Seginer, R. (1992). Future orientation: Age-related differences among adolescent females. *Journal of Youth and: Adolescence* 21: 421–37.

Seiffge-Krenke, I. (1995). *Stress Coping and Relationships in Adolescence*. Mahwah, N.J.: Lawrence Erlbaum.

Seltzer, V. (1982). *Adolescent Social Development: Dynamic Functional Interaction*. Lexington, Mass.: Lexington Books.

Seltzer, V. (1989). *The Psychosocial Worlds of the Adolescent: Public and Private*. New York: John Wiley.

——— (1990). Adolescent future perception index. Unpublished questionnaire, University of Pennsylvania, Philadelphia.

Smith-Rosenberg, C. (1985). *Disorderly Conduct: Visions of Gender in Victorian America*. New York: Knopf.

Spindler; G. (1974). The transmission of culture. In G. Spindler, ed., *Education and Cultural Process: Toward an Anthropology of Education*. New York: Holt, Rinehart and Winston. 279–310.

Suls, J., and R. Miller, eds. (1977). *Social Comparison Processes: Theoretical and Empirical Perspectives*. Washington, D.C.: Hemisphere.

Tanner, J. (1972). Sequence, tempo and individual variation of growth and development of boys and girls aged twelve to sixteen. In J. Kagan and R. Coles, eds., *Twelve to Sixteen: Early Adolescence*. New York: Norton. 1–24.

Tanner, J. (1974). *Physical Aspects of Adolescence*. London: University of London Press.

Trommsdorff, G. (1983). Future orientation and socialization. *International Journal of Psychology* 18: 381–406.

West, M., and A. Sheldon-Keller (1994). *Patterns of Relating: An Adult Attachment Perspective*. New York: Guilford.

Commentary

Vivian C. Seltzer

Currents of the Twentieth Century

While "adolescence" has been regarded as a unique period of development since ancient times (Kleijwegt 1991), more recent interest in this developmental stage was mild to say the least until the beginning of the twentieth century. G. Stanley Hall's Clarke University Lectures (1908) and two-volume work *Adolescence* (1916) within which he depicted emotional life during adolescence as oscillating between contradictory trends kindled strong interest in the field and earned him the title of "father of adolescence." He related the stage of adolescence to a turbulent transitional period during the last decades of the eighteenth century characterized as "Sturm und Drang." It is no coincidence that his work coincided with Freud's dramatic structural theory of mental functioning. Freud shocked Victorian Vienna with concepts like unconsciously motivated behavior and drives searching for satisfaction present at birth. Furthermore, he theorized an unconscious sexual desire for the parent of the opposite sex surfacing at the end of early childhood (Oedipus Complex) only to be repressed, shut off to consciousness, during middle childhood but churning up again with increased drive and intensity at puberty, marking entry into adolescence (1905). Although Freud paid scant attention to adolescence preferring to concentrate on the prior four stages, he did accord it a unique status. Freud's developmental theory assigns to adolescence the final period of psychological growth and accords the developing individual a second chance—an opportunity to resolve unfinished psychological work of earlier stages and enter early adulthood less psychologically handicapped, if at all. The adolescent stage was studied in depth by Sigmund Freud's daughter Anna. She carried her father's work on adolescence to a deeper level contributing new insights. For example, she argued that behavior during this period might reach almost psychotic proportions and still be regarded as within a normative passage. In fact, she worried that youth experiencing a smooth passage might enter adulthood with an inhibited or a restricted "self" (1948).

Erik Erikson, one of Freud's disciples, deviated from strict psychoanalytic principles in his embrace of the impact of the social environment. He went beyond agreeing that age-mates were the "safe others" to replace parents as objects of libido, but that they were important also important for the safe haven their peer gatherings offered during this turbulent period. Here, agemates had a place to "try out" characteristics and abilities modeled by others as they struggled psychologically to arrive at what Erikson introduced to the literature as a "sense of identity" (1960, 1963).

As the social context entered the debate on what influenced adolescent growth and behavior, the extent of peer influence so impressed John Coleman that he coined the concept of an *adolescent society* with attitudes and mores quite separate from those of the parenting generation (1972). Prior to this organizing conception, other scholars had worried. Bandura saw division between the generations so dramatic as to coin it *a split level society* (1963). Others worried about impact of a developing technological world of specialization as encouraging parental abdication (Friedenberg 1963; Goodman 1956). Concern was raised as to potential dire consequences of peers as a default destination. David Ausubel identified peer groups as satellite peer societies and worried that an overabundance of modeling by peers could stimulate wide-scale development of immature adults (1954).

Origins of My Interest in Adolescence and Adolescents

As I engaged the adolescent literature in my pursuit of a Ph.D. in child development and clinical evaluation, this above type of literature raised questions for me. I thought about my own prior social work practice. I wondered how one identified irregular behaviors without knowledge of what the normative behavior is. Furthermore, just how do growth experiences immediately impact observable behaviors? To begin, I stepped up the frequency of my observation of adolescents. This gave rise to a question which would not go away. *Why did I observe adolescents socializing in large groups far more frequently than in small groups, especially younger adolescents?* A second question arose as I read further. At that same time (the 1970s), when influence sources of adolescents were discussed, the literature spoke in dichotomous terms only. "Parent, or peer?" Yet, as I spoke with adolescents and observed even more, I found it hard to understand how all varieties of peers could possibly be combined into one category. My curiosity evolved into two questions I investigated in my Ph.D. dissertation work.

Pertinent Empirical Studies

Findings from dissertation studies supported my hunch. Lumping agemates within a general category of "peers" was both a conceptual error and a pragmatic disservice. Rather, adolescents needed to differentiate their influence world in order to use it. Findings disclosed sufficient cognitive differentiation by early adolescence to distinguish between categories of peers, different types of adults and transition groups like older siblings regarded as best suited to ask opinions of those. These studies were my first contribution to literature on workings of the adolescent mind (Seltzer 1980).

The Question of Congregating in Large Groups? It Did Not Go Away

Just as Erikson had suggested, peers assembled to try out characteristics and abilities. What he did not study, however, was which psychological dynamics they utilized. In asking why adolescents needed to be with so many others while they "tried out", my dissertation studies supported a concept Leon Festinger contributed in the 1950s to the social psychology literature. In his theory of social comparison and subsequent studies, he argued that to feel confident about opinions and actions, people compare with others they judge to be similar (1954). He did not apply this psychological interaction to adolescents, but to me it seemed to fit. I found it did. However, my studies revealed they needed many, many others to compare with since they asked not one, but a series of questions. A lot a information is necessary to resolve the quest of "who am I" and to resolve "identity." These 1976 findings were published in 1980.

The Next Step—A Theory of Adolescent Psychosocial Development

Since new knowledge derives from what already exists in the literature, my new insights built on work of developmental theorists mentioned above as well as others from the field of social psychology. My theoretical model continued on where Erik Erikson stopped. Erikson identified the relevance of peers and peer groups in the search to resolve one's own identity. *My work specified the process, particulars, and sequence.* It argued an adolescent period of two stages with the end goal of identity resolution. It identified beginning and ending of adolescence according to arousal and satiation of the need for comparison. In modern times, computers give scholars a powerful tool for empirical analyses. The era of theorizing without support from empirical findings in the behavioral and social sciences is over. Accordingly, I published *a second book of empirical studies* whose findings did support major premises of DFI (1989).

The Twenty-First Century

Today's world is a global world. Just as the time arrived when theory alone could not survive without supporting empirical findings, domestic findings alone no longer suffice. Now, it is essential to study whether a phenomenon is local or global. Accordingly, in 1990 I began pilot studies in several overseas locations and in 1992 began a series of overseas studies to determine whether what U.S. studies revealed was culture specific or did it portend of a universal tendency. The purpose of the Seltzer and Waterman analysis which follows this introduction and the first to be published was to investigate this overriding question of culture specificity or universality and to examine three basic questions: 1) Do adolescents in other nations occupy the central position of relevance to one another as do U.S. youth, as will be evidenced by the closeness of views on matters of the future? 2) Are age-related patterns of peer relevance found in all countries? 3) Are age-related patterns the same in all countries or do they vary as to country?

Seltzer and Waterman report findings from a study of four countries: Costa Rica (Central America), Philippines (East Asia), Scotland (Northern Europe), USA (North American). Findings from subsequent studies where two additional countries were added—Malaysia (Asia) and South Africa (Africa)—have been completed but are yet unpublished. Analyses to date reveal generally similar findings.

Note on Current Activities

I am preparing a book for practice with adolescents. It will be based in the application of my prior books of theory and empirical exploration, domestic and global. It is intended to complete a cycle of work following the model set by the social psychologist Kurt Lewin, father of group dynamics. He held that theory and experimentation is of most utility when it can be practically applied since application stimulates new questions which in turn drive development of new theory and empirical investigation—a cycle of knowledge building. Thus, I intend for this last of three books to be a text for graduate students and for academics and practicing professionals in the fields of mental health, family life and education.

My View of Adolescent Development and Behavior and My MSW Education

The organizing power of "function" was as great a gem in my MSW education at the Pennsylvania School of Social Work as was the school's overarching concept of "process." I found each concept remarkable in its contribution to enlarging my understanding of the psychological dynamics at work during the adolescent stage.

Could it be accident that my theory of development, Dynamic Functional Interaction, argues that peers and peer groups are not for fun and games. They are *functional*. Peers engage in "deep structure" functional social comparison. The *process* is long . . . ten years or more. The product? An "Identity"!

A Final Personal Comment

During the period I pursued my MSW at Penn, I had the good fortune to be student to some of the "greats"—Goldie Basch Faith, Rosa Wessel, Ruth Smalley. I was lucky enough to have "gems of knowledge" strewn before me—among them concepts of process, function, beginning middle and end, will, choice, etc. Most of all, a deep respect for the strengths in each individual. As is the case for most students, it was not until long after my graduation that I came to understand the depth and force of these teachings. With considerable awe, I also acknowledge the gifts of the pen from Virginia Robinson and Jessie Taft. I always regretted not having arrived soon enough to be their student.

References

Ausubel, D. (1954). *Theory and Problems of Adolescent Development.* New York: Grune and Stratton.

Coleman, J. (1961). *The Adolescent Society: The Social Life of the Teenager and its Impact on Education.* New York: Free Press.

Erikson, E. (1963). *Youth, Change and Challenge.* New York: Basic Books.

Freud, A. (1948). *The Ego and the Mechanisms of Defense.* London: Hogarth.

Freud, S. (1905). The transformations of puberty. In J. Strachey, ed., *The Standard Edition of the Complete Psychological Works of Sigmund Freud.* London: Hogarth.

Friedenberg, E. Z. (1963). *The Vanishing Adolescent.* Boston: Beacon Press.

Goodman, P. (1956). *Growing Up Absurd.* New York: Random House.

Hall, G. S. (1916). *Adolescence.* New York: Appleton Press.

Kleigwegt, M. (1991). *Ancient Youth: The Ambiguity of Youth and the Absence of Adolescence in Greco-Roman Society.* Amsterdam: Gieben.

Chapter 33
The Journey Toward Intercultural Sensitivity: A Non-Linear Process

Joretha N. Bourjolly, Roberta G. Sands, Phyllis Solomon, Victoria Stanhope, Anita Pernell-Arnold, and Laurene Finley

Introduction

Over the past two decades, increasing attention has been given to the importance of intercultural competence in the human services. Health and mental health researchers have identified disparities among cultural groups in diagnosis, resource utilization, and treatment (Jackson 2002; Robinson and Morris 2000). In a special 1999 mental health supplement, the Surgeon General's Report highlighted inequities based on culture, race, and ethnicity in the delivery and utilization of mental health services (Department of Health and Human Services 1999). These findings highlight the need for education and training programs that help providers develop sensitivity and skills for serving diverse ethnic, racial, and cultural groups.

With the development of intercultural training programs, the need to evaluate participants' growth of interpersonal competence has become apparent. This paper demonstrates the use of Milton Bennett's Developmental Model of Intercultural Sensitivity as a tool for assessing changes in trainees' intercultural sensitivity over the course of a training program and analyzes the results of this application. The authors employ the term intercultural sensitivity here to mean the "ability to discriminate and experience relevant cultural differences," in contrast to intercultural competence, which describe "the ability to think and act in interculturally appropriate ways" (Hammer, Bennett, and Wiseman 2003, 422). Hammer and his colleagues (2003) state that greater intercultural sensitivity is related to a greater potential for intercultural competence.

The program, Partners Reaching to Improve Multicultural Effectiveness (PRIME), is funded by the Substance Abuse and Mental Health Services Administration as a Multicultural Workforce Training program. PRIME is a statewide intensive training course in Pennsylvania, which aims to reduce culturally based disparities in the provision of mental health services. Trainees attended two consecutive all-day sessions for nine months in which they were presented content on such topics as worldviews, specific cultures and ethnicities, communication styles, oppression and racism, and managing discrimination, diagnosis and assessment, treatment/rehabilitation/recovery planning, groups and social network support. Training goals were targeted toward improving participants' awareness, knowledge, and skills as culturally competent mental health service providers. The training had both didactic and experiential components with opportunities to examine one's own culture and the culture of others.

The evaluation of the training had quantitative and qualitative components. The quantitative component employed a pre-posttest design. Data were collected on sociodemographic characteristics of the trainees, their knowledge of culture, their cultural adaptability, and their cultural competency skills at the beginning and end of the PRIME training. A description of quantitative component of this evaluation, including the measures that were used, is reported elsewhere (Stanhope et al. 2005). The qualitative component of the evaluation consisted of evaluators' observation of the process of the training sessions and their fidelity, an assessment of the accomplishment of outcome objectives, and an examination of the written logs that participants submitted in which they reflected on their between-session cultural experiences. In this paper, the authors focus on the logs, which the participants submitted, one at each two-day session throughout the training. Lopez and his colleagues describe the utility of using logs to examine the development of cultural sensitivity (Lopez et al. 1989). The Bennett Developmental Model of Intercultural Sensitivity (DMIS) was used as the framework for analyzing the logs.

The Bennett Developmental Model

Bennett (1986a, 1993) created a model of intercultural competence in his developmental model of intercultural sensitivity (DMIS) (Hammer, Bennett, and Wiseman 2003). The DMIS explains how people construe cultural difference and is based on the assumptions that one's experience is a function of the meaning one ascribes to phenomena. There are many levels at which one experiences cultural difference and ethical choices must be made for intercultural sensitivity to develop (Bennett 1993). As one's experience of cultural difference becomes more complex and sophisticated, one's potential competence in intercultural relations increases (Hammer, Bennett, and Wiseman 2003). Bennett states that there is a linear assumption built into the model, but it is not assumed that progression is one way or permanent (Bennett 1993). Nevertheless, Bennett presents the stages in hierarchical order and sees "retreats" as occasional; people do not tend to move from more to less complex experiences of cultural difference (Hammer, Bennett, and Wiseman 2003).

The model is divided into six "stages of development," which correspond to how one experiences difference (Bennett 1986a). These stages are on a continuum spanning three ethnocentric to three ethnorelative stages (see Table 1). The shift from the first three (ethnocentric) stages to the second three (ethnorelative) stages represents a change of a deeply seated worldview (Bennett 1993).

TABLE 1. Bennett's Model of Stages of Intercultural Sensitivity

Stage and subcategories	Characteristics
Ethnocentric Stages	Using the worldview of one's own culture is the basis for defining reality and making judgments of others.
Denial of difference	One's own worldview is the only one that exists or matters. This perception may be due to full or partial isolation or social or physical barriers. May dehumanize others.
Defense against difference	Cultural differences are recognized but because they are threatening, they are resisted. Three common strategies are denigration, assumption of cultural superiority, and reversal.
Minimization of difference	Cultural differences are acknowledged and are not denigrated, but they are not considered important. The focus is on similarities as a way of obfuscating differences. Strategies include trivialization of differences and the assumption of universality.
Ethnorelative Stages	Comfort with a variety of customs and standards and the ability to adapt judgments and behavior to many different interpersonal settings without considering one's own culture as any more central than others.
Acceptance of difference	Cultural differences are acknowledged and appreciated. Acceptance occurs on two levels: respect for behavioral differences and respect for underlying value differences.
Adaptation to difference	Suspending value judgments based on one's own culture, one evaluates behavior from the perspective of another's culture. One develops communication skills that are attuned to another's culture, e.g., empathy and pluralism (the internalization of bicultural or multicultural frames of reference).
Integration of difference	The application of ethnorelativism to one's own identity. One evaluates experience using an understanding of multiple frames of reference and is able to act as an insider and outsider. It includes contextual evaluation and constructive marginality.

Sources: Bennett (1986b); http://www.cocc.edu/cagatucci/asa/MCsources/intercultdev.htm

Literature Review

Research Using the Bennett's DMIS

Prior research using Bennett's model has used the Intercultural Development Inventory (IDI), a quantitative instrument developed to assess an individual's response to cultural difference. The IDI consists of six subscales that reflect Bennett's ethnocentric and ethnorelative stages of intercultural sensitivity (Altshuler, Sussman, and Kachur 2003; Endicott, Bock, and Narvaez 2003; Hammer, Bennett, and Wiseman 2003). There are a few studies that have used this model and the IDI instrument. One study examined shifts in students' attitudes toward cultural difference, while participating in Latin American cultural events and readings about intercultural difference.

Sixty-three undergraduate students enrolled in geography courses at Miami University completed pre- and posttests using the IDI. Students completed the IDI in the beginning and end of the courses. During the period after the pretest, they were required to read material on intercultural difference and attend related lectures and the university-wide Latin American cultural events. While results show that participation in planned university-wide cultural programs can increase intercultural sensitivity among college students, the authors caution that there may have been some selection bias. Those students who completed both pre- and posttests appeared to have been more motivated about cultural issues (Klak and Martin 2003).

Other research found that gender and multicultural experiences can influence one's level of intercultural sensitivity (Altshuler, Sussman, and Kachur 2003). Twenty-four pediatric resident trainees had their stage of intercultural sensitivity assessed using the IDI before and after their participation in an intercultural training intervention. Demographic information was also collected from the participants. The results showed that the female residents exhibited lower Denial and Defense (DD factor) and higher Acceptance, Cognitive Adaptation, and Behavioral Adaptation (AA factor) compared to their pre-training scores. Males, however, showed an increase in DD and a decrease in AA. In addition, the results also suggest that cultural training increased intercultural sensitivity (Altshuler, Sussman, and Kachur 2003).

Another study, conducted among high school students attending an international school in Southeast Asia, found a positive relationship between the length of time spent at the school and the level of intercultural sensitivity. Three hundred and thirty-six high school students participated in the study. The IDI were distributed to students with parent consent forms in the students' English classes. Those students who returned signed consent forms were administered the IDI. The results showed that the longer students were at the school, the lower their scores on Denial and Defense and the higher their scores on Acceptance and Cognitive Adaptation (Straffon, 2003). Considering these findings, the authors will explore the impact of the training over time on intercultural sensitivity for the PRIME participants. Applied to the present study, these findings suggest that PRIME trainees will likely decrease their ethnocentricity and increase their ethnorelativity over the course of the training program.

Research by Endicott, Bock, and Narvaez (2003) explored the relationship among moral reasoning, intercultural development, and multicultural experiences. Seventy undergraduate students from a large Midwestern university were administered the Multicultural Experiences Questionnaire (MEXQ), the Defining Issues Test-2, and the IDI. Bivariate correlational analyses showed that there were significant associations (1) between moral and intercultural development, (2) between multicultural experiences and intercultural development, (3) between depth of multicultural experiences and intercultural development, and (4) between depth of multicultural experiences and moral development. These results suggest that moral and intercultural development were positively related, likely due to their common reliance on cognitive flexibility which enables one to integrate and consider multiple frameworks (Endicott, Bock, and Narvaez 2003).

Bennett's model, along with empirical research applying the model, provide a theoretical basis for the development of intercultural sensitivity as well as a methodology for assessing this complex process. The present study attempts to expand the knowledge base by examining the development of intercultural sensitivity over a longer period of time and by utilizing a qualitative approach as a means for assessing this development for individuals participating in intercultural competency training.

Methods

Participants

Initially 46 individuals enrolled in the PRIME training program. This analysis, however, is limited to the 34 who remained in the program and submitted logs on a consistent basis. Of the 34, 32 completed demographic profile forms. Of these, 72% were female and the average age was 46. Fifty-three percent were below the age of 45 and 47% were age 45 and older. Fifty-nine percent identified as European or American White 13 % defined themselves as American Black, and 16% said that they were multiracial. Large proportions reported their religion as Christian (75%) and their sexual orientation as heterosexual (94%). Thirty-eight percent had completed college, with an additional 15% having completed some years of college. Forty-one percent had graduate degrees. Sixty-nine percent of the training participants, all of whom were mental health providers, had some prior multicultural competency training.

Procedures

As mentioned earlier, participants in the PRIME training were required to write reflection papers (logs) on their cultural experiences between sessions and to submit them at the next training session. No page limit was specified; most were 1–3 pages. The logs were assigned the first month with the first log entry due at the second month of the training session. Therefore, each participant was to submit a log at each session. The logs reflected their experiences over 10 months of training, as there was a two-month break over the summer. After reviewing the literature on assessing intercultural sensitivity, the authors concluded that Bennett's framework best lent itself to assessing the evolution of cultural sensitivity over time when the group itself was diverse. Two members of the evaluation team (JNB and RGS) read the logs, which, to ensure anonymity, were categorized and organized according to code numbers. Initially, they read the first three logs of each participant; then they met and checked their codes for inter-rater reliability. Subsequently, they read the next three logs followed by the last two logs. They coded each participant's log for each session separately and met subsequently to share their results. They discussed places where they disagreed on the codes and came to a consensus about the appropriate code. This discussion involved reviewing the Bennett Model and relevant stages that were being considered as the codes for the log. At times one or both of the evaluators assigned more than one code to the same log. When this was the case, they used the code for the highest level of intercultural sensitivity development. Initially, the names of the codes were entered

TABLE 2. PRIME Training—Coding for Logs

Code #	Log 1	Log 2	Log 3	Log 4	Log 5	Log 6	Log 7	Log 8
01	2	2	4	2	5	5	3	4
02	4	4	4	4	3	4	4	
03	4	4	4	5	3	3	4	4
04	5	3	2	4	2	4	2	4
05	3	1	5	2	2	2	4	4
06	2	2	1	3	1	1	3	3
07	1	3	2	1	1	1	1	
08	3	2	3	3	2	2	4	3
09	4	6	5	4		4	3	5
10	2	5	2	2	2	2	2	5
11	2	4	4	4	5	3	3	2
12	2	1	3	2	3	3	3	4
13	4	3	3	4	3	2	5	4
14	4	4	4	4	5	5	4	4
15	4	4	4	4	4	4	4	5
16	3	3	3	5	5	2	3	4
17	2	1	3	4	4	4	2	3
18	4	2	4	3	3	4	4	4
19	4	4	4	4	4	4	4	4
20	2	2	3	3	3	4	3	3
21	1	2	4	3	2	2	3	4
22	2	1	2	3	4	3	4	5
23	4	2	2	4	2	5	4	4
24	2	3	5	3	3	2	3	4
25	2	3	2	2	3	2		4
26	2	2	3	2	4		4	4
27	3	3	4	5	4	5	2	4
28	2	4	4	2	2	3	5	4
29	5	4	4	2	5	2	2	3
30	3	3	3	4	4	4	3	4
31	5	6	6	4	4	4	4	
32	3	2	2	4	2	2	4	4
33	2	2	2	2	2	3	4	
34	1	3	3	3	3	3	3	4

Key
1 = Denial   4 = Acceptance
2 = Defense   5 = Adaptation
3 = Minimization   6 = Integration

into a table that displayed codes by each participant for each of the eight logs he or she submitted.

Data Analysis

Subsequently a new table was constructed in which the six code names were converted into numbers (1 through 6) (see Table 2). The numerical assignments followed Bennett's sequence of development, that is: Denial = 1, Defense = 2, Minimization = 3, Acceptance = 4, Adaptation = 5, and Integration = 6. In order to have sufficient data to evaluate changes over time, logs from participants who submitted fewer than

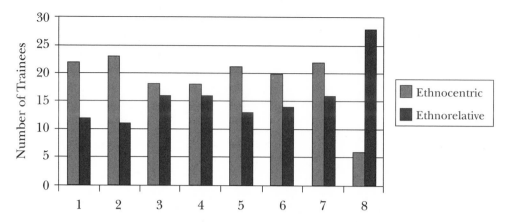

Figure 1. Cultural competence across logs.

7 logs were excluded from the analyses. The numerical format made it possible to use SPSS to examine the results, create bar graphs, and to test for the impact of sociodemographic characteristics and prior multicultural training on log scores.

Findings

Examining the sequence of codes for the 34 participants who submitted all or all but one of their logs, the authors identified two sets of patterns. The first set had to do with linearity, with the most pervasive configuration being nonlinear ($n = 32$). For these participants, the development of intercultural sensitivity appears to involve a combination of regressions to earlier stages while progressing to more ethnorelative stages. Only two participants developed cultural sensitivity in a linear manner.

Other patterns emerged from an examination of movement from ethnocentric to ethnorelative groups over time. Among the trainees, 28 participants moved from ethnocentric to ethnorelative positions, two remained ethnocentric, and four remained ethnorelative.

As Figure 1 shows, by the time log #8 was submitted, most of the participants were in one of the ethnorelative stages. For logs #1 through #6, the majority was in the ethnocentric stages. For log #7, there are more logs in the ethnocentric stages but the numbers are close, with 18 ethnocentric and 16 ethnorelative. By log #8, 28 of the 34 participants were in the ethnorelative stages. Figure 1 compares the relative changes in the proportion of the logs that were ethnocentric vs. ethnorelative over time.

An examination of logs of those trainees who stayed in the ethnorelative stages were qualitatively different from those trainees who remained in the ethnocentric stages, as well as other PRIME trainees who went back and forth between ethnocentric and ethnorelative stages. This difference had to do with the manner in which they described their cultural experiences in their personal and professional lives. It was apparent that those individuals who remained ethnorelative had begun a journey of

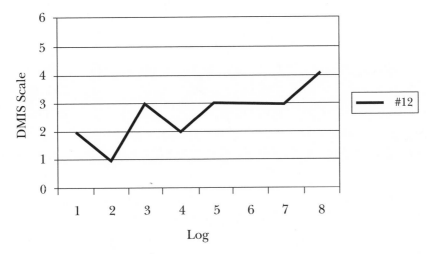

Figure 2. Non-linear progression (#12).

self-exploration of their culture or those of family members before the PRIME training. They lived bicultural or multicultural lives and gained a great deal of insight from
the struggles they have had and currently face from cultural encounters. The next
section will demonstrate the major patterns found in the logs.

Examples from the Logs

Logs Showing Non-Linear Development. The majority of individuals who attended the
PRIME training submitted logs that had a non-linear development in intercultural
sensitivity during the training period. Examples from two training participants' logs
12 and 18 (see Figures 2 and 3) will be used to show the nature of their development.
Participant #12 is a 38-year-old American White male. The trainee's first log, coded
as *defense against differences* showed that he had some difficulty with the cultural difference of the trainers and the manner in which they communicated and conducted the
training. The two trainers were African American females. He wrote, "During the
training I felt like the 'troubled' child. I was the one who questioned the trainers on
following an outline among other things." In log 2, the trainee showed *denial of difference* in his log as evidenced by the following quote:

Prior to the first PRIME training session, I was riding somewhere in Philadelphia when a
thought came to me that has made me question my cultural awareness. This thought focused
on my comfort level with other culturally different groups. I realized that I would be more cautious and concerned if I came upon an unknown Black group of young men than any other
group of people I did not know. . . . On the job and in my personal life I believe I treat everyone
the same way. I believe that my becoming friends with someone is based on mutual respect and
trust in that person regardless of their race/ethnicity/sex. NOW am not sure how open I have
been because I am less likely to get to know people within a group, especially if the group is
young Black men.

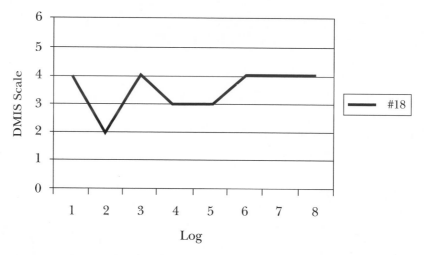

Figure 3. Non-linear progression (#18).

It appeared as though the PRIME training helped this trainee to realize that although he initially thought he was open to forming relationships based on nonracial factors, he had separated himself from African American males, because of his lack of comfort with this group. His third log, however, shows *minimization of difference* with an attempt to "bury differences under the weight of similarity" (Bennett 1986b, 2). This excerpt from the trainee's log 3 demonstrates this stage:

My belief that "similarities" among people can be the key to navigate through culture (personal/professional) differences appears to be similar to this training's concept of a shared "spiritual core." I am thinking if I can tap the treatment team's "spiritual core" the team can better serve the client. We'll see if I can!

In log 4, the trainee shared that he has a talent for sarcastic humor. This is also a trait that his family values among its members and is often a means of relating to other people. He has begun to question, however, in this log, whether this means of interacting with other people may be counterproductive to becoming culturally competent. He conveys some *defense against difference* in changing this behavior in his comment, "At the same time I realize that this sarcastic humor is most often how I relate to people. If I move from it who am I?"

In the next three logs, 5, 6, and 7, he goes back to using *minimization*. For example, in log 5, he poses the question, "What are some similarities (core principles?) that can lead us to equality, understanding, and even acceptance of that which is different?" In the subsequent log, he made reference to a video clip shown in the training of an African American retired police officer who was physically abused by White policemen for a supposed traffic violation. The trainee stated in his log that, "I began to see similarities between myself and the retired police officer." By log 8, there was a move toward the ethnorelative stage of *acceptance*. He began to have contact with a brother whom he described as being very different from himself; he has gotten more involved with researching his own family history; and has recognized the link between understanding "the importance of one's own family history and the ability to be empathic good mental health providers."

Another trainee whose development of intercultural sensitivity was non-linear is participant #18. This trainee is a 35-year-old American White female. In her first log, coded as *acceptance*, the trainee wrote about her realization that culture encompasses more than what can be seen on the surface, "that unseen components of one's culture need to be 'seen' as well." She has also been involved in her own process of cultural self-exploration and sees this as important for providing effective services to clients. In log 2, however, she reverts to *defense against difference*. The trainee described a couple of cultural encounters that made her feel uncomfortable. One was with a co-worker who was of a different religion. The trainee stated:

I learned about the Baptist faith and the traditions my coworker's family had. I had feelings that some of my beliefs were "right" and her beliefs were "wrong." This was most prominent when she shared information about her beliefs and traditions that differed from mine. In addition, this created some turmoil for me since it made me reflect upon my own beliefs, traditions, and their origins.

This was an example of *defense*, in that the differences in religious beliefs were recognized, but were perceived as threatening. Another section of the log described the trainee's emotional reaction to an incident that happened in the training. She did not provide details, but it appeared to be a conflict among some of the training participants in which "hot buttons" were pushed. As a result, this trainee said, "I am more cautious of expressing my own opinions and beliefs because I am concerned with having another cultural encounter. I'm not sure if this is good or bad, but it fits into my comfort zone at this time." It appears as though the *acceptance* that was evident in the first log may have changed to *defense* due to "new" experiences in which the trainee had not developed cultural competency.

In the subsequent log, she moved back to *acceptance*. She recounted a recent trip she and her family made to Florida. While eating at a restaurant there, they were served by a waitress who appeared to be Greek and spoke "broken English." The waitress's manner of relating and speaking was culturally different from that of the trainee and her family. The trainee realized that she was gaining an increased respect for cultural differences. This awareness is exemplified in an excerpt from log 3:

To be honest, in the past, I would have been annoyed and tolerated these incidents. Instead, I was grabbing napkins and jotting down all of the observations so I wouldn't forget them for this log entry. I am surprised that I found myself interested in the waitress's comments and mannerisms and how they revealed things about her ethnicity and culture. I was not so quick to judge her based upon communication barriers, and I was curious about her heritage. In hindsight, I wish I had asked about her ethnicity, as it would have painted a better picture of her for me.

Logs 4 and 5, however, show a regression back to an earlier stage of *minimization*. Although she recognized cultural differences between herself and other individuals with whom she came in contact, there was an internal struggle to accept and understand these differences. For example in log 4, she noted she felt uncomfortable with unfamiliar practices at a funeral. She recorded in her log, "I attended a funeral recently and was subjected to some cultural experiences that differed from my own. . . . However, after some time, I have been able to accept the fact that my attitude toward the proceedings was interfering with my understanding of the overall purpose of the process." In log 5, she wrote again about these feelings when she met a new co-worker who was of a different culture, a vegetarian and a PETA (People for the Ethical Treatment of Animals, an animal rights organization) activist. Although she was able to have a conversation with her co-worker about their differences, she experienced some internal conflict after the conversation. The following passage from the log reflects these feelings:

Personally, I am not a vegetarian, I occasionally wear animal skin clothing, I support hunting, and I have used products that are tested on animals—all of which her culture is opposed to. However, this did not inhibit us from having a nice, respectful conversation. I think some of this was due, in part, to me not passing judgment and accepting her beliefs as her own. In addition, I wanted to learn more about her culture and she enjoyed relaying her knowledge. My internal conflict occurred after the conversation. Specifically, I realized how frustrating it is to feel that you have to explain and defend your culture to those from a different culture. . . . I struggle with wanting to maintain my position within my culture. Yet, I want to be strong enough to be supportive to the new employee's culture. I don't want my culture to impact my ability to "treat people how they want to be treated" but it does.

Part of the content of the PRIME training focused on racial and cultural identity development. In this same log, the trainee expressed that she was questioning where she was in relation to this development. She wrote, "I had a thought: where do I stand with my identity development? Am I making movement? Every time I think that I am in one stage, I have doubts." It is likely that her internal conflicts during cultural encounters are related to her racial and cultural identity development.

Logs 6, 7, and 8 were coded in the *acceptance* stage. In these logs, the trainee's narratives illustrate continued attention to cultural differences but not in a defensive manner or with internal conflict. She described incidents in her logs as learning experiences and ones that gave her greater understanding and respect for these differences. For example, in log 7, she described a visit to someone she knew in prison.

I learned about the "rules." . . . The visit left me with a new perspective. I always felt that a person must be punished for a crime they commit, and I still do. However, being within that culture has made me more sensitive to how this way of life can make a person feel.

In her final log, the trainee described a cultural encounter between a waitress, who was biracial, and a White American couple. Apparently, the couple had made a comment about the waitress' complexion, and she responded in an irritated voice that she had a Black and a White parent. She also described an incident at her work where staff were joking with each other and calling each other racial slurs. This happened when she was on vacation, but was apprised of it when she returned. Although these

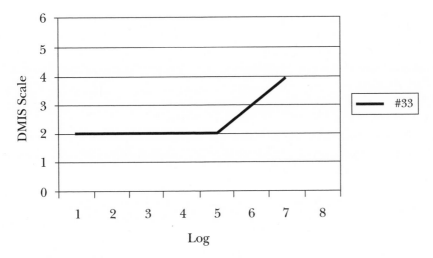

Figure 4. Linear progression (#33).

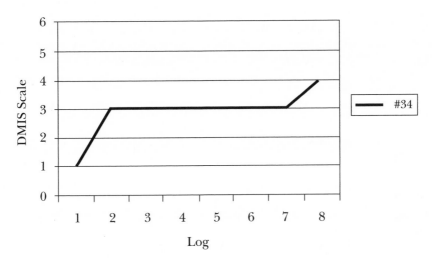

Figure 5. Linear progression (#34).

two incidents produced feelings of anger, worry, and resentment, she felt that she gained a better understanding of "hot buttons" among different cultural groups and that the PRIME training had given her the coping skills to get through these types of situations in a positive manner.

Logs Showing Linear Development. The two participants whose logs reflected a linear development in intercultural sensitivity were #33 and #34 (see Figures 4 and 5). Examples from #34's logs will be used to demonstrate this linear progression. Individual's first log, coded as *denial*, revealed that she had very little contact working with mental health service consumers for several years and had forgotten the challenges they face on a daily basis. She wrote, "I have not worked this closely with consumers for several years, and besides missing that contact, I may have forgotten what it is like to work side by side with the consumers." The form of denial this log conveyed was isolation.

Content in the next six logs were coded as *minimization*. The logs described the recognition of cultural differences, but on a superficial level. For example, in log 2, this trainee shared her feelings about being excluded from attending a conference for a specifically targeted population dealing with mental health and substance abuse issues. The following quote portrays these feelings:

I participated in a committee for my county to work on a conference for a specifically targeted population, dealing with MH and D and A issues. I was a member of this committee for four months, until the actual event was held. When the event happened, I was told I could not attend because I was not of the same culture that the conference was addressing, and the facilitators of the committee felt it would be best for the participants to see that people of their same culture work in the fields of MH and D and A. I understand the concept, but I was disappointed after all of the contribution I personally made.

A later log (log 6) also showed the trainee minimizing the significance of race in her conversation with a client who did not want her son sharing a room with someone of a different race: "I listened and we briefly discussed that she may have these feelings due to her upbringing, and that the race of her son's roommate is not relevant in how her son feels and does. (He just happened to do better when he was alone for a few weeks)." It appears as though the client struggled with her feelings of racial prejudice, which she learned from her father. The trainee's reluctance to explore the potential impact of amother's feelings on her son may perhaps reflect the trainee's preference to focus on nonracial issues.

The final log was coded in the stage of *acceptance*. In this log, the trainee showed that she gained a deep respect for cultural differences and saw the importance of developing cultural competency in her work. In addition, she is currently in a position within her agency to help others in her organization gain knowledge and skills in becoming culturally sensitive and competent. She expressed these feeling in the following manner:

What I have learned since our last training is that culture and cultural competence is a much needed area to focus on as a provider of services. I am very fortunate that our organization values diversity and cultural competence. I am the chair of our organization's Cultural Awareness Team (CAT). We have been recruiting new members to make our internal committee diverse and working diligently on informing the rest of the organization on what our goals and mission are. . . . We are continuing training for all employees as sort of an orientation or paradigm shift training.

This trainee's log described her greater appreciation and respect for cultural differences and the importance of using this knowledge in the provision of mental health services. She is also playing an instrumental role in her position by having others in her organization receive the PRIME training so that there is greater support in her efforts in providing culturally sensitive and competent services.

Discussion and Implications

Previous research has described the utility of Bennett's Developmental Model of Intercultural Sensitivity. This is the first documented attempt to examine this process using the logs from trainees in cultural competency training over a period of several months. Whereas other studies used pre- and posttest assessments, the authors were able to observe this process qualitatively for each individual monthly, over a period of 10 months. It was observed that the stages in the Bennett model were applicable to the individual's cultural experiences; however, this process occurred in a non-linear fashion for most of the participants in the training program. The results also did not show a correlation of the stages with sociodemographic characteristics of the participants. According to the analysis of the logs, as well as other measures, however, the PRIME training appeared to have a positive impact on the trainees. By the eighth log, the majority of participants were in one of the ethnorelative stages of intercultural sensitivity.

A look at the group results showing the proportion of ethnocentric to ethnorelative logs in Figure 1 indicates that this relationship varies. However, starting with log 6, there is a gradual increment in the proportion of logs coded as ethnorelative from 6 to 7 and then a sharp increase from logs 7 to 8. A possible explanation for this finding can be derived from adult learning theory. Adults need to learn experientially and have opportunities to apply new knowledge and practice new skills (Zemke and Zemke 1984). In the PRIME training, this was facilitated by providing the participants with several opportunities to integrate what they learned in the training by conducting comprehensive cultural assessments and developing treatment/rehabilitation plans.

The curriculum was designed to have an emphasis on knowledge in the first part with application in the second part. Participants were given tasks in the second part that increased their ability to integrate and apply the information they received earlier. For example, in the fifth training session, content focused on discrimination, including strategies for addressing and managing the social and psychological effects of various types of discrimination (racial, religious, sexual orientation, etc.). The participants gave examples of situations in which they or their clients experienced discrimination, and they practiced role-play re-enactments, using the strategies they had learned in the previous didactic portions of the training to address these problems. The increase in ethnorelativity at log 6 may have resulted from this opportunity for knowledge application.

Opportunities for the PRIME participants to apply what they learned in the training continued to increase over the subsequent sessions. In session 6, the trainees were presented with content on cross-cultural diagnosis and assessment. In small groups, they discussed culturally diverse case examples and practiced how to identify cultural factors in making a culturally informed diagnosis and assessment. In session 7, training participants worked in teams with other trainees from their respective agencies to develop a culturally competent treatment/rehabilitation/recovery plan for a person-in-recovery. Each team developed a treatment/rehabilitation/recovery plan that emanated from a comprehensive biopsychosocial cultural assessment. These plans were presented orally to all of the PRIME training participants and feedback was given by the trainers. In the eighth session, the trainees submitted ethnographies of an elder adult in their social network. Again, this experience allowed each individual to apply what was learned and to take a personal multicultural journey into his/her own family and heritage. Considering the implications for multicultural training, it appears that designing opportunities for knowledge application in different contexts helps in the integration of learning.

In addition, the results also show that positive change toward intercultural sensitivity does not develop quickly; there needs to be time for individuals to learn and integrate new information, as well as an appropriate amount of time to practice new skills. Reversions to earlier stages of intercultural sensitivity may be indicative of integrating information that challenges one's cognitive and affective schemas toward certain cultural groups. Perhaps the principle from adult learning theory applies, that new information which conflicts significantly with what is already known is integrated more slowly (Zembe and Zembe 1984). For example, it may take a long time for individuals to change beliefs they have had for most of their lives about their own and other people's race, ethnicities, and cultures, even when they are inaccurate. The implication here for multicultural training is that this type of training cannot be done in a short period of time. Sufficient sessions need to be offered for knowledge integration and skill development with repeated opportunities for practice. It is also important for the training to take place in a trusted and supportive environment, as trainees take risks in revealing their beliefs and trying new behaviors.

Another interesting observation made in reading the logs of participant #18 was that in her fifth log she shared her responses to cultural encounters and connected this to questioning her own stage of racial identity development. Ottavi, Pope-Davis, and Dings (1994) explored the possible relationship between one's development of intercultural sensitivity and racial identity development. They found that White racial identity development has its own unique relationship to multicultural counseling competencies and concluded that racial identity attitude formation needs to be considered as an integral part of multicultural counseling training. Carter, Helms, and Juby (2004) show that racist attitudes influence White racial identity development and conclude that more research is needed to explore exactly how racism relates to the development of intercultural sensitivity (cultural competence). Resistance and defensiveness among Whites about racism during cultural competence trainings may contribute to differences in Whites' development of intercultural insensitivity compared with other races, and may also explain non-linear patterns of development among Whites. Carter and his colleagues (2004) also questioned the use of the linear concept "stages" in terms of racial identity development and proposed that examining one's "status profile" may offer a richer understanding of the process of developing a racial identity.

In a few instances, an individual's log could have been coded in more than one stage, but the authors decided to assign the highest stage to the log. Perhaps, developing profiles that combined multiple stages would have provided us a more nuanced understanding of the trainee's intercultural sensitivity development. Future research needs to examine the relationship between intercultural sensitivity development and racial/cultural identity development. Also, consideration of the relationship between these two factors is essential in planning multicultural competency trainings.

Limitations

Although the findings provide useful information on the development of intercultural sensitivity among individuals who participated in an intensive training program on intercultural competency, one must use caution in interpreting the results for a number of reasons. The sample size was small and individuals who dropped out of the training or those who did not complete at least 7 logs were excluded from the analyses. Therefore, the results are more reflective of those who followed through with the training and did what was expected in terms of the log assignment. In addition, the data were analyzed using only one model. There are other areas of growth and cultural competency that could be included, but were not, given the resources for the evaluation. Furthermore, it is unclear to what extent one's ethnorelative stage of intercultural sensitivity lasts over time and in multiple settings. The results are limited by the period of time individuals participated in the PRIME training.

Reprinted from Joretha N. Bourjolly, Roberta G. Sands, Phyllis Solomon, Victoria Stanhope, Anita Pernell-Arnold, and Laurene Finley, The journey toward intercultural sensitivity: A non-linear process, *Journal of Ethnic and Cultural Diversity in Social Work* 14 (2005): 41–62. Reprinted by permission.

References

Altshuler, L., N. M. Sussman, and E. Kachur (2003). Assessing changes in intercultural sensitivity among physician trainees using the intercultural development inventory. *International Journal of Intercultural Relations* 27 (4): 387–401.

Bennett, M. J. (1986a). A developmental approach to training for intercultural sensitivity. *International Journal of Intercultural Relations* 10: 179–96.

——— (1986b). http://www.cocc.edu/cagatucci/asa/MCsources/intercultdev.htm, Accessed January 31, 2005.

——— (1993). Towards ethnorelativism: A developmental model of intercultural sensitivity. In R. M. Paige, ed., *Education for the Intercultural Experience*. Yarmouth, Me.: Intercultural Press. 21–71.

Carter, R. T., J. E. Helms, and H. L. Juby (2004). The relationship between racism and racial identity for White Americans: A profile analysis. *Journal of Multicultural Counseling and Development* 32: 2–17.

DHHS (1999). *Mental Health: Culture, Race, and Ethnicity: A Supplement to Mental Health: A Report of the Surgeon General.* Rockville, Md.: U.S. Department of Health and Human Services, Substance Abuse and Mental Health Services Administration, Center for Mental Health Services, National Institutes of Health, National Institute of Mental Health.

Endicott, L., T. Bock, and D. Narvaez (2003). Moral reasoning, intercultural development, and multicultural experiences: Relations and cognitive underpinnings. *International Journal of Intercultural Relations* 27 (4): 403–19.

Hammer, M. R., M. J. Bennett, and R. Wiseman (2003). Measuring intercultural sensitivity: The intercultural development inventory. *International Journal of Intercultural Relations* 27 (4): 421–43.

Jackson, V. H. (2002). Cultural competency: The challenges posed by a culturally diverse society and steps toward meeting them. *Behavioral Health Management* 22 (2): 20.

Klak, T. and P. Martin (2003). Do university-sponsored international cultural events help students to appreciate "difference"? *International Journal of Intercultural Relations* 27 (4): 445–65.

Lopez, S. R., K. P. Grover, D. Holland, M. J. Johnson, C. D. Kain, K. Kanel, C. A. Mellins, and M. C. Rhyne (1989). Development of culturally sensitive psychotherapists. *Professional Psychology: Research and Practice* 20 (6): 369–76.

Ottavi, T. M., D. B. Pope-Davis, and J. G. Dings (1994). Relationship between White racial identity attitudes and self-reported multicultural competencies. *Journal of Counseling Psychology* 41: 149–54.

Robinson, D. T., and J. R. Morris (2000). Multicultural counseling: Historical context and current training considerations. *Western Journal of Black Studiesi* 24 (4): 239–53.

Stanhope, V., P. Solomon, A. Pernell-Arnold, R. G. Sands, and J. N. Bourjolly (2005). Evaluating cultural competency among behavioral health professionals. *Psychiatric Rehabilitation* 28 (3): 225–33.

Straffon, D. A. (2003). Assessing the intercultural sensitivity of high school students attending an international school. *International Journal of Intercultural Relations* 27 (4): 487–501.

Zembe, R. and S. Zembe (1984). 30 things we know for sure about adult learning. http://honolulu.hawaii.edu/intranet/committees/FacDevCom/guidebk/teachtip/adults-3.htm. Accessed January 31, 2005.

Commentary

Joretha N. Bourjolly

The Penn School of Social Policy & Practice has a strong history of promoting social justice for populations oppressed due to economic inequities, racial and ethnic discrimination, sexual orientation, age, religious beliefs, and physical and mental disabilities. Since it's inception in 1908, the School has implemented this philosophical approach through its curriculum and field internships for students and the scholarly endeavors of its faculty. I am honored to be a member of the faculty and administration of a school with this legacy, which has framed my scholarship, and to participate in commemorating the School's centennial year.

I selected the article, "The Journey Toward Intercultural Sensitivity: A Nonlinear Process," for inclusion in the centennial book because it reflects the School's tradition and goal of social work to improve the welfare and social functioning of individuals. This article also reflects the central theme of my research, which has been examining individual and social factors that impact access and use of health care for vulnerable populations. There has been growing evidence that differences in diagnosis, treatment, and service provision among racial and ethnic groups contribute to disparities health outcomes. These findings highlight the need for social work education and training programs that help students and social service providers develop awareness, knowledge, and skills for serving diverse racial and cultural groups. With the subsequent development of multicultural training and educational programs, the need to evaluate student and providers' growth and level of multicultural competence has become apparent.

"The Journey Toward Intercultural Sensitivity" reports on one aspect of an evaluation that was done of an intensive multicultural training program to reduce culturally based disparities in the provision of mental health services. This evaluation was the result of team effort among several faculty from the School of Social Policy & Practice, Dr. Phyllis Solomon, Dr. Roberta Sands, myself, and a doctoral student, Victoria Standhope. The evaluation consisted of several components. We used a mixed methods approach to assess both outcomes and process of cultural competence and intercultural sensitivity development. In regard to outcomes, we utilized a pre-post test design. The design was chosen to answer whether the training increase the trainees' knowledge and awareness of culture and cultural competency skills as a result of the training. We also collected demographic and employment information, as well as racial and ethnic information on the populations that the trainees served. Quantitative cultural competency instruments included several standardized self-report measures and we designed a Person-in-Recovery Survey to assess the impact of the providers' cultural competency training on the clients they served.

The qualitative component of the evaluation consisted of evaluators' observation of the process of the training sessions and their fidelity, an assessment of the accomplishment of outcome objectives, an analysis of critical incidents, and an examination of written logs that participants submitted in which they reflected on their between-session cultural experiences over a ten-month period.

The article discusses our use of Milton Bennett's Developmental Model of Intercultural Sensitivity (DMIS) as a framework to analyze the logs. Reading and coding the logs allowed us to assess how the training participants applied knowledge and skills gained from the training in their personal and professional lives. Our results showed that the process of intercultural sensitivity was for the most part a nonlinear process and that it can take several months to develop. In addition, the majority of trainees demonstrated positive outcomes from the training in terms of intercultural development. This qualitative component to the evaluation of the training added to the findings of the pre- and posttest measures because they allowed us to observe the participants process of change over the course of the training.

As a team, we have reflected on our successes and challenges in measuring the complex phenomenon of cultural competency. With our use of standardized self-report measures, we have observed that they are limited in assessing cultural competence across broad categories of diverse populations. The majority of measures focus attention on competence in working with nonwhite ethnic and racial populations and not other groups such as people who live in rural areas, women, religious and sexual minorities, and people with disabilities. This limitation is rooted in the larger conceptual issue of deciding the extent of cultural competence.

One of the most difficult challenges in evaluating cultural competences is that measures are limited by disagreements at the conceptual level on the factors that constitute cultural competence. There are several theoretical frameworks on what factors comprise cultural competence. In terms of one's intercultural sensitivity development, we have not fully explored the possibility of one being in multiple stages of development at the same time and what factors contribute to this occurrence. Another difficulty is measuring the impact of the providers' cultural competency on the clients they served.

In terms of my future development as a researcher in this area and avenues for advancement in the field of measuring cultural competency, a combination of different strategies or mixed methods may offer us greater understanding of the process and outcomes of interventions designed to increase cultural competency. My colleagues and I have begun to utilize this approach in the work we have done in this area. In addition, we are developing a vignette-based instrument to assess the transfer of skills participants gain in cultural competency training and social work education to their work in conducting culturally based assessments with clients. We hope that our efforts in this direction will move us closer to understanding how successful we are in preparing social work students and providers to be culturally competent in providing appropriate and meaningful services.

Chapter 34
Occupational Social Work for the Twenty-First Century

Roberta R. Iversen

Work is an essential, defining component of most people's lives, serving both instrumental and expressive purposes among individuals and their families. As the 20th century ends, economic restructuring and radical changes in welfare policy are producing increasing social dislocation and disadvantage among both employed and unemployed people in the United States. Such disadvantage is experienced particularly strongly by women, members of racial and ethnic minority groups, and youths (Blank 1997; Hale 1997; Holzer 1996b; Jargowsky 1997; Wilson 1996). Despite the fact that social workers historically have focused their practice acumen on the needs of poor and oppressed people, occupational social work practice is not reported in evaluations of welfare-to-work or employment and job training programs (Besharov, Germanis, and Rossi 1997; Herr, Halpern, and Wagner 1995; Quint, Musick, and Ladner 1994). Although some social workers practice occupational social work in varied government, school, and medical settings (Bargal and Katan 1998), most of the literature in this field of specialization is directed at practice with employed people in work organizations (Kurzman and Akabas 1993; Straussner 1990), not with unemployed people in work-enhancement programs.

This article follows the direction of Lewis (1997) and Ozawa (1980) to suggest that the social work profession is missing the opportunity to have a significant practice effect on the increasingly dire occupational needs of poor people. Specifically, occupational social workers should apply systematically the specialized knowledge and skills they have accumulated in workplace practice to practice in welfare-to-work and other work-program settings. This occupational practitioner would enact multiple work-specific roles concurrently at multiple systems levels. Although this reformulation focuses occupational social work practice on the work-related needs of unemployed and newly employed people, such practice would also pertain to the work needs of underemployed, dislocated, and working poor people, as well as to the needs of those who are comfortably employed.

Economic Restructuring and Welfare Policy Change

Economic Restructuring

National and global economic forces are associated with widespread worker dislocation and disadvantage, particularly among poor residents of beleaguered inner cities. First, technological advancements and reductions in entry-level manufacturing positions continue to necessitate a more educated workforce. In the next 10 years, occupations requiring at least an associate's degree are expected to grow faster than those requiring less education and training (Silvestri 1997). At the same time, inner-city schools, in particular, are inadequate for providing the complex knowledge and skills needed for this educated workforce (Danziger, Sandefur, and Weinberg 1994). Among other reasons, most urban schools have difficulty drawing a cadre of qualified teachers, and most lack adequate science and mathematics materials for their students (Murnane 1994). Moreover, educational disadvantage varies by gender as well as socioeconomic status. Although men and women realize wage returns from increased education (Herman 1997), with few exceptions men still outearn women at all educational levels (Blank 1995; Hecker 1998).

Second, expanded foreign production sites have lowered labor needs and opportunities in the United States for both entry-level and middle management workers (Blank 1995; Silvestri 1997; Tausky 1996). One recent analysis of inner-city employment advertisements found that only 433 jobs of more than 6,300 offered were appropriate for entry-level applicants (Binzen 1998). In the same city, 65,000 adults on welfare faced a regional economy that expected to absorb 7,500 new workers a year at most (Parmley 1998). A similar analysis reported that only 13 percent of all vacancies and 8 percent of all fulltime vacancies offered work for unemployed poor people (Pease and Martin 1997).

Third, in recent decades the postindustrial economic structure has changed from a manufacturing to an information and service base (Rifkin 1995; Tilly 1996). This change resulted in increased numbers of involuntary part-time, temporary, and contingent (without an explicit or implicit contract for ongoing employment) jobs (Economic Policy Institute 1997). Such jobs, and many others in the service sector, offer low or below-poverty wages, few or no nonwage benefits, geographic mismatches between jobs and residents, and more frequent layoffs and plant closings. Median weekly earnings of $417 among full-time contingent workers in 1997 amounted to only 82 percent of those of noncontingent workers (Bureau of Labor Statistics 1997. Real earnings for male high school graduates and dropouts have declined by 13 percent and 21 percent, respectively, since 1979, whereas earnings for their female counterparts have remained flat (Herman 1997). Pensions and health insurance benefits fell during the 1980s for all wage earners, but they fell the most among the lowest fifth (Mishel and Bernstein 1994), and there is no evidence that this decline has reversed in the 1990s. Regarding geographic location, Jargowsky (1997) reported that housing program participants in Chicago were 13 percent more likely to be employed if they relocated to the suburbs than if they stayed in the central city. Finally, in 1995, 42 percent of the *working poor*, defined as people who worked or looked for work for 27 weeks or more during the year and whose incomes fell below the poverty threshold, experienced at least one spell of unemployment (Hale 1997). Despite rates of metropolitan area unemployment that declined to below 5 percent during the 1990s, the unemployment rate in many inner cities has remained well above 10 percent (Danziger and Lehman 1996).

These ramifications of structural change are predicted to increase well into the 21st century (Franklin 1997; Rothman 1998), continuing to exert disproportionate negative impact on poor urban workers and new labor market entrants. One leading labor economist foresees ample jobs for unskilled workers but sees hourly wages dipping below $6 because of worker oversupply (Burtless 1997). Moreover, potential dislocation will occur increasingly frequently as the average person in the United States works for 8.6 different employers between ages 18 and 32 (Bureau of Labor Statistics 1998), rather than having a single employer for life, as was the case in earlier decades (Foster and Schore 1990).

Welfare Policy Change

Recent changes in welfare policy are a second major contributor to worker disadvantage. As part of the Personal Responsibility and Work Opportunity Reconciliation Act of 1996 (P.L. 104–193), block grants called Temporary Assistance to Needy Families (TANF) are now allocated to states to develop, finance, and run their own assistance programs for low-income families, replacing 60 years of federally funded Aid to Families with Dependent Children (AFDC). The initial AFDC legislation was called Aid to Dependent Children (ADC), Title IV of the Social Security Act of 1935 (U.S. Congress 1935). In 1962 the program name was changed to AFDC to emphasize the family unit (Karger and Stoesz 1998). Most critical to the discussion here, TANF programs are mandated to move increasing percentages of women into the workplace, or they face federal economic sanctions. The programs also are mandated to devise lifetime limits for public assistance aid to individuals. In addition, employment and training programs for poor men and women that are not solely AFDC-related, such as those sponsored by Job Opportunities and Basic Skills and Job Training Partnership Act legislation, which include Opportunities Industrialization Center (OIC) programs and the Summer Youth Employment and Training program, will be phased out under TANF. Although definitive evaluation results of TANF programs are not yet available (Besharov et al. 1997), early reports suggest at least three reasons that this policy change will not result in widespread economic self-sufficiency among poor women. First, the mandated replacement of postsecondary educational investment by work in most states (Pierre 1997) is completely counter to the body of research that documents the importance of education to income. Second, although the initial wave of women exiting welfare was believed to be more "employable" than waves to come, only one-quarter to one-third of women leaving welfare in New York City in the first several months after P.L. 104–193 found jobs (Hernandez 1998). Such women typically earned more than their public assistance allotment, but not enough to raise their income above the poverty level (Harris 1996; Maryland Department of Human

Resources 1997). In addition, employment differentials by race or ethnicity persist. African American and Hispanic women remain disproportionately disadvantaged compared with white women in both wage income (Holzer 1996a) and rates of unemployment ("Current Labor Statistics," 1998). These conditions exist despite relatively strong national economic conditions. Many scholars caution that an economic downturn could provide additional occupational disadvantage for low-income workers and welfare recipients who have reached their time hmits On public assistance (Blank 1997; Wilson 1996).

Third, high rates of job loss—between 25 percent and 40 percent—are reported among workers just off welfare (Berg, Olson, and Conrad 1991; Hershey and Pavetti 1997). However, welfare to work and job training programs generally have focused on how to get, rather than keep, jobs. A small set of demonstration programs emphasized job retention support services (Haimson, Hershey, and Rangarajan 1995; Herr and Halpern 1991), and some urban centers now plan a retention focus (City of Philadelphia 1998). Given the increasing numbers of people who will need such supports because of economic and welfare changes, this article advances the position that work-enhancement sites provide a natural domain for systematic expansion of occupational social work practice. The successes of earlier work programs and the development of occupational social work frame this reformulation.

Background and Reformulation

Research Evaluation of Work Programs

Most analyses of welfare-to-work and work-enhancement programs concluded that program characteristics, participant characteristics and needs, historical and geographic context, local labor market conditions, and evaluation methods combined to produce varied results about program success and failure (Hollister 1997). Nevertheless, the most successful work programs shared one critical component: intensive, long-term, individualized, multilevel services (see full discussion in Gueron and Pauly 1991; Herr and Halpern 1991; Hollister, Kemper, and Maynard 1984; LaLonde 1995; Rangarajan, Meckstroth, and Novak 1998). These programs were financed by varying combinations of federal, state, and local funding streams, not unlike states' welfare-to-work efforts under TANF.

Welfare-to-Work Programs. Closely supervised work experience by supervisors who had workplace-related knowledge and skills, sensitivity to individual rates of progress, and attention to work-related ancillary supports such as job search assistance, counseling, or driver's license training were centerpieces of the National Supported Work demonstration program (Hollister et al. 1984). Such individually tailored supports—the pillars of social work practice—contributed to job attainment, retention, and gains in earnings that persisted for at least eight years after the program ended (Couch 1992). Similarly, San Diego's Saturation Work Initiative Model and its successor, California's Greater Avenues for Independence (GAIN), were successful efforts under federal Work Incentive Program legislation (Friedlander and Burtless 1995). The greater success of Riverside County GAIN in raising earnings and reducing AFDC payments, compared with other county GAIN programs, was attributed to small caseloads, job-specific skill training, and individualized job search activities (Mead 1996).

Finally, Project Match, a demonstration project serving some 600 voluntary AFDC participants in Chicago in the 1980s (Herr and Halpern 1991), and its sequel in the 1990s, the Postemployment Services Demonstration (PESD) programs (Rangarajan et al. 1998), were successful welfare-to-work efforts that maximized job retention through intensive supports. Project Match and PESD supports were based on a person-in-environment perspective, paralleling the fundamental social work practice focus on the interface between human behavior and environmental context (Austin 1997). For example, both viewed job attainment and retention as processes. At the individual level, assessment and goal-setting in both projects were continuous processes facilitated by the development of trusted relationships between program participants and workers. At the organizational level the job retention services of both included financial and social supports such as child and health care subsidies, help moving from one career step to another, and open-ended post-employment monitoring. Despite program successes in job attainment, retention, and earnings. Project Match and PESD researchers concluded that the process of leaving welfare is long and complex and that many need even more intensive support services over time.

Work-Enhancement Programs for Men and Youths. Job training programs in the early 1960s were targeted primarily at unemployed white male heads of households, although the development of antipoverty policies later in the decade broadened the focus to African American men and youths (Rose 1995). OIC offered skill training and prevocational training for entry- level jobs. Rose reported that counseling and outreach contributed significantly to program enrollment in these centers. Furthermore, personally supervised employment and life skill development contributed to the success of OIC efforts among male and female participants (Belden 1997).

Generally, however, evaluations of job training and employment program efforts among men and youths reported mixed results. Job attainment and retention outcomes among extremely disadvantaged men (ex-offenders and former drug addicts) and youths (school dropouts) in the National Supported Work program were less notable than those among AFDC participants (Maynard 1984). Maynard hypothesized that "a more comprehensive package of services" might have led to greater program participation and success among youths (233). Maynard (1998) reiterated this view more recently, stressing that the case management and support services found to be essential to the success of AFDC recipients in welfare-to-work programs are equally critical to the potential success of youths. Job Corps evaluation results support Maynard's conclusions. Intensive employment, training, and personal services in a residential format were associated with long-term earnings benefits for Job Corps participants (LaLonde 1995).

Moreover, whether work programs are aimed at men, women, or youths, results may be severely limited by staff inability to manage both the training and personal concerns of the participants. A cooperative venture involving the state, American Express, the National Retail Federation, and the Kravco development company (Valbrun 1997) to prepare underemployed and unemployed people for sales careers was unable to realize its placement goals because staff members were not trained to deal with the interaction between complex personal problems and program structure. For example, a participant's medical treatments for high blood pressure conflicted with several program sessions. The participant surpassed the program allowance for absences, and, because staff members did not pursue her reasons for the absences, she dropped out of the program.

For men, women, and youths, the core services leading to program success—multiple and individualized employment goals and objectives, interventions based on "where the client is," development of a trusted relationship base, long-term postemployment services, and local job development—match those suggested here for reformulated occupational social work.

Occupational Social Work in the 1980s and 1990s

Scholars Googins and Godfrey (1987) defined *occupational social work* as "a field of practice in which social workers attend to the human and social needs of the work community by designing and executing appropriate interventions to insure healthier individuals and environments" (5). In an earlier period, social workers engaged in employment-related direct services and reform efforts among poor people at individual, organizational, and community levels through settlement houses (Addams 1910; Brieland 1990) and union-based member assistance programs (Molloy and Kurzman 1993). However, over time the dominant model for occupational social work became individual-level intervention among employed people through employee assistance programs (EAPs) within work organizations (Balgopal 1989; Kurzman and Akabas 1993; Root 1997). By now, almost two-thirds of the employees working in medium-sized or large firms are covered under EAPs (Root 1997).

Occupational social workers used the EAP model to develop and provide significant employee services for personal or relational problems (Yamatani 1988), substance abuse (Hanson 1993), disability (Mudrick 1991), worksite health and safety (Lewis 1990), and corporate job relocation (Anderson and Stark 1988). EAPs also provided employers and managers with training about diversity, sexual harassment, and AIDS, although such training often stemmed from management concern about legal liability instead of employee well-being. Even so, occupational practitioners were able to build skills in strategic planning, labor-management relations, policy formation, and organizational reform (Googins and Davidson 1993).

However, attending to the dual purpose of human service and organizational stability and profitability also raised professional concerns (Bargal and Katan 1998; Gould and Smith 1988; Kurzman and Akabas 1981). Although social workers in host settings such as schools and most hospitals faced similar practice dilemmas in regard to client definition, decision making, and authority for service provision, the essential mission of these settings was client centered. Conversely, in spite of the significant service component of EAPs, organizational survival was business's primary concern (Ozawa 1980 1985). As a result, occupational social workers gained considerable expertise in resolving conflicts between professional emphases on individual worth, self-determination, equality, and social justice, and organizational emphases on commodities and profits (Bakalinsky 1980).

Thus, it is the position in this article that systematic application of specialized occupational social work knowledge and skills to job retention among work-program constituents would refocus practice on the employment needs of poor people, thereby furthering the mission of the profession to increase equality and social justice. This expanded formulation of occupational social work would be evidenced by work-specific, multilevel role definitions, work-program practice settings, and the application of workplace-derived knowledge and skills.

Occupational Social Work Reformulated

Work-Specific Role Definitions

The reformulation of occupational social work calls for defining multiple work-focused roles (**Table 1**). This definition forwards the vision of earlier occupational social work scholars who emphasized social as well as interpersonal change functions (Gould and Smith 1988; Kurzman 1993; Ozawa 1980; Root 1993). Although similar to advanced generalist practice in expanding the practice focus to group, organization, and policy levels (Schatz, Jenkins, and Sheafor 1990), this formulation specifies work programs as the particular practice domain. Similar also to policy practice in emphasizing interactional, analytical, political, and value clarification skills (Jansson 1990), this formulation specifies a broader range of employment-specific practice skills and identifies multiple levels of intervention, about which policy-practice theorists have different views (Wyers 1991). Practitioners in work programs will have titles such as job developer, job coach, employment advisor, retention support worker, and job placement advisor, but I use the more general title "occupational social worker" or "occupational practitioner" here to emphasize the substance of the reformulation.

Work-Focused Assessment, Brief Counseling, and Referral. In a work-focused assessment role, occupational social workers would conduct a contextualized assessment of the meaning of work and employment dynamics with each work program participant (Vigilante 1982), similar to the traditional examination of family and interpersonal dynamics. Beginning "where the client is" would mean examining attitudes and values about education and work in the family of origin (Farber and Iversen 1998; Iversen and Farber 1996); work experiences in youths (Rich 1996); networks and information sources about work, early and future goals, consistency in the content of high school goals, postsecondary education and job characteristics (Iversen 1995); conflictual or discriminatory experiences in the workplace; and workplace-relevant physical abilities and disabilities (Estes 1987). Assessment would also address how personal and family issues, such as substance abuse, health and mental health, and needs of children or extended family members, influence work attitudes and experience. Brief counseling or referral might mediate differences that arise in these areas among new workers, their coworkers, and employers.

Work-Focused Advocacy. Occupational social workers in a work-focused advocacy role

TABLE 1. Occupational Social Work in Welfare-to-Work and Work-Enhancement Programs: Roles, Functions, and Levels of Practice

Work-related practice role	Work-program functions	Multilevel work-related practice examples

Assessment, brief counseling, and referral	Assessment of
	  meaning of work
	  attitude, values, and goals about
	    work
	  youth work experience
	  sources of information
	  educational attainment
	  content consistency of work
	  pathway discrimination
	  physical ability
	Brief counseling and referral
	  coworker relations
	  substance abuse
	  mental health
	Collect individual- and
	  organizational-level data
		Example One
		
		Assess meaning of work (micro)
		Collaborate with corporate occupational social worker (micro/meso)
		Advocate for nondiscriminatory hiring procedures (meso/macro)

Advocacy	Collaborate with corporate
	  occupational social workers
	Evaluate recruitment and hiring
	  procedures
	Educate businesses about tax issues
	Forward family-sensitive policies
	  and programs
	Collect employment data
		Example Two
		
		Assess adolescent work experience (micro)
		Evaluate youth experience of company employees (meso)
		Plan training with employer (micro/meso)
		Lobby for summer youth employment funding (macro)

Program development	Establish career enrichment and
	  school-to-work programs
	Initiate mentorship training
	Form business-community
	  collaboratives
		Example Three
		
		Asessment of brief counseling for feelings of depression (micro)
		Match program participant with workplace mentor (micro/meso)

Social activist	Organize policy support at local,
	  state, and national levels for
	  wages, workplace practices, and
	  form and content of TANF
	  programs
	Lobby for job creation
	Counter declassification of social
	  service jobs
	Collect individual- and program-
	  level data
		Advocate for peer support groups inworksite (meso)

could team with corporate counterparts to facilitate improvements in organizational structure and resource management (Googins and Davidson 1993) appropriate to poor and dislocated workers. Hiring mechanisms, such as informal recruitment channels and relative weighting of credentials and face-to-face interviews, can be examined for their discriminatory potential (Holzer 1996b). The occupational practitioner might educate and advocate with businesses to increase hiring of unemployed and working poor clients to take advantage of tax breaks for doing so and to set up support services for employees making the transition from welfare to work. Gender-related policies can also be examined, because work issues related to women are particularly neglected or minimized in most models of social work intervention (Vigilante 1993). The practitioner would gather data on workers disadvantaged by factors such as insufficient or poor quality child care, problematic transportation, inhospitable hours, and inadequate wages to influence institutional and government policy in these areas.

Work-Focused Program Development. Occupational social workers in a work-focused program development role could initiate community-wide prevention and amelioration efforts, such as career enrichment and mentorship activities with high schools, skills development centers, and local social services organizations. Such collaboratives would mutually benefit youths, businesses, and community groups. Today, such initiation stems mainly from the corporate arena as U.S. businesses invest in public education to prepare children for workforce futures. Development of partnerships among businesses, work-enhancement programs, and community and four-year colleges would increase individual human capital and provide an enriched hiring pool for employers at the same time. Such partnerships are essential for job skills training, because workplace-specific training is most economically productive for employers and new workers (U.S. Department of Labor 1996).

Work-Focused Social Activist. Finally, occupational social workers could use an employment-focused social activist role to initiate and support policy changes essential to poor workers, such as the Earned Income Tax Credit, the American Family Fair Minimum Wage Act ("Wage Increase Backed," 1998), flextime, and flexplace. They could also mobilize appropriate stakeholders to promote employment-enhancing policy changes. One such change would be for TANF regulations to consider education, training, community volunteer activities, and social service-related efforts equivalent to paid employment among recipients not ready for full labor-market participation. This change could be patterned after Project Match's "incremental ladder to self-sufficiency" model (Herr and Halpern 1991, p. 24). Another policy direction would be the development of time-limited community services employment programs (Savner and Greenberg 1997) with concomitant union or union-like benefits and on-the-job training opportunities, in the absence of sufficient opportunities in local labor markets. Work-program social activists could use testifying, lobbying, and coalition-building skills (Jansson 1990) to reclassify employment-focused social services jobs as needing the particular knowledge and skills of advanced occupational social work practitioners (Meyer 1983; Pecora and Austin 1983). Targets for such activism include local professional organizations, NASW, and government task forces on job creation and workforce development.

Concurrent Multilevel Practice. Individual practitioners will engage in these roles concurrently at micro (individual), meso (small group and family), and macro (organization and community) levels. To accomplish practices and changes, the occupational worker in each role would gather and use data about the work-related needs of people at all levels of practice. Three brief examples of multilevel practice follow. In the first case a job developer found that a work-program participant wanted to work but feared face-to-face interviews because of racial discrimination in earlier interviews. The job developer contacted the potential employer's occupational social worker to discuss interview procedures, and they advocated together with the employer for changes in hiring procedures. In the second case an employment advisor noted that a work-program participant had no high school work experience, yet the advisor had examined a particular workplace for this participant and knew that the longest-tenured employees had such experience. The advisor collaborated with the employer to see what remedial training might suffice. The advisor also lobbied at the state level for continued funding for summer youth employment. In the third case an occupational practitioner engaged in brief counseling with a work-program participant who expressed feelings of depression. Finding that the participant felt alienated in her new work role, the practitioner matched the participant with a workplace mentor through a mentoring agency. Together, the practitioner, mentor, and new worker advocated for the establishment of peer support groups in the worksite.

Work-Program Practice Settings

Settings that can benefit from reformulated occupational practice will be expanded under TANF, and their funding sources will vary. This listing of work-program possibilities is only approximate, because states are in the process of selecting their TANF program providers. Settings such as community jobs programs, community service employment programs, community work-experience programs, transitional work programs or supervised worksites, and job-readiness programs are likely to be funded predominantly through federal TANF block grant and welfare-to-work grant funds. Other locations such as skills development centers, one-stop job centers, mentoring agencies, and job clubs might be supported by discretionary state TANF funds and foundation or business contributions. Last, employee training programs and employee support programs might receive tax credit for hiring former welfare recipients, wage subsidies, or grant diversions (funds that would otherwise be paid directly to a program participant's family) or be funded collaboratively by another community organization, such as a university or church, and the employer.

Although some work programs will highlight job retention features described earlier in the article, different funding sources may mean differences in program construction. A full discussion of such differences is beyond the scope of this article, but length of program, content of program, nature of clientele, amount of post-employment follow-up, ratio of program workers to participants, and professional background and characteristics of program workers are possible variations. As these settings emerge, occupational practitioners can be vigilant in assessing and asserting the program participants' perspectives and needs.

Application of Specialized Occupational Knowledge and Skills

Relocation Knowledge and Skills. Relocation services within businesses are addressed now by occupational social workers from a managerial perspective, which incorporates not only counseling and services for personal and relational stresses of moving and change, but also often offers financial incentives to facilitate family moves. Such services frequently include interpreting corporate relocation benefits and policy to employees and enabling them to use benefits best, providing information about possible stressors, providing information about the new community, arranging helping networks in the new location, providing counseling to address individual adjustment problems, and providing career assistance to spouses (Siegel 1988).

Most of these service components pertain also to the needs of unemployed and new workers. First, occupational social work practitioners can help entrants and re-entrants learn about the range of non-wage benefits available in different organizations, understand specific offerings among potential employers, and assess the implications of the presence or absence of particular benefits in relation to each individual's needs. Such practitioners would draw on workplace knowledge about inflation, wages, pension vestiture, profit sharing (Root 1993), and insurance coverage. The Index of Job Desirability (IJD) (Jencks, Perman, and Rainwater 1988) could be a useful tool to help clients assess non-wage characteristics of previous jobs to maximize the fit between such characteristics and their needs in the future. The IJD was designed to discriminate between monetary and non-monetary characteristics of jobs and to determine differences among jobs with the same and different occupational titles. Information about the validity and reliability of the index and justification for use of a slightly modified version that may be even more relevant to work program participants (Iversen 1995) is presented in Jencks et al. (1988).

Second, occupationally oriented practitioners can draw on workplace experience with downsizing to educate new workers, re-entrants, and their employers about potential psychosocial ramifications of unemployment. Such byproducts might include depression, anxiety, learned helplessness, substance abuse, and violence. If needed, practitioners can link workers with resources in these domains and mediate at individual, organizational, and policy levels to resolve multiple, and possibly competing, demands between workers' service needs, such as flextime to attend counseling, and workplace performance requirements, such as uniform, fixed hours.

Third, with knowledge gained from relationships developed with local businesses, occupational practitioners can educate work-program participants about differing workplace climates, structure, and organizational format to maximize the fit between worker and employer.

Last, practitioners can draw on organizational outreach experience to encourage legislatures and organizations to fund long-term transitional services for new workers. Services such as post-employment counseling, after-hours child care programs, moving expenses, and short-term no-interest loans for emergencies (Herman 1998) would likely maximize job retention as well as attainment, as evidenced by the welfare-to-work and work-enhancement program successes discussed earlier.

Outplacement Knowledge and Skills. Outplacement counseling and services, such as personal counseling, career and interest assessment, strategy development for the job search, and skill development and encouragement, (Smith, Gould, and Hosang 1988) are offered free to many corporate employees, frequently by occupational social workers (Foster and Schore 1990). Similar services are needed in welfare-to-work programs to maximize job retention. More than 20 million Americans, roughly one-sixth of the workforce, change their jobs each year; half of them involuntarily (Foster and Schore 1990). Whereas many quickly attained new employment, others cycled back onto welfare or general assistance for short interim spells (Bane and Ellwood 1994).

Knowledge about making alliances and collaborating with other community organizations to maximize job creation are also outplacement skills that pertain to work-enhancement settings. Practitioners, workers, and community stakeholders can develop sites to provide resources that will counter the deleterious byproducts of unemployment and speed employment re-entry. Such resources might include job clubs, skill development groups, public assistance services, activist efforts to expand transportation and child care subsidies, and entrepreneurial outreach to create more jobs. Federal and state job training dollars and university and corporate money could be used to back the recent federal/state mandate for such centers, because funding reportedly is not following the legislation (personal communication with Michael Mink, Planning Division, Private Industry Council of Philadelphia, March 4 1998). Similar group and individual services could lead to job advancement as well as job retention. These resources can be offered through community human services centers, job training programs and agencies, vocational institutions, and one-stop employment centers, among other potential sites. Such sites might be funded by federal vocational dollars and contributions that satisfy corporate social responsibility. The cost of such efforts would not be insignificant, but data from successful job creation initiatives show that financial benefits to both employee and employer exceed program costs (Johnson and Lopez 1997).

Practitioners can also forge alliances with grassroots employment programs such as the Philadelphia Unemployment Project (PUP), a nonprofit membership organization of unemployed people that offers free financial, legal, health, and job-search services. PUP is a good example of how local government, business, industry, and community organizations cooperate as a funding stream. In settings like PUP, practitioners can learn about client needs through direct contact with the staff and participants and mobilize both groups in advocacy and policy efforts to broaden the base of available jobs. Other alliances with advocacy groups such as the Working Women's Department of the AFL-CIO, particularly concerned with issues of comparable wages and provision of adequate non-wage benefits, could help to counter the persistence of below-poverty wages among TANF recipients entering the labor market.

Unions afford an additional collaborative venue. Whereas approximately 16 percent of the labor force is represented by a trade union (Molloy and Kurzman 1993), public reports suggest that unionization or union-related efforts on behalf of wages and benefits for welfare-to-work clients is increasing (Goldman 1997). Collaboration also could give practitioners and unions a joint constituent base to protect low-wage workers from displacement by TANF recipients. Study of the historic alliances between occupational social workers and unions could guide the collaborative efforts, because such alliances traditionally blended advocacy with service provision (Molloy and Kurzman 1993).

Implications for Social Work

Systematic expansion of occupational social work practice to welfare-to-work and other work-enhancement settings suggests a number of implications for the profession. Reformulation would promote the historic mission; it could broaden the domain of professional service; it might slow or reverse declassification of advanced social work positions; and it could provide a model for resolving practice dilemmas.

First, reformulation systematically expands the practice domain to the full spectrum of individuals' work situations: unemployed, underemployed, dislocated, working poor, and comfortably employed. Thus, reformulation fulfills the mission of the profession to serve people who are economically disadvantaged: unemployed, low-wage, and new workers. The intellectual stimulation and societal reinforcement that occupationally oriented social workers would receive from fulfilling multiple roles at multiple levels in work-program settings might help counter professional disinterest in poverty issues and practice with poor individuals and families (Hagen 1992). Moreover, in keeping with the traditional dual focus of occupational social work on employees and employers, businesses should benefit from this reformulated practice as well. For example, skills training and better matching of workers' skills and employers' needs through job-retention services should boost employee morale and productivity. Also, hiring and initial training costs should be lessened, because occupational social work services aimed at job retention would lengthen work attachment and reduce turnover.

Second, reformulation could broaden the domain of professional service. Because work is central to all individuals' lives, the knowledge base of this expanded practice specialization could be applied productively to economically disadvantaged clients at places other than work-related service sites. Knowledge about how transitional and institutional services support employment, how to collaborate with local businesses for job creation, and legislative rights of workers through the Community Mental Health Centers Act (P.L. 88-164) and the Occupational Health and Safety Act of 1970 (OSHA) (PL 91-596) would help occupational social workers negotiate and mediate with employers to maximize the work efforts of people with chronic mental illnesses. Such services, together with family outreach, collaboration with medical facilities, and knowledge of the Americans with Disabilities Act of 1990 (ADA) (PL 101-336) would enable employment-focused practitioners to expand work opportunities for people with physical disabilities. Similar knowledge and services would enable social workers in urban high schools to augment school-to-career efforts mandated by the School-to-Work Opportunities Act of 1994 (P.L. 103-239).

Third, when businesses, community organizations such as social services agencies and universities, and taxpayers benefit economically from occupationally focused social work with disadvantaged clients, the contribution of professional expertise will be reinforced. One consequence might be a slowing or reversal of the trend to declassify professional social work positions. Integrated occupational curricular offerings in more graduate programs (Mor-Barak et al. 1993), instead of individual elective courses (Ramanathan 1992), would buttress the professional domain. Specialized content focused on job retention practices could form a set of graduate-level continuing education offerings to work-program staff, job developers, and employers (Iversen, Rich, and Lewis 1998). Under TANF, public assistance caseworkers could benefit from such education to meet clients' work-related needs—knowledge and skills many reportedly lack (Valbrun 1998). Broadened collaborative efforts between practitioners, work programs, and schools of social work might reintegrate professional social services and welfare organizations, counteracting the separation between these groups that has prevailed since the 1970s (Wyers 1983). Increased employment of master's-level social workers with an occupational focus, together with staff development of public assistance caseworkers, might bridge the historic separation, provide more substantive work-focused service, and broaden the recipient base for social work education.

Finally, as privatization, bureaucratization, and entrepreneurial activities increase in social services organizations, traditional occupational social workers have a head start in addressing the concomitant practice dilemmas. Conflicts between managers and professionals have arisen frequently in relation to prioritizing goals, protecting confidentiality, facing incompatibility in client definition and purview of service, and mediating divided loyalties. How occupational practitioners traditionally maintained both service delivery and advocacy roles; honed their negotiation, mediation, and conflict-resolution skills; and resolved characteristics and limits of confidentiality in situations of disparate rights and obligations (Kurzman 1988) can guide new occupational practitioners' efforts on behalf of unemployed clients. Devising models to forward organizational diversity (Mor-Barak 1998) and active curricular and field practicum involvement in work-program settings (Iversen et al. 1998) also should contribute to resolving such dilemmas. The occupational social worker can draw on these experiences to establish socially just guidelines for public and private ventures as these new alliances change the nature, funding, and structure of employment-focused service delivery in the 21st century.

Reprinted from Roberta Rehner Iversen, Occupational social work for the 21st century, *Social Work* 43 (6) (1998): 551–66. Copyright 1998 National Association of Social Workers, Inc.; reprinted by permission.

References

Addams, J. (1910). *Twenty Years at Hull-House.* New York: New American Library.

Anderson, C., and C. Stark (1988). Psychosocial problems of job relocation: Preventive roles in industry. *Social Work* 33: 3841.

Austin, D. M. (1997). The profession of social work in the second century. In M. Reisch and E. Gambrill, eds., *Social Work in the 21st Century.* Thousand Oaks, Calif.: Pine Forge. 396–407.

Bakalinsky, R. (1980). People vs. profits: Social work in industry. *Social Work* 25: 471–75.

Balgopal, P. R. (1989). Occupational social work: An expanded clinical perspective. *Social Work* 34: 437–42.

Bane, M. I., and D. T. Ellwood (1994). *Welfare Realities: From Rhetoric to Reform.* Cambridge, Mass.: Harvard University Press.

Bargal, D., and Y. Katan (1998). Social work in the world of work: The Israeli case. In F. M.

Loewenberg, ed., *Meeting the Challenges of a Changing Society: Fifty Years of Social Work in Israel.* Jerusalem: Magnes Press, Hebrew University. 275–78.

Belden, T. (1997). Opportunities knock: Training institute prepares students to work in the hospitality industry. *Philadelphia Inquirer,* November 13, D1, D2.

Berg, L., L. Olson, and A. Conrad (1991). *Causes and Implications of Rapid Job Loss Among Participants in a Welfare-to-Work Program.* Evanston, Ill.: Northwestern University, Center for Urban Affairs and Policy Research.

Besharov, D. J., P. Germanis, and P. H. Rossi (1997). *Evaluating Welfare Reform.* College Park: University of Maryland.

Binzen, P. (1998). Amid the boom times, he foresees a deepening of misery. *Philadelphia Inquirer,* January 5, E1, E3.

Blank, R. M. (1995). Outlook for the U.S. labor market and prospects for low-wage entry jobs. In D. S. Nightingale and R. H. Haveman, eds., *The Work Alternative: Welfare Reform and the Realities of the Job Market.* Washington, D.C.: Urban Institute. 33–69.

Blank, R. M. (1997). *It Takes a Nation: A New Agenda for Fighting Poverty.* New York: Sage.

Brieland, D. (1990). The Hull-House tradition and the contemporary social worker: Was Jane Addams really a social worker? *Social Work* 35: 134–38.

Bureau of Labor Statistics (1997). *Contingent and alternative employment arrangements.* Washington, D.C.: U.S. Department of Labor.

——— (1998). *Number of jobs, labor market experience, and earnings growth: Results from a longitudinal survey.* Washington, DC: U.S. Department of Labor.

Burtless, G. T. (1997). Welfare recipients' job skills and employment prospects. *Future of Children* 7: 39–51.

City of Philadelphia. (1998, March 24). *The City of Philadelphia's Welfare to Work Strategy.* Report from Donna Cooper, Deputy Mayor for Policy and Planning. Philadelphia: City of Philadelphis

Couch, K. A. (1992). New evidence on the long-term effects of employment training programs. *Journal of Labor Economics* 10: 380–88.

Current Labor Statistics. (1998). Selected unemployment indicators, monthly data seasonally adjusted. *Monthly Labor Review* 121: 70.

Danziger, S., and J. Lehman (1996). How will welfare recipients fare in the labor market? *Challenge* (March–April): 30–35.

Danziger, S. H., G. D. Sandefur, and D. H. Weinberg, eds. (1994). *Confronting Poverty: Prescriptions for Change.* Cambridge, Mass.: Harvard University Press.

Economic Policy Institute (1997). *Nonstandard Work, Substandard Jobs: Flexible Work Arrangements in the U.S.* Washington, D.C.: the Institute.

Estes, R. J. (1987). Assessing the employability of disabled adults. *Public Welfare* (Spring): 29–46.

Farber, N. B., and R. R. Iversen (1998). Family values about education and their transmission among black inner-city young women. In A. Colby, J. James, and D. Hart , eds., *The Development of Competence and Character Through Life.* Chicago: University of Chicago Press. 141–67.

Foster, B., and L. Schore (1990). Job loss and the occupational social worker. In S. L. A. Straussner, ed., *Occupational Social Work Today.* New York: Haworth Press. 77–97.

Franklin, J. C. (1997). Industry output and employment projections to 2006. *Monthly Labor Review* 120: 39–57.

Friedlander, D., and G. Burtless (1995). *Five Years After: The Long-Term Effects of Welfare-to-Work Programs.* New York: Sage.

Goldman, H. (1997). N.Y. touts workfare; critics see problems. *Philadelphia Inquirer,* March 12, A1, A16.

Googins, B., and B. N. Davidson (1993). The organization as client: Broadening the concept of employee assistance programs. *Social Work* 38: 477–84.

Googins, B., and J. Godfrey (1987). *Occupational Social Work.* Englewood Cliffs, N.J.: Prentice-Hall.

Gould, G. M., and M. L. Smith, eds.. (1988). *Social Work in the Workplace*. New York: Springer.

Gueron, J. M., and E. Pauly (1991). *From Welfare to Work*. New York: Sage.

Hagen, J. L. (1992). Women, work, and welfare: Is there a role for social work? *Social Work* 37: 9–14.

Haimson, J., A. Hershey, and A. Rangarajan, (1995). *Providing Services to Promote Job Retention*. Report series of the Postemployment Services Demonstration. Princeton, NJ: Mathematica Policy Research.

Hale, T. W. (1997). The working poor. *Monthly Labor Review* 20: 47–48.

Hanson, M. (1993). Se, eds., *Work and Well-Being*. Washington, D.C.: NASW Press. 218–38.

Harris, K. M. (1996). Life after welfare: Women, work and repeat dependency. *American Sociological Review* 61: 407–26.

Hecker, D. E. (1998). Earnings of college graduates: Women compared with men. *Monthly Labor Review* 121: 62–71.

Herman, A. M. (1997). *Report on the American Workforce*. Washington, D.C.: U.S. Department of Labor.

——— (1998). Speech, National Press Club, February 17, http://wtw.doleta.gov/resources/secspch.htm.

Hernandez, R. (1998). Most dropped from welfare don't get jobs. *New York Times*, March 23, A1, B6.

Herr, T., and R. Halpern (1991). *Changing What Counts: Rethinking the Journey Out of Welfare*. Evanston, Ill.: Northwestern University, Center for Urban Affairs and Policy Research.

Herr, T., R. Halpern, and S. L.Wagner (1995). *Something Old, Something New*. Chicago: Project Match, Erikson Institute.

Hershey, A. M., and L. A. Pavetti (1997). Turning job finders into job keepers. *Future of Children* 7: 74–86.

Hollister, R. (1997). What works, for whom? Learning from the experience of welfare reform. *Poverty Research News* 1: 3–6.

Hollister, R. G., Jr., P. Kemper, and R. A. Maynard, eds. (1984). *The National Supported Work Demonstration*. Madison: University of Wisconsin Press.

Holzer, H. J. (1996a). *Employer demand, AFDC recipients, and labor market policy*. Discussion Paper DP 115–96. Madison: University of Wisconsin Institute for Research on Poverty.

Holzer, H. J. (1996b). *What Employers Want*. New York: Sage.

Iversen, R. R. (1995). Poor African-American women and work: The occupational attainment process. *Social Problems* 42: 554–73.

Iversen, R. R., and N. B. Farber (1996). Transmission of family values, work and welfare among poor urban black women. *Work and Occupations* 23: 437–60.

Iversen, R. R., L. M. Rich, and B. M. Lewis (1998). Job retention and post-employment support in Greater Philadelphia Works programs. Proposal under consideration, July.

Jansson, B. S. (1990). *Social Welfare Policy: From Theory to Practice*. Belmont, Calif.: Wadsworth.

Jargowsky, P. A. (1997). *Poverty and Pace*. New York: Sage.

Jencks, C., L. Perman, and L. Rainwater (1988). What is a good job? A new measure of labor-market success. *American Journal of Sociology* 93: 1322–57.

Johnson, C. M., and A. C. Lopez (1997). Shattering the myth of failure: Promising findings from ten public job creation initiatives, http://www.cbpp.org/1222jobcr.htm.

Karger, H. J., and D. Stoesz (1998). *American Social Welfare Policy*. 3rd ed. New York: Longman.

Kurzman, P. A. (1988). The ethical base for social work in the workplace. In G. M. Gould and M. L. Smith, eds., *Social Work in the Workplace*. New York: Springer. 16–27.

Kurzman, P. A. (1993). Employee assistance programs. In P. A. Kurzman and S. H. Akabas, eds., *Work and Well-Being*. Washington, D.C.: NASW Press. 26–45.

Kurzman, P. A., and S. H. Akabas (1981). Industrial social work as an arena for practice. *Social Work* 26: 52–60.

Kurzman, P. A., and S. H. Akabas, eds. (1993). *Work and Well-Being*. Washington, D.C.: NASW Press.

LaLonde, R. J. (1995). The promise of public sector-sponsored training programs. *Journal of Economic Perspectives* 9: 149–68.

Lewis, B. (1997). Occupational social work practice. In M. Reisch and E. Gambrill, eds, *Social Wrk in the 21st Century*. Thousand Oaks, Calif.: Pine Forge. 226–38.

Lewis, B. M. (1990). Social workers' role in promoting occupational health and safety. In S. L. A. Straussner, ed., *Occupational Social Work Today*. New York: Haworth. 99–118.

Maryland Department of Human Resources (1997. *Life After Welfare: An Interim Report*. Baltimore: Department and University of Maryland School of Social Work, September.

Maynard, R. A. (1984). The impacts of supported work on youth. In R. G. Hollister, P. Kemper, and R. A. Maynard, eds., *The National Supported Work demonstration*. Madison: University of Wisconsin Press. 205–38

———— (1998). Rigorous research to improve policy and practice: Lessons from welfare reform demonstrations. Talk, University of Pennsylvania School of Social Work, January.

Mead, L. M. (1996). Are welfare employment programs effective? Institute for Research on Poverty Discussion Paper 1096–96. Madison: University of Wisconsin.

Meyer, C. H. (1983). Declassification: Assault on social workers and social services. *Social Work* 28: 419.

Mishel, L., and J. Bernstein (1994). *The State of Working America 1994–95*. Armonk, N.Y.: M.E. Sharpe.

Molloy, D. J., and P. A, Kurzman, (1993). Practice with unions. In P. A. Kurzman and S. H. Akabas, eds,, *Work and Well-Being*. Washington, D.C.: NASW Press. 46–60.

Mor-Barak, M. E. (1998). The inclusive work place: An ecosystems approach to organizational diversity. Paper presented at the Joint World Congress of the International Federation of Social Workers and the International Association of Schools of Social Work, Jerusalem, July.

Mor-Barak, M. E., L. M. Poverny, W. A. Finch, Jr., J. McCroskey, H. L. Nedelman, E. T. Seek, and R. Sullivan (1993). A model curriculum for occupational social work. *Journal of Social Work Education* 29: 63–77.

Mudrick, N. R. (1991). An underdeveloped role for occupational social work: Facilitating the employment of people with disabilities. *Social Work* 36: 490–95.

Murnane, R. J. (1994). Education and the well-being of the next generation. In S. H. Danziger, G. D. Sandefur, and D. H. Weinberg, eds., *Confronting Poverty: Prescriptions for Change*. Cambridge, Mass.: Harvard University Press. 289–307.

Ozawa, M. N. (1980). Development of social services in industry: Why and how? *Social Work* 25: 464–70.

———— (1985). Economics of occupational social work. *Social Work* 30: 442–44.

Parmley, S. (1998). Rendell to outline job plan for poor. *Philadelphia Inquirer,* April 12, Bl, B4.

Pease, J., and L. Martin (1997). Want ads and jobs for the poor: A glaring mismatch. *Sociological Forum* 12: 545–64.

Pecora, P. J., and M. J. Austin (1983). Declassification of social service jobs: Issues and strategies. *Social Work* 28: 421–26.

Pierre, R. E. (1997). New rules are blamed as welfare recipients stop taking courses. *Philadelphia Inquirer,* December 31, Al0.

Quint, J. C,, J. S. Musick, and J. Ladner (1994). *Lives of Promise, Lives of Pain: Young Mothers After New Chance*. New York: Manpower Demonstration Research Corporation.

Ramanathan, C. S. (1992). EAP's response to personal stress and productivity: Implications for occupational social work. *Social Work* 37: 234–39.

Rangarajan, A., A. Meckstroth, and T. Novak (1998). *The Effectiveness of the Postemployment Services Demonstration: Preliminary Findings*. Princeton, N.J.: Mathematica Policy Research.

Rich, L. M. (1996). The long-run impact of teenage work experience: A reexamination. *Review of Black Political Economy* 25: 11–36.

Rifkin, J. (1995). *The End of Work*. New York: Putnam.

Root, L. S. (1993). Unemployment and underemployment. In P. A. Kurzman and S. H. Akabas, eds., *Work and Well-Being*. Washington, D.C.: NASW Press. 332–49.

———— (1997). Social work and the workplace. In M. Reisch and E. Cambrill, eds., *Social Work in the 21st Century*. Thousand Oaks, Calif.: Pine Forge. 134–42.

Rose, N. E. (1995). *Workfare or Fair Work*. New Brunswick, N.J.: Rutgers University Press.

Rothman, R. A. (1998). *Working: Sociological Perspectives*. Upper Saddle River, N.J.: Simon and Schuster.

Savner, S., and M. Greenberg, (1997). Community service employment: A new opportunity under TANF. *CLASP*, http://epn.org.

Schatz, M. S., L. E. Jenkins, and B. W. Sheafor (1990). Milford redefined: A model of initial and advanced generalist social work. *Journal of Social Work Education* 26: 217–31.

Siegel, D. I. (1988). Relocation counseling and services. In G. M. Gould and M. L. Smith, eds., *Social Work in the Workplace*. New York: Springer. 109–22.

Silvestri, G. T. (1997). Occupational employment projections to 2006. *Monthly Labor Review* 120: 58–83.

Smith, M. L, G. M. Gould, and M. A. Hosang (1988). The outplacement process. In G. M. Gould and M. L. Smith, eds., *Social Work in the Workplace*. New York: Springer. 185–99.

Straussner, S. L. A., ed. (1990). *Occupational Social Work Today*. New York: Haworth.

Tausky, C. (1996). *Work and Society: An Introduction to Industrial Sociology*. 2nd ed. Itasca, Ill.: Peacock.

Tilly, C. (1996). *Half a Job*. Philadelphia: Temple University.

U.S. Department of Labor. (1996). Involving employers in training: Best practices. http://wtw .doleta.gov/bestpractice/reportbp.htm.

Valbrun, M. (1997). Fear of failure vs. desire to work. *Philadelphia Inquirer*, September 10, Bl, B4.

———— (1998). State welfare workers now pushing jobs, not paper. *Philadelphia Inquirer*, April 12 Al, A18.

Vigilante, F. W. (1982). Use of work in the assessment and intervention process. *Social Casework* 63: 296–300.

Vigilante, F. W. (1993). Work. In P. A. Kurzman and S. H. Akabas, eds., *Work and Well-Being*. Washington, D.C.: NASW Press. 179–99.

Wage increase backed (1998). *NASW News*, February 1, 10.

Wilson, W. J. (1996). *When Work Disappears*. New York: Knopf.

Wyers, N. L. (1983). Income maintenance and social work: A broken tie. *Social Work* 28: 261–68.

———— (1991). Policy-practice in social work: Models and issues. *Journal of Social Work Education* 27: 241–50.

Yamatani, H. (1988). Client assessment in an industrial setting: A cross-sectional method. *Social Work* 33: 34–37.

Commentary

Roberta R. Iversen

I am honored to contribute to this book commemorating the centennial of the Penn School of Social Policy & Practice as I was to contribute to the special centennial issue of the journal *Social Work* at the dawn of the twenty-first century. I draw the following parallels between these two contributions. First, "Occupational Social Work for the Twenty-First Century" is in concert with Penn's historic dual focus on both people and organizations or institutions—in short, on both micro- and macro-levels of social action. Second, the article's incorporation of theory, empirical examination and application lodge it in the School's history as a forerunner of theory- and research-based knowledge production for practice. Third, the article's primary orientation to the particular challenges of post-industrial urban environments mirror the School's historic attention to the challenges faced by residents, neighborhoods, and communities in Philadelphia—both as an end goal and as a model for the role that university-based schools of social work and social welfare can play in urban social and economic development writ large.

My reflections in this commentary on the occupational social work article ten years later, and on the social environment in which its ideas and urgings are embedded, are both heartening and disheartening.

As background, the article was written during a period of impassioned social work outrage at the passage of the Personal Responsibility and Work Opportunity Reconciliation Act of 1996, commonly known as "welfare reform." Given my prior scholarly work in the area of occupational and economic mobility, one of my responses to the new legislation was that the profession should seize the opportunity to make a significant contribution to its historic target population—poor persons who contend with economic and employment disadvantage. I offered "Occupational Social Work in the 21st Century" as a model or template to that end.

Although the field of occupational social work shifted during the twentieth century from its origins in the settlement movement to institutional and business environments, welfare reform provided an opportunity to redeploy the field's philosophy, tenets, and expertise to the historic population of social work. In addition, the legislative upheaval and its programmatic aftermath provided new impetus to incorporate subject matter about urban poverty, economics, and the labor market into social work curricula, preparing students more fully for varied practice domains and populations.

The heartening aspect of my reflection is that over the ten years since welfare reform spawned a new landscape of employment-focused programs, many ideas in "Occupational Social Work for the 21st Century" have been implemented. For example, in 2005, a Penn colleague, Dr. Lina Hartocollis, and I were awarded a grant to design a case management training program for an innovative welfare-to-work demonstration based on the model in this and a commissioned article that we wrote with another colleague (Iversen, Lewis, and Hartocollis 1998). The city's central welfare/workforce development intermediary subsequently invited us to design training modules based on the model for all welfare and workforce program supervisors. Dishearteningly, administrators at the state level overrode this invitation with their particular agenda.

More broadly, the ideas in the occupational social work article informed my subsequent research and publications, with a heartening impact on welfare and workforce development policy and programs. As a result of independent research grants from the Annie E. Casey Foundation for a five-city, five-year ethnographic study of low-income families trying to move up through work (Iversen 2002; Iversen and Armstrong 2006), I used the findings from that research, together with the ideas in the occupational social work article, to redesign components of workforce and welfare-to-work programs locally, nationally and globally (Iversen 2001). For example, preemployment assessment procedures came to include inquiry about how housing, debt, and depression might impact job training participation and performance. New post-employment and job retention designs laid out procedures for program staff to advocate with employers on behalf of new workers, develop mentor programs in firms, and collaboratively engage with a broader array of workforce intermediaries and organizations. The article and subsequent research also led to improvements in housing and living wage policies that benefited low-income workers in a number of cities across the country. Dishearteningly, even the best programs and policies cannot eradicate urban poverty on their own. Massive investment in multi-institutional change and significant reformulation of the worldviews of the populace are needed to realize that goal.

Returning to the School and the profession, "Occupational Social Work in the 21st Century" is required reading for social work students in our School and others, aimed at extending their awareness of the reach of the social work profession. Most recently, the article and my subsequent scholarly work formed the framework for a course on urban poverty, welfare and work that I designed and offered for the first time in Fall 2005. Hearteningly, the second-year MSW students responded to this course with extended understanding of the interplay between persons, poverty, and poverty remediation strategies such as welfare and employment. As one student reported in the evaluation of the course: "I will never forget my county assistance [office] observation experience and my wage-earning assignment. The wage analysis convinced me more about institutional discrimination, poverty and negative effects of capitalism than years of reading from textbooks." Another's feedback was "The assignment to visit the CAO [County Assistance Office] and write a paper about the experience, and the logging of people's wages assignment and paper, were amazing learning experiences. It forced my eyes open to the disparity of our welfare/wage system." The students also reported renewed dedication to using the competencies they gained from their Penn SP2 education to dedicate their professional futures to further eradication of poverty and economic inequality.

References

Iversen, R. R. (2001). Occupational social work and job retention supports: An international perspective. *International Social Work* 44 (3): 329–42.
——— (2002). *Moving Up Is a Steep Climb.* Baltimore: Annie E. Casey Foundation.
Iversen, R. R., and A. L. Armstrong (2006) *Jobs Aren't Enough: Toward a New Economic Mobility for Low-Income Families.* Philadelphia: Temple University Press.
Iversen, R.R., B. M. Lewis, L. Hartocollis (1998). Occupational social work and welfare reform: Directions for continuing social work education. *Professional Development: The International Journal of Continuing Social Work Education* 1 (3): 12–17.

Chapter 35
Where the Homeless Come From: A Study of the Prior Address Distribution of Families Admitted to Public Shelters in New York City and Philadelphia

Dennis P. Culhane, Chang-Moo Lee, and
Susan M. Wachter

Introduction

Researchers and policy makers have increasingly emphasized the structural and dynamic nature of the homelessness problem (Burt 1992; Interagency Council for the Homeless 1994; Piliavin et al. 1993). Research on the structural factors associated with homelessness has used primarily intercity homelessness rates (point prevalence) as the dependent measure, attempting to identify the associated housing, population, income, and policy factors (Applebaum et al. 1991, 1992; Burt 1992; Elliot and Krivo 1991; Quigley 1991; Tucker 1987). This research has yielded significant though inconsistent results, particularly regarding many predicted housing and income variables. This article addresses the same issue, using intracity data, aggregated by census tract, based on the prior addresses of homeless families in two large U.S. cities.

Literature Review

Basic research on contemporary homelessness has employed primarily cross-sectional survey methods designed to enumerate the population and document its demographic characteristics. While providing a detailed profile of the population and many of its needs, this method has had limitations. It has produced a static representation of a dynamic problem; it has identified where and in what condition people end up as homeless, but not where they come from or go to; and while it has identified the characteristics of individuals that increase their vulnerability to the condition, the data have not been well suited to assessing the social processes that contribute to that vulnerability. To some extent, public policies and programs designed to address homelessness have shared these limitations. Most homelessness program development has focused on expanding the availability of residential and supportive services that target currently homeless persons and families. Program development has focused less on forestalling the housing emergencies of the many more individuals and families who, without intervening assistance, will move in and out of homelessness over time. Homelessness programs have also targeted individuals for intervention, and not the communities or institutions from which they come or the social and economic forces that have put these individuals at risk. However, evidence has emerged of a shift in both the research and policy sectors toward a greater understanding of the structural and dynamic nature of the homelessness problem.

In the research sector, several investigators have applied or argued for the use of geographic methods to study structural aspects of the homelessness problem (Kearns and Smith 1994; Wallace 1989, 1990; Wolch and Dear 1993). Most commonly, researchers have attempted to identify the socioeconomic factors that correspond to the spatial distribution of homelessness, using data on intercity homelessness rates as the dependent variable (Applebaum et al. 1991, 1992; Burt 1992; Elliot and Krivo 1991; Quigley 1991; Ringheim 1990; Tucker 1987). Based on this research, homelessness appears to vary by socioeconomic conditions, although specific study findings have been inconsistent. Tucker (1987), in one of the first applications of this method, argued that cities with rent control had higher homelessness rates, based on data from an early survey of city shelter capacity by the U.S. Department of Housing and Urban Development (HUD 1984). Applebaum and colleagues (1991, 1992) identified major flaws in Tucker's approach and provided counterevidence that low vacancy rates, as a proxy for tight housing markets, were more closely related to HUD's intercity homelessness rates. Elliot and Krivo (1991), using the same data, found that the availability of low-income housing and lower per capita expenditures on mental health care were significantly related to homelessness rates but that poverty and unemployment rates were not. In a test of several more carefully specified models of intercity homelessness rates, Burt (1992) found that per capita income, the poverty rate, and the proportion of single person households combined to explain more than half the variation in homelessness rates in high-growth cities, interpreted as evidence that more affluent households and a greater number of households with single people put pressure on the housing choices of poorer people.

A limitation of this research, and perhaps an explanation for study differences, is the reliability and validity of the dependent variable. While perhaps the most widely attainable proxy for the size of the homelessness problem across locales, point prevalence measures are difficult to obtain reliably from place to place. The HUD estimates (1984) used by Tucker (1987), Applebaum et al. (1991), Elliot and Krivo (1991), and Quigley (1991) were based on a key informant survey in 60 cities. HUD officials asked field staff to report on the capacity of localities' emergency shelters and the estimated number of street homeless in their areas; thus, these estimates were not based on a systematic count. The comparability of study findings based on the HUD estimates is further complicated by the various authors' use of different jurisdictional boundaries in calculating rates. The Urban Institute estimates used by Burt (1992) were derived from results of a larger, more systematic survey of shelter providers and based on a hypothetical ratio of street homeless to sheltered homeless; but again, they were not derived from an actual count.

Even if estimates were reliably obtained across jurisdictions, their validity as comparable measures of the extent of homelessness across locales would be confounded by the highly variant responses of those locales to the problem of homelessness. To a significant degree, the daily size of the sheltered population, typically the largest component of the homeless count, is supply and policy-driven (Burt 1994; Culhane 1992). The elasticity of the supply of shelter beds defines access to the shelter system, which in turn is a function of local policies governing admission criteria, length-of-stay limits, and the flexibility of resources to meet demand. Other policies, such as co-payment requirements, sobriety checks, and treatment mandates, as well as the overall quality of facilities, are also likely to influence some clients' perceptions of whether accepting accommodations in a shelter has relative appeal over other options, and for what duration.

Likewise, opportunities for exiting homelessness will affect the duration of episodes; in general, more programs to facilitate exit from homelessness should decrease time to exit and correspondingly produce a lower daily census.[1] Each of these factors is likely to exercise a systematic influence on a city's average shelter stay and shelter capacity, which in turn will playa determining role in the point prevalence of homelessness.

Recent longitudinal research has suggested the potential relevance of a structural and dynamic model of homelessness and has raised questions about the adequacy of point prevalence data for measuring the homelessness problem. Analyses of administrative data (Burt 1994; Culhane et al. 1994), a national telephone survey (Link et al. 1994), and a housing survey in New York City (Stegman 1993) have all found that as much as 3 percent of the population experienced an episode of "literal" homelessness between 1988 and 1992, suggesting a high degree of turnover in the homeless population. Longitudinal research based on tracked samples of homeless persons (Fournier et al. 1994; Koegel and Burnam 1994; Piliavin et al. 1993; Robertson, Zlotnick, and Westerfelt 1994; Wright and Devine 1995) has also documented the often transitory, intermittent nature of homelessness. Most shelter users appear to mobilize resources and community ties to avoid the shelters most of the time. Hopper (1990, 1995) has characterized these informal networks as the "economies of makeshift." Unfortunately, the nature of these support systems, and the factors that strain or enhance their supportive capacity, are not well understood (see related discussions in Burt [1994], Piliavin et al. [1993], and Rossi [1994]).

In the policy sector, recent proposals have discussed the dynamic and structural aspects of the homelessness problem. Most recently, the Clinton administration's plan *Priority Home: The Federal Plan to Break the Cycle of Homelessness* (Interagency Council for the Homeless 1994) offers a social and economic analysis of the causes of homelessness, as well as a distinction between chronic and episodic homelessness.[2] Based on this analysis, the plan argues for making homelessness prevention a priority for future federal policy. The Clinton plan describes broad legislative initiatives intended to approach that goal, such as the administration's health care and welfare-reform proposals, expansion of the earned-income tax credit, and increased homeownership and rental-assistance opportunities.[3] In addition, the plan's core policy objective—that localities establish an organized "continuum of care" for the homeless service system—acknowledges the need for preventive and long-term housing stabilization efforts, as well as traditional remedial strategies, to reduce the prevalence of homelessness.

The plan does not address how localities might plan for prevention programs and offers few specifics regarding implementation other than in the broad terms of the major legislative initiatives described above. Given that many of the proposals in the federal plan are placed in the context of the scientific literature, the gap in the plan could well be a reflection of a gap in prior research. Some conceptual elaboration of homelessness prevention programming has appeared in the literature (Jahiel 1992; Lindblom 1991), but the available empirical literature is limited (U.S. Department of Health and Human Services 1991). The literature on program targeting has been comparably sparse (Knickman and Weitzman 1989). Researchers have not provided a method for helping policy makers to determine where homelessness prevention resources should be targeted, nor have they clearly documented the factors they should focus on.

Our present study is an attempt to contribute to the continuing integration of a structural and dynamic model of homelessness in the research and policy sectors, both by beginning to answer the "where to target" question facing the planners of homelessness prevention programs and by adding to researchers' tools for investigating the structural correlates of homelessness (or the "what to target" question facing planners). This study uses the prior-address information reported by persons admitted to the Philadelphia and New York City shelter systems to construct an intracity index for the rate of homelessness by census tract and identifies census tract variables that correspond to that distribution. An intracity measure has the following methodological advantages over the intercity point prevalence measures described above: (1) in general, it is concerned not with the exactness of a count for a given day but with identifying a representative sample of persons from whom prior-address information can be obtained over a given period of time; and (2) it is not confounded by local policies and regulations that affect shelter supply and stay patterns because those factors would presumably have a similar impact across a city's jurisdiction, particularly in centrally administered shelter systems such as those studied here. While intercity analyses permit researchers to assess the policy and social factors that vary in relation to homelessness rates among cities, an intracity approach allows them to characterize spatial variations within a city. Thus, an intracity approach may contribute to an understanding of the "makeshift economies" that beget homelessness and of the processes that contribute to the success or failure of the makeshift economies in mediating housing instability.

Social Selection Processes of Homelessness

To develop a theory for generating hypotheses, our study builds on previous theoretical work (Blau 1992; Burt 1992; Culhane 1990; Hopper and Hamberg 1986; Jahiel

1992; Rossi 1989; among others). Briefly, the model argues that homelessness is a consequence of a combination of housing, income, population, and policy factors that have significantly increased the probability that poor persons will live in precarious housing arrangements. Among the precariously housed, a shelter admission is most likely to occur following some household crisis (e.g., job loss, marital separation, benefit termination, utility disconnection, hospitalization, incarceration, family conflict) and most frequently occurs among persons who have the least amount of familial, social, or public support. These people include unemployed single mothers who are caring for young children and do not receive child support payments; adults with disabilities, including people with mental disorders and people addicted to drugs or alcohol; the undereducated and underemployed, particularly those ineligible for unemployment insurance or general assistance welfare programs; and people with weak familial supports, such as those fleeing abusive families and individuals who were reared in foster care or otherwise unsupportive family environments. The precariously housed are expected to be concentrated in certain areas, because of both selective migration and restrictions on their housing choice.

A family crisis or household disruption does not necessarily lead to shelter use, but such a result is more likely in the context of shortages of affordable and suitable housing for people with very low incomes. The risk of homelessness would likely be greater if the disruption were preceded by residence in poor-quality housing or if it resulted in a subsequent move to such housing.

Thus, one would expect to find that public-shelter admissions are most often generated in the lowest rent neighborhoods where poor people exhaust the opportunities most accessible to them. Such areas are more likely to have generally distressed housing conditions, as indicated by more vacancies and abandonment. Moreover, despite having the lowest-cost housing available, such areas may nevertheless be "unaffordable" to the people who live in them, leading some to live in crowded or doubled-up arrangements (in subfamilies).

The relevance of the other major component to the housing affordability problem—low income—is likely to be evident by the higher rates of poverty and joblessness in such neighborhoods. Problems with access to the labor market are indicated by higher rates of unemployment, less full-time employment, and less participation in the labor force. Public assistance presumably reduces the risk of homelessness in an area (compared with poor areas where people receive less public assistance), but it also may be associated with an increased risk of homelessness to the extent that receipt of public assistance indicates very low income and less participation in the labor market.

It is presumed that the housing and income problems described above have differentially affected African Americans because of historical patterns of migration, economic development, residential segregation, and discrimination. Other ethnic minorities, such as Hispanics and immigrant groups, may also face increased risk of homelessness due to poverty, restricted labor market access, and segregation in poorer-quality housing.

Hypotheses and Research Questions

First, our study explores the spatial distribution of the residential origins of homeless families through spatial statistics and thematic maps, permitting us to compare the degree of clustering and segregation in those distributions between cities and among boroughs within New York City. The descriptive analyses also identify the degree to which the homeless and poverty distributions differ in their concentration, unevenness, and clustering, to further qualify the nature of the prior address distribution of homeless families.

To understand the marginal effect of various factors on the spatial distribution of homeless families' prior addresses, we used cross-sectional data from the 1990 decennial census (measuring demographic composition, economic status, and housing and neighborhood factors) in a regression analysis to test some of the assumptions of the theoretical model regarding an area's potential risk. We hypothesize that the variables defined in Table 1 will be significantly associated with the rate of family shelter admission by census tract. We expected variations by city to affect our results, given known differences in several housing market factors such as population loss, a much higher proportion of single-family housing, and overall lower housing costs in Philadelphia. We also explored differences between low- and higher-income areas to test for factors that may differentially expose persons to homelessness in areas disaggregated by median income.

Procedures

Database Development

Data sources. New York City and Philadelphia systematically register all users of public shelters through automated client management information systems (see Culhane et al. 1994). As part of the shelter admission process, families in New York City and all households in Philadelphia are asked to report their "last address." This question may be variously interpreted by families requesting shelter. For purposes of the present study, we assume the addresses, through their aggregation, to be a proxy for the areas in which families entering the shelter have had some recent residence. For consistency between sites, only data on families were included in the study. To create an admission record in Philadelphia, clients must present two forms of identification that together must include a social security number and a Philadelphia street address.[4] The Philadelphia database begins December 21, 1989, and is current to April 1, 1994. It includes records for 9,160 families. In New York City, shelter admission information for families may be verified against a family's information in the New York State Welfare Management System at the time of admission, if the family is registered in that system. The data from New York used for this study begin April 1, 1987, and are current to April 1, 1994. They include records for 71,035 households.

Geocoding procedures. To construct a database of addresses aggregated by census tract, we overlaid the addresses from the Philadelphia data set with the census tract coverage from the TIGERJLine file (U.S. Department of Commerce 1993). We processed the

TABLE 1. Variable Definitions and Hypotheses

Variable	Definition	Expected sign
Demographic		
RBLACK	Ratio of black persons	+
RSPAN	Ratio of Hispanic persons	+
RUNDER18	Ratio of persons under 18	+
ROVER64	Ratio of persons over 64	+
RNOHIGH	Ratio of persons without high school diploma	+
RFHHOLD	Ratio of female-headed households	+
RFYOUCHD	Ratio of female-headed households with children under six years old	+
ROLDFAM	Ratio of families with householder over 64 years old	+
RSUBFAM	Ratio of subfamilies	+
RGRPQUAT	Ratio of noninstitutionalized persons in group quarters	+
RFRBRN70	Ratio of the foreign-born who immigrated after 1970	+
Economic		
RUNEMP	Ratio of unemployment	+
MNHHPAI	Mean household public assistance income	+
MEDHHINC	Median household income	−
RNOPOV	Ratio of persons below poverty level	+
RNOWORK	Ratio of persons not in labor force	+
RTMPWORK	Ratio of persons working under 18 hours per week	+
Housing and neighborhood quality		
MEWDVALUE	Median property value	−
MEWDCOREN	Median contract rent	−
RRENT	Ratio of rental units	+
RENTHINC	Ratio of median contract rent to median household income	+
RCROWD	Ratio of housing units with more than two persons per room	+
RVAC	Ratio of vacant units	+
RBOARDUP	Ratio of boarded-up housing units	+

Dependent variable is log (ratio of homelessness occurrence + 1). All ratios are in percent.

address data from New York City through Geo-support, a program for normalizing street addresses and for producing geo-codes for census-blocks and tracts maintained by the New York City Department of City Planning.

For both cities, we first matched client address data to the respective base map files (see Table 2). For New York City, 70 percent of the cases had an address that matched the Department of City Planning's geographic files. Shelter addresses were removed to produce the study population. The unmatched cases constitute 30 percent of the total and include rejected in-city addresses, in-state non-New York City addresses, out-of-state addresses, and missing addresses. In Philadelphia, 59 percent of the cases had an address that matched the TIGER file. Again, shelter addresses were removed to produce the study population. The unmatched cases (41 percent) include rejected in-

TABLE 2. Qualification of Study Populations

	New York	Philadelphia
Address-matched sample	49,604	5,375
Shelter addresses	481	319
Family	49,123	5,056
Nonmatched sample	21,431	3,785
In city[a]	9,990	858
In-state (not in city)[b]	429	24
Out-of-state[c]	2,120	42
Missing[d]	8,892	2,861
Total households	71,035	9,160

[a] In-city rejected addresses represent 16.8 percent of the total in-city addresses reported in New York City. The rejected addresses correlate with the matched addresses by zip code at $r = 0.877$. For Philadelphia, the rejected addresses represent 13.8 percent of the in-city addresses and correlate at $r = 0.972$ with the matched addresses by zip code.
[b] In New York, the most frequent counties of origin outside New York City are Westchester (48 cases), Suffolk (46 cases), and Ulster (20 cases).
[c] Outside of New York, the most frequent states/territories of origin are Puerto Rico (422 cases), New Jersey (244 cases), Pennsylvania (137 cases), California (117 cases), South Carolina (93 cases), North Carolina (90 cases), Connecticut (83 cases), and Massachusetts (81 cases).
[d] 12.5 percent missing in New York City, and 31.2 percent missing in Philadelphia.

city addresses, in-state non-Philadelphia addresses, and out-of-state addresses, but are composed largely of missing addresses. We conducted further analyses to determine the representativeness of the study population, including comparing the race and ethnicity of matched versus unmatched cases, comparing the geographicdistribution of in-city addresses (both those that did and those that did not match the respective base maps by zip code), and comparing the prior addresses of households with single and multiple admissions to shelter (see appendix for a more complete discussion).

Descriptive Measures of Area Variations in Homelessness Rates

Concentration by census tract. To analyze the two-dimensional concentration of the prior addresses of homeless households with thematic maps by census tract, we used the location quotient (LQ). The LQ is frequently used to identify the proportionate distribution of a given object group among areas (Bendavid-Val 1983). The LQ refers to the ratio of the fractional share of the subject of interest at the local level to the same ratio at the regional level (see appendix). This article uses the census tract as the equivalent of the local unit and the city or borough as the equivalent of the regional unit.[5]

Although the LQ is used to examine the two-dimensional aspects of a spatial distribution, other indices are required to quantify the relational aspects of that spatial distribution within and among jurisdictions. For this study, we selected three additional indices to measure these relational aspects: unevenness, contiguity, and clustering.

Unevenness. Unevenness refers to how unequally an object or social group is distributed among defined areas in a given jurisdiction. For example, a minority group is said to be "segregated" if it is unevenly distributed over census tracts in segregation studies (Massey and Denton 1988; White 1983). The most widely used measure of unevenness is the index of dissimilarity. It measures departure from evenness by taking the absolute deviation of the population-weighted mean of every census tract's object-group proportion from the city's object-group proportion and expressing that quantity as a proportion of its theoretical maximum (James and Taeuber 1985) (see Appendix).

Contiguity. A second distributional attribute is the degree of spatial contiguity. While unevenness deals with the distribution of an object group within a set of areal units overall, contiguity is concerned with the similarity in concentration between adjoining areal units. In this study, we used an index of spatial autocorrelation, Moran's *I* (Odland 1988), to measure the degree of contiguity (see Appendix).

Clustering. The third dimension to the spatial distribution of an object group is clustering. The contiguity index captures some aspects of clustering because it identifies the extent to which adjoining areas have similar concentrations of a given phenomenon. However, when the object group forms highly segregated enclaves in space, the contiguity index would fail to distinguish that type of clustering. Unfortunately, a proper measure of clustering for lattice data is not available in the literature. Therefore, we developed a clustering index based on our own definition of clustering, referring to the close spatial association of areas with a high concentration of that object group (see Appendix).

Regression Analyses

As stated in the conceptual model, we assume the number of the prior addresses of the shelter users in each census tract to be a function of demographic composition, economic factors, and housing and neighborhood characteristics in the census tract. The mathematical form of the model can be denoted as follows:

$$(1) \quad \log{(\mathrm{HR}_i)} = a + b(X_{1i}) + c(X_{2i}) + d(X_{3i}) + \epsilon_i,$$

where HR_i is the rate of shelter admission with the number of households in tract i; X_{1i} is the set of demographic variables in tract i; X_{2i} is the set of economic variables in tract i; X_{3i} is the set of housing and neighborhood variables in tract i; a is intercept; b, c, and d are sets of the coefficients corresponding to the sets of the explanatory variables X_1, X_2, and X_3 respectively; and ϵ_i is the error disturbance in tract i. Sample statistics for the variables are shown in Table 3.[6]

The ordinary least square (OLS) estimation is based on the assumption of constant error variance. However, data based on census tract contain sources of unequal error variance. Every census tract does not have the same physical size or equal population. Therefore, the shelter-admission rate in less-populated census tracts tends to fluctuate more than the rate in more populated census tracts. This situation can worsen when sheltered households are concentrated in smaller census tracts.

To test the existence of heteroskedasticity, we assumed the error variance to be a decreasing function (negative exponential) of the number of households in each cen-

TABLE 3. Sample Statistics

Variable	New York			Philadelphia		
	N	Mean	Corr.*	N	Mean	Corr.*
Demographic						
RBLACK	2,107	28,675	0.67	342	39,712	0.71
RSPAN	2,107	21,985	0.46	342	4,990	0.06
RUNDER18	2,107	21,823	0.64	342	22,027	0.46
ROVER64	2,107	13,427	−0.50	342	15,523	−0.24
RNOHIGH	2,107	21,433	0.46	342	22,225	0.36
RFHHOLD	2,107	19,325	0.82	342	31,992	0.79
RFYOUCHD	2,107	5,352	0.76	342	9,167	0.64
ROLDFAM	2,107	10,451	−0.44	342	18,676	−0.24
RSUBFAM	2,107	5,193	0.58	342	8,562	0.69
RGRPQUAT	2,107	1,000	0.09	342	2,507	−0.04
RFRBRN70	2,107	18,912	−0.05	342	3,810	−0.22
Economic						
RUNEMP	2,107	9,632	0.63	342	11,079	0.67
MNHHPAI	2,107	1,986	−0.52	342	3,897	−0.21
MEDHHINC	2,107	31,532	−0.58	342	25,783	−0.51
RNOPOV	2,107	19,268	0.75	342	20,028	0.68
RNOWORK	2,107	2,321	0.47	342	2,383	0.54
RTMPWORK	2,107	1,773	−0.11	342	2,101	−0.08
Housing and neighborhood quality						
MEDVALUE	2,008	203,004	−0.48	337	65,580	−0.45
MEDCOREN	2,107	489,000	−0.57	341	364,173	−0.56
RRENT	2,107	65,143	0.42	342	39,669	0.24
RENTHINC	2,107	1,720	0.54	341	1,542	0.15
RCROWD	2,107	1,657	0.34	342	0,383	0.31
RVAC	2,107	5,367	0.12	342	10,875	0.54
RBOARDUP	2,107	0,336	0.36	342	2,378	0.72
RNOHMLS	2,107	1,530	NA	342	1,239	NA
LRNOHMLS**	2,107	1,812	1.00	342	0,495	1.00

NA = not applicable.
* Correlation coefficient with the dependent variable (LRNOHMLS).
** LRNOHMLS is calculated as log (RNOHMLS + 1) to avoid missing values.

sus tract. Technically, the log of squared residuals from the OLS estimation is regressed with the number of households. The White test for the pooled OLS estimations reveals the existence of heteroskedasticity (New York: $\chi_2 = 35.6$, $p = 0.00$; Philadelphia: $\chi_2 = 2.66$, $p = 0.10$). To overcome heteroskedasticity, we used the square root of the estimated error variance for the weight for the final weighted least square (WLS) estimations.

Results

Descriptive Measures

In both cities in the aggregate, the distribution of homeless origins is more highly concentrated than the poverty distribution. Both cities have a lower proportion of cen-

TABLE 4. Shares of the Homeless Among Boroughs in New York (1987–1994) and Philadelphia (1990–1994)

| | New York | | | | | | Phila-delphia |
	Man-hattan	Bronx	Brooklyn	Queens	Staten Island	Total	
Number of families	305,368	291,978	563,283	495,625	99,464	1,755,718	381,339
Number of homeless families	11,207	15,475	16,875	4,927	639	49,123	5,056
Homeless/families (%)	3.67	5.30	2.99	0.99	0.64	2.80	1.33
Location quotient	1.31	1.89	1.07	0.36	0.23	NA	NA

NA = not available.

TABLE 5. Location Quotients of the Homeless (Number of Tracts and Percent of Total)

| | New York | | | | | | Phila-delphia |
Location quotient	Man-hattan	Bronx	Brooklyn	Queens	Staten Island	Total	
Zero	40	50	162	192	30	474	229
	13.84%	14.84%	21.07%	29.31%	30.61%	22.07%	65.62%
≤1.00	151	154	381	257	39	1,048	8
	52.25%	45.70%	49.54%	39.24%	39.80%	48.79%	2.29%
≥1.01	98	133	226	206	29	626	112
	33.91%	39.47%	29.39%	31.45%	29.59%	29.14%	32.09%
Total	289	337	769	655	98	2,148	349
Missing*	7	18	19	18	3	65	18

* Number of census tracts with population under 100.

sus tracts with an LQ greater than or equal to 1.01 for homelessness than for poverty, but a higher proportion of tracts with an LQ greater than 2.00 for homelessness than for poverty (see Tables 4, 5, and 6. Thus, while the poverty distributions are characterized by areas that are more broadly distributed but have moderately high concentration (LQ ≥ 1.01), the homeless distributions are characterized by areas that are less broadly distributed but have higher concentration (LQ > 2.00). Accordingly, poverty is a modest proxy for homelessness. The correlation coefficient between the two distributions (by LQ by census tract) is 0.558 in New York City and 0.640 in Philadelphia, as the relative shares of poverty are more widely distributed than the relative shares of homeless origins.

Within each city, the concentrations of homeless origins yield visually evident clusters as well. Nearly two-thirds (61 percent) of all homeless families from New York City from 1987 to 1994 were from the three major clusters: Harlem (15 percent of total), South Bronx (25 percent), and the Bedford-Stuyvesant-East New York neighborhoods (21 percent). Philadelphia also has three major clusters accounting for 67 percent of the homeless families' prior addresses: North Philadelphia (primarily west of Broad Street) (38 percent), West Philadelphia (20 percent), and South Philadelphia (primarily west of Broad Street) (9 percent).

TABLE 6. Location of Quotients of the Poor (below Poverty Level) (Number of Tracts and Pecent of Total)

Location quotient	New York City						Phila-delphia
	Man-hattan	Bronx	Brooklyn	Queens	Staten Island	Total	
Zero	7	12	13	20	4	56	15
	2.36%	3.45%	1.66%	2.99%	4.00%	2.55%	4.18%
≤1.00	152	185	483	413	87	1,387	198
	51.18%	53.16%	61.84%	61.83%	87.00%	63.22%	55.15%
≥1.01	138	151	285	235	9	751	146
	46.46%	43.39%	36.49%	35.18%	9.00%	34.23%	40.67%
Total	297	348	781	668	100	2,194	359
Missing*	1	7	8	5	1	22	8

* Number of census tracts with population of zero.

TABLE 7. Indices of Unevenness, Contiguity, and Clustering of the Homeless and the Poor

	New York						Philadelphia
	Manhattan	Bronx	Brooklyn	Queens	Staten Island	Total	
Unevenness							
Homeless	0.56	0.40	0.49	0.56	0.63	0.54	0.58
Poor	0.39	0.40	0.33	0.29	0.36	0.40	0.37
Contiguity							
Homeless	0.59	0.61	0.21	0.63	0.59	0.62	0.52
Poor	0.50	0.64	0.59	0.31	0.37	0.65	0.54
Clustering							
Homeless	0.81	0.84	0.87	0.83	0.80	0.86	0.85
Poor	0.75	0.84	0.79	0.73	0.72	0.80	0.72

The calculated indices of unevenness, contiguity, and clustering are given in Table 7. For unevenness, Staten Island scores the highest, and the Bronx scores the lowest among the five boroughs in New York. The homeless families' addresses are highly segregated in Staten Island, whereas in the Bronx, where a broad set of areas is affected, homeless origins are not highly segregated. With the exception of the Bronx, each of the boroughs has much higher unevenness, or more segregation, in the distribution of the homeless than of the poor. In New York overall, the unevenness index is 35 percent higher for the homeless distribution than for the poverty distribution, and in Philadelphia, the index is 57 percent higher for the distribution of homelessness than for poverty.

According to the clustering index created for this study, in four of the boroughs (Manhattan, Brooklyn, Queens, and Staten Island) and in both cities overall, origins of the homeless are, again, more clustered than those of the poor. The Bronx is the only jurisdiction with an equal clustering score for poverty and homelessness, again consistent with the other evidence showing a more widespread area of risk of homelessness that more closely parallels the poverty distribution.

TABLE 8. WLS Estimation Results for Pooled Samples

Variable	New York I		New York II		Philadelphia	
	Standard coefficient	p	Standard coefficient	p	Standard coefficient	p
Demographic						
RBLACK	0.363***	0.000	0.342***	0.000	0.219***	0.001
RSPAN	0.098***	0.000	0.081***	0.000	0.029	0.594
RUNDER18	−0.038**	0.033	−0.058***	0.001	−0.041	0.525
ROVER64	−0.121***	0.000	−0.124***	0.000	−0.025	0.771
RNOHIGH	0.080	0.000	0.057***	0.000	0.016	0.833
RFHHOLD	0.040	0.110	0.085***	0.001	0.201**	0.042
RFYOUCHD	0.186***	0.000	0.196***	0.000	0.007	0.928
ROLDFAM	0.014	0.448	0.008	0.659	0.050	0.449
RSUBFAM	0.091***	0.000	0.083***	0.000	0.089	0.121
RGRPQUAT	−0.003	0.791	−0.002	0.831	−0.047	0.234
RFRBNRN70	−0.148***	0.000			0.013	0.699
Economic						
RUNEMP	−0.001	0.980	0.018	0.472	0.201**	0.022
MNHHPAI	0.040*	0.072	0.064***	0.005	−0.024	0.701
MEDHHINC	0.062**	0.023	0.095***	0.001	−0.066	0.465
RNOPOV	0.204***	0.000	0.248***	0.000	0.264***	0.007
RNOWORK	0.042***	0.050	0.024	0.272	−0.181**	0.013
RTMPWORK	0.006	0.565	0.006	0.553	0.084*	0.051
Housing and neighborhood quality						
MEDCOREN	−0.080***	0.001	−0.128***	0.000	0.029	0.723
RRENT	0.008	0.666	−0.025	0.183	0.034	0.573
RENTHINC	0.072***	0.000	0.082***	0.000	−0.150**	0.027
RCROWD	0.049***	0.001	−0.034***	0.005	−0.135**	0.031

Regression Results

New York, pooled sample. Among the demographic variables, indeed among all variables in the model, the proportion of African-American persons in a tract is the most important predictor, in terms of the standardized coefficient (Table 8). The ratio of female-headed households with children under age six is the second strongest predictor among demographic variables, even though a variable for the ratio of female-headed households is included and is nearly significant in the predicted direction βi = 0.040, p = 0.110). Contrary to our hypothesis, tracts with more immigrant households are less likely to have shelter admissions. When this variable is removed in New York Model II, the sign for crowding reverses to become negative, suggesting that there is a positive relationship between immigrant communities and crowding that reduces the likelihood of shelter admissions. Coefficients for other demographic variables—such as the ratio of persons without a high school diploma, the ratio of subfamilies (families with children who are part of a larger household), and the ratio of Hispanic households—are significant and in the predicted positive direction, though of relatively lower magnitude. The ratio of persons under 18 was negatively associated with shelter admissions (opposite the predicted direction), as was the ratio of persons over the age of 64. The coefficient for the variable for older families with children is in the predicted direction, and the coefficient for the variable for persons in group quarters is opposite the predicted direction, but neither is statistically significant.

Among economic variables, the ratio of poor households is the most important factor. The coefficient for the rate of labor force nonparticipation is also significant and in the predicted direction. The effect of the ratio of temporarily employed persons is not significant but is in the predicted direction. Effects of the ratio of unemployed persons and the mean household public assistance income variables are not significant, although the public assistance variable is nearly significant in the positive direction. The effect of median household income, which is opposite the predicted direction and statistically significant, may proxy for housing market tightness.

Among the housing and neighborhood quality factors, the rent-to-income ratio is significant and positively associated with the rate of shelter admission. The association of median contract rent is negative and significant, as expected. The effect of the ratio of rental units in an area is not significant. All of the other neighborhood quality variables are significant and positively associated with the rate of shelter admission, including the vacancy rate, the ratio of boarded-up buildings, and the ratio of housing crowding.

Philadelphia. In general, the Philadelphia regression results produced findings qualitatively similar to those of New York, though fewer variables achieved a level of statistical significance. Once again, the proportion of African-American persons produced the most significant positive coefficient among demographic variables and, in Philadelphia, is the second most important predictor as measured by the standardized coefficient. The effect of the ratio of female-headed households is also significant and positive. Coefficients for the other variables are in the same direction as in New York (with the exception of percent foreign born) but do not reach statistical significance.

Among the economic factors, again, the ratio of poor persons is an important predictor (and the largest standardized coefficient in the Philadelphia model). Median household income is negatively associated but not significant. The impacts of the unemployment rate and the proportion of temporary workers are also significant (nearly significant in the case of temporary workers, $p = 0.051$) and positively correspond to the rate of shelter admission, although neither was significant in New York. The coefficient for mean public assistance income is not significant. The coefficient for persons not in the labor force is negative, opposite that found in New York.

Among the housing and neighborhood variables (including median contract rent as a control variable), the most significant predictor (and among the most important variables in the Philadelphia model overall) is the proportion of boarded-up buildings. Coefficients for both the crowding and the rent-to-income ratio variables are significant, but with negative signs (opposite that found for New York), suggesting that homeless families in Philadelphia come from areas that are less crowded and more "affordable" than other parts of the city, perhaps because of the low neighborhood quality and the comparatively lower cost of housing in Philadelphia. Coefficients for the vacancy rate and proportion of rental units variables are not significant.

New York, comparison between low-income and higher income areas. We used median household income to define low- and higher-income areas in New York, with the city-

TABLE 9 WLS Estimation Resuls for Low- and Higher-Income Areas in New York

Variable	Higher-Income Tracts		Low-Income Tracts	
	Standard coefficient	p	Standard coefficient	p
Demographic				
RBLACK	0.567***	0.000	0.362***	0.000
RSPAN	0.150***	0.000	0.096***	0.000
RUNDER18	−0.015	0.553	−0.038	0.158
ROVER64	−0.173***	0.000	−0.104***	0.001
RNOHIGH	0.068***	0.007	0.075***	0.000
RFHHOLD	−0.015	0.663	0.037	0.325
RFYOUCHD	0.079***	0.001	0.187***	0.000
ROLDFAM	−0.019	0.570	0.031	0.213
RSUBFAM	0.226***	0.000	0.082***	0.000
RGRPQUAT	−0.050**	0.026	0.030*	0.053
RFRBRN70	−0.203***	0.000	−0.130***	0.000
Economic				
RUNEMP	−0.058	0.208	−0.050	0.151
MNHHPAI	0.168***	0.000	−0.041	0.231
MEDHHINC	−0.028	0.660	0.045	0.429
RNOPOV	0.120***	0.000	0.149***	0.000
RNOWORK	0.100**	0.025	0.077**	0.012
RTMPWORK	−0.002	0.916	0.002	0.901
Housing and neighborhood quality				
MEDCOREN	0.053	0.380	−0.161***	0.000
RRENT	0.076***	0.007	−0.064***	0.004
RENTHINC	−0.028	0.616	0.091**	0.011
RCROWD	0.069***	0.007	0.043**	0.029
RVAC	0.051**	0.020	0.093***	0.000
RBOARDUP	0.096***	0.000	0.041**	0.016
N	1,031		1,030	
R^2	0.704		0.809	

* $p < 0.10$. ** $p < 0.05$. *** $p < 0.01$.

wide median value of each tract's median household income as the break point. In New York, census tracts that have a median household income lower than \$30,609 are categorized as low-income neighborhoods and the remainder as higher-income.[7]

Results for most demographic variables are similar to those of the pooled sample (Table 9). Coefficients relating to the proportion of African American persons, Hispanics, female-headed households with young children, subfamilies, immigrants, and persons lacking a high school education are all significant and have the same sign in both areas as in the pooled sample.

Among economic factors, effects of the poverty rate and the rate of labor force nonparticipation are also positive and significant in both areas. However, the mean household public assistance income is now significant and positive in predicting shelter admissions in high-income areas, but negative (though not significant) in low-income areas. Unemployment and temporary work remain not significant.

Among the housing and neighborhood variables, the impact of the proportion of rental units is now significant in both areas, though positively associated in high-income tracts and negatively associated in low-income tracts. The positive association of homelessness to an area's rent-to-income ratio holds only in low-income tracts. The neighborhood quality variables (crowding, vacancy, boarded-up buildings) are all positively associated and significant.

Discussion

While homeless households appear to come from areas with high rates of poverty, areas with the greatest risk of homelessness are generally more densely clustered than poor areas. In both cities, the distribution of homeless families' prior addresses is more highly segregated than the poverty distributions. An exception to this pattern is the Bronx, where the rate of shelter admissions is more evenly distributed among the borough's poor neighborhoods, and where the level of risk appears generally high. But, in general, homeless families come primarily from a subset of poor neighborhoods where some additional set factors contribute to their increased risk of public shelter admission.

The regression results support several of the hypotheses concerning the neighborhood characteristics associated with the rate of public-shelter admissions among families. We will focus primarily on the New York regression results, which benefited from more observations (census tracts) and thus greater statistical power. We will discuss the Philadelphia results in light of differences between the two cities.

The rate of public-shelter admissions from an area increases with the proportion of African Americans and female-headed households (FHH), particularly those with young children, and to a lesser extent with Hispanic households. These results were predicted, based on previous research, which has shown that homeless families are disproportionately composed of minorities and FHH. Variables for race and FHH with young children continue to be strongly associated with the rate of shelter admission, even controlling for the rate of poverty, welfare receipt, educational attainment, and various housing and labor market variables, which indicates that such households face additional barriers to residential stability not specified in this model.

Areas with high concentrations of FHH may be at greater risk because of a higher level of risk among individuals in those areas, such as having more limited social network size, higher rates of substance abuse and mental-health problems, and other individual risk factors. However, research comparing housed and homeless Aid to Families with Dependent Children recipients in New York City has shown that there are few such differences in individual risk factors among public assistance recipients and that such individual risk factors affect a relatively small proportion of families entering shelters (Knickman and Weitzman 1989). In addition to these individual-level effects, it is likely that other social and economic barriers, such as restricted residential mobility, limited labor-market access, and various neighborhood effects, have a differential negative impact on FHH with young children and contribute to both their concentration in low-rent areas and their increased risk of public-shelter admission.

A similar set of dynamics may contribute to race and poverty concentrations in a neighborhood, which are among the most significant predictors of shelter admissions for both cities. Again, the increased risk of shelter admission may be partially attributable to a larger number of individual-level risk factors among such groups. However, research has found that race has an additional positive effect on public-shelter use that has not been explained by individual risk factors. For example, African American single adults in Philadelphia have been found to have a significantly longer homelessness duration (controlling for history of mental health and substance-abuse treatment), and African American homeless families in New York City have been found to have a significantly higher probability of readmission to shelters (controlling for homelessness and type of shelter discharge) (Culhane and Kuhn 1995; Wong, Culhane, and Kuhn forthcoming). Thus, apart from individual risk factors, other social and economic factors are likely to contribute to the differential exposure of predominantly African-American and poor neighborhoods to the risk of public-shelter admission. For example, the high degree of spatial clustering among homeless families' prior addresses found in the descriptive results and the significance of the effects of race and poverty concentration suggest that processes of racial and economic segregation contribute to the increased risk of shelter admission. Such an effect would be consistent with research on the impact of segregation on housing and neighborhood quality. Massey and Denton (1993) have found that increasing racial segregation has interacted with declining income to produce higher poverty concentrations among African Americans over the past two decades, which the authors argue has promoted disinvestment in these communities by concentrating tenants with a decreasing ability to pay market rents in financially distressed buildings. This concentration can produce a "hollowing out" effect, in which units and buildings are more likely to be left vacant or abandoned, a portrait consistent with the neighborhoods identified in this study as being at greatest risk of generating homelessness. Housing market forces and government policies may contribute to increases in spatial stratification by income and race (Schill and Wachter 1995).

The finding that homeless families come from areas with more subfamilies, together with the significance of the crowding variable, provides empirical support for the hypothesis that homelessness is one consequence of "doubling up" in an area. Families doubling up are presumably doing so because of a lack of income for independent household formation. Aside from being at greater risk of a housing emergency because of crowding, people in doubled-up arrangements may also expend sources of social support more quickly in the event of a crisis. For example, people in subfamilies are often already living with parents or other family members prior to public-shelter admission; thus, they have exhausted some of the housing alternatives to which others might have access in the event of a housing emergency.

The interesting exception to the heightened risk associated with crowding is found among recent immigrants. The reversal of the sign relating to the crowding variable in the New York Model II, when the ratio for foreign-born persons is excluded from the regression analysis, suggests that immigrant groups mitigate the risk of homelessness by increased crowding. Such groups may have developed adaptations to crowding that prevent or resolve housing emergencies. Alternatively, such persons may be less willing to seek the support of the public-shelter system, even though they may need its services. This area deserves further study, as immigrant communities' accommodations to crowding may help to inform the design of prevention efforts for other communities and families confronting crowding or, alternatively, may reveal a greater need for outreach to immigrant families in need of public shelter. Further research on accommodations to housing distress may also help to explain differences in shelter admissions by race and ethnicity.

The results provide support for hypotheses that family homelessness is related to housing and neighborhood conditions. Homeless families often come from deteriorated and low-rent neighborhoods, as measured by the ratio of boarded-up buildings (among the most important variables in the Philadelphia model) and the median contract rent. Homeless families are also more likely to come from neighborhoods with higher vacancy rates, suggesting that these areas are viewed as relatively undesirable and that the rental housing in these areas is at risk of undermaintenance and abandonment. Affordability matters as well, as indicated by the positive effect of the rent-to-income ratio, confirming the hypothesis that shelter admissions are more likely to occur in areas with a relatively greater rent burden.

The Philadelphia data generally support the findings from New York, though with less statistical significance. Some differences are worth noting, particularly because they might be a function of differences in housing and labor markets, as well as in public policies between the two cities. Among the demographic variables, the effect of the ratio of foreign-born persons immigrating since 1970 is not significant in Philadelphia, nor is the effect of the Hispanic variable. Hispanics constitute a relatively small proportion of the population in Philadelphia (5.6 percent versus 24.4 percent in New York) and are known to be underrepresented among shelter users there. Hispanics and recent immigrants in Philadelphia may be subject to dynamics similar to those of the recent immigrants in New York, whose relatively greater crowding may be an alternate accommodation to housing distress.

Among economic variables, unemployment is significantly related to shelter admission rates in Philadelphia but not in New York. This finding may indicate a relatively greater problem of unemployment in some of that city's neighborhoods. (However, the effect of the rate of labor force nonparticipation is significant and positively related to shelter admissions in New York.) The importance of labor market opportunities as a contributing factor in Philadelphia is amplified by the added positive significance of persons temporarily employed.

Finally, among the housing and neighborhood variables, the negative association between the rent-to-income ratio and the rate of shelter admission likely reflects the comparatively lower cost of housing in low-rent areas in Philadelphia (compared with New York), because population loss has resulted in higher vacancy rates. The relatively greater importance of abandonment as a predictor in Philadelphia compared with New York could also be related to Philadelphia's continuing population loss, as well as the higher rate of immigration in New York, where immigrants fill some of the low-cost housing that might otherwise have been left vacant. Differences between cities in the disposition of abandoned and tax-foreclosed properties may also help to explain the more limited effect of abandonment in New York, where local government has assumed more direct responsibility for the management and rehabilitation of tax-foreclosed properties.

Separating tracts by median income in New York also produced some interesting differences from the pooled sample. First, the model performed better for low-income than for higher-income tracts. However, among higher-income tracts, the ratio of African-American persons increases in importance in terms of the standardized coefficient, again raising concerns about the increased risk of homelessness among African-American communities, even those with relatively higher income. The effect of the proportion of rental units also appears more significant in these models, tending to be positive in the case of higher-income areas and significantly negative in low-income areas. This finding may suggest that in low-income areas, homeowner-related housing problems, such as the inability of aging parents or their adult children to maintain the costs of the home, may play a role in increasing the risk of homelessness. In higher-income areas, homelessness is more often related to problems with rental housing and its unaffordability.

From a policy perspective, this research offers two broad insights. First, because the risk of family homelessness is spatially and demographically concentrated, homelessness prevention and outreach efforts would likely benefit from a geographic- and population-targeted strategy. Policies designed to counteract residential segregation, concentrated poverty, and poor housing and neighborhood conditions, as well as more narrowly defined homelessness-prevention programs, could target the neighborhoods found to be at greatest risk for generating shelter admissions in this study and the population groups they over-represent. Second, this study has identified some of the associated factors that could guide the substance of a prevention-oriented policy strategy. For example, improved household income, through expanded rental assistance, improved access to employment income, or increased public assistance benefits, would reduce the poverty and housing unaffordability that this study found to be associated with a higher rate of shelter admission. An income support or housing-subsidy program could also reduce crowding, vacancies, and possibly abandonment, as well as the potential reinforcing effect of these problems on the risk of shelter admissions. Further research is needed to model and test the impact of such policy strategies.

Our study was limited in that the dependent variable represented an aggregation of homeless families' responses to a single query regarding their prior address. Although intake forms for both cities' systems provide some standardization for collecting information, there are no scripts for collecting information from people seeking shelter admission. Some unknown rate of false reporting could also occur because people are responding to questions that partly determine their access to or eligibility for services. Moreover, having found significant and theoretically consistent associations among neighborhood-level variables, the study's results do not diminish the importance of other levels of causal influence, such as intercity effects, emergency-assistance policies, household dynamics, behavioral adaptations, or other individual risk variables. Each of these may influence who among the persons in these areas is at greatest risk of shelter admission and how that risk is distributed geographically. A multilevel or hierarchical analysis would be necessary to examine the differential impact of these factors in a more systematic manner.

Finally, future research should further develop and refine this analytic approach for studying homelessness. This study was limited in treating shelter-admission data and predictive variables cross-sectionally, whereas a more time-sensitive treatment of these variables would be better able to capture the dynamics of change, including population composition, neighborhood quality, and housing conditions. This study was also limited by an aggregation of variables at the level of the census tract, whereas further analyses could examine the block-group-level predictors or even the characteristics of specific properties associated with the risk of shelter admission. The analysis could also be further refined by including various spatial measures in the specification of the regression model: Researchers should consider replicating this work in other localities. Such research could be undertaken in areas without computerized shelter-tracking systems by selecting a representative sample of shelter admissions over a given period of time and surveying people about their housing history. The prior-address data could be enhanced by including more detailed questions regarding the housing arrangements of clients. Such an approach would bring greater depth to the understanding of the interaction of neighborhood- and household-level dynamics of housing instability than we could discern with the data available for this study.

Conclusion

This study has provided empirical support for several hypotheses regarding the influence of housing and income problems in generating homelessness in New York City and Philadelphia, particularly as they disproportionately affect women with young children and Mexican Americans. The rate of public shelter admission was found to be associated with housing crowding, residence in subfamilies, poverty, restricted access to the labor market, rent burden, and poor neighborhood quality. Future public policies should consider the role of geographic and demographic variations in the risk of homelessness in designing interventions to reduce that risk.

Appendix

Qualifications of the study population. To assess the degree of bias in the selection of the matched versus unmatched cases, we conducted t tests comparing the groups in each respective city by race and gender of household head (see Table A-I). In New York, the matched addresses were significantly more likely to be composed of African-American households ($t = 11.445$, $p < 0.0001$). The matched addresses were also significantly less likely to be composed of Hispanic households ($t = -7.851$, $p < 0.0001$). However, as shown in Table A-I, none of the mean differences between groups was large enough to warrant great concern with the representative ness of the study population ($+5.8$ percentage point difference for African American and -3.9 for Hispanic). Neverthe-

TABLE A-1. Demographics of Matched and Nonmatched Samples in Philadelphia and New York

		African American	Hispanic
Philadelphia			
Matched sample	Proportion	0.917	0.036
	N	5,332	5,098
Nonmatched sample	Proportion	0.875	0.058
	N	3,745	3,497
t test for H0	t	41,897	23,181
	p	0.000	0.000
	Result	Can reject H0	Can reject H0
New York			
Matched sample	Proportion	0.651	0.325
	N	36,296	36,296
Nonmatched sample	Proportion	0.593	0.364
	N	12,427	12,417
t test for H0	t	11,445	−7,851
	p	0.000	0.000
	Result	Can reject H0	Can reject H0

Notes: Total number of observations varies due to missing values. H0 = null hypothesis. The means between matched and nonmatched samples are the same.

TABLE A-2. Correlations Between the Number of Homeless Families in Each Zip Code in New York and Philadelphia

Pair of comparison	New York	Philadelphia
Address-matched and nonmatched sample	0.877	0.972
Single and multiple admissions	0.992	0.999

less, study findings will remain qualified by the fact that the study population for New York City is slightly more likely to represent African American households and slightly less likely to represent Hispanics than the overall homeless family population.

In Philadelphia, the address-matched group (the study population) is more likely to include African-American households $(t = 41.897, p < 0.0001)$ and to under represent Hispanic households $(t = 23.181, p < 0.0001)$. Again, the mean differences are not large ($+4.2$ percentage points for African American and -2.2 for Hispanic).

We undertook an additional procedure to assess whether a geographically distributed bias operated in the matching and rejection of reported addresses *within* each city by the geo-coding procedures. It is possible that inaccurate base maps or systematically unconventional address reporting resulted in a biased distribution of matched versus rejected in-city addresses. Matched and rejected addresses within each city were thus geo-coded by zip code, and the correlation coefficient was computed between the distributions (see Table A-2). The matched and rejected addresses are highly similar in distribution in New York City ($r = 0.877$) and nearly identical in Philadelphia ($r = 0.972$), showing that the geographic distribution of the study population in both cities is highly representative of all households reporting in-city addresses, at the zip code level (see Table A-2).

Finally, because these systems were designed for management and not research purposes, both systems are limited in that households with multiple admissions to shelters have their prior address information overwritten at the time of subsequent readmissions. In other words, an address history is not retained for households with multiple shelter admissions. It is conceivable that households readmitted to shelters may have a significantly different locational distribution than households presenting to shelters for the first time. For example, households with multiple admissions may be disproportionately discharged by shelter programs to housing in more or less stable areas relative to the locational origins of households with a single admission. To assess the degree of bias introduced by this possibility, and to assess whether single- and multiple-admission households should be separated for the purposes of the distributional measurements for this study, the correlation between the distribution of prior addresses for households with single versus multiple admissions by zip code for all matched addresses was computed in both cities. Again, however, the distributions are highly similar in New York City ($r = 0.992$) and Philadelphia ($r = 0.999$), suggesting that such a locational difference does not occur at the zip code level and would not warrant further adjustment (see Table A-2). Measures of area variations in homelessness rates include the location quotient, unevenness, contiguity, and clustering.

The location quotient (LQ). The LQ cannot have a value less than zero. When the LQ in a locality is greater than 1.00, the locality has a higher concentration of the subject of interest relative to the other localities of the region combined. Thus, the LQ is used to identify census tracts that contain a higher percentage share of the prior addresses of the homeless, the poor (people below poverty level, as reported in 1990 census), and minority poor than that of Philadelphia or New York as a whole. Because of its unitlessness and absolutivity, the LQ also permits intercity and interborough comparisons of the spatial distribution of the subject of interest.

Unevenness. The dissimilarity index varies between 0 and 1, and conceptually it represents the proportion of an object group that would have to change its location to achieve an even distribution. The dissimilarity index is calculated as follows:

$$(A.1) \quad \text{Dissimilarity} = \sum_i \left[\frac{t_i |r_i - R|}{2TR(1 - R)} \right],$$

where t_i is population of areal unit i; r_i is homeless proportion of areal unit i; and T and R are the total population and the proportion of an object group in the whole, respectively.

Contiguity. The difference between contiguity and unevenness is well illustrated by comparing the case of the "checkerboard problem" (White 1983); highly concentrated areas are located in a scattered fashion like the dark squares on a checkerboard, with a pattern in which the dark and light areas are each clustered together to form two halves on the board (one light, one dark). Both patterns yield the same unevenness index value, although they clearly have different distributional patterns in terms of spatial association. A contiguity index is used to capture this difference in spatial association. In this study, we used an index of spatial autocorrelation to measure the degree of contiguity. If objects that are similar in location also tend to be similar in attributes, the pattern as a whole is said to show positive autocorrelation. Conversely, if objects that are close together in space tend to be more dissimilar in attributes than objects that are farther apart, then negative spatial autocorrelation is displayed (Shen 1994). Moran's I is used to calculate spatial autocorrelation, and its mathematical notation is as follows (Odland 1988):

$$(A.2) \quad I = \frac{n}{\sum_i \sum_j w_{ij}} \frac{\sum_i \sum_j w_{ij}(p_i - \bar{p})(p_j - \bar{p})}{\sum_i (p_i - \bar{p})^2}.$$

where n is the number of census tracts; the double summation indicates summation over all pairs of tracts; p_i is the ratio of an object group of tract i to the population of tract i; p is the mean of p_i; and w_{ij} is a proximity weight for the pair of tract i and tract j, which is 0 when i equals j.

In the geographic literature, the quantity w_{ij} refers to an element in the "contiguity matrix" that equals 1 when census tracts i and j are contiguous and 0 otherwise. In this article, adjacent tracts of every census tract were identified by using a geographic information system.

Clustering. As a first step in creating a clustering index, we divided census tracts into two groups, based on the LQ: highly concentrated census tracts and census tracts with low concentrations. When two highly concentrated tracts are adjacent to each other, the common boundary lines are deleted and the two polygons of the tracts are merged to form one polygon. If this merging process keeps going, a few polygons that represent highly concentrated areas are obtained. The more unevenly distributed an object group is, the smaller number of tracts categorized as the highly concentrated area will be. The more clustered the highly concentrated tracts are, the more common boundaries are erased, and the smaller the ratio of the sum of the perimeters of the merged polygons to the sum of the perimeters of the original areal units will be. In this concept, the clustering index (CI) can be denoted as follows:

$$(A.3) \quad \text{CI} = 1 - \frac{\sum_{i'} \sum_{j'} b_{i'j'}}{\sum_i \sum_j b_{ij}},$$

where b_{ij} is the length of common boundary between census tracts i and j before polygon merging; i' and j' are a pair of census tracts that form the boundaries between the highly concentrated areas and the sparsely concentrated areas.

In the checkerboard example, the sum of the perimeters of highly concentrated polygons persists after the merging process, and CI will be 0. In the opposite extreme, when the object group is concentrated in a few census tracts adjacent to one another, a single highly concentrated polygon will remain after the polygon merging process, and CI will be close to 1 but not exceed 1 (see Lee and Culhane 1995 for diagrammatic examples).

Recently, Wong (1993) formulated a new segregation index that uses the length of the common boundary of two areas as an indicator of the degree of social interaction between the residents of the two areas. In a similar context, the total length of common boundaries between the two areal groups (for racial segregation, minority area, and majority area) may be interpreted as the total possibility of social interaction between the two groups. The total length of the common boundaries between the areas belonging to the same areal group may be interpreted as the total possibility of social interaction within a group. Therefore, the clustering index measures how small total social interaction between the two groups is compared to the sum of total interaction between the two groups and total interaction within groups.

Reprinted from Dennis P. Culhane, Chang-Moo Lee, and Susan M. Wachter, Where the homeless come from: A study of the prior address distribution of families admitted to public shelters in New York City and Philadelphia. *Housing Policy Debate* 7 (1996): 327–65. ©1996 Fannie Mae Foundation, Washington, D.C.; reprinted by permission.

Notes

1. Paradoxically, the opposite could also occur, as may occur in some programs that require a minimum stay to become eligible for exit programs, or as may occur as a result of increased demand for emergency shelter to obtain access to exit programs.

2. Kondratas (1994) observed that the Bush administration plan also emphasized homelessness prevention and the integration of homeless populations into mainstream social programs.

3. Regardless of the particular merits or shortcomings of many in those proposals, their future in uncertain in light of recent changes in the composition of the U.S. Congress.

4. Some persons may be admitted to a shelter with a non-Philadelphia street address because they can otherwise prove that they have been in Philadelphia for a minimum of six weeks (thereby meeting the residency requirement), because they are sheltered as part of the mandatory shelter provision policy in effect on extremely cold or hot days, or because they have been admitted in violation of policy. Some persons do not report a prior address because they enter the shelter system after-hours (after 5 P.M.), thereby avoiding the complete intake interview. Families are permitted to avoid the intake interview if they stay for only one night; they are required to complete the intake interview if they stay for consecutive nights.

5. Census tracts with populations under 100 were omitted from both the descriptive and the regression analyses to avoid the outlier effects produced by small denominators.

6. In terms of explanatory variables, median property value (MEDVALUE) is missing in 99 census tracts in New York. The census tracts are mostly low-income neighborhoods that are our main areas of interest (the mean of MEDHHINC in the 99 tracts is $20,090, while the mean of all the tracts is $31,532). MEDVALUE is presumably missing in these tracts because it measures owner-occupied property values, and these areas may have too few owner-occupied properties. We dropped MEDVALUE in the final model specification, since MEDVALUE was not statistically significant in the exploratory model specifications and the loss of the observations is so large that it may produce a biased result.

7. We did not make a similar comparison for Philadelphia because there were too few observations. We used the Chow test to check for structural differences with the null hypothesis that the regressions of the low- and high-income groups are identical. The results show that there are structural differences at a statistically significant level ($F_{22, 2107} = 6.12$, $p = 0.00$).

References

Applebaum, Richard, M. Dolny, Peter Dreier, and John Gilberbloom (1991). Scapegoating Rent Control: Masking the Causes of Homelessness. *Journal of the American Planning Association* 57: 153–64.

———— (1992). Sham Rent Control Research: A Further Reply. *Journal of the American Planning Association* 58: 220–24.

Bendavid-Val, Avrom. 1983. *Regional and Local Economic Analysis for Practitioners*. New York: Praeger.

Blau, Joel (1992). *The Visible Poor: Homelessness in the United States*. New York: Oxford University Press.

Burt, Martha (1992). *Over the Edge: The Growth of Homelessness in the 1980s*. New York and Washington: Sage and Urban Institute Press.

———— (1994). Comment. *Housing Policy Debate* 5 (2): 141–52.

Culhane, Dennis P. (1990). The Social Selection Processes of Homelessness. In On Becoming Homeless: The Structural and Experiential Dynamics of Residential Instability, Ph.D. dissertation, Boston College. 135–47.

———— (1992). The Quandaries of Shelter Reform: An Appraisal of Efforts to "Manage" Homelessness. *Social Service Review* 66 (3): 428–40.

Culhane, Dennis P., Edmund F. Dejowski, Julie Ibanez, Elizabeth Needham, and Irene Macchia (1994). Public Shelter Admission Rates in Philadelphia and New York City: The Implications of Turnover for Sheltered Population Counts. *Housing Policy Debate* 5 (2): 107–40.

Culhane, Dennis P., and Randall Kuhn (1995) Patterns and Determinants of Shelter Utilization Among Single Adults in New York City and Philadelphia: A Longitudinal Analysis of Homelessness. Paper presented at the Annual Meeting of the Eastern Sociological Association, March 31, Philadelphia.

Elliot, Marta, and Lauren J. Krivo (1991). Structural Determinants of Homelessness in the U.S. *Social Problems* 38 (1): 113–31.

Fournier, Louise, Malijai Caulet, Gilles Cote, Jean Toupin, Maurice Ohayon, Micheline Ostoj, and Isabelle Laurin (1994). Longitudinal Study of the New Homeless: Preliminary Results. Paper presented at the Annual Meeting of the American Public Health Association, November 1, Washington, D.C.

Hopper, Kim (1990). The New Urban Niche of Homelessness: New York City in the Late 1980s. *Bulletin of the New York Academy of Medicine* 66 (5): 435–50.

———— (1995). Definitional Quandaries and Other Hazards in Counting the Homeless: An Invited Commentary. *American Journal of Orthopsychiatry* 65 (3): 340–46.

Hopper, Kim, and Jill Hamberg (1986). The Making of America's Homeless: From Skid Row to New Poor, 1945–1986. In Rachel Bratt, Chester Hartman, and Ann Meyerson *Critical Perspectives on Housing*, 12–40. Philadelphia: Temple University Press.

Interagency Council for the Homeless (1994). *Priority Home: The Federal Plan to Break the Cycle of Homelessness*. Washington, D.C.: U.S. Department of Housing and Urban Development.

Jahiel, Rene (1992). Toward the Prevention of Homelessness. In Rene Jahiel, ed., *Homelessness: A Prevention Oriented Approach*, 315–36. Baltimore: Johns Hopkins University Press.

James, David R., and Karl E. Taeuber. 1985. Measures of Segregation. In Nancy Tuma, ed., *Sociological Methodology 1985*, 1–32. San Francisco: Jossey-Bass.

Kearns, Robin A., and Christopher J. Smith (1994). Housing, Homelessness and Mental Health: Mapping an Agenda for Geographical Inquiry. *Professional Geographer* 46 (4): 418–24.

Knickman, James, and Beth Weitzman (1989). *Forecasting Models to Target Families at High Risk of Homelessness*. New York: New York University Health Research Program.

Koegel, Paul, and M. Audrey Burnam (1994). The Course of Homelessness Among Homeless Adults in Los Angeles. Paper presented at the Annual Meeting of the American Public Health Association, November 1, Washington, D.C.

Kondratas, Anna (1994). Comment. *Housing Policy Debate* 5 (2): 153–62.

Lee, Chang-Moo, and Dennis P. Culhane (1995). The Spatial Distribution of Homelessness Occurrence and the Efficacy of Shelter Programs in Philadelphia. Wharton Real Estate Center Working Paper 213, University of Pennsylvania.

Lindblom, Eric N. (1991). Toward a Comprehensive Homelessness-Prevention Strategy. *Housing Policy Debate* 2 (3): 631–47.

Link, Bruce G., Ezra Susser, Anne Stueve, Jo Phelan, Robert E. Moore, and Elmer Struening (1994). Lifetime and Five-Year Prevalence of Homelessness in the United States. *American Journal of Public Health* 84: 1907–12.

Massey, Douglas S., and Nancy A. Denton (1988). The Dimensions of Residential Segregation. *Social Forces* 67 (2): 281–315.

——— (1993). *American Apartheid: Segregation and the Making of the American Underclass*. Cambridge, Mass.: Harvard University Press.

Odland, John. (1988). *Spatial Autocorrelation*. New York: Sage.

Piliavin, Irving, Michael Sosin, Alex H. Westerfelt, and Ross L. Matsueda (1993). The Duration of Homeless Careers: An Exploratory Study. *Social Service Review* 67: 576–98.

Quigley, J. (1991). Does Rent Control Cause Homelessness? Taking the Claim Seriously. *Journal of Policy Analysis and Management* 9: 89–93.

Ringheim, Karen (1990). *At Risk of Homelessness: The Roles of Income and Rent*. New York: Praeger.

Robertson, Marjorie J., Cheryl Zlotnick, and Alex Westerfelt (1994). The Course of Homelessness Among Adults and Families in Alameda County. Paper presented at the Annual Meeting of the American Public Health Association, November 1, Washington, D.C.

Rossi, Peter (1989). *Down and Out in America*. Chicago: University of Chicago Press.

——— (1994). Comment on Dennis P. Culhane et al.'s "Public Shelter Admission Rates in Philadelphia and New York City: The Implications of Turnover for Sheltered Population Counts." *Housing Policy Debate* 5 (2): 163–76.

Schill, Michael H., and Susan M. Wachter (1995). Housing Market Constraints and Spatial Stratification by Income and Race. *Housing Policy Debate* 6 (1): 141–67.

Shen, Qing (1994). An Application of GIS to the Measurement of Spatial Autocorrelation. *Computer, Environment, and Urban Systems* 18 (3): 167–91.

Stegman, Michael A. 1993. *Housing and Vacancy Report: New York City, 1991*. New York: Department of Housing Preservation and Development.

Tucker, W. (1987). Where Do the Homeless Come From? *National Review*, September, 32–45.

U.S. Department of Commerce. 1993. *TIGER/Line 1992*. Washington, DC: Bureau of Data User Services Division.

U.S. Department of Health and Human Services (1991). *Homelessness Prevention Programs*. Washington, D.C.: Office of the Inspector General.

U.S. Department of Housing and Urban Development. (1984). *A Report to the Secretary on the Homeless and Emergency Shelters*. Washington, D.C.: Office of Policy Development and Research.

Wallace, Roderick (1989). "Homelessness," Contagious Destruction of Housing and Municipal Service Cuts in New York City: 1. Demographics of a Housing Deficit. *Environment and Planning A* 21: 1585–1603.

Wallace, Roderick (1990). "Homelessness," Contagious Destruction of Housing and Municipal Service Cuts in New York City: 2. Dynamics of a Housing Famine. *Environment and Planning A* 22: 5–15.

White, Michael J. (1983). The Measurement of Spatial Segregation. *American Journal of Sociology* 88 (5):1008–18.

Wolch, Jennifer, and Michael Dear (1993). *Malign Neglect*. San Francisco: Jossey-Bass.

Wong, David W. S. 1993. Spatial Indices of Segregation. *Urban Studies* 30 (3): 559–72.

Wong, Irene, Dennis P. Culhane, and Randall Kuhn. Forthcoming. Predictors of Shelter Exit and Return Among Homeless Families in New York City. Available from authors, University of Pennsylvania.

Wright, James D., and Joel A. Devine (1995). Housing Dynamics of the Homeless: Implicationsor a Count. *American Journal of Orthopsychiatry* 65 (3): 320–29.

Commentary

Dennis P. Culhane

For much of the last decade, my work has focused on the integration of administrative data, or records which are gathered by public agencies as part of their regular business activities, to better understand both homelessness and measures of neighborhood environments. When I joined the School of Social Policy & Practice (then the School of Social Work) in 1995, I had just begun this line of research and could not have predicted the many different forms it would take. The resulting approach has since been the basis of a broad set of partnerships with the City of Philadelphia and the School District of Philadelphia, and among a variety of academic collaborators at the School, throughout Penn, and among other institutions. What began as a series of discrete projects in 1995 has developed into an active interdisciplinary research center, and has begun to serve as a model for other universities and communities seeking to establish policy research partnerships through the use administrative records. A brief history of these efforts is described here.

My initial work on homelessness at Penn was based on merging administrative records that track shelter utilization with those that track health and mental health services. The Center for Mental Health Policy and Services Research in the School of Medicine has been a longstanding collaborator with the School, and includes five of the School's faculty (Rothbard, Wong, Solomon, Draine, and Culhane) among its own participating faculty. The Center's historical strength has been its use of administrative records from Philadelphia's public mental health system to study the dynamics of the treatment system, and the costs and effectiveness of various models of care. I was able to build on this approach as a means of studying homelessness because Philadelphia was one of the few cities at the time to track use of nearly all of its homeless shelter beds in a computerized database. This database represented a longitudinal archive of all of the city's shelter users and their patterns of entry and exit from the shelter system. This enabled my collaborators and me to examine homelessness from a dynamic, citywide perspective for the first time nationally.

Even the most basic analyses of Philadelphia's shelter data were of interest, given the uniqueness of these data nationally. For example, we discovered that although relatively few people are homeless on a given day (about 0.3%, or 3,400 people), the population turned over about five times per year, affecting 1% of the city's population and about 6% of its poor population annually. Further analysis showed that some subpopulations of the city were particularly vulnerable to homelessness, including poor

African American men in their 30s and 40s (20% annually). Other analyses of shelter utilization patterns helped to identify a subpopulation of people experiencing "chronic homelessness," or those who live in shelters or on the streets for years at a time, but who represent a relatively small proportion of shelter users annually. This group has recently been targeted for various federal housing initiatives in recognition of their high costs to society, but relatively small population size overall.

The research on homelessness that has been based on merging the shelter data with other administrative records is too numerous and detailed to summarize adequately here. But the range of projects that these data have enabled has been quite broad, including studies of arrests and incarcerations, hospital admissions and discharge patterns, births and birth outcomes, foster care placement and the aging out of foster care youth, rates of AIDS and HIV risk behaviors, the effectiveness of housing interventions for the street homeless, the impact of welfare reform, and the role of the affordable housing crisis. Most of these projects have involved merging data through the linkage of personal identifiers, such as names, birthdates, and social security numbers. (Such research requires careful legal protections and authorizations.) In effect, most of this research has tracked *people* as they move through or encounter various public systems. However, one study deviated from this pattern, and in so doing, helped to launch a broader set of data integration efforts at our School.

Paradoxically, although most homelessness researchers would argue that the homelessness problem is fundamentally a housing problem, very, very few studies have actually examined the nature of the housing problems that are associated with homelessness. I suspect that one reason for this is that homeless people are much more readily available for study than are the conditions that render them homeless. Nevertheless, it is striking how little of the research literature has looked directly at the housing issues so widely presumed to underlie the problem. At Penn, we were once again for—their prior addresses. While it is an admittedly limited piece of information, the "prior address" is collected for all people admitted to public shelters in Philadelphia, and represents the only piece of information about these individuals that connects them to some meaningful place. Given that housing market factors are driven to a great extent by location, this piece of information became an important piece of connecting tissue to a series of inquiries about the types of housing market conditions that generated homelessness. Beginning with this address information, my colleagues and I began to assemble a variety of other administrative databases that track addresses, rather than people, in the City of Philadelphia. These data included utilities (water and gas shutoffs), housing code enforcement, building permits, tax delinquency, tax foreclosure, real estate sales, and fires. In addition, we were able to geocode the person-level data and aggregate it such that it provided area measures of the social environment as well. These included crime data, as well as school records, child welfare, health, mental health, etc. Thus, our shift in focus to neighborhoods and to environmental factors associated with homelessness led us to envision a broader set of ecological factors that could be derived from these new data sources, as well as from our existing person-level data sources.

The article reproduced here was our first attempt to develop an ecological model of homelessness and was the springboard for the collaboration between the Graduate School of Design and our School that would result in our now joint sponsorship of the Cartographic Modeling Lab. The Cartographic Modeling Lab now supports a broad array of projects, and works on issues beyond homelessness and the City of Philadelphia. However, we continue to develop and enrich our data resources for Philadelphia, given both our School's continuing commitment to help the City address its needs, and to the fact that many researchers on campus are conducting research in the city. The Lab also continues to work with researchers to find better ways of modeling how the built and social environments impact health, development and behavior. Our collaborations involve researchers from the Graduate School of Education, the School of Medicine, the School of Arts and Sciences, the School of Nursing, the Wharton School, and the School of Engineering and Applied Sciences. We also work with many community organizations, schools, and public agencies, as they seek to better understand needs in their communities and how to better fulfill their missions. Finally, we support instruction and the needs of our students as they seek to integrate spatial analysis and mapping into their own research, planning, and policy analysis projects.

Part VI
Recent Former Faculty

Chapter 36
Risk Classification and Juvenile Dispositions: What Is the State of the Art?

Peter R. Jones, David R. Schwartz, Ira M. Schwartz, Zoran Obradovic, and Joseph Jupin

I. Introduction

The past two decades have witnessed increased concern with the problem of serious and violent juvenile crime.[1] The juvenile justice and child welfare public policy response has varied across the states, with some adopting a get-tough stance involving increased supervision, incapacitation, and waiver, and others looking to improve the effectiveness of rehabilitative and preventive strategies.[2] Increased attention has focused on the ability of both the juvenile justice and child welfare systems to make the most appropriate decisions on placement. There is some consensus that the most appropriate decision involves an informed matching of youth needs with system responses.[3] Of course, this requires an ability to appropriately assess youth needs for control, supervision, and intervention, and the availability of a comprehensive continuum of care from which decision makers can select. Increasingly, these assessments of youth needs involve the classification of juvenile risk.[4]

The methods of risk assessment currently used in juvenile justice and child welfare cover an enormous spectrum, from highly informal "clinical" decisions to sophisticated actuarial risk assessments that reflect best practice for the field.[5] Research studies have repeatedly demonstrated that empirically derived and validated risk assessment tools can efficiently estimate the risk of reoffending or maltreatment and substantially improve upon clinical risk assessment performed by individual caseworkers or even by clinically based assessment tools. Consequently, actuarial risk assessment is increasingly supplanting clinical practices that are widely perceived as being overly subjective and discretionary. Many jurisdictions have worked with agencies such as the National Council on Crime and Delinquency ("NCCD") and the National Institute of Corrections ("NIC") to develop, introduce, or validate actuarial risk assessment tools.[6] Those that use actuarial models are generally convinced of the models' superior performance, pointing to attributes of objectivity, nonarbitrariness, efficiency, and consistency as the main benefits.[7] Unfortunately, there is only a very limited understanding of what constitutes best practice in risk assessment, and consequently, risk assessment in the field is often woefully short of what should be considered acceptable.

Researchers in the field of risk assessment understand that the superior performance of actuarial over clinical risk assessment is to be earned rather than simply assumed.[8] Developing ineffective actuarial assessment tools by using poor and inappropriate methodological or statistical techniques that produce risk assessments with little or no predictive validity is quite possible. Such tools not only possess none of the implied advantages of actuarial assessment but have the danger of "laundering" poor and inappropriate assessments as scientific, objective results. Poorly developed or inappropriately employed actuarial risk assessment is damaging because it contributes to poor decision making and gives the decision maker an unwarranted optimism and faith about the validity and utility of the estimates of risk that buttress their decisions. The consequences of poor risk assessment in juvenile justice and child welfare are serious and far reaching, leading to inappropriate or inequitable decisions that significantly undermine the chances of successful treatment in any given case. Poor risk assessment can place a child at risk of abuse or neglect, justify removal from a home, or place in the community a youth at significant risk of continued delinquency.

Given these potential problems, the increased use of risk assessment tools raises concern about the issue of standards of quality and appropriateness. No clear set of minimum standards by which risk assessment tools may be evaluated exists. Studies have compared clinical and empirical approaches and demonstrated the greater effectiveness and validity of the latter type.[9] Other, more recent studies have tested the validity of existing actuarial assessment tools in different settings—sometimes finding that they work well and on occasion showing that risk assessments do not travel well.[10] There are to our knowledge, however, no studies that compare different types of actuarial risk assessment to ascertain the variability and the predictive validity of the classifications.

Absent clear guidelines about best practice or minimal standards, the superiority of actuarial over clinical approaches is assumed but rarely demonstrated. This absence of standards may explain why there is very little case law that challenges the admissibility of actuarial risk assessments as a scientific basis for decision making. The paucity of case law is somewhat surprising—aside from challenges to child welfare placement decisions or juvenile delinquency detention decisions based on risk, there are potential claims of immunity from liability in cases where juveniles remain in or are removed from the community based on a risk score.

This article addresses the lacuna in the actuarial risk assessment literature by comparing the performance of three actuarial risk assessment tools that represent three different levels of sophistication.[11] It examines the extent to which juveniles are placed in the same risk category irrespective of the method used.[12] The Article also examines the ability of each method to accurately predict reoffending.[13] For both these issues, it reviews performance across key demographic criteria such as gender and race.[14]

The study utilizes a rich and unique data source as the basis for developing the actuarial risk assessment classifications. The first assessment classifies juveniles using a long-established and frequently validated generic risk assessment method—the Wisconsin Delinquency Risk Assessment Tool. Although now very dated and obsolete, the tool is currently used either in its original or revised version in many settings across the United States.[15] The second approach utilizes a customized risk assessment tool developed specifically for the juvenile sample being studied.[16] It uses configural analysis techniques that have been employed previously in risk assessment research and offers several advantages over more traditional regression-based approaches. The third approach also develops a customized actuarial risk assessment for the juvenile sample studied, using an extremely powerful and sophisticated neural networks approach.[17] By comparing the results of each of the approaches, it is possible to establish the extent to which risk classification remains—as earlier studies suggested—stable across methodologies. If the results indicate different classifications or predictive validities across assessment types, however, it undermines the confidence currently placed in actuarial risk assessment. It also begs two additional questions. First, how should minimal standards of performance for actuarial risk assessment in the juvenile justice and child welfare fields be established? Second, who will provide the impetus for establishing and maintaining such standards?

A. Risk Assessment in Juvenile Justice and Child Welfare

The development and utilization of formal risk assessment tools in juvenile justice and child welfare decision making has been a relatively recent but increasingly widespread phenomenon.[18] The types of assessment tools currently used in juvenile justice and child welfare fall into one of two broad categories—clinically based tools relying on the professional judgment and expertise of clinicians, and empirically derived actuarial tools that identify statistically significant predictors of the risk outcome and create a scoring mechanism that allows for classification of the youth.

Clinical assessment tools tend to perform poorly in comparison to empirical tools largely because they allow for widely differential selection and weighting of information about the subject.[19] Factors that intuitively and theoretically appear to be associated with risk may in fact have little or no predictive validity. Similarly, two or more factors assumed to have an independent impact on risk may be highly intercorrelated so that their combined inclusion effectively biases the risk assessment in one particular direction. From a purely methodological perspective, therefore, one reason why the research repeatedly demonstrates the greater predictive validity of empirical tools is that hypothesized predictors of risk have to be both statistically significant and theoretically independent.[20]

Recognition of the superiority of actuarial approaches to risk assessment has prompted state and local jurisdictions, as well as many public and private agencies, to integrate standardized risk assessment into the decision-making stages of juvenile justice and child welfare processes.[21] This process has been aided and facilitated by research and technical assistance programs involving agencies such as the Office of Juvenile Justice and Delinquency Prevention ("OJJDP"), the NIC, and the NCCD. One example of the process is the widely used Wisconsin Delinquency Risk Assessment

Tool. This actuarial-based risk assessment tool, developed by the Wisconsin Department of Juvenile Corrections with assistance from NCCD in the late 1970s, has been revised and revalidated.[22] One version or other of the assessment tool is found in current use in many juvenile justice agencies nationally. The original Wisconsin Risk Assessment Tool attempts to measure the risk of recidivism through an objective assessment of eight factors determined to be statistically significant predictors of reoffending.[23] Based on the total scores across all items, a juvenile is classified into a risk category. The original and the revised Wisconsin Risk Assessment Tool are examples of established risk tools that are adopted or adapted for use nationwide. Other well-known and similar types of assessment include the Washington State Juvenile Court Risk Assessment, Orange County Risk Assessment, Missouri Risk Assessment Scale, Global Risk Assessment Device, and from Canada, the Youth Level of Service/Case Management Inventory ("YLS/CMI"). A body of research validates these assessment tools[24]—particularly in Canadian applications[25]—but the fact remains that in the majority of settings where these tools are used, their predictive validity is assumed rather than demonstrated.

The growth in use of actuarial risk assessment is fueled by the fact that it is considered "good practice" in juvenile justice and child welfare. OJJDP's Comprehensive Strategy for Serious, Violent, and Chronic Juvenile Offenders states that the use of risk and needs assessment tools is a critical component of an effective juvenile justice system.[26] Unfortunately, the statements supporting the use of empirical risk assessment are broadly philosophical rather than specifically methodological, and they do not make clear that the potential benefits and advantages of the approach are contingent on the integrity and quality of both the development and implementation of the tool. Most likely, many jurisdictions as well as juvenile justice and child welfare programs are using forms of actuarial risk assessment that are simply not valid for their setting or population. In these cases, it is a mistake to assume any "good practice" benefits accrue, and it is possible that serious errors of classification are being made.

B. Evaluating Risk Assessments

The existing methodological literature on risk assessment tends to divide into three categories. There are studies that compare clinical and empirical risk instruments in terms of their predictive validity, studies that validate existing actuarial risk assessments, and studies that compare the performance of different forms of empirically based risk assessment.[27]

Almost all studies in the first category reach the conclusion that actuarial risk outperforms clinical assessment tools.[28] A review by Professors Don Gottfredson and Stephen Gottfredson of such comparisons concluded that "in virtually every decision-making situation for which the issue has been studied, it has been found that statistically developed predictive devices outperform human judgments."[29]

In addition to outperforming clinical decision making, actuarial assessment tools have the distinct advantage of providing an explicit basis for the risk decision.[30] Unlike clinical risk assessment, actuarial models do not require one to accept classification decisions on faith.[31] Professors Eileen Gambrill and Aron Shlonsky warn against over confidence in actuarial models within the field of child welfare, pointing out that "actuarial models are rarely able to predict reabuse at acceptable levels of sensitivity (correctly classifying those children who will be reabused)."[32] They further note that "although actuarial models tend to be the best predictors of future maltreatment, they are far from perfect."[33]

The research literature on validation of existing assessment tools is rapidly expanding.[34] Unfortunately, government or contract researchers, rather than independent researchers with no stake in the performance of the instruments, produced many of these studies.[35]

The literature on the comparative performance of different actuarial approaches suggests that the type of method makes little difference.[36] There are several reasons why this is possible. The first is that theory in the field of juvenile justice and child welfare is still developing when compared with applications of prediction studies in fields such as medicine, econometrics, and engineering. The second is the constraint of poor data. Existing limitations on the range of available measures added to problems of reliability and validity of the data and therefore limited the ability of more sophisticated statistical approaches to achieve their potential. Professor Peter Jones argues that "without better and different data we simply cannot improve on the basic analytic approaches of the past."[37] Similarly, Professor Stephen Gottfredson warns that limited and generally poor quality data combined with the highly random nature of delinquent behavior ensures that prediction research will rarely explain more than fifteen to twenty percent of the outcome variance and may never do better than thirty percent.[38] Professors Peter Schmidt and Ann Witte concur and caution against overly optimistic goals for prediction studies in the field of delinquency, pointing to the fact that even in disciplines with well-developed, specific theories and relatively accurate data, prediction instruments struggle to explain more than half the variation in the outcome measure.[39] A third reason why researchers expect little variation across statistical approaches is that the lack of differentiation is more apparent during the validation than the construction of a risk instrument so that apparent gains in the creation of an assessment tool will disappear upon testing. Professor Roger Tarling and Analyst John Perry warned of this when they completed their review of seven different statistical approaches by concluding that "no method is consistently better than any other in validation samples."[40] A fourth reason is that the methods being compared are often basic, regression-based techniques that share similar assumptions about the data.[41]

Most of the comparative studies use traditional, statistical methodologies, and it is rare to find contributions from nontraditional disciplines such as engineering or bioinformatics.[42] For this reason, it is premature to assume that the type of actuarial assessment tool is of little importance. The present study employs three different actuarial assessment tools that are founded upon widely different mathematical platforms and vary enormously in their range of sophistication and power. If these approaches yield divergent results for the same sample of juveniles—in terms of both classification and predictive validity—then we are forced beyond the generic label of actuarial assessment to determine the quality of the tool and the results it yields.

II. Developing Risk Assessments

Before examining in more detail the three approaches compared in the present study, it is worth outlining some methodological issues that affect the quality of any actuarial risk assessment study. These issues include sample size, quality and range of available data, and the statistical basis of the assessment tool itself.

A. Sample Size

Sample size is important for several reasons. It affects the ability of the assessment tool to identify important patterns among subgroups defined by factors such as race and gender. For example, if the etiology of offending for females is different from that of males, then small delinquent samples that are predominantly male will not yield enough female cases for their specific patterns of offending to be recognized. The resulting assessment tool will likely perform poorly for females.

Roger Tarling and John Perry cautioned that most of the variation in the performance of different statistical approaches to assessment disappears upon validation.[43] Therefore, it is critical that any risk tool development includes validation—preferably on an independent, randomly selected sample. This requires that the available sample is divided into construction (training) and validation (testing) subsamples, with the actual proportions determined by the investigator. For small samples, this is a difficult trade-off because the benefits of validation are potentially outweighed by the decreased ability to identify significant predictors from the reduced sample.

Finally, the lower the base rate for the outcome—for example, violent offending and sexual offending can have base rates of less than five percent even for delinquents—the larger the sample necessary to develop reliable risk assessments. In a sample of five hundred delinquents, there may be only twenty-five individuals who commit a sexual offense, and this inevitably restricts the ability of any assessment device to reach its full potential. There is no required sample size for the development of a risk assessment model, but for the reasons outlined here, samples of less than five hundred should be treated with extreme caution.

B. Quality of Data

Empirical risk models require the analysis of numeric values. These numeric values signify objective measures such as age, gender, race, or the number of prior arrests. They also signify more subjective measures that reflect second-party assessments of behavior or personality. Reviews of risk assessments identify the use of highly subjective measures such as "could make better use of time," "non-rewarding parental relations," "inconsistent parenting," "poor social skills," and "inadequate supervision."[44] For such measures, it is difficult if not impossible to determine the consistency of interpretation and measurement. Inevitably, measures vary along a spectrum from the value free to those that involve "substantial speculation and morally laden subjective assessments."[45] The reliability and validity of such data are dependent on quality of training by those making the assessments.

Data quality is affected significantly by the prevalence and source of missing data. At its simplest, the problem of missing data means values are unavailable for varying proportions of cases on different measures. A more complex issue involves the process that gives rise to the missing data. To the extent that the underlying process is biased in some way, and that bias is associated with specific attributes of the sample, then the resulting model will be inappropriately shaped by the missing data. An example will illustrate. In juvenile justice files, it is common to find information on whether a female has a child of her own. Comparison of different sources of such information—official files, staff reports, and self-report—will often be highly correlated. The same is not true for males. Analyses for the data set used in the present study show that reports of delinquent males with children of their own increase quite significantly when one compares official file, staff report, and self-report sources. The availability of this information increases respectively with each of these sources.

For the investigator, there are several options to dealing with the missing values problem. One may remove variables with excessive proportions of missing data—the actual threshold usually being determined by the investigator. An alternative is to adopt one of several forms of missing value substitution—a process that can range from simplistic mean substitution to sophisticated missing data estimation algorithms that learn from patterns of data among the remaining good data.[46]

Despite its significance, the issue of missing data is treated as almost inconsequential in many studies.[47] It represents one of the most serious threats to the validity of any risk assessment, however, and represents an essential indicator of quality control. Recognition of the problem is dependent on the expertise of the researcher. In inexperienced hands, it is possible for an investigator to believe they are studying hundreds of cases with dozens of potential measures when in fact the effective sample is a small portion of the whole and several important predictors are missed through the lack of information.

C. Theoretical Understanding: How Should We Select and Measure the Predictors?

Scholarly interest in risk assessment within justice and welfare disciplines has a long history.[48] In the 1920s, Ernest Burgess completed his famous prediction study on parole decision making,[49] and subsequent work by Lloyd Ohlin[50] in the 1950s, as well as Don Gottfredson, Leslie Wilkins, and Peter Hoffman in the late 1970s, further refined risk classification through work on "salient factor scores" and "parole guidelines."[51] The work of Steven and Eleanor Glueck is one of the best-known prediction studies in the history of delinquency[52] and was so influential that President Richard Nixon was advised that the Gluecks' Social Prediction Table enabled "9 out of 10 delinquents [to be] correctly identified at the age of 6."[53]

Review of the theoretical literature in the justice and welfare disciplines generates a very wide array of potential predictors. Unfortunately, most of these are not available among the usually constrained range of measures routinely maintained by programs or agencies. The list of potential predictors that can be found in a juvenile court or child welfare agency includes such factors as gender, race, age, family relations, living arrangements, degree of family involvement, substance abuse, and past offending record.[54]

Less commonly found are important predictors such as early problem behavior,[55] parenting and family management techniques,[56] family disruption and family size or structure,[57] parental or sibling criminality or delinquency,[58] delinquent peers,[59] alcohol abuse,[60] personality,[61] self-esteem,[62] attitudes,[63] family bonding,[64] and school bonding.[65] Most of the available measures pertain to the individual rather than the family or the community. This unavailability is being seen as an increasing limitation as the literature continues to demonstrate the importance of predictors incorporating familial, peer, and environmental measures such as household violence,[66] gang membership,[67] and neighborhood.[68]

Finally, almost all the measures used in risk assessment are "static"—gender, race, number of prior arrests, etc.—and cannot change or decrease over time.[69] The recent risk assessment literature points to the importance of "dynamic" risk factors that indicate temporal trends in behavior and personality rather than snapshot measures frozen in time.[70] For example, a juvenile with poor school grades may behave differently if poor grades are the norm rather than a very recent development.

D. Methods of Developing a Risk Assessment Tool

The goal of most actuarial prediction studies is to select and combine a small number of predictors into a parsimonious model that will maximize predictive efficiency in terms of validity, cost, and utility. As noted above, that type of statistical approach has been found to have limited impact on overall predictive validity. Francis Simon compared seven different statistical techniques and concluded that all worked equally well.[71] Subsequent criticism of Simon's analysis prompted Roger Tarling and John Perry to extend the examination of alternate methods by submitting the same data to analysis by two more sophisticated and appropriate prediction methods—Automatic Interaction Detection and Logistic Regression.[72] They concluded that both methods performed equally well but not significantly better than Simon's other approaches.[73] Stephen Gottfredson and Michael Gottfredson completed a similar comparative study involving several analytic methods—linear additive models (OLS Multiple Regression and unweighted Burgess Method), clustering models (Predictive Attribute Analysis and Association Analysis), and multidimensional contingency table analysis.[74] They too concluded that "simpler and more easily understood and implemented statistical prediction devices may work as well as those based on more complex techniques."[75]

In summary, the juvenile justice and child welfare fields are experiencing significant development in the methods of actuarial risk prediction. There is slow but steady progress in the theoretical understanding of the behavior to be predicted—especially as the realm of measures expands to include the family, peer groups, and the community—but very limited development in the range or quality of available data. These weaknesses suggest that confidence in actuarial risk assessment is perhaps exceeding what is reasonable. We are in danger of creating a seriously misplaced and misleading aura of utility, accuracy, and validity among actuarial risk assessments in delinquency and child welfare. An international literature search conducted by Kelly Hannah-Moffat and Paula Maurutto revealed few published peer-reviewed academic studies of youth risk assessments, especially by investigators with no vested interest in the promotion of the tools.[76]

After several decades of research on actuarial risk assessment, there is need for the development of minimum standards and external regulation to ensure that these standards are met. To achieve the potential advantages of actuarial risk assessment we must do more than pay lip service to the process—we must ensure its validity and its integrity. As Leslie Wilkins reminds us, "the ultimate test of predictive methods is . . . neither the scientific nor the statistical nature of the exercises, but their honesty, rigor and moral underpinnings."[77]

III. Current Study: Comparing Risk Assessment Tools

The present study employs three assessment tools, each based on a different methodological approach. The first—the Wisconsin Risk Assessment Tool—was developed using multivariate logistic regression techniques.[78] The second approach employs configural analysis, an improved version of the automatic interaction detector method utilized by Tarling and Perry.[79] The third approach involves neural network analysis.

The comparative analysis poses a number of important questions. First, has the field progressed beyond the studies of Francis Simon,[80] Stephen Gottfredson and Don Gottfredson,[81] and Roger Tarling and John Perry[82] to the point where it is possible to identify significant differences in the predictive validity of different statistical approaches? Second, do these differences translate into differential classifications of juveniles based on the type of assessment tool being used? For example, will a juvenile classified low risk by one model be classified high risk by another? Depending on these results, the analysis poses several secondary questions. What are appropriate minimal standards for actuarial risk classification? Where will the impetus for change be found? Ultimately, the study seeks to examine the extent to which actuarial tools deserve the methodological "high ground" they currently inhabit.

A. Data

The study utilizes data from the ProDES database of juvenile delinquents processed by Family Court in Philadelphia from 2000 to 2002.[83] The ProDES database comprises data on all juveniles whose Family Court disposition involved more than regular probation—either probation with the condition of attending a treatment program or placement in a state juvenile correctional facility. The dataset provides a wide array of measures including official records, staff assessments, and self-reported data. For this

TABLE 1. Characteristics of Sample

Variable	% in Sample	Variable	% in Sample
Gender		Type of offense	
Males	87.6	Drugs	24.6
Females	12.4	Personal (e.g., assault)	38.5
Race		Property (e.g., theft)	28.9
White	13.1	Weapons	6.0
Black	70.9	Other	1.9
Hispanic	14.2	Injury to Victim	
Asian	1.5	No	80.3
Other	0.3	Yes	19.7
Age			
10	0.2	IQ	
11	1.1	Mentally deficient	6.7
12	2.7	Borderline	15.5
13	6.7	Low average	16.1
14	13.1	Average	21.6
15	20.0	High average	4.6
16	24.6	Missing	35.5
17	22.1	Prior arrests	
18	7.9	None	51.2
19	1.3	1	25.8
20	0.2	2	12.1
		3 or more	10.9
History of drug abuse			
None	47.2		
Occasional	22.6		
Chronic	30.2		

study, the available measures include the eight variables that comprised the original Wisconsin Risk Assessment Tool and a wide range of additional measures pertaining to the juvenile, his or her family, his or her school, and his or her peers. All cases were screened for missing data on the Wisconsin Risk Assessment Tool measures and all cases missing these risk scores were removed.[84] The effective sample comprises 8,239 juveniles that are primarily male, African American, and between ages fourteen and seventeen (see Table 1). Additional attributes show almost forty percent of the juveniles in the sample have dispositions for personal offenses, twenty percent injured a victim, and twenty-three percent have two or more prior arrests. Approximately thirty percent of juveniles have a history of chronic drug abuse, and over twenty-two percent have IQ scores that classify them as "borderline" or "mentally deficient."

All juveniles in the ProDES system are monitored during their program placement (involving a variable program length of stay—sample average thirty-two weeks) and for six months following program discharge. The outcome measure for the study is juvenile rearrests leading to new court petitions during the combined in-program and post-program periods. In total, almost thirty percent of the sample reoffended, though the figure varies by gender—31.9% for males and 12.7% for females.

B. Modeling Risk I: The Wisconsin Risk Assessment Model

The Wisconsin Risk Assessment Model was developed in the late 1970s and remains widely used in its original form, its revised form, or in some site-specific adaptation that reflects local needs and data availability. The assessment tool yields risk scores based on information derived from official records and interviews conducted by case management staff. The assessment should be completed within thirty days of a juvenile's assignment to a placement, and the ProDES system required this of all programs.

Risk classification is based on a total risk score calculated by simple summation of the eight risk items.[85] Though the risk assessment tool has undergone revision, the one employed here comprises the following items:

1. Age at first adjudication,
2. Prior delinquent behavior,
3. Prior institutional commitments of thirty-plus days,
4. Drug or chemical abuse,
5. Alcohol abuse,
6. Quality of parental control,
7. Evidence of school disciplinary problems, and
8. Quality of peer relationships.

The attributes of each item are weighted to reflect the magnitude of their association with recidivism. For example, "quality of parental control" involves a risk score of zero for "generally effective," two for "inconsistent," and four for "little or none." Other risk items have different weights to reflect their specific correlation to reoffending. The procedure for determining a juvenile's risk classification involves summation of total score and classification into low, low-medium, medium-high, and high risk using cutoff scores of six, twelve, and nineteen, respectively.[86]

The Wisconsin Risk Assessment Tool has been validated in different settings both in its original and various revised formats. Christopher Baird, Richard Heinz, and Brian Bemus reported on the validity of the original model, and using a three-level categorization based on total risk score, were able to predict rates of probation and parole revocations for a Wisconsin sample of over four thousand cases.[87] The overall base rate for revocations was eleven percent, and they identified rates of two, nine, and twenty-six percent for low-, medium-, and high-risk cases, respectively.[88] Professors Kevin Wright, Todd Clear, and Paul Dickson reported less favorable results for a New York sample of 366 probationers for which in-program information on a variety of indices of recidivism were available.[89]

The in-program "failure" rate, as defined by the above indicators, was thirty percent.[90] The New York study found no significant relationship between overall risk scores and recidivism, and only three of the eleven components of risk individually predicted failures at levels above chance. Other studies, such as Professors Eileen

TABLE 2. Wisconsin Risk Classification

Risk	%	N
Low	14.7	1215
Low-medium	31.6	2603
Medium-high	32.4	2669
High	21.3	1752
Total	100	8239

TABLE 3. Wisconsin Risk Classification by Gender

	Males		Females	
Risk	%	N	%	N
Low	14.2	1022	18.9	193
Low-medium	31.6	2277	31.8	326
Medium-high	32.7	2362	30.0	307
High	21.5	1554	19.3	198
Total	100	7215	100	1024

Chi-square 17.51; df = 3; $p < 0.001$

TABLE 4. Wisconsin Risk Classification by Race

	White		Non-White	
Risk	%	N	%	N
Low	11.3	122	15.3	1091
Low-medium	25.1	270	32.62	329
Medium-high	33.7	363	32.2	2306
High	30.0	323	20.0	1428
Total	100	1078	100	7154

Chi-square 71.25; df = 3; $p < 0.001$

Gambrill and Aron Shlonsky's work in child welfare, have shown that actuarial risk assessments such as the Wisconsin Risk Assessment Tool do not perform adequately.[91]

The Wisconsin assessment-based risk classification of the juveniles in the ProDES sample is presented in Table 2. The cutoffs provided in the original study create four risk groups with almost fifteen percent of juveniles considered low risk, sixty-four percent low-medium or medium-high risk, and twenty-one percent high risk. The overall risk classification clearly varies by gender (see Table 3) and by race (see Table 4) with males and whites overrepresented in the high-risk category.

C. Modeling Risk II: Customized Model Using Configural Analysis

The second approach to assessing risk involves the use of configural analysis on the Philadelphia sample itself. The method uses tree induction algorithms or nonparametric classification procedures to subdivide a sample into significant groupings on the basis of specific statistical and theoretical conditions.[92] The predictor variables used in the model are related to the outcome variable (reoffending) by a set of rules. As Professor Irene Casas notes,

These methods do not require a functional form specification, thus allowing situations to be revealed by the data with minimum interference of the analyst. [Such] decision tree induction systems are under the supervised learning category techniques, which have as [their] purpose producing general rules from externally supplied examples.[93]

Configural analysis techniques are rarely found in the juvenile justice or child welfare literature, but they are more commonly used in other social science and business disciplines. They are often used when an analyst seeks to identify the optimal predictor from a wide range of competing options. They can be used as an alternative or as an adjunct to traditional regression-based techniques and offer considerable advantages when interested in identifying complex interactions among predictors.

The research reported here makes use of a segmentation technique called Answer Tree that is available within the software package, Statistical Package for the Social Scientist.[94]

Answer Tree is a set of statistical algorithms, designed to select patterns of variables [that] are especially predictive of a pre-defined criterion variable. The methods are . . . ideal for use in relatively large samples, where the cases are characterized by many variables and where a multitude of different . . . variable patterns are expected to occur.[95]

Published risk assessment research involving this technique is found in many disciplines, including the health sciences,[96] marketing,[97] psychology,[98] geography and regional planning,[99] criminal justice,[100] and education.[101] From an analytic perspective, Answer Tree begins by dividing the initial sample (preferably a randomly selected construction subsample) into smaller first-order subgroups, which seek to maximize the variability of the criterion variable. Each first-order subgroup is then analyzed independently to identify the optimal predictor that maximizes the variability of the criterion variable for that subgroup. Each new category is similarly subdivided until one of several "stopping rules" are met. This process produces a tree-like structure (dendogram) with the initial sample at the top and a series of "branches" extending downward to the terminal subgroups. Each subdivision is based on the analyst's selection of the predictor variable that is considered the best predictor of the criterion variable for that sample. In the "exhaustive chaid" algorithm used in this study, the selection of the optimal predictor is based on a combination of the analyst's assessment of the quality of the predictor variables involved and their probability scores or effect sizes (Cohen's d) based on chi-squared tests. At each selection point, Answer Tree arranges the potential predictors by effect size and the analyst is free to select that predictor that best meets his requirements.[102] Model development ends when all remaining subgroups fail to meet analyst specified stopping rules based on either a minimal subgroup size or probability level.[103]

In the current study, Answer Tree repeatedly divides the initial construction sample into mutually exclusive and exhaustive subgroups on the basis of the criterion mea-

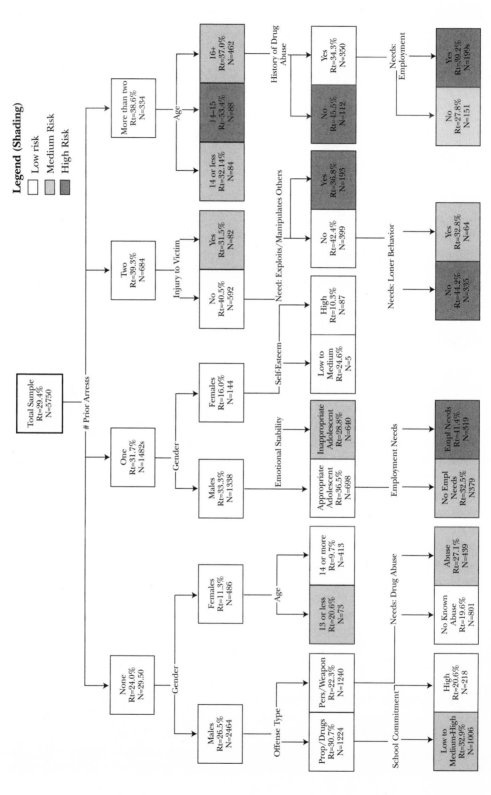

Figure 1. Dendrogram of predictors of rearrest.

TABLE 5. Configural Risk Classification

Risk	%	N
Low	28.5	2349
Medium	53.0	4369
High	18.5	1521
Total	100	8239

TABLE 6. Configural Risk Classification by Gender

	Males		Females	
Risk	%	N	%	N
Low	19.7	1420	90.7	929
Medium	59.8	4313	5.5	56
High	20.5	1482	3.8	39
Total	100	7215	100	1024

Chi-square 2222.131; df = 2; $p < 0.001$

sure of reoffending.[104] As a result, the predictors identified do not always apply to the entire sample (as would be the case with more common regression-based approaches). For example, the number of prior arrests is identified as the most significant initial predictor (see results for construction sample in Figure 1). The model subsequently searches for the next best predictor among the subgroups with no prior arrests, one prior, two priors, or more than two priors. For the first two of these subgroups, the second predictor is gender, for those with two priors the next predictor is "injury to victim" during commission of the current offense, and for those with more than two prior arrests the next predictor is the juvenile's age. The model adds predictors of different types to each of these subgroups, creating "branches" of different length, size, and composition for different types of juveniles.

Each of the individual variables that comprise the Wisconsin Risk Assessment Tool was available to the configural analysis for inclusion in the model, but none was selected. Interestingly, several of the variables included in the Wisconsin needs assessment—a set of variables not considered to have predictive criminogenic value—were selected and included in the configural model. These "need" based variables included staff assessments of whether the juvenile was manipulative of others, was a loner, had employment needs, or had a drug or alcohol abuse problem.

The resulting risk classification is presented in Table 5, and the relationship of risk to gender and race is presented in Tables 6 and 7, respectively. When compared with the Wisconsin classification, it is evident that the configural analysis—which has three risk groups—places far more juveniles in the low-risk group and slightly fewer in the high-risk group. The distributions also vary significantly by gender and race. In the configural model, very few females are placed in the high-risk category, and the proportion of high-risk whites and non-whites are more comparable than is found in the Wisconsin classification.

TABLE 7. Configural Risk Classification by Race

Risk	White		Non-White	
	%	N	%	N
Low	26.5	286	28.8	2060
Medium	57.7	622	52.3	3743
High	15.8	170	18.9	1351
Total	100	1078	100	7154

Chi-square 11.72; df = 2; $p < 0.01$

D. Modeling Risk III: Customized Model Using Neural Networks

The third approach uses artificial neural networks "because of their ability to learn from databases and build predictive models that can evolve and update themselves using random selections of case file data."[105] The potential of this type of statistical technique has been demonstrated in the child welfare arena where the final trained network was able to successfully categorize 89.6% of the cases in the testing population.[106]

Neural networks offer an appropriate statistical approach to risk assessment because they "are not organized around rules or programming, but learn the underlying behaviors of a model by analyzing its input and output values and adjusting the weights between neuron layers. In this respect the behavior of a neural network is trained using supervised or unsupervised techniques."[107] This type of "soft computing" methodology is widely used in research and practice by other fields because it is highly adaptive and robust. For example, "neural networks have performed well as risk assessment and classification tools . . . in the medical decision-making literature."[108] Felipe Atienza developed a network to correctly classify 123 of 132 patients,[109] and Richard Orr trained a network to estimate mortality following cardiac surgery to the point where he achieved 91.5% accuracy for the training set and 92.3% accuracy for the validation set.[110] Though the prediction of health outcomes is quite different from the prediction of actual human behavior, the fact remains that the existing actuarial models used to predict human behavior are an adaptation of the health and life insurance models developed in the past.[111] Child welfare literature discusses neural networks, but with the exception of David Schwartz, they have not been implemented in the field.[112] David Marshall and Diana English compared "logistic and linear multiple regression to neural networks using child protective service data from the State of Washington's risk assessment model. . . . [and] concluded that the neural network produced superior prediction and classification results."[113]

For the present study, the neural network analysis was run on the same ProDES database as produced the Wisconsin and configural analysis results. Though the neural network could in theory work with a wide array of potential predictor variables, it was decided, for purposes of this analysis, to restrict the model to those variables that had previously been identified as predictors in the configural analysis. The utilization of the configural model to constrain the array of potential predictors for neural networks

TABLE 8. Neural Network Risk Classification

Risk	%	N
Low	65.8	5424
High	34.2	2815
Total	100	8239

TABLE 9. Neural Network Risk Classification by Gender

	Males		Females	
Risk	%	N	%	N
Low	62.8	4532	87.1	892
High	37.2	2683	12.9	132
Total	100	7215	100	1024

Chi-square 235.32; df $= 1$; $p < 0.001$

TABLE 10. Neural Network Risk Classification by Race

	White		Non-White	
Risk	%	N	%	N
Low	72.8	785	64.8	4634
High	27.2	293	35.2	2520
Total	100	1078	100	7154

Chi-square 26.96; df $= 1$; $p < 0.001$

analysis is an unusual but appropriate application of a preliminary noise reduction strategy. Indirectly, it also enhances direct comparison with the results of the configural model.

Classification of the dataset was undertaken using a multilayer perceptron ("MLP"), which is a feed-forward neural network model trained using the backpropagation algorithm. Such models are very powerful and suitable for learning highly complex concepts given sufficiently large data in training time that scales linearly with data size.[114] The MLPs were trained with seventy percent of the sample and tested with a thirty percent validation sample that was disjointed and randomly generated. This methodology is used for predictive purposes to test the accuracy of the model on unseen instances. For purposes of this study, the analysis was performed with a general purpose machine learning suite with mostly default parameters. Training MLPs is a computationally expensive and complex process that requires a large number of trials to identify the optimal set of parameters to produce the most accurate model. The training data are processed hundreds to thousands or more times to obtain the final model. The model was initially run on the entire sample, but because of the importance of gender differences with regard to reoffending, separate models were also run for the male and female sample subsets. See Tables 8, 9, and 10.

TABLE 11. Wisconsin by Configural Risk Classification (%)

Wisconsin Risk Classification	Configural Risk Classification			
	Low risk	Medium risk	High risk	Total
Low	25.4	10.6	10.2	14.7
Low-medium	40.8	28.2	27.2	31.6
Medium-high	23.5	35.3	37.9	32.4
High	10.3	25.9	24.7	21.3
Total	100	100	100	100

TABLE 12. Wisconsin by Neural Network Risk Classification (%)

Wisconsin Risk Classification	Neural Network Risk Classification		
	Low risk	High risk	Total
Low	15.9	12.5	14.7
Low-medium	31.4	32.0	31.6
Medium-high	31.3	34.5	32.4
High	21.4	21.0	21.3
Total	100	100	100

E. The Risk Classifications Compared

In theory, even though the three risk assessment tools combine different types of measures in different ways, it is possible that the same juveniles will be identified as high or low risk by all three methods. Table 11 compares Wisconsin and configural classifications. If one combines the "low-medium" and "medium-high" categories of the Wisconsin Tool, the Wisconsin Tool classifies about twenty-five percent of the configural classification's low-risk youth as low risk, it classifies sixty-four percent of medium-risk juveniles as medium risk, and it classifies twenty-five percent of high-risk juveniles as high risk. There are also instances where the two classifications are at odds—ten percent of the configural classification's low-risk youth are assessed high risk by the Wisconsin classification and, similarly, ten percent of the configural high-risk youth are assessed low risk by the Wisconsin classification.

Comparing the neural network with the Wisconsin classification indicates even less agreement (see Table 12). Of the juveniles assessed low risk by neural networks, only fifteen percent were low risk in the Wisconsin classification and twenty-one percent were assessed high risk. Similarly, of the juveniles assessed high risk by neural networks, twenty-one percent were also assessed high risk by the Wisconsin analysis, and over twelve percent were assessed to be low risk.

Comparing the third pair of assessments—configural and neural networks—shows greater agreement (see Table 13). Of the juveniles assessed low risk by neural networks, thirty-five percent were also low risk in the configural analysis; of those assessed high risk by neural networks, twenty-seven percent were similarly assessed by the configural model.

These results provide definitive proof that type of assessment does matter. Table 14

TABLE 13. Configural by Neural Network Risk Classification (%)

Configural risk Classification	Neural Network Risk Classification		
	Low risk	High risk	Total
Low	34.7	16.6	28.5
Medium	51.3	56.3	53.0
High	14.0	27.0	18.5
Total	100	100	100

TABLE 14. Comparing Risk Classifications: High Risk Juveniles

Classification	N	%	% Reoffend
Agreement			
None high	4664	56.6	3.0
One high	2185	26.5	59.1
Two high	1221	14.8	69.2
Three high	169	2.1	91.1
Total	8239	100	29.5

TABLE 15. Wisconsin Risk Classification by Reoffending Rate (%)

Risk	No	Reoffend
Low	75.6	24.4
Low-medium	71.4	28.6
Medium-high	67.6	32.4
High	70.0	30.0
Total	70.5	29.5

focuses solely on juveniles classified as high risk by each of the assessment tools. Over half the juveniles in the sample were assessed high risk by one or other of the tools, and yet less than two percent were assessed high risk by all three tools.

F. Predictive Validity

The risk assessments can be tested by comparing the predicted risk classification with actual reoffending patterns. The results for the Wisconsin Risk Assessment Tool show that 24.4% of the low-risk juveniles reoffended during the follow-up period compared with 30.0% of the high-risk juveniles (see Table 15). The results for the two medium-risk categories are similar—28.6% and 32.4%, respectively. Nonetheless, the fact that the medium-high-risk group reoffended at a higher rate than the high-risk group suggests the classification is not discriminating well on the basis of risk.

Separating the results by gender highlights the poor overall discrimination of the Wisconsin Tool, and the higher rate of reoffending for medium-high-risk group compared with the high-risk group is replicated for both males and females (see Table 16). Indeed, for females the rate of reoffending is also lower for the low-medium than the low-risk group (10.4% to 13.0%, respectively).

TABLE 16. Wisconsin Risk Classification by Gender and Reoffending Rate (%)

	Males		Females	
Risk	*No*	*Reoffend*	*No*	*Reoffend*
Low	73.5	26.5	87.0	13.0
Low-medium	68.8	31.2	89.6	10.4
Medium-high	65.4	34.6	84.7	15.3
High	67.7	32.3	87.9	12.1
Total	68.1	31.9	87.3	12.7

TABLE 17. Wisconsin Risk Classification by Race and Reoffending Rate (%)

	White		Non-White	
Risk	*No*	*Reoffend*	*No*	*Reoffend*
Low	78.8	21.3	75.3	24.7
Low-medium	71.9	28.1	71.3	28.7
Medium-high	75.5	24.5	66.3	33.7
High	76.2	23.8	68.6	31.4
Total	75.1	24.9	69.8	30.2

TABLE 18. Configural Risk Classification by Reoffending Rate (%)

Risk	*No*	*Reoffend*
Low	82.6	17.4
Medium	68.8	31.2
High	56.7	43.4
Total	70.5	29.5

Repeating the analysis for race indicates poor overall discrimination for both whites and non-whites. For white juveniles, the low-medium-risk group had the highest actual rate of reoffending (28.1%), though all groups differed only slightly from the overall average of 24.9% (see Table 17). For non-whites, the separation of reoffending rates is a little more marked, but the highest rate of reoffending remains with the medium-high-risk group (33.7% compared with 31.4% for the high-risk group).

The results for the configural assessment represent an improvement, with 17.4% of low-risk juveniles reoffending compared with 31.2% of medium-risk juveniles and 43.3% of the high-risk juveniles (see Table 18). The configural risk tool achieves considerably better discrimination among the risk categories in terms of reoffending. Moreover, the model places a similar proportion of juveniles into the high-risk category (18.5% compared with 21.3% for the Wisconsin Risk Assessment Tool) and almost twice as many juveniles into the low-risk category (28.5% compared with 14.7%). From a decision-making perspective, the configural model is superior—it allows for the identification of a larger group of low-risk juveniles whose actual reoffending rate is lower than that for low-risk juveniles identified by the Wisconsin Risk Assessment Tool (17.4% compared with 24.4%), and it is correct more often for the

TABLE 19. Configural Risk Classification by Gender and Reoffending Rate

Risk	Males		Females	
	No	*Reoffend*	*No*	*Reoffend*
Low	79.0	21.0	88.1	11.9
Medium	68.6	31.4	83.9	16.1
High	56.2	43.8	74.4	25.6
Total	68.1	31.9	87.3	12.7

high-risk juveniles. If the configural assessment was used as part of dispositional decisions, a larger proportion of juveniles would be considered for less intrusive interventions, and a larger proportion of those individuals would remain delinquency free for the period of study. Among the high-risk juveniles, there would be a lower rate of false positives.

Separate analysis by gender shows that the improved discrimination of reoffending is evident both for males and females (see Table 19). The actual reoffending rate for high-risk males is twice that for low-risk males (43.8% to 21.0%, respectively) and for females the differences are even greater (25.6% to 11.9%). The most striking contrast between the two models is found in classification of females. The Wisconsin Risk Assessment Tool places 193 females in the low-risk category and, for this group, the reoffending rate is 13.0%. If one combines the low-and low-medium-risk categories the figures become 519 and 11.4%, respectively. The configural analysis places 929 females in the low-risk category and their reoffending rate is 11.9%.

This contrast in models reflects a common problem in risk-prediction modeling, where male-dominated samples are analyzed with statistical techniques that prioritize predictors with explanatory power for the entire sample. Such an approach fails to recognize that the predictors of reoffending for females may have a different etiology to those for males. This problem is compounded when the resulting risk model—dominated as it is by male predictors—is applied to females. The model incorrectly places some females in medium-and even high-risk categories and simultaneously fails to identify females with the highest risk of reoffending. The Wisconsin Risk Assessment Tool shows a 12.1% reoffending rate for its high-risk females whereas the configural model identifies a smaller but more at-risk group, with an actual reoffending rate of 25.6%, or twice the female base rate.

The results by race reveal superior statistical discrimination of reoffending rates by risk category for both whites and non-whites (see Table 20). For white juveniles, the low-risk group in the configural assessment is larger in size (26.5% of juveniles) than the Wisconsin low-risk category (11.3%), yet has a lower rate of reoffending (14.0% compared to 21.3%). In contrast, the configural assessment high-risk white group is half the size of the Wisconsin high-risk group (15.8% to 30.0%, respectively) and has a higher rate of reoffending (36.5% to 23.8%, respectively).

For non-whites, the results are slightly different. The low-risk non-white group in the configural assessment is larger in size (28.8% of juveniles) than the Wisconsin low-risk category (15.3%) and has a lower rate of reoffending (17.9% compared to

TABLE 20. Configural Risk Classification by Race and Reoffending Rate (%)

| | White | | Non-White | |
Risk	No	Reoffend	No	Reoffend
Low	86.0	14.0	82.1	17.9
Medium	73.3	26.7	68.0	32.0
High	63.5	36.5	55.8	44.2
Total	75.1	24.9	69.8	30.2

TABLE 21. Neural Network Risk Classification by Reoffending Rate (%)

Risk	No	Reoffend
Low	97.0	3.0
High	19.4	80.6
Total	70.5	29.5

TABLE 22. Neural Network Risk Classification by Gender and Reoffending Rate (%)

| | Males | | Females | |
Risk	No	Reoffend	No	Reoffend
Low	96.9	3.1	97.5	2.5
High	19.5	80.5	18.2	81.8
Total	68.1	31.9	87.3	12.7

24.7%). The configural assessment non-white high-risk group is about the same size as the Wisconsin high-risk group (18.9% to 20.0%, respectively) and has a higher actual rate of reoffending (44.2% to 31.4%, respectively).

Though race is not a predictor in either model, it is likely that many of the predictors identified are themselves closely correlated with race and therefore act as proxy measures for race in the assessment models. The results presented here suggest that the Wisconsin Risk Assessment Tool is not recognizing those variables that affect reoffending differentially for whites and non-whites or for females compared with males. As a result, the Wisconsin Risk Assessment Tool reflects very little discrimination of reoffending rates by risk group for either gender or racial groups. The configural model has superior performance for gender—which is included in the model—and for race, even though race is not directly included in the model.

The results for the neural networks assessment represent a significant improvement over both the Wisconsin and the configural models (see Table 21). Creating only two categories, it identifies a group of low-risk juveniles for whom the reoffending rate is three percent and a high-risk group for which it is almost eighty-one percent. The predictive validity of this model far exceeds the estimated prediction capabilities forecast by Stephen Gottfredson[115] and Peter Schmidt and Ann Witte[116] less than twenty years ago. The predictive validities vary slightly by gender (see Table 22) and race (see

TABLE 23. Neural Network Risk Classification by Race and Reoffending Rate (%)

	White		Non-White	
Risk	No	Reoffend	No	Reoffend
Low	98.6	1.4	96.7	3.3
High	12.3	87.7	20.2	79.8
Total	75.1	24.9	69.8	30.2

Table 23), but it is evident that the neural networks model is far superior to either of the two other classifications.

IV. Discussion

During the past several decades, there has been a large body of research that has established the superior predictive validity of actuarial compared with clinical risk models.[117] This research has also established many features of best practice in the field of risk prediction. Samples need to be large enough to sustain multivariate analyses and division into construction and validation subsamples.[118] Appropriate multivariate techniques need to be employed and the researcher must be guided either by theory or by the data to identify and include complex interactions among predictor variables—gender being a primary example. The quality of the data used is vital to the reliability of the final results—analyses that are seriously compromised by copious missing data are simply not to be trusted. And finally, the samples being used to develop a risk instrument will inevitably place some constraints on the range of applications for which the resulting risk assessment tools can be used—a model developed on a Midwestern, primarily white urban or rural sample cannot be transferred to an urban, inner city, predominantly minority setting with any sense of confidence.

Despite this growing body of knowledge, the fact remains that many of the risk assessments being utilized in juvenile justice and child welfare settings leave a great deal to be desired. Risk assessments are borrowed, adapted to fit local data conditions (by adding or excluding carefully identified predictors or by changing the risk scores associated with established predictors), and then utilized without validation to produce risk classifications to support potentially life-changing decisions. There is a general but misplaced sense that actuarial risk assessment is so robust, so superior to clinical decision making, that it can sustain these modifications without being seriously compromised.

The data presented here examines the classifications and the predictive validity of three risk assessments—all of which could easily be employed in the field. The data indicates that the tools do not produce the same classifications—very few juveniles would be placed in the same risk category if assessed by all three tools. The data further indicate that the Wisconsin Risk Assessment Tool performs poorly, displaying little predictive validity overall, and particularly poor validity for females. The configural assessment represents an improvement, and the neural network assessment sets a new and higher standard.

The implications of the disparity among these three assessment models are not trivial. Actuarial risk instruments—even the very poor ones—have an aura of objectivity and general superiority to clinical decision making. They appear "scientific." The results of this study demonstrate that such assumptions need to be justified. The predictive validity of actuarial tools must be examined, especially when they are used in settings other than those where they were developed. For example, if a low-risk classification was a factor in securing a less intrusive response from the juvenile justice system, then the Wisconsin Risk Assessment Tool would classify 1,215 of the current sample as low risk, and it would be correct in about seventy-five percent of cases (i.e., they would not reoffend during the study period). The configural model would identify 2,349 as low risk and get eighty-three percent of them correct. The neural networks model would identify 5,424 as low risk and get ninety-seven percent correct.

The appropriateness and predictive validity of risk assessment tools is clearly an issue that will continue to generate considerable research activity. The degree to which these instruments shape the rights and freedoms of juveniles is less well-known. This becomes particularly pertinent when it involves predictions of high risk that result in more intrusive interventions requiring juveniles to be removed from their home and school communities. Also pertinent is the risk instruments contributing directly or indirectly to discriminatory decisions based on such factors as gender and race. The Canadian Human Rights Commission has provided evidence that actuarial tools discriminate against women in general, and Aboriginal women and women with disabilities in particular.[119] Such criticism is found increasingly in Canadian research,[120] but is not as evident in the United States. Professor Ivan Zinger cites critics who argue that actuarial risk assessment not only reflects, but also contributes to, the overrepresentation of minorities in the juvenile and criminal justice systems[121] and states that "the enthusiasm demonstrated by its promoters is "cult-like.' "[122]

Actuarial risk assessment has not yet become the target of legalistic scrutiny and challenge, and there is little existing case law that addresses the problems identified in the present study. Judge David P. Cole and Former Director of Special Projects for the Corrections Branch of the Solicitor General Glenn Angus identify a few Canadian cases and one American case that directly questioned the scientific validity of actuarial risk assessment.[123] Ivan Zinger reports a review of Canadian case law as revealing no cases arguing that actuarial risk assessment violated individual rights.[124]

A review of federal and state case law in the United States does show that actuarial risk assessment is facing some legal challenge. A recent Illinois Supreme Court decision addressed a case where the respondent initially argued that actuarial risk assessment is "a novel scientific methodology that has yet to gain general acceptance in the psychological and psychiatric communities."[125] The respondent further argued that any expert testimony based on actuarial risk assessment must be excluded under Frye v. United States.[126] "The State argued that (1) actuarial principles are not the least bit novel and therefore are not subject to Frye; and (2) even if the particular actuarial instruments at issue are novel, they have gained general acceptance in the relevant psychological and psychiatric communities."[127] After conflicting opinions by the circuit and appellate courts, the Illinois Supreme Court ruled that actuarial risk assessment of a sexually violent offender meets the Frye general acceptance test and is admissible evidence in an Illinois court of law.[128]

As Ivan Zinger notes, most criticism of actuarial risk assessment fails to offer any reasonable alternative, and a return to clinical assessment takes us in the direction of increased and less explicit and recognizable bias.[129] The answer is not to throw the baby out with the bathwater—it is to recognize the gap that exists between theory and practice in the field of actuarial risk assessment in the United States and to move quickly to establish minimum quality control standards. The present study has established that actuarial risk assessments can vary enormously in terms of where they place juveniles and how accurate their predictions can be. For change to occur, there needs to be explicit recognition that the potential benefits of actuarial risk assessment can be achieved only by carefully maintaining the integrity of the risk prediction process. The methodological "high ground" needs to be earned and not simply assumed.

The analyses presented in this Article show the variation that exists between a reputable, widely recognized and commonly used tool such as the Wisconsin Risk Assessment Tool and alternative risk models developed for a specific sample.[130] For Philadelphia's delinquent population, the Wisconsin Risk Assessment Tool performed only slightly better than chance (the relative improvement over chance ("RIOC") statistic is seven percent). The configural model provided modest improvement (RIOC = twenty percent), and the neural networks model a very significant improvement (RIOC = ninety percent).

Neural networks represent a level of analysis that is not presently available on a widespread basis. Immediate improvements to the field of risk assessment are possible, however, with the application of several quality control measures. The benefits of a "scientific" label should adhere only if actuarial risk assessments meet or exceed the following criteria:

1. The risk assessment should have been tested for reliability and validated at the time of development. Both indicators should be reassessed at least every three years.
2. If a risk assessment developed for a specific population is being used in a different setting—whether this be defined by geography, race, gender, age, etc.—then it must be validated prior to implementation where data allow, or within two years of implementation if required historic data are not available.
3. If a risk assessment of a specific outcome is being used for a different purpose, its predictive validity needs to be established—e.g., an assessment of general reoffending likely has little predictive validity for outcomes such as dangerousness, violent reoffending, or sexual reoffending.
4. The tests of reliability and validity need to be conducted by researchers who do not have a vested interest in the promotion of the assessment tools.[131]
5. The content or format of a risk assessment should match the original risk assessment—it must be recognized that any unauthorized deletions or additions may not only render the assessment tool invalid but introduce inappropriate, and not always recognizable, bias.

6. Risk assessments should be required to identify any possible gender and racial bias—i.e., tests that the predictive validity is comparable for appropriate subgroups of the population.
7. Risk assessment tools should have a clearly defined and reasonable articulation of the number of risk levels it produces and the cutoff scores for those categories (i.e., the risk score that moves a juvenile from medium to high risk).
8. All risk assessments are dependent on the quality and availability of the risk measures. Data quality should be explicitly reviewed and reported—e.g., adequate reliability and psychometric validity of the risk variables employed and, for each risk item, the proportion of cases for which data are missing.

This article clearly demonstrates the importance and value of using more sophisticated research protocols in juvenile justice and child welfare. The results presented also have implications for the professional development of many of the criminal justice and juvenile justice researchers in academic and practice settings. Configural analysis is rarely used and neural networks are something about which many researchers are quite unfamiliar. The results also demonstrate the value of enlisting support and participation of professionals from disciplines outside the traditional social and behavioral science fields. We must reach out to well-trained experts in computer and information sciences, engineering, and bioinformatics—experts trained and familiar with the advanced research protocols that are needed to advance the quality of work currently being completed in the field.

There is a desperate need to inform and educate practitioners in the field of juvenile justice and child welfare—particularly judges and administrators—about new advances that can significantly improve the quality of services and decision making. If they remain uninformed about new developments—particularly ones that involve advanced research protocols—they are unlikely to embrace promising practices anytime soon. This may explain why there continues to be widespread use and abuse of actuarial models of risk assessment despite their limited utility, and the fact that, while vintage for their time, they are based on obsolete technology.

Maintaining the integrity of the risk assessment process by identifying and requiring adherence to minimal standards of quality is imperative. After more than two decades of relative neglect, it is unlikely that sufficient impetus for improvement will come solely from the researchers and statisticians who develop the models, or even from decision makers who use the models. There is an opportunity for lawyers and child advocates to inject increased rigor into the use of actuarial risk assessment practices of the field. Given the current poor standards of risk assessment applications and the significant potential for improvement, there is no time for delay.

Reprinted from Peter R. Jones, David R. Schwartz, Ira M. Schwartz, Zoran Obradovic, and Joseph Jupin, Risk classification and juvenile dispositions: What is the state of the art? *Temple Law Review* 79 (2000): 461–98. Reprinted by permission.

Notes

1. Ilyse Grinberg et al., Adolescents at Risk for Violence: An Initial Validation of the Life Challenges Questionnaire and Risk Assessment Index, 40 *Adolescence* 573, 573–74 (2005).

2. See Office of Juvenile Justice & Delinquency Prevention, Comprehensive Strategy for Serious, Violent, and Chronic Juvenile Offenders 7 (1998) (discussing states' responses in attempting to fulfill responsibilities of juvenile justice system).

3. See Ted Palmer, *The Re-emergence of Correctional Intervention* 35–39 (1992) (discussing studies that show effectiveness of treatments where specific programs are chosen depending on certain characteristics of an offender).

4. See Kelly Hannah-Moffat & Paula Maurutto, Dep't of Justice Can., Youth Risk/Need Assessment: An Overview of Issues and Practices §1.0, at 1 (2003), http://www.justice.gc.ca/en/ps/rs/rep/2003/rr03yj-4/rr03yj-4_1.html (noting that classifying risks and needs of youths using "new actuarial and quasi-actuarial techniques" is growing trend among researchers).

5. For a review of literature dealing with methods of risk assessment currently used in juvenile justice and child welfare, see generally Tim Brennan, Classification: An Overview of Selected Methodological Issues, in *Prediction & Classification: Criminal Justice Decision Making* 201 (Don M. Gottfredson & Michael Tonry eds., 1987) (calling for upgrade in quality of classification methods by integrating interdisciplinary methodological frameworks); Stephen D. Gottfredson, Prediction: An Overview of Selected Methodological Issues, in *Prediction & Classification: Criminal Justice Decision Making*, supra, at 21 (discussing why actuarial approach methods are superior and describing methods of analysis); Roger Tarling & John A. Perry, Statistical Methods in Criminological Prediction, in *Prediction in Criminology* 210 (David P. Farrington & Roger Tarling eds., 1985) (comparing various statistical predictive techniques); Leslie T. Wilkins, The Politics of Prediction, in *Prediction in Criminology*, supra, at 34 (discussing superiority of statistical over clinical analyses and moral implications of predictive assessments); Christopher Baird et al., Risk Assessment in Child Protective Services: Consensus and Actuarial Model Reliability, 78 *Child Welfare* 723 (1999) (comparing actuarial-based systems with consensus-based systems); Robyn M. Dawes et al., Clinical Versus Actuarial Judgment, 243 *Sci.* 1668 (1989) (finding actuarial methods superior at predicting human behavior over clinical methods); Robert D. Hoge, Standardized Instruments for Assessing Risk and Need in Youthful Offenders, 29 *Crim. Just. & Behav.* 380 (2002) (comparing three standardized risk assessment measures and explaining why they are preferred over clinical methods). See also Peter R. Jones, Risk Prediction in Criminal Justice, in *Choosing Correctional Options That Work* 33, 35 (Alan T. Harland ed., 1995) (stating that evidence points to success of statistical over clinical prediction methods); D.A. Andrews et al., Does Correctional Treatment Work? A Clinically Relevant and Psychologically Informed Meta-Analysis, 28 *Criminology* 369, 377–80 (1990) (providing examples of statistical analyses); Christopher Baird & Dennis Wagner, The Relative Validity of Actuarial-and Consensus-Based Risk Assessment Systems, 22 *Child. & Youth Servs. Rev.* 839, 867 (2000) (finding actuarial-based systems more accurate than consensus-based systems).

6. According to the NCCD website, the organization has collaborated with over seventy-five state and local jurisdictions as well as with the United States Department of Justice. More information about the NCCD can be found at The National Council on Crime and Delinquency, http://www.nccd-crc.org/nccd/n_index_main.html (last visited Jan. 2, 2007).

7. See Baird & Wagner, supra note 5, at 842–43 (discussing accuracy of actuarial risk assessment systems); Dawes et al., supra note 5, at 1673 (determining that actuarial method of predicting human behavior is superior to clinical method because its accuracy can be more easily monitored); Jones, supra note 5, at 35 (stating that evidence points to success of statistical over clinical prediction methods); David R. Schwartz et al., Computational Intelligence Techniques for Risk Assessment and Decision Support, 26 *Child. & Youth Servs. Rev.* 1081, 1082–83 (2004) (suggesting that actuarial risk assessment methods are more reliable than consensus or clinical methods).

8. See Dawes et al., supra note 5, at 1673 (explaining that although actuarial methods have great benefits, "quality controls" should be used to ensure that actuarial method is appropriately working).

9. For a discussion of studies that have demonstrated the greater effectiveness of empirical approaches over clinical approaches, see generally John Monahan, The Scientific Status of Research on Clinical and Actuarial Predictions of Violence, in 2 *Science in the Law: Social and Behavioral Science* Issues §2–2.1.1(2); (David L. Faigman et al. eds., 2002); Tarling & Perry, supra note 5; Dawes et al., supra note 5; William M. Grove & Paul E. Meehl, Comparative Efficiency of Informal (Subjective, Impressionistic) and Formal (Mechanical, Algorithmic) Prediction Procedure: The Clinical-Statistical Controversy, 2 *Psychol. Pub. Pol'y & L.* 293 (1996).

10. For more recent reviews of evaluations of actuarial assessment tools, see generally Grinberg et al., supra note 1; Shane R. Jimerson et al., The Santa Barbara Assets and Risks Assessment to Predict Recidivism Among Male and Female Juveniles: An Investigation of Inter-Rater Reliability and Predictive Validity, 27 *Educ. & Treatment Child.* 353 (2004); Cornelis Stadtland et al., Risk Assessment and Prediction of Violent and Sexual Recidivism in Sex Offenders: Long-term Predictive Validity of Four Risk Assessment Instruments, 16 J. *Forensic Psychiatry & Psychol.* 92 (2005).

11. See infra Parts III.B–D for a comparison of the performance of the Wisconsin Delinquency Risk Assessment, the customized model using configural analysis, and the customized model using neural networks.

12. See infra Part III.E for an examination of results of the comparison in relation to juvenile risk placement.

13. See infra Part III.F for an examination of the accuracy of each method in predicting reoffenders.

14. See infra Part III.A for an overview of the demographic data used in these assessments.

15. Seventy-three agencies representing forty-four states and twenty-four localities, collectively supervising well over half that nation's probationers and parolees, reported that just over one-third of agencies used the Wisconsin instrument or an instrument based on the Wisconsin model. U.S. Dep't of Justice, Nat'l Inst. of Corr., Topics in Community Corrections: Offender Assessment 4 (2003).

16. See infra Part III.C for an analysis of the customized model using configural analysis.

17. See infra Part III.D for an analysis of the customized model using neural networks.

18. See Baird & Wagner, supra note 5, at 840 (stating that, as of 1996, at least thirty-eight out of fifty-four U.S. states and territories used formal risk assessment tools; twenty-six implemented tools after 1987).

19. Id. at 842; Dawes et al., supra note 5, at 1671–72; Grove & Meehl, supra note 9, at 293–95.

20. See Paul E. Meehl, Clinical Versus Statistical Prediction: A Theoretical Analysis and a Review of the Evidence 3–4, 136 (1954) (labeling clinical methods as hypothesizing predictors of risk as opposed to actuarial methods that use statistics and concluding that use of actuarial method is "unavoidable" because clinical methods are untrustworthy); Baird et al., supra note 5, at 743 (finding that actuarial methods are more consistent and reliable than consensus, or clinical, methods); Dawes et al., supra note 5, at 1671 (finding that actuarial methods are more accurate than clinical judgment methods because clinical methods rely on independent judgments that can dramatically fluctuate and are not statistically significant).

21. Baird & Wagner, supra note 5, at 839–40.

22. See Jones, supra note 5, at 43 (discussing programs developed through assistance from the NIC); Baird & Wagner, supra note 5, at 842 (stating that NCCD has conducted actuarial research in at least seven states since 1989). See generally Office of Juvenile Justice & Delinquency Prevention, supra note 2 (introducing its strategy for dealing with varying degrees of juvenile offenders).

23. See infra Part III.B for a list of the eight factors.

24. See generally Baird & Wagner, supra note 5 (comparing Washington Risk Assessment

Matrix with California Family Assessment Factor Analysis and Michigan Structured Decision Making System's Family Risk Assessment of Abuse and Neglect); Peter R. Jones et al., Identifying Chronic Juvenile Offenders, 18 *Just. Q.* 479 (2001) (describing study identifying chronic juvenile offenders in Orange County, California).

25. See Hoge, supra note 5, at 390–91 (explaining YLS/CMI method). See generally Hannah-Moffat & Maurutto, supra note 4, §4.0, at 9–13 (reviewing and critiquing risk assessment procedures in Canada, including YLS/CMI); David P. Cole & Glenn Angus, Using Pre-Sentence Reports to Evaluate and Respond to Risk, 47 *Crim. L.Q.* 302 (2003) (describing benefits of presentence reports in risk assessment); Ivan Zinger, Actuarial Risk Assessment and Human Rights: A Commentary, 46 *Canadian J. Criminology & Crim. Just.* 607, 609 (2004) (commenting on accuracy of third-generation actuarial risk assessment techniques, particularly Canada's LSI-R, in predicting recidivism).

26. Office of Juvenile Justice & Delinquency Prevention, supra note 2, at 13–14.

27. For examples of each type of study, see generally D.A. Andrews et al., The Recent Past and Near Future of Risk and/or Need Assessment, 52 *Crime & Delinq.* 7 (2006) (comparing performance of different types of empirical methods); Baird & Wagner, supra note 5 (comparing predictive validity of actuarial-and consensus-based or clinical methods); Grinberg et al., supra note 1 (validating existing actuarial method).

28. See Stephen D. Gottfredson & Don M. Gottfredson, Accuracy of Prediction Models, in 2 *Criminal Careers and "Career Criminals"* 212, 247 (Alfred Blumstein et al. eds., 1986) (explaining that various studies have determined statistical predictive devices are more accurate than clinical methods); Jones, supra note 5, at 35–36 (suggesting that all available evidence regards statistical predictive devices over clinical devices); Baird & Wagner, supra note 5, at 842–43 (noting that research has shown superiority of actuarial method over clinical method); Dawes et al., supra note 5, at 1673 (reviewing research that propels theory that actuarial assessment is as accurate or more accurate at prediction than clinical assessment).

29. Gottfredson & Gottfredson, supra note 28, at 247.

30. See Monahan, supra note 9, §2–2.1.1(2), at 102–3 (discussing actuarial study indicating that substance abuse, prior arrests for violent crimes, and young age were significant predictors of future violence); Tarling & Perry, supra note 5, at 212–13 (explaining that variables used to predict reconviction can remain relatively constant); Dawes et al., supra note 5, at 1671 (stating that actuarial tools are effective in identifying significant variables that contributed to a decision); Grove & Meehl, supra note 9, at 317 (stating that actuarial data allows most influential variables to be identified).

31. See Gottfredson & Gottfredson, supra note 28, at 247–48 (citing various studies in which results from actuarial devices were superior to individual human's judgment).

32. Eileen Gambrill & Aron Shlonsky, Risk Assessment in Context, 22 *Child. & Youth Servs. Rev.* 813, 825 (2000).

33. Id. at 826.

34. For a review of such literature, see Jess McDonald & John Goad, Ill. Dep't of Children & Family Servs., Illinois Child Endangerment Risk Assessment Protocol 10 (2002), available at http://www.state.il.us/dcfs/docs/cerap2002.pdf (concluding that Child Endangerment Risk Assessment Protocol reduced recurrence rates of maltreatment for at-risk children); Grinberg et al., supra note 1, at 598 (finding "initial support" for validity of The Life-Challenges Questionnaire and Risk Assessment Index as a risk assessment measure); Jimerson et al., supra note 10, at 370 (concluding that Santa Barbara Assets and Risks Assessment provides enhanced assessment of juveniles for both males and females); Stadtland et al., supra note 10, at 105–6 (finding that various assessment tools efficiently predicted violent nonsexual, noncontact sexual, and contact sexual recidivism).

35. See, e.g., Hannah-Moffat & Maurutto, supra note 4, §4.0, at 9–10, §6.1, at 27 (noting that government and contract researchers conducted many of these studies and suggesting that independent researchers should be conducting these studies to ensure lack of bias).

36. Tarling & Perry, supra note 5, at 211 ("On the basis of her results and those of other prediction studies that she reviewed, Simon argued that no method was greatly superior to any other and concluded that "from this examination of statistical methods for combining data . . . in practice all of them work about equally well.'" (quoting Frances H. Simon, Home Office Research Study No. 7, Prediction Methods in Criminology: Including a Prediction Study of Young Men on Probation 154 (1971)).

37. Jones, supra note 5, at 43–44.

38. Gottfredson, supra note 5, at 24–25.

39. Peter Schmidt & Ann Dryden Witte, *Predicting Recidivism Using Survival Models* 13–14 (1988).

40. David P. Farrington & Roger Tarling, Criminological Prediction: The Way Forward, in *Prediction in Criminology*, supra note 5, at 264.

41. See Gottfredson, supra note 5, at 26–27 (explaining how statistical methods sometimes assume that results from one sample can explain results from similar sample).

42. For examples of studies of human behavior from nontraditional disciplines, see generally Albert Nigrin, *Neural Networks for Pattern Recognition* (1993) (studying frameworks of pattern recognition by neural networks); T.A. Arentze et al., Using Decision Tree Induction Systems for Modeling Space-Time Behavior, 32 *Geographical Analysis* 330 (2000) (discussing use of decision tree induction systems to predict an individual's activity and travel choices).

43. Tarling & Perry, supra note 5, at 227.

44. Hannah-Moffat & Maurutto, supra note 4, §4.1, at 12–13.

45. Id.

46. Roderick J.A. Little & Donald B. Rubin, *Statistical Analysis with Missing Data* 60–61 (1987).

47. See generally Dean J. Champion, *Measuring Offender Risk: A Criminal Justice Sourcebook* (1994) (reviewing thoroughly a range of issues pertaining to development and application of risk assessment within criminal and juvenile justice without once referring to problems of missing data). But see Don M. Gottfredson & Howard M. Snyder, Office of Juvenile Justice & Delinquency Prevention, National Center for Juvenile Justice Report, The Mathematics of Risk Classification: Changing Data into Valid Instruments for Juvenile Courts 6 (2005), available at http://www.ncjrs.gov/ html/ojjdp/209158 (dealing specifically with the mathematical aspects of risk assessment and stating that "missing data cause great problems").

48. See Jones, supra note 5, at 36 (detailing various studies attempting to predict criminality since the 1920s).

49. See generally Ernest W. Burgess, Factors Determining Success or Failure on Parole, in *The Workings of the Indeterminate-Sentence Law and the Parole System in Illinois* 205 (Andrew A. Bruce et al. eds., 1928) (discussing factors that may help determine whether an individual is more or less likely to violate his or her parole).

50. See generally Lloyd E. Ohlin, *Selection for Parole: A Manual of Parole Prediction* (1951) (discussing factors that may help determine whether an individual is likely to violate his or her parole and how to utilize these factors).

51. Don M. Gottfredson et al., *Guidelines for Parole & Sentencing* 17–36 (1978).

52. David P. Farrington & Roger Tarling, Criminological Prediction: An Introduction, in *Prediction in Criminology*, supra note 5, at 7 (citing Steven Glueck & Eleanor T. Glueck, Unraveling Juvenile Delinquency (1950)).

53. Farrington & Tarling, supra note 52, at 8.

54. For a discussion of potential predictors typically used in a juvenile court or welfare agency, see generally Gwen A. Kutz & Louis E. Moore, *The "8% Problem": Chronic Juvenile Offender Recidivism* (1994); Charles W. Dean et al., Criminal Propensities, Discrete Groups of Offenders, and Persistence in Crime, 34 *Criminology* 547 (1996); Christy A. Visher et al., Predicting the Recidivism of Serious Youthful Offenders Using Survival Models, 29 *Criminology* 329 (1991).

55. See Sheila Mitchell & Peter Rosa, Boyhood Behaviour Problems as Precursors of Criminality: A Fifteen-Year Follow-Up Study, 22 J. *Child Psychol. & Psychiatry & Allied Disciplines* 19, 33

(1981) (finding that a child is more likely to be convicted of crime later in life if he or she has previously exhibited "anti-social behavior (stealing, lying, destructiveness and wandering from home)").

56. See David Riley & Margaret Shaw, Home Office Research Study No. 83, Parental Supervision and Juvenile Delinquency 1, 2 (1985) (noting that child offenders "tend to come from large families, to have parents with a criminal record, to have poor or erratic discipline at home, conflict between parents, and poor supervision by their parents").

57. See Donald J. West, *Delinquency: Its Roots, Careers & Prospects* 29–30 (1982) (finding that juveniles are twice as likely to become delinquent if their parents have a low income, come from a large family, have a criminal record, or are "unsatisfactory" with "below-average intelligence").

58. See David P. Farrington, Nat'l Inst. of Justice, Further Analyses of a Longitudinal Survey of Crime and Delinquency: Final Report to the National Institute of Justice 68–80 (1983) (discussing correlation between troubled youths and families with convicted parents).

59. Albert I. Reiss, Jr., Co-Offender Influences on Criminal Careers, in 2 Criminal Careers and "Career Criminals," supra note 28, at 122–23.

60. See Michael R. Gottfredson, Home Office Research Study No. 81, Victims of Crime: The Dimensions of Risk 14–15 (1984) (finding that self-reported drinking correlates with risk of personal victimization).

61. See William McCord & Joan McCord, *The Psychopath: An Essay on the Criminal Mind* 8–17 (1964) (discussing personality traits that can characterize individual as psychopath, including being asocial, having uncontrollable desires, being impulsive, being aggressive, feeling little guilt, and not having capacity to develop lasting, loving relationships).

62. See David Thornton et al., Pretreatment Self-Esteem and Posttreatment Sexual Recidivism, 48 *Int'l J. Offender Therapy & Comp. Criminology* 587, 587 (2004) (finding a correlation between low self-esteem and higher sexual recidivism).

63. See Andrews et al., supra note 27, at 7 (stating that treatment strategies for juvenile criminals should be matched to motivation of participants).

64. See Stephen A. Cernkovich & Peggy C. Giordano, Family Relationships and Delinquency, 25 *Criminology* 295, 297 (1987) (discussing that children in homes in which family members get along well with one another are less likely to have delinquency problems, even if parents are separated or divorced).

65. See Steven A. Cernkovich & Peggy C. Giordano, School Bonding, Race and Delinquency, 30 *Criminology* 261, 261 (1992) (noting that juvenile delinquency increases when juvenile's bond to school is low).

66. See Richard Dembo et al., The Role of Family Factors, Physical Abuse and Sexual Victimization Experiences in High-Risk Youths' Alcohol and Other Drug Use and Delinquency: A Longitudinal Model, 7 *Violence & Victims* 245, 245 (1992) (finding significant relationship between physical abuse or sexual victimization and juvenile delinquency).

67. See Pamela K. Lattimore et al., Risk of Death Among Serious Young Offenders, 34 J. Res. Crime & Delinq. 187, 188 (1997) (noting that gang involvement, a factor that leads to victimization, may also lead to criminality).

68. Jones et al., supra note 24, at 480; Robert J. Sampson et al., Assessing "Neighborhood Effects": Social Processes and New Directions in Research, 28 *Ann. Rev. Soc.* 443, 443–45 (2002).

69. See Hannah-Moffat & Maurutto, supra note 4, §2.0, at 3 (noting that risk assessments traditionally receiving the most attention stress "static historic factors, such as age, number and type of convictions, sexual offending, and relationship to victim").

70. See id. at 2–4 (discussing distinctiveness of "third-generation risk assessment" that takes into account both static and dynamic risk factors).

71. Simon, supra note 36, at 154.

72. Simon used Predictive Attribute Analysis and OLS Multiple Regression in her work. Id. at 80, 91.

73. Tarling & Perry, supra note 5, at 214–26.

74. See generally Steven D. Gottfredson & Michael D. Gottfredson, *Screening for Risk: A Comparison of Methods* 62–63 (1979) (determining analytic methods examined produced same degree of predictive efficiency).

75. Steven D. Gottfredson & Don M. Gottfredson, Screening for Risk Among Parolees: Policy, Practice and Method, in Prediction in Criminology, supra note 5, at 54, 75; see also Don M. Gottfredson et al., The Utilization of Experience in Parole Decision-Making: Summary Report 18 (1974) (suggesting that less powerful and more simple prediction techniques may produce better predictive validity than more complex techniques given insufficient data).

76. Hannah-Moffat & Maurutto, supra note 4, §4.0, at 10.

77. Wilkins, supra note 5, at 50.

78. S. Christopher Baird et al., Wis. Div. of Corr., The Wisconsin Case Classification/Staff Deployment Project: A Two Year Follow-Up Report 9 (1979).

79. Tarling & Perry, supra note 5, at 215–16.

80. See Simon, supra note 36, at 72–134 (comparing several statistical techniques for their predictability).

81. See Gottfredson & Gottfredson, supra note 75, at 54 (comparing statistical efficiency of five methods for predicting parole risk).

82. See Tarling & Perry, supra note 5, at 212–26 (studying whether social and criminal histories of individuals were predictive of future criminal convictions using the Automatic Interaction Detection and Logistic Regression methods of analysis).

83. Peter R. Jones et al., Evaluating Services to Delinquent Youth in Philadelphia: The Pro-DES Information System, 59 *J. Pa. Ass'n Probation, Parole & Corrections* 10, 10–13 (1999).

84. Removal of cases with missing data is not a problem in the present study since its function is solely to compare different methods of assessment for the same juveniles rather than build a risk assessment tool for use in the field.

85. Prorated total risk scores were calculated in cases involving any missing data.

86. Alternative cutoff points were evaluated but none provided improvement.

87. Baird et al., supra note 78, at 10 tbl.1, 21.

88. Id. at 10 tbl.1, 11 tbl.2.

89. K. N. Wright, T. R. Clear & P. Dickinson, Universal Applicability of Probation Risk-Assessment Instruments: A Critique, 22 *Criminology* 113–34 (1984).

90. Id.

91. Gambrill & Shlonsky, supra note 32, at 825–26.

92. Arentze et al., supra note 42, at 336–38. A tree induction algorithm, or nonparametric classification procedure, is a "discrete choice model" that predicts an individual's behavior and choices. Id. at 330. These algorithms "assume that individuals compare a number of choice alternatives on relevant attributes and choose the alternative that maximizes some measure of utility." Id.

93. Irene Casas, Evaluating the Importance of Accessibility to Congestion Response Using a GIS-Based Travel Simulator, 5 *J. Geographical Sys.* 109, 119 (2003).

94. See R. Gnanadesikan, Methods for Statistical Data Analysis of Multivariate Observations 333 (1997) (stating that since the late 1970s researchers have widely used the Statistical Package for the Social Scientist to perform data analysis).

95. Emma C. Smith & Klaus Grawe, What Makes Psychotherapy Sessions Productive? A New Approach to Bridging the Gap Between Process Research and Practice, 10 *Clinical Psychol. & Psychotherapy* 275, 278 (2003).

96. John Welte et al., Risk Factors for Pathological Gambling, 29 *Addictive Behav.* 323, 329 (2004).

97. Jedid-Jah Jonker et al., Joint Optimization of Customer Segmentation and Marketing Policy to Maximize Long-term Profitability, 27 *Expert Systems with Applications* 159, 159–60 (2004).

98. Smith & Grawe, supra note 95, at 279.

99. See Casas, supra note 93, at 119–24 (using the CHAID method of risk assessment research for geographical planning of transportation system).

100. Jones et al., supra note 24, at 490.

101. Bennie R. Grobler et al., The Chaid-Technique and the Relationship Between School Effectiveness and Various Independent Variables, 30 *Int'l Stud. Educ. Admin.* 49, 49–50 (2002).

102. Smith & Grawe, supra note 95, at 278.

103. Id. at 279.

104. Jay Magidson, The CHAID Approach to Segmentation Modeling: Chi-squared Automatic Interaction Detection, in *Advanced Methods of Marketing Research* 118, 156–57 (Richard P. Bagozzi ed., 1994) (discussing that CHAID segmentation algorithm is superior to the previously used models when desired result is clusters with differing criterion).

105. Schwartz et al., supra note 7, at 1082.

106. Id. at 1091.

107. Earl Cox, *Fuzzy Logic for Business and Industry* 582 (1995).

108. Schwartz et al., supra note 7, at 1084.

109. Felipe Atienza et al., Risk Stratification in Heart Failure Using Artificial Neural Networks, *Proc. AMIA Ann. Symp.* 32, 34 (2000), available at http://www.amia.org/pubs/proceedings/symposia/2000/ D200367.pdf.

110. Richard K. Orr, Use of Probabilistic Neural Network to Estimate the Risk of Mortality After Cardiac Surgery, 17 *Med. Decision Making* 178, 178 (1997).

111. Schwartz et al., supra note 7, at 1084.

112. For a discussion of Schwartz's work with neural networks, see supra note 7, at 1081.

113. Schwartz et al, supra note 7, at 1092; see also David B. Marshall & Diana J. English, Neural Network Modeling of Risk Assessment in Child Protective Services, 5 *Psychol. Methods* 102, 103 (2000) (concluding that under certain conditions linear decision making is superior to clinical judgments).

114. Nigrin, supra note 42, at 107–8.

115. See Gottfredson, supra note 5, at 24 (suggesting that "no clear-cut empirical advantages of selecting one prediction method over another" exist).

116. See Schmidt & Witte, supra note 39, at 15 (finding it encouraging that research studies kept false positives and false negatives below fifty percent).

117. See, e.g., Eileen Gambrill, *Critical Thinking in Clinical Practice: Improving the Quality of Judgments & Decisions* 442–43 (2d ed. 2005) (stating that actuarial model is superior because it can better integrate substantial amounts of diverse data).

118. See id. at 234–35 (suggesting that relying on small sample sizes may cause inaccurate estimates).

119. Canadian Human Rights Comm'n, Protecting Their Rights: A Systemic Review of Human Rights in Correctional Services for Federally Sentenced Women 24–25 (2003).

120. See Zinger, supra note 25, at 610 (citing series of criticisms of actuarial tools for discrimination against women).

121. Id. at 613.

122. Id. at 613–14 (quoting Kelly Hannah-Moffat & Margaret Shaw, Situation risquée: Le risque et les services correctionnels au Canada, 34 *Criminologie* 47 (2001)).

123. David P. Cole & Glenn Angus, Using Pre-Sentence Reports to Evaluate and Respond to Risk, 47 *Crim. L.Q.* 302, 313–14 (2003) (citing, among other cases, Bains v. Canada (Nat'l Parole Bd.), [1989] 3 F.C. 450; Moore v. Valdez, unreported op. (Fla. C.I. Aug. 21, 2000)).

124. Zinger, supra note 25, at 615.

125. In re Commitment of Simons, 821 N.E.2d 1184, 1186 (Ill. 2004).

126. Simons, 821 N.E.2d at 1186. Frye provides that scientific evidence is an admissible methodology if it has gained mainstream, general acceptance. Frye v. United States, 293 F. 1013, 1014 (D.C. Cir. 1923).

127. Simons, 821 N.E.2d at 1186–87.

128. Id. at 1196.

129. Zinger, supra note 25, at 615–16.

130. See supra Part III.E for a comparison of the three models discussed.

131. As Ivan Zinger notes, risk assessment has become big business and independent evaluations are required to support those of the individuals or companies that developed the tools. Zinger, supra note 25, at 608.

Commentary: My Life at Penn

Ira M. Schwartz

I became the dean of the (then) School of Social Work at the University of Pennsylvania in July 1993. This was an exciting time at Penn. The University was in the final throes of a $1.5 billion dollar campaign, and had just recruited a new, and its first woman, president. Dr. Judith Rodin was committed to excellence and catapulting the university into becoming a truly world class academic and research institution.

The School of Social Work had fallen on hard times. Although enrollments were strong, the quality of the students was weak in comparison to the rest of the University. The faculty, with a few notable exceptions, were not actively engaged in research, did not have much in the way of research funding, and were not contributing to the scholarly literature.

In many respects, the School was out of step with the rest of the university. In fact, I learned after I arrived that the Board of Trustees of the university had actually explored the possibility of closing the School but decided against doing so. Penn was only one of two Ivy League universities with a school of social work, and the trustees felt it should be one of the leading schools of social work in the country. Also, because Penn is located in the city of Philadelphia, it was felt that this was the ideal environment for a school of social work to flourish.

The plan to revitalize the School was relatively clear and straightforward. The first order of business was that the faculty needed to be rebuilt. Fortunately, there were a number of vacant positions. The initial goal was to aggressively recruit distinguished and highly productive senior faculty, particularly faculty with external funding and who were not yet at the peak of their careers. We also wanted to recruit senior faculty who could help attract promising junior faculty and serve as their mentors.

The second part of the strategy consisted of developing incentives for existing faculty to be more productive and to reward faculty based upon performance. At the same time, standards for promotion and tenure were strengthened and faculty had to demonstrate that they were outstanding educators as well as outstanding researchers and scholars.

The third component consisted of raising the standards for admission to both the master's and doctoral programs.

The last component consisted of building a stronger constituency for the School.

The School had a Board of Overseers, but it was weak and made up largely of social workers in the community. While important people in the social work profession locally, they were not the kind of people who could generate resources for the School, resources it desperately needed. Consequently, the Board was changed and the membership made up of prominent university alumni and people from the community, and people with significant capability.

In general this strategy proved to be highly successful. As the record will show, the faculty who were recruited in the mid and late 1990s were strong and helped to advance the reputation and standing of the School. The volume of externally funded research increased greatly, and the numbers of articles, book chapters and books authored and co-authored by Penn School of Social Work faculty increased dramatically as well. In fact, independent studies show that the School ranks in the top three of all schools of social work in the country with respect to the volume publications appearing in respected academic journals. Also, and just as important, the quality of professional education at the School improved significantly.

I left the deanship at the end of June 2001. While I believe my tenure as dean was successful, my one regret is that I was not able to leave the School with a larger endowment. Had I stayed, raising more endowment resources, particularly for endowment professorships and student financial aid, would have been the next items on my agenda.

From a personal perspective, I have no doubt that my experience at Penn, both as a dean and as an administrator, prepared me well for my next position, provost at Temple University.

Chapter 37
Organizational Learning and Change in a Public Child Welfare Agency

Burton J. Cohen and Michael J. Austin

There is general agreement today among researchers and practitioners that our large public child welfare agencies are in trouble. Faced with more severe cases, fewer resources, and conflicting mandates, they have come under attack from the media, from advocacy groups, and from the social work profession itself. In a comprehensive study of child and family service systems around the country, Kamerman and Kahn (1989) concluded that

During the 1980s, social services for children, youth, and families underwent a series of changes as a result of both federal policies and developments in society. These changes, imposed on what appeared to be an increasingly overburdened system, created crises in some places, uncertainty in others, and pressure everywhere.

In order to respond to these changes, Kamerman and Kahn call for a reformulation of social policies, such as a larger role for government requirements for strong professional child protective services more public funding and more cross-system cooperation.

Other critics have called for changes in how programs and services are delivered. For instance, child welfare agencies have been asked to become more prevention oriented, more family focused, more decentralized, and more connected to their communities. As appealing as these recommendations may be, they are typically directed towards organizational settings that have been notoriously poor at adapting to changing conditions, encouraging new ideas and creative solutions, experimenting with new approaches, and managing major organizational transformations. Most public child welfare agencies still operate as monolithic bureaucracies with rigid lines of authority and top-down decision making that is often uninformed by the experience of line workers (Hegar and Hunzeker 1988; Thomas 1990; Weatherley 1980). Change often comes slowly in such systems, if at all and is typically accompanied by frustration and resistance. Public child welfare bureaucracies, for the most part, simply have not built the internal or external structures for promoting continuous learning and improvement. Yet, this is precisely what is required if major transformations are to occur in the delivery of services.

Producing substantial change in child welfare systems requires changes in how we think about and utilize human resources, especially the staff who work most closely with clients of the child welfare system. We are just beginning to acknowledge that most child welfare organizations are not "good places to work," and that poor working conditions add to the already existing stress and frustration among the workers. These conditions include neglected and unsafe physical plants, lack of clerical assistance, excessive workloads, inadequate supervision, and excessive paperwork, regulations, and monitoring (Bramhall and Ezell 1981; Pecora et al. 1989; Woolverton 1989). The transformation of the workplace in public child welfare organizations requires a recognition that top-down centrally mandated change efforts in human service settings, as in other large organizations, usually fail to produce the changes they espouse (Beer, Eisenstat, and Spector 1991).

In order to illustrate and refine how organizational change can take place in human service organizations through staff empowerment and collaborative action research, a case study is presented and discussed. A key feature of the change strategy is the process of creating "learning laboratories" where new approaches can be identified and tested in sheltered settings through intensive involvement of line workers and shared decision making. It contrasts with the more typical approach of trying to change the whole organization at once, or through top-down mandates. By undertaking experimental efforts and reflecting on the results, innovations can be spread to other parts of the organization or can stimulate alternative experiments and solutions.

Child Welfare and the Quality of Working Life

Efforts to transform the child welfare workplace will require giving more of a voice to workers and middle managers, experimenting with ways to redesign the work itself, and promoting continuous learning and improvement. The Quality of Working Life (QWL) movement which emerged in the 1970s is concerned with creating organizations that "more effectively deliver services and products valued by society, while simultaneously being rewarding stimulating places for employees to work" (Camman 1984). Pioneering efforts in industrial settings in England, have led to the identification of six intrinsic requirements for satisfying work regardless of the level of employment (Emery 1964):

1. For the content of the job to provide *variety and challenge.*
2. To be able to *learn on the job* and go on learning.
3. For an *area of decision making* that the worker can call his own.
4. For a certain degree of *social support and recognition* from colleagues in the workplace.
5. To be able to see a *tasks from start to finish* and how one's job contributes to a larger and meaningful whole.

6. Believing that one's job will continue to allow for *personal growth* and some sort of desirable future.

The challenge facing public child welfare organizations is how to create work settings and organizational structures that will promote the above six requirements. Just as the human services field and the social work profession have strongly advocated for the empowerment of clients and consumers of services, it is now time to address the need for empowerment of social services staff.

Efforts to redesign work and restructure the workplace also involve the sharing of power and decision making. This entails moving from a system of centralized decision making, to one that encourages initiative and innovation from individuals and units that are willing to assume more responsibility. It also implies a need to reframe the relationship between management and labor from an adversarial relationship to one that is more collaborative (Henrick 1990).

Action Research as an Approach to Organizational Change

Our approach to understanding the problem of organizational change in a public child welfare agency has been through action research, which was first developed by Kurt Lewin (1948) as a way to combine theory and practice, or experimentation and application. It was formulated as an approach that would be ideal "for scientists whose chief concern was geared toward action, toward changing the world while simultaneously contributing to the advance of scientific knowledge" (Marrow 1969). The major distinguishing feature of action research is the collaborative relationship between the researcher and the "client system," which may be an individual, a group or an organization that is in a problem situation. The researcher becomes involved in the action setting and the action process, which is directed towards producing some change. The researcher must therefore start with the problem situation as it is experienced by the client, and must take into account the action setting in all its complexity and turbulence.

The action research process bears some similarities to "social R&D" which Rothman (1982) has proposed as a systematic process for using scientific knowledge and methods to solve real world problems. This model, assumes that innovative ideas and practices can be designed, tested and diffused in a relatively stable host system through centrally managed processes. However, complex organizations often resist or ignore such efforts. In these instances, introducing innovation is not a linear sequence of events leading to discrete changes in programs; rather it involves a major transformation of the host organization itself. Such has been found to be the case in efforts to transform the public schools (Olson 1988) and the business corporation (Kanter 1985).

A Case Study of Organizational Change

When public child welfare agencies seek assistance from schools of social work, the interests usually focus on training. It was no different in 1985 when the Philadelphia

Department of Human Services Children and Youth Division agreed to support a special training program on ethnically sensitive social work practice. This successful training program for direct service staff evolved into an expanded program of supervisory management training and teambuilding for top administrative personnel. By 1988, a new commissioner and deputy commissioner requested an external independent assessment of the organization. The School of Social Work's Center for Research and Education on the Workplace was awarded the contract and completed the study in the Spring of 1989.

The Children and Youth Division (CYD) is the public child welfare agency for the city and county of Philadelphia. It receives federal, state, and local funding as part of a county-administered, state-supported system. The organizational study was one of the first efforts to assess how well the agency functioned from the staff's perspective. The Division had been operating under significant duress created by the rapid increase in very serious child abuse cases and the results of a state-mandated review team which had issued a report critical of its accountability processes and procedures. The process of identifying the key problems began with the work of an employee task force representing different levels and programs in CYD which had 650 employees. The task force identified the following major issues: (1) managing the inadequate service delivery resources, especially in the area of foster care for seriously abused children, (2) working in difficult conditions without sufficient workplace supports and resources, especially the lack of cars to make home visits, office space to work, and supplies, and (3) insufficient clarity about what should be the content of the case records and ways to simplify multiple reporting requirements. From the perspective of senior management, the major problems included the uncontrollable rise in cases which overwhelmed the organization, the difficulty in meeting state standards in the light of inadequate resources, and low staff morale caused, in part, by the local media attention and accusations blaming the organization for not preventing the deaths of abused children.

As part of the design of the organizational assessment, the employee task force was expanded into three design groups which met over a three-month period devoting their attention to the key issues of service delivery resources, workplace supports, and case record content. Each design group was assisted by a member of the consulting group and developed a set of recommendations for inclusion in the final report. The cabinet of senior management also served as an important partner in the study process by evaluating the standardized questionnaire and recommending customized questions as well as participating in in-depth interviews sharing their views of the organization.

The standardized questionnaire (Metrix 1987) of 122 items which included seven customized items was group-administered to 403 of the 650 employees for a 62% return rate. The instrument included items on job component, work relationships, organizational structure, organizational effectiveness, and planning.

The findings and recommendations were organized into four major themes (Cohen 1992; Austin and Cohen, pending review). The first theme related to the need to reassess the overall direction of the Division in relationship to its vision, mission, and organizational credo. The second theme involved the need to transform the organizational culture from one of rigidity and blaming to one of more flexibility and cooperation in managing change. The third theme addressed the need to clarify organizational structures, systems, and roles. And the fourth theme stressed the importance of actively managing the implementation process with respect to all the recommendations.

The recommendations served as the foundation for promoting change and increasing internal communications. Staff opinions on the study were solicited and passed up through the organization to top management for priority setting. In addition, intensive management team-building sessions were led by the consultants along with training sessions to clarify and explore the roles of middle-management administrators and supervisors. A six session training program was conducted for all 90 supervisors. It included further analysis of the organizational study for implications at the supervisory level. Supervisors were encouraged to share their interpretation of the study findings and recommendations. A second training program included all 18 senior administrators in order to address one of the key findings of the study, namely that the role of administrator needed more definition and clarification. While these training strategies provided an important step in clarifying the implementation issues identified in the recommendations, it was clear that lasting organization change could not rely solely on cross divisional training strategies aimed at individuals.

Although communication was increased, the study only heightened some existing conflicts about how to proceed and did little to achieve agency-wide consensus. The implementation process was further affected by several factors. First, a press conference announcing the results of the study resulted in news stories which emphasized and distorted one of the twenty recommendations, namely that more autonomous work units might serve to improve staff workflow and morale. This recommendation was interpreted as a statement that the only way to improve the agency was to decentralize the bulk of the operations into community-based service centers. Second, most of the top executive staff, who each had many years of experience in the agency, felt that the study did not tell them anything new, was viewed as superficial, and was simply a political act taken by the deputy commissioner to take off some of the pressure of the state office related to pending recertification. Third, the recommendation related to team-building at the top was seen as irrelevant by many senior staff members who attributed problems at the top to a lack of decisiveness and direction by the new deputy commissioner and commissioner (each had been in office one year). Fourth, nearly six months after the completion of the study, the deputy commissioner died unexpectedly at the age of 52.

While the consultants who conducted the study continued to serve as facilitators for the implementation phase, it was clear that the tension expressed in the interactions among senior staff would greatly slow and possibly impede the implementation process. It became clear to the consultants that a different approach would be needed in order to prevent the study findings from being ignored or buried by the inertia associated with the highly politicized crisis management environment of public child welfare administration.

Reformulating Our Approach

Nearly one year after the Organizational Study was completed, cynicism within the organization was still widespread and there was little to show in terms of actual changes in staff attitudes or behaviors. It seemed clear that there would need to be some fundamental shift in the organizational change strategy *and* that this would have to be accompanied by a change in the relationship between the University and the Department. If these changes could not occur, then the continuation of the project would be in serious doubt.

Up until this point, the University was viewed by the Department as an outside provider of training, not as a collaborator involved in the real work of the agency. While this may be a typical role for a University, it was seen by the consultants as an insufficient foundation for jointly bringing about fundamental organizational change. Training groups of supervisors and administrators in order to raise the capacity of individuals to improve the overall performance of the organization simply did not work. In a highly victimized and stalemated setting, individuals acting on their own can do little to induce change. In order to be an effective partner with the Department, the University consultants had to reconceptualize their role from that of a provider of training to being an active partner engaged with the agency in the change process. There were three major shifts associated with this reconceptualization.

The first shift was from focusing on individuals as the targets of intervention to whole work units. Without the support of others on whom they depend, individuals' efforts to produce organizational change were likely to be frustrating. Also, many of the recommended changes involved a system of interrelated tasks and roles. Therefore, efforts to produce change required a redesign of the work system. The target of intervention needed to embody major aspects of this work system.

The second shift was from providing training and technical assistance across the board (e.g., to all supervisors, or to all units) to focusing on *selected* work units. In particular, these units needed to be committed to engaging in a change process and willing to view themselves as experimental.

The third shift was from expecting training by itself to produce improvements in organizational performance to viewing training as a means to implementing new initiatives which had some commitment within the organization.

As the University consultants began to formulate this new approach, they proposed to the Department that the focus of the contracted work shift from training to that of assisting the Department in its efforts to institute change in two strategic areas. The areas were identified as (1) moving toward community based delivery of services, and (2) changing the work environment by moving from a rigid bureaucratic structure to a more open and participative organizational culture.

Another factor supported the shift away from organization wide change towards more localized change efforts contained within smaller units. There had been a growing awareness of the need to rethink the role of the senior mid-level managers known as Social Work Administrators (SWAs). In the Organizational Study, these individuals had expressed the most dissatisfaction with their jobs and the most cynicism about the possibilities for change. This was at first surprising, since there was a general perception among lower level staff that the SWAs were in a powerful position, although they were also perceived as being out of touch with what was actually happening on the line and with clients. Upon reflection, there are several possible explanations. One is that the Administrators face the classic dilemma of the "second floor bureaucrat," (Havassy 1990) of being too far from the line to experience the satisfaction of working with clients, and too removed from top management to feel that they have a real say in policymaking. In fact, interviews with several SWAs revealed the following perceptions of their role:

"We're a link in a chain; it feels like a production line."
"Our primary role is quality control—reviewing cases to ensure compliance; I'm the one who is held responsible."
"I'm just a conduit for upper management and the regulatory agencies."
"I feel powerless, isolated, and abandoned; people think I have control and I don't."

In contrast, when asked what they would like their role to be. those interviewed responded:

"More ability to do things with my own Section—to make changes, decisions, to do planning."
"More responsible for training of supervisors and direct service staff."
"More in control of the workflow."
"More involvement in policy making."

A key theme of the new change strategy was to shift the role of the Administrator from being someone who is responsible for reviewing and inspecting the work of thirty workers and over 750 cases to being the leader of a coherent work group known as a Section. Until this time, a Section had been a somewhat artificial group with little cohesiveness or identity of its own. Workers generally did not know all of the workers in their Section. nor did they see the Section as a place where their needs could be met. Under the new strategy, a Section would be acknowledged as the appropriate level for worker participation and shared decision making within CYD.

In order to test out the new approach, one experimental Section (consisting of an Administrator, five supervisors, and 25 line workers) was selected from among the eighteen Sections that carry out the operations of CYD. This Section (one of five that conducts Intake investigations) was chosen because the Administrator was excited about the prospects of involving the whole Section in a work improvement effort, and was also open to exploring her own role and how it might change. The experimental Intake Section was charged by the Commissioner of the Department with designing and carrying out a pilot effort "to test the feasibility of developing and implementing a staff development and workplace improvement plan at the level of a Section." The Section was to be viewed as a "laboratory" in which new ideas and approaches could be invented and tried out without trying to change the whole organization. The vehicle for planning and organizing the initiative was to be a representative governance group that came to be known as the Task Force on Staff Development and Workplace Supports. It consisted of the Administrator, each of the Supervisors, one worker selected from each of the five units, the Administrator's secretary, and a union representative.

A second arena for testing the new approach was an initiative to design a pilot project for delivering children and youth services from a field office to be located in a selected neighborhood. Up to this point in time, all of CYD's services were delivered from one central location with all Sections handling cases throughout the entire City. The Department had often been criticized for not having a more decentralized or community based approach, but previous efforts to consider decentralizing the entire agency had not been well-planned and had met with considerable staff resistance. Under the new initiative, a representative Task Force chaired by two Administrators was created and charged by the Commissioner with "designing a pilot project to test the feasibility of delivering child welfare services through a community based approach." In addition to the Administrators, the Task Force consisted of supervisors, line workers, clerical staff, and union representatives. The Task Force was encouraged to think as broadly and as creatively as possible.

After five months, the Task Force on Community Based Services designed a pilot program to be located in a specified part of the City and addressing all of the concerns that staff had previously expressed. The final report was accepted by the Commissioner and plans are now underway for implementation. The work improvement initiative, focusing on the experimental Intake Section, has resulted in several proposals which were approved and are currently being tested. These included a process for workers to assist each other in special circumstances, the assignment of a car from the city carpool exclusively to the Section, and taking responsibility for the planning and delivering of staff development for the Section as a whole. The Section recently voted to continue the initiative for a second year and they have been joined by a second experimental Section.

Spreading New Ideas Through Organizational Learning

These initiatives have been viewed as laboratories in which "sheltered" experiments could be conducted without necessarily involving or disrupting the rest of the Department. The participants were encouraged to design and try out the new approaches, reflect on the results, and then help to spread what was learned throughout the Department. They received support when needed from top management, but were as much as possible left alone to develop their own ideas.

There were several similarities between the two initiatives. Each was chaired by one or two Administrators in order to demonstrate that leadership and planning were appropriate roles for an Administrator. Each initiative was to be contained within one work group or part of the organization so as to shelter it from the complexity of trying to change the whole agency at once. Each was conceived of as a "laboratory" in which new ideas could be developed, nurtured, and tried out before attempting to spread them to other places. Each was given strong support from top management, but also given sufficient space and flexibility in which to innovate. Finally, each invited broad based participation from those who would be affected by the initiatives.

After an idea has been successfully developed in a "sheltered setting," how does it influence behavior throughout the larger organization? The process by which innovations developed and tested in one place are then spread to other places is commonly called "diffusion." Schön (1971) describes the way we typically think about diffusion as resting on three assumptions:

1. The innovation to be diffused exists fully realized in its essentials prior to its diffusion.
2. Diffusion is the movement of an innovation from a center out to its ultimate users.
3. Directed diffusion is a centrally managed process of dissemination, training, and provision of resources and incentives.

He then indicates that in cases of substantial organizational transformation, diffusion is much more disruptive and unpredictable, often leading to new organizational configurations. In these cases:

the problem of directed diffusion is to set in motion and guide a chain of related processes of social learning in which sequences of deliberate entrepreneurial intervention interact with unanticipated and inadvert processes, all more adequately treated under the metaphor of battle than communication. (108)

Our experiences with the spread of innovations in CYD tends to support this view. In organizations that are rigid and where change has been difficult, diffusion will seldom be an orderly process. We therefore have chosen to use the term "organizational learning" (Argyris and Schon 1978; Bunker and Wijnberg 1988) instead of diffusion to describe the processes by which new ideas and practices are spread throughout an organization and compete with the conventional ways of operating. Organizational learning is the process through which an organization continuously improves its performance over time, and through experience. The learning process is interactive and purposeful, not simply the receiving of information or ideas from a central source. Learning takes place as the parts of an organization struggle to make sense of current practices or conditions that are considered problematic, and to invent more effective practices.

A concrete example of organizational learning in CYD occurred in the area of staff development. The experimental Intake Section decided to develop a staff development plan for the whole Section as an alternative to the established practice of each worker attempting individually to meet the agency's annual training requirement. In order to experiment with this approach, a committee planned one training session based on an overall need that had been identified: the need for a theoretical framework that would define intake and its function, and promote more consistency, objectivity and self-awareness in completing investigations.

Arrangements were made with a faculty member from the School of Social Work to conduct this session, and the planning committee met with him twice to plan the session and ways to utilize some actual cases that Section members would present. The session was enthusiastically received and the members of the Section decided to proceed with developing more Section-wide training activities. The perceived benefits were that this model more effectively addressed the practice needs of the Section, and helped to create more of a Section identity.

A supervisor in the agency's Staff Development Unit heard about this effort and thought that other Sections might benefit from a similar approach. He had been concerned that the established approach to training put the workers in too reactive a position, and also led to sessions that were too global and not focused enough on the actual experience of the workers. He was impressed that in this case the initiative came from the workers in the Section and that the Administrator had assumed leadership in designing staff development activities for a whole work unit.

The supervisor discussed this with his Director and then met with all of the Administrators in small groups and presented the following offer. Each Administrator could propose a full day of training for his/her entire Section on a topic of their choosing. The training unit would make training resources available through a private contractor to meet the needs of each Section that responded. Administrators could submit a proposal individually or in conjunction with another Administrator. After a follow-up meeting with all of the Administrators, he sent them forms to fill out and set a deadline for submitting proposals. In the end, he received seven proposals for programs involving 13 of the 18 Administrators. The other five Administrators declined the offer. The contractor was excited about this new approach and efforts are currently underway to respond to the proposals.

In the above example, the spread of the new idea occurred through the initiative of the supervisor and the request for proposals, not through the chain of command. The supervisor initially heard about the innovation through casual conversation and modified it to fit the circumstances, as he saw them.

A second example concerns the formation of Section based councils to promote employee involvement in decision making. The experimental Intake Section created a representative Task Force as described previously to manage the change process within the Section. A second experimental Section has recently been added to the Project and has created a similar structure which it calls the Section Management Team. The two Administrators involved recently distributed a report on these efforts and called a meeting of their colleagues who wanted to hear more about how it was working. As a result, several other Administrators have expressed an interest in this mechanism and are considering creating a governance council for their own Sections.

Creating a Learning Organization

Public child welfare agencies are faced with constant changes in their client populations, in the social and political environments that surround them, and in the expectations placed upon them by the public, the courts, and others. In this context, no set of programs or policies can be viewed as permanent. A premium must be placed on the organization's capacity to engage in continuous learning and adaptation. This requires the strengthening of four capabilities:

1. *Diagnosis/Problem Definition*—the ability to question current organizational realities. In child welfare organizations, this might mean questioning why family service plans are incomplete, why intake workers and ongoing case workers don't seem to trust each other, or why large numbers of children are being placed out-of-state.

2. *Invention*—the ability to imagine alternatives to the *status quo*. This includes redefining roles or responsibilities, redesigning the way cases are assigned or grouped, or redistributing power and authority for making decisions.

3. *Action*—the ability to test ideas in practice. Learning occurs through the experience of change. Change typically begins with local experimentation, or pilot testing, since in large organizations, change rarely occurs everywhere at once.

4. *Generalization*—the ability to examine sincerely the results and then to apply them to the wider organization and its environment; in other words, moving from experiment to policy.

In a "learning organization," this process takes place over and over again, with initiatives occurring throughout the organization. At times, the learning process through which innovations spread can be directed and managed. At other times, it occurs or erupts spontaneously. Over time, an organizational learning approach responds to several of the requirements for satisfying work and for improving the quality of work life. It addresses the need "to learn on the job and go on learning." It allows staff to receive recognition from their colleagues. It also provides a way to see how one's work can contribute to the larger organization and its overall mission. Over a sustained period, numerous episodes of experience based learning can lead to significant organizational transformation. In the Department of Human Services, the process of locally initiated change has begun to raise some hopes. It has produced some "small victories" and provided a model for how workers, supervisors, and administrators can take more control of their work lives.

Based on our experience, an organizational learning system for an organization like DHS should have the following features:

1. Support from the top that learning is valued in the organization and should be continuous.

2. Encouragement of local experimentation. Any place in the organization can become a "laboratory" where learning can take place.

3. A variety of ways to promote and facilitate dialogue, or active exchange of information. Learning involves interaction among those who initially have diffluent perspectives that change over time through the interaction and dialogue.

4. Constant efforts to integrate research and practice. Ultimately, reflection and learning can't be separated from doing, and have to involve the workers themselves as well as the research unit or the academic minded.

5. Examining the results of experiments in terms of their wider implications for agency structure, agency activities, and agency relationships. This should be followed by providing opportunities to spread the results of experiments across the organization.

Conclusion

Our investigation began with a focus on the public child welfare organization as a workplace that was not adequately responding to the needs of its *workers* or its *clients*. We were drawn to the Quality of Working Life approach as a "paradigm shift" that represented a "challenge to the established, conventional views of management and organization" (Mohrman and Lawler 1985) in the field of child welfare. Our efforts to bring a QWL perspective to child welfare were coupled with the desire to work collaboratively with a "client organization" in order to create learning opportunities for both researchers and practitioners. The difficulties in trying to introduce organization wide change, led us to adopt an action research approach and the organizational learning model. "Sheltered experiments" have been used to stimulate learning and the further questioning of the conventional organizational paradigm. Every part of the organization is encouraged to become a "learning laboratory" where workers and managers jointly develop ideas for experimentation.

The major conclusions drawn from this program of action research include the following:

1. Organizational change in a public child welfare agency is like a long distance run where patience and perseverance are essential. It cannot be expected to occur overnight or through a centrally mandated and orderly sequence of events.
2. Vision and leadership at the top of the organization should be coupled with giving middle level managers the space and encouragement to be innovative and display leadership within their domains.
3. Involving child welfare staff in the restructuring of the workplace can be a way of energizing workers, promoting staff retention, and enhancing staff learning through hands-on experience and job relevant training.
4. Effective organizational intervention requires moving from an individual focus (changing the behavior of individuals through training) to a focus on whole work units that are representative of the complexity and different levels of the organization.
5. Collaborative action research is driven by problems that emerge in actual practice, not by the research agendas of academicians. This partnership requires mutual trust between researchers and agency staff and acknowledgement that each has something to learn from the other.

Reprinted from Burton J. Cohen and Michael J. Austin, Organizational learning and change in a public child welfare agency. *Administration in Social Work* 18 (1994): 1–19. Reprinted by permission.

References

Argyris, C., and D. Schon (1978). *Organizational Learning: A Theory of Action Perspective.* Reading, Mass.: Addison-Wesley.

Austin, M. J., and B. J. Cohen (1992). Revitalizing public child welfare organizations: Implications for staff development. Pending review.

Beer, M., R. A. Eisenstat, and B. Spector (1990). Why change programs don't produce change. *Harvard Business Review* (November/December).

Bramhall, M., and S. Ezell (1981). Working your way out of burnout. *Public Welfare* 39 (2).

Bunker, D. R., and M. H. Wijnberg (1988). *Supervision and Performance: Managing Professional Work in Human Service Organizations.* San Francisco: Jossey-Bass.

Camman, C. (1984). Productivity of management through QWL programs. In C. J. Fombrun, ed., *Strategic Human Resource Management.* New York: John Wiley.

Cohen, B. J. (1992). Quality of working life in a public child welfare agency. *Journal of Health and Human Resource Administration* (Fall).

Emery, F. E. (1964). *Report on the Hunsfoss Project.* London: Tavistock Document Series.

Havassy, H. M. (1990). Effective second-story bureaucrats: Mastering the paradox of diversity. *Social Work* 35: 103–11.

Hegar, R. L., and J. M. Hunzeker (1988). Moving toward empowerment-based practice in public child welfare. *Social Work* 33 (6): 499–502.

Henick, N. (1990). *Joint Management and Employee Participation.* San Francisco: Jossey-Bass.

Kamerman, S. B., and A. J. Kahn (1989). *Social Services for Children, Youth, and Families in the United States.* New York: Columbia University Press.

Kanter, R. M. (1980). *The Change Masters.* New York: Simon and Schuster.

Lewin, K. (1947). Group decision and social change. In T. M. Newcomb and E. L. Hartley, eds., *Readings in Social Psychology.* New York: Holt, Rinehart and Winston.

———— (1948). *Resolving Social Conflicts.* New York: Harper and Brothers.

Marrow, A. J. (1969). *The Practical Theorist: The Life and Work of Kurt Lewin.* New York: Basic Books.

Metrex Associates (1987). *Human Resource Audit.* Tryon, N.C.

Mohrman, A. M., and E. E. Lawler (1985). The diffusion of QWL as a paradigm shift. In W. B. Bennis, K. D. Benne, and R. Chin, eds., *The Planning of change.* 3rd ed. New York: Holt, Rinehart and Winston.

Olson, L. (1988). The restructuring puzzle. *Education Week*, November 2.

Pecora, P., H. Briar H., and J. Zlotnick (1989). *Addressing the Program and Personnel Crisis in Child Welfare: A Social Work Response.* Silver Spring, Md.: National Association of Social Workers.

Rothman, J. (1982). *Research and Development in the Human Services.* Englewood Cliffs, N.J: Prentice-Hall.

Schön, D. (1971). *Beyond the Stable State.* New York: Norton.

Susman, G. I. (1983). Action research: A sociotechnical systems perspective. In G. Morgan, ed., *Beyond Method: Strategies for Social Research.* Beverly Hills, Calif.: Sage.

Thomas, E. J. (1989). Advances in developmental research. *Social Service Review* 63: 578–97.

Thomas, G. (1990). "Bottomed out" in a "bottom up" society: Social work education and the default and recapture of professional leadership in child welfare. Paper presented at Council of Social Work Education, Annual Program Meeting, Reno, Nevada.

Weatherley, R., C. B. Kottwitz, D. Lishner, K Reid, G. Roset, and K. Wong (1980). Accountability of social service workers at the front line. *Social Service Review* 54: 556–71.

Woolverton, C. (1989). *Child Welfare Staffing Crisis.* Silver Spring, Md.: National Association of Social Workers.

Commentary: Reflections of a Former Dean

Michael J. Austin

One gray, drizzly Seattle day in December 1984, I received a call from Professor Al Hersh, chair of the Dean Search Committee at the Penn School of Social Work. He wanted to know if I was interested in the deanship. I told him that I would be willing to explore the possibility if I knew more. My only familiarity with Penn was through my son's freshman application, mailed the previous month. After a campus visit and the opportunity to learn more about the School's rich history, I was indeed interested. When the call and offer finally came later that spring from Provost Tom Ehrlich, I was excited about being a part of one of our pioneering schools of social work.

Since I was the first dean of the School who had not been educated in the context of functional social work, I knew that I had much to learn, especially about the early days of the 1920s and 1930s. During that period the Penn School was one of the national big three that included Columbia University (psychodynamic approach), University of Chicago (social reform approach), and the University of Pennsylvania's functional approach. I immediately enrolled in a tutorial with our able associate dean, Howard Arnold, to learn more about the principles of functional social work practice. The next step was to publish a brochure entitled *The Penn Approach*, which, to my delight, continues to appear on the School's website. This brochure proved to be extremely helpful to those of us who had not learned and experienced the Penn Approach to functional social work practice, to future applicants to the School who needed to know why Penn's Ivy League program offered them a unique opportunity, and to alums who appreciated the clear documentation of the approach they had learned and highly valued.

Early in my tenure as dean I discovered that my job included the responsibilities of a restoration architect. The Penn School, one of the oldest schools of social work in the nation, had been built by the likes of Jessie Taft, Virginia Robinson, and Kenneth Pray. Like a neglected grand Victorian home, the School was in need of repair, due in part to the massive cutbacks of federal traineeships in the early 1980s of the Reagan administration. In addition, the graduate school marketplace had become extremely competitive with public university tuitions far below those of private universities. By 1986, enrollments had plummeted from an average of 100+ entering students to 40. The School bulletin was in need of significant updating, new hires were needed to replenish the faculty, a new development program needed to be created, the building needed upgrading along with new classrooms needed in the basement area. Finally, the university expected the School to rebalance its heavy focus on education with equal attention to research. There was a similar call to play a more active role in the community, beyond all the excellent fieldwork agencies that had been part of the Penn tradition.

Within the context of these challenges, it is important to identify some of the accomplishments that resulted from both administrative staff and faculty efforts. These included converting the DSW to a Ph.D., establishing a Clinician Educator track for faculty, building a computer lab, creating new certificate programs with various religious institutions of higher education, developing several dual degree programs of campus, and developing joint research appointments with several nationally recognized agencies in Philadelphia. It was clear that creating the first-rate research climate and culture would take time, given the fiscal crisis caused by low enrollment. One of the biggest accomplishments achieved by the staff and faculty was the significant surplus of tuition funds from increased enrollments at the end of my seven-year tenure as dean.

I am particularly proud of the groundwork that Burt Cohen and I laid with a program of applied research at the Philadelphia Department of Human Services. I have always been deeply committed to linking our schools of social work with the publicly supported social services that serve the most vulnerable in our society. Burt and I were able to demonstrate this commitment in our collaboration with the Department of Human Services. The Department faced enormous challenges. One of the articles that grew out of our work is reprinted here. It focuses on organizational learning and describes innovations in the context of organizational change. In retrospect, it reflects some contemporary enhancements of Penn's historical foundation of functional social work practice, namely, moving from client empowerment to staff empowerment, moving from mutual respect between practitioners and clients to mutual respect between line workers and administrators, moving from group-based social inequalities among clients to those among staff, and moving from client problem-solving to organizational problem-solving that includes beginnings, middles, and ends. The article also features other Penn principles of functional social work including the importance of:

- understanding that agency purpose not only guides practice but also informs organizational learning,
- seeing that planned change not only involves cooperation and needs assessment but also a focus on relationship-building, especially between staff members inside and outside the organization,
- recognizing that the monitoring of change in clients also includes monitoring change in organizations in order to develop learning organizations that support evidence-informed practice,
- understanding that advocating for clients also includes advocating for staff, and
- demonstrating that creating a climate of inquiry relates not only to the management

I learned a great deal from my Penn experience. Some of my learning is captured in a publication with other deans at the time, *The Professional School Dean: Meeting the Leadership Challenges.* Other aspects of my learning are seen in my current work related to transforming public social service agencies into learning organizations. This work is being expanded by an endowment to create a new Mack Center on Nonprofit Management in the Human Services at the University of California, School of Social Welfare.

My experience at Penn provided a foundation for many of the initiatives that emerged following my departure in 1992. I shall always be grateful for the opportunity to play a role in the first 100 years of one of our premier schools of social work.

Reference

Austin, M. J., F. Ahearn, and R. English (1997). *The Professional School Dean: Meeting the Leadership Challenges.* San Francisco: Jossey-Bass.

Chapter 38
Lessons Learned About Working with Men: A Prison Memoir

Jack Sternbach

The last few chords of Dylan's *The Times They Are A-Changin'* were still vibrating in the air. I hit the stop button on the cassette player, and some 30 bemused, confused, and a few angry correctional officers, social workers, administrators, cooks, and clerks at Foothills Correctional Institution got ready to end another training session with the professor from the university—me. It was early in the 1970s and a reform-oriented correctional administration had appointed the first black warden in the history of the state. I had also been taken on as consultant and staff trainer as part of the effort to restructure and humanize this minimum security institution. Later, as we deepened our relationship, superintendent (his official title) Henry broadened my role to include administration-inmate liaison and trouble shooter.

The whole situation was a bit bizarre—I felt the ghosts of generations of tough (mostly white) security minded officers wailing in the walls as Superintendent Ed Henry, a few years older than myself and I walked down the main corridor together on my first visit to the prison. The fact that I was decked out in my finest hippie splendor added to the effect: beads, leather vest, laceless low-cut sneakers, long hair, and a red bandana. My arrogance was matched only by my ignorance, and both were balanced by my innocence. I had done prison work previously in Wisconsin, but always within a traditional social work service structure and never with the kind of administrative entry and backing for system change as at Foothills.

I could say much about the social function of prison—that is, in defining and justifying the "otherness" on which cultural and socioeconomic hierarchy is based. Men with low socioeconomic status who fill our prisons, these days overwhelmingly black and Latino are necessary for the maintenance of white male entitlement. The racial and socioeconomic disparity in apprehension, adjudication, and sentencing helps to justify hierarchy and privilege for the rest of us. And, these days, in a time of conservatism and economic plenty, to justify the wholesale neglect of housing, job, and public health programs for either the inner-city or the hardscrabble impoverished rural areas. I also could speak of the vital role prisons play in small-town economic life, how they are a part of a multimillion-dollar correctional industry, of theories of rehabilitation and other related matters. As I rewrite this article, in 2000, prisons are again very much in the headlines. We note that more black young men are incarcerated than are in college. We also observe how prison construction and management have become a growth industry, attracting capital from seemingly unrelated sources (for example, American Express) and becoming privatized for profit undertakings.

In this article, however, I want to focus on what I learned about men together with other men under conditions so oppressive and brutal, you would expect to find the worst kinds of male aggression, dominance, and exploitation. There was that, in abundance. What is more important is how much I learned of the positive and affirming ways so many men found to be with each other even under such conditions. I learned lessons about manhood that shook and shaped me then and provided the ground for much of my subsequent life work and personal development.

The Institution—Foothills

Foothills, pre-Henry, exemplified an approach to prison management that was medieval, brutal, and totalitarian. In the words of a former administrator: "Discipline is peremptory, privileges are a matter of grace." An inmate brought up for a disciplinary infraction might be ordered to stand with his back to the panel of officers hearing his case with his face pressed to the wall. If he moved his head to either side, he might be cuffed on the side of his head. Visitors were not allowed any physical contact with inmates; they sat across from each other with a wire mesh grill in between. Racism was rampant everywhere and affected both inmates and staff. There was a sizable contingent of very competent black officers. Some of the officers had served for 20 years. None of them had ever achieved a rank higher than sergeant in a hierarchy that included positions such as lieutenant, captain, major, and so forth. Black Muslims had been actively organizing their religious observances themselves in U.S. prisons for a decade or more. in Foothills as elsewhere. They were refused the right of religious observance, and it was only after several court cases that they finally were recognized as a legitimate religious group.

If the prison system was unsparing for inmates, it was no more forgiving for staff. There was one innocuous white guard in his mid-50s, nicknamed "Strawberry Sam," who had served for 30 years. Indeed his name was Sam, but the "Strawberry'" part came from one of the first days on the job when he was told to take canteen orders on the cell block. A bunch of inmates ordered ice cream, which this poor fellow procured for them. Only then was he told that his wages would be docked because such an order was against the rules. The other guards on duty as well as the inmates knew this at the time but let him fall into the trap. This poor guy had labored under that nickname all these years; he still winced and cast his eyes down when called by that name. What a humiliating and shaming way for a man to have to spend his working life!

Most of the white officers were, like Sam, simple country guys from an impoverished rural background, trying to make a living at a steady civil service job. Yes, many were racist, and some were brutal; all of them were trying to survive.

Reform and Change

Ed Henry had vision, courage, and intelligence. He set right to work to change many of the policies and practices described. He also had a presence that quickly won regard and respect from even the old-timers at the prison.

One event that reverberated through the prison and earned Henry the greatest credits occurred when a prisoner, in the main hall, in the hearing of other prisoners and various staff, called him a "m———r f———r." The deputy warden, Tom, a huge and very tough guy who had been there for decades, gave a signal and moved with several officers to administer a beating to the man. Henry put a gentle hand on Tom's arm and said words to the effect, "I don't want any man ever beaten on my account— besides, maybe he really does believe that's what I am, and I don't think it's right to punish a man for his beliefs." The deputy warden, the inmate, and everyone within hearing were left speechless as Ed continued on his jaunty way with his warm and slightly ironic smile intact.

As Warden Henry's changes took hold, there was a renaissance of creativity and cooperation in the prison. Inmates, officers, and other staff as well, who had labored quietly for years in behalf of constructive programs and decent relationships, were identified, supported, and rewarded. Inmates Fred Pissano and Antoine Samuels formed their inmate-run paralegal law clinic, which came to be recognized for its excellence in legal circles beyond the prison. Inmate Victor Jones developed more openly a number of consciousness-raising groups geared to helping young, angry black prisoners substitute dialogue for fratricidal violence. Aaron, a black officer in his late forties who could alone command a mess hall of 300 men by virtue of the kind of respect and integrity he conveyed, was prompted and given a staff-training role. Other officers who had labored under a Jim Crow system for years also emerged in creative leadership roles. And many white officers as well gave support.

It is important to record the fact that many of the officers, black and white, were decent, humane, and generous human beings doing their best at a difficult job. One of my mentors was Jim Sergeant, a white officer in his forties who also held the rank of sergeant. Everyone, including him, had fun with this. He was well regarded by the inmates. He played it straight, was fair, wise, and incorruptible. He also was funny as hell. Staff or other inmates would direct a new inmate with a question to ask the "Sergeant." When so addressed, Ed would put on a scowl and say, "Watch it, don't get personal with me, call me by my rank!" The fuddled inmate would then say, "Well uh, OK, Sergeant." Ed would then smile and say: "That's better!" That initiation had more fun than bite in it. Actually, if he thought the inmate could handle it, he might say, "You know, I have a name as well as a rank." The inmate by then would usually figure it out and say with a laugh, "OK Sergeant Sergeant.'" Jim used humor to establish mutuality and defuse the authority intrinsic in his position and to secure the willing cooperation of the inmates. I think one reason he was so well liked was the absence of self-serving ego or malice in his humor.

Previously, requests from prisoners for alleviation of even a modest kind were ignored with contempt. In our second year we developed the first graduate social work intern program in any of the state's correctional facilities, consisting of four student interns whom I supervised. One intern became aware of how resentful men in one dining area were that coffee was always served with milk mixed in. As we all know, it is the little things that can get to you! This had gone on for years, but now this intern was able to take a petition to the warden who was receptive. From then on coffee was served with milk on the side. This was more than an indicator of Ed Henry's openness. It also spoke to a basic principle—that of redress of grievances and the participation by the governed in their own affairs. Warden Henry did not simply issue an edict. He went into the dining hall and interviewed several prisoners himself on the subject. He also took care to meet with the dining room stewards, who, like Aaron, had the responsibility for organizing mealtime, to make sure they felt acknowledged and included.

The petition event caused considerable controversy on higher levels in the state correctional bureaucracy, including several meetings and memoranda. I remember the dean at the School of Social Work nervously asking me if I was making trouble. Given the hierarchical structure of the school, I could see where the idea of participatory democracy would be troublesome to her. Warden Ed Henry stood by that principle and also with the student and me, as his supervisor.

He also planted several trees in a fenced-in compound, easily visible to all the men on the yard. He relaxed visiting rules. Sometimes the visiting room did get a bit steamy, but the consensus was that no harm was done as lovers and married folks embraced and kissed during visiting hours. He also developed a community relations program, which brought interested people into the prison. He also arranged for weekend furloughs, which provided inmates with opportunities to taste a bit of freedom outside the walls.

In the second year he and I were able to organize a graduate social work course, which met on alternate weeks at the prison and at the university with a number of prisoners and officers as noncredit students. The sessions at the School of Social Work were wonderful social events. Prisoners' families would join the class session, often bringing picnics to share with all. It reminded me of a Joan Baez song that had the refrain "We'll tear down the prison walls."

He was an unafraid man, able to look truth in its face. Several inmates had complained that a particularly "effeminate" flamboyant gay inmate on their cell block was teasing and enticing them. Rather than dismissing their complaint Ed went on to the block and observed the situation. I asked him what happened. Ed laughed and said he thought the gay prisoner was actually "kinda cute" and told the men he thought so. He arranged to have the two complainers housed elsewhere, which seemed to take care of the situation.

This action may have sounded routine, maybe trivial, but it was not. Tom, the deputy warden, told me of a time not that long ago when two inmates had thrown an officer off a catwalk to the cement floor 20 feet below, injuring him severely, in their attempt to rape another prisoner.

The spirit of cooperation released by Warden Henry received its most profound test early in his first year. It was during this time that the Attica uprising was quelled with the loss of many lives, both inmates and guards. Attica was a maximum-security prison in the New York State system. There was a prisoner rebellion. After several days of impasse in the negotiations, the governor, Nelson Rockefeller, ordered an armed response from the state police. State troopers killed more than 30 prisoners and correctional officer hostages in the hail of gunfire as they took control of the prison from the inmates.

The tension in the prison was tangible as the news spread. Warden Henry was urged to lock down the men in their cells and curtail all special programs, classes, therapy, and so forth. While he studied the situation, I received word that one of the inmates I had gotten close to, Antoine Samuels, wanted to see me. When I got to his cell, he gave me a note for the warden. In it he recommended that the warden announce over the prison speaker system that a fund was being established for the families of the Attica victims, both guards and inmates. Antoine had been busy talking up this idea and was sure it would get widespread support. Warden Henry did just that. The prison community rallied together, the contributions came from staff and inmates alike, and the tension dissipated. Restrictions were not imposed, the liberalization continued. I was an enthusiastic and, I hope, effective participant in this change process. However, from the beginning I found that my contribution would be enhanced by my willingness to be a student as well as a teacher, a trainee as well as a trainer.

Lesson 1: Vulnerability. Mutuality, Willingness to Learn from Clients

My deepest initiation and first lessons came early in the prison yard. Consider for a moment a vast expanse of hard packed earth, not a flower or a tree or a blade of grass anywhere. Although the prison was located in the country, the walls had been built so high that they blotted out anything but the sky. There were bleachers on one side by an athletic field and some weight lifting equipment, but mostly just space, with men moving or standing around in twosomes or small groups. When I checked with the warden to get permission, I did not know I was the first "civilian" to go out on the yard. The specialized staff (teachers, counselors, medical personnel, and so forth) stayed put, and the inmates came to them. When Warden Henry told me to go ahead, I wondered a little about his smile. He knew I was in for a little education.

As I strolled the yard saying hello to some of the men I knew, I noticed a group of about 30 black inmates giving off an energy that drew me. I gave no consideration to whether I was welcome. After all, I was the expert, committed to racial equality, working for their welfare. What possible problem could there be! I walked over, joined the group, and stood bewildered while the conversation flowed around me. I did not understand a thing that was said. I became inwardly defensive and paranoid, and my discomfort was obvious. One of the men, Marvin, asked me why I looked so unhappy. I told him I was missing most of the dialogue and couldn't figure out what was going on. To which he replied, "And you're the man whose gonna teach the guards to understand US!"

A brief comment on this exchange. In an environment as routinized and predictable as the prison, anything or anybody new drew considerable attention. I found that anywhere I went in the prison news of my arrival and my function always preceded me. Inmates and sometimes staff often made themselves and their concerns known without my asking.

There I stood, feeling naked and exposed. Being unable to control the situation with words, I suddenly felt weak and powerless. I have to admit I was relieved to notice one of the larger correctional officers amble over to monitor the situation as I received the ragging I deserved. It took some work with myself for me to return to the yard the next week. The same group was assembled, and I joined them. Marvin, who had delivered the pithy rejoinder the week before, asked me why I was back. I told him, "For me." He and the others laughed, and he said how could I justify coming back for what I would get when I was being paid good money to learn useful things to teach the guards? I was quiet for a while and then I said. "Look, you gave me a lot of yourself last time, and I'm back because I need that for my own growth as a man."

Rereading this, I have a number of complex responses, not all of them particularly positive. There was a sense in which I, as a white man, was feeding off the energy of black men, and without invitation or sanction. Rather like young white boys digging "gangsta rap." At the same time I think I was working from a basic commitment to openness and mutuality—perhaps that came through and mitigated my racism.

What I took away from this encounter, as contradictory and multilayered as it might be, was to reaffirm my belief that what I have to offer others has little value unless it is embedded in mutuality. There was also a corollary piece of learning—that an admission of my vulnerability and human need more often than not closes the gap and permits the relationship to proceed with greater trust. And this, of course, cannot happen unless I am able to acknowledge my ignorance and openness to being tutored and educated by my clients.

Lesson 2: Let the People Speak for Themselves

On a practical level, all future staff training I led always included both staff and inmates together in the same group. I had learned enough from Marvin to know that I had best let others speak for themselves. This principle worked well both in the prison community and in prison-community and prison-university contacts that I later helped initiate and nourish.

It also works in workshops and conferences today as I often ask some of the men in the groups I lead client and colleague, to bear witness to their lives by becoming coparticipants with me in professional presentations.

Lesson 3: Respecting Limits

Marvin became a friend and confidant, and as with so many men that I became close to—inmates then, therapy clients now—I had to learn about boundaries and limits. A year or so after our first meeting, Marvin approached me in the corridor and asked me to carry a letter out to his son because he was concerned that mail was not getting through. Now this was against prison regulations, and he knew it and I knew it. I tried to explain, but he said. "It's OK, man," and went down the corridor.

We both understood that the tightly regulated prison society functioned through an informal system of rule bending, bribery, manipulation, "special" arrangements, and understanding. Although that code of conduct may have succeeded for some people in the prison environment, my participation in this behavior would have been fatal to my role. The men had to know I could not be manipulated through our relationships. Analogously, the prison staff knew that I would not report minor rule infractions or irregularities that came to my attention in the course of moving around the prison. I could be neither a purveyor of favors nor a snitch.

I experienced considerable guilt at refusing Marvin. I had to struggle within myself to approach him when we saw each other again. I did check to find out if there was a problem with mail delivery. Apparently there was not. At the same time, as a father separated from several of my children, I could really understand the powerlessness and frustration Marvin felt, locked away, having to depend on the efficiency and goodwill of the impersonal prison administration. Marvin did remain open to me.

Lesson 4: Start Where the Other Man Is Right Now

Antoine Samuels was one of the men who reminded me of yet another lesson that has proved useful since that time—that is, the importance of accepting men where they are in the present moment, rather than focusing first on the past. And Antoine in the present was a courageous, highly conscious, and giving black man, who wrote writs and petitions as a service for other inmates. Only later did he tell me that he was in for homicide, the results of a bar fight a dozen years before. I was reminded of a doctrine, which lies at the heart of social work practice: "of starting where the client is." I have found, over the years, that if I can open myself to how a man presents himself, he will sooner or later bring me his past as well, especially when the past may include shameful behaviors.

Lesson 5: Taking the First Step by Revealing Myself

Another event from my early days in the prison reinforced what I had learned on the prison yard with Marvin and his buddies. This new event also generated another powerful realization—that I must risk revealing something of my inner thoughts and beliefs as a way of facilitating open and honest interaction. This lesson began a week or so after the incident with Marvin on the prison yard.

Tough Freddy Pissano, the most powerful and highly respected prison inmate, white or black, approached me. (Freddy was white.) His nickname came from a highly publicized series of criminal acts committed years before culminating in the murder of one of the victims. By the time I met him, Tough Freddy was a soft spoken scholarly man who had spent all those years in an isolation building used for discipline and for prisoners, like Freddy, under the death sentence. Most of the time he was in solitary confinement. During those years he had taught others in that building to read and write, had become a legal expert, and had climbed to the top of inmate leadership.

He and another inmate, Antoine Samuels, had organized an informal legal group, which served other prisoners without charge. He had only recently, when Ed Henry became warden, been allowed into the general population.

Freddy asked me, because I was offering group process consultation to staff, if I would also be willing to offer the same to his group of prisoners. I agreed, and with the warden's permission soon found myself in one of the treatment-wing therapy rooms with a dozen or so inmate leaders. These men had gathered together to try to organize prisoner support for the new warden, who they believed was their first and best chance for some constructive change in the prison situation. He had already, in a series of bold and courageous actions established his credentials, especially the hallway interaction with the inmate who had called him an "MF."

I was nervous about being in the same room with some of these men, for instance, Bernie, who was known to have killed one guard and at least two other inmates over the years, with a homemade knife. Appearances are deceiving—Bernie was about 5' 6", slightly built with a little paunch, wore thick glasses, spoke softly, and was almost bald. He looked more like a convenience store clerk or lower-level civil servant than a dangerous convict.

During our third meeting I was puzzled by the absence of dynamic interaction in the group. Although the men said they wanted my consultation, they were not forthcoming with anything of their own. I pointed that out, and one of the men, maybe Kareem, a Black Muslim leader, said, "Jack, you can walk out of here tonight, but we have to live with each other, so you have to make the first move."

Although I did not figure out the full significance of that statement until later, I could intuitively grant the absolute rightness of his words. I had not appreciated how much these men might risk by exposing themselves, given their history of antagonism and violence, and with their status in the prison community at stake.

So I swallowed, took my courage in my hand, and tried to respond as best I could. What I did was to offer my deepest beliefs, without ornamentation or apology. I raised the question of whether these men could achieve their goals without a fundamental shift toward nonviolence within the inmate community. And, furthermore, might they have to consider a comparable shift in the ways in which they related to the correctional officers? One may imagine how foolish and exposed I felt, a white middle-class guy trying to tell this collection of extraordinary men how to relate and work with each other on principles. I felt separate from them, vulnerable, and afraid of appearing foolish, with nothing of relevance to offer.

To my surprise my words were received thoughtfully, I wasn't razzed or dismissed, and the group got down to business. After all, they said they had come together to figure out a way to give the new warden support in his reform efforts, and what I told them seemed to make sense. As it turned out, my words fell on very fertile ground.

Several weeks later the warden was taken hostage by a group of inmates on one of the cell blocks when he was hearing their grievances. The situation was nasty; there were some out-of-control men threatening to do him physical harm. Two of the men from "my" group, Freddy, and Peters, a black inmate with considerable status, persuaded the rebellious group to accept them as hostages in return for the warden's release—pledging that if the warden didn't come through they could do anything they wanted to them. They risked their lives and their reputations in the process, but it all worked out well. No one was hurt, there were no reprisals, and the process of reform went forward. My facilitative role in all this was made known by Freddy and Peters, and it was after this point that the warden asked me to take on expanded duties to act as an "honest broker" and roving communicator in the prison. The lesson I learned remains at the heart of my practice. I must often take the risk first. No matter who I am working with, he has a lot more to lose than I do. If I expect him to reveal himself, then I must first find a way to let him experience me as fully human and as transparent as the situation permits. He may not be in as desperate a situation as the Foothills inmates, but he certainly is operating within a much more constricted psychological space than that which I occupy in my life. Although there have been times in my therapy practice that men could not hear me, I am convinced that my willingness to take that first step has been a vital, energizing factor between us and perhaps freed them to become more self-revealing in their lives.

Lesson 6: Physical Affection Between Men

During the months our group met, Freddy sat next to Bo, a solidly built, warm, and friendly black inmate. They had been in the solitary building together. Freddy had taught Bo, along with other illiterate inmates, to read and write over several years by copying passages from Shakespeare and passing them down the corridor. He also had filed a legal writ that was soon to bring Bo his freedom. During these group meetings Bo and Freddy sat thigh to thigh, most of the time with their inside hands on each other's knee or inner thigh. The current of love between them was palpable.

On another occasion a year or so later, Freddy was one of a number of prisoners who were in the combined prisoner, graduate social work student seminar I mentioned earlier, which met on alternate weeks at the prison and the university. It was Freddy's first time out of the "joint" in 16 years. When we entered the seminar room and sat down, he turned to me and said, "Jack man, hold my hand, I'm so nervous I don't know what to do." I obliged him, not without discomfort.

I doubt very much that Freddy was gay. At the same time I imagine he had sex, at times, with other prisoners. That and a myriad other adaptations were part of doing time in this kind of setting. I remember very clearly, especially in the early days, coming across many twosomes of lovers, some of them very purposefully, through posture and eye contact, making sure I saw and understood their relationship—part of educating this professor man about the joint. At times, especially in the first year, I was discomfited and felt awkward under their gaze. I was fascinated and drawn to their connection, and my homophobia surfaced simultaneously.

There was a wide range of sexual adaptation including celibacy, loving partnership, sexual predation, rape, and exchange of favors in the prison. For instance, Peters, who so courageously stood with Freddy in the warden's behalf, was a notorious "wolf," that is, he preyed on other men and used them sexually. Freddy was inclusive when he put together the inmate group that met with me. With Peters he included Gerry, a white, principled, gay man who refused to sexually "service" other men. His survival in such a violent environment was in large part due to Freddy and Victor protecting him.

I do not think Freddy and Bo were sexual lovers. At the same time the current of love between them was unmistakable, and they were not afraid to show it. Since then I am always delighted in my men's groups, when after some time together the men almost always develop a goodbye ritual of hand holding or a group hug. It feels right. Being with Freddy and Bo helped me, over the years, to relax a bit about close physical contact with other men.

Lesson 7: Hubris Deflated; I Am Not Invulnerable or Special

The regulation and management of violence was a shared concern of both officers and prisoners. Although the intervention by Freddy and Peters was dramatic and public, it was only one of many occasions when prisoners intervened to contain the violence and make the prison bearable. Most often guards and prisoners worked together toward that end. After all, the prison simply could not function without the participation of inmates. They not only did the work that maintained the infrastructure, they also gave assent to many of the practices by which they were governed. After all, the correctional officers carried no weapons, not even nightsticks or batons. The staffing was minimal; four correctional officers would be in charge of a cellblock of 400 prisoners. Clearly, without the cooperation and consent of the inmates the correctional officers could not have maintained even a semblance of control.

The prisoners also often worked with the guards to prevent greater evils from occurring. The system of inmate-officer relationships was full of delicately balanced protocols and understandings. It was simply a matter of the most psychologically intact individuals agreeing on rules of mutual conduct to prevent a descent into barbarism even well beyond what already characterized the prison.

An example of one such informal agreement was conveyed to me in a conversation with Tom, the deputy superintendent for control, who told me of dressing down an officer who had in the past brought Freddy Pissano into the main building improperly shackled. That is, he had chained Freddy's hands behind his back, and Tom told me of his concern about that infraction. After all, a man should be chained with his wrists together, chest high, so that if attacked by another inmate with a knife, for example, he could use the chains to fight him off and defend himself. When I asked Tom what would prevent Freddy from using the chains aggressively, Tom simply said that Freddy "knew the rules." (This was before Ed Henry's time. One of his first acts was to order that no man ever again be chained like an animal.)

I soon had the opportunity, in the two events that follow, to experience first hand the capacity for violence, from both an inmate and a correctional officer. Part of what I did was roam the prison, sometimes at night, to try to pick up what was going on and act as a vehicle for information exchange between the warden and the inmates. Many times I was out of view of guards in highly exposed situations. This never bothered me; I thought my good intentions provided magical protection. I also tended to romanticize my role and to idealize the inmates. However, one evening I got a clearer picture of what was going on.

I found myself standing in the doorway of Chuck's cell, a very hard guy, a career armed robber, a man about my age, and a member of my inmate consultation group. He was talking funny, and I realized he was high on something. His "punk," a younger, smallish man who provided Chuck with sex (maybe there was affection also?) in exchange for physical protection, was visiting in the cell with him. Chuck started ragging on me, and I turned to leave. He stepped up close, his hands were in his pants, I think he was playing with himself, and he demanded I give him a beautiful set of beads my kids had made for me. I was terrified at his sexual aggression. I gave him the beads, got off the block, and told no one. The next visit Freddy handed me the beads and said he and a few other men had told Chuck to behave himself. After that I continued my all block activities, but with no illusion that there was anything special about me personally. I was useful, I was part of several networks of prisoners, I had connections with the warden, and I certainly was not invulnerable. This too was an important lesson. From that time on, I also made doubly sure the officers on duty knew more or, less where I was when I roamed around.

At that time the word "punk" seemed natural, part of prison argot. Now I want to distance myself from it—from all that it carries of male cruelty and domination. I use it deliberately as a way of contextualizing the event and to convey to the reader my realization of how easily I could have been the "punk." Why Chuck did what he did I don't know, but I surely was on his turf, without invitation, and maybe he picked up intuitively my "attitude" toward his young lover. Maybe he was simply showing off that he could overcome a self-important man like me in a head-on encounter.

Lesson 8: Goodbye Lone Ranger—Ask for Help—Use Your Networks

The truth was you hardly ever saw a man by himself in the prison except perhaps in transit, let's say, from cell block to infirmary. In all other continuously occupied spaces every man had at least one "homey," who might be different in each area—someone on the block, someone in the work area, and so forth. You see, if you're alone you are vulnerable, easy prey. But two men can stand together and protect each other. It was a very sobering piece of understanding a lesson in interdependence and the phoniness of the hero myth and rugged individualism.

For instance, one part of staff training for new officers concerned rape prevention. Some of these new guards might be inclined to doubt the masculinity or courage of an inmate who "allowed" himself to be raped. At that point two of the trainers, both medium-sized men, would pounce on him, put him down on the door on his stomach, spread his legs, and tell him. "Baby, you've just been raped."

Violent tendencies were not restricted to inmates. There were correctional officers whose willingness to use any terrorist devices against inmates was barely contained. These officers could turn that wrath against fellow staff just as easily.

I remember one time after I was let through a locked gate by one of the officers hearing him say something I couldn't catch. When I checked it out with several inmates whom I had walked back to the block, I was told that he had said, " 'Guys like this Sternbach make you realize Hitler did a lot of things the right way." I later had occasion to verify the accuracy of the story. Later he was in a combined officer-inmate training group I was leading. He not only verified the "Hitler" story but told me, openly and dearly, in the group, that anytime I wanted to take it further he would meet me outside the prison gate with '45s (handguns) to settle the matter. Afterward two of the officers told me not to take him seriously; everyone knew him for what he was, and no one ever let him handle a situation alone. Looking back on it, at the stage of awareness I was at then, I felt shamed by his aggression and would have fantasies of calling him out and facing him down.

Word of his threat got around, and both officers and inmates asked me about it. Warden Henry even queried me. In all instances I shrugged nonchalantly and mini-mized it. Looking back on it, I think I should have seriously considering filing a com-plaint. Perhaps this would have permitted some kind of intervention and corrective action with an officer known to be out of control and a threat to everyone around him. Such was my individualism I had lost sight of the need to stay within some system of support, both for my sake and for my clients as well. I think I deprived Warden Henry of information he could have used to intervene effectively with his guard, who was a very dangerous man. Since then, even as an independent practitioner, I try to remember to make use of collegial and community resources—I really can not do the job alone.

Democracy and Its Discontents

Ed Henry lasted four years; I lasted three. Ironically, the guards had unionized, the most reactionary of them had taken control, and they did their best to block further reform. One of the first union demands was that no personnel be required to attend "Sternbach's training groups"!

Several years later, after Ed Henry's tenure ended, I read that an inmate had beaten Wassily Losko, a grandfatherly captain of the guards, to death. He did not deserve such an ending. It reminded me of what could happen when hope was dimmed and aspects of rigid authoritarianism again became ascendant. It is important to record that while Ed Henry was warden the incidence of violence and assault within the prison, on all levels, was reduced considerably.

Conclusion

I have written of knowledge gained and false consciousness exposed. I have tried to convey some sense of a number of extraordinary men who were my teachers. The prison was in a sense a compressed world, but in essence not much different from the one we all live our lives out the imperatives of the male role in extremis.

I have never again had the illusion that I can afford rest time from a conscious living of life, that somehow the absence of prison walls allows me "down time" in how I live. That illusion was unmasked for me because I know that we are all prone to the same consequences of becoming self-destructive, mad, or exploiters of others.

What was remarkable about so many of these men is how they learned to make use of the very lack of freedom they were experiencing as a vehicle for personal transcendence. Victor Jones told me of a time early in his incarceration when he realized the environment had overwhelmed him. He asked for and was granted time in solitary confinement. He was there for six months, during which he was able to focus and center himself to work with his circumstances in a creative way over the next 10 years, becoming a leader, organizer, spokesman, and model for other energetic, younger black prisoners interested in collective consciousness and self-regarded.

I learned, at Foothills, that it is only by a focused act of consciousness, shared and shaped in a loving way with others, that we can locate our freedom and our humanity.

I have tried to make clear the life lessons I was privileged to learn in this crucible of suffering and transcendence. This experience came at a pivotal point in my life: I had turned 40, moved from the Midwest, completed my doctorate, and my marriage had ended. My political beliefs had been revitalized by the antiwar movement at the University of Wisconsin, and I was trying, in the words of one of the younger men in that movement who served as a mentor, "to make my life and my work one." Shortly after Foothills, I left the cocoon of academia in behalf of greater engagement as a practitioner. I choose to work primarily with men—to struggle against sexism, to bring forth men's capacity for more loving connection, and to sustain my own growth as a man.

Much of what I do derives from what I learned at Foothills prison. Much of the person I have become likewise derives from the same place. Although I have become more conventional in attire and personal grooming (no more long hair and laceless sneakers), I hope that the capacity for connection and caring deeper. I have found since then that when I have the courage to be transparent, honest, and open to a mutual relationship my work and my life are deepened and made more meaningful.

When I can remember to stay connected to others and to ask for the support I need, my work and my life are enhanced. I thank those amazing men for how much of themselves they gave me and hope I have continued to earn their trust. Perhaps the best summary is in the words of Warden Ed Henry, said to me during one of our many conversations: "You grow or you die."

Reprinted from Jack Sternbach, Lessons learned about working with men: A prison memoir. *Social Work* 45 (2000): 413–23. Reprinted by permission.

Commentary: The Times, They Are A-Changin'

Jeffrey Draine

In addition to what I do professionally as a researcher, I have always tried to be involved in change work and awareness building around jail and prison issues. One of those activities has been my sometime involvement with a group of mostly lifers and academics that meet at Graterford Prison every Wednesday Night called the Inside Out Think Tank—its a group that thinks and does projects related to the criminal justice system. I was telling Max Silverstein—one of our alumni and former faculty members from years gone by—about this and he asked me if I had ever heard of Jack Sternbach. I hadn't. Jack Sternbach was a maverick of a professor who would go to Graterford and take students there, and in some cases, have Graterford prisoners come to campus. Well, I started asking around about this Jack Sternbach guy. Sandie Bauman and Nancy Rogers told me that on his first day of work as a faculty member, he rode his motorcycle up the front steps of Caster and into the lobby and put his motorcycle helmet on June Axinn's head! Max also told me that there was a *Gazette* piece done about him back in the early 1970s. I contacted the *Gazette* and they sent me a copy.

It all seemed to be true. The *Gazette* piece showed a guy with the long hair and beard of the time—a vest of course, "rapping" with a prisoner at Graterford. The fact that a photo was taken of this inside Graterford, now the fifth largest maximum security prison in the U.S., is remarkable—that would rarely be allowed today. Even more unusual were some of the other things Jack did. He was seemingly able to roam the prison cellblocks, even at night—"rapping" in the yard and in cellblocks. He held what amounted to encounter groups—and brought students in to share the experiences. All these are things one would never see in the Graterford of today.

What is different today? First of all, all prisons are much more crowded. Since 1970 we have experienced a fourfold increase in the imprisonment rate in the U.S.—a social experiment unprecedented anytime in U.S. history, war or peace. Also—today there is far less violence than recent past in most prisons. This is on one hand a good thing—but one of the things that explains this is that prisons and the criminal "justice" system in general have become far more repressive and controlling in their tactics and in how they maintain control. This is part of a growing security state mentality that was begun way before 9/11; but clearly was accelerated by those events.

What does this have to do with mental illness, my main research interest? Many have argued that in the time span between Jack Sternbach's time and mine, that mental illness has been "criminalized"—moved from the hospitals to the jails by deinstitutionalization, restrictive civil commitment laws and ineffective community mental health infrastructure. The premise is that people with mental illness are going to jail because they lack treatment. I think it's far more complicated than that. A lot of what explains why people with mental illness are in jails more than ever before is because lots of people are in jails more than ever before—and that poor people are there more than ever before.

Which doesn't mean that those with mental illness don't need treatment. What it does mean is that we can't treat ourselves out of the problem of people with mental illness in jails. In the current criminal justice system, people on probation and parole have on average 11 conditions or stipulated requirements to comply with in exchange for serving time in the community instead of behind bars. Growing caseloads and growing restrictions have led probation officers to place more of the burden of supervision on probationers without providing opportunity to create the capacity to meet these demands. Mental health services per se do not necessarily help this matter for people with mental illness. In three studies in the Philadelphia area, Phyllis Solomon and I have shown that a greater intensity of mental health treatment services can be associated with more, not less recidivism. In our study of Philadelphia probation and parole, if the probation officer was in contact with an intensive case manager, that increased the odds of being sent to jail for violating your probation.

You see, the mental health system risks being a part of the problem it is trying to solve. The services that are being provided are largely monitoring to increase medication compliance and adherence to services—services that are less and less accessible to those in the community as resources become scarcer and the numbers of people needing services become larger. Thus, in the rationing of these services, those with fewer connections and even less tenacity lose out the fastest, even though they are arguably the ones that need help the most. Or perhaps these supposedly treatment-needy individuals think it's not worth the effort.

Where the mental health system fails is not just in offering too little treatment—but in not offering up the most effective forms of treatment it has to offer for this population. Such treatment provides real supports for housing, employment and community life. We have models that effectively provide these—they are very difficult to implement—but we know they can be effective. What keeps us from implementing them is the political will to provide resources (like housing) for these services. What helps mental illness, in the end, are the same things that help reduce criminal recidivism—a place to live, a place to work, and meaningful social relations. In this article by Jack Sternbach in *Social Work* a few years back, he reviews an approach to social and mental health that is more humanistic than evidence based, but it also reflects an approach that is more consistent with effective treatment than what is often offered to those who are least able to pay for services themselves. The consistency lies in the effort expended for thorough and deliberate practice. Such practice, whether "evidence based" or not, is grounded in the idea that every individual is worth the effort expended to practice well.

Jack Sternbach died in 2004. Part of his life work was to maintain the humanity of those we isolate as prisoners. While many think that rehabilitation is an old fashioned word in the justice system of today—perhaps we social workers need to be a bit old fashioned in showing how rehab can be seen to actually increase our security in society while also enhancing human dignity. I wonder if Jack might like that.

Contributors and Their Relationships to the School

Howard Arnold (MSW 1963, former faculty)
Michael J. Austin (former professor and dean)
Stephen J. Betchen (MSW/DSW 1986)
Tybel Bloom (MSW 1995, DSW 1960, former faculty)
Stephanie C. Boddie (MSW 1997, PhD 2002)
Joretha N. Bourjolly (current faculty, associate dean for academic affairs)
Anthony F. Bruno (DSW 1984, current adjunct faculty)
Louis H. Carter (MSW 1962, former faculty)
Ram A. Cnaan (current faculty, associate dean for research and doctoral education)
Burton Cohen (former adjunct faculty)
Ira Colby (DSW 1984)
Dennis P. Culhane (current faculty)
Karl de Schweinitz (former faculty)
Melissa E. Dichter (MSW 2002, doctoral candidate, adjunct faculty)
Martha M. Dore (former faculty)
Jeffrey N. Draine (Ph.D. 1995, current faculty)
Richard J. Estes (MSW 1967, current faculty)
Gerald L. Euster (DSW 1969)
Zvi Feine (DSW 1974)
Rich Furman (MSW 1993)
Richard J. Gelles (current faculty and dean)
David G. Gil (DSW 1963)
Kevin Grigsby (DSW 1990)
Roberta R. Iversen (current faculty)
Toba S. Kerson (DSW 1976)
Porter R. Lee (former faculty)
Beth Lewis (former faculty)
Harold Lewis (DSW 1959, former faculty)
Mark Frazier Lloyd (historian)
Jacqueline B. Mondros (DSW 1981)

J. Prentice Murphy (former faculty)
Kenneth Pray (former faculty)
Mary E. Richmond (former faculty)
Virginia P. Robinson (former faculty)
Kathryn Rossé (MSW 1966, former adjunct faculty)
Nicholas Roush (MSW 1979)
Roberta G. Sands (current faculty)
Ira M. Schwartz (former faculty and dean)
Vivian C. Seltzer (MSW 1953, current faculty)
William Silver (MSW 1968, DSW 1976, current adjunct faculty)
Ruth E. Smalley (former Dean)
Kenwyn K. Smith (current faculty)
SaraKay Smullens (MSW 1965)
Phyllis Solomon (current faculty)
Carol W. Spigner (current faculty)
Victoria Stanhope (Ph.D. 2007)
Mark J. Stern (current faculty)
Jack Sternbach (MSW 1955, former faculty)
Jessie Taft (former faculty)
Frank D. Watson (former faculty)

Contributors Not Affiliated with the School

Jamie J. Fader
Laurene Finley
Trevor R. Hadley
Peter R. Jones
Joseph Jupin
Michael B. Katz
Chang-Moo Lee
Kathleen Nuccio
Zoran Obradovic
Anita Pernell-Arnold
David R. Schwartz
Mark S. Salzer
Susan M. Wachter
Richard P. Waterman

Index

Abramowitz, Ira A., 455
actuarial risk assessment. *See* "Risk Classification and Juvenile Dispositions" (Jones et al.)
Addams, Jane, 159
Adler, Alfred, 83
adolescent peer concordance. *See* "A Cross-National Study of Adolescent Peer Concordance" (Seltzer and Waterman)
Adoption and Safe Families Act (1997), 407
Adoption Assistance and Child Welfare Act (1980), 395
African Americans. *See* "The Black Instructor" (Carter); "Institutional Change as a Creative Process" (Arnold and Bloom); "The New African American Inequality" (Katz et al.); "Social Services of African American Congregations" (Boddie)
Age Discrimination in Employment Act (ADEA), 221–22
agency function and functional approach, 75, 171–72, 204
Aid to Families with Dependent Children (AFDC), 521, 554
Alexander, Franz, 178n.75
Allen, Sue Ann, 436
Allen-Meares, Paula, 233
American Association for Marriage and Family Therapy (AAMFT) Supervision Committee, 216, 220; Approved Supervisor certification, 220
American Association of Social Workers, 158
American Jewish Joint Distribution Committee (AJJDC/JDC), 272–84, 286–87
Americans with Disabilities Act (ADA) (1990), 239, 531
Angus, Glenn, 594
Antonescu, Ion, 272
Aponte, Harry, 219
Applebaum, Richard, 540
Argyris, Chris, 235

Arnold, Howard, 4, 619. *See also* "Institutional Change as a Creative Process" (Arnold and Bloom)
Artigues, Roland, 190–91, 230
Ashenfelter, Orley, 222
Association for Gerontology in Higher Education, Annual Conference (2003), 222
Association of Training Schools for Professional Social Work (ATSPSW), 35, 49, 56
Atchley, Robert C., 227
Atienza, Felipe, 586
Austin, Lucille, 178n.71
Austin, Michael J., 7–8, 618–20; on becoming dean at Penn, 618–19; and Dore, 175, 180; and functional approach, 619–20; on School restoration, 619. *See also* "Organizational Learning and Change" (Cohen and Austin)
Ausubel, David, 496
"Avocational Guidance" (de Schweinitz), 26–37; alternative perspective, 35–36; overview, 34–35; social/cultural context, 32–34; and World War I era women's roles, 34
Axinn, June, 7, 634

Baird, Christopher, 581
Baltes, Margert M., 228
Baltes, Paul B., 228
Baltimore City Hospitals, 244–45
Bandura, Albert, 496
Barusch, Amanda S., 227
Bauman, Sandie, 634
Beck, Aaron, 186
Becker, James, 272
Bemus, Brian, 581
Bennett Development Model of Intercultural Sensitivity (DMIS), 500–504, 513, 517
Berg, David, 411–12, 416
Berlin, Sharon B., 468

Berzoff, Joan, 468

Betchen, Stephen J., 6, 218–20; on Drenk and therapeutic model, 219–20; on training at Penn, 219–20. *See also* "An Integrative, Intersystemic Approach" (Betchen)

Billingsley, Andrew, 128

Birchwood, Max, 455

Bishop, Julia Ann, 186, 193, 198n.1

Bishop, Margaret, 78, 185, 195, 198n.1

Black Faculty and Administrators (BFA), 142–43

"The Black Instructor: An Essential Dimension to the Content and Structure of the Social Work Curriculum" (Carter), 114–22; and belief change is possible, 115–16, 121n.6; racism course and black instructor, 114–17; social work practice course, 117–20; and white suspicion of delegation of power, 115, 121n.3; Roush's commentary, 4, 121–22

Blatch, Harriot Stanton, 34

Blau, Peter, 432

Bloom, Tybel, 4, 6; on functional approach, 148. *See also* "Institutional Change as a Creative Process" (Arnold and Bloom)

Blum, Arthur, 433, 437–38

Bock, Tonia, 503

Boddie, Stephanie C., 7; on arriving at Penn, 330; biology and social work, 329; black church from functional perspective, 328–32; on Du Bois's study, 329–30; on functional approach, 328–30; recent research on black congregations, 330–31. *See also* "Social Services of African American Congregations" (Boddie)

Bolduc, Vincent, 434–38

Bombyk, Marcia J. C., 468

Bonacich, Edna, 384n.14

Boston Children's Aid Society, 23

Boston School of Social Work, 87

"Boundary Spanning: An Ecological Reinterpretation of Social Work Practice in Health and Mental Health Systems" (Kerson), 232–47; and business management frameworks, 235; definitions of health-related settings, 236–37; development, 232–33; ecological perspective, 233–36; expanding knowledge bases, 237; and general systems theory, 233–36; health/mental health care, 23; levels of practice, 237; methods, 237–41

Bourjolly, Joretha N., 8. *See also* "The Journey Toward Intercultural Sensitivity" (Bourjolly et al.)

Bowen, Murray, 209, 211–12, 412

Bowen, William G., 424

Bowlby, John, 479

Boyte, Harry, 441

Brager, George, 130

Bricker-Jenkins, Mary, 468

Brill, Abraham A., 166

Brody, Morris, 195

Bronfenbrenner, Uri, 440

Bruno, Anthony F., commentary on Arnold and Bloom, 4, 147–48

Bruton, Paul W., 79

Bryn Mawr College, 84, 245

Buber, Martin, 70

Buel, Estelle, 100

Bureau of Child Guidance (New York), 78

Burgess, Ernest, 577

Burnside, Irene, 226

Burt, Martha, 540

Bush administration, 322, 330, 562n.1

business management frameworks and boundary spanning, 235

Butcher, Hugh, 435,–37

Butler, Evelyn, 190

Butler, Robert N., 226

Cabot, Richard C., 53

Cajal, Nicolae, 276

Camberwell Family Interview, 451–52

Card, David, 222

Carter, Isabel, 5

Carter, Louis H., 4. *See also* "The Black Instructor" (Carter)

Carter, Robert T., 514

Cartographic Modeling Lab, 8, 567

Casas, Irene, 583

Catt, Carrie Chapman, 34, 86

"The Cause in Function" (Lewis), 4, 105–13; analogic reasoning in practice, 111, 113n.3; emphasis on client activity, 112–13; and Faatz on helping process, 105, 107, 109–11; and Lee hypothesis, 105–7, 109; cause and function in helping act, 106–8, 112–13

Cavendish, James C., 324

Ceausescu, Nicolae, 274–76

Center for Mental Health Policy, 319–20, 565

Center for Research and Education in the Workplace, Penn School, 608–10

"Challenging Injustice and Oppression" (Gil), 248–70; changing behavior and institutions, 262–65; conventional politics to politics of common human needs, 262; critical consciousness (key to social change), 259–61; critical consciousness (strategies), 261–62; historical notes, 251–53; key social institutions in just and free/ unjust and oppressive societies, 250–51; long-range visions/transformation strategies, 256–58; meaning of social justice/injustice and oppression, 248–49, 268–70; perpetuation of inequality, 255–56; pre- and post-agricultural societies, 251–53; short-range, 256; theoretical perspectives on transformation, 258–59; types of oppression and injustice, 251, 253–55; violence and social change, 264–65; and "war on terrorism," 267–68

Charity Organization Societies (COS): and helping model, 165–66; and neighborhood-representing organizations, 428; and Lee, 48; and Richmond, 166; and social casework as method, 73

Chaves, Mark, 323–24

Chernesky, Roslyn H., 468

Child Abuse Prevention and Treatment Act (1974), 394

Children's Aid Society of Pennsylvania, 2, 21

Children's Bureau (Philadelphia), 21, 23, 87, 175n.7

Children's Hospital of Boston, Family Development Study, 406–7

Child Welfare League of America, 23

child welfare system's crisis, 391–95, 606–7. *See also* "How Evaluation Research Can Help" (Gelles); "Organizational Learning and Change" (Cohen and Austin)

Chodorow, Nancy J., 468

Cixous, Hélène, 471

Clear, Todd, 581

Clinton plan on homelessness, 541–42

Cloward, Richard J., 297

Cnaan, Ram A., 8, 330; commentary on Lee, 3, 48–50; commentary on Murphy, 3, 23–25; commentary on Watson," 3, 56–57; director of social planning for State of Israel, 446–47; doctoral program experience, 446–47; "Neighborhood-Representing Organizations: How Democratic Are They?" 428–49; *Handbook of Community Movements and Local Organizations*, 448; *The Invisible Caring Hand: American Congregations and the Provision of Welfare*, 449; *The Newer Deal: Social Work and Religion in Partnership*, 449; *The Other Philadelphia Story: How Local Congregations Support Quality of Life in Urban America*, 449

Cohen, Burton J., 8. *See also* "Organizational Learning and Change" (Cohen and Austin)

Cohen, Carl I., 305–6

Colby, Ira, 3, 6; commentary on de Schweinitz, 3, 32–37

Cole, David P., 594

Coleman, John, 479, 496

Coles, Robert, 125

College Association of Woman Suffrage, 85–86

Collis, Patricia, 435, 436, 437

Columbia University School of Social Work, 49, 76, 179–80, 619

Commonwealth Fund, 166

Communism. *See* "Partnering with the Jewish Community of Romania" (Feine)

Community Mental Health Centers Act (1963), 230, 531

community organizations. *See* "Introduction to a Dissertation" (Mondros); "Neighborhood-Representing Organizations" (Cnaan)

"A Community Program for Child Care" (Murphy),

3, 20–25; Children's Bureau, 21; Philadelphia Children's Aid Society, 21; Philadelphia Society for the Protection of Children from Cruelty, 21; Seybert Institution, 20, 22; Cnaan's commentary, 3, 23–25

A Comparison of Diagnostic and Functional Casework Concepts (Cora Kasius, ed.), 173

Conley, Dalton, 377

"The Contributions of American Social Agencies to Social Progress and Democracy" (Watson), 51–57; as free lances, standard bearers, critics, 54–55; and public opinion, 53; and "social exploring," 51–53; and social legislation, 53–54; Cnaan on Watson, 3, 56–57

Cooper, Terry, 433–34, 437, 440

Cordray, David S., 311

Cornell Clinic of Psychopathology, 86

Cornell University, 48

Corner, George, 329

Council for Relationships. *See* Marriage Council of Philadelphia

Council on Social Work Education: Curriculum Policy Statement (1962), 72; and Harold Lewis, 111; and Penn 1963 reaccreditation, 79–80; and Lee, 49; and Smalley, 79–80; use of categories, 473; and Watson, 57

couple therapy. *See* "An Integrative, Intersystemic Approach" (Betchen)

Coursey, Robert D., 455

Cox, Fred, 289

Coyle, Grace, 120, 121n.11

Crenson, Matthew, 435

crime. *See* "Risk Classification and Juvenile Dispositions" (Jones et al.); "The Role of Social Disadvantage" (Draine et al.)

Cross, William, 33

"A Cross-National Study of Adolescent Peer Concordance on Issues of the Future" (Seltzer and Waterman), 478–99; Adolescent Future Perception Index (AFPI), 483–84; age differences, 481–82, 491; cross-national dimensions, 482, 491; Dynamic Functional Interaction (DFI) model, 479, 481, 491; gender differences, 482, 491; hypotheses, 482; literature on future and adolescents, 480; methods, 482–85; participants, 482–83; peer groups, 478–80; pertinent empirical studies, 497; research issues/questions, 481–82; results, 485–91; summary, 491–92; and theory of psychosocial development, 497–98; twentieth-century interest, 495–96; twenty-first century, 498

Crystal Stair Award, 197

Culhane, Dennis P., 8, 565–67; and Cartographic Modeling Lab, 8, 567. *See also* "The Role of Social Disadvantage" (Draine et al.); "Where the Homeless Come From" (Culhane et al.)

Dahl, Robert, 430

Davis, Katharine Bement, 86

Davis, Liane V., 468

Dawley, Almena, 75

Delworth, Ursula, 211

Denton, Nancy A., 357–58, 555

Derrida, Jacques, 469, 471

de Saussure, Ferdinand, 469

de Schweinitz, Karl, 3, 32–33; *Growing Up*, 33; recruited to Philadelphia Training School, 57. *See also* "Avocational Guidance" (de Schweinitz)

Devine, Edward T., 55

Dewey, John, 85, 178n.75

Diagnostic and Statistical Manual of Mental Disorders, Third Edition Revised, 473–74

diagnostic approach: Columbia, 76, 179, 619; Freudian interpretation of human nature, 75–76; New York School of Social Work, 95, 96; psychodynamic theory, 75–76, 159, 166, 175n.7, 619; Taft's departure, 200–202. *See also* diagnostic/functional debates

diagnostic/functional debates, 3–4, 95–97, 169, 171–73, 177n.47, 178n.71; and Dore, 179–81; and ego psychology, 173, 178n.75; and Pray, 95–96, 172; and Robinson, 4, 172; Smalley on, 76–77; and Smullens, 185, 195

Dicks, Henry V., 212

Dickson, Paul, 581

Dings, Jonathan G., 514

Dix, Dorothea, 159

Dixon Lisa B., 460

DMIS. *See* Bennett Development Model of Intercultural Sensitivity

Dore, Martha M., 4; and diagnostic/functional debate, 179–81; joining Penn School, 179–80; on Taft and Robinson, 181. *See also* "Functional Theory" (Dore)

Dorfman, Lorraine T., 222

Downes, Laura, 185, 189–90, 195–97

Downs, Anthony, 428, 436

Draine, Jeffrey N., 7, 8, 462; commentary on Sternbach, 8–9, 633–35; and mental illness issues, 634–35; and prison issues, 633–34; and Social Work Mental Health Research Center, 319–20. *See also* "The Role of Social Disadvantage" (Draine et al.)

Drenk Memorial Guidance Center (New Jersey), 219

Droegmueller, W., 394

Drucker, Peter, 235

DSW program, 5–7; clinical program (2007/8), 7, 199; Doctoral Council and Admissions Committee, 5–6; early, 5–6; functionalist approach, 6; and today's leaders in social work education, 6; and Turner, 5

Du Bois, W. E. B., 329–30, 389

Duhl, Bunny S., 215

Duncan, Barry, 215

Dupont, Robert, 438

Durkheim, Emile, 428

ecological perspective: and boundary spanning, 233–36; and business management frameworks, 235; and functional theory, 174; and general systems theory, 233–36; Germain Life Model, 219–20; and time, 174. *See also* "Boundary Spanning" (Kerson)

"Education for Social Development: Curricular Issues and Models" (Estes), 333–53; assumptions of social development practice, 334–35; "concentrated" approach, 343–46, 347n.4; and curricular intensity, 343–46; goals, 334; "integrated" approach, 344–46; levels of practice, 336–37; models of education, 337–43, 347n.3; new world order model (NWOM), 339–42; paradigm for international social work, 351; personal social services model (PSSM), 338, 340–42; sectors of practice, 337–38; "selective" approach, 343–46; social development, social work, and social change, 333–37; knowledge base, 335–36; social development model (SDM), 339–42; social welfare model (SWM), 338, 340–42

ego psychology, 173, 178n.75

Ehrenreich, John H., 3–4

Ehrlich, Tom, 619

Elion, Sandra, 435

Elliot, Marta, 540

Ellmann, Richard, 223

Endicott, Leilani, 503

English, Diana, 586

Epstein, Laura, 174

Erikson, Erik: and adolescence, 478–79, 496–98; and ego psychology, 178n.75

Estes, Richard J., 7; and Euster coursework, 230; on Penn's interdisciplinary and international environment, 351–52. *See also* "Education for Social Development" (Estes)

Euster, Gerald L., 6; dissertation research at Philadelphia State Hospital, 230–31; education at Penn, 230; gerontology courses, 229; at Menninger Clinic, 230–31; at University of South Carolina, 229–31. *See also* "Reflections upon University Retirement"

evaluation research. *See* "How Evaluation Research Can Help" (Gelles)

evidence-based practice movement, 205–6

Faatz, Anita, 102, 105; concept of social casework, 75, 93–94; first candidate in DSW program, 5–6; and Harold Lewis, 105, 107, 109–11; and Smullens, 186, 196–97

Faculty Retirement Survey, 222

Fader, Jamie J.. *See* "The New African American Inequality" (Katz et al.)

Faith, Goldie Basch, 5–6

Faith-Based Initiative, 322, 330

"The Family and the Social Worker" (Richmond), 3, 13–19; address to National Conference on Social Welfare (1908), 16–17; issue of education, 17; issue of parental responsibility, 17; Richmond influence on profession, 2, 16–19

family education, 452–56; conceptual base, 453; program evaluation, 454–56; program formats, 453–54. *See also* "Moving from Psychoeducation to Family Education" (Solomon)

Family Service Association of America, 95, 172–73

family therapy, 218–19. *See also* "An Integrative, Intersystemic Approach" (Betchen)

Fatley, Reynolds, 371

Feder, Ted, 286

Feine, Zvi, 6, 285–87. *See also* "Partnering with the Jewish Community of Romania" (Feine)

Fels Master of Government Administration program, 420

feminist theory. *See* "Postmodern Feminist Theory and Social Work" (Sands and Nuccio)

Ferenczi, Sándor, 89–90

Festinger, Leon, 497

Finley, Laurene. *See* "The Journey Toward Intercultural Sensitivity" (Bourjolly et al.)

Fishman, H. Charles, 209

Fishtown Civil Association (FCA), 292–93, 296–97

Flexner, Abraham, 49

Florin, Paul, 436–37, 438

Foucault, Michel, 469–71

Framo, James L., 209, 212

Frankel, Victor, 70

Fraser, J. Scott, 215

Frazier, E. Franklin, 323

Freeman, Anne, 441

Freeman, Miriam L., 467

Freire, Paolo., 297

French, Thomas, 178n.75

Freud, Anna, 496

Freud, Sigmund: developmental theory and adolescence, 496; *The Interpretation of Dreams*, 186; and 1930s, 166–67; Rank's break, 83, 89–90, 168, 172, 186–87; and structuralism, 469

Friedmann, Robert, 436–38

functional approach, 3–4, 167–71, 200–206, 619; adolescent development and behavior, 499; agency function, 75, 171–72, 204; Austin on, 619, 620; and black church, 328–32; Bloom on, 148; Boddie on, 328–30; client participation, 169–70, 173–74, 201, 204; and contemporary theory/practice, 3, 173–74, 203–6; controversiality, 172; core principles, 203–4; early years, 165–67; and ecological perspective, 174; and helping relationship, 75, 165–66, 170–71, 201, 204, 206; Penn

pioneers, 167–71, 203; and postmodernism, 476–77; and Pray, 95–96, 167, 170, 203; and Rank, 3–4, 76, 92–95, 167–71; Richmond and history of casework, 73–75; and Robinson, 3–4, 75, 168–69, 171, 203; Rossé on influence, 4, 102–4; Smalley on, 723–77; and social casework, 72–77; and Taft, 75, 200–203, 206; and time as therapeutic tool, 61–70, 168, 170–71, 174, 179n.82. *See also* "The Cause in Function" (Lewis); diagnostic/functional debates; "Functional Theory" (Dore)

"Functional Theory: Its History and Influence on Contemporary Social Work Practice" (Dore), 165–81; and agency function, 171–72; and client participation, 169–70, 173–74; contemporary practice, 173–74; development of functional theory at Penn, 167–71; diagnostic/functional debates, 3–4, 169, 171–73, 177n.47, 178n.71; early years, 165–67; functional theory and Rank, 167, 168–71; and helping relationship, 165–66, 170–71; post-World War I/Progressive era and psychodynamic theory, 159, 166; Rank's concept of Will, 168, 176nn.28, 36, 203; and time, 168, 170–71, 174, 179n.82; treatment relationship, 168

Furman, Rich, 4. *See also* "Jessie Taft and the Functional School" (Furman)

Gambrill, Eileen, 575, 581–82

Gelles, Richard J., 7, 406–8, 422; ASA Congressional Fellow, 407; clinical training and fellowship, 406–7; career and influence, 406–8; and School Transformation Committee, 422. *See also* "How Evaluation Research Can Help" (Gelles)

Geographic Information Systems (GIS) technology, 8, 298

Gerlach, Luther P., 297, 299

Germain, Carel, 174, 219–20, 233

Gil, David G., 6; and Gelles, 406–7. *See also* "Challenging Injustice and Oppression" (Gil)

Gilligan, Carol, 468

Gitterman, Alex, 174, 233

Gittle, Marlyn, 440

Glen, Andrew, 435, 436

Glueck, Bernard, 176n.22

Glueck, Eleanor, 577

Glueck, Steven, 577

Godfrey, Joline, 524

Golan, Naomi, 179n.82

Goldstein, Hoard, 201–2

Goldstein, Michael J., 451

Goleman, Daniel, 192

Gomberg, Robert, 73

Googins, Bradley, 524

Gottfredson, Don, 574, 577, 579

Gottfredson, Michael, 578

Gottfredson, Stephen, 574–75, 578–79

Goucher College, 183
Graduate School for Jewish Social Work, 83, 96–98
Green, Rose, 96–97
Grigsby, Kevin, 3, 18–19; commentary on Richmond, 3, 16–19
Guarnaccia, Peter J., 457
Gurteen, S. Humphreys, 48
Gutmann, Amy, 422

Hacker, Andrew, 355
Hackney, Sheldon, 424
Hacohen, Orly, 434, 435
Hadley, Trevor R., seminar in mental health services, 319. *See also* "The Role of Social Disadvantage" (Draine et al.)
Haeberle, Steven, 436
Haight, Barbara K., 226
Haley, Jay, 209, 219
Hall, G. Stanley, 496
Hallman, Howard, 434
Hamilton, Gordon, 169, 172, 178n.71, 180
Hammer, Mitchell R., 500
Handy, Femida, 8
Hannah-Moffat, Kelly, 579
Harnwell, Gaylord P., 78–79
Hartman, Ann, 178n.71
Hartocollis, Lina, 537
Harvey, Margaret, 198n.2
Hatfield, Agnes, 452, 460–61
Haverford College, 56, 57
health-related social work. *See* "Boundary Spanning" (Kerson)
Healy, William, 166
Heinz, Richard, 581
Helms, Janet E., 514
helping relationship and functional approach, 75, 165–66, 170–71, 201, 204, 206
Hersh, Al, 618–19
Higgins, Lynn M., 323–24
Hillier, Amy, 331
Hine, Virginia H., 297, 299
Hoffman, Peter, 577
Hollis, Florence, 169, 174, 180
Holloway, Stephen, 130
homelessness. *See* "The Role of Social Disadvantage" (Draine et al.); "Where the Homeless Come From" (Culhane et al.)
Hooyman, Nancy R., 223, 468
Hopper, Kim, 541
Howard University, 424
"How Evaluation Research Can Help Reform and Improve the Child Welfare System" (Gelles), 391–408; considering why so few evaluations are made, 400–403; crisis, 391–95; evaluation data and findings, 396–98; "gold standard" for evaluation research, 402, 403–4; National Research Council Committee on the Assessment of Family

Violence Interventions, 396–98, 403; reasons for crisis, 392–93; reasons research is unable to find evidence of program effectiveness, 398–400; and standard interventions (typical "tool box"), 394–95; three basic steps for better evaluation research, 403–4
Hudson, Walter, 18, 19
Hughes, Langston, 197
Hunter College School of Social Work, 111

Iadicola, Peter, 467
Index of Job Desirability, 529
"The Influence of Otto Rank in Social Work: A Journey into a Past" (Robinson), 82–104; and development of social casework at Penn, 92–95; diagnostic/functional debate, 95–97; differentiation from Freud's circle, 83, 90; early influence, 83, 89–90, 97; popular lectures, 83, 89–90, 96–100; Robinson's first meetings with Rank, 90–91; Taft's first meeting with Rank, 88–90; use of word "functional," 94. *See also* Rank, Otto
injustice. *See* "Challenging Injustice and Oppression" (Gil)
Institute for Child Guidance (New York)y, 166
"Institutional Change as a Creative Process: Some Educational and Practice Considerations" (Arnold and Bloom), 123–48; intentional change/nature of change in human systems, 124–25; learning environment, 126–27; Penn and change orientation, 123–24; racism sequence/courses and learning process, 128–38, 146n.2; relating social work practice knowledge to institutional change, 144–45; self-knowledge/knowledge of self for professional use, 125–26; seminar for field instructors, 140–42; social change efforts by faculty, 142–44; social work practice for social change case illustration, 138–40; term "institutional change," 146n.3; understanding organizational structure, 144
"An Integrative, Intersystemic Approach to Supervision of Couple Therapy" (Betchen), 209–20; development of supervisory model, 220; family therapy and social work, 218–19; limitations of model, 216; the Marriage Council Intersystem Model, 209–10, 215–16; models introduced in 1980s, 209, 215, 220; supervision case, 212–15; and systems therapy, 220
intercultural sensitivity. *See* "The Journey Toward Intercultural Sensitivity" (Bourjolly et al.)
"Introduction to a Dissertation: Posing Questions on Perceived Empowerment and Community Problem Solving" (Mondros), 288–301; Alinsky style organizations, 289, 296, 298; categorizing organizations, 288–90; contribution to literature on community organization, 291–92; defining community organizations, 289; defining neighborhood/neighborhood organization, 289,

296nn.18–19; empowerment of participants in neighborhood organizations, 291; innovations in studying community organizations, 298–300; Philadelphia neighborhood organizations, 292–93, 296–97; resolution of neighborhood issues, 290; study plan, 292–95

Ionaid, Radu, 273

Irigaray, Luce, 471

Iron Law of Oligarchy (Michels), 429, 440, 447–48

Israel neighborhood-representing organizations, 429, 433–39

Iversen, Roberta R., 8; research and publications, 537–38. *See also* "Occupational Social Work for the Twenty-First Century" (Iverson)

Jahn, Julius, 230

James, William, 85

Jargowsky, Paul A., 520

Jarrett, Mary, 166

"Jessie Taft and the Functional School: The Impact of Our History" (Furman), 4, 200–206; concept of emotions, 202–3; contribution to social work values, 203; formative association with Rank, 200–202; functional movement and contemporary theory, 3, 203–4; functional paradigm, 200–202; helping relationship, 201, 206; Penn pioneers in functional approach, 203; and twenty-first century, 204–6

Jewish community. *See* "Partnering with the Jewish Community of Romania" (Feine)

Jockel, Else, 177n.47

Jones, Martyn, 468

Jones, Peter R. *See* "Risk Classification and Juvenile Dispositions" (Jones et al.)

"The Journey Toward Intercultural Sensitivity: A Non-Linear Process" (Bourjolly, Sands, Solomon, Stanhope, Pernell-Arnold, Finley), 500–518; DMIS, 500, 501–4, 513, 517; data analysis, 505–6; discussion and implications, 513–15; findings, 506–13; Intercultural Developmental Inventory (IDI), 502–3; limitations, 515, 517; literature review, 502–4; logs of linear, nonlinear development, 507–13; methods, 504–6; Multicultural Experiences Questionnaire (MEXQ), 503; participants, 504; and Penn tradition, 516; PRIME training program, 500–501, 503–15; racism and intercultural sensitivity, 507–12, 514

Joyce, James, 223

Juby, Heather L., 514

Jung, Carl, 83, 186

Jupin, Joseph. *See* "Risk Classification and Juvenile Dispositions" (Jones et al.)

juvenile crime/delinquency. *See* "Risk Classification and Juvenile Dispositions" (Jones et al.)

Kahn, Alfred J., 606

Kahn, Robert L., 228

Kamerman, Sheila B., 606

Kaplan, Alexandra G., 468

Karls, James M., 233

Katan, Joseph, 433, 435–36, 438–39

Katz, Michael B. *See* "The New African American Inequality" (Katz et al.)

Keith, David V., 209

Keller, James F., 215

Kelsey, Carl, 23

Kempe, C. Henry, 394

Kensington Action Now (KAN), 292–93, 296–98

Kenworthy, Marion E., 50, 166–67

Kerson, Toba S., 6; and doctoral program, 245. *See also* "Boundary Spanning" (Kerson)

King, Paul, 434–35

Kirk, Stuart A., 473–74

Kiyak, H. Asuman, 223

Klein, Melanie, 212

Kondratas, Anna, 562n.1

Kotter, John, 235

Kristeva, Julia, 469, 471

Krivo, Lauren J., 540

Kuroda, Yasumasa, 437

Kusmer, Kenneth L., 57

Kutchins, Herb, 473–74

Lacan, Jacques, 469, 471

Lamb, Curt, 434

Lane, Bruce A., 233

Lane, W. Clayton, 222

Langer, Suzanne, 125

Langstroth, Lovell, 100

Lawder, Elizabeth Alston, 6

Lawrence, D. H., 101, 191

Lawton, Ruth, 23

Lebow, Jay L., 209, 215

Lee, Chang-Moo. *See* "Where the Homeless Come From" (Culhane et al.)

Lee, Porter R., 3; and COS of Buffalo, 48; foundation course "Human Behavior and the Social Environment," 50; influence on education standards, 49–50; and Lewis, "The Cause in Function," 105–7, 109; *Mental Hygiene and Social Work*, 50, 166–67; Philadelphia Training School, 49–50; pioneer in seeing the person in environment, 50; pioneer of the "case method," 49; *Social Salvage*, 50; *Social Work Cause and Functions*, 50. *See also* "Personality in Social Work" (Lee)

Lehman, Anthony F., 311, 460

Leiberg, Leon, 286

"Lessons Learned About Working with Men: A Prison Memoir" (Sternbach), 621–35; blocks to further reform, 632; changes since Sternbach wrote, 634; Foothills Correctional Institution, 621–28; gay inmates, 624, 629–30; and graduate sessions at Penn School, 624; inmate-run programs, 623, 628; lesson about violence/informal

Lessons Learned About Working with Men
(*continued*)
    containment, 630–32; lessons about letting peo-
    ple speak for themselves, 626; lessons about phys-
    ical affection between men, 629–30; lessons
    about protection and violence, 631–32; lessons
    about respecting limits, 626–27; lessons about
    revealing oneself, 627–29; lessons about starting
    where the other man is, 627; lessons about vul-
    nerability, mutuality, willingness to learn from
    clients, 625–26; and news of Attica uprising, 625;
    prison management, 622; racism, 622; reform
    and change, 623–25; staff/officers, 621–25, 632
Levi, Margaret, 434
Levin, Herman, 102
Levine, Moe, 274, 286
Lévi-Strauss, Claude., 469
Lewin, Kurt, 498, 608
Lewis, Beth, 4, 110–13, 519
Lewis, Harold, 4, 6, 191–92; courses at Penn, 111;
    and nature of social work, 18; and self-knowl-
    edge/knowledge of self, 126; and research cur-
    riculum, 111; speeches following departure,
    111–12. *See also* "The Cause in Function" (Lewis)
Lewis, Michael I., 226
Liddle, Howard A., 211
Lieberman, Alice, 321
Lincoln, C. Eric., 323, 326
Lindbo, Tracy L., 223
Lipsky, Michael, 434
Liron, Ruth, 433, 435
Lloyd, Mark Frazier, commentary on Smalley, 4,
    78–81
Lodge, Richard, 191, 230
Loeffler, Diane N., 299–300
Lopez, Steven Regeser, 501
Lubove, Roy, 3–5; *The Professional Altruist*, 3

Mack Center on Nonprofit Management in the
    Human Services, 620
MacNair, Ray H., 233
Madanes, Cloe, 209
Maluccio, Anthony N., 204
Mamiya, Lawrence. H., 323, 326
Mandela, Nelson, 424
MANNA. *See* Metropolitan Aids Neighborhood
    Nutrition Alliance
Mansfield, Katherine, 191
Marcovitz, Eli, 196
Marcus, Grace F., 178n.62
Mark, Yecheskiel, 276
Marriage Council of Philadelphia (Council for Rela-
    tionships): and Betchen, 219–20; Intersystem
    Model, 209–10, 215–16; supervision case, 212–15
Marshall, David, 586
Marx, Karl, 250, 469
Massey, Douglas S., 357–58, 555

Masterson, Michael, 433
Mauratto, Paula, 579
May, Rollo, 186
Maybon, Linda, 198n.2
Maynard, Robert A., 523
McCarthy, John, 440
McClelland, George, 5
McCrohan, Nancy M., 310
McFarlane, William, 451, 457
McGoldrick, Monica, 219
McKnight, John L., 430, 436
McLean, Francis H., 54–55
McNamee, Stephen, 434, 439
Mead, George Herbert, 181
Meier, Ron, 436–38
Menninger Clinic (Topeka), 230–31; Retirement
    and Geriatric Center, 230
mental health care. *See* "Boundary Spanning"
    (Kerson)
mental hygiene, 61–70, 86–88, 166
Mental Hygiene and Social Work (Lee and Kenworthy),
    50, 166–67
mental illness. *See* "Moving from Psychoeducation
    to Family Education" (Solomon); "The Role of
    Social Disadvantage" (Draine et al.)
Meyer, Carol, 173, 180; ecological perspective, 233
Metropolitan Aids Neighborhood Nutrition Alli-
    ance (MANNA), 415, 423
Milford Conference Report Social Case Work,
    Generic and Specific, 49–50, 74
Milofsky, Carl, 429–30, 435, 448
Mintzberg, Henry, 235, 238
Minuchin, Salvador, 186, 195–95, 209, 219
Mishkin, Harriet, 198n.2
Mizrachi, Cecille, 274
Moi, Toril, 472
Mondros, Jacqueline B., 6. *See also* "Introduction to
    a Dissertation" (Mondros)
"Moving from Psychoeducation to Family Educa-
    tion for Families of Adults with Serious Mental
    Illness" (Solomon), 450–65; Assertive Commu-
    nity Treatment (ACT), 463; Evidence Based Prac-
    tices (EBPs), 464; family education, 452–56;
    family education program evaluation, 454–56;
    family education program formats, 453–54;
    future directions, 456–60; psychoeducation
    interventions, 450–52
Moynihan, Daniel, 401–2
Mudd, Emily, 219
Mukenge, Ida Rousseau, 322–23
Multi-Ethnic Placement Act (1994), 407
Murphy, J. Prentice, 2–3, 23–24; first course at
    Penn, 23; on illegitimate children, 23; legacy,
    23–24; on Depression, 24. *See also* "A Community
    Program for Child Care" (Murphy)
Murphy, Michael, 433, 437–38

Narvaez, Darcia, 503

National Advisory Committee of the Social Work Research Group, 111

National Alliance for the Mentally Ill (NAMI), Journey of Hope family education program, 457, 459–60

National Association of Social Workers (NASW): *Code of Ethics*, 160, 173–74; and Pray, 95; and Smalley, 80; Watson on, 51, 52

National Child Abuse and Neglect Data System, 394

National Commission on Neighborhoods, 429

National Committee for Mental Hygiene, 166

National Conference of Charities and Correction (1915), 49

National Conference of Social Work: and diagnostic/functional debate, 95; and Murphy, 23, 24; Pray 1945 address, 149–61; Pray 1947 address, 95–96, 170; Taft 1919 address, 166; Watson on, 51

National Conference on Social Welfare (1908), Richmond address, 16–17

National Council of Social Work Conference (1917), 33

National Council on Crime and Delinquency (NCCD), 571–74

National Institute of Corrections (NIC), 571–74

National Institute of Justice, 307

National Research Council Committee on the Assessment of Family Violence Interventions, 396–98, 403

National Supported Work program, 522–23

neighborhood organizations. *See* "Introduction to a Dissertation" (Mondros); "Neighborhood-Representing Organizations" (Cnaan)

"Neighborhood-Representing Organizations: How Democratic Are They?" (Cnaan), 428–49, 439–41; accountability, 431, 435; competition among organizations, 432–33, 439; cui bono, 438; defining democracy in, 430–33; and due process, 431, 436; and free, open elections, 430–31, 433–34; and informed membership, 431, 434–35; member participation, 431, 434; and Michels's Iron Law of Oligarchy, 429, 440, 447–48; similarity between leaders and members, 431–32, 436–37; similarity in perceived needs, 432, 437–38; successful advocacy, 432, 438–39; ten criteria for democracy in, 430–39

Nelsen, Hart M., 322–23

Nelson, Scott, 320

Nes, Janet A., 467

"The New African American Inequality" (Katz, Stern, and Fader), 354–90; and assets (home ownership), 377–79; census data and Minnesota IPUMS, 354; changes in racism since paper was written, 390; civil rights movement/affirmative action, 370, 387n.39; differentiation, 379–82; distribution/occupational mobility, 362; earnings,

371–79, 387nn. 42, 47; education, 368–71, 375, 377, 380–81, 387nn.37, 39, 388n.49; geography (segregation and redistribution), 357–58, 379–80; Hacker-Thernstrom debate, 355; industry (employment), 362–65, 380, 385nn.20, 22, 23; occupation trends, 365–68, 380, 386n.29; participation in employment, 358–62, 380; Penn racism emphasis, 389–90; poverty, 371–72; rewards (relative income), 371; twentieth-century programs and policies, 364

Newberger, Eli, 407

New York City Conference of Charities and Corrections (1926), 86

New York homeless. *See* "Where the Homeless Come From" (Culhane et al.)

New York School of Philanthropy, 48–49

New York School of Social Work, 49, 87, 166–67; diagnostic orientation, 95, 96; Rank lectures at, 83, 89–90, 97

New York State Laboratory of Social Hygiene, 86

New York State Reformatory for Women, 86

Nin, Anaïs, 101

Nonprofit/NGO Leadership (NPL) graduate program, 422, 427

North Carolina School of Social Work, 96

Nuccio, Kathleen. *See* "Postmodern Feminist Theory and Social Work" (Sands and Nuccio)

Nurmi, Jari-Erik, 480

Obradovic, Zoran. *See* "Risk Classification and Juvenile Dispositions" (Jones et al.)

Occupational Health and Safety Act (OSHA) (1970), 531

"Occupational Social Work for the Twenty-First Century" (Iversen), 519–38; application of specialized knowledge and skills, 528–30; background and reformulation, 522–25; defining occupational social work, 524; employee assistance program (EAP), 524–25; economic restructuring, 520–21; implications for social work, 531–32; occupational social work in 1980s/1990s, 524–25; Penn orientation, 537–38; reformulating, 525–30; research evaluation of work programs, 522–24; TANF grants and regulations, 521, 527–28, 530, 532; welfare policy change, 521–22; welfare-to-work, 522–23; work-enhancement programs, 523–24; work-program practice settings, 528; work-specific role definitions, 525–28

Office of Juvenile Justice and Delinquency Prevention (OJJDP), 573–74

Ohio State University, 476

Ohlin, Lloyd, 577

Olds, David., 398

Oliver, Melvin L., 377

Oliver, Pamela, 434

Olson, Mancur, 429, 438

"On Becoming a Scholar-Practitioner" (Smith), 409–27; on becoming a community builder, 421–23; on becoming an educator, 417–21; on becoming a researcher, 409–17; and Center for Workplace Studies, 421; childhood/youth and ongoing "becoming," 425–27; on developing an integrated persona, 423–25; faculty master of Ware College House, 421–22; Fels MGA program, 420; joining Penn, 414; MANNA projects, 415, 420, 423; Nonprofit/NGO Leadership (NPL) graduate program, 422, 427; nonprofit volunteer-based organizations, 423; Penn course, "Group Dynamics and Organizational Politics," 417–19; professional world, 422–23; research on conflict, 411–13; research on group and intergroup relations, 409–11; research on organizational change, 413–14; journal reviews/editorial boards, 422–23; School Transformation Committee, 422; and Wharton senior executive education programs, 420, 424–25

Opportunities Industrialization Center (OIC) programs, 521, 523

oppression. *See* "Challenging Injustice and Oppression" (Gil)

organizational change, 413–14. *See also* "Institutional Change as a Creative Process" (Arnold and Bloom); "Organizational Learning and Chang" (Cohen and Austin)

"Organizational Learning and Change in a Public Child Welfare Agency" (Cohen and Austin), 606–20; action research as approach to organizational change, 608; case study (Philadelphia program), 608–13; child welfare organizations and Quality of Working Life (QWL) movement, 607–8, 617; creating a learning organization, 615–16; crisis in child welfare system, 606–7; DHS and Children and Youth Division (CYD), 609, 612–15; experimental Intake Section (at CYD), 612–15; Philadelphia DHS, 608–10, 616; reformulation of case study approach, 611–13; rethinking roles of Social Work Administrators, 611–12; spreading new ideas through organizational learning, 613–15; strengthening four capabilities of learning organizations, 615–16; Task Force on Community Based Services, 613; Task Force on Staff Development and Workplace Supports, 612–13

Orlin, Malinda, 239

Orr, Richard, 586

Oshry, Barry, 410

Ottavi, Thoams M., 514

Ozawa, Martha N., 519

Parra, Pilar, 457

"Partnering with the Jewish Community of Romania and Transitioning from Holocaust and Communism to Modernity" (Feine), 271–87; American Jewish Joint Distribution Committee, 272–84, 286–87; and Communist government, 273–77; community building and leadership development, 282–84; Federation of Jewish Communities of Romania (FEDROM), 274–84, 286; informal education, 281–82; and Rabbi Rosen, 274–77, 286–87; social welfare and medical programs (SMAD), 277–81; transition, 1990–2006, 277–84, 287; World War I, 272–73; World War II and Holocaust, 272–73

Pecorella, Robert, 434, 437, 440

Penn School of Medicine, 565

Penn School of Social Work. *See* University of Pennsylvania School of Social Work/School of Social Policy & Practice

Pennsylvania Society for the Protection of Children from Cruelty, 21

Pepper, Benjamin Franklin, 2

Perlman, Helen Harris, 173, 178n.75, 180

Perlman, Janice, 429

Pernell-Arnold, Anita. *See* "The Journey Toward Intercultural Sensitivity" (Bourjolly et al.)

Perry, John, 575–79

"Personality in Social Work" (Lee), 38–50; adjustment, 44–45; development of personality for social work, 43–44; leadership, 45–47; personality and civilization, 47–48; Cnaan on Lee's career, 3, 48–50

Personal Responsibility and Work Opportunity Reconciliation Act (1996), 521, 537. *See also* welfare reform legislation (1996)

Petit, Michael, 400

Pettit, Walter William, 50

Philadelphia: crime and mental illness, 319; shelter data, 311–12, 565–66. *See also* "Where the Homeless Come From" (Culhane et al.)

Philadelphia Child Guidance Clinic, 75, 166, 194, 219

Philadelphia Department of Human Services (DHS), 608–10, 616, 620; Children and Youth Division (CYD), 609, 612–15

Philadelphia Psychiatric Hospital, 195

Philadelphia Society for Organizing Charity, 2, 49

Philadelphia Society to Protect Children, 186, 193, 195

Philadelphia State Hospital, 230–31

Philadelphia Training School for Social Work, 2, 49, 56–57, 166, 175n.7

Philadelphia Unemployment Project, 530

Piaget, Jean, 469

Pitkin, Hanna, 430–32

Piven, Frances F., 297

Protinsky, Howard, 215

Pollak, Otto, 230

Pope-Davis, Donald B., 514

Posner, Craig M., 455

"Postmodern Feminist Theory and Social Work"

(Sands and Nuccio), 466–77; and categories, 473–74; feminist theory and social work, 466–68; French feminism, 471; postmodernism and functionalist orientation, 476–77; postmodernism and research orientation, 477; social work implications, 473–74; structuralism and poststructuralism, 469–70

Pray, Kenneth L. M., 4, 158, 167; address to 1947 National Conference of Social Work, 95–96, 170; and diagnostic/functional debate, 95–96, 172; efforts to define community organizations, 289; and functional model, 95–96, 167, 170, 203; lasting influence, 159–60; philosophy of profession of social work, 160; and Philadelphia Training School for Social Work, 57, 87. *See also* "Social Work and Social Action" (Pray)

PRIME (Partners Reaching to Improve Multicultural Effectiveness) training, 500–501, 503–15

prisons and incarceration: and black men's labor-force nonparticipation/unemployment, 359–61, 384n.15; the mentally ill, 634–35. *See also* "Lessons Learned About Working with Men" (Sternbach)

Prochaska, James O., 400

Proctor, Enola, 19

ProDES database of juvenile delinquents by Family Court of Philadelphia, 579–80, 582

The Professional School Dean (Austin et al.), 620

Progoff, Ira, 94–95

Protinsky, Howard O., 209, 215

psychodynamic theory, 75–76, 159, 166, 175n.7, 619. *See also* diagnostic approach

psychoeducation, 450–52. *See also* "Moving from Psychoeducation to Family Education" (Solomon)

Psychological Center, Paris, 97, 99–100

Public Education Association of New York, 86–87

Putnam, Robert, 299

Quality of Working Life (QWL) movement, 607–8, 617

Quigley, John, 540

Quinn, Joseph F., 221

Rabinowitz, Barbara, 198n.2

racism: Carter course of social work practice and racism, 117–20; Carter course on institutional racism, 114–17; definitions, 128, 146n.4; and intercultural sensitivity, 507–12, 514; Penn sequence/courses, 128–38, 146n.2. *See also* "The Black Instructor" (Carter); "Institutional Change as a Creative Process" (Arnold and Bloom); "The Journey Toward Intercultural Sensitivity" (Bourjolly et al.); "The New African American Inequality" (Katz et al.)

Radloff, Roland, 481

Rank, Otto, 3; on activity versus passivity of analyst, 98–99; and American psychoanalytic community, 168–69, 176n.36; *The Artist*, 186; *Beyond Psychology*, 100; break with Freudian circle, 83, 89–90, 168, 172, 186–87; concept of Will, 168, 176nn.28, 36, 186, 201, 203; death, 100; definition of therapy, 99; emphasis on treatment relationship, 168; emphasis on time as therapeutic tool, 168, 170–71; and functional theory at Penn, 3–4, 76, 92–95, 167–72; *Genetic Psychology*, 83, 90; popular lectures, 83, 89–90, 96–100; and Robinson, 83–101, 167–69, 186–87; and Taft, 88–90, 167–69, 176n.36, 185–86, 200–202; Taft translations, 90, 186–87; *Technique of Psychoanalysis*, 83, 90; *Trauma of Birth*, 83, 168, 186; use of word "functional," 94. *See also* "The Influence of Otto Rank" (Robinson)

Rankin, Jeanette, 33, 36n.1

Rebecca Gratz Club, 229, 230

"Reflections upon University Retirement: With Thanks and Apologies to James Joyce" (Euster), 221–31; age discrimination and ADEA, 221–22; factors influencing retirement decisions, 222–23; Faculty Retirement Survey data, 222; impact of elimination of mandatory retirement, 222; retirement as social process, 222

Regab, Ibrahim, 433, 437–38

Regensburg, Jeanette, 145

Reid, William, 174

Reilly, James, 454

Reimer, Michele S., 468

retirement. *See* "Reflections upon University Retirement" (Euster)

Rhoads, Jonathan E., 79

Rhodes, Margaret L., 468

Rich, Richard, 432–36, 438

Richmond, Mary, 2–3; and COS model, 166; and ecological perspective, 233; *The Good Neighbor*, 166; social casework as functional method, 73–75; *Social Diagnosis*, 74, 92, 166. *See also* "The Family and the Social Worker" (Richmond)

Riis, Jacob A., 53

"Risk Classification and Juvenile Dispositions" (Jones, Schwartz, Schwartz, Obradovic, and Jupin), 571–605; actuarial risk assessment tools, 571–72, 593–96; Answer Tree segmentation technique, 583–85; attempts to standardize risk assessment, 573–74; comparing tools, 579–93; configural analysis model, 573, 582–86, 588–92, 595; developing risk assessments, 576–79; evaluating risk assessments, 574–76; juvenile justice/child welfare public policy response to juvenile crime, 571; neural network model, 573, 586–89, 592–93, 595; predictive validity, 589–93; ProDES database of juvenile delinquents, 579–80, 582; risk classifications compared, 588–89; Wisconsin Risk Assessment Tool, 573–74, 579–82, 585, 588–95

Robinson, Virginia P.: applying for "therapy"/analysis with Rank, 91, 167; Associate Director of Penn School, 87; attending University of Chicago, 85–86; *A Changing Psychology in Social Work*, 4; decision to seek doctorate at Penn, 92; and diagnostic/functional debates, 4, 172; dissertation, 92; early education, 83–85; first jobs, 86–88; first meetings with Rank, 90–91; and functional model, 3–4, 75, 168–69, 171, 203; functional theory and Rank, 168–69; functional theory and agency function, 171; life partnership with Taft, 85, 88, 181, 186; and Penn Doctoral Council/ Admissions Committee, 5–6; Philadelphia Training School, 57; and social casework, 75; study of development of social work practice (1930), 166; and woman suffrage issue, 85–86. *See also* "The Influence of Otto Rank" (Robinson).

Rockefeller, John D., Jr., 31

Rodin, Judith, 604

Rogers, Carl, 186, 425–26; *On Becoming a Person*, 425

Rogers, Nancy, 634

Rogerson, Ann, 420

"The Role of Social Disadvantage in Crime, Joblessness, and Homelessness Among Persons with Serious Mental Illness" (Draine, Salzer, Culhane, and Hadley), 305–21; crime and people with mental illness, 306–8, 319; diagnostic definition of mental illness, 314; employment rates of people with mental illness, 308–10; homelessness and mental illness, 311–13; implications for policy, 315–16; implications for research, 314–15; implications for services, 313–14; public responses/critiques of paper, 320–21; and substance abuse, 320; and Supplemental Security Income, 312

Romania. *See* "Partnering with the Jewish Community of Romania" (Feine)

Rose, Nancy E., 523

Rosen, Rabbi Moses, 274–77, 286–87

Rosen, Robert, 106, 108

Rosenbloom, Robert, 432

Rossé, Kathryn: commentary on Robinson, 4, 102–4; on functional approach in her professional development, 4, 102–4

Rothman, Jack, 608

Rothschild, Joyce, 430–31

Roundtree, Bettie, Bassett, 198n.2

Roush, Nicholas, commentary on Carter, 4, 121–22

Rowe, John W., 228

Russell Sage Foundation, 79

Sacks, Patricia, 95

Saegart, Susan, 299–300

Sager, Clifford J., 211

Salzer, Mark S. *See* "The Role of Social Disadvantage" (Draine et al.)

Sanders, Daniel, 334

Sands, Roberta G., 8; on postmodernism and functionalism, 476–77; "The Journey Toward Intercultural Sensitivity" (Bourjolly et al.); "Postmodern Feminist Theory and Social Work" (Sands and Nuccio).

Satir, Virginia, 219

Schachter, Stanley, 481

Scharff, David E., 212

Scharff, Jill S., 212

Schmidt, Peter, 575

Schön, Donald, 614

Schultz, Kenneth S., 223

Schumpeter, Joseph, 430

Schwartz, David R. *See* "Risk Classification and Juvenile Dispositions" (Jones et al.)

Schwartz, Ira M., 7, 8; as dean, 604–5; and Gelles, 407. *See also* "Risk Classification and Juvenile Dispositions" (Jones et al.)

Schwartz, Richard C., 211

Scott, Richard, 432

Scott, Ruth, 192

Seider, Violet, 289

Self, Robert, 363

Seltzer, Vivian C., 8. *See also* "A Cross-National Study of Adolescent Peer Concordance (Seltzer and Waterman)

Senge, Peter, 235

Sentencing Project, 360

Setleis, Lloyd, 230

settlement house movement, 428

Severson, Margaret, 321

Seybert Institution, 2, 20, 22–23, 167

Shapiro, Thomas M., 377

Sheldon, Eleanor, 95

Shlonsky, Aron, 575, 582

Shoemaker, Louise, 230

Shulman, Lawrence, 233

Shyne, Ann, 174

Sills, Patrick, 435–37

Silver, Bill, commentary on Taft, 4, 69–71

Silver, Henry K., 394

Silverman, Frederic N., 394

Silverstein, Max, 230, 634

Silverstein, Olga, 219

Simon, Bernece K., 180

Simon, Francis, 578–79

Singer, Betty, 407

Sinnot, Edmund, 329

Siporin, Max, 233

Slavin, Betty, 198n.2

Smalley, Ruth, 3, 4; acting dean, 79–80; awards and recognitions, 81; connections of biology and social work, 329; country differences in social work profession, 81; and "Educational Survey," 78–79; and functional model, 3, 78–80, 127–28, 203; human behavior course with Euster, 230; joining Penn, 78, 97; leading School through